Australian Anglicans
WORSHIP
performing APBA

CHARLES SHERLOCK

Australian Anglicans Worship performing APBA
First published in 2020
by Broughton Publishing Pty Ltd
32 Glenvale Crescent Mulgrave VIC 3170

Copyright © Charles Sherlock 2020

All rights reserved. No part of this publication
may be reproduced, stored in a retrieval system or
transmitted, in any form or by any means electronic,
photocopying, recording or otherwise, without the
prior written permission of the publisher.

ISBN
Print 978-0-6482659-6-2
ebook 978-0-6482659-7-9

Foreword

"A form of words is only a means to an act of worship" was John Grindrod's last word at the publication of *An Australian Prayer Book* (*AAPB*, 1978). However, much of the liturgical debate and practice in Australia since has fallen into the trap that he identified.

In this lively publication, Charles Sherlock invites Australian Anglicans (and others in a liturgical tradition) to engage with liturgical texts in a more wholistic way. *Australian Anglicans Worship performing APBA* invites us to consider not just words, but context, time, season, movement, ministers, space, light and sound – in short, all the performance aspects of liturgy that constitute a meaningful act of worship.

Charles Sherlock brings to this volume, and to its predecessor, *Performing the Gospel in Liturgy and Lifestyle*, a lifetime of academic and practical liturgical thinking. Between them, these two books explore not only the text of *APBA* but also its performance. Two features in them stand out.

First, Dr Sherlock traces the rich heritage of the *Books of Common Prayer* and how the 1662 version, authoritative for the Anglican Church of Australia, was revised for *AAPB*. This heritage is assessed in the light of the scriptures and ancient Christian sources, and against the ecumenical and missional context in which we live today.

Second, Dr Sherlock is sensitive to the theological and contextual issues faced in preparing *APBA*. While never afraid to state his own convictions clearly, he is generous to other positions, and carefully articulates the way in which the Liturgical Commission decided on a particular point.

Charles Sherlock has made a major contribution to the liturgical life of Australian Anglicans for over four decades. Alongside teaching Theology and Worship at Ridley and Trinity Colleges, he participated in the *Anglican-Roman Catholic International Commission* from 1991 to 2016, was a member of the General Synod Liturgical Commission that drafted *APBA*, and saw to the issuing of its electronic version, *ePray*.

Through all this time, Dr Sherlock has been an active and exuberant participant in "doing" local church, and in engaging with his local community. This is all part of the rich gift that he brings to this wise and practical guide for all involved in preparing, leading and participating in worship.

+ Garry Weatherill,
Chair, Liturgy Commission, Anglican Church of Australia

Abbreviations

A Practical Commentary
          Ronald Dowling, David Richardson and Gillian Varcoe (edd), *A Prayer Book for Australia. A Practical Commentary* (Alexandria: EJ Dwyer, 1997)
AAPB   An Australian Prayer Book (1978)
APBA   A Prayer Book for Australia (1995)
ARCIC   Anglican-Roman Catholic International Commission
BCP   The Book of Common Prayer [preceded or followed by date]
BEM   Baptism, Eucharist and Ministry (Geneva: WCC, 1982)
CCP   Society of St Francis, *Celebrating Common Prayer, A Version of the Daily Office SSF* (London: Mowbray, 1992)
ELLC   English Language Liturgical Consultation
HC1   Holy Communion (First Order)
HC2   Holy Communion (Second Order)
HC3   Holy Communion (Third Order)
IALC   International Anglican Liturgical Consultation
ICEL   International Council on English in the Liturgy [Roman Catholic]
M&EP1   Morning and Evening Prayer (First Order)
M&EP2   Morning and Evening Prayer (Second Order)
PPP   Prayer, Praise and Proclamation
RCL   Revised Common Lectionary (1992)
WCC   The World Council of Churches

The Commission appointed to prepare liturgical resources for Australian Anglicans has had a variety of names since it was established in 1962:

1962–1997   Liturgical Commission
1997–2001   Liturgy Panel
2001–   Liturgy Commission

In this book, 'Liturgical Commission' is used for the groups that prepared liturgical material up to and including *APBA*. 'Liturgy Commission' is used for the group that prepares materials since *APBA* was issued.

Acknowledgements

Three members of the Liturgical Commission that drafted *APBA* who have departed this earthly life and are with Christ were significant for my ongoing learning: Canon Dr Lawrence Bartlett (Sydney), Canon Dr Evan Burge (Melbourne), and the Revd Dr Ronald Dowling (Melbourne, Adelaide and Perth). It was a privilege to work closely with each of them in the communion that is God's gift and being. Their insights – though not always adopted – have given focus to this book.

I also want to acknowledge (then) Brother Gilbert Sinden, who edited *An Australian Anglican Prayer Book* (1978) and its accompanying *Collects and Readings at the Holy Communion on Weekdays*, and penned his detailed commentary on *AAPB*, *When we meet for Worship* (Adelaide: Lutheran Press, 1978). Without his liturgical insight, care for detail, sensitivity to doctrinal questions and willingness to work with others, notably (then) Bishop Donald Robinson, Australian Anglicans would be much the poorer.

As *APBA* was at the printer in 1995, *Church Scene*, the national Anglican weekly, published six articles written or commissioned by myself as the Editor. These were revised and extended in *A Practical Commentary on A Prayer Book for Australia*, edited by Gillian Varcoe, Ronald Dowling and David Richardson (Sydney: EJ Dwyer, 1997). Some of this material is taken up here: where the original chapter was not written by me, kind permission has been given by the author, or those responsible for their estate.

A Pastoral Handbook for Anglicans (Canberra: Acorn, 2001) was a thorough revision of a similar book issued in 1998 by the Diocese of Melbourne. Both were drafted by myself, working with experienced clergy, and approved by the Archbishop of Melbourne as offering "guidelines for the conduct of baptisms, weddings and funerals". This work is also drawn upon, especially its suggestions for liturgical practice.

Bob Andersen of Broughton Books has been a constant encourager. I am grateful to Robyn O'Sullivan for her editorial insights, and Rhys Bezzant for his proof-reading.

This book represents what I have struggled with over six decades, as an Australian man of Irish descent, raised on the *Book of Common Prayer* by devout parents, called to the work of teaching Theology, liturgical revision and ecumenical engagement.

I acknowledge with particular thanks ongoing reflection and engagement with the Revd Dr Peta Sherlock of every aspect of *APBA*: its texts, rubrics – and limitations.

CONTENTS

Foreword
Abbreviations
Acknowledgements
Introduction *APBA* – why bother? 1

Part A ***APBA* – background and features** 7

Chapter 1 From *BCP* to *AAPB* and *APBA* and beyond …
Beginnings
The 60s and 70s: worshipping in a culture of change
The path to *APBA* (1995)
APBA: from uniformity to coherent diversity
What's next?
Further reading

Chapter 2 *APBA* – Coherent diversity for common prayer 28
Coherent diversity of language
Coherent diversity and structure
Further reading

Part B **Resources for every Christian liturgy** 43

Chapter 3 According to the Scriptures 44
Planning liturgy: what comes first?
Patterns of scripture reading in *APBA*
Scripture readings for weekdays
The Ministry of the Word in practice
Bible translations for use in church
Further reading

Chapter 4 The Church's Year 'down under' 63
History: times and seasons in Christian perspective
Context: seasons 'down under'
Further reading

Chapter 5 Seasons and Saints in *APBA* 80
The Calendar in *APBA*
Marking time in *APBA*
The Calendar and the diary
Further reading

Chapter 6	Singing the Lord's Song	96
	The Psalms in Christian worship	
	Musical settings for *APBA* services	
	Further reading	
Chapter 7	The Ministry of Prayer	110
	What makes prayer Christian?	
	Aspects of prayer in *APBA*	
	Forms of prayer in *APBA*	
	Further reading	
Part C	**Services of the Word**	**129**
Chapter 8	Services of the Word, mainly for Sundays	132
	Background	
	Morning and Evening Prayer (First Order)	
	Morning and Evening Prayer (Second Order)	
	A Service of Praise, Prayer and Proclamation	
Chapter 9	Services of the Word, mainly for weekdays	149
	Background	
	Daily Morning and Evening Prayer in *APBA*	
	The Service of Light, and Prayer at the End of the Day	
	Further reading	
Part D	**"Go and make disciples": Christian initiation**	**161**
Chapter 10	Initiating Christians: theology and practice	164
	Prologue: terms that may matter	
	Christian initiation: what is involved?	
	Christian initiation: some issues of context	
	Further reading	
Chapter 11	Initiating Christians: preparing the way	181
	Preparing the people	
	The Catechism	
	Preparing for the service	
	Further reading	
Chapter 12	Initiating Christians using *APBA*	195
	Holy Baptism	
	Holy Baptism for an infant (2009)	
	Confirmation and Re-affirmation	
	Further reading	

Part E	Holy Communion / Eucharist / Lord's Supper	211
	A rose by any other name?	
	Resources and works cited	
	How these chapters are structured	
	Bibliography for Part E	
Chapter 13	'Do this for my remembrance': theological foundations	217
	Last Supper and Lord's Supper	
	The presence of Christ	
	Sacrifice and the Eucharist	
	The 'episcopal-diaconal' dialogue in liturgy	
	Conclusion	
Chapter 14	'Do this for my remembrance': liturgical implications	235
	The 'four fold shape'	
	Presiding at the eucharist	
	Familiar elements in *APBA* Eucharists	
	Sensitive issues in eucharistic celebration	
	Sensitive issues in administering Holy Communion	
	Conclusion	
Chapter 15	Celebrating Holy Communion using First Order	262
	The structure of the service	
	Commentary	
	A final note	
Chapter 16	Celebrating Holy Communion using Second Order	273
	The structure of the service	
	Commentary	
	A final note	
Chapter 17	Celebrating Holy Communion using Third Order	297
	Why a Third Order?	
	Commentary	
	A final note	
Chapter 18	Celebrating Holy Communion in Pastoral Services	303
	Holy Communion: Outline Order	
	Holy Communion in a Wedding	
	Holy Communion in Ministry with the Sick and Dying	
	Holy Communion on the Day of the Funeral	
Chapter 19	Celebrating Holy Communion in post-*APBA* rites	313
	Lent, Holy Week and Easter	
	Celebrating Holy Communion using post-APBA rites	

| Part F | **Marking Rites of Passage using *APBA*** | **325** |

                  Four needs for pastoral liturgy

| Chapter 20 | Thanksgiving for a Child | 328 |

                  Rites marking childbirth
                  Commentary

| Chapter 21 | Celebrating Marriage using *APBA* | 336 |

                  Solemnising Holy Matrimony in Australia today
                  The wedding services in *APBA*

| Chapter 22 | Ministries of Wholeness in *APBA* | 351 |

                  Christian understandings of wholeness
                  Ministry with the Sick
                  Ministry with the Dying
                  Reconciliation of a Penitent
                  Post-*APBA* resources from the Liturgy Commission
                  Further reading

| Chapter 23 | Funeral Services and Resources in *APBA* | 374 |

                  Funeral ministry in perspective
                  A Funeral Service
                  Funeral Services for Children
                  A final comment
                  Further reading

| **Part G** | **Other Resources in *APBA*** | **397** |

| Chapter 24 | The Ordinal | 398 |

                  Ordination in Australian Anglican contexts
                  Theological issues around ordination
                  Commentary
                  Re-arranging the Ordinal
                  Further reading

| Chapter 25 | Supplementary material | 418 |

                  The Articles of Religion
                  The Athanasian Creed
                  Index of Prayers
                  Acknowledgements

Back to the future: The Preface to *APBA*   427

Index   428

Introduction: *APBA* - why bother?

Australian society has changed a good deal since *APBA* was issued in 1995 – the NBN and smartphones, Facebook, the global financial crisis, a succession of Royal Commissions, 'church' online … And the life of many congregations has changed, not least as they seek to be 'mission-shaped'. So why bother writing about a prayer book published before John Howard was Prime Minister? I've asked myself this question often, especially as chapter has succeeded chapter, and raised it with others. But responses have been warmly positive. People have said they'd welcome insights into using *APBA*, and ideas to support 'mission-shaped liturgy'.

The challenges of taking part in God's mission grow daily. 'Fresh expressions' of church have emerged as cultures shift around us. My experience in inner-city, suburban, regional city and small town congregations, however, tells me that 'holding our liturgical nerve' is a key aspect of mission. What Christians do when we meet together regularly forms 'godly ruts' in our innermost selves – our 'hearts', as Cranmer would express this. So I believe that *APBA*, used flexibly and creatively, is a sound platform for performing the gospel 'in church'. Doing this well equips and shapes us to take our part in God's mission 'in the world'.

Moreover, another hard-copy 'prayer book' is unlikely: electronic distribution is the future. The risk is that a congregation can end up with a limited range of liturgical resources that lose touch with the 'mainstream'. Since *APBA* is probably the final 'prayer book' to be issued nationally for Australian Anglicans, a commentary on it offers long-term support for new resources. Those issued so far by the Liturgy Commission offer 'bridge' to the future, and are included here: prayers for particular situations, services for Lent and Holy Week, Blessing of a Civil Marriage and new resources for celebrating Holy Communion.

But back to the opening question: *APBA* – why bother? For a variety of reasons:

- First, it offers 'Liturgical Resources' approved by the General Synod of the Anglican Church of Australia. Being **canonically authorised**, they should be taken seriously.
- Secondly, *APBA* provides **scripturally grounded, doctrinally sound, historically aware** and **culturally sensitive** resources for performing the gospel in Australian conditions, with contributions from Indigenous and immigrant Anglicans.

- Thirdly, *APBA* is a ***flexible*** book. One wit calculated that if you used daily every variation of Holy Communion (Second Order), you would pass 2100AD before all the permutations were exhausted. There is plenty of room for creative adaptation.
- Fourthly, using shared resources such as those offered in *APBA* helps congregations in different settings have an ***affective communion*** as well as 'legal' or 'organisational' relationships with one another.
- Finally, *APBA* takes account of prayer books from across the Anglican Communion, and is ***ecumenically open***. This maximises the potential for liturgy being shared across Christian traditions.

But how Australian is *APBA*?

The prayer books of every Christian tradition draw on its age-long heritage. *APBA* is grounded in the 'catholic and reformed' Anglican heritage of Word and sacrament. This embraces rites of sacred passage, time-honoured prayers, responses and songs, little of which is specifically 'Aussie'. But all liturgies are shaped by the cultural, linguistic and church contexts in which they are performed. Each does its part in passing on the Christian heritage, yet each inevitably dates.

APBA is no different. Some features follow on from its immediate predecessors, the *Book of Common Prayer* (*BCP*, 1662) and *An Australian Prayer Book* (*AAPB*, 1978). *APBA* offers greater flexibility than these, plus new resources arising from the liturgical, ecumenical and charismatic movements. It responds to cultural shifts felt across all Australian churches, notably around gender and electronic communication. Further, especially since the 'Bicentennial' year, 1988, Australians of immigrant background have become more aware of the heritage of this land's Indigenous peoples.

One critic described *AAPB* as an English prayer book with wattle illustrations. Yet how 'Australian' is the Bible, containing the Hebrew and Aramaic First Testament and *koiné* Greek New Testament? These must be translated to be used, which brings in cultural issues – and the versions Australians read were prepared by scholars from the other side of the world. The Bible story began with God's promise to Abram and Sarai in a country far, far away – yet tens of thousands of years after human beings occupied this ancient land as their 'country'.

Christian existence in every nation inevitably transcends its local culture, since believers are 'citizens of heaven' (Philippians 3.20). Given the English / Scottish / Irish origins of Australia as a modern nation, it was cultures from these lands that new arrivals brought with them. More than half the population adhered to the Church of England for the first century or more of European settlement, so services from *BCP* were well known and widely welcomed, and fostered cultural continuity with the 'mother country'. Indeed, when revision of *BCP* began in the 1960s, little attention was given to inculturation beyond using modern English: doctrinal continuity was seen as more important than cultural adaptation.

The Liturgical Commission which drafted *APBA* in the 1990s sought to lend Australian accents to their work. But the burgeoning insights of emerging liturgical scholarship were just as significant. So it is not surprising that for theological, cultural and liturgical reasons, much of *APBA* could be used in any English-speaking country.

Even so, *APBA* does include significant echoes of living in this 'wide brown land'. A prime example is Thanksgiving 2 in Holy Communion (Second Order), whose Preface (page 130) includes the generations of this land's Indigenous peoples in the history of God's people. The story of God's work opens with "At the dawn of time", and comes to its climax in the phrase "the new day dawned". All English speakers understand this imagery, but to Australian ears it carries distinct echoes.

Furthermore, 'direct' language is used in several places, reflecting Australian impatience with fuss and bother: a good example is Occasional Prayer 6 (page 203), sent in by a Melbourne handyman.[1] And Australian occasions and people are included in the Calendar: William Grant Broughton, Mother Esther, Anzac Day, the Week of Prayer for Reconciliation, Georgiana Molloy for example.

A major concern of the Commission was recognizing the heritage and experience of Indigenous Australians. Several contributions were received from Aboriginal Anglicans, who insisted that these should be useable by all. Thus Occasional Prayer 7 (page 203) came from Bishop Arthur Malcolm, then chair of the *National Aboriginal and Torres Strait Islander Commission*. Its reconciliation focus arises from Indigenous experience, but is open to many situations. Similarly, Thanksgiving 3 (pages 218-9), written by Ms Lenore Parker during a Women's Commission meeting, acknowledges the joys and struggles of Australia's Indigenous people alongside those of new arrivals: "the convicts, the hunted, and the dispossessed … as we gather from the four corners of the earth".[2] In like manner, Confession 3 (page 199), drafted by the Koori Commission of the Diocese of Canberra and Goulburn, can be used in any Australian Christian community. The Calendar was enriched by the inclusion of 'The Coming of the Light', the major Christian festival celebrated on July 1 by Torres Strait Islanders.

1　My memory is that the final line of this prayer, as received, was "for Christ's sake": but since this echoes a familiar Australian blasphemy, the Liturgical Commission changed it to "for Jesus Christ's sake".

2　For discussion at the 1995 General Synod of the phrase 'Mother Earth' in this inspired prayer, see page 122 in this book.

In sum, *APBA* is not – and could not be – an 'Aussie' prayer book. The gospel it seeks to see performed arose in a particular time and place, yet transcends every culture. It arrived in this land in Anglo-Irish dress, far distant from the cultures of its Indigenous peoples, and of many later arrivals. Sadly, much Australian Anglican energy has been spent on issues arising from the sectarian bitterness between English and Irish Christians, Protestants and Roman Catholics, and more recently on issues around gender. **The concern of the Liturgical Commission which drafted APBA, however, was to offer 'Liturgical Resources' which all Australian Anglicans could use together to perform the gospel authentically.**

A trilogy of books

The book you are reading complements two accompanying volumes.

Australian Anglicans Remember (Melbourne: Broughton, 2016) gives information, and resources for use in services, for all entries related to Australian and New Zealand events and holy people in the Calendar of *APBA* .

Performing the Gospel in Liturgy and Lifestyle (Melbourne: Broughton, 2017) explores aspects of Christian worship that lie behind and go beyond words: space, music, screens, time, planning, leading and so on. *APBA* in large part consists of text. Canon Lawrence Bartlett, who chaired the Liturgical Commission that drafted *APBA* wrote in its Preface, "Liturgy is more than words. Words provide a framework to encourage worship, but the important thing is the spirit in which the words are used."

Liturgy takes place in varied settings: church door, font, caravan park, aisles, lectern, garden, nursing home, sports ground and more. There could be a screen, organ or band, prayer desk, seats and pews, pulpit, vestry, bishop's chair, stained glass windows – or not. Each aspect affects the way that a particular service is prepared and performed. *Performing the Gospel* addresses these dimensions of worship, as well as issues around using words, notably how language and gender interact.

This trilogy of books works together. *Australian Anglicans Remember* familiarizes today's Anglicans with the heritage of holy people in this land, so equipping them better to take part in civic events. *Performing the Gospel* explores the wider canvas of Christian worship, our Spirit-inspired service of God in liturgy and lifestyle alike. *Australian Anglicans Worship performing APBA* introduces *APBA* as a whole, and explores each service and the 'liturgical resources' within it. All three books take up the theme of 'performance' that undergirds Christian worship, which entails far more than what we do as churches on Sunday.

Australian Anglicans Worship performing APBA in overview

This book is arranged in seven Parts.

- Part A (Chapters 1 and 2) tells the *APBA* 'story', notably areas debated by the Liturgical Commission and at the 1995 General Synod. This leads to an analysis of the guiding '**principle of coherent diversity**' (my phrase) which undergirds *APBA*.
- Part B (Chapters 3 to 7) explores **resources for all services**: Lectionary (Bible reading pattern); Calendar (the Christian year); Psalter and music; and Prayers.
- Part C (Chapters 8 and 9) covers **Services of the Word** for Sundays and daily use.
- Part D (Chapters 10 to 12) takes up **Christian initiation**. Attention is paid to the theological, liturgical and pastoral dimensions of Holy Baptism, Confirmation and Reaffirmation, as well as Reception into the Anglican Communion.
- Part E (Chapters 13 to 19) opens up the theological, liturgical and pastoral issues around **Holy Communion**. Attention is paid to how the Liturgical Commission faced areas of debate, and learnt from the post-World War II Liturgical Movement and ecumenical dialogue, notably *ARCIC*. As well as commentary on the *APBA* services, eucharistic resources issued since *APBA* was published are considered.
- Part F (Chapters 20 to 23) brings together services which take up major '**rites of passage**' in human life: birth, marriage, ill-health, dying and death.
- Part G (Chapters 24 and 25) takes up resources that are not strictly part of 'common prayer': the **Ordinal** ('attached' to the *Book of Common Prayer*), and **Supplementary Materials** not covered elsewhere in this book.

But before you proceed to read further, let me be clear about the approach taken throughout this book.

The core theological, liturgical and pastoral 'positions' taken in *Australian Anglicans Worship performing APBA* inevitably reflect my own perspectives. The intention, however, is to show the rationale for the Liturgical Commission's work – why we did what we did. That said, most of the practical suggestions offered arise from my own experience – other Commission members might not go along with these.

However you assess this book, its focus and aim is to help Australian Anglicans reflect on how best we may perform the gospel of Christ 'in church'. Which is but one part of living out God's mission in the changing contexts of third millennium Australia, and beyond. After all, as spelled out in *Performing the Gospel*, Christian worship involves the interaction of liturgy and lifestyle.

Charles Sherlock

The Liturgical Commission for *APBA*

The list below is in alphabetical order; diocesan locations are as in 1993–1995. Skills brought to the work are noted underneath each person's name. Most portfolios had a 'lead' drafter and a 'support' person: the latter is indicated in [square brackets]. Executive members at the time of the July 1995 General Synod are marked #.

Name / Skill	Diocese	Portfolio
Bartlett, Lawrence # *Music, BCP, diplomacy*	Sydney	Chair (from 1993) *Preface; First and Third Order services;* *Supplementary Material [Psalms]*
Burge, Evan *Liturgy, BCP, original languages*	Melbourne	*Collects, Psalms* *[Third Order services; In Living Use*]*
Collison, Margaret *English*	Sydney	*English usage; Thanksgiving for a Child* *[Prayers]*
Dowling, Ron # *Liturgy, parish ministry*	Perth	*Christian Initiation; Calendar; Reconciliation* *[Holy Communion (Second Order)]*
Dowling, Owen *Pastoral care*	Canberra & Goulburn	Chair (to 1993); *Ministry with the Sick*
Hearn, George *Episcopal and rural ministry*	Rockhampton	*Daily Services* *[Ministry with the Sick, Ordinal]*
Lawton, William *Pastoral theology, Australian Studies*	Sydney	*Marriage* *[Holy Communion (Second Order)]*
Peterson, David *New Testament*	Sydney	Consultant *[Holy Communion (Third Order)]*
Richardson, David # *New Testament, Theology*	Adelaide	Executive Secretary *Holy Communion (Second Order)* *[Ordinal, Christian Initiation]*
Sherlock, Charles # *Theology, BCP, Liturgy,* *Ministry Studies*	Melbourne	Minutes Secretary *Lectionary & Sentences; Prayers;* *Morning & Evening Prayer (Second Order)* *Ministry with the Dying; Funerals; Ordinal* *[First Orders; Reconciliation; In Living Use*]*
Varcoe, Gillian # *Liturgy, Editing*	Canberra & Goulburn	Editor; *Prayers* *[Holy Communion Second Order]*

The voices of these Australian Anglicans often came to mind while writing, especially Lawrie Bartlett, with whom I shared General Synod 1995 and more besides.

* *In Living Use*, services from the *Book of Common Prayer* rendered in modern English and taking account of typical *BCP* usage.

Part A

APBA – the background story

A commentary on any book of prayers and rituals cannot be made effectively without an account of its origins and context. Further, only rarely does such a book emerge without controversy, as was the case with *An Australian Prayer Book* (AAPB, 1978).

APBA was drafted in the midst of debates about mission strategy, gender issues and even the nature of Christian worship. This book therefore opens with two chapters on the background of *APBA*, the first revision of a modern-language prayer book in the Anglican Communion.

Chapter One sets out the longer-term background to *APBA*, from the arrival of the *Book of Common Prayer (BCP)* on Australian soil, to the debates around its revision and the issuing of *AAPB*, and the 1995 General Synod which authorised *APBA*.

Chapter Two offers an analysis of the underlying 'principle of coherent diversity' that – with the exception of pages 133-135 – shapes *APBA* from cover to cover.

Chapter One

From BCP *to* AAPB *and* APBA

Beginnings

Australia's Christian origins

In 1788, when England set up a penal colony in what was named New South Wales, conditions for Christian beginnings were far from promising. The Church of England was in a parlous state – it was the 'Barchester Chronicles' era. A chaplain, the Revd Richard Johnston, accompanied the 'First Fleet' under sufferance, while Roman Catholics among the convicts had no priest. Most of those on board belonged to the established Church of England and Ireland. The flagship, *HMS Sirius*, carried hundreds of copies of its *Book of Common Prayer (BCP)* and the *King James Bible*. Services on board were taken from *BCP*, as was the first Christian service on shore, on February 3, 1788.[1] Johnston ministered under great difficulties: though he gained the respect of many convicts, his first chapel was burnt down. Christian faith was tolerated as a useful way to instil moral order.

Despite these difficult beginnings, until the 1960s the *BCP* and the *King James Bible* had a deep and lasting influence in Australian society. This extended beyond adherents of the 'CofE' – the majority of the population – to Australians generally, including many Aboriginal people.[2] Torres Strait Islanders took on Christian faith in its Anglican form from the 'Coming of the Light' in 1871.[3]

As the six Australian colonies grew and (eventually) prospered, the churches, rather than living as brothers and sisters in Christ, treated one another as spiritual rivals.

---

1. Charles Sherlock, *Australian Anglicans Remember* (Mulgrave: Broughton, 2015), entry for February 3. Bruce Kaye (ed), *Anglicanism in Australia. A History* (Melbourne: Melbourne University Press, 2002) is an accessible collection of essays covering what the title describes. Chapters One and Six are of particular relevance to the current book.

2. With his wife Mary, Johnston sought to minister to Aboriginal people: they adopted an Aboriginal girl, Boo-ron, and he once stood as hostage to allow Bennelong to visit Governor Phillip. The English *Church Missionary Society* initiated missions among Aboriginal people from 1825. By the end of the nineteenth century several Anglican mission stations had been established.

3. See *Australian Anglicans Remember,* entry for July 1.

Anglicans from England, Presbyterians from Scotland and Roman Catholics from Ireland each assumed they should run the religious show, as at home. Their proper concern for all souls in a nation – the 'parish' rather than 'gathered church' mentality – became competition for spiritual control. The forms of worship brought from Europe became the sign of the churches' differences – the (Roman Catholic) Latin mass, (Church of England) *Book of Common Prayer*, (Presbyterian) *Directory of Divine Service*, and the Methodist Hymn Book, whose influence spread far beyond Methodists.

Many men and women of all Christian traditions nevertheless gave sterling service for Christ in the cities, towns, country and outback areas of this 'wide brown land'. Yet it was not until the 1960s that liturgical changes, many arising from cultural shifts in society, helped lower the barriers between the churches. Most notable were the shift from Latin to English by Roman Catholics, and the move away from Elizabethan English among Protestants.

Australian Anglican worship 1788-1962

Australian Anglicans used *BCP* services from 1788 until the 1960s with little variation beyond hymns. A typical Sunday in the suburbs would see well-attended services of Morning Prayer around 11am, preceded by a smaller Holy Communion service at 8am, with Evening Prayer at 7pm or so. In rural settings, Morning Prayer was likely to be taken by a Lay Reader, perhaps not every week, with Holy Communion only when a priest could visit, often just once a quarter. Baptisms typically took place on Sunday afternoons, when a dozen or so infants might be 'done'. Weddings filled Saturday afternoons for many city clergy, while funerals were held on weekdays. All this said, the biblical depth and pastoral orientation of *BCP* served well the cycles of community life.

Yet the revision of *BCP* was not at first sought in response to changes in society, the challenges of science or biblical scholarship. Rather, it was to widen its eucharistic doctrine, one outcome of the Anglo-Catholic movement. Changes were strongly resisted by Protestant Anglicans: divisions became so great in England that in 1906 Parliament called a Royal Commission. Its Report lead to a revised *BCP* being approved by church authorities, but failing to pass Parliament in 1927 – and failing again in 1928. Faced with a major crisis, the English bishops agreed not to take action against any priest who used services from the 'Deposited Book (1928)', its official name.[4]

---

4   Donald Gray, *The 1927-28 Prayer Book Crisis*. Alcuin / GROW Joint Liturgical Series 60 and 61 (London: SCM-Canterbury, 2005) gives a careful analysis. The revision method was itself problematic: texts were debated in committee, but not given 'trial use' in congregational life.

The Anglo-Catholic movement spread steadily across the Australian colonies. In part this was due to the 'churchmanship' of the initial bishops of the Dioceses of Adelaide (Short) and Newcastle, which then included Queensland (Tyrrell). Holy Communion services became more frequent, with richer ceremonial and greater emphasis on the priest. The 1927–28 debate in England flowed over to Australia: a few bishops took action against 'ritualist' practices, several allowed the 1928 book to be used, and a few supported the new ways, especially where parish life was vibrant.

The issue came to a head in the 'Red Book' case of 1943–47, when a group of laymen took the Bishop of Bathurst to court over his authorising a 'ritualist' Holy Communion service, printed in a red-covered booklet. The (then young) Revd Dr Broughton Knox, later Principal of Moore College, was the group's chief witness, arguing that the *Church Trust Act* permitted only *BCP* to be used on church property. The judge agreed, but made sharp comments about doctrinal issues coming to civil courts. Divisions among Australia Anglicans sharpened, delayed the adoption of a Constitution for the national Church until 1962, and took prayer book revision off the table for decades.

The 60s and 70s: worshipping in a culture of change

The cultural changes of the 1960s made everyday Anglicans aware of the growing gap between Sunday church and daily life. The 'pill' altered gender relations profoundly, and rising affluence fostered a consumerist culture. On the other hand, the Billy Graham campaign of 1959 saw Protestant churches open up to one another. Modern English, through Bible translations among Protestants and in the Mass for Roman Catholics, arrived a decade later. The advent of television in 1956 (in time for the Melbourne Olympics), in colour from 1977, exposed people to worlds wider than those experienced in daily life, and led them to expect colour and movement in services. Revision of '1662' was clearly desirable, but the process was full of pitfalls.

How then did Australian Anglicans respond to this multitude of challenges, and the opportunities they offered for fresh approaches to liturgy?

A national church: liturgical revision begins

A Constitution for a national 'Church of England in Australia' was finally agreed in 1962 after decades of debate.[5] Sections 1–4, the 'Fundamental Declarations' and 'Ruling Principles', enshrine *BCP* (1662), with the Articles and Ordinal, as "the standard of doctrine and worship". Unlike other Anglican Provinces, the power of the Australian General Synod is permissive: its agreement is needed for any major change,

---

5   See John Davis, *Australian Anglicans and their Constitution* (Canberra: Acorn, 1993). The Constitution is available at https://www.anglican.org.au/constitution

but a decision takes effect in a diocese only when the diocesan synod accepts it. Further, votes on a major matter require two-thirds majorities in each 'House' (Laity, Clergy, Bishops) in successive General Synods, usually held every three or four years: a majority of dioceses, and all metropolitan ones (Sydney, Melbourne, Brisbane, Adelaide, Perth), must then agree with the change. Alternatively, 75% majorities in each House will carry a major matter forthwith.

So liturgical change, though widely sought, could not take place lightly. Yet the first major decision of the first General Synod in 1962 under the new Constitution, was to set up a Commission "to consider whether revision of the *Book of Common Prayer* was needed".[6] Given the history of sharp division, and the sensitivity at local level to changing a dearly-loved prayer book, a representative body of scholars from across the national church was needed.[7] The initial Commission comprised a large body of men: six bishops, four deans, five archdeacons, eight canons, five priests and five laymen. Despite ongoing suspicions, limited meeting time and vigorous letter-writing in church papers, the Commission worked. As its chairman, Bishop R.G. Arthur (Grafton), concluded in his introduction to its Report to the 1966 General Synod, *Prayer Book Revision in Australia*:

> We have experienced a remarkable openness to one another. We have seen our various traditional positions in new perspectives. We have become more clearly aware of our unity in Christ and in his mission to the world of our time. We are confident that the task of revising the Prayer Book can be carried forward, provided that we proceed "with patience, forbearing one another in love, eager to maintain the unity of the Spirit in the bond of peace."

The Commission's Report not only made a firm 'Yes' to the question put, but included a set of services in modern English! These were in two forms: 'conservative' services (effectively *BCP* translated) and 'radical' ones that employed insights from the Liturgical Movement. General Synod accepted the Report, and asked the Liturgical Commission, as it was called from then on, to work towards a revised book.

---

6   The Church of England had set up a Liturgical Commission in 1955, which in 1958 issued *Liturgical Revision in the Church of England*. Colin Buchanan and Trevor Lloyd, *The Church of England Eucharist 1958–2012*. Alcuin / GROW Join Liturgical Studies 87/88 (Norwich: Hymns Ancient & Modern, 2019) tells the story of the Commission until 1980, when *The Alternative Service Book* was published, in many ways the English equivalent to *AAPB*. Beyond several visits to Australia by Colin Buchanan, however, there was little contact between the English and Australian Commissions until *IALC* formed in 1985.

7   For details of its members and meetings, see Gilbert Sinden, *When We Meet for Worship. A manual for using An Australian Prayer Book 1978* (Adelaide: Lutheran Publishing House, 1978) Chapter Two.

An Australian Prayer Book (AAPB, 1978)

In the ferment of liturgical experiment and revision, the question on many Anglican lips was "How do we stay faithful to 1662?" After a decade of trial services – the 1966, 1969 and 1973 Holy Communion services, *Sunday Services Revised,* trial uses for weddings, Ministry with the Sick, Funerals and more besides – a draft prayer book came to the 1977 General Synod.[8] The Primate and Archbishop of Sydney, Sir Marcus Loane, a conservative Evangelical, gave his strong support to the project, travelling around the nation to encourage use of the draft services. Proposing changes to the draft book in the Synod was seen as risky, lest the project fail. In the event, just one was made: in the Lord's Prayer, the ecumenical text, "save us from the time of trial" reverted to "lead us not into temptation".

With one dissenting vote (by an unidentified bishop), all Houses voted to adopt *An Australian Prayer Book (AAPB),* and it was published the following year. Legally, *AAPB* did not replace *BCP,* but stood 'under' it: in practice, however, it quickly came to stand 'alongside' *BCP.* Beyond cathedrals and a few parishes, the use of *BCP* declined, prompting the formation of Prayer Book Societies in Sydney and Melbourne.

The new book spread rapidly, going through several printings, and bringing welcome capital to the General Synod office. It was a breath of fresh air for Australian Anglicans: by 1980 most were worshipping in contemporary English, using modern service structures, and exploring the flexibility that the new book allowed. Fussy ritual and 'low-church' stiffness alike declined in favour of a more relaxed ethos, as rigid adherence to text and rubrics lessened. Parishes experienced more lay participation in reading the scriptures, taking the intercessions, administering communion, and participating in 'worship committees'. All of which was aided by the advent of photocopiers and overhead (not yet data) projectors.

These positive outcomes owed much to two men who came from different geographical, spiritual and theological places: Brother Gilbert Sinden, a *Society of the Sacred Mission* member and liturgical scholar, based at its priory in Adelaide, and the (then) Revd Donald Robinson, Vice-Principal of Moore College, Sydney.[9] A New Testament

---

8   A full account of the Commission's work and the 1977 General Synod debate can be found in John Grindrod, 'The Story of the Draft Book', in *When we Meet for Worship,* 17–29. A noticeable absence is contributions reflecting Indigenous perspectives.

9   Andrew Judd, "Donald Robinson and the Imperfect Unity of *An Australian Prayer Book* (1978)", *Integrity* 1/1, analyses Robinson's contributions to *AAPB* and the debates around its formulation: http://integrity.moore.edu.au/article/view/1/1. It is surprising that none of the essays in the Festschrift for Donald Robinson, *In the Fullness of Time* (Sydney: Lancer, 1992) reflect on his scholarly work on prayer book revision, though its importance is noted in the chapters outlining his ministry.

scholar whose teaching on 'church' would play a part in significant changes in Sydney, Robinson would become its Archbishop a decade later. Both men risked considerable misunderstanding by cooperating, but their careful work, accompanied by the Revd Dr Evan Burge, a priest-scholar in Melbourne who drafted Holy Communion (Second Order), saw suspicions largely set aside. Sinden undertook the mammoth task of editing the draft book, and completed his detailed 'manual' on it, **When we meet for Worship,** in time for it to come out with *AAPB*. And this was before word processors: it is said that he typed the 700-page volume half a dozen times.

Developments in the wake of *AAPB*

In subsequent years General Synod approved several Liturgical Commission texts: Ministry with the Sick, including anointing (too controversial for inclusion in *AAPB*), Alternative Collects, a revised Ordinal for Deacons (given the prospect of women being deaconed), and an Outline Order of Holy Communion.

Liturgy Committees emerged in many dioceses to help parishes with the new book. Some members of the Melbourne committee, notably Ronald Dowling, were able to participate in the *Inter-Anglican Liturgical Consultation (IALC)* that formed in 1985.[10] Its initial work was on Christian initiation, which led the Melbourne group to draft a service that integrated Baptism (of any age), Confirmation, Reception and Re-affirmation in the context of Holy Communion. Revised and published by the Liturgical Commission in 1990, it would become the first draft text for inclusion in *APBA*.

One criticism voiced about *AAPB* was its seeming lack of 'Australianness', and that at a time when Australians were vigorously exploring their post-British identity, and Indigenous issues were coming to the fore in public consciousness. Further, the effort employed in forging agreement in doctrinally-sensitive areas – notably Holy Communion and Marriage – had restricted the energy for revision of other services, which were largely translations of *BCP* with some pastoral adjustments. Moreover, contact with Provinces and scholars overseas was difficult in the 70s, so developments elsewhere in the Anglican Communion, and ecumenically, played minor roles in *AAPB*'s formation.

But such criticisms were minor compared to the effect of the protracted debates on the ordination of women as priests. General Synod authorised the ordination of women as deacons in 1985, but at successive meetings (1981, 1985, 1987, 1989) a Canon to allow women to be ordained priest, though gaining the required two-thirds majorities in the House of Bishops and the House of Laity, failed by the narrowest

---

10 See David Holeton (ed), *Christian Initiation in the Anglican Communion. The Toronto Statement* (Nottingham: Grove Worship Series 118, 1991).

margin in the House of Clergy. The protracted debate deepened the increasingly distinctive approach of the Diocese of Sydney to 'church', 'ministry' and 'worship', and sharpened it opposition to women as priests or bishops. The issue was not synodically resolved until late 1992, and only after the Diocese of Perth used its distinctive Constitutional position to ordain women as priests in March 1992.[11]

Closely associated with the ordination debate was concern around gender-exclusive language. *AAPB* has a few places where this is a problem in relation to humans, notably "for us men and our salvation" in the Nicene Creed. But the Tudor/Caroline heritage of *BCP* saw God frequently addressed using royal imagery. The widespread desire in the 60s for more intimate forms of divine address led to many prayers in *AAPB* beginning with 'Father' rather than 'Almighty God' – which reinforced growing concern about using male language for God, a far more sensitive issue.

Meanwhile music in church was moving from classical and brass band styles to folk, pop, film themes and soft rock. The churches' life was affected by the charismatic movement, increasing distance from mainstream society, ecumenical openness – with a growing impatience of 'denominational loyalty' – alongside theological uncertainty and plurality. Few Australian Christians born after 1960 have access to what 'church' in any tradition was like before these changes took hold. Change was now part of the furniture.

These issues around flexibility, gender and the increasing gap between the churches and Australian society, form the background to the request by the 1989 General Synod for the Liturgical Commission to consider whether revision of *AAPB* was needed.

The path to *APBA* (1995)

The Liturgical Commission 1989–95

The 1989 Liturgical Commission appointed by General Synod had ten members, of whom Evan Burge and Lawrence Bartlett had been drafters of *AAPB*.[12] It was a representative group theologically and geographically, though just two women were included. Sydney had three members (Lawrence Bartlett, Bill Lawton, Margaret

---

11 A month earlier, the Diocese of Canberra & Goulburn had been prevented from ordaining women as priests due to court action in NSW: a restraining order came down as the ordinands' retreat was under way. The initiative was led by the diocesan bishop, Owen Dowling, who chaired the Liturgical Commission at the time. Several court hearings interrupted its meetings; work was once suspended so Bishop Owen could be interviewed for television in the meeting room. Late in 1992 he handed the chair's baton to Canon Lawrence Bartlett.

12 On the development of *APBA*, see David Richardson, "*A Prayer Book for Australia*: Historical Background", in Ronald Dowling, David Richardson and Gillian Varcoe (edd), *A Prayer Book for Australia. A Practical Commentary* (Alexandria: EJ Dwyer, 1997) 6–12.

Collison), plus a consultant (David Peterson); Melbourne two (Evan Burge, Charles Sherlock); Canberra & Goulburn one (Bishop Owen Dowling) plus the Editor (Gillian Varcoe); Adelaide (David Richardson), Perth (Ron Dowling) and Rockhampton (Bishop George Hearn) one each.

Noting criticisms such as those mentioned above, the Commission agreed that revision of *AAPB* was needed. The 1992 General Synod accepted this recommendation, and work began in earnest. It commenced with a light revision of Melbourne's 'Holy Baptism with the Laying on of Hands', issuing it as a booklet in 1990: this became the draft for the 'page 51' service in *APBA*. 'Trial use' booklets of other services appeared steadily, and consultations were held in each state.[13] David Richardson, then the Commission's Executive Secretary, describes how it worked:

> Responsibility for particular liturgies was given to a specific member who undertook research in the area before bringing an outline procedure and philosophy to the full Commission ... Having received the proposed procedure and the philosophy undergirding it, the Commission would debate the principles, modifying them, challenging the assumptions—liturgical, pastoral, theological—and bring forward suggestions for consideration which may hitherto have been overlooked. Only at the conclusion of that process would the member responsible be invited to bring a draft, preliminary text.

> The draft once brought would itself undergo rigorous examination, being assessed for its theology as well as its liturgical usefulness and simplicity and its linguistic felicity. In certain cases—the Ordinal is a prime example—the work of the Liturgical Commission was forwarded to the Doctrine Commission for critical appraisal and comment.[14]

---

13   Booklets published included:

    1992 A Service for Marriage (became Second Order)
        Ministry with the Dying and Bereaved
    1993 Funeral Services and Resources
    1993 The Holy Commuion, Lord's Supper or Eucharist (became Second Order)
    1994 Sunday Services of the Word (became Second and Third Orders)

    In addition to these 'trial use' booklets, drafts of Confirmation, Reconciliation of a Penitent, The Catechism and The Ordinal were sent to the House of Bishops and Doctrine Commission for response, while Thanksgiving for a Child was sent to the Women's Commission. Drafts of Occasional Prayers, and papers on the Calendar and Lectionary proposals, were provided for the Pronvincial Consultations which took place in 1994. 'First Order' services were drafted following the Consultations.

14   *A Practical Commentary*, 6, comments included by David in the Commission's Report to the 1995 General Synod. A list of members and their portfolios can be found on page 6 of this book.

The Commission aimed to reach a consistency across all services in shape, scholarship, literary style and merit, as well as doctrine. However, as David Richardson writes, "This process of revision took place at a time when the Australian Church ... had other significant issues on its agenda, issues to fire the imagination and summon up the blood in a way that liturgical reform would not."[15] But –

> Late in 1993 the work of revision undertaken by the Liturgical Commission gained support from an unexpected quarter. An article in *Southern Cross* [the monthly magazine of the Diocese of Sydney] appeared, criticising the published work of the Commission and warning the Church against indecent haste in moving further in the direction of reform. That one article achieved what regular press releases from the Commission for over ten years had not: it demanded that the Church take seriously the process of revision and invited participation in it ... Suddenly liturgical revision was on the agenda.

Meanwhile David Silk, a former member of the Liturgical Commission of the Church of England, arrived in Australia early in 1994 to become the Bishop of Ballarat, a diocese then strongly opposed to women being ordained. He took up vigorously the concerns of 'traditional Anglo-Catholics', meeting with the Commission for a whole day.[16] Bishop Silk's contributions improved the draft book in a number of places, but his support for the Church of England practice of employing language tolerable of varied doctrinal positions was rejected by all Liturgical Commission members.[17]

In Sydney, Archbishop Harry Goodhew had set up a Liturgical Committee to consider how best to respond to the growing variety of practice in that diocese. One outcome was *Experimental Sunday Services* 1993, reflecting 'Sydney' emphases, but continuing the ethos of *AAPB*. Its 'Service of the Word' was close to the Liturgical Commission's drafting, and 'The Lord's Supper' drew on the Commission's *Outline Order* (1988). The Sydney Committee and the national Commission met together twice, with the Revd Dr David Peterson participating in both bodies as an active Consultant.

---

15   *A Practical Commentary*, 3.
16   The Commission had independently considered over two meetings a Thanksgiving Prayer based on one from the (Roman Catholic) *International Council on English in the Liturgy* (ICEL), and sought responses to the resulting draft from diocesan bishops and liturgical scholars. Worthwhile agreement was unable to be reached, and work continued on a Thanksgiving based on Hippolytus.
17   Buchanan and Lloyd, 23 note that the Church of England Liturgical Commission opposes this approach, seeing it as 'horse-trading'. It emerged from negotiations related to General Synod and House of Bishops debates, affected by the Church being 'established'.

Ecumenically, the *Australian Consultation on Liturgy (ACOL)* had emerged in the wake of *AAPB*, in large part from the initiative of Evan Burge and Lawrence Bartlett. *ACOL* brings together scholars from most of Australia's churches for an annual two-day meeting. It is linked with the *English Language Liturgical Consultation*, the international ecumenical body which prepares agreed liturgical texts in English. In Melbourne, the *Ecumenical Liturgical Centre* was active, with Liturgical Commission member Ron Dowling as its Executive Officer: in 1982 it had amalgamated with the *Australian Academy of Liturgy*. Ron went on to chair the *International Anglican Liturgical Consultation*: several Liturgical Commission members were able to take part in its conferences on Christian initiation (1991) and Eucharist (1993, 1995).

The draft book put before General Synod in 1995 thus drew on a wider range of resources and insights than was possible in the lead-up to 1977. In several areas it represented movement beyond 'churchmanship' debates of the past, and offered a more flexible approach to services' structure, language and ethos than its predecessor.

The 1995 General Synod debate

The draft of *APBA,* coming in at 910 elegantly printed pages – and weighing over a kilogram – was published in January 1995. It was a remarkable achievement after just three years' work, undertaken by Commission members alongside their other ministries: only the Editor was stipended. General Synod members were required to submit proposed amendments well ahead of its week-long meeting at Melbourne Grammar School in July 1995. Some 418 requests arrived, which the Commission sorted into five groups to clarify which needed discussion by the Synod.[18]

The 1995 debate was in marked contrast to that of 1977, running for more than 15 hours over three days.[19] So was the outcome: the Liturgical Commission believed

18   Group A was typological and trivial changes, passed without debate. Group B was minor changes, passed (with a few amendments) in a series of motions. Group C set out nine changes which the Liturgical Commission recommended, but believed needed discussion by the General Synod. Group D listed 17 changes which the Liturgical Commission believed could only be decided by the General Synod. These, including the debate on Thanksgiving 3, took up most of the debate time. Group E was changes opposed by the Liturgical Commission: as far as I recall, none were passed.

19   Dean David Richardson (Executive Secretary), Bp George Hearn and Dr Evan Burge were the only Liturgical Commission members on General Synod. Canon Lawrence Bartlett (Chair), and the Revd Dr Charles Sherlock (Minutes Secretary), having failed to be re-elected in Sydney and Melbourne respectively, were given permission to speak in the debate. In the event, Lawrie and myself, sitting together for the three days of discussion, found ourselves speaking often, explaining the Commission's work and responding to questions. We were seated adjacent to the small delegations from Armidale and Willochra dioceses, whose personal support was deeply appreciated. And that we could not vote meant that we could offer responses as 'outside' experts, without perceptions of 'political' bias.

that the book would get at least a 'triple 66.7%' vote (two-thirds majorities in each of the Houses of Bishops, Clergy and Laity). This would see it needing to be considered by all dioceses, before coming back to another General Synod.[20] But would the 75% level be reached, that would authorise the book for dioceses to consider immediately? When the final vote was taken at the end of Thursday, it was overwhelmingly in favour: 22 of 23 bishops, 87 of 99 clergy, 84 of 99 laity – an overwhelming endorsement by 193 out of 221 members, 87.3% overall.[21]

This outcome gave APBA a high level of spiritual authority, leading to its acceptance in almost all dioceses by the end of the year. Two versions were agreed: the 'green' (Sunday and Daily Services) and 'red' (full) books. As a publishing venture, *APBA* was a major success: the 'green' book had three printings in six months.[22]

Canon Dr Evan Burge included an account of the Synod debate on *APBA* in his 1995 Austin James Lecture: this is reproduced on the next two pages, with kind permission of his estate.[23] Dr Burge had drafted the most used service in *AAPB*, Holy Communion (Second Order), on which the similar rite in *APBA* was closely based. He also worked with me on the 'Hippolytus' Third Thanksgiving in the draft of *APBA* presented to General Synod, which was set aside in favour of the current one.[24]

---

20 Constitution #27. This was the procedure followed in relation to the ordination of women as priests.
21 Almost all of the 12 clergy and 13 laypeople who voted against *APBA*'s acceptance came from the Diocese of Sydney, but a majority of its clergy and lay delegations voted 'Yes'. Sydney's members took a helpful interest in the draft book: small groups were allocated sections to consider and make responses to the Commission in the months leading up to the 1995 General Synod.
22 The resulting funds, which the Commission hoped would be used to workshop the new book at local levels, nevertheless went to a missional use by supporting the 'Engaging Australia' project. When E.J. Dwyer ceased operation in 1998, the Prayer Book Publishing Committee took over distribution until Broughton Publishing was established by the 2001 General Synod. Its first project was developing *ePray*, the electronic version of *APBA* in association with *Duplo Data*, a Norwegian company that specialises in electronic liturgical publishing. Their key staff, Per Halverson and Dagfinn Skogoy, were of indispensable assistance in enabling this ground-breaking project to come to completion.
23 A personal note. At the time of the 1995 General Synod I was a member of the Liturgical Commission, and Editor of *Church Scene*, the national Anglican weekly. My accounts of the Synod can be found in its issues of July 7 and 14, 1995. During 2014-15 Bishop David Silk would frequently call in at my home when visiting from Ballarat to commend the changes he was urging. As Minutes Secretary, it was my uncomfortable task to communicate with him during the Synod about the work going on behind the scenes. More positively, in 1998–2000 we were able to work together on the daily lectionary, on aspects of the implementation of the ordination of women as priests, and on Anglican-Roman Catholic relationships. Some years after he retired to England, David Silk was received into the Roman Catholic Church.
24 The text was issued on the General Synod website by the Liturgy Commission in 2009, available at https://anglican.org.au/our-work/liturgy-worship/holy-communion/.

The Austin James Lecture (1995): an excerpt

When the 1995 General Synod of about 220 members assembled at the Melbourne Grammar School, the first time the General Synod had not been in Sydney, the general desire for the success of the new book and the atmosphere of goodwill were almost palpable. The Primate, Archbishop Keith Rayner, interpreted this feeling in his Presidential Address: "We need a liturgy ... which while sound in theology yet allows reasonable freedom for the different strands of Anglican tradition to be able to use the book with full integrity." Later speeches were often passionate but they lacked courtesy never, and good humour seldom.

On the Monday night was a helpfully low-key but significant presentation arranged by Dr Charles Sherlock on behalf of the Liturgical Commission. After an anthology of liturgical readings spanning the centuries from St Paul to **AAPB**, short unscripted interviews conducted by Mrs Margaret Collinson, a member of the Commission, with members of different Melbourne parishes, revealed how great was the diversity, even within one metropolis, of the needs we were trying to meet. Attention was thus focussed on the needs of parishioners, not on entrenched positions.

The next day, the debate opened with two strong speeches from different ends of the spectrum, as Bishop Phillip Newell of Tasmania moved the adoption of the Canon to authorize the new book, and Dean Boak Jobbins of Sydney seconded the motion. Significantly, Bishop Newell referred to the desire for "a liturgical resource that would keep us in touch with Anglican liturgies round the world".

The Synod then moved into the Committee stage to consider over 400 proposed amendments received in response to the draft book. The Liturgical Committee helped by classifying these into five groups, ranging from (A) typographical and (B) other changes that could be accepted without discussion, through (C) changes it endorsed and (D) changes which it opposed, in both cases but raised matters on which Synod needed to decide, to (E) changes it did not commend. Synod readily endorsed most of the first two groups *en bloc* and settled down to three days – twice the allotted time – debating the points in groups C, D and E. Many proposals were withdrawn to expedite the business. Before it could be discussed and put to the vote, an amendment required the consent of 70 members, estimated on a show of hands.

Some of the most substantial amendments proposed for the Second Order of the Eucharist were the result of a prior consultation initiated by Bishop Silk with the blessing of the Primate. Bishops Silk, Curnow and McCall met in Sydney with Dean Jobbins and Bishop Donald Robinson; Dr David Peterson called in for lunch. This informal but significant consultation was chaired by Archbishop Harry Goodhew of Sydney. Its proposals were forwarded by Bishop Silk and duly considered by the Liturgical Commission. The Commission adopted a few points and recommended against most of them. The decision was left in the hands of the Synod.

As well as the long official lists of amendments, members of Synod received an unofficial four-page document from Bishops Silk, Curnow and McCall under the headline 'A Fair Go'. It urged that because the Third Order for the Holy Communion (which originated in Sydney) met the needs of evangelicals, changes should be made in the Second Order to provide at least one Thanksgiving that catholics could use with a clear conscience. Bishop Silk had drafted such a Thanksgiving in the light of the Sydney consultation. It contained the requisite *epiclesis* (divided in the modern Roman fashion) and expression of offering. In addition it affirmed the sufficiency of Christ's sacrificial death and our acceptance by grace alone.

Liturgical Commission members were variously bemused or irritated by what followed. They felt sidelined. Discussions were going on outside the Synod until late at night, as Bishop Silk and his supporters negotiated with an evangelical group in an attempt to achieve agreement on a modified version of the new Thanksgiving. On Tuesday evening, Commission members were shown the developing new version, and suggested further changes – removal of heavily masculine language (especially 'Almighty Father', which can be a terrifying phrase for victims of sexual abuse) and simplification of the style. By Thursday morning, agreement had been reached in private. Soon after, the new Thanksgiving was welcomed, with relief, by the Synod, despite reservations about including a prayer that had never been prayed and was the result of back-room negotiations. Hippolytus went out in favour of the new Thanksgiving.

The Archbishop of Sydney, Harry Goodhew at a later stage helped many evangelicals to accept the book as a whole by proposing that it be given an additional subtitle: "Liturgical resources authorised by the General Synod." This development and the new subtitle illustrate why *A Prayer Book for Australia* is a watershed.

APBA and the Diocese of Sydney

The 'Liturgical resources ...' subtitle reassured those concerned that the new book would displace *BCP*, but has led some to see it giving the book less 'authority'. Liturgical Commission members welcomed it, however, since the notion of a single 'prayer book' is an Anglican distinctive. *BCP* (1549) was the first example in Christian history of one book containing all that was needed for public worship. *BCP* arose from the particular circumstances of the Church of England, and was made possible by the new technology of printing. That this tradition was formally left behind for Australian

Anglicans by the subtitle 'Liturgical Resources' marked a significant shift in self-understanding, indicating an openness to a diversity of liturgical resources.

The major exception to *APBA*'s acceptance was in the Diocese of Sydney. Early in the Synod debate, Bishop David Silk (Ballarat) persuaded members to allow Archbishop Harry Goodhew to work with him on a new eucharistic prayer.[25] The outcome – not supported by the Liturgical Commission – was voted into the book as the Third Thanksgiving in HC2. Wider issues were involved, but this new Thanksgiving prayer became the focus of contention in the Diocese of Sydney. When a motion for the *formal* acceptance of *APBA* came before its Sydney Synod in October 1995, it was phrasing in the Third Thanksgiving that saw the motion fail narrowly. The following motion, however, allowed parishes to request the Archbishop to permit its use – a *material* acceptance of *APBA*. Some four dozen parishes took up this opportunity.

APBA: from uniformity to coherent diversity

Behind the formal rejection of *APBA* by Sydney's synod lay this question: does *APBA* conform to the Constitution of the Anglican Church of Australia? Paragraph 4 of Part I, the 'Ruling Principles', enshrines *BCP* (1662) as

> the authorised standard of worship and doctrine in this Church, and no alteration in or permitted variations from the services or Articles therein contained shall contravene any principle of doctrine or worship laid down in such standard.

The national Church thus has limited room to move when it comes to new questions. Elsewhere in the Anglican Communion, including the Church of England, canons have been adopted that allow for greater flexibility. What then of Australia? To consider the issues further, attention needs to be given to the period before 1962, when Australian Anglicans took on their own identity, distinct from the 'mother' Church of England.

---

25 The 'parallel' discussions were initiated by the General Secretary, Bruce Kaye, and the Deputy Chair of Committees, Peter Young (Newcastle), who believed that without them the Synod would fracture, and the book fail. Bishop Bruce Wilson (seen as 'neutral') chaired the group, which included Archbishop Harry Goodhew and Bishop David Silk.

As Minutes Secretary, I received the resulting text from the group after dinner time on the Tuesday; the Commission met until 10.40pm to edit it to conform to the principles under which it worked. (It was particularly unhappy about the Synod considering a eucharistic prayer which had never been tested or prayed.) I handed the revision to Bishop David Silk early the next morning, with "fellowship strained but unbroken" (as I wrote in my *Church Scene* coverage). The 'parallel' group continued to work behind the scenes all day Wednesday: a final text was submitted to the Liturgical Commission chair, Lawrence Bartlett, after dinner. Regrettably, the Synod voted to have the new Thanksgiving replace one based on the *Apostolic Tradition* of Hippolytus (but see pages 322-323 in this book).

The 'principle of uniformity'

Successive editions of the *Book of Common Prayer* from 1549 to 1662 were authorised by English sovereigns (Edward VI, Elizabeth I, James I and Charles II), to provide uniform "rites and ceremonies" across England and its "catholic and reformed" established Church. As 'Concerning the Service of the Church', the introduction to the 1552 book, states, "from henceforth all the whole Realm shall have but one Use" (i.e. the same set of services). This 'principle of uniformity' sought to let the land live "in godly peace and quietness", an understandable aim given the 15C Wars of the Roses, the 16C persecution of Catholic and Protestant in turn, and the 17C Civil War. The modern notions of more than one church in a place, or diverse patterns of worship, was inconceivable. Church and state were indivisible: *eius regio, cuius religio* (location determines religious practice) was taken for granted on all sides. Christian liturgical practice was inseparable from political allegiance.

Elizabeth I and James I exercised some prudence as regards the toleration of those who resisted the imposition of *BCP*. Charles I's attempt to impose a version of *BCP* on Scotland in 1637, however, was seen by the Scots as tyranny.[26] A major factor in the outbreak of the two English Civil Wars and King Charles' eventual execution, it fostered the Puritans' exodus to found the North American colonies of New England. During the Commonwealth (1647–1661), bishops were rejected along with the monarchy, and *BCP* was outlawed, though Oliver Cromwell allowed its covert use.

Tragically, the Restoration of the monarchy, bishops and *BCP* under Charles II in 1661–2 was accompanied by the 'Clarendon Code'. This applied the 'principle of uniformity' harshly: some 2000 'Dissenting' clergy were ejected from the Church of England, and the Code saw the persecution of Dissenters, notably John Bunyan, until the 'Glorious Revolution' of 1689, when 'constitutional monarchy' was accepted by William and Mary. This allowed some freedom of public worship in England, but the Test Act (1672) continued to exclude Dissenters and Roman Catholics from the universities, Civil Service and Parliament until the Reform Acts of the 1830s.

---

26 The established Church of Scotland is Presbyterian; the Scottish Episcopal Church, much fewer in number, is independent of the state. Its *BCP* largely continued the 1637 book, based on 1549 rather than 1552, on which 1662 is based. The Scottish *BCP*, lightly amended, was adopted in 1784 by the Protestant Episcopal Church in the USA (now The Episcopal Church), and in churches arising from its missionary work. There have thus been two *BCP* traditions in the Anglican Communion since 1637.

In the 1927–28 debates, and in the lead-up to *AAPB*, doctrinal debate among Australian Anglicans often reflected the differences between these two traditions: see the relevant chapters in Charles Hefling & Cynthia Shattuck (edd), *The Oxford Guide to the Book of Common Prayer. A Worldwide Survey* (Oxford: OUP, 2006). This superb volume considers all modern prayer books, not just *BCP*.

Corresponding to this political stiffness, minimal variation is allowed in *BCP* (1662). In Morning and Evening Prayer an 'anthem' may be sung – adding hymns and metrical psalms began a century later – and a little choice is allowed in the prayers read. In Holy Communion, the minister can announce banns and official notices, read an Exhortation (from three options, rarely used) and has a choice of offertory sentences and two post-communion prayers. All else is specified. Even fewer variations are permitted in pastoral services.

To contemporary minds, this inflexibility is intolerable, even 'unAnglican'. Those who see 'tolerance' and 'inclusiveness' as marking the Anglican tradition do not know their history. But until recent decades, few saw this lack of flexibility as problematic. Indeed, *BCP*'s memorable words, spiritual depth and doctrinal consistency were evidenced as its enduring worth, sustaining 'common prayer' for English-speaking Christians. It was taken into colonies and mission fields in the Caribbean, India, Africa, Canada, Asia and Australasia.

But the 'principle of uniformity', intended to bring harmony to a dislocated island realm, saw *BCP* become an instrument of colonial power as well as spiritual resource. Its services were translated into local languages, but little cultural adaptation took place until after World War II, when former colonies emerged into modern nations.

– and its demise

The Church of South India (CSI) formed from Anglican and other churches in April 1947, a month after India became independent from Britain. The Lambeth Conference met a year later, but failed to recognise CSI as part of the Anglican Communion, since all clergy from CSI's former churches had been accepted, some of whom had not been ordained by a bishop (all future ones have been).[27] But this exclusion freed the new church from the 'principle of uniformity'. Led by scholars of the calibre of Bishops Azariah and Stephen Neill, it proceeded to shape its own forms of worship. These drew on its local ecumenical heritage and the wider Liturgical Movement, notably adopting the 'four-fold shape' for the Eucharist, but continued to use 'thee/thy' English, though only in 1985 would elements of Indian culture be taken up officially.

In English-speaking nations of the developing Anglican Communion, the ongoing use of *BCP* brought a strong sense of communion in culture as well as faith with the Church of England. World War I led to fundamental changes in western societies, including sharp declines in church attendance, and awareness of the growing

---

27 That said, Lambeth 1948 Resolutions 52–55 specify that hospitality is to be given to all CSI clergy and people, and look forward to the time when it would be a full member of the Communion. CSI bishops have participated in Lambeth Conferences from the 1978 meeting.

gap between church and society, especially in the 'working classes' of the cities. Yet until the 1960s, debate about prayer book revision – in Australia as well as England and elsewhere – focussed on doctrinal differences, rather than on how best to perform the gospel as society changed.[28]

It was the genius of the Commission set up by the 1962 General Synod that its members interpreted the question put to them, "whether revision of the *Book of Common Prayer* was needed", as giving implicit permission to vary its text and rubrics, within the limits set by the Constitution. Evan Burge, in a lecture given soon after the publication of *APBA*, wrote

> The Liturgical Commission which produced *AAPB* in 1978 was adamant that it should not contain anything that others would find doctrinally offensive. It resisted pressures to include any prayer in order to gratify a particular party. If a dispute arose, it was resolved by returning to the judiciously balanced words of 1662.[29]

AAPB was to be a book that all Anglicans could use in good conscience. The changes made to *BCP* involved a move away from the 'principle of uniformity', but not from the Ruling Principles. The flexibility it introduced, most notably for intercessions, was motivated by the need for rites for an Australia very different from England in 1662. But the Church's doctrine was to be maintained without favour to any party.

A 'principle of coherent diversity'

The Liturgical Commission that drafted *APBA* took a similar approach to its work. *AAPB* had opened the doors to flexibility, and modern English had seen 'churchmanship' differences lessened, but not removed. Post-*AAPB* debates around gender issues, and the emergence of 'Sydney' understandings of 'church' and 'worship', saw new tensions arise, as the 1995 General Synod debate showed. But had that Synod

---

28 The 1988 Lambeth Conference, a decade after *AAPB*, passed a Resolution affirming the importance of culture and then this Resolution (47):

> *Liturgical Freedom.* This Conference resolves that each province should be free, subject to essential universal Anglican norms of worship, and to a valuing of traditional liturgical materials, to seek that expression of worship which is appropriate to its Christian people in their cultural context.

But the Conference did not spell out what is meant by "essential universal Anglican norms of worship". This was the focus of the 2005 *IALC* held in Prague. Its statement, 'Liturgy and Anglican Identity', outlines 'elements' and 'characteristics' that are 'valued'. This excellent resource raises many of the questions that Christians – not just Anglicans – face in seeking to offer authentic worship in today's culturally plural societies. It is available at https://anglicanliturgy.org/documents.

29 Evan Burge, "The Austin James Lecture (1995)", *Australian Journal of Liturgy* 5/1 (October 1995). Only once in *AAPB* was resort to *BCP*'s wording needed: the prayer over the water in Baptism remained, "Sanctify this water to the mystical washing away of sin".

not approved *APBA*, the liturgical life of many congregations would likely have developed in idiosyncratic and overly 'local' ways. Two decades and more on, that has happened in some places.

The Liturgical Commission for *APBA* believed that, well done, a new prayer book would foster coherence across an increasingly diverse Church. The chapters that follow here note issues raised in the various services, how they were resolved, and what this means for their use. **The 'principle of uniformity' thus gave way to a 'principle of coherent diversity'.**[30] It might run the risk of too many options being offered, but its aim is both to sustain and develop the heritage of *BCP* and the wider Christian tradition in performing the gospel in today's diverse Australian social contexts.

A note on terminology

'Minister' in *APBA*, following the usage of *BCP* and *AAPB*, means any Anglican communicant, ordained or not, authorised to take a public role in liturgy. Such ministers normally hold a 'license' from the bishop.

A congregational exercise: change at your local church

What is the situation in your home congregation? Here are some ideas for following up the ideas put forward in this chapter:

1. Talk with older parishioners who can remember Anglican services in Australia before 1977. Ask them to recall the pattern of a typical Sunday, the types of services, and the role of ministers and people. What differences do they see today?
2. Identify parishioners who have come from Christian traditions other than Anglican. (First check that they are happy to discuss this.) Ask them to describe the typical liturgical pattern of their previous adherence, and how similar or otherwise this is to the Anglican services they experience today.
3. Consider having a small group attend the main Sunday service in a neighbouring Anglican parish. What similarities or otherwise did the group find to your congregation's usual performance of the Gospel?
4. Looking back over these accounts, what stands out as being closely similar across the times and places encountered? Were there things that were very different and, if so, what do you believe the reasons are? What do you think these differences reflect about the gospel, culture, worship, circumstances of the occasion, people's tastes and so on? And how does this affect performing the gospel in church?

---

30 This term is my own: it was never identified or documented, but having participated in every meeting of the *APBA* Liturgical Commission, I believe that it represents a fair summary of how we worked.

What's next?

APBA is now a quarter-century old, but there seems to be little pressure for it to be further revised. The web more than the printed page will carry the future: *ePray* makes all the resources in *APBA* readily available, and on the General Synod website new resources are added regularly by the Liturgy Commission. A wide range of other liturgical resources is available online, whether from Anglican Provinces, other Christian traditions – notably Lutheran, Presbyterian and Roman Catholic – liturgy scholars, or idiosyncratic enthusiasts. Australian Anglicans in the third millennium are most unlikely to produce another 'prayer book': indeed, the Liturgy Commission recommended against this in its Report to the 2017 General Synod.[31]

Planning and leading a service today is more like directing, producing and playing a lead in a drama in which all present have parts. But Christian worship is far more than a 'concert' in which just a few perform 'on stage' (see *Performing the Gospel*). A modern-day analogy would be to view liturgy planning as designing a 'role playing' game that enables all members of Christ to participate in performing the Gospel, in liturgy and lifestyle.

What then are the key features and themes of *APBA*? And how do they affect the way Australian Anglicans worship "not only with their lips, but in their lives"? That is the subject of the next chapter.

---

[31] This Report lists an exciting range of projects, from wider resources for use with *APBA* to pastoral rites in more accessible English: see https://www.anglican.org.au/general-synod-sessions, Book 4.

Further reading

Burge, Evan, "*A Prayer Book for Australia* – a watershed for Australian Anglicans. The Austin James Lecture 1995", *Australian Journal of Liturgy* 5/1 (October 1995)

Earey, Mark, *Beyond Common Worship. Anglican Identity and Liturgical Diversity* (London: SCM, 2013): Chapter Four explores liturgical challenges in the Church of England in the wake of *Common Worship* (2000)

Galbraith, Douglas (ed.), *Worship in the Wide Red Land* (Melbourne: JBCE, 1981): essays on liturgy in Australian contexts for lay leaders of the Uniting Church

IALC, *Liturgy and Anglican Identity* (2005). The Prague Statement, available at https://anglicanliturgy.org/documents

Kaye, Bruce (ed), *Anglicanism in Australia. A History* (Melbourne: Melbourne University Press, 2002), especially Chapters One and Six

Neill, Stephen, *Anglicanism* (Harmondsworth: Penguin, 1966): a still relevant classic

Richardson, David, "*A Prayer Book for Australia:* Historical Background", in Ronald Dowling, David Richardson and Gilliam Varcoe (edd), *A Prayer Book for Australia. A Practical Commentary* (Alexandria: EJ Dwyer, 1997)

Sherlock, Charles, "The Anglican Church of Australia", in Charles Hefling & Cynthia Shattuck (edd), *The Oxford Guide to the Book of Common Prayer. A Worldwide Survey* (Oxford: OUP, 2006) 324–332

Sinden, Gilbert, *When we Meet for Worship. A manual for using An Australian Prayer Book 1978* (Adelaide: Lutheran Publishing House, 1978): a still useful *tour de force*

Chapter Two

APBA – *coherent diversity for common prayer*

A 'principle of coherent diversity' undergirds *APBA*, rather than *BCP*'s 'principle of uniformity': that is the argument made in Chapter One. In making this shift, the Liturgical Commission worked within the 'Ruling Principles' of our Constitution, as recognised by *APBA* being "authorised by General Synod", the book's 'formal' authority. What then of its 'material' authority, its actual contents, text and rubrics?

How does the 'principle of coherent diversity' sustain common prayer among Australian Anglicans in the post-modern cultural air that western Christians breathe today? Two strategies are adopted in *APBA*: coherent diversities of **language**, and of service **structure**: both have wider application across the body of Christ as a whole.[1]

Coherent diversity of language

A 'common words' strategy

Only 50 or so years ago, nearly all the words in a service, beyond readings and sermon, were the same for English-speakers across the Anglican Communion. All shared a similar vocabulary and experience of worship, reinforced by the *King James Bible* being the dominant English version in use. But by the late twentieth century, 'olde English' had become less and less familiar. Having identical words across all congregations made sense in past ages: today it belongs to history.

How then is common prayer supported through language? One strategy is to have **common words** for elements of Christian identity – the Lord's Prayer, Apostles' and Nicene Creeds, Gloria and familiar psalms, and responses such as "Lift up your hearts! / **We lift them to the Lord!**" The *English Language Liturgical Consultation (ELLC)* has issued a range of ecumenically agreed modern-language texts, many of which are used in *APBA*.[2] Deeply familiar words embrace worshippers in mind and spirit: they become 'heart-felt', enabling *Praying Together*, the title of *ELLC*'s work.

---

1   *Performing the Gospel* Chapter Nine sets these issues against a wider background.
2   See Notes 1 and 2 in the full edition of *APBA*, pages 820–822.
    Praying Together is available at http://englishtexts.org/Portals/11/Assets/praying.pdf

But this does not resolve all the issues. In particular, agreement on the wording of the Lord's Prayer is yet to be found. Roman Catholics and some Protestants continue to use a 'traditional' form—'Our Father, which / who art in heaven …', though with different pronouns and ending ('doxology').[3] Most Anglicans and mainline Protestants, however, use the *ELLC* version, 'Our Father in heaven …', though 'Save us for the time of trial' sometimes stays as 'Lead us not into temptation' (in the Church of England, for example). The wider public, however, is likely to only know a 'traditional' form, if at all. So at a civic service or funeral, or when different Christian traditions meet together, a useful practice is to encourage people to pray using the version with which they are most familiar (whether in English or otherwise). Indeed, such disciplined variety models undue uniformity being imposed, while sustaining the sense of praying together in heart and mind.

Language in liturgy: from *BCP* to *AAPB* and *APBA*

Worship, whether in liturgy or lifestyle, involves far more than words, but it is nigh impossible to do without them. Speaking of or to God touches on profound mystery: it lies at the limits of human expression.[4] But unless the language of liturgy is accessible to worshippers, it cannot do its job. Many people told the Liturgical Commission that 'prayer book' words are too complex, while others said that language in church should retain a sense of dignity. The Commission also heard from people who disliked flexibility and wanted more 'direct' language and structures; some for whom gender-inclusive language was a major concern; a few who sought a return to 'thee / thy' forms; and groups looking for other than English language rites.[5] The challenge is to find language which is meaningful for today's varied Australians, but stretches us to transcend the words employed.

BCP used the same 'court register' throughout, as did the *King James Bible*.[6] But the language of these classic texts functions in more subtle ways than their uniformity of

---

3 *BCP* has 'Our Father which art in heaven' (implying that the Father is 'at least' personal, i.e. more than 'a person'); 'them' rather than 'those' who trespass against us; and ends "for thine is the kingdom, the power and the glory". Roman Catholics use 'who' and 'those', with the ending (in the Eucharist, after a response), "for the kingdom, the power and the glory are yours".

4 *Performing the Gospel* Chapter Four considers issues around how words work as 'sacraments of meaning', with fuller discussion of the place of gendered and military language in liturgy.

5 As the official language of Australia, and the most commonly used, English is the only living language used in *APBA*. Following Article XXIV (*APBA* page 830), other languages are not only permitted when English is not understood by those present, but required. *APBA* services in have been translated into Indigenous languages, as well as Chinese, Japanese, Vietnamese and Tamil amongst others.

6 On the deliberate 'Jacobean' (rather than 'everyday') register of *KJB*, see Adam Nicholson, *Power and Glory* (London: Harper Perennial, 2003) Chapter Ten.

style might suggest. In particular, they were written to be *heard* rather than read – one reason for their being so memorable. Many phrases in *BCP* are repeated using variations of metaphor or imagery, as in the Psalter, with its frequent 'parallelism' in verses. This has the benefit for hearers that, if one does not immediately catch what was said, the repetition offers a second chance. And the pairing of metaphors allows a 'conversation' between them, thus avoiding simplistic ideas and offering deeper insights into God's truth. So in Morning and Evening Prayer the congregation is invited "to *acknowledge* and *confess* our manifold *sins* and *wickedness*," and later the minister prays, "Fulfil now, O Lord, the *desires* and *petitions* of thy servants". None of the words in these pairs are exact equivalents: 'sins' tends to focus on individual behaviour, whereas 'wickedness' is typical of communal life. Again, while 'desires' relates to our inner selves, 'petitions' involve outward expression. Such combinations have both aural and semantic advantages, though they can seem repetitious to us moderns.

AAPB employed what some have called a 'staff common room' register: clear modern English, with occasional excitements (e.g. the post-communion prayer 'Father, when we were still far off'). Many of the language-pairs of *BCP* were pruned in *AAPB*, while reaction against authoritarian social structures grew in favour of participatory ones. The dominant use in *BCP* of terms like 'Almighty' was felt to set God unduly apart from human beings, for example. To balance this, as noted earlier, dozens of new prayers in *AAPB* address God simply as 'Father', thus increasing the proportion of male imagery for God, just as this was emerging as an issue for English-speakers.

Gendered language in liturgy

Divine names

The scriptures use an astonishingly wide range of metaphors and images to describe God, and God's work. Consider those used by Melchizedek ("El 'Elyon: God Most High', Genesis 14.19–20); Abram ('Shield', Genesis 15.1; "El Shaddai: God Almighty', Genesis 17.1, also used by Isaac and Jacob); Abraham ('God of the heavens', Genesis 24.7); Hagar ("El Roi: God who sees', Genesis 16.13); David ('LORD of hosts', 1 Samuel 17.45); Daniel ('Ancient of Days', Daniel 7.9,13) as well as by the prophets of Israel ('Holy One', 'Redeemer', 'Mighty One of Israel'). Yet the meaning of the divine Name revealed to Moses (Exodus 3.15), YHWH, remains unknown: no naming can contain God.[7]

---

7 'Lord' or 'GOD' is used in *BCP* for YHWH. When a Jewish reader encounters this term, out of respect he or she sounds *'adonai*, 'sovereign'. Before the time of Jesus, no vowels were provided in Hebrew: so when vowels were later added to YHWH, those for *'adonai* were used, leading to the mistaken rendering 'Jehovah' in the *King James Bible*. Modern versions in this tradition, such as the *NRSV*, use 'LORD'.

Most liturgical traditions, however, use but a small sample of those available. As noted above, regal images for God predominate in *BCP,* as in the First Testament, especially the Psalms. This partly undergirded, partly relativised, the social context of Tudor and Stuart England. To address God as "King of kings, Lord of lords, the only ruler of princes" was both relevant to the times, and also made the point that earthly kings, especially those claiming to rule by 'divine right', are accountable to *the* King.

All these are masculine images, however, supplemented by a few non-personal ones, notably 'Light' and 'Rock'. As Lawrence Bartlett noted in the Preface to ***APBA***, inclusive language was of major concern to the Liturgical Commission. Adjusting words about human beings (e.g. avoiding 'man' used generically) raised few challenges, but translating the Psalter posed sharp questions, notably the frequency of masculine pronouns used for God.

The Psalter

Commission members examined thirteen different translations of the Psalms, seeking to find one that was a) appropriate for liturgical use, b) able to be readily said or sung, and c) respected inclusive language issues. On the first two points, it found that the ***Liturgical Psalter*** included in ***AAPB*** was the best available: it therefore requested its editors to prepare a new version which took the third point into account. After protracted negotiations with the Commission's Chair, and some public discussion, they agreed to do so.[8] However, whether the work would be completed in time for inclusion in the draft book remained in doubt: it was completed less than a month before General Synod was scheduled to meet. In case it did not eventuate, Evan Burge, who had portfolio responsibility for the Psalter, drafted most of a new translation: it is his version that is used for psalms elsewhere in ***APBA*** than the ***Liturgical Psalter***.

A condition of including the revised Psalter was that this acknowledgment must be included when a psalm from it was reproduced, typically on service sheets:

From *The Psalms: New Inclusive-Language Version* © English text 1976, 1977, © 'inclusive language' version 1995 David L. Frost, John A. Emerton, Andrew A. Macintosh, all rights reserved.[9]

Copyright normally belongs to the publisher of a work, in this case HarperCollins. When the 'inclusive language' version was issued, HarperCollins released its

---

8   See Charles Sherlock, "Language Catholic and Reformed: a response to David Frost", *Australian Church Union*, October 1992, recording an ACU-sponsored public meeting at Ridley College.

9   See General Note 8 (***APBA*** page x) and the statement in the Acknowledgements (page 847), "One psalm only may be reproduced on a non-commercial basis for single occasions, within the guidelines for reproduction from this book."

copyright on *The Liturgical Psalter* to the three editors. In 2000, when electronic production of *APBA* was in train, leading to *ePray*, the editors eased these copyright and reproduction restrictions. So Note 8 in *ePray* states about the Psalter,

> It is the work of David Frost, John Emerton and Andrew MacIntosh, to whom HarperCollins have released the copyright. The authors have generously given permission for this Psalter to be used in the Australian Anglican edition of *ePray*.

As a result, psalms from *The Liturgical Psalter* in *APBA* may now be reproduced without restriction (while respecting the integrity of the translation).[10]

But the use of inclusive language in the Psalter continues to pose significant challenges for English-speaking Christian traditions.[11] As Evan Burge wrote,

> In the revised *Liturgical Psalter*, there are many occurrences of the pronoun he / him / his referring to God – more than the Liturgical Commission would have wished. Most can be justified on the grounds of accurate, or literal, translation. Outside the *Liturgical Psalter*, [in *APBA*] masculine pronouns referring to God are avoided whenever possible. This is why the Psalms in the Daily Offices and Occasional Services are not always identical with those in the Psalter.[12]

The Report of the Liturgy Commission to the 2017 General Synod recommended that a new translation of the Psalter be prepared.

Gender and God

So what *does* *APBA* do with masculine images for God?[13] That these are overwhelmingly employed in the scriptures is not contested, nor is the reality that the eternal Word of God was incarnate as a male human (evidenced primarily by Jesus being circumcised). But these realities do not close the discussion.

After careful consideration, the Commission made no changes to the way God is spoken of in sentences from the scriptures. In prayers whose heritage is from *BCP*, royal, family and impersonal metaphors continue to be employed (notably Lord, Father and Light). The classical Christian naming of God as "Father, Son and Spirit"

---

10   The Acknowledgements (page 847) statement thus no longer applies.
11   A Liturgical Psalter prepared in 1995 by the (Roman Catholic) *International Council on English in the Liturgy* adopted some inclusive language strategies. Initially it received an *imprimatur* (authorisation) for liturgical use, but this was withdrawn in 1998.
12   Evan Burge, Austin James Lecture (1995), Note 41.
13   There is a large literature on this topic. My contributions include "Gendered Language in Corporate Worship", *Australian Journal of Liturgy* 1/3 (1988) 84–94; *God on the Inside: Trinitarian Spirituality* (Melbourne: Acorn, 1991) Chapters Five to Nine; *Words and the Word*, Chapter Six; and *The Doctrine of Humanity* (Leicester/ Downers Grove: IVP, 1996) Appendix II.

is retained, but also varied, for example in some Daily Morning and Evening Prayer psalm prayers, and a few blessings (e.g. pages 221–222).[14] But the frequency of masculine pronouns referring to God was reduced in comparison to *BCP* and *AAPB*, though removing them was beyond the Liturgical Commission's scope and ability.[15]

APBA employs a much wider range of images for God than *BCP* or *AAPB*. This can be seen in the opening of many prayers, especially in seasonal material, Occasional Prayers, and pastoral services. As Evan Burge summarizes,

> We find God addressed not only as almighty and everlasting but also as life-giving, righteous, bountiful, generous, loving, caring, gentle, forgiving and many more. Prayers with feminine imagery for God are introduced as optional alternatives, notably about twenty Collects by Janet Morley from her book *All Desires Known*.[16] Some will find that these prayers add greatly to the sensitivity and intimacy of the worship. Others, who find them alienating or unsuited to public worship, will not have to use them. Perhaps some men who feel discomfort may gain insight into how many women have felt when exposed only to the traditional male-dominated images of the past.

A less obvious feature is the care taken in combining images for God. Many are linked with God's power, notably the Abrahamic *'El Shaddai* (Genesis 17.1), traditionally rendered 'God Almighty' in English and 'Almighty God' in prayers. On the other hand, Jesus initiated the practice of disciples addressing God as 'our Father', shown in the retention of the Aramaic *'Abba*, 'father', among Greek speaking churches (Romans 8.15, Galatians 4.6, and most significantly, Mark 14.36). In *BCP* and *AAPB*, these two ranges of imagery are often combined, typically as 'Almighty Father'. However, this bringing together of power and paternal imagery, *which appears nowhere in the scriptures*, undergirds 'patriarchy', systems of human organisation which privilege men over women. In *APBA*, both power and paternal imagery for God is used – but they are not combined.[17]

---

14 For further discussion, see pages 117–118 in this book.

15 *A personal note.* On study leave from Ridley College, in 1982 I was a Research Fellow at Yale Divinity School, where serious discussion of gender and Christian theology was under way. One personal outcome was ceasing to use masculine pronouns for God, in ways which did not draw attention to this.

16 Evan Burge notes that these prayers "have been used with generous permission of the author. Understandably, she was unwilling to accept the numerous 'improvements' that were proposed."

17 Two possible exceptions come in ecumenically agreed texts. In the 'Hymn of Praise' (*APBA* pages 53, 85, 115, 121, 179), the fourth line is "almighty God and Father". In the Nicene Creed (pages 103, 123, 170) a comma was introduced in the second line, so that it reads "We believe in one God, the Father, the Almighty", thus putting the Christian and Abrahamic naming of the one God in parallel.

Feminine images of God and of God's work was a sensitive issue in the 1995 General Synod debate over **APBA**. In the draft book, Additional Canticle #9 from Julian of Norwich began "God chose to be our mother in all things" (page 427), and went on to speak of Christ's work in maternal terms: it was excluded by the Synod. 'A Thanksgiving for Australia' (#3 on **APBA** page 218), composed by Lenore Parker, an Aboriginal Anglican, includes reference to 'Mother Earth'. This was contested in the Synod, but when its meaning for Indigenous Christians was explained, the objection was withdrawn.[18] Examples of divine feminine imagery remain in **APBA**, where scriptural evidence supports it. So God's work is compared to a mother's care (Isaiah 66.13), as is Jesus' heartbreak over Jerusalem (Matthew 23.37), while 'Wisdom' is portrayed in Proverbs and elsewhere as a woman doing God's creative work. Such biblical usage is taken up in a few prayers in **APBA** (e.g. #1 on page 46), and in Additional Canticles #6, #7 (pages 428–429).

No doubt the conservate approach taken in **APBA** to divine gendered imagery will disappoint some. Even so, that, on the basis of the scriptures, the door was opened at all is significant. The General Synod debate was a good example of how **APBA** takes up new learning while being consistent with the Constitution, and is a useful example of the shift from 'uniformity' to 'coherent diversity'.

Four styles – one book

This shift is clearly seen in the variety of language styles employed in **APBA**. When the Commission began its work, it was assumed that a single modern style would continue, similar to that employed in **AAPB**. Responses to 'trial use' services, however, questioned whether this could work for all Australians. Four distinct linguistic registers emerged as different services were drafted and revised. Such 'coherent diversity' moves well away from the uniformity of language style in **BCP** and **AAPB**.[19]

Book of Common Prayer style

BCP (1662) has given a classical tone to much English language. The works of Jane Austen, Agatha Christie, T.S. Eliot, Manning Clark, Dorothy L. Sayers and more are shot through with phrases from it and the **King James Bible**. Though less familiar today, this style continues in **APBA**, especially in First Order services. It has three broad characteristics, related to the fact that **BCP** was written for 'clerks' to read the service aloud to people who generally could not read.

---

18 See pages 120–127 in this book.

19 **BCP** could be thought of as essentially 'pre-modern', **AAPB** as culturally 'modern' and **APBA** as typically 'post-modern' in its acceptance of diversity, though coherent: **APBA** is far from the 'anything goes' ethos associated by some with post-modernity.

1. Sentences are generally long, divided by commas and semi-colons to mark breathing points rather than grammar. For people used to hearing rather than reading, such sentences and punctuation work well.
2. There is significant repetition, to assist hearing and deepen meaning. This lends a distinct 'feel' to *BCP* language, which those who love it miss in the terser rhythms of modern language. This repetition remains in **APBA** First Order services, though reduced somewhat: see #4 (page 4) for example.
3. Relative clauses, beginning with who / which, are used a great deal: "our Father *which* art in heaven" is a familiar example. "Almighty and everlasting God, *who* alone workest great marvels ..." is another. This style suggests a descriptive rather than definitive naming of God, and evokes a sense of respectful 'distance' between creatures and our Creator. It undergirds an ethos – typically English – of understatement and objectivity.

For examples of this *BCP* style in **APBA**, see #18–21 on pages 13–16.

Modern English (AAPB) style

Given text messaging, tweeting and the like, many Australians today find long sentences hard to follow, and the *BCP* 'say it twice' habit confusing. In **AAPB,** especially in Second Order/Form services, these features were reduced, but 'who' clauses often became 'you' clauses: the metaphor is unchanged, but the grammar shifts from the third to the second person. Thus "Almighty and everlasting God, *who* alone workest great marvels," became "... *you* alone work great marvels ...". *Describing* God became *address to* God, a change today felt as more personal than the more 'objective' tone of *BCP.*

Such a 'modern English' pattern continues in **APBA**, especially in the Prayers for Various Occasions. This 'you' rather than 'who' style is also employed in some canticles, to avoid an overly 'objective' feel, and the multiplication of masculine pronouns for God.[20] Notable examples are the Song of Mary and the Song of Zechariah: compare the versions on pages 9 and 31 (third person) and page 425 (second person).

'Direct' style

Several books of prayers in modern 'terse' styles have been published in recent years: Janet Morley's ***All Desires Known*** has already been mentioned.[21] These typically use

---

20 As Evan Burge, in Austin James Lecture (1995) note 41 states:
In Hebrew, God can be praised in both the second and the third person with little or no apparent difference in effect. There are many examples of alternation between the two in the Psalms; for instance, Psalm 104.6-15. Even Psalm 23 contains such a switch from 'he' to 'you' at verse 3. For purposes of worship in modern English, many psalms can be translated inclusively by replacing 'he/him' by 'you'.
21 A decade after **AAPB**, the Church of England's *Patterns of Worship* (London: Church House, 1989) broke new ground with rites wholly in 'direct' style, notably 'A Service of the Word'.

brief sentences, direct and bold metaphors. Some speak to the highly literate; others appeal to people with less formal education.

In *APBA*, direct style is notably evident in shorter sentences. Punctuation is affected, too: First Orders aside, full stops and commas are the most frequent punctuation, with colons used sparingly (apart from the Psalms, where they have a special function), and semi-colons rarely. Unlike *BCP*, punctuation in *APBA* follows the rules of English grammar and syntax, rather than indicating breathing points. On the other hand, care was taken with the lineation of prayers, so that their structure can be readily seen on the printed page, and so they can more easily be read aloud.

Thanksgiving 5 of Holy Communion (Second Order) is a good example of 'direct' style. Many prayers take up aspects of this style, some through the images employed (e.g. prayers #3, #17, #25 of Occasional Prayers, pages 202–217), others through their verbs (e.g. #29, #30, #38) or brevity (#6, #49).

NB: it might be expected that 'direct' style is used in 'Prayer, Praise and Proclamation'. This employs modern (*AAPB*) *language*, however, while adopting a direct *structure*, in which few alternatives are offered.

Intimate style

A felt need for intimacy in some official texts was a growing trend in the 1970s. In some situations 'objective' language may not work well: a more personal or speaking style is needed. Intimate language can be appropriate not only in prayers, but in scripture sentences offered for use, and in affirmations of personal faith.

Intimate language is notably found in *APBA* in 'Ministry with the Dying' (e.g. page 697), and 'Funeral for an Infant who has died near the Time of Birth' (e.g. #11 on page 763). But aspects of this style are also found elsewhere.

Coherent diversity of language: some exercises

APBA contains a range of language styles because no one style fits every situation. The challenge for ministers is to sense the style that best enables divine worship for those present on a particular occasion. Beyond the words themselves, how they are spoken matters: rushed reading, putting on a 'churchy' accent, sounding uninterested or being inaudible all get in the way of good communication. Words spoken 'in church' need to be consonant with the way we speak and communicate in daily life, using language that enlivens, and does not demean others.

These exercises are best done in a group setting, including those who regularly engage in ministries that involve using words in services. Though the focus is on language in liturgy, the exercises also apply to the way we use words in daily life.

1. In what way(s) do you think language factors affect how prayer is made 'real' in corporate worship? Here are some examples:
   sentence length, repetition of metaphors, 'who' or 'you' grammar,
   layout of lines, combining images of God's work
2. Look up some of the prayers in *APBA* noted above, and compare them with others on the pages around them.
   What styles, metaphors and grammar do you see at work?
   Some may speak more to you than others. Can you say why this might be so?
3. How might language factors apply to different occasions?
   Here are some examples: 8am Holy Communion, a healing service,
     Sung Eucharist, 'Messy church', a youth celebration, a baptism
   What factors might need to be adapted for different congregations?
4. How do language factors apply to intercessions prepared by parishioners?

Coherent diversity and structure

The 'principle of coherent diversity' has been traced in terms of language, the 'micro' level of liturgy. What of the 'macro' level, the structure of services? A familiar structure helps us sense 'where we are' in a service, allowing for flexibility without losing its overall shape. Yet it can be taken so badly that everyone is lost, and little if any structure can be detected. Too many (or too few) directions, chatty comments, omissions without warning and so on are typical. But there is a better way.

Scholars have come to see that a flexible shared structure for Sunday services can help sustain common prayer across diverse churches. This development can be seen through the use of headings. Each *BCP* service has an unvarying structure, so no headings are needed. When *AAPB* was being drafted, a few headings were introduced so people knew when something different from *BCP* was coming up. Most headings were needed in what became *AAPB*'s most used service, Holy Communion (Second Order). This brought together the three services that *BCP* rubrics specified were to be taken together on Sundays: Morning Prayer, the Litany, and Holy Communion. Using all three together had not happened for generations: Morning Prayer and Holy Communion were celebated as distinct services, and the Litany used only occasionally.

The 1969 Liturgical Commission report *Prayer Book Revision in Australia* included 'A Modern Liturgy', which folded *BCP*'s three rites back together. Tightened and smoothed in two stages, *Australia '69* and *'73*, this became Holy Communion (Second Order) in *AAPB*. Headings were needed to guide participants in the new structure, the beginnings of a shift towards services with a shared shape.

Classical liturgical shapes

Two basic patterns have emerged in western Christian traditions, complemented by 'rites of passage' patterns of human behaviour identified in cultural anthropology.[22]

Office and eucharistic shapes

The first shape derives from daily Morning and Evening Prayer – the 'office' shape. On Sundays, such a 'Service of the Word' often begins with confession and absolution, includes a creed and prayers, and is typically followed by a sermon. From the people's point of view, the climax towards which this shape moves is preaching.

The second is the 'eucharistic' shape, with two main parts. The Ministry of the Word, responded to in creed, sermon, and intercessions, forms the 'synaxis' or 'ante-communion'. It leads into the second part, the Lord's Supper.[23] These two parts are sometimes spoken of as 'two tables' – the table of the Word and the table of the Lord – or (as Augustine of Hippo loved to say) the Word 'audible' (heard) and 'visible' (seen). From the people's point of view, the climax towards which this shape moves is receiving communion.

A significant difference between these two shapes is the way the scriptures are heard. Instruction in and meditation upon them is to the fore in the 'office'; biblically grounded gospel proclamation in the eucharist. These two approaches are not opposed, but complementary, as the images of the two tables, the Word heard and seen, imply.

Pilgrimage and liminality

Some services do not quite 'fit' neatly into either shape, however – weddings and funerals for example, or community services like Anzac or Remembrance Day. A third structure from the Christian tradition that serves well here is 'pilgrimage', in which participants journey together from one place to another, whether literally or symbolically.

Insights from 'rites of passage / liminality' analysis in cultural anthropology tie in with this. When facing major life-changes, we humans tend to do so in three stages. A group 'separates' from regular life, to cross a significant boundary or threshold (*limen*) in safety, before resuming daily living as people 're-incorporated' into a renewed identity. For example, marriage rites can be seen overall as a process of engagement (separation), wedding (*limen*) and honeymoon (re-incorporation), and the wedding service itself by the couple making separate entrances; exchanging vows; and exiting together.

---

22 For fuller discussion, see *Performing the Gospel* Chapter Nine, which offers a range of practical ideas for each of the five 'sections' of Sunday services (see below).

23 Holy Communion Outline Order (*APBA* page 813) shows this structure on a single page.

Rites of passage analysis is particularly helpful in planning events that relate to birth, maturity, marriage and death (whether individual or communal). A clear example is the Funeral Service in **APBA.** At a macro level it offers a 'vigil' (pages 708-9); funeral (pages 712-729, itself in pilgrimage shape); and burial or interment (pages 730-737). In this way typical human responses to grief and the gospel of Christ's life-transforming ministry are performed in ways that seek to respect and integrate both truths (see 'For the congregation', page 711).

The shape of God's mission in liturgy

The mission of God and liturgy

But what might the best shape for a typical Sunday service look like? After research and creative reflection by scholars and churches, wide agreement is found across the western Christian world to this outline: ***gather, listen, pray, do, go.***

Behind this structure lies the conviction that it corresponds to the 'shape' of the mission of God, beginning with the Old Covenant ('First Testament') described in Exodus. The people of God, ***gathered*** by God at Sinai to ***listen*** to the words of the covenant, to offer three-dimensional ***prayers*** of dedication and well-being ('peace') offerings (Exodus 20.18-26; 23.14-19), to ***celebrate*** the covenant and ***live it out*** in fairness (Exodus 21.1-22.27; 23.1-9) and in harmony with the land (Exodus 23.10): this was Israel's calling, their 'worship' of God as "a people consecrated to me" (Exodus 23.31).

A similar shape undergirds the New Covenant. Jesus called people to ***gather*** as disciples, to ***listen*** to his teaching, and to follow his example of ***prayer*** and holy living. He assured them of his living presence as they obeyed his command to "***do this*** for my remembrance", and commissioned them to ***go out*** into all the world. This remains the basic shape for all Christian worship, whether in life-style or liturgy. It begins with God's call, attends to God's Word, responds in prayer and action and issues in our being sent out to perform the gospel. In short, it is the shape of God's mission.

Each of the five parts matters. But trying to make each as significant as the others in any one service is likely to lead to spiritual indigestion. Each occasion, no matter how 'regular', calls for varying emphasis on different parts. In a service that includes baptism, for example, the gathering can include introducing the candidate and sponsors, and the 'doing' will be the natural focus. But the prayers can be minimal (e.g. ***APBA*** page 56), trusting that baptism itself is a way of bringing all of life before God.

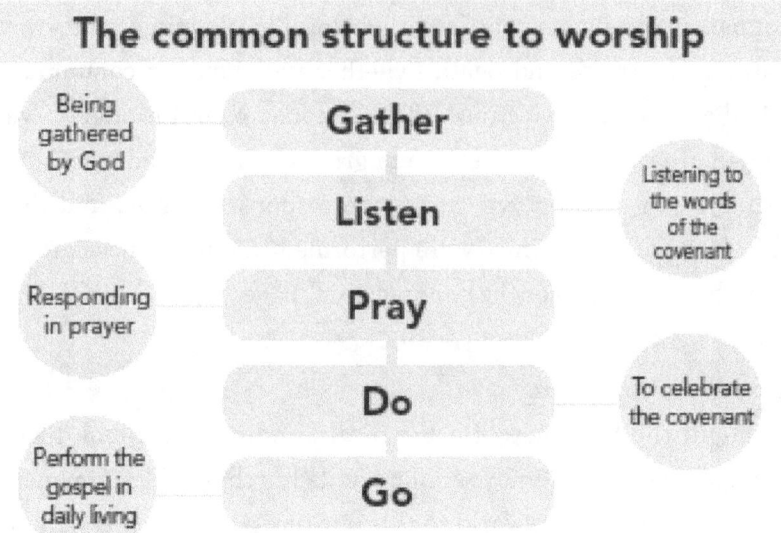

This structure is not the only one possible for Christian worship.[24] But since it is based on the shape of God's mission, a Sunday service without each of these elements would be significantly impoverished. As week by week passes, this common structure shapes the perfomance of the gospel in ways that promote 'common prayer', adapted flexibly to different needs, times and circumstances. Behind this concept of a five-part shape is the importance of disciplined flexibility: like playing an accordion, it only works by being expanded and contracted. So it is with liturgy in the shape of God's mission. As each part is expanded and contracted in relation to the context, the Spirit breathes all the more among those present.

What's in a heading?

Many modern prayer books have adopted this 'gather / listen / pray / do / go' structure.[25] It is evident in *APBA*'s Sunday services, the outcome of the Liturgical Commission's commitment to a 'principle of coherent diversity'. Each of the five sections is explored in the commentaries on services in later chapters.

What heading should be used for the first part of a Sunday service?[26] In the initial draft of *APBA*, 'Gathering of the People' was used, reflecting the biblical picture of the 'people of God' being gathered by God to be 'church' – '*ek-klesia*, 'assembly', from *'ek* (out) and *kaleo* (call). But it was soon realised that many would read this as a gathering that we the people initiate. So, noting that those gathered

---

24 The graphic was drawn by Sarah Crutch, Bishop's Assistant, Anglican Diocese of Bendigo..

25 *New Patterns of Worship* (2002) from England is an example: https://www.churchofengland.org/prayer-and-worship/worship-texts-and-resources/common-worship/common-material/new-patterns-worshp.

26 Morning & Evening Prayer (First Order) are translations into moden English of the respective *BCP* services, in 'office' shape. The only heading is 'Introduction', to clarify what is to be used on Sundays.

in Christ are baptised "into the Name of Father, Son and Holy Spirit" (Matthew 28.19), 'Gathering in God's Name' emerged. God gathers us together as those baptised "in God's Name", now assembling – 'churching' – to engage with God and one another in worship.[27]

Coherent diversity and structure: some exercises

A common structure that arises from the shape of God's mission is how the diversity of rites and options in *APBA* is kept coherent. To explore what this looks like in practice, here are some exercises. While they can be done individually, they work best in a small group.

a) Look at how the three 'Services of the Word' begin (pages 3–5, 19–22, 35–36). Which 'gathering' style do you think would be best for particular situations?

Now compare these with the way Holy Baptism begins (pages 51–53).
What does explaining why God has gathered us for this occasion add?

b) Why do you think the Ministry of the Word is near the beginning of each of these three services?

Are there circumstances in which it might come at another point?

What might be the consequences of such a change?

c) Morning and Evening Prayer Second Order #24–29 (pages 27–28) give a number of suggestions for the 'dismissal'.

Which might you want to use every week in your parish?

Which occasionally? Some never?

d) Consider the overall pattern of Thanksgiving for a Child (pages 43–47).
Why do you think some of the usual titles are not used, but others are added?

---

27 David Peterson, *Engaging with God. A Biblical Theology of Worship* (Leicester: IVP, 2002) provides a thoughtful account of New Testament patterns, concluding with some practical implications for today.

Further reading

Austin, J.L., *How to Do Things with Words* (Oxford: Clarendon, 1952): a classic analysis, introducing the concept of 'performative language'

Mascall, Eric, *Words and Images. A study in theological discourse* (London: Longmans, Green 1957): a key contribution to the mid-twentieth century debate in philosophy and theology on language and God

Morley, Janet, *All Desires Known* (SPCK, 1992): beautifully creative prayers, mostly in collect form

Dix, Gregory, *The Shape of the Liturgy* (London: Dacre Press, Adam and Charles Black, 2nd Edition, 1945): a long, highly readable (if sometimes annoying) work of enduring significance, focussed around the theme of the title

ELLC, *Praying Together:* http://englishtexts.org/Portals/11/Assets/praying.pdf

David Peterson, *Engaging with God. A Biblical Theology of Worship* (Leicester: IVP, 2002): David was a Consultant to the Liturgical Commission for *APBA*

Sherlock, Charles, *Words and the Word. Case Studies in using Scripture today* (Melbourne: Mosaic / Morningstar, 2013): Chapter Four is on gender and theology, Chapter Five on language and power

Sherlock, Charles, *God on the Inside: Trinitarian Spirituality* (Melbourne: Acorn, 1991): Chapters Five to Nine consider God and gender

Turner, Victor, *The Ritual Process* (London: Penguin, 1969): a basic sociological text on rites of passage

Part B

Resources for every Christian liturgy

Any and every Christian liturgy draws on some 'basics', without which the service would not be Christian. It is these that this Part explores.

First cab off the rank is the scriptures, heard in the context of the seasons of nature, society and church - the Calendar. The music performed and songs sung are likely to feature in many services. And the concerns worshippers bring, or sense in the world around, will spur on the way God is praised and intercessions are offered.

So the next Chapters are:

Chapter 3	According to the Scriptures
Chapter 4	The Christian Year 'down under'
Chapter 5	Seasons and Saints in *APBA*
Chapter 6	Singing the Lord's Song
Chapter 7	The Ministry of Prayer

Chapter Three

According to the Scriptures

Attending to the scriptures has been at the heart of Christian worship from the beginning. This practice derived from the Jewish synagogue, in which the main part of a service consisted of "readings from the Torah, the law of Moses, succeeded by a reading from the prophets which in turn was followed by the teaching of the rabbi, who sought to tease out the significance of the readings for the current community."[1]

Over the centuries churches have developed a variety of 'lectionaries', systems of readings from the scriptures. There are clear advantages in different congregations hearing the same scripture passages each Sunday.[2] Not only are preaching and educational resources made more feasible, but individual Christians share the sense of listening to the scriptures with the wider people of God.

But why begin a commentary on *APBA* with lectionaries?[3]

Planning liturgy: what comes first?

Beginnings in the *Books of Common Prayer*

The first-ever 'all-in-one' prayer book was the 1549 *BCP* prepared by Thomas Cranmer, Archbishop of Canterbury (1533–1553).[4] You might think that it would have begun with the Eucharist: after all, only the previous year 'The Order for Communion', in English, had been inserted into the Sarum (i.e. from Salisbury) Mass in Latin.[5] But no: the 1549 *BCP*, and the editions that followed over the next century (1552, 1559, 1604, 1662) each begin with 'Lessons Proper for Sundays and

---

1 *A Practical Commentary*, 68.
2 Sunday is assumed here to be when regular church services take place. Some churches have their main service on another day, e.g. in aged care homes, or in a 'fresh expressions' congregation. Where this is the case, it is presumed that the readings for the following Sunday or Principal Festival are used.
3 *Performing the Gospel* Chapter Six gives a wider perspective on the scriptures and their use in liturgy, especially their being 'performed' though varied forms of public reading.
4 This innovation was made technically possible thanks to printing, and politically possible by Edward VI coming to the throne, wanting a reformed Church of England.
5 This 'Order' was the second liturgical text in English: the first was the Litany, issued by Henry VIII in 1544 to gather prayer support for his war with France. Cranmer took the opportunity to purge it of invocations of the saints, and ground all petitions in Christ and the Spirit.

Holy Days', followed by 'The Calendar, with the Table of Lessons' for every day of the year.[6] The First Testament is read once each year (less some genealogies and cultic regulations), the New Testament twice (except Revelation 9 and 13), and the Psalms recited twelve times.

This system comes close to a full coverage of the Bible, immersing people in the scriptures rather than selecting 'purple passages', let alone proof texts. As Cranmer wrote in the introduction to the 1549 book, 'Concerning the Service of the Church', the ancient Fathers, in contrast to the medieval western Church,

> so ordered the matter, that all the whole Bible (or the greatest part of it) should be read over once every year; intending thereby, that the Clergy ... should (by often reading, and meditating in God's word) be stirred up to godliness; ... and further, that the people (by daily hearing of holy Scripture read in the Church) might continually profit more and more in the knowledge of God.

The scriptures – or better, hearing and reading them – are here thought of as the *matter* of divine worship. Everyone agreed that the Bible was important, and authoritative in some way. All the Reformers thought of it as the *formal* authority in the Church, rather than Church Councils or the Pope. Cranmer, however, believed that the pastoral *use* of the scriptures, their *material* authority, was of critical importance. Therefore its public reading was to form the substance of 'common prayer'. This ethos can readily be sensed by using Morning or Evening Prayer for a few days as *BCP* sets out these services. Some 50% of the time is devoted to hearing the scriptures, 15% with reciting psalms, and 15% with scriptural songs. A mere 20% is left for exhortation, confession, absolution and written prayers, all of which are woven from a tissue of scriptural allusions and citations.

So, according to *BCP*, the greater part of performing the Gospel in liturgy involves engaging with the scriptures – which is why each edition opens with tables setting out the daily and Sunday readings. A firm precedent is thus set: in preparing for any service, from 'fresh expressions' to a big cathedral celebration, begin by checking out the scripture readings allocated to the occasion.

What then of the tables of readings in *APBA?* Before looking at these, some attention to *performing* the scriptures will set them in context.

---

6   The 'Deposited Book' of 1927–28 included a revised Calendar and Tables, still at the front of the book. *AAPB* (1977) was the first modern prayer book to move the Calendar and Tables away from the front: the tables of readings for Holy Communion, with the Calendar, come between the main services and the Psalter. The daily reading Tables (unfortunately) are only included in the (black) 'Ministers' Edition', printed after the Acknowledgements and Articles of Religion, effectively forming an Appendix.

Eating and drinking: the 'sacramental Word'

Putting the scripture readings in first place in planning is not just about ensuring correct teaching, though this matters: poor instruction breeds weak disciples. Rather than images from the schoolroom, *BCP* typically uses images of eating and drinking about engaging with the scriptures. This 'sacramental' approach is seen in the *Homily on the Reading of Scripture*, written by Cranmer to help clergy with limited skills to preach.[7]

> And as drink is pleasant to them that be dry, and meat to them that be hungry; so is the reading, hearing, searching and studying of holy scripture, to them that desirous to know God, themselves, and to do his will.

The Homily concludes with these words:

> Let us ruminate, and, as it were, chew the cud, that we may have the sweet juice, spiritual effect, marrow, honey, kernel, taste, comfort and consolation of them.

Rather a mixture of agricultural metaphors! Yet they point to the 'sacramental' nature of the ministry of the Word as the primary means of grace. The feeding images evoke the Lord's Supper, in which Christ, our food and drink for eternal life, is offered to us. "Feed upon him in your hearts by faith, with thanksgiving" could be as much an exhortation before a scripture reading as before receiving the sacrament. The English Reformers drew on this approach from Augustine: it unites the ministries of book (the Word audible – heard) and table (the Word visible – seen).

Considering the scriptures as the 'sacramental Word' brings us back to performance. A sacrament is something *done* as well as said. This draws attention to *how* the scriptures are read, for example using several voices. Effective performance calls for preparation, and discernment as to what methods are most appropriate for the service concerned. Several extremes need to be avoided, not least as regards preaching.

- Some preachers use the scriptures in a merely intellectual way, giving Bible lectures, but neglecting their function to feed God's people, to ***trans*form** as well as ***in*form**.
- Others cite the scriptures, but as only one resource alongside other texts, prayers or spiritual thoughts.
- Still others might refer to the scriptures, but only to legitimate or express insights arising from elsewhere, typically from their personal experience.

Such practices set aside or dilute the scriptures' function as the primary means of grace, 'authoring' God's healing work in us. Approaches like these ignore the strong words of the *Homily on the Reading of Scripture*:

---

7   This, the first of the Homilies, is available at www.anglicanlibrary.org/homilies/bk1hom01.htm

Let us reverently hear and read holy scriptures, which is the food of the soul (Matthew 4.4). Let us diligently search for the well of life in the books of the Old and New Testaments, and not run to the stinking puddles of men's traditions, devised by men's imaginations for our justification and salvation.

But now it is time to turn to the system of scripture-reading used in **APBA**.

Patterns of scripture reading in *APBA*

Lectionaries: some history

The lectionary that opens each edition of *BCP* assumes that people begin and end the day in church, before heading for the field or returning from trade. With the Industrial Revolution spreading across England, housing and work patterns changed. Sunday-only worship became the norm, complemented by personal prayer and reflection on weekdays: hearing just the Sunday readings raised problems of understanding, since large gaps were left between them.

So in 1871 the Church of England produced separate lectionaries for Morning and Evening Prayer: one for Sundays and festivals, the other for weekdays. Holy Communion was allowed to be celebrated by itself, but its readings, an epistle and gospel, the same each year, remained unchanged. Despite these changes, only a very limited range of readings was heard at the Eucharist until recent times, and then from the New Testament only.

The Second Vatican Council (1962–65) of the Roman Catholic Church placed a strong emphasis on 'the faithful' engaging with the scriptures 'afresh'. So, as well as services being translated into local languages, a new English translation of the Bible was made, the Jerusalem Bible, and a new pattern of readings was adopted.[8] For weekday Eucharists, this reading scheme ran over two years, covering much of the New Testament and some of the First. For Sundays, however, a three-year system was developed, based around the gospels of Matthew, Mark and Luke in Years A, B and C respectively: the 'Three-Year Lectionary'. It included semi-continuous reading of other New Testament books, with a First Testament reading and psalm chosen to match the gospel reading.

The Three-Year Lectionary brought a welcome breadth of readings to Sundays, and gained ready acceptance in other western churches. Resources to support the resulting Ministry of the Word were developed and shared ecumenically. The new Lectionary worked nicely with the Liturgical Commission's combination of Morning Prayer, Litany and Holy Communion in *A Modern Liturgy* (1966). As noted above, this service

---

8   The Jerusalem Bible was the work of the lively English Benedictine scholar, Dom Henry Wansbrough. It was my privilege to meet and engage with him, then in his eighties. on ARCIC III.

would become Holy Communion (Second Order) in *AAPB*, in which the Three-Year Lectionary was adopted (with minor changes) for Sundays and festivals, together with a revision of the 1871 lectionary for daily Morning and Evening Prayer.[9]

Significant criticisms arose, however. One was the use of the First Testament only to support the gospel reading, rather than letting this, the Jewish Bible (Tanach), be read in its own right.[10] The ecumenical *Common Lectionary*, developed in North America, attended to this issue by providing a systematic series of First Testament readings in 'ordinary' time: the link with the gospel reading was retained in Advent, Christmas / Epiphany, Lent and Easter.[11] Other criticisms included women's participation in the biblical story being minimised: Ruth and Esther get no mention, for example, and Anna is left out of the Presentation gospel (Luke 2.25-35, rather than 25-38). Some passages heard by many as carrying anti-Semitic overtones were not used sensitively, and some biblical books were unduly fragmented, notably John's gospel. In the New Testament letters, the omission of names and places gave the impression that they teach 'abstract' truths, rather than God's wisdom for a particular context.

The *Revised Common Lectionary*

In the light of critiques like these, the *Revised Common Lectionary (RCL)* was published in 1992, after considerable research by liturgical and scripture scholars working ecumenically.[12] *RCL* includes three years of readings for Sundays and Holy Week, providing both the *Common Lectionary* (semi-continuous) and Three-Year Lectionary (gospel-

---

9 The Church of England, rather than adopt the Three-Year Lectionary in its first revision of *BCP*, the *Alternative Service Book* (*ASB* 1990), created its own two-year 'thematic' system, the readings being printed in *ASB* from several translations. The British ecumenical *Joint Liturgical Group* (*JLG*) had in 1967 issued a two-year *Calendar and Lectionary* with one reading 'controlling' the choice of others: this seems to have influenced the 'thematic' lectionary in *ASB*. *JLG* issued a revision in *A Four Year Lectionary* (Norwich: Canterbury, 1990), with the Gospel of John as the base for a Year D: this proved to be unworkable.

That the 1969-77 Australian Liturgical Commission included the Three-Year Lectionary in *AAPB* thus reflected a growing sense of independence from its 'mother' Church of England.

10 Jews refer to the Hebrew/Aramaic Bible as 'Tanach', a word that combines the Hebrew names T (*Torah* – law), N (*Nevi'im* – prophets), and Ch (*Chethivim* – Writings).

11 Fritz West, *Scripture and Memory. The Ecumenical Hermeneutic of the Three-Year Lectionaries* (Collegeville MN: Liturgical Press, 1997) offers a superb analysis of the differing Protestant and Roman Catholic approaches to the way scripture 'works' in church, and how the new lectionaries seek to integrate these. (My thanks to the Revd Dr Elizabeth Smith for pointing me to this book.)

12 The Consultation on Common Texts, *The Revised Common Lectionary* (Norwich: The Canterbury Press, 1992). This book includes the history and principles of *RCL*, as well as tables of readings and full Indices. A wealth of web resources is available: the Wikipedia article on *RCL* is excellent.

The Church of England, with *ASB* no longer authorised beyond Advent 2001, included an *RCL*-based lectionary in *Common Worship*.

RCL is now the base for Sunday lectionaries across the Anglican Communion.

linked) sets of First Testament readings (and psalms). In Australia, *RCL* was taken up by the Churches of Christ, Lutheran, Uniting and some Baptist churches, and forms the basis for the readings for Sundays listed in *APBA* pages 462-642.[13] The Roman Catholic Church continues with the Three-Year Lectionary, so that disagreement over how the First Testament is read continues.[14] Even so, that a high proportion of Australian Christian congregations share both readings from the New Testament on Sundays is a significant ecumenical achievement.[15]

But *RCL* did not do the whole job. Fifty years ago many Anglicans were 'twicers', typically being in church on Sundays for Holy Communion and Morning Prayer, or for a morning service and Evening Prayer. Few do so now, but provision for those that do was needed. So, rather than thinking in terms of morning and evening, or Morning Prayer and Eucharist, in *APBA* the *RCL* set of readings is used for the 'Main' service, whether Holy Communion or a Service of the Word. A 'supplementary' set of readings is provided for a second Sunday service, using passages which complement the *RCL* ones, but which also form a reasonably coherent system in its own right. (This 'Main / Supplementary' system is now used in other parts of the Anglican Communion.) After *APBA* was authorised, a few requests were made for a 'third service' (e.g. early Morning Prayer prior to an 8am Eucharist). In response, the Liturgical Commission added a set of two readings plus a psalm for 'trial use' (§ in *An Australian Lectionary*).

---

13   *RCL* also includes 'Special Days' observed across the churches involved: Ascension (either on the seventh Thursday after Easter, or the next Sunday); January 1 (with readings for both New Year's Day and Holy Name [Mary Mother of God], a Roman Catholic Solemnity; February 2 (Presentation); March 25 (Annunciation); May 31 (Visitation); September 14 (Holy Cross); November 1 or the next Sunday (All Saints); and Thanksgiving (second Monday in October – Canada; fourth Thursday in November – USA).
Minor changes were made to *RCL* for *APBA*, most commonly extensions to bracketed verses, or to allow readings to be (optionally) more continuous. Two significant changes are the inclusion of James 2:18-26 (fragmented in *RCL*), with a consequent re-arrangement of New Testament readings in Sundays 23-25 in Year B, and the optional extension of Ephesians 5:11-21 to include verses 22-33.

14   When Transfiguration is observed is a further area of incomplete ecumenical agreement. In *BCP*, it is marked on August 6 as a 'black-letter' day (i.e. without readings or collect). In *RCL*, Epiphany becomes a season in its own right, beginning with Baptism of the Lord and then exploring the 'signs' which explicate the identity of Jesus as the Christ, concluding with the Last Sunday before Lent being optionally observed as Transfiguration. An older tradition, reflected in the Three-Year Lectionary and *AAPB*, marks Transfiguration on Lent 2. All three possibilities are found in *APBA*, with the *RCL* proposal preferred. A Transfiguration gospel is offered as an alternative on Lent 2, while the observance of Transfiguration on August 6 is kept as a Festival, not least due to its post-1945 association with Hiroshima Day.

15   There are numerous commentaries to assist the Ministry of the Word based on *RCL*, notably the gospels. Two by Australian authors are Frank Moloney's, *This is the Gospel of the Lord*, and Peta Sherlock's, *Inside the Sunday Gospels*. Australian internet resources include www.mediacom.org.au (UCA), www.laughingbird.net/LaughingBird/Welcome.html (Baptist), and https://shop.liturgybrisbane.net.au/ (Roman Catholic).

Now would be a good time to turn to page 462 in *APBA* (the full red edition) and read the notes on 'The Readings'. These explain this Main / Supplementary process, and the biblical versification that is followed in the tables.

What then of the psalms? In each set of *RCL* readings, the psalm (or scripture canticle) is chosen to foster the response of the congregation to the First Reading. It would be tempting to have only 'nice' psalms chosen – a criticism of some substance for the Three-Year Lectionary and *AAPB*. The *RCL / APBA* system cannot be so accused: portions from 117 psalms are used, including laments, praise, royal, personal and penitential psalms.[16]

The Lectionary in *APBA* – and 'themes'

Ever searched for a 'theme' across the three readings and psalm? It won't work for most Sundays. Why not? In *RCL* and *APBA*, each First Testament, New Testament and Gospel reading follows its own course from week to week in Epiphany, and for Sundays after Pentecost ('ordinary' time). **No 'theme' is intended, and each reading speaks for itself.** So, when preparing for these Sundays, rather than trying to 'smooth out' the readings, best practice is to explore one as a 'base', referring to the others when a clear link emerges for that particular time, place and occasion.

On the other hand, the readings for Sundays in the major seasons are chosen to relate to the flavour of these special times. The ethos of Advent, Christmas-Epiphany, Lent and Easter is reflected in the readings chosen, which *might* then relate to one another. As Evan Burge notes,[17]

> For major festivals and in Advent, Lent, and the Easter season, the readings are chosen, with due regard for long-standing tradition, to be in keeping with the atmosphere and main themes of the day or season.

How then do the readings for 162 distinct Sundays over three years hang together?[18]

Gospels

Years A, B and C focus on the Gospels of Matthew, Mark and Luke respectively, with John read across the years. As Evan Burge continues, this system has as its

> foundation the proclamation of the central mystery of the Christian faith: the life, death, resurrection and continuing presence of Jesus Christ, and the work

---

16 Settings for singing all psalms in the *RCL* system can be found in *Together in Song: the Australian Hymn Book II*, using including metrical, chanted, cantor-and-refrain methods: see further Chapter Six.

17 *A Practical Handbook*, Chapter Fourteen, 'The Readings for Sundays and Holy Days'.

18 Readings for 162 rather than 156 Sundays are provided since two are omitted each year due to Easter being movable. Details of the readings (Advent to Advent inclusive), with supporting tables, are set out in the Introduction to *An Australian Lectionary* (Melbourne: Broughton, annually).

of the Holy Spirit. Each Lord's Day, the first day of the week, we recall and proclaim Christ's resurrection and triumph over sin and death.

First Readings

The alternative First Readings (and psalm), shown in square brackets underneath the *RCL*-based set, are chosen to link with the gospel passage (as in the Three-Year Lectionary). In 'ordinary' time, however, a more systematic approach is taken, following the major divisions of the Jewish Bible [Tanach, First Testament]:

Year A:	*Law /lore*:		Genesis–Deuteronomy
Year B:	*Former Prophets*:		Joshua–2 Kings; and
	Writings:		Ruth, 1 Chronicles–Songs, Lamentations
Year C:	*Latter Prophets*:		Isaiah–Malachi

Selections from Isaiah are read in Advent (Years A and B) and each Holy Week. During the Easter season, selections from Acts 1–15 are used for the First Reading.

New Testament letters ('Epistles' in BCP)

These are read continuously in 'ordinary' time, though their length means that a full coverage is impracticable. The readings are selected from the following books:

Year A	*After Epiphany*	1 Corinthians 1–4
	After Pentecost	Romans, Philippians, 1 Thessalonians
Year B	*After Epiphany*	1 Corinthians 6–9, 2 Corinthians 1–4
	After Pentecost	2 Cor 5–12, Ephesians, James, Hebrews 1–10
Year C	*After Epiphany*	1 Corinthians 12–15
	After Pentecost	Galatians, Colossians, Hebrews 11–12, Philemon, 1 & 2 Timothy, 2 Thessalonians

In the Easter Season, the following books are read semi-continuously:

Year A	1 Peter
Year B	1 John
Year C	Revelation 1, 5, 7, 21

Sentences

A scripture sentence is provided for each set of Sunday and Festival readings. They are chosen to relate to the season, or highlight one of the readings – but not to set out a 'theme'. Each is edited so that it can be used in a variety of places in a service, and also to ensure that, when read aloud, it makes sense. Someone saying, "I am the resurrection and the life" by itself makes rather a large claim. So a verse like this is introduced, "Jesus / the Lord said, 'I am ... '.".

Scripture readings for weekdays

Several issues arise in constructing a daily lectionary that covers the Bible as a whole. Some First Testament material does not lend itself to public reading – genealogies and cultic regulations for example, that are omitted from the *BCP* Tables. What do you do for the days around Christmas, which vary depending on which day it falls? What about the yearly 'major chasm' that results from how early or late Easter falls – readings for 54 weeks turn out to be needed to meet all possibilities. Thought must be given as to how longer books like Luke, John and Acts are read: experience shows that reading them in several 'blocks' is helpful (but not so for Job). And the length of each reading needs consideration, without impairing the passage concerned: how is the Joseph narrative (Genesis 37–50) to be divided up, for example, or the long reflections of Jesus in John 5 and 8? It's actually quite fun to work with all these variables, while paying close attention to the scriptural text.[19]

Readings at the daily Eucharist

General Synod agreed that the *AAPB* practice of using the Roman Catholic *Ordo* for readings at the daily Eucharist would continue, as is the case across much of the Anglican Communion. This provides two short readings daily: one from the gospels, broadly covered over two years, and one other reading, plus a psalm portion.

Readings at daily Morning and Evening Prayer

When General Synod considered the draft of *APBA* in 1995, it judged that the tables for readings at daily Morning and Evening Prayer had not had sufficient trial to have settled down, so these were published separately. They provided for three readings each weekday, one from the First and two from the New Testament. This recognised that one daily service is held in most places, and followed well-tried systems in the Anglican Church of Canada and The Episcopal Church (USA).

Over three years, the scheme could cover almost all the First Testament and much of the Apocrypha, taking account of what was being read on Sundays. It was put in place in *An Australian Lectionary* from 1996, but after a couple of years the House of Bishops instructed the Liturgical Commission to revert to a four-reading system (one from each Testament at Morning and Evening Prayer). While new tables were being prepared, the change sought was managed by using the 1995 First Testament readings for Years A and B, then B and C, for mornings and evenings respectively, though this made them overly long.

---

19   *An Australian Lectionary*, issued by AIO for *AAPB* and Broughton Publications for *APBA*, was prepared for 40 years until 2017 by Pamela Raff (Rockhampton, Queensland), and now by Susan Bassett (Castlemaine, Victoria). I held the Lectionary 'portfolio' for *APBA*, so have worked with them both.

In 2001, after extensive trial in some seventy parishes and agencies, General Synod approved tables of readings for daily Morning and Evening Prayer, and Festivals. A feature of this set is its taking account of the season of the Christian year in which books are placed. Thus Isaiah and Revelation are read in Advent, while Jeremiah and Genesis / Exodus run from Epiphany into Lent, in which Hebrews is read. The New Testament is read through in full each year (including all of Revelation).

First Testament readings run over two years: as with the daily Eucharist readings, they are the same from Advent to Trinity each year, with a two-year cycle for 'ordinary' time, including readings from the Apocrypha. In Year 1, Israel's story is told from Ruth to 2 Kings; in Year 2, from 1 Chronicles to Ezra. The prophets and wisdom are distributed over both years. Each cycle alternates between morning and evening in odd and even years, so that people using one reading each day will work though the First Testament over four years. Omissions are made from Leviticus, Numbers, Joshua and Judges, but these books are read more fully than in *BCP*. Significant genealogies are included (e.g. Genesis 5.1-5), along with lists of prominent court officers (e.g. 2 Samuel 8.15-18), and key cultic regulations (e.g. Number 3.40-51). Some 'less attractive' texts are retained (e.g. Ezekiel 25-33) but allocated to 'ordinary / proper' weeks 6-9, which do not occur every year. Readings for days like January 7-12 may not all be used, depending on the weekday on which Christmas falls, so they run from morning to evening rather than day to day.

The Psalms in daily services

The Psalms have formed the core of prayer and praise from the earliest days of the people of God, and continue to be foundational for Jewish and Christian practice. In monastic communities the psalms came to be recited and sung 'in course' over a week. Archbishop Cranmer, in reshaping daily Morning and Evening Prayer for use by everyone, continued this pattern, though spreading the psalms over a month. *BCP*'s Psalter thus includes headings before the psalms for a particular day and time – 'Day Four, Morning Prayer', for example. Such a scheme calls for 50-60 verses to be recited each morning and evening, a bit much. So in *AAPB* this pattern was extended to run over six weeks: each Psalm fell on the same weekday, however, so if you missed Saturday Evening Prayer, you never encountered Psalm 119.

The table of daily psalms associated with *APBA* returned to the *BCP* practice of allocating them to days of the month rather than weekdays, but over two months. As far as possible, they are read in sequence: the few exceptions are due to length (e.g. putting Psalm 144 with 150). Where a psalm is too long to be read as one portion, it is read at Morning and Evening Prayer in sequence (notably Psalms 78 and 89). Psalm 119, allocated to Saturdays in *AAPB,* is read on seventh evenings, days 7, 14, 21 and 28.[20]

A pastoral issue is passages that express anger or vengeance – 'imprecatory' psalms. For daily services the full Psalter is used, since "all scripture is useful" (1 Timothy 3:15–16). The strongest 'imprecatory' psalms (58, 58, 79, 83.9–18, 109.6–14) are read on Day 31 in Odd Months, which lessens their frequency, but does not remove them. Suggestions that offending verses be put in brackets in the *APBA's* Psalter were rejected by General Synod, but it was agreed that brackets could be used in the Table of Psalms, indicating that the verses concerned may be omitted "at the discretion of the minister".

The Ministry of the Word in practice

How many readings?

More than arithmetic is at stake here. Behind the numbers lies a 'principle of worship', that the scriptures are to be heard in 'stereo'. Having more than one reading means that a passage is not heard in isolation, and that dialogue or conversation is invited between them. This discourages the preacher's temptation to lay down "what the Bible *really* means". Thus, following *BCP,* the rubrics for all Sunday services in *APBA* specify a minimum of two readings, one being from the gospels in Holy Communion.

In Holy Communion (Second and Third Orders), three readings plus a psalm are offered – a substantial provision, but sometimes too rich a diet. In what situations are all four passages appropriate? Or a lesser number, for example one from each Testament, as at Morning and Evening Prayer? And what about the psalms: when are they essential, when not? What you would regard as helpful on occasions like these:

- a 'traditional' 8am Holy Communion with no music?
- a choral Eucharist with a robed choir?
- a family service that includes infant and primary-school children?
- a 'fresh expressions' service in a public place, designed for young adults?
- a small congregation in a village, where everyone knows each other well?
- a Eucharist held outside during a parish camp?
- a youth celebration with a band?

The point is not to come up with 'solutions', but to encourage reflection on context.

---

20 After the 2001 Tables were issued, requests were made for a selection of psalms that follow the major seasons of the Church year ('cathedral' use). *An Australian Lectionary* now includes a table of psalms (for 'trial use') related to Advent, Christmas, Lent and Easter on a weekly cycle: this allows a seasonal focus to balance the systematic ('monastic') use of the Psalter in 'ordinary' time.

Sermon series

Sermon series which work their way through a particular book of the Bible, or a range of related passages, are a familiar practice in many places. Sustained exposition of the scriptures has a lot going for it: indeed, without being exposed to something like it, few adult Christians will grow to mature faith in Christ. But when is the most appropriate time and place?

The Christian year, grounded in Israel's annual festival of Passover / Unleavened Bread and Weeks, arose in the northern hemisphere. In those climes, the long summer break of July–September is taken up by the Sundays after Pentecost. Much of the work-year falls in the seasons of Advent to Epiphany (December–February), and Lent to Trinity (March–May). This leaves only October as 'ordinary time', free of seasonal commitments. In the southern hemisphere, however, the central months of the year (May–November) are available for planning of services with 'sermon series', especially as the Sunday readings run continuously week by week. So here are some ideas:

a) Adult education experts advise that the ideal number of sessions on any topic for most adults is five or six, with a break of at least three weeks between topics. And preparation takes time and energy – so don't overcrowd May–November.

b) Series planning is an opportunity to involve more than just you. The scriptures 'speak' with a variety of voices, and so should the ministry of the Word. Consider the 'patriarchal' stories of Genesis 12–50: without input from both men and women a lot of insights will be missed. Likewise, in working through Paul's letters, who in the congregation might most be affected by his argument? Get them involved in the planning, and perhaps in presentation (e.g. by an interview).

c) The liturgy / worship / preaching team needs to understand and agree on the series plan, who will do what, and when. If it entails sermons over successive Sunday services, who will preach can be complemented by who will read, and how other elements of the service can be shaped around the ministry of the Word.

d) It is unwise to announce a series ahead of time: better to just let it emerge. This may seem odd advice, but as the series goes on, it is likely (and desirable) that the ministry which has taken place will call for adjustments, and sickness or unexpected events can intervene. Having a public plan that has to be to adhered to can be a rod for your back. Also, some 'regulars' will not be there every week, and public announcements can make them feel guilty: having realised that the series is happening, many will welcome having tapes or YouTube videos to catch up.

e) Finally, as with all ministry of the Word, review and evaluation is important. In the case of a series, doing so at least once during its course can open up room for responses and adjustments. In this way, all involved can better "hear what the Spirit is saying to the churches".

The ministry of the Word – in season and out

What then of preaching in the main seasons of the Christian year? Rather than just changing the dates on last year's booklets, good practice is to start by working through all the scripture readings for the Year concerned (A, B or C). Explore how the readings for each Sunday engage one another (they are likely to in seasonal time), the 'progressions' from week to week, and the way the 'feel' of the season affects how the scriptures are heard and received. And it is wise to reflect on how the season 'sits' in the civic year: Advent in church is surrounded by 'Xma$ shopping' in society, for example.

What follows are some suggestions that may prove helpful.

1) Read through the introduction to The Readings on page 462 of **APBA,** then the readings for the first four weeks. These cover the Sundays of Advent.
Look up the four readings for one Sunday. How do they relate to the seasonal 'flavour' of Advent? What 'theme(s)' can you discern across them?
Repeat this process for an Advent Sunday in a different Year. What differences / similarities do you find? How might these affect preparation?

2) Now turn to a Sunday after Pentecost, and consider the readings offered: these are not chosen to relate to one another, but continue week by week.
How does each Main reading relate to those of the previous week?
How do they relate to the Supplementary set?
In what ways does the Prayer of the Day pick up one or more of the readings?

3a) Look at the sequence of First Testament readings over the Sundays on either side of the one you have chosen. Take a few minutes to read them through aloud. Some passages will be omitted between each Sunday, given their length. How might 'filling in' the missing part of the ongoing story or message affect the way these readings are used 'in church'?

3b) Now look up the bracketed First Testament reading for the same Sunday, chosen to relate to the gospel reading. In what ways do you think it does this? How helpful / confusing / artificial / illuminating do you find this pairing?

3c) Look up the psalm for each Sunday you have considered and have it read aloud. In what way does it form a response (or not) to the First Testament reading?

4) Go back to the 'Sundays after Pentecost' in *APBA,* and find a set of Sundays that work through a New Testament letter (e.g. Romans, Year A June–July; Ephesians, Year B July–August; 1 & 2 Timothy, Year C September–October). How adequate do you think is the coverage of the letter concerned?
What changes (if any) might improve the way its overall message is communicated in your congregation?

5) How might your liturgy / worship / preaching team work out a 'series' based on one of the cycles of readings you have explored?
Are there possibilities of marking the series by using visual or dramatic aids?

Scripture readings for special occasions

Three types of special occasions have provision made for them in *APBA* and the 2001 Tables: **Principal Festivals / Principal Holy Days** (e.g. Christmas), **Festivals / Holy Days** (e.g. Peter and Paul, Apostles and Martyrs, June 29) and **Lesser Festivals / Commemorations.**

- Principal Festival and Festival readings employ the same 'Main / Supplementary' system as on Sundays. However, which readings are to be used for Morning or Evening Prayer for Festivals is not clear in *APBA*. So for saints' days and special occasions the tables in *An Australian Lectionary* are set out in the 'traditional' pattern of Morning Prayer (two), Evening Prayer (two), plus psalms (and First Evensongs where specified).

- Some Lesser Festivals / Commemorations have readings provided in *APBA*, though not always a full set (e.g. First Service at Sydney Cove, February 3). A few others (e.g. For a Theologian, Thanksgiving or Baptism) have readings appropriate to the overall category.

- Most Lesser Festivals / Commemorations, however, have no provision made for readings or sentences in *APBA* or the 2001 Tables. Since then, requests for these have been made, especially for days commemorating Australians and New Zealanders (e.g. Mother Esther, William Broughton, Bishop Patteson). This gap is met in *Australian Anglicans Remember* (Broughton, 2016).

- *An Australian Lectionary* also includes 'watch-night' readings for December 31, and useful tables at the end, including 'Readings for Certain Lesser Festivals', dates for the following year, and the daily and seasonal Psalms patterns: consulting its closing pages will repay dividends.

Some occasions, however, call for the readings to be chosen afresh. The temptation is to find (brief) passages which seem to 'prove' whatever is wanting to be celebrated or commemorated. This needs to be resisted. In particular, **the 'principle of worship' that the scriptures should always be heard in 'stereo' needs to be adhered to. This means that at least two readings should always be heard, preferably from both Testaments, so that a dialogue or conversation is set up between them.** Further, each passage should be long enough to say something, and not be 'filleted' to remove any 'awkward' bits (as happens occasionally even in official lectionaries). When this is done, preacher(s) and intercessors will face the challenge of having to struggle with the text, rather than find a snippet as a launch pad for their own ideas.

Bible translations for use in church

Overarching issues

What is the best translation of the Bible to use in a service conducted in English?[21] There are so many versions available that a simple response is difficult.[22] Every translation is already an act of interpretation: there is no such thing as a 'pure' version of the scriptures. Indeed, no single tongue is used for the whole Bible – Hebrew, Aramaic and *koine* Greek are employed. The question of a 'best' version raises several issues.

- What type of translation will be best understood by those hearing it aloud in a service, or reading it privately – a 'reader-response' approach? (*The Amplified Bible* is a good example of a version taking this approach.) The risk here is so shaping the translation to bridge the cultural gap between the varied contexts of biblical times and today that the 'sharp edges' of scriptural meaning are softened – or explained – too much.

- Should a translation focus on following as closely as possible the words, grammar and syntax of the original text – a 'literary' ('formal') method? No translation can avoid the necessary discipline of seeking to be faithful to the original. Yet without significant adaptation to the ways in which the varieties of English language work, the outcome will be a text which few can understand (as was the case with *The Revised Version*, 1881–1884).

---

21 https://www.biblegateway.com offers a wide range of translations that can be downloaded.
22 English-speakers have a veritable glut of translations, as the publication of Curtis Vaughan, *The New Testament from Twenty-Six Translations* (Zondervan, 1967) shows. Other global languages have many less versions available, notably Spanish and Chinese, which only in recent decades have modern-language versions become available. Many Indigenous languages are yet to have a translation of more than a book or two: in Australia, the Kriol Bible is a significant 'half-way' step forward for Aboriginal Christians.

- How helpful is translating 'thought by thought', seeking to bridge the gap between original text and today's Bible hearers and readers – 'dynamic equivalence'? This was the method adopted for the *Good News Bible*, designed for people for whom English is a second language (an aim not always appreciated). Its vocabulary was limited to a thousand words (plus names): so "you are the apple of my eye" (Deuteronomy 32.10; Psalm 17.8; Proverbs 7.2; Zechariah 2.8) is left out, or rephrased as "protect me as you would your eyes" – not untrue, but far less expressive.

Across all these issues is the question of theological interpretation. Every group of translators faces this at some point. How is Romans 9.5 to be punctuated? What tenses will be inserted in Romans 5.11ff and 1 Corinthians 15.20ff (the Greek has few)? What do you do with the gender biases of English?

Translations and gendered language

Gender language issues are present in the opening chapter of the Bible. Is Genesis 1.26 better rendered "Let us make man in our image" or "Let us make humankind in our image"? The word concerned, *'adamah,* refers to the human race as a whole, and the account continues "Let *them* have dominion …"[23] Similar issues arise in the New Testament. Translating the Greek *'adelphoi* (brothers / brethren) as 'brothers and sisters' (e.g. 1 Corinthians 15.1) recognizes that the original writer addressed women and men, yet in this expansion of *'adelphoi* an interpretive step is taken.[24]

A more complex example is how to render Jesus' favourite self-description, *'uios tou 'anthropou.* Usually translated 'son of man', it is literally 'son of humanity', a corporate term. Further, behind the Greek lies Aramaic, the language Jesus spoke, which (like Hebrew) forms adjectives using son of …' (*bar* …). So Bar-nabas is a 'son of encouragement', an encourager – and a 'son of man' (*bar/ben-'adam*) is a 'mere mortal' (as the *NRSV* renders it in Ezekiel). In Daniel, however, this Aramaic phrase is used for one given rule over all things by the Ancient of Days (Daniel 7.13-14), a divine figure. Jesus, in using this phrase for himself, thus poses the question to listeners: do you see me as mere mortal, or God in human flesh? As well as the gender issues involved, how to render the theological 'double meaning' of *'uios tou 'anthropou* poses quite a challenge.

When it comes to passages reflecting gender relations, using inclusive language – or *not* doing so – means taking sides in the 'complementarian / egalitarian' debates

---

23 The English Standard Version (2001) uses 'man' but with a footnote, "The Hebrew word for man (adamah) is the generic term for mankind and becomes the proper name *Adam*."
24 This is the consistent practice of the *New Revised Standard Version*.

about male-female relationships. Thus Ephesians 5.21 instructs wives and husbands "to submit to one another," but no verb is supplied in the next verse: so should it continue "wives, to your husbands, as to the Lord", or "wives, submit to your husbands as to the Lord", repeating the earlier verb? Sharp debate has taken place about this in modern translations, even leading to some versions being replaced or banned.

Which Bible version?

Which translation, then, best helps congregations hear and respond to the word of God, rather than (unintentionally) distort it?

Have it both ways: use two or more translations, for example 'formal' and 'dynamic equivalence' ones. A 'standard' version for liturgy and congregational study (for example the *NRSV*) is helpfully complemented by another for personal use, and occasional reading in church (for example *The Message*). This position may not see agreement with everyone, so some background is needed to help in a church's choice.

For decades after World War 2, the *Revised Standard Version* (of the *King James Bible – RSV*) was used across many English-speaking churches, and favoured by scholars.[25] After several editions, it has been updated in two newer translations, continuing the 'feel' of the *KJB*. Both use 'you/your' rather than 'thee/thy' pronouns throughout, and pay close attention to manuscript research, notably the Dead Sea Scrolls, unknown when the *RSV* was translated, which shed light on many First Testament passages.

- *The New Revised Standard Version (NRSV*, 1989) is a project of the *National Council of Churches in the USA.* The mandate given to the ecumenical committee which did the work was, "As literal as possible, as free as necessary". The *NRSV* employs inclusive language for humans, while retaining masculine images and pronouns for God. It is approved for church use by many English-speaking Anglican Provinces and Protestant churches, and in several Episcopal Conferences of the Roman Catholic Church. The *NRSV* is my preferred version for study purposes.

- *The English Standard Version (ESV*, 2001, 2016) is a revision of the *RSV* prepared by scholars with a firm commitment to "historic evangelical orthodoxy, and to the authority and sufficiency of the inerrant Scriptures." It retains a higher proportion of older terms than other modern translations, and takes some account of gender-neutral terms. It has been adopted by the Lutheran Church–Missouri Synod (USA), and has become popular among some evangelical Christians.

---

25 The *RSV* was published in stages by the Division of Christian Education of the *National Council of Churches* (USA): New Testament in 1946, Old Testament in 1952, Apocrypha in 1957, A Roman Catholic version was issued in 1965, and the 'Common Bible', including Greek and Slavonic additional passages in 1973.

While not directly related to the *RSV* lineage, two further translations are significant.

- *The New International Version (NIV*, 1984, 2011) was translated from the original languages, aiming to bridge 'word for word' and 'thought by thought' approaches. Prepared by over 100 international evangelical scholars, it has become the most used English translation among Protestants, until controversy over a 2005 'inclusive language' version (*Today's NIV*) saw it rejected by some churches. A 2011 revision took a more conservative approach.

- *The New Jerusalem Bible (NJB,* 1985), translated from the original texts, draws on the English translation of the French *Bible de Jérusalem* (1973). Given its French and Roman Catholic provenance, the *NJB* has a distinctive 'feel' in comparison to the *KJB* heritage. It takes a 'formal' approach, and employs limited gender-neutral language, but leaves some Hebrew names for God untranslated (e.g. 'El Shaddai rather than 'Almighty'), and renders the divine Name as 'Yahweh' (rather than 'Jehovah' (*KJB*) or 'Lord' (*RSV* and successors). As well as in Roman Catholic English-speaking churches, the *NJB* is approved for use in The Episcopal Church and in some Anglican Provinces.

Alongside one of these generally 'literary' (word for word) translations, I warmly encourage use of a 'dynamic equivalence' (thought for thought) version for personal reading, and sometimes for public reading in church. Given the traditional respect for the Bible in English-speaking societies, and public familiarity with the language of the *KJB*, only in recent times have such translations been attempted. The first was by J.B. Phillips, who during the London Blitz began to translate the scriptures for young people for whom the *KJB* was difficult: his full New Testament was published in 1958. In my opinion, two 'dynamic equivalence' versions stand out today – one from the Bible Society, the other from an American minister.

- *The Contemporary English Version (CEV,* 1991) is issued by the American Bible Society. It takes a similar approach to the Society's *Good News for Modern Man / Good News Bible / Today's English Version* (*GNB / TEV*: New Testament 1966, First Testament 1976). The *GNB / TEV* arose from requests in 'mission' areas for a version suited to readers for whom English is not a first language – and sold in the millions in English–speaking countries. By their very nature, both versions 'flatten' many metaphors, as noted earlier, but they are easy to read and understand. A fresh translation from the original languages, the *CEV* takes account of issues of gendered language, anti-Semitism, and 'post-television' English. It is particularly suitable for reading aloud to children.

- *The Message: The Bible in Contemporary Language* (Colorado Springs: NavPress, 2002) is the outcome of translations made by Eugene H. Peterson during his decades of pastoral ministry. Though based on the original languages, it is refreshingly startling at points, using the grammar of speech and a fair bit of slang. Its strength is in the Bible's stories, especially 1 Samuel – Nehemiah and the Gospels. Its rendition of the prophets and New Testament letters might not major on doctrinal precision, but you sure know the point being conveyed! I read The *Message* New Testament against the Greek text one year, and despite a few queries came away most impressed. This is the version I would give to someone enquiring about Christian faith.

Further reading

An Australian Lectionary (Melbourne: Broughton, annual)

The Consultation on Common Texts, *The Revised Common Lectionary* (Norwich: The Canterbury Press, 1992)

West, Fritz, *Scripture and Memory. The Ecumenical Hermeneutic of the Three-Year Lectionaries* (Collegeville MN: Liturgical Press, 1997)

Websites:

https://www.biblegateway.com/ allows downloads from numerous Bible versions

https://www.englishtexts.org/is the website of *ELLC*

Australian church resources:

www.mediacom.org.au/

www.laughingbird.net/LaughingBird/Welcome.html

https://shop.liturgybrisbane.net.au/

Chapter Four

The Church's Year 'down under'

The times and seasons in which a congregation worships play key parts in shaping the ethos and context for what is done. Several 'rhythms' exist in any calendar: the cycles of nature, civic celebrations and public holidays, the sporting, work and school years. These interact with the Church's Year in a variety of ways in different places. The financial year in our personal lives is less significant than for businesses, for example, and ends on June 30 in Australia, but April 15 in the USA. Importantly for Austalian Anglicans, the 'Kalendar' in *BCP* interacts with northern temperate climes, while we experience tropical or southern temperate zones.

The Calendar gives shape to the Church's Year, while engaging with human experience. This chapter takes up the perspectives of the Christian tradition on time – the day, week, year and seasons – and how these work in Australian contexts.[1]

History: times and seasons in Christian perspective

Day by day

In traditional Jewish and Christian practice, the day begins at sunset. This puts rest ahead of our human endeavours, preparing us for work rather than being its aftermath or reward.[2] But sin came in, distorting our perception of time: by the era of Jesus and Paul, night had come to be known for "works of darkness" (John 12.35; 1 Thessalonians 5.4–8). Yet night and day continue to be graced, according to the biblical ideal that rest undergirds work.

Most Australians, Christians included, live the other way around, from day to night. Some do so by choice, but many because their work is toil, and rest is relief. And electric lighting has changed how we view day and night: for shift workers they are indistinguishable. Whatever our way of life, performing the gospel daily calls us to live out of grace rather than effort.

Sleeping and eating are daily universal human experiences. Both have Christian customs associated with them. Bedtime prayers may be offered by mum and

---

1. *Performing the Gospel* Chapter Eight discusses wider questions around time, from Plato to Einstein, Gregory of Nyssa to Karl Barth, via the feasts of Israel, 'BC' and 'AD' and Holy Week.
2. This concept of 'day' remains in having 'First Evensongs' for major Festivals: see page 87 in this book.

dad with a young child: I still pray "Now I lay me down to sleep, I pray you, Lord, my life to keep ..." before closing my eyes each night. *APBA* provides 'Prayer at the End of the Day' (pages 439–446) for group or personal use, as well as daily Evening Prayer and A Service of the Light.

At each meal, Christian practice is to offer thanks to God ('saying grace'): a familiar formula helps children take this on board, and works when we don't feel like praying. On Sundays, in our house we often use the opening responses of the Great Thanksgiving, "Lift up your hearts / **we lift them to the Lord** ...", to begin the main meal. It leads in to a brief prayer appropriate to the occasion (including remembrance of those who hunger and thirst). This responsive form enables all at the table to join in, and connects household and church life.

Week by week

If God rested from creative activity (Genesis 2.1–4a), so should God's creatures. The seven-day rhythm of the week is shaped by the sabbath, its concluding day. This cycle does not arise from the rhythms of nature, but is God's gift to meet the human tendency to stretch our creative capacity beyond its limits. Observing this weekly gift of rest keeps us from imagining that we humans create our world, and that everything depends on our efforts.

In Christ, the first day of the week became the day of resurrection, pointing to the new creation, the "life of the ages" ('eternal life' in Greek). The first and seventh days of the week thus have different foci: the first is "the Lord's day" (Revelation 1.10) and centres on Easter; the seventh is one of rest (Exodus 20.11) and centres on re-creation. And both look forward (Hebrews 4.1–11). As Gilbert Sinden has written,

> The Sabbath is not only a day of rest; it is, more importantly, a day when God's people recall the completeness, totality, and consummation of all God's creative work ... It is also a sign, a foretaste, of the kingdom of God. Its celebration sanctifies the whole week and the whole of life.

For Christians, the Sabbath is also the weekly celebration of that Sabbath (the first Easter Eve) when Christ rested from the labours of the new creation on the cross. The observance of the Lord's Day was not in its origin an alternative to the Sabbath observance, but an addition to it and its fulfilment. It was not a day of rest, but of work, on which we contemplate and are caught up in the work of the new creation.[3]

---

3   Gilbert Sinden, *Times and Seasons* (Sydney: AIO, 1980) 8, exploring the Calendar in *AAPB*.

Bodies such as *The Lord's Day Observance Society* have defended Sunday as the Christian sabbath, supporting laws that forbid work or leisure activities.[4] A famous example is Eric Liddell's refusal to run in the Olympics on Sunday, the basis for the film 'Chariots of Fire'. In the scriptures, however, the evidence for the sabbath and Sunday being the same day is weak, as any Seventh Day Adventist will soon tell you.[5] But practicing both sabbath and Sunday remains important, whether together or separately. The one points to the priority of grace, living a 'sabbatical lifestyle'; the other witnesses to Christ's resurrection: living in the hope of new creation.

Sunday: first day – and eighth

Sunday is special for Christian faith and living, just as Saturdays are for Jewish believers.[6] As the day of resurrection, it points us forward to the new creation, and so for Christian faith Sunday is also the eighth day.[7] It was on the eighth day that the child born to Mary was circumcised, grafted into the First Covenant / Testament and named 'Jesus', Saviour (Luke 2.21). It was on the eighth day that this Jesus was transfigured, displaying the reality of the New Covenant / Testament (Luke 9.28). Baptism fonts traditionally have eight sides, signifying that we are baptised into Christ's death in the hope of being raised to live in "newness of life" (Romans 6.3-4).

Sunday is a day of joy, "the day that the Lord has made – we shall rejoice and be glad in it." (Psalm 118.24 – see *APBA* page 19 #2 and page 383 #1).[8] There is a profound paradox in this joy, however: our eighth-day anticipation of the new creation is all of a piece with commemorating the victory of Christ's passion. This paradox lies at the heart of Baptism and the Eucharist, with their imagery of burial and death, of *costly* hope. It is easily obscured or forgotten in places where Christians meet in comfortable places on Sunday, commencing a week without having to worry about the next meal, whether children can get to school, or gravely ill friends can find a doctor. All such privileges are outcomes of God's generous provision, but can cloud the truth that Christian liturgy are celebrates matters of death and life. Many believers gather in places where despair, injustice and sheer ordinary meanness are everyday realities.

---

4 Sunday was first legislated as a day of rest by the Emperor Constantine c. 330, thus conflating it with sabbath observance: Eusebius, *Life of Constantine* 4.18.

5 See further Roger Beckwith, *Daily and Weekly Worship: Jewish to Christian* (Alcuin/GROW Liturgical Study 1. Nottingham: Grove, 1987).

6 The debates in the Gospels about sabbath observance (e.g. Mark 2.23 – 3.6) may reflect controversy in early Christian communities around how much of the Law was to be retained (see Galatians 4.8-11).

7 *The Epistle of Barnabas* 15.8 (c. 100AD) is the earliest known citation of Sunday as 'eighth day', as part of arguing that Sunday be kept and not the Sabbath.

8 So Sundays are not 'of' but 'in' Lent: there are 47 days from Ash Wednesday to Easter, not 40.

I once heard lectures on liturgy from an Afro-American professor about the characteristics of 'black' worship in the USA. He made the telling point that in the centuries of slavery, the only ones allowed by their white masters to learn to read were preachers. Sunday was the only day free from unrelenting toil, a day of rest indeed. The preacher was called to give people enough hope to stay alive until the next Sunday. Western Christians – not least laid-back Australians – easily forget the importance of living in hope, rather than just the present. On the other hand, failing to live out our Sunday hope in the realities of daily life is 'pie in the sky when you die' religion.

Seeing Sunday as the eighth day does not set aside the challenges of living in this age. Rather, it offers the hope of time renewed, the whole week transformed – Sunday to Saturday and all in between. An 'eighth day' outlook suggests that the new creation might be like the ideal Australian weekend: free of toil, open to endless opportunities of creative activity, renewed relationships, eating and drinking with all God's people, as together we are "transformed from one degree of glory to another" (2 Corinthians 3.18). Yet Christ's 'glory' was the cross (John 12.23ff), whose power is displayed in weakness, the only thing of which Paul would boast (Romans 5.2-3; Galatians 6.14). In short, Sunday, the first and eighth day of Christian faith, calls and shapes us to live out the gospel of hope in the realities of this age and world.

Year by year: Lent, Holy Week and Easter – the Christian Passover

Christ's atoning death, rest and being raised to new life were the turning point of history, when the "life of the ages" broke in decisively. Just as being a Jew is inextricably tied up with Passover, being a Christian is inseparable from Easter, the Christian Passover (*pasch*: 1 Corinthians 5.7-8). So Holy Week and Easter form the hinge around which the Christian year revolves. Lent leads into this crucial time – 'crux' is Latin for 'cross' – and the fifty days of Easter find their climax at Pentecost ('fifty' in Greek).[9]

This near-century of days is the core of the Christian Calendar, setting Christ crucified and risen at the year's centre. Ron Dowling, who drafted the Calendar in *APBA*, notes that Easter, "the original Christian feast", was for some time kept as a "one-night liturgy", but "gradually the idea of historical commemoration began to dominate, and the main parts of this saving event were assigned to the various days".[10]

---

9   Lent began soon after the 'peace' of Constantine (312AD): Gregory Dix suggests that it commenced as a preparation for the multitude seeking baptism once persecution had ceased, and continued as a season of repentance and renewal for all the baptised.

10 Ronald Dowling, 'The Calendar' in *A Practical Commentary*, 93-94. The change seems to have begun in the late third century, and spread quickly after the Peace of Constantine: *Egeria's Journal*, documenting her visit to Jerusalem in Holy Week c. 380, was influential in this spread.

Human beings find it helpful to enter into the unfolding events around Christ's passion by marking them in succession. Many Christians feel betrayed on Maundy Thursday, heart-broken on Good Friday, empty on Holy Saturday and joyful on Easter morning. The western Christian tradition came to mark these truths in successive days, the *triduum* ('of three days' in Latin). The eastern tradition, however, keeps them as an integrated celebration of the Christian Passover, climaxed with the 'new fire' lit at midnight on Easter Eve. Whether celebrated together or over a few days, the various aspects of Christ's victorious passion belong together. We cannot *re-enact* God's saving work, but are *re-membered* by entering once more into the once-for-all saving events of Holy Week.[11]

Passover is associated not only with God's historic acts of rescue, but also with northern hemisphere spring (Leviticus 23, Deuteronomy 16). Yet classical Christian service texts link Easter to God's acts in history, rather than spring. Nevertheless, Christian celebrations often include springtime elements, such as Australian church buildings being lavishly decorated with flowers, despite it being autumn. Likewise, Israel's festival of Weeks, a 'week of weeks' plus one day, Pentecost, marks both the giving of the Law and the wheat harvest (Exodus 34.22; Leviticus 34.15).

There are dangers in confusing cyclic fertility celebrations with God's once-for-all historic rescue operation in Christ, made over to us in the gift of the Spirit. A better way, however, is to view these Passover / springtime, harvest / Pentecost pairings as reflecting the integration of God's work in creation and re-creation, anticipations of the reconciliation of "all things, whether on earth or in the heavens" in Christ (Colossians 1.20). Performing the gospel in Christian liturgy can thus fold in what is true from the seasons of nature and human life-cycles.

Year by year: the 'great cloud of witnesses'

Christ's paschal victory over death, with its hope of new creation, was soon linked with commemorating the witness (*marturia*) to death of faithful believers, their 'birthday' into the new creation.[12] On such saints' days, believers celebrate the grace of God in a particular Christian's distinctive witness to Christ, one of the "great cloud of witnesses" who have run the race of faith before us (Hebrews 12.1-2).

---

11 For fuller discussion see *Performing the Gospel*, 228–232; Peter Akehurst, *Keeping Holy Week*. Grove Worship Series 41 (Bramcote: Grove, 1976); and Trevor Lloyd, *Celebrating Lent, Holy Week and Easter*. Grove Worship Series 93 (Nottingham: Grove, 1985).

12 Thus the *Martyrdom of Polycarp* #18 records that, after this Bishop of Smyrna was killed in 156AD, local Christians took his bones to "a fitting place" where they would pray on the anniversary of his being burnt and stabbed to death.

Traditionally, church buildings are named after a holy person, giving those who worship there a particular example of following Jesus as a disciple. The date of a saint's day is normally the day of their 'falling asleep' in Christ, their 'patronal festival'. So Vincent is remembered on 22 January, Thomas Cranmer on 21 March and James Noble on 25 November. Indeed, until government authorites took over the task of recording births, each person in Christendom was named after a saint, and celebrated their 'feast day' rather than their (often unknown) 'birthday', as many Greek, Italian and other Australians still do.

Year by year: Advent / Christmas / Epiphany

The Advent / Christmas / Epiphany group is the third main cycle in the Calendar: its focus is the revelation of God in our human flesh. As with Passover / Weeks and Easter / Pentecost, these seasons interact with the cycles of nature, though through links with solstices and equinoxes rather than harvests.[13] Each year has a pair of 'solstices', the longest (summer) and shortest (winter) days, and a pair of 'equinoxes', autumn and spring, when day and night are the same length. Days lengthen from the winter solstice and spring equinox, shorten from the summer solstice and autumn equinox.

The date of Christmas Day

Christmas Day came later than Easter, as reflection on the mystery of Incarnation deepened. In northern Europe, how – but not *why* – it was observed was shaped by its nearness to the winter solstice, when the sun's light was least, and people feared the dark. But this was not why December 25 became Christmas Day.

March 25 is the (northern) equinox in the Julian calendar, the opening of spring.[14] It was observed as New Year's Day in Britain until the Gregorian calendar was adopted in 1752, when the year's beginning reverted to January 1. Western society had long marked March 25 as 'Lady Day', the historical beginning of God's new creation, when the eternal Word was conceived by the Spirit in Mary's womb (Luke 1.20-38) – the 'Annunciation' (announcement) by Gabriel to the Blessed Virgin Mary that she would bear Jesus, the "first-born of the new creation" (Colossians 1.15).[15] Christmas Day, 25 December, falls nine months after March 25: that

---

13 Human societies, including Israel, have based their calendars on both the solar (annual) and lunar (monthly) cycles, which do not readily 'fit': see *Performing the Gospel*, 216–217. The 'Gregorian' calendar brings them together: since its adoption world-wide, the differences minimally affect the Church year.

14 March 25 often falls close to Passover, which led Augustine of Hippo (amongst others) to believe that it was on that day that "Christ our Passover" (1 Corinthians 5.7) died.

15 Late medieval art (e.g. paintings by Giotto and Botticelli) delights to portray the Annunciation as the Word of God coming on a scroll from Gabriel's lips to Mary's womb, where a tiny baby already rests.

date was not chosen to counterbalance winter solstice celebrations around the Roman Saturnalia or Germanic Yuletide feasts, but because Christians knew how long a pregnancy lasted.

What then of the "twelve days of Christmas"? Eastern Christians celebrate the incarnation on January 6–7, near the winter solstice in Egypt. The emphasis falls on the incarnation as a doctrinal truth: January 6 is Eastern Christmas Day, explicating the meaning of the Saviour's coming. In the West, on the other hand, telling the story is the great delight, and this is the focus of December 25: January 6 became Epiphany, the "Manifestation of Christ to the Gentiles" (**BCP**), 'showing meaning' day. English tradition blended both approaches, thus creating the 'twelve days of Christmas' from December 25 to January 6.

Other solar-influenced days

The solar cycles also influence other Christian commemorations. June 24 is the Julian (northern) summer solstice, after which days shorten. The Church year marks it as 'Birth of John the Baptist': "he must increase, I must decrease" (John 3.30) as John said of his cousin, Jesus. September 29 is the Julian (northern) autumn equinox, the beginning of autumn: the Church year keeps it in honour of Michael and All Angels, spiritual protectors in darker times.

What then of Halloween, 31 October? All Saints' Day began to be observed from the fourth century, soon after Pentecost. Pope Gregory III set its observance on November 1 in 835, the date followed by the West thereafter. All Saints' (Hallows') Eve, Hallowe'en, may go back to a Celtic feast, Samhain, marking the start of the long northern winter, when it was thought that the 'spirit world' impinged on ordinary life. In popular Irish culture it came to be marked as a time to repudiate the demonic by 'sending it up'. Hallowe'en in its modern form is thought to have been brought by Irish immigrants to the USA, from where it slowly spread in the West with little if any reference to Christian faith.

Advent: why does it begin the Christian year?

Advent sets before Christians the biblical vision of the 'end' of all things, centred around the return of Christ. Why then does the Christian year open with Advent'?

The day of judgement linked with Christ's return can be felt as deeply threatening, bringing about a prevalent fear of dying unprepared. Human beings are accountable to God, both as persons and peoples: for those who refuse to recognise this, the day of judgement is to be feared (cf Matthew 25.32ff). But God's judgement is a liberating truth for believers: Christ is our "advocate with the Father" (1 John 2.1), affirming that in Christ we are in the right, and so have peace with God (Romans 5.1–2). We look to hear from God's mouth those blessed words: "well done, good and faithful servant: enter into the joy of your Lord." (Matthew 25.21). Advent thus points to the day of judgement as one of hope, when all in Christ will be vindicated. But this does not explain why Advent begins the Christian year.

Advent is seen by many as preparing for Christmas, a bit like Lent preparing for Easter. The prophets are heard in Advent, especially Isaiah and John the Baptist, but their message is about the 'end', the goal of God's work, not Christ's birth in isolation from this. An ancient custom is to turn towards Christmas in Advent's final 'octave' (eight days from December 17, as in *An Australian Lectionary*). In similar vein is the tradition of the third Advent wreath candle being pink, for 'Rejoice' Sunday (from the opening word of the Latin service, 'gaudete'). Rather than preparing for Christmas, these traditions do not obscure the main focus of Advent on the 'end' that God is bringing about in Christ. So this is not why Advent begins the Christian year.

Christmas and Xma$

Christmas is today celebrated across much of the globe without little reference to Christ's birth: Xma$, ending by noon on December 25. Even so, this has some positive aspects: families and work colleagues get together, children's eyes widen in excitement, there is community singing, leaders reflect on the year past and ahead, peace and goodwill are commended. Such good things reflect the grace of God which undergirds all living.

But there are dangers in focussing on December's days as just "getting ready for Christmas". Advent calendars covering the month's first 25 days traditionally gave space for a daily gift to be shared with those in need. Today many provide a daily gift for children, often promoting chocolate consumption, feeding the 'NN shopping days left' mentality that views Xma$ as the climax of the retail year. Its patron saint is $anta Claus, the re-invention of the slim and green Saint Nicholas into the well-fed man in the red and white of Coca-Cola.

A whole Xma$ mythology has grown up around reindeer, elves, chimneys, the North Pole, $anta circling the globe in a day and so on. Singing 'Jingle Bells', 'Rudolph' and similar ditties may be innocent enough. But feeding youngsters blatant lies about flying sleighs and a fat man coming down chimneys is cruel. Tears abound when a child realises that the $anta legend has no reality – and the experience may train them to see the story of Christ's birth as just another fairy tale.

At the core of this myth lies another heresy, perpetuated in the song 'Santa Claus is Coming to Town' (written at the heart of the Depression in 1934). Children are not to cry or pout, must be naughty or nice, because Santa is making a list, checking it over, and watching them even when they are asleep. This seemingly harmless ditty is not funny: being 'good' is in order to get lots of presents. And it promotes fear in children: Advent is overshadowed by the dread of being judged by $anta. Quite a contrast to the Christian hope of God's judgement, bringing vindication and new life.

NB: telling children to be 'good' because God is watching their every moment is even worse than this Xma$ 'anti-theology'.

Advent: on earth as it is in heaven

So why *does* Advent begin the Christian year? Jesus taught us to pray, "Your kingdom come, your will be done, on earth as it is in heaven" (Matthew 6.10). We pray to live 'on earth' as citizens of the new creation (Philippians 3.20).

Advent opens the Christian year because it calls us to live from God's future backwards, rather than just from our human past forwards. It involves the disciplined work of re-visioning our living, seeing everything in the light of the 'reign of Christ the king' (as the Sunday before Advent has been named since the 1970s). Advent calls us to delight in the 'blessed hope' of the full presence of Christ, our judge and vindicator (Titus 2.13), our advocate with the Father (1 John 2.1). We stand in awe of the age-old prophets, who saw these things from afar, and indicted those who practised oppression and lived unjustly. Only with the return of Christ, "who is coming to call all to account", will we be able to truly celebrate the first 'advent' of our Lord, the amazing gift of God's eternal Word enfleshed in Mary's womb by the Holy Spirit, who "brings all things to their true end",[16] anticipating God's future in our present (cf 2 Corinthians 5.5).

Advent is thus a time of serious joy. That is why the traditional colour for the season is purple or blue, the ancient colour of royalty, and why an Advent carol service is more than a 'Christmas singalong'. The Nine Lessons & Carols service from King's College Cambridge, drawn up by Eric Milner-White in 1913 and broadcast from 1918, sets the Christmas story within the scope of God's saving work. A wide range of 'carol services' is available that work for regular worshippers and the public alike.[17]

---

16 The last two citations are from the 'Affirmation of Faith', *APBA* page 37.

17 Australian ones include Elizabeth Smith, *Prayers and Plays for Christmas and Holy Week* (Mulgrave: Broughton, 2007), and Peta Sherlock, *Six Carol Services* (Melbourne: JBCE, 1990). These resources relate strongly to contemporary culture, and involve a range of participants. A web search will find more.

Context: seasons 'down under'

Three major 'cycles' thus shape the Christian year:
>the Easter cycle (96 days from Ash Wednesday to Pentecost);
>the cycle of saints' and special days spread across the year; and
>the Incarnation cycle (Advent to Epiphany).

Each has the Lord Jesus Christ at its centre; each celebrates God's presence, grace and activity in nature, history and human societies.

But how do these cycles work out 'down under', helping Australians perform the gospel under the Southern Cross? I vividly remember a European scholar at an international liturgy conference in Sydney being amazed when he realised that Easter is kept in autumn here. "Heretical!" he cried. Australians responded that seeing Easter as a spring fertility rite was scarcely orthodox. On the other hand, a new minister in a country town cancelled the long-standing 'Christmas in July' meal because having Christmas other than in December was unorthodox. A better way is taking positive approaches to our 'inverse' seasons. Australia's southern latitudes experience the 'four seasons' known in Europe and North America, while our northern climes are tropical, akin to much of Asia. That Christian festivals here fall in 'opposite' seasons to northern hemisphere invites a re-working of their 'nature-related' aspects.

More challenging than the 'seasons swap', however, is the reality that the Christian year 'down under' mixes with holidays and special days only related to it indirectly, if at all. Before reflecting on the Christian year in Australia, attention to this wider context is needed.

The Australian weekend

Saturday and Sunday have become the 'weekend', centred around leisure more than rest or worship, though for many these too are work days. Seeing Sunday as sabbath means that employment and public sporting events are regulated by law. 'Penalty rates' are paid to people in 'essential services' like hospitals, where work must be done '24/7'. 'Sunday trading' laws have now been rescinded, though there is firm resistance to 'penalty rates' being removed.

For many Australians Sunday is a hectic day. Apart from shopping or eating out, Sunday morning may be taken up with sport, the afternoon by professional games, and the evening by television. Finding ways to enable Christians to worship if they cannot attend on Sundays, for whatever reason, can be challenging. Many churches have changed service times, and Saturday evening services are common: in the Roman Catholic Church, participation in a 'vigil mass' on Saturday evening was in

1947 accepted as fulfilling the obligation to worship on Sunday. And there are circumstances in which it is best for a church to meet on a weekday: a midweek service for shift workers, for example, or one for people on the autism spectrum, or a congregation in a nursing home.

Observing Sunday as a day of rest, 'sabbath', may not be a Christian essential, but it is not wrong. The growing habit of putting Monday rather than Sunday as the first day of the week – as in many diaries – sees human existence in terms of work rather than rest and hope. I grew up in a clergy home, where 'church' dominated Sundays. Dad took three services in the morning, often one in the afternoon, and one in the evening: we went to at least two (plus Sunday school). Mum was determined that we should enjoy this special day: so we had guests to (midday) dinner, afternoon 'Sunday surprises', and joined in supper after evening church. My highlight was breakfast with a lively bunch of Sunday school teachers, and Milo on my cereal (which I still have). Homework on Sundays was discouraged: in my university years Sunday brought the gift of guilt-free freedom from the hard work of study.

Sunday is special, the ideal day to celebrate the resurrection: but it is not sacrosanct (cf Romans 14.5-6). And setting aside funds for the weekly collection (cf 1 Corinthians 16.1-2) can happen at any time with electronic banking and direct debit giving.

The Australian year: civic holidays

What then of the 'Australian year', shaped by a dozen or more civic holidays? Some are national (Australia Day and Anzac Day), others sporting (the various Cup, Show and Grand Final days) or global (New Year's Day). Some have been around for a while, such as Mothers' Day, started in the USA by Anna Jarvis in 1908. Other days are more recent, for example 'Jane McGrath' day at Sydney's Test cricket match, supporting breast cancer nurses. None make explicit reference to Christian faith, but God's grace undergirds all that is good in these celebrations: 'holiday' is a contraction of 'holy day'. Churches that play active and imaginative parts in local celebrations bear witness to God's grace beyond individual Christians' involvement as citizens. Hospitality can be offered, practical assistance given to people in need, patient hope given to those wrestling with addiction, and opportunity taken for occasions of prayer.

APBA offers resources for national days (e.g. pages 161-162, 628-629) and the 'Week of Prayer for Reconciliation' (May 27 – June 3) . The 'Occasional Prayers' (pages 202-210) include several that relate to national life. *APBA* also notes the blessing of animals (near October 4, St Francis' Day) and harvest festivals ('Rogationtide', *APBA* page 451, open to blessings of the fleece or fleet).

But these holidays also call for bearing witness against ungodly social trends: untruths about *terra nullius*, false nationalism, consumer-driven values and hopes in 'lady luck', the sexualisation of women and relationships ... and refusal to face the ambiguities of Anglican participation in the shadow side of our history. This is recognised in Confession #3 (*APBA* page 199, which should only be used after preparation), and A Thanksgiving for Australia (#3 on *APBA* pages 218–219). One national day in particular calls for further comment: Anzac Day.[18]

Anzac Day

Anzac Day, the most widely observed national day for Australians and New Zealanders, carries ambiguities, not least for Christians. Its celebration of bravery and dedication in and through defeat echoes Christ's victory through suffering and death. But it also runs the risk of seeing the suffering of combatants and civilians as likewise redemptive. Jesus' words, "Greater love hath no man than this, to lay down his life for his friends" (John 15.13, the sentence for the day in *APBA*) are placed on many memorials and stained glass windows, and often cited on April 25 without reference to Christ. As I have written elsewhere,

> There are dangers involved, not so much of glorifying war, as of confusing ideas about 'sacrifice', notably overly close parallels between the atoning death of Christ and the tragic death of military forces. Soldiers do not go to war looking to die, to 'sacrifice themselves', but rather look to return home safely. Yet the willingness to face danger, becoming disabled or even dying is profoundly praiseworthy.[19]

Anzac Day rites are dignified and impressive, especially the minute's silence and the Last Post / Reveille. But Binyon's Ode speaks of the fallen as "they shall not grow old", imprisoning them in an unchanging youth. The Christian hope, with its dynamic of growth "from one degree of glory to another"(2 Corinthians 3.18), is liberating. The ethos of Anzac Day is one of recalling the past as left in the past (*mimesis*), rather than the Easter sense of remembering the past as illuminating the present (*anamnesis*). Which is why Jesus' command for disciples to "do this for the *anamnesis* of me" leads us to "proclaim the Lord's death until he comes" (1 Corinthians 11.23–26) as an act of hope.[20] The good news? April 25 always falls in Eastertide: resurrection hope can thus embrace the sombre Anzac Day commemoration of the disaster that is war.

---

18 Australia Day, the other civic event added to the Calendar in *AAPB*, was retained in *APBA* but with resources that underline its ambiguity. See further *Australian Anglicans Remember*, 18–20.

19 *Australian Anglicans Remember*, 49.

20 See Charles Sherlock, "ANZAC and Easter Dawn: *mimesis* and *anamnesis*", *Australian Journal of Liturgy* (May 2010) 3–11, and *Studia Liturgica* 40/1–2 (2010) 102–109.

What then should clergy do if asked to take part in an Anzac Day service? Accept gladly: Christian ministers are not always asked to take part in civic events, and that resources are provided in *APBA* gives you official permission to do so. 'Best practice' (and good manners) will see you ask to see the order of service ahead of time so you know what your part is. Robes must be clean and on hand for changing into: this is an occasion where the wider public expect to see a minister looking like one. Cassock, surplice and scarf are acceptable, with medals on the scarf if you are entitled to them, or at least 'dog-collar' and suit. Prepare and write down any words you will say, to avoid any misunderstandings and keep to time. Anazc Day is an opportunity to reflect on the serious issues of life, both for parishioners and those who may rarely walk through the doors of a church.

The Easter long weekend – before and beyond

The Easter long weekend sees some churches with low attendance, as people take the opportunity to have a break before the weather worsens and winter begins to set in the south. Good Friday is less and less observed as a day for quiet reflection: sporting events, the Easter Show in Sydney and the Royal Melbourne hospital appeal in Victoria, are the focus for many people. And the 'paschal sacrament' for children – of any age – is chocolate. In contrast, for police, ambulance and emergency services the Easter road toll looms large. Culturally appropriate public Christian witness is possible, however. In Bendigo, Easter marks the city's Chinese heritage: local Christians set up a labyrinth in the gardens at the town centre, inviting all to meditate as they walk its circles.

Lent in autumn

Taking Lent seriously is a good start to entering deeply into Holy Week and Easter. The practice of parishioners engaging in Lenten study groups is widely accepted: resources are issued by mission agencies (e.g. ABM-A and TEAR) and educational bodies (e.g. the Roman Catholic Archdiocese of Brisbane). Such reflection, with special services, personal disciplines and giving, are the 'stuff' of parishioners preparing for Easter.

But what of the wider population? Lent opens on Ash Wednesday, remembered in South Australia and Victoria as a terrible day of dust-storms and bushfires in 1983, a sobering reminder of mortality, both personal and social. The custom of burning last year's palm crosses to create the ashes to be imposed evokes similar ideas.[21] In

---

21 The symbol of burning is brought out when the old palms are set alight in a steel vessel (on a table mat) on the holy table: sprinkled with shellac or similar, they will burn quickly with visible flames. Adding a small amount of cold water will result in a paste, cool enough to use for ashing by the end of Psalm 51.

Australia's southern climes, Lent runs its course as autumn deepens, supporting its reflective ethos. Embracing people's memories of fire and flood, and allowing the autumnal cycle to shape the journey to Easter, can help 'down under' folk sense God's call to be accountable in all of living – and avoid running the northern hemisphere risk of fertility religion.

Above all, however, Lent moves faithful Christians towards the centre of the Christian year – Holy Week, and its climax on Easter Day, THE Sunday of Sundays.

Holy Week: re-enacting or re-membering?

Holy Week offers opportunities for 'fringe' as well as 'committed' parishioners to be called back to their roots in Christ. On the Sunday before Easter the whole gospel of Christ's passion is read, so that we enter Holy Week shaped by the story as a whole. (This is an opportunity for 'dialogue' or dramatic reading by several voices.)

Hearing the whole passion read avoids the temptation to 're-enact' the last week of Jesus' earthly life. Christ's saving work was unique, 'once for all' (Hebrews 9.26-28): it can and must be commemorated, but cannot be repeated or re-enacted. So in Holy Week we gather, not to re-enact his final week, but to be 're-membered' in Christ.[22] This is why 'The Sunday next before Easter' is named that in *BCP*. In *APBA* and other modern prayer books, it is called 'Passion Sunday'. For most people, however, it is 'Palm Sunday': human nature loves to enact a story, and starting the service with a procession of palms into the building, and distributing palm crosses to worshippers, enables all to take part in celebrating Christ's once-for-all work. So *APBA* adds 'Palm Sunday' in brackets after 'Passion Sunday', and provides a 'Liturgy of the Palms' (pages 493–4). But the main focus falls on our hearing the whole story, not beginning a week of re-enactment.

Similar comments apply to Maundy ('new commandment') Thursday. A quiet meal can be shared on Thursday evening, during which Eucharist is celebrated. A stark cross can be carried into church on Good Friday for all to acknowledge in some way. Symbolic actions like these are 'effectual means of grace' to support believers' participation in Holy Week. On Good (God's) Friday, ecumenical 'stations of the cross' processions make the gospel 'public', and bring Christians from different churches together in serious witness.[23] Easter services that are readily followed fold in visitors, while the renewal of baptism promises deepens the faith of disciples. An Easter Vigil

---

22 The 'Last Supper' pointed forward towards Christ's atoning death, and is unrepeatable: the Christian celebration of the Lord's Supper (1 Corinthians 11.20) points both back towards that sacrificial act, and forwards to the new creation when Christ comes (1 Corinthians 11.26): see pages 223–224 in this book.

23 On Holy Saturday, which has no civic reference, see page 322 in this book

Eucharist commencing in the dark, coming to its conclusion as dawn breaks, can be unforgettable – and champagne and croissants to follow does no harm. Activities involving children engage older people too: everyone enjoys an Easter egg hunt.

A big challenge for celebrating Easter is how to mark its jubilee of fifty days, running through to Pentecost. For most Australians Easter ends on Easter Day, a sense not helped by its seven weeks falling in autumn and early winter. Unlike England, where Whitsun means a long weekend in early summer, Pentecost has not entered Australian culture. But it does offer opportunities for ecumenical celebrations that, with some imagination, can tap into widespread interest in 'spirituality'.

Christmas down under

Like Easter, for most Australians the Christmas season closes by noon on December 25, with relief that the annual hectic Xma$ rush is over. Many who hum along to 'On the first day of Christmas' have little idea that December 25 *opens* twelve days of celebration. The 'spirit of Christmas' is increasingly diluted to a general sense of well-being: no bad thing, but my suspicious mind senses that people are being softened up to open wide their wallets in honour of Xma$ (as considered earlier). But some Australian Christmas customs deserve comment.

Australian Christmas customs

'Carols by Candlelight' is one such, enabled by the summer weather. Begun on Christmas Eve 1938 by Norman Banks, a well-known radio broadcaster in Melbourne, it was initially resisted by church leaders. It is now the most-watched Christmas event on television, and has spread globally. In my town, 'Carols in the Park' takes place on the first Friday in December, a lovely event, with family groups gathered at the lake in the middle of town on a (hopefully) balmy evening. Well-known carols are included alongside 'holiday songs' that make no reference to the birth of Christ. Even so, a local Anglican priest has compered it, Santa is usually one of our churchwardens, and I've been one of his elves (i.e. child controller). There is no future in ignoring or despising events such as these: far better to join in and sing up.

For wider society, Advent may well be a lost cause in terms of 'keeping awake' for Christ's return, the 'end' of all things. But when Christians avoid these realities the gospel is diluted, and we run the danger of offering 'cheap grace'. Even so, as Christmas Day draws near, activities such as 'dress up' nativity scenes, 'give a goat' campaigns, supporting people in need (especially refugees), social media greetings and carol singing in nursing homes, give opportunities for 'ordinary' Christians to play their part in commending the gospel in public.

Christmas and Epiphany: story and meaning

Schools, colleges and many businesses are in recess for the summer holidays, and sporting events cluster around the Christmas–New Year week: the Boxing Day Test in Melbourne, Sydney to Hobart yacht race and so on. Nothing wrong with these – God's grace undergirds all that is good in human life. Yet for many these events are the exclusive focus of the first days of the Christmas season.

The Christmas season's twelve days include the commemoration of Stephen the first martyr, John the Divine, and the Holy Innocents (December 26, 27 and 28). People of faith can live out the truths of these Festivals alongside the week's other events: quite a few will take part in 'beach missions' where holiday-makers gather. The choice is not between God's gifts of holidays and Christ, but how the Spirit integrates life and faith when society is in holiday mode. These special days bring a more realistic tone to a merely 'happy' Christmas. Pennyweight Flat in the Diocese of Bendigo is where many children were buried in gold rush days: the parish holds a service there on Holy Innocents Day, remembering all taken from life before their time.

January 1 marks the circumcision of Christ, for which resources are provided in *APBA*. It is rather a challenge to blend in with New Year celebrations, which give opportunities for churches to take part in community gatherings, and offer quieter ways to mark the changing of the year. Where crowds gather, practical support can be provided (ecumenically) for those who go too far in celebrating. In John and Charles Wesley's day, many workers wasted their money on strong drink on New Year's Eve. So they provided a 'watchnight service' for the public, and on the first Sunday of the new year a 'covenant service' for Methodists to consecrate themselves to Christian service. *An Australian Lectionary* offers 'watchnight' readings, while *Uniting in Worship* includes a modern covenant service.

Epiphany themes can be taken up by exploring Christ through the 'signs' of his ministry.[24] Eastern and Western churches now mark the Sunday after January 6 as 'Baptism of the Lord', the beginning of Christ's public ministry: Greek Christians 'bless the waters' on this day, gaining widespread media coverage. The second Sunday marks Jesus' first 'sign', the wedding at Cana: but please don't repeat the 'drink sermon' my family came to dread on our annual vacation. Epiphany is holiday time: using the 'signs' Jesus performed in holiday-type ways offers creative possibilities.

---

24 In *BCP* Epiphany is a 'filler' season. The three Sundays before Lent look to Easter: Septuagesima, Sexagesima and Quinquagesima (i.e. roughly 70, 60 and 50 days before it). The number of other Sundays needed before Lent depends on the date of Easter: *BCP* adds extra ones from the final Sundays of the year, which would then not be needed.

Further reading

Akehurst, Peter, *Keeping Holy Week.* Grove Worship Series 41 (Bramcote: Grove, 1976): an excellent resource for a liturgy planning team

Alexander, J. Neil, *Waiting for the Coming: the liturgical meaning of Advent, Christmas, Epiphany* (Pastoral Press: Washington DC, 1993)

Beckwith, Roger, *Daily and Weekly Worship: Jewish to Christian* Alcuin/GROW Liturgical Study 1 (Bramcote: Grove, 1987)

Dershowitz, Nachan & Reingold, Edward, *Calendrical Calculations* (Cambridge: CUP, 1997): a detailed and fascinating account of fourteen calendars from past and present, written to assist software developers, but with many insights into the development of holy/idays

Lloyd, Trevor, *Celebrating Lent, Holy Week and Easter,* Grove Worship Series 93 (Bramcote: Grove, 1985): an excellent planning resource, widening the scope of Peter Akehurst's work

McGowan, Andrew, *Ancient Christian Worship* (Grand Rapids: Baker Academic, 2014): Chapter Seven gathers together the available evidence relating to the development of the Christian year

Talley, Thomas J., *The Origins of the Liturgical Year* (Pueblo Publishing, New York: 1986): a ground-breaking and influential work by a Texas Anglican scholar

Vasey, Michael, (ed) *Family Festivals*, Grove Worship Series 73 (Bramcote: Grove, 1983): lots of creative, well-grounded ideas for bringing church and home together

Webber, Robert, 'The Services of the Christian Year', Chapter Twenty in *Worship Old and New* (Grand Rapids: Zondervan, 1994): a highly readable guide

Chapter Five

Seasons and Saints in APBA

Christian understandings of time revolve around Jesus Christ: that we date history in terms of BC and AD witnesses to God's gracing of all time. Human beings are creatures of space and time, yet destined for eternity: 'earthlings' called in Christ to be citizens of heaven. We live 'between the times', this present age interweaving with God's new creation, the 'ages of ages' (the Greek often rendered 'for ever and ever'). Our experience, personal and communal, of the basic rhythms of day / night, sabbath / Sunday and the cycles of salvation, Christmas, Easter, and the saints, tunes our innermost selves to God's 'rhythm' of work and rest, gracing nature and history alike.

The Calendar in *APBA* is a basic resource to assist Australian Anglicans to perform the gospel in the context of southern hemisphere life. It is grounded in the biblical witness to the focal points of God's work in ancient Israel, Christ and the Spirit. It is shaped by generation upon generation of Christian experience, transmitted and reformed in successive *BCPs*. It recognizes the need to face this nation's 'original sin' and work for reconciliation between Indigenous and immigrant citizens. It takes ecumenically sensitive steps towards performing the gospel in our Australian social, historical and cultural settings. And it leaves open many opportunities for participating in God's mission though local 'times and seasons'.

The Calendar in *APBA*

The Calendar in *APBA* is preceded by 'Directions' (pages 450–451). These contain significant instructions for Anglican clergy, who agree to live within the discipline of the Church, including the Church's Year. This imposes no great burden: the Calendar in *APBA* is a simplified version of the one in *BCP*, and represents an ecumenically-informed 'placing' of this heritage in an Australian setting. Most feasts belong to the worldwide Church, and are complemented by events and holy persons distinctive to our story (see *Australian Anglicans Remember*).

The Calendar continues with notes on two times that blend the cycles of nature, society and the Church's Year: Ember and Rogation days.

Ember Days

These days originated in the agricultural calendar of the northern hemisphere. They are interesting examples of Christian faith taking on board existing customs and shaping them in the light of the gospel. In *BCP*, following the long-term practice of the Western Church, four three-day 'ember' periods are provided: the Wednesdays, Fridays and Saturdays after Lent 1, Pentecost, September 14 (Holy Cross) and December 13 (St Lucy). They are designated as 'days of fasting, or abstinence', calling Christians to mark the change of the seasons by a serious discipline. Their observance was made optional in the Anglican Communion from 1976.

Where the term 'ember' comes from is a bit of a puzzle. It is not a Latin word, but some scholars think it is an abbreviation of 'quattuor tempora' (four seasons) via the German 'Quatember'. More scholars prefer the Anglo-Saxon *ymbre* ('around', or 'circuit'), reflecting the centuries-old practice of holding processions on these days. Among the ancient Romans it was customary to observe the sowing and harvest times each year with petitions to the relevant deities. The Church in Rome marked these days of seasonal change as Christian from around 200AD, and the custom spread across Europe. One of the instructions given to Augustine of Canterbury for his mission to Britain (597AD) was to ensure that Ember Days were observed there.

The practice of ordaining clergy at Embertide began in the fifth century in Rome: it was made a rule in Britain by Archbishop Ecgbert of York in the eighth century. The Preface to the Ordinal attached to *BCP* refers to Canon XXXI (1603), which specifies that ordinations take place on a Sunday after an Ember Day, but allows the bishop "for urgent reason" to ordain on a "Sunday or holy-day". In practice, ordinations have often taken place at the end of the academic year: in England on June 29 (Peter and Paul) and in Australia on November 30 (Andrew) or December 21 (Thomas), so new priests can preside at Christmas communions.

APBA adapts the Embertide tradition to relate it to Australian conditions. They are reduced from four to two, following Pentecost and St Andrew's Day, and the three days are extended to a week. These changes orient their meaning to the mission of God, and links with the English meaning of 'ember' as 'burning fuel'. As one diocese's publicity for an Embertide ordination enquirer's day runs:

> If Pentecost offers fresh inspiration from the Holy Spirit, November 30 draws us towards Andrew's example of personal evangelism. Fanned by the wind, embers flame into fire. Ember Days call us to pray for God's Spirit-wind to inflame us to discern the men and women God calls to the ministry of Word and sacrament.

APBA contains sentences, prayers and readings for use on Ember Days (pages 635-636). Other appropriate prayers can be found on pages 210-215, and the Exhortations in each of the Ordinals can be used as a guide for reflection.

Rogation Days

On 'rogation' days (Latin *rogare*, 'to ask'), God's blessing is sought for a fruitful harvest. As with Ember days, their observance goes back to agricultural festivals of ancient times. *BCP* provides for two three-day times of 'rogation': the Mondays-Wednesdays in Holy Week, and preceding Ascension Day (always a Thursday). These dates set 'harvest festivals' within the celebration of the ministry of Christ, especially of intercession, a further example of nature and history being integrated rather than separated.

In the nineteenth century, the 'arts and crafts' movement in England saw harvest festivals and customs such as 'Blessing of the Fleece' revived. In Australia these were common by World War I, but the *BCP* dates do not fit the nature cycle of the southern hemisphere. So, as with Ember days, *APBA* updates Rogation days in several ways:

a) The focus shifts beyond harvest to an ecological perspective: "Prayers of thanksgiving for the whole created order and for the right use of the resources of the earth, its conservation and for the abundance of its fruits."

b) A suggested time is "the days around the commemoration of Francis of Assisi (4 October)", widely kept as the 'Blessing of the Animals'. Since 2001, October 4 has been observed as World Animal Day (with no reference to Francis).[1]

c) The animal kingdom includes human beings, whose harvest includes the fruits of industry, caring and learning. So "it is also appropriate that thanksgiving and prayer be offered for all human wisdom, imagination, skill and labour."

Harvest Festival is typically celebrated on a Sunday, which runs the risk of displacing its focus on the resurrection of Christ. *APBA* permits this, but adds that it "should not replace any Sunday in the seasons of Lent and Easter".

The Liturgy Commission has issued a variety of resources relating to harvest and ecology. A preliminary question was, "What exactly are people looking for here, and how do their desires engage with the wide range of social, moral and political issues involved?" A start was made with 'Thanksgiving for gardens', then a form of confession for our abuse of God's creation, before moving to prayers around farming and so on.[2]

---

1 See https://www.worldanimalday.org.uk/about_us.
2 These resources are available on the General Synod Liturgy page under 'Themes': https://www.anglican.org.au/thematic-resources.

Observing Sunday

In *APBA*, pages 452ff set out an overview of the Calendar. Most is probably familiar, but it should be read through carefully. Overall, it is similar to the 'Kalendar' that opens *BCP*, but its 'shape' is clearer, with three 'levels' of celebration: Principal Holy Days / Festivals; Holy Days / Festivals; and Lesser Festivals / Commemorations.

The first sentence under Principal Holy Days (page 452) is of high importance: **Every Sunday is a Holy Day, being a celebration of the resurrection of our Lord.**

Especially since 2000, civic days, weeks, years and decades related to 'issues' have proliferated, increasingly supplanting days and seasons from the Christian tradition.[3] It is tempting to fill up Sundays with 'special' celebrations of things good in themselves, but this runs the risk of supplanting its central focus on the risen Lord Jesus Christ. So General Synod adopted this policy, prepared by the Liturgy Commission:

Special Observances on Sunday

In the course of each year, various agencies prepare and distribute resources for parishes, including material for use during Sunday services.

The Liturgy Commission offers these Guidelines to assist groups preparing such materials in order that any references to special observances will be well integrated with other elements of the Sunday liturgy.

Guidelines for Groups preparing Liturgical Resources for Special Observances on Sunday

1. The faith-narrative unfolded through the Sunday lectionary, texts and feasts is of primary importance for a principal Sunday service. Material relating to a special observance should be seen in the context of the overall purpose of the Sunday celebration – to recall the life, death and resurrection of Christ and offer praise and thanksgiving to God who "has begotten us again, through the resurrection of Jesus Christ from the dead, into a living hope" (1 Peter 1:3).

    The primary purpose of the Sunday assembly is not to promote or educate people about a particular cause, however worthwhile it may be. Any special observance during the principal Sunday liturgy needs to be well-integrated into the service, and its main purpose.

2. The Sunday Lectionary readings and Prayers of the Day are basic components of our common worship, both within the Anglican Church and

---

3   The United Nations list of Days, Weeks, Years and Decades is available at www.un.org/en/sections/observances/united-nations-observances/

amongst other Churches. The message of these texts should not be replaced by references to special observances, for instance by the substitution of prayers or Scripture passages related to these observances.

3. It may be appropriate to refer to the special observance in the words of welcome. Agencies might provide a short text giving an example of such introductory words, without ignoring the celebration of the day or season.

4. Special observations can be recognised during the sermon. While the sermon is normally based on the Scriptures for the day, the special observance can be referred to in the course of the preaching, but this should flow from the proclamation of the word.

   Agencies may wish to provide a brief text (perhaps of one or two paragraphs) which the preacher could use as the basis for a reference to the special observance. A full sample sermon gives the impression that the preacher is being invited to preach on a particular cause or observance.

5. The special observance could be included in the Prayers of the People. Whilst it would not be appropriate for a particular topic to dominate these intercessions, it would be appropriate to include a petition or two related to the special observance as one of the elements in the community's prayer.

   Agencies may wish to provide a few examples of petition, but not a complete set of Prayers: again, this would give the impression that one observance alone was important to the exclusion of all others.

6. There might also be mention of the special observance in the notices. Agencies might provide a text for such a notice.

7. In addition to these references within the liturgy itself, there are other avenues that can by employed to publicise a special observance or cause. These include a notice for the parish bulletin and posters for display. Agencies may wish to provide these items amongst the resources they distribute. Study materials for use outside Sunday services in homes or small groups are always a welcome possibility.

So take care that the gospel is not unintentionally shoved aside on Sundays. Note that *APBA* provides that "a Festival may displace a Sunday in the season after Epiphany and the season after Pentecost, but not the Sundays of Advent, Lent or Easter".

Marking time in APBA

From *AAPB* to *APBA*

When *AAPB* was being prepared in the 1970s, Gilbert Sinden records that there was sensitivity around how much of the British and European oriented 'Kalendar' in *BCP* should be retained. Two 'levels' of observation were employed in *AAPB*, corresponding to *BCP*'s 'red' and 'black' letter days.[4] All 'red letter' days were retained, with 'black letter' days pruned and added to; prayers or readings were only provided for 'red letter' days. A few steps were taken in *AAPB* towards including 'down under' commemorations: Australia and Anzac Days were added, as well as First Christian Service in Australia and Martyrs of New Guinea.

However, the then Liturgical Commission, believing (as Sinden states) that "a multiplicity of saints days lessens the significance of their observance", decided to include 'group commemorations'. The traditional criterion for inclusion in the Calendar, however, is that the person's life shows distinctive marks of God's grace. This cannot be guaranteed for groups, and the inclusion of some might be seen as partisan. In *APBA*, therefore, as Ron Dowling explained, "group commemorations were dropped in favour of a representative individual". So **the criterion for inclusion in *APBA*'s Calendar is "the victory and holiness of Christ shown in a particular person"**.[5]

In preparing the Calendar, work from the Liturgical Movement and other Anglican Provinces was drawn on.[6] The outcome was to give greater clarity to its overall shape:

- the priority of Sunday;
- the cycles of Easter, Christmas / Epiphany and the saints;
- three 'levels' of commemoration; and
- greater attention being paid to our Australian context.

Overall, as Ron Dowling notes, "New commemorations, with a number of significant Australians, have been added. The number of women has been increased, and there has been an emphasis on lay persons in the new inclusions."[7] Alongside this,

---

4   Major feasts were called 'red letter' days because their names were printed in red in *BCP*'s Kalendar, while others were left in black. Likewise, directions and instructions in *BCP* came to be called 'rubrics' (from Latin *ruber*, red) since they were printed in red to distinguish them from text to be read aloud. This practice continues in *AAPB* and *APBA*, though some printings used green.
5   *A Practical Commentary*, 97. Dr Dowling held the Calendar portfolio for *APBA*.
6   See Leonel Mitchell, 'Sanctifying Time: The Calendar', in Charles Hefling and Cynthia Shattuck (edd.), *The Oxford Guide to the Book of Common Prayer* (Oxford: OUP, 2006) 476–481 for details.
7   *A Practical Commentary*, 97. Paul Couturier, ecumenist (d. 1853), commemorated on March 24, is a unique inclusion in *APBA* among Anglican Provinces, though he may have been added in other Anglican Calendars issued since 1995.

- Resources to enrich the celebration of times and seasons are enlarged, in both the Readings and Collects (pages 608–642) and liturgical elements (pages 147–163).
- Two significant inclusions are the Week of Prayer for Christian Unity (Ascension Day to Pentecost) and the Week of Prayer for Reconciliation (May 27 to June 3): these often overlap, encouraging intersections in our prayers for this land.
- New Festivals are Joseph (March 19) and Mary, Mother of Our Lord (August 15).
- June 29 reverts to the ancient Festival of 'Peter and Paul'. Correspondingly, the Conversion of Paul (January 25) is made a Lesser Festival (with readings), linked with a new inclusion, Confession of Peter (January 18, with readings). This pairing bookmarks the Week of Prayer for Christian Unity in the northern hemisphere.
- Two potentially controversial days were accepted as Lesser Festivals: Thanksgiving for Holy Communion (Thursday after Trinity, 'Corpus Christi') and All Souls Day (November 2). Believing that it is wiser to provide resources that all can use rather than foster division, both Commemorations were provided with sentence, collect and readings (*APBA* pages 636, 633).

The Calendar in *APBA* is the outcome of a thorough review of every aspect of how the times and seasons of the Church's Year can be observed by Australian Christians. Its focus is on clarity about what matters, combined with openness to changes in the Australian context.

'Levels' of feasting

The two-level system of 'red' and 'black' letter days is replaced in *APBA* by the three distinct 'levels' noted above: Principal Festivals; Festivals / Holy Days; and Lesser Festivals or Commemorations.

Principal Festivals

These focus on the central realities of Christian faith: they are listed on *APBA* page 452. The choice was made as a "realistic statement of the occasions when church people should regard it as a duty to attend public worship".[8] In earlier ages church attendance was required by law, and so holy days were free from work – 'holi-days'. Beyond adjustments in pay for Christmas and Good Friday, this practice has long disappeared in Australia. Lent, Holy Week and Easter are defined by the Principal Festivals that surround them.

---

8 Sinden, *When we meet for Worship*, 187, citing a statement of the principles guiding the 1970s English Liturgical Commission. The statement was used in the preparation of both *AAPB* and *APBA*.

Reflecting older understandings of 'day', Principal Festivals (except for Easter Day) and a few Festivals begin at sunset on the preceding evening, with a 'First Evensong'.[9] Two Principal Festivals call for further comment:

- **Baptism of the Lord** adds to the 'red letter' days of *BCP*. As the first Sunday after Epiphany, it gives a greater 'shape' to this season, and takes note of its importance in the Eastern Churches, many of which are present in Australia.

- **Ascension Day** is sometimes 'skipped' because it falls on a Thursday, though no Anglican Province provides for this. In the Roman Catholic Church, after the Second Vatican Council, it was moved to the next Sunday. However, this means missing 'The Sunday after Ascension', when we are faced with the challenge of the 'spiritual hole' between Christ's departure and Spirit's coming – the experience of 'divine absence' that not a few Christians endure.

   Sometimes, however, Ascension Day is skipped because what took place on the Mount of Olives remains a mystery, despite artistic depictions of rising feet in stained glass windows. But the truth of Christ taking our human nature into God's full presence, being exalted as Lord to the Father's side to reign and intercede for us, is affirmed over and over in the letters of the New Testament.

The General Synod website's Liturgy page offers excellent resources for Ash Wednesday, Passion / Palm Sunday, Holy Week and Easter Day.[10] As well as texts for these once-a-year services, full introductions are provided that explore issues around preparation, uses of symbols, participation by the congregation, and the practical matters involved: see further Chapter Nineteen in this book.

Festivals / Holy Days

These mark key events in Christ's earthly life (Annunciation, Naming and Circumcision, Presentation, Transfiguration), and God's grace shown in believers of apostolic times. None must be observed. Where one falls on a Sunday in Advent, Lent or Easter, it is moved to the next available weekday, since each Sunday is a Principal Festival.

---

9 The list of First Evensongs in early editions of *APBA* was incorrect. The 2004 General Synod, on the advice of the Liturgy Commission, amended the list to this:

All Saints' Day	Christmas Day	Naming and Circumcision
Epiphany	Baptism of the Lord	Presentation
Annunciation	Ascension Day	Day of Pentecost
Trinity Sunday	Birth of John Baptist	Peter and Paul
Mary, Mother of our Lord		

10 Available at https://www.anglican.org.au/lent-holy-week-and-easter – see Chapter 19 in ths book.

Lesser Festivals / Commemorations

These celebrate God's grace in the lives of Christian disciples of every age, along with some days of civic significance. Again, none is required to be observed, but where an event or person is significant locally, commemoration will be natural.

APBA provides sentences, prayers and readings for several Lesser Festivals which are of wider significance, and for various categories of holy persons: a missionary, theologian, bishop and so on. *An Australian Lectionary* includes a full list of readings for all Lesser Festivals / Commemorations.

Informal commemorations

As well as the people and events in *APBA*'s Calendar, there will be local Christians, anniversaries and occasions to celebrate. Just as no Festival or Lesser Festival *must* be observed, there is no prohibition on celebrating the witness to Christ borne by another person or group. When St George's Trentham turned 150, for example, a play (with some less serious moments) covering its history was written and performed in public by parishioners in the local park. Resources for anniversaries can be gained from the local Historical Society or found on the web, and long-term parishioners will almost certainly have insights to share.

'Ordinary' time

In *AAPB*, the Sundays outside the Advent / Epiphany and Lent / Easter cycles are termed 'Ordinary Sundays', since they fall in 'ordinary time'. But no Sunday is 'ordinary'. As Ron Dowling notes,

> Many people objected to the name 'ordinary Sunday' … *APBA* has adopted the names 'Sundays after Epiphany' and 'Sundays after Pentecost'. The former 'ordinary Sunday' number is printed on the right hand margin.

In 'The Readings and Collects', *APBA* uses the range of possible dates for each of these Sundays, rather than numbering them 'after Trinity' (as in *BCP*), because the dates on which they fall vary from year to year. Each is given a 'Proper' number, following *RCL* and Roman Catholic usage: this eases knowing which Sundays fall into the 'major chasm' around Easter. *An Australian Lectionary* takes care of all these matters.

How can these Sundays be used fruitfully? In the northern hemisphere, the period between Trinity Sunday and Advent ('ordinary' time) is mostly taken up by the summer holidays. 'Down under', the long run of 'ordinary' time is only interrupted by the Queen's Birthday long weekend, which has the advantage of allowing for 'sermon series' and the like. But week after week without a distinctive Sunday or two runs the risk of liturgy being so routine that a sense of 'sameness' sets in.

This is where creative planning will balance forming 'godly ruts' through routine, with changes that disturb spiritual complacency. Both routine and variety are important, whether in a 'straight *APBA*' service or a 'fresh expression' one. One way forward is to take seriously the Festivals and Lesser Festivals in the Calendar, especially those of particular relevance to the congregation concerned: 'saints days'.

Saints and other special days

What is a 'saint'?

'Saint' means 'holy person', and in the New Testament this term is used for disciples of Christ. Paul typically addressed his letters "to the saints that are at …" (Romans 1.7, 1 Corinthians 1.2, Ephesians 1.1, Philippians 1.1 and more). Christians who bore witness (*marturia*) to Christ even to death, and those whose lives exhibited a special grace of God in following Christ, came to be called 'saint' in a distinctive sense. So *BCP* recognises Saint Peter, Saint Irenaeus, Saint Lucy, Saint Athanasius and Saint Augustine, taking examples from each of the first five centuries.

In medieval times, just as Christians would ask for favours from their feudal 'patron' in society, many came to ask their 'patron' saint to pray for them: such 'invocation' was officially approved. But as God gradually came to be seen as distant, and Christ as a stern judge, invocation of a saint moved to praying ***to*** a saint, especially the Blessed Virgin Mary. This practice was never officially supported, though it was rarely contradicted. Affirming that prayer directed to other than God is idolatrous, some Reformation traditions came to reject 'saints days' altogether.

Archbishop Thomas Cranmer, however, when revising the Calendar for the Church of England, retained feast days for saints significant in passing on the Gospel, whether biblical (e.g. Andrew) or historic (e.g. Monica). But he rejected false understandings of invocation: as Article XXII states, "The Romish Doctrine concerning … invocation of Saints, is a fond thing vainly invented, and grounded upon no warranty of Scripture, but rather repugnant to the Word of God."

Christians in whom God's special grace was seen continued to be added to the Calendar of the Church of England after 1662, though 'Saint' before their name was discontinued.[11] In the Anglican Communion, a person is added to the Calendar of a Province by a resolution of its General Synod, based on a recommendation from a diocese that the person is commemorated locally. Australian examples include William Broughton (February 20), Georgiana Molloy (April 8) and James Noble

---

11   The term 'Heroes' is used by Anglicans in places such as The Episcopal Church in Cuba, where the term 'saints' can raise cultural difficulties.

(November 25).[12] In all Christian traditions, the commemorated person's feast day is the date when they 'fell asleep' in Christ.[13] The official position of the Anglican Communion on 'saints' is set out in Resolution 79 of the 1958 Lambeth Conference:

Saints and Heroes of the Christian Church in the Anglican Communion
- In the case of scriptural saints, care should be taken to commemorate men or women in terms that are in strict accord with the facts made known in Holy Scripture.
- In the case of other names, the Calendar should be limited to those whose historical character and devotion are beyond doubt.
- In the choice of new names, economy should be observed and controversial names should not be inserted until they can be seen in the perspective of history.
- The addition of a new name should normally result from a widespread desire expressed in the region concerned over a reasonable period of time.

These principles were followed in preparing the Calendar in *APBA*, especially as regards Australian 'saints' and events.

A significant addition to the *APBA* Calendar was the inclusion of 'Mary, Mother of Our Lord' as a Festival on August 15. This gives Our Lady a feast day in her own right, on the date traditionally marking the end of her earthly life.[14]

---

12 There are some errors in the Calendar of the first printing of *APBA*: please check your copy.

    March 1:   David of Menevia (not Minevia)
    March 24:   Oscar Romero is commemorated on March 24, not April 24.
    May 11: add Catherine of Siena, spiritual teacher (d. 1380)
    September 30: John Patteson (not Patterson)
    November 25: When *APBA* was drafted, James Noble was believed to be the "first indigenous Australian ordained". It was soon learnt that a Torres Strait Islander had been ordained earlier. General Synod 2001, on the basis of the Liturgical Commission's affirmation of James' saintly life, changed his commemoration to "pioneer Aboriginal deacon". See *Australian Anglican Remember*, 99–102.

13 The Roman Catholic Church teaches that prayer can rightly be directed only to God. Further,
    The liturgical implementation of the Second Vatican Council included a drastic cull of saints, particularly those of dubious reputation or existence, but partly also to avoid the fact that almost every day of the year directed the commemoration of at least one saint, which was rightly deemed to be particularly unhelpful in Advent, Lent and the Easter season.

    Benjamin Gordon Taylor, 'Time', in Juliette Day & Benjamin Gordon-Taylor, *The Study of Liturgy and Worship* (London: SPCK, 2013) 115.

    Rome adds to its Calendar in two stages, beatification and sanctification, after which the person is termed 'The Blessed' and 'Saint' respectively. A miracle must be confirmed as a result of their invocation: see further ARCIC, *Mary: Grace and Hope in Christ* (London: SPCK / CTS, 1995) #67–70.

14 Other Festivals linked with Mary have a Christological focus: Presentation (February 2) and Annunciation (March 25). *APBA* continues to include Visitation (with collect and readings, May 31), the Conception of Mary (December 8) and Birth of Mary (September 8) from *BCP*, while adding a full set of 'propers' for the Blessed Virgin Mary: pages 160, 617–618.

The Calendar and the diary

The 'church diary'

The 'church diary' belongs to the faith community overall. Planning, drawing up, implementing and reviewing it engages the range of leaders in the congregation concerned, not just the minister 'in charge'. Paul, while insisting on his distinctive authority, time and again emphasises the importance of his 'fellow-workers' (Romans 16.21; 2 Corinthians 8.23; Philippians 2.25; 1 Thessalonians 3.2 and more), women and men alike (notably Romans 16.1–15). Taking care to include stalwarts and newer folk, women and men, as well a range of ages, pays dividends. Clergy come and go: parishioners stay the course for decades.

Diverse settings

The 'church diary' will look quite different in a school, hospital, prison or the defence forces context from that in a cathedral or parish.[15] In country areas, life will be linked to the rhythms of the agricultural year and tourist season. Significant variations are likely between single-centre (typically urban) and multi-centre parishes (typically regional or rural). Stipended clergy have different demands on their time, notably around travel, and the distinct culture of each congregation in a multi-church parish must be taken seriously. Some city parishes may have congregations meeting at different times; many country ones will have congregations meeting in discrete localities. Parish structures exist primarily to enable effective clergy deployment and financial administration. In a multi-congregation parish, people typically identify in the first place with their congregation rather than 'the parish': clergy who impose a 'parish comes first' mentality will find deep resistance, especially from smaller centres. A better way is to encourage all centres to see themselves as 'congregations in communion' to serve God's mission.

A 'future backwards' outlook

Every diary has entries added as time goes on: it grows 'forwards'. Using it 'backwards' is also important. It is good practice to spend a few minutes after each major event jotting down immediate reactions and responses. What was 'spot on'? What did not 'work' as well as planned? Were there 'godly surprises', and what did they communicate? What could be done differently next time around?

This task is not only the priest's responsibility. Other leaders reviewing the past year's diary can lead to more multi-faceted reflection and review, and generate ideas for the future. Communication works best when diaries are shared.

---

15 By 'parish' here is meant any organisational unit that is served by stipendiary ministers, including clusters, ministering communities and so on.

Initial planning

Winter or the wet season is drawing to a close, and thoughts are turning to next year: getting the process going is a clergy responsibily. An initial task is to mark in key dates: Ash Wednesday and Lent, Holy Week and the Easter weeks to Pentecost and Trinity, Advent and Christmas. Then there is the patronal festival, AGM, and other 'set' times: synod, clergy conference and retreat, parish fair or houseparty and so on. What about clergy's annual holidays? What civic events impinge on the faith community's life: Anzac Day, Mothers' Day, St Francis' Day, local festivals, long weekends? This initial work is likely to take some time: it is best done over two or three sessions to give space for reflection.

NB: The third millennium diary may be electronic, but whether you plan on paper, screen or phone, without hard copy, times and rosters will soon be muddled.

Planning together

Now is a good time to share priorities and ideas with Wardens, Parish Council, sacristan, music, youth and other leaders. Reflecting on the year past will help focus attention on changes needed, opportunities missed, and what did not go well. Particularly important are things such as the following.

- How will Lent to Trinity be observed? What study groups might be helpful? What ecumenical opportunities exist? When more than one centre is involved, reaching agreement on the 'when/where/what' of Holy Week services is important.[16]

- What Christian education processes (for all ages) should continue?[17] Which need review? How does their ethos work with the 'learning lens' and 'spiritual personalities' of different folk?[18]

- If a parish camp / houseparty is in view, have the date, place and theme set early. What might be the best approach to using the opportunities it offers: guest speaker(s)? videos? panel of locals? small groups?

- When will the bishop come, whether for baptisms / confirmation / reception, or for a general visit? What subject(s) would it be good to explore with him/her?

---

16 *Performing the Gospel*, Chapter Nine, Part C outlines a process for planning a particular service.

17 Programmes for high school students and adults supported in Australia include *Australis*, *Education for Ministry (EFM)* and *Christianity Explored*.

18 In Lent in one parish, a group walked quietly around the local lake on a weekday afternoons, starting and ending with prayer. Another met to read and meditate on the gospel for the following Sunday. A Saturday afternoon 'God at the movies' group reflected on general-release films: one year it was six directed by Clint Eastwood; another year, six starring George Clooney. There are many possibilities.

The outcomes of this initial meeting should put participants in a good place to work on creative aspects of the coming year: 'fresh expressions', engagement with issues of the day, events of public witness, times of teaching. It will also help with the 'must-do' aspects of the Church's Year. How will children and young people be engaged in worship? What regular 'sick communions' and nursing home services are needed? Do home groups need renewal?

By now it may be November. Allow Advent, with its focus on "living from God's future backwards", to calm things down when they get hectic, and bring its prophetic challenges to parish planning. January, if not taken as annual leave, a necessity for clergy with children at home, can be a good time to mix some visiting with reading and reflection on the year ahead. Holiday meals with local leaders can stimulate the 'little grey cells', while a games night can build relationships.

The trans-parish ('chaplaincy') diary

Much of what is written above will apply in other settings, notably schools, hospitals, prisons and military establishments. But significant differences exist in the ways that the year in such places interacts with the Calendar in *APBA*.

A timetable that governs the institution's meeting and activities routine will already be drawn up. So analyse the institution's calendar for the year ahead. How do the dates for Holy Week / Easter and Christmas / Epiphany relate to the institution's timetable? For hospitals, prisons, military establishments and the like, matters such as staffing and major events will already be in place.

In hospitals, services are often held to remember people who have died in the year past, whether near All Saints / All Souls (November 1-2) or in December, with Christmas Day on the horizon. Sensitive input is rarely knocked back: see *APBA* pages 689-706, 719-720, 745-746, 758-762, 765-770 for resources.

In schools and colleges, Holy Week / Easter and Christmas / Epiphany nearly always fall out of term time. Finding ways to work these focal seasons with school life calls for thoughtful creativity, not least where a significant proportion of students and staff do not adhere to Christian faith. Ash Wednesday can be important, because it falls in a regular school week, and in Victoria at least carries the memory of catastrophic bushfires. A significant psychological and spiritual challenge exists for chaplains preparing and leading Easter and Christmas events prior to their actual Calendar dates. Significant energy will have been expended in these ministries, leaving little for celebrating with their local congregation, for whom these festivals will be fresh.

Different issues arise in prison ministry, where Christmas means limited contact with family and friends for inmates, and the easy happiness of Xma$ stands in stark contrast to jail life. The refugee experience of Mary, Joseph and Jesus, or the sombre stories of Stephen (December 26) and Holy Innocents (December 28) may be helpful. But the message of hope in God's incarnated love and grace can never be dimmed.

The diary and the Ministry of the Word

The Ordinal sees the 'ministry of the Word' as the central responsibility of ordained ministers. Sustained, informed and engaging preaching is demanding: but if scripture speaks with a variety of voices, why not the pulpit? Where only the priest is available to preach, having a guest preacher occasionally can be enriching: theological college staff see this as part of their calling, for example.[19] But many parishes and institutions are in a good position to spread the Ministy of the Word around.

In a variety of settings I have been part of a 'preaching group' that included perceptive women and men, who contribute different insights, some of whom might preach occasionally. The priest having the 'cure of souls' led the group, and preached at least half the time. Meetings took place every six weeks or so, a typical one including

- honest responses to services since the last meeting, not just the sermon;
- a look ahead at readings for the next month or so, reaching consensus on which passages will be the main focus for preaching, and common approaches to them;
- agreeing on a 'preaching roster', taking account of occasions such as a family service or baptism Sunday, as well as the highlights of the Christian year; and
- ideas for liturgical elements other than the sermon: each group was effectively a 'worship committee' but the focus on the ministry of the Word gave it direction.

Once allocated, each preacher was free to take an approach that she or he believed was best for the sermon concerned. The benefit was not only preaching of a higher standard, but greater variety of style, better feedback, and a ministry of the Word more closely related to the life-setting of the congregation.

NB: Anyone who preaches regularly, even if not often, needs to hold the bishop's licence. But not all in the group need preach: the committed listener is a gift.

---

[19] The occasional mission agency deputation can be helpful, but this tends to complement rather than replace a varied Ministry of the Word.

Further reading

Bradshaw, Paul and Johnson, Matthew, *The Origins of Feasts, Fasts and Seasons in Early Christianity*. Alcuin Club Collections 86 (London: SPCK, 2011)

Mitchell, Leonel, 'Sanctifying Time: The Calendar', in Charles Hefling and Cynthia Shattuck (edd.), *The Oxford Guide to the Book of Common Prayer* (Oxford: OUP, 2006) 476–481

Sherlock, Charles, *Australian Anglicans Remember* (Melbourne: Broughton, 2016)

The following website, from the Anglican Church of Aotearoa New Zealand, carries information on holy persons from across the Christian tradition:

www.anglican.org.nz/Resources/Lectionary-and-Worship/For-All-the-Saints-A-Resource-for-the-Commemorations-of-the-Calendar/For-All-the-Saints

Chapter Six

Singing the Lord's Song[1]

Music is an integral part of human life. Men and women, boys and girls, find it natural to use music in worship. From the exuberance of Miriam's dance through the highs and lows of the Hebrew Psalter, human beings have expressed their faith and fear of Almighty God through music. Our Lord often quoted the Psalter. The early Church found many references to the Messiah in it. The last thing our Lord did with his disciples before his arrest was to sing a hymn.[2]

"How can we sing the Lord's song in a strange land?" was a cry of mourning for Israel of old, exiled to a foreign land far, far from home (Psalm 137.4). Similar feelings were no doubt felt by the first Europeans who came to Australia, many against their will – let alone by the original inhabitants, for whom the consequences would be catastrophic.

Music is a major shaper of culture, especially since the coming of radio, recording devices and music galore online. Songs dominate much church culture today, with an explosion of new ones in recent decades. In the scriptures, however, and in the Christian tradition until around 1800, the psalms dominated Christian praise and reflection. In *BCP* (1662), the Psalter is used in full monthly,[3] with only a few other songs included: Te Deum and Benedicite (Morning Prayer), Magnificat and Nunc Dimittis (Evening Prayer), the Gloria (Holy Communion), and the 'Easter Anthems'.[4] Other singing is an 'Anthem' after the third collect in Morning and Evening Prayer.

---

1. In *APBA*, 'hymn' and 'song' mean words which can be sung. A 'canticle' is a song from the scriptures or Christian tradition set out for responsive saying or singing. An 'anthem' is words sung to rather than by the people, usually by a choir.

    General Notes 4 and 6 (*APBA* page x) allow a wide scope for music. General Notes 7, 8 and 9 explain the translations of the psalms employed.
2. The opening words of 'Music and APBA', *A Practical Commentary*, Chapter Four by Canon Lawrence Bartlett. Dr Bartlett worked on every aspect of church music, as parish priest, cathedral precentor, music editor of the *Australian Hymn Book* and *Together in Song*, composer and arranger.
3. The *BCP* Psalter is that of Miles Coverdale, continued in the 1662 edition from earlier books. The 1611 *King James Bible* was not then in widespread use, and was not translated with liturgical use to the fore.
4. These Latin terms are the opening words of each song, and have become their technical names: thus 'Benedicite' means 'youse - bless!' (a plural imperative). In *APBA*, English names are used (e.g. 'Song of Creation' for the *Benedicite*), with the Latin name being placed in parentheses in First Order services.

APBA offers a much greater provision for singing.[5] Though services suggest hymn placement, Note 6 (page x) states that songs "may be sung otherwise than where provision is made for them". Along with a variety of 'canticles' in the services, full use of the Psalter continues.

The Psalms in Christian worship

The Psalter as 'hymn book'

The Psalter has classically been at the heart of the songs of God's people, both Jewish and Christian. It is hard to better Evan Burge's words about the Psalter:[6]

> The Psalter is the oldest hymn book of the Church. It also approximates to a Jewish 'hymn book' and forms the basis of much of the synagogue worship of Jews today. The Psalter is a sign of the continuity of Christianity with its Jewish origins; its piety transcends the divisions of the Jewish-Christian faith communities and overarches their history.

Christian interpretations

From an early date, Christians have made the Psalter their own. No other book is quoted so frequently by the New Testament writers. In Acts 13.30–39, for instance, Psalms 2 and 16 are used as the basis of a developing Christology, as is Psalm 8 in Hebrews 2. Later Christian piety has often treated all the psalms in this way, as descriptions of Christ, as prayers to Christ, and as the voice of Christ speaking to his people or to the Father on behalf of his people.

Thus the psalms of lament (2, 22, 38, 59, 69, 88) provide vivid images for reflection on the cross and passion. The penitential psalms (6, 32, 38, 51, 102, 133, 143) have traditionally been used as prayers of Christ bearing the sins of the world. Similarly, the messianic psalms (2, 16, 22, 45, 110) and various psalms referring to the Davidic monarchy have their fulfilment in the sovereignty of Christ. However, the psalms also have their own life and integrity. Their openness to one kind of interpretation does not exclude other interpretations.

The voice of a people

The origin of many psalms was liturgical, since they presuppose a corporate setting. In them, the pronoun *I* may refer not to an individual but to the nation as a whole. Here is the voice of a people in its experience of life: moments of

---

5   *Performing the Gospel* Chapter Six considers the wide range of questions around contemporary culture and music in church, and explores the choice and placement of songs and music in services.

6   Canon Dr Evan Burge held the Psalter 'portfolio' on the Liturgical Commission that drafted *APBA*. Kind permission was given by his family for the use of his Chapter Eleven in *A Practical Commentary*.

aspiration, degradation, joy and hope. Those who read the psalms, even alone, are accompanied by a host of voices stretching across two-and-a-half millennia.

The psalms began as the cry of a people in moments of pain and joy. They are an intensely human cry. When Christians use the psalms they do not leave their Christianity behind, nor do they abandon their humanity. Christians experience doubt and anger as well as joy and hope. To give expression to those realities is not to fail in faith or love but to recognise that faith and love cannot be claimed as mere palliatives of present pain. Present pain and anger must be owned and brought before God if life is to be transformed.

Until fifty years or so ago, Morning and Evening Prayer were the most frequently used services among Australian Anglicans. In these the Psalms hold a prominent place, with the responsive prayers, both at the beginning and before the third collect, also being taken from them. Many choirs and congregations sang the psalms (and canticles) to 'Anglican chant', *The Parish Psalter* being a typical version.[7] But from the time of Queen Elizabeth I, singing 'metrical' psalms – translated into rhyming poetry – was popular in English-speaking churches. The 'Old Version', brought together by Thomas Sternhold and John Hopkins (1562), "became the people's music of the Church of England, and for three hundred years 'Psalmody' meant singing metrical psalms, not reciting the psalms from the *Book of Common Prayer*."[8]

After the Restoration in 1661, 'Sternhold and Hopkins' was significantly improved by Nahum Tate (the poet laureate) and Nicholas Brady in 1696: the 'New Version'. These Versions' "chief virtue was homeliness, which brought religious expression within the reach of ordinary people" (Box). For many years copies of *BCP* were printed with the Old or New Versions bound in. Several of the metrical psalms found their into the hymnbooks that emerged from the mid-1800s: 'All people that on earth do dwell' and 'O God, our help in ages past' for example. Anglican chant, used in cathedrals and larger parishes, spread steadily in the nineteenth century. In a few places plainsong chanting was employed, a simpler form of chanting based on medieval practice.

---

7   Sydney H. Nicholson, *The Parish Psalter* (London: Royal Society for Church Music [RSCM], 1932). The RSCM updated this in 1989 to emphasise 'speech rhythm', i.e. the music supporting the way words are said. An online version is available at www.big-english-cheese.com/psalm/psalms.html.

8   Reginald Box SSF, *Make Music to our God. How we sing the Psalms* (London: SPCK, 1996) 48. Box's volume gives a detailed account of the history of psalm-singing in English, with particular attention to how the psalms' words interact with the method of singing employed.
See also Bryan D. Spinks, *The Rise and Fall of the Incomparable Liturgy. The Book of Common Prayer 1559-1906*. Alcuin Club Collections 92 (London: SPCK, 2017) 17-22, 97-99, 114-117, 135-137.

New challenges for the Psalter

In the 1960s three shifts in church life saw significant changes in the way psalms are used in Sunday worship.

Reduced use

The first shift was reduced use of the Psalter on Sundays, as the Eucharist became the main service in many Anglican congregations.

Until the law changed in 1872 to allow them to be celebrated separately, the usual Sunday service was Morning Prayer (including significant psalmody), Litany and Holy Communion. *BCP* Holy Communion makes no provision for psalmody, so it was never encountered by congregations that only experienced the Eucharist. When, following the Second Vatican Council, a psalm portion was restored to the Eucharist in the Roman Catholic Church, Anglican revisions followed suit, notably Holy Communion (Second Order) in *AAPB* and then *APBA*. But by then many congregations had lost the facility to sing psalms using Anglican chant.

New ways to sing the psalms

The second shift was changes in the way the psalms were sung. Chant, plainsong and even metrical psalms were becoming outdated. A 1951 Report of the Church of England on music concluded "that the psalms, whether they are sung to plainsong tones or Anglican chants, do not lend themselves readily to singing by the average congregation."[9] Several responses to this admission have emerged.

Joseph Gelineau translated the Psalter from Hebrew into French for the (Roman Catholic) *Bible de Jérusalem* (1966), with a view to their being sung. Box describes his work as "a gust of fresh air," and notes that "An English translation, based on Gelineau's principles, was published by Grail, who also began to publish his music." The Grail version arranges each Psalm into two to four short stanzas, which can be sung by all, or by a cantor followed by the congregation singing a response. This method became well-known in Anglican circles: the Grail versification was included in *Collects and Readings for Sundays and Saints Days*, issued in conjunction with *AAPB*.

A 'responsive' method of singing developed from this, involving a reader singing one or more verses, the people (or choir) joining in with a response. This is particularly useful when the congregation includes people from a variety of churches. It is why responses are provided for the psalms printed in the Funeral Services in *APBA*, since people are unlikely to have prayer books or full service sheets. The responsive method also lends itself to local composition of music to accompany the response.

---

9   Cited in Box, 69.

New metrical translations have also been issued. A major project of the English Jubilate Group was *Psalm Praise* (76 psalms, plus canticles) and then *Psalms for Today* (1990: 133 psalms and scripture songs, some with more than one method of singing). These collections, together with psalm-based songs from other writers and composers, are gradually transforming the offerings available in hymn-books.

In Australia's ecumenical hymnbook, *Together in Song* (1999) the first 97 entries provide settings for all the psalms in *RCL*. Australian (and other) Christians thus have ready access to a sung version of every psalm (or psalm portion) in the readings for each Sunday. *Together in Song* also employs a range of musical styles: chant and plainsong, Gelineau and responsive, old and new metrical versions.

Language issues

A third shift was a growing concern about gendered language in the Psalter.[10] The version in *AAPB* 1978, *The Liturgical Psalter*, included many terms such as 'man', 'men' and 'sons of men' referring to members of the human race.[11] A dozen or more translations of the Psalter use modern pronouns and verb forms, some paying attention to 'inclusive' language. Liturgical Commission members used a total of thirteen Psalters published between 1970 and 1994 to find one that was suitable for inclusion in the new book. All had issues, however: it was agreed that *The Liturgical Psalter* was the most usable version for an Anglican prayer book, and that an inclusive language version would do the job best.

Therefore, on behalf of the Commission, Dr Evan Burge was asked to contact Professor David Frost, then at the University of Newcastle NSW, to ask whether he and his team would be prepared to undertake this task in time for it to be included in *APBA*. At the time, Professor Frost was actively engaged in public discussion about gendered language, so some diplomacy was needed involving Dr Burge and Canon Bartlett, as Chair of the Commission.[12]

As time drew near to the 1995 General Synod, however, the Liturgical Commission became concerned lest the project fail to be completed on time. So Dr Burge

---

10 The Liturgical Commission in 1991 issued a list of a dozen 'fixes' for *AAPB*, the most notable being changing to 'for us and our salvation' in the Nicene Creed. The changes, recommended by several diocesan bishops, needed to be adopted by a Parish Meeting before being adopted locally.

11 As Dr Burge explains, this "was produced by Professor David L. Frost on the basis of a scholarly translation of the original Hebrew by John A. Emerton and Andrew A. Macintosh. Its style is suitable for corporate recitation or singing according to Anglican traditions based on the sixteenth century version by Miles Coverdale, which was retained in *BCP* 1662." From Chapter Thirteen in *A Practical Commentary*.

12 See, for example, the articles by David Frost and Charles Sherlock in the *Australian Church Union*, October 1992. These arose from a public lecture at Ridley College, Melbourne.

began his own version, based on a light revision of the Psalter in the *Book of Common Prayer* of The Episcopal Church, which had been placed in the public domain. In the event, Professor Frost and his team came good, sending off the 'inclusive language version' of *The Liturgical Psalter* (APBA pages 224-380) a month before the last date for inclusion in the book to be distributed to General Synod members.

NB: No attempt has been made in the complete Psalter to revise masculine language referring to God. In some psalms included in the Daily Services and Pastoral Services, another translation, used for reasons of copyright, has reduced the number of specifically masculine references to God.[13]

A note on 'Glory to God: Father, Son and Holy Spirit'

> In *BCP,* psalms and canticles were followed by the doxology *Gloria Patri*:
> Glory be to the Father, and to the Son, and to the Holy Spirit:
> as it was in the beginning so now and ever shall be. Amen.
>
> In *AAPB (1978),* the first modern English prayer book in the Anglican Communion, this was changed to
> Glory to God: Father, Son and Holy Spirit:
> as in the beginning so now and for ever. Amen.
>
> This change was done both to simplify the text, and express trinitarian faith more clearly. In drafting *APBA*, consideration was given to returning to the fuller form, but the shorter one, distinctive to the Anglican Church of Australia, had become so well known across the national church that it was retained.

The Psalms in the *APBA* Lectionary

APBA continues the *BCP* practice of using the full Psalter for daily services, though over two months rather than one. The choice of Psalms for Sundays and Principal Festivals was made from *RCL*. How this works in *APBA* is set out by Evan Burge:

> The entire Psalter is included in *APBA* for reflection and study, and for use in worship when appropriate ... The Sunday lectionary passes over some that are generally unsuitable for congregational worship, obvious examples being the 'imprecatory psalms' in which the psalmist curses his enemies. A number of the longer historical psalms also do not appear in the Sunday lectionary because of their length. A Table of Psalms for use in the Daily Services was adopted by General Synod in 1995 for a three-year trial period ... This table provides for recitation of the full Psalter over two calendar months, with the imprecatory

---

13 *A Practical Commentary*, Chapter Eleven.

psalms on the 31st day of the month. They may be replaced by repeating some of the psalms of praise used on the 29th or 30th day (Psalms 145–150), somewhat in the manner prescribed in the *Book of Common Prayer*.

After extensive trial in parishes, cathedrals and colleges, in 2001 General Synod approved the daily Tables for ongoing use, and particular psalms for Morning and Evening Prayer on all Festivals and Lesser Festivals with readings.

A note on 'pointing'

The psalms in *APBA* are not 'pointed': no marks indicate where the chant changes. Lawrence Bartlett, the music expert on the Liturgical Commissions that drafted *AAPB* and *APBA*, explains the issues:[14]

> In *AAPB*, in response to a request by local representatives from the *Royal School of Church Music*, the psalms were pointed according to speech rhythm … The request was motivated by a desire to assist congregations join in the singing. It was a brave initiative. Unfortunately, in between the request to the Liturgical Commission and the publication of the book in 1978, a great deal happened. Many congregations were experimenting with trial services in contemporary language. To them, it did not seem appropriate to sing psalms from *BCP* as part of a liturgy in contemporary language … Thus, when the prayer book was published in 1978, many congregations had already lost the facility for Anglican chant and have not returned to it since then.
>
> For 1995, the question was whether it was reasonable to point psalms for a minority of congregations, thus requiring all to pay for the few. The matter was discussed by a representative of the Liturgical Commission with a gathering of Anglican church musicians at the Summer School of the *Royal School of Church Music* in 1994. It was pointed out that many who sing the psalms now use responsorial psalmody rather than Anglican chant. Some are exploring a renaissance of plainsong. Many of the experts (cathedral choirs and the like) who have maintained Anglican chant use much more sophisticated pointing than *AAPB*. In short, it was suggested that it was not necessary or reasonable to provide pointing in *APBA*. Those wishing to continue chanting the psalms are able to do so in the short term by recourse to *AAPB*. The pointing is unchanged as the majority of the psalms are the same in *APBA* as they were in *AAPB*. Where verses vary, it is to be hoped that the local choirmaster is able to repoint that particular verse.

---

14 *A Practical Commentary*, 20-21. As noted in the Introduction, kind permission was given by Dr Bartlett's family for the use of his contributions in this book.

Singing the Psalms

Reginald Box ends his chapter 'Singing a new song' with these points about singing:

> First, congregations are not the same as crowds. Large gatherings need a regular beat to keep them together. Smaller groups can manage simple recitative if they have competent leaders.
>
> Second, instant participation is more likely when there are simple responses for the people. But congregational music does not have to be so immediate that no effort is needed to learn it and get it right ... But nothing is so instant that it requires no practice.
>
> Third, our concern should not be to get people to sing psalms at any cost, but to find methods which enable the psalms to be sung with correct verbal emphasis as in good clear reading.[15]

He concludes the book with these admirable words:

> The psalms can lift us above ourselves and draw us into that eternal stream of adoration which is the prayer of the whole church and of the Lord Christ himself. That is what liturgy is about.[16]

Saying the psalms

How the psalms are best *sung* has been touched on above. But in most places, on weekdays and in Sunday services, psalms are *said* not *sung*. So Lawrence Bartlett argues that

> If it is not possible to sing the psalms, they should be said in the most imaginative and rhythmically poetic way possible. Just 'getting through' the psalms is not sufficient. The parallelism of Hebrew poetry is best reflected antiphonally.[17]

But why read 'antiphonally' ('voice over against voice')? This is because they are set out like this in the Hebrew Psalter: an idea is stated, then said again in different terms, engaging readers and listeners in a 'two-dimensional' way:

> O save me from the lion's mouth:
>
> and my afflicted soul from the horns of the wild oxen. (Psalm 22.22)

The 'conversation' between different metaphors or images (lion's mouth // ox horns) gives a 'three-dimensional' effect that enables language, especially about God, to be 'stretched' beyond its literal sense. Sometimes the parallel is one of contrast, often a repeated one:

---

15 Box, 85.
16 Box, 119.
17 *A Practical Commentary*, 22.

Some put their trust in chariots and some in horses:
but we will trust in the name of the Lord our God.
They are brought down and fallen:
but we are made strong and stand upright. (Psalm 20.7-8)

In Jewish tradition, the psalms are proclaimed by the two halves of the congregation taking each half verse alternately (as indicated by the colon). The first half verse can be said by a minister, the people responding with the second half: however, as Lawrence Bartlett notes, this can become an "unequal dialogue between minister and people".

Another method is for alternate verses to be recited by the minister and congregation in turn, or each half of the congregation. If a pause is left at the colon, it is best 'timed' by breathing in, breathing out and breathing in before continuing, rather than people trying to guess when to start again! A slight pause should then be left before the next verse is begun, rather than rushing on. The aim is a communal 'taking in' of the psalm, following the bodily rhythm set by the lungs.

Good antiphonal reading sees one group active in proclaiming while the other is active in listening – and then these roles switch, making a congregational *conversation* in performing the psalms. This is also why psalms are not set as 'readings' in lectionaries: their distinctive literary form leads them to be given a distinctive place in liturgy, both Jewish and Christian.

Musical settings for *APBA* services

Beyond psalms and hymns, several liturgical texts are often sung: the Lord's Prayer, creeds, canticles and responses, especially those in the Great Thanksgiving. Lawrence Bartlett, writing on 'notes and rubrics' in *APBA*, states:

> A number of rubrics refer to musical matters. For example, #11 on page 7 specifies the kind of metrical hymn which may replace the Te Deum. #3 on page 36 sets the tone for music chosen at this point. #6 on page 712 allows a wide range of music here ...
>
> Notes after services also deal with music. For example, note 4 on page 164 provides advice on the use of the Gloria or its equivalent in a service of Holy Communion.[18]

---

18   *A Practical Commentary*, 20.

Music in Services of the Word

For generations of Anglicans, Morning and Evening Prayer were the *BCP* services in which congregations enjoyed singing. Whatever method is used, the canticles and psalms, supplemented by hymns, make up a high percentage of these services. The opening responses, and those after the Creed, are suitable for singing, as is 'Glory to God' (see the discussion on page 101). Especially in large buildings such as cathedrals, a minister singing the collects enables them to be heard clearly.

Similar patterns of song can be used with Services of the Word in *APBA*. Musical settings for M&EP1 can readily be taken over from those composed for use with *BCP*. If Anglican chant is used, the pointing in *AAPB* can be used, or constructed locally. In M&EP2, rubrics at the bottom of pages 29-32 note metrical versions of the canticles, while *Together in Song* includes versions of these and the psalms in the Sunday Lectionary, as noted above.

The Apostles' Creed is less sung today, but metrical versions can be found on the internet.[19] *APBA* allows it to be replaced by the Song of the Church (Note 2, page 17) "or another hymn declaring the Christian faith" (#17, page 24).

The Litany for Ministry (pages 192-193) is traditionally sung in ordination services, the people responding with a memorable response. The Great Litany (pages 188-191) and other Litanies (pages 194-196) can be similarly sung.

The lovely evening hymn 'Hail Gladdening Light' comes near the beginning of A Service of Light (page 434) and Prayer at the End of the Day (page 439). The tune usually used (*Together in Song* 191) is based on plainsong, so may take a little learning for people used to metrical songs. But the effort is well repaid: this ancient song fits any evening service.

Musical settings for the Holy Communion
Ths historical background

Singing the congregational parts of the Eucharist goes back to the Church's earliest days. Texts varied until doctrinal issues in the Western Church saw the Latin text increasingly fixed from the eighth century on, a trend reinforced by the coming of printing, and Reformation controversies. The text of the Latin Mass was fixed from 1571, while successive *BCP*s saw the Holy Communion service defined from 1549.

Further, singing involving harmonies was for centuries seen as unsuitable for Christian use, since these could arouse passions. So singing was restricted to a limited number of notes in unison: plainsong or 'Gregorian' chant. The Renaissance

---

19 Several songs based on the Apostles' Creed are offered at https://cardiphonia.org/2014/06/24/sung-versions-of-the-apostles-creed/, though some vary the text unhelpfully.

saw this begin to change: it became a major project for musicians to compose 'mass settings' rich in harmony, though these were for choirs rather than congregations to sing.[20]

The Reformation in England found expression in Cranmer's liturgical work, in which a major emphasis was enabling all to participate. Musical settings for the new English texts soon emerged, notably by John Merbecke, who in 1550 issued *The Booke of Common Praier Noted*. Revived in the nineteenth century, it was used across the Anglican Communion: it remains familiar from my days as a choir boy in a Sydney parish.

Eucharistic settings and APBA

All Holy Communion services in *APBA* use modern English translations for parts traditionally sung: 'Glory to God in the highest', 'Lord have mercy / Kyrie eleison', the Lord's Prayer, 'Holy, holy holy …', communion acclamations and anthems (pages 144-146), and (less often today) the Lord's Prayer and Nicene Creed.

The texts follow the ecumenically agreed wording of *Praying Together*, with small changes in the Creeds (see Note 1 on page 820). This means that settings from overseas as well as Australia can be considered, as can (pre-2015) Roman Catholic settings in English. Composers have been active in writing new music for these new English translations: Australian composers include Lawrence Bartlett, Geoffrey Cox, Michael Dudman, Philip Matthias, Beverley Phillips and Christopher Willcock.

NB: *APBA* page x, Note 4 gives permission for traditional settings of traditional words to be used when the words vary from those set in *APBA*. Thus, cathedral choirs and others may continue to sing familiar settings of the canticles. However, new settings are being provided for the new words and the best of these will eventually become part of the cathedral repertoire.[21]

Many congregations have a standard set of communion settings, but special occasions warrant extra effort. A season may be illuminated by using something different, for example, the 'Kyrie eleison' from the Ukrainian Orthodox community (*Together in Song* 736) is easily learnt and builds up into wonderful six-part harmony. When a setting seems tired, learning a new one can be a staged process, a new section being gradually introduced over several weeks.

---

20 Music for the Latin Mass continues to be composed: *Gloria, Sanctus, Benedictus, Agnus Dei* and sometimes *Pater Noster*: classical and new versions are performed in concert halls as well as church.

21 *A Practical Commentary*, 20.

Complex communion settings are not for every congregation, especially "churches without strong choral leadership, for whom singing the eucharist can be daunting," as Lawrence Bartlett has acknowledged. Nevertheless, as he explains,

> Most settings have thematic relationships between the movements. That is, themes are used in varied forms throughout the settings. This assists the congregation to learn the music. It also means that a setting can be memorised gradually. For example, the Sanctus ('Holy, holy, holy...') could be a good starting point. Then the acclamations could follow, and the Gloria would then be learnt more easily. Having learnt one Communion setting, it is good to try others, one at a time. The rotation could be annual (Year A, B, C with the three-year lectionary) or seasonal (Lent, Easter, etc.). When choosing a setting, be practical and ask what the people can learn. In addition, look for settings which take the words seriously. The rhythm of the new texts is quite different from that of *BCP*. Composers who don't take that seriously spoil the new words with inappropriate emphases. The new words can sing beautifully when the right music is provided.[22]

As well as songs and music settings, music and / or singing can be helpful – or distracting – during the administration of communion. Canon Bartlett continues:

> Some people like words sung during the Communion. Others find it distinctly distracting and intrusive. An imaginative organist can provide reflective music at that time as an aid to meditation. In addition, times of silence can play their part. There is no need for continuous sound.

Two final matters

Music involves more than the minister

Lawrence Bartlett, writing from long experience, urges that

> The musicians in a congregation should get together to plan the way forward. They need to assess the musical skills and tastes of their people, and then look carefully at the liturgy. There is a great deal of music available today. The needs of no two congregations will be exactly the same. Thus, it is imperative that local musicians be set free to take initiative.

> On the other hand, musicians tend to think in terms of their favourite styles. Give them space to be themselves as Christian disciples with particular skills. For their part, they need to work with local leaders, especially clergy who have

---

22   *A Practical Commentary*, 24-25. *Together in Song* Section XV provides a range of user-friendly and singable communion settings.

spiritual responsibility for the congregation to ensure that music used in liturgy supports performing the gospel.[23]

Who is likely to be present?

For most Sundays it will be 'the usual suspects', but when there is a baptism, for example, people who are unfamiliar with church will be present. The songs, as well as any musical setting, need to be considered. It may well be that the regulars will 'carry' these in such a way that visitors find their singing helpful: over-simplifying a a service is not always the best strategy.

For most weddings and funerals, however, many of those present will expect to be an 'audience' rather than a congregation. This is especially so when the service does not take place in a church building: particularly in the open air, accompaniment for singing is likely to be an issue. Songs for such situations need to be well-known and carefully chosen.

The closing words of *Performing the Gospel* Chapter Six are a fitting end to this chapter also:

> Music in worship is often a contentious area, where trends and tastes will ebb and flow, empires rise and fall. The challenge for those entrusted to choose, lead and perform music is to be so immersed in the flow of a service as to sense the best ways and means for the gospel to be performed. There are so many rich angles from which to explore the ways in which music can contribute to this ministry. Along and together with the words used in liturgy, music shapes us, and forms (or deforms) our insights into the wisdom and ways of God.

---

23 *A Practical Commentary*, 20.

Further reading

The Australian Hymn Book Company, *Together in Song. The Australian Hymn Book II* (Sydney: AHBC, 1999), especially the Introduction and Indexes

Box, Reginald SSF, *Make Music to our God. How we sing the Psalms* (London: SPCK, 1996)

Witvliet, John D., *The Biblical Psalms in Christian Worship* (Grand Rapids; Eerdmans, 2007)

Wood, D'Arcy, *A Companion to Together in Song: The Australian Hymn Book II* (Sydney: AHBC, 2006): includes notes on every hymn, composer and lyricist

Chapter Seven

The Ministry of Prayer

What makes prayer Christian?

The short answer? Belief in the Holy Trinity. A little unpacking will explain this succinct claim, and set the background for considering the ministries of prayer in *APBA*.

From First to New Covenant

Intercessory prayer was the new reality that the Holy Spirit brought to the disciples of Christ. Believers certainly prayed before the Spirit's coming: the psalms are half praise, half lament or thereabouts, and confessions of faith and of sin are plentiful in the First Testament. Intercessory prayer is rare, however, and taken up with hesitation. It was the courageous act of but a few: Abraham, Moses, David, Ezra and some prophets.[1] The design of the Tabernacle and Temple, where Israel delighted to know God's presence, reinforced such a sensibility. The ordinary Israelite mostly stayed in the outer of three courts, passed into the next occasionally, and the inner shrine never. Intercession was possible before the coming of Christ, but only entered into with great reserve.

A similar attitude is seen in Jesus' disciples: they were struck by the distinctive freshness in Jesus' praying. His intimacy with God gave them a new standard and hope for such praying – a hope opened in Christ's death and resurrection. Respect

---

1 Explicit intercessory prayers in the First Testament are:
   Genesis 18:27 (Abraham)
   Exodus 32:11–14, 33:12–23, Numbers 12:13, 14:13–19 (Moses)
   1 Samuel 12:19–23 (Samuel)
   2 Samuel 7:18–29 and 1 Chronicles 17:16–27; 29:10–19 (David)
   1 Kings 8:22–53 and 2 Chronicles 6:14–42 (Solomon)
   2 Chronicles 20: 6–12 (Jehoshaphat)
   1 Kings 17:20–21, 18:36–37 (Elijah)
   2 Kings 19:14–19 // Isaiah 37:14–20, 20:2–3 // Isaiah 38:2–3, 2 Chronicles 30:18–19 (Hezekiah)
   2 Chronicles 33:12–13, 18–19 (Manasseh)
   Ezra 9:6–15, Nehemiah 9:6–38 (Ezra)
   Daniel 9:4–19 (Daniel).
   In each case the prayer is offered in distinctive circumstances, with considerable trepidation. Alongside these are many calls for divine help, especially in the psalms.

and awe at the majesty of God is allied with a sense of personal relationship with God. This is portrayed vividly by the curtain that separated the inner shrine in the Temple being torn down (Matthew 27:51, Mark 15:38, Luke 23:45). Hebrews thus depicts Jesus as the great High Priest, who entered the inner shrine of God's presence through his obedient death, to intercede for believers (Hebrews 9:24–26).

The atmosphere changes after Pentecost, when the ascended Lord poured out the Spirit on believers. Knowing the presence of God in a new way, they prayed in a new way. The disciples had earlier implored Jesus to teach them to pray as he did. In response, Jesus said, "Your Father knows what you need before you ask" (Matthew 6.7), which might seem a reason not to pray. But this teaching introduces the Lord's prayer: if God did *not* know our needs before we asked, we would be helpless indeed. Jesus went on to encourage the disciples to address God in prayer as their 'Father' (Luke 11.1; Matthew 6.9–13), though there is no record of the disciples doing so while Jesus was with them.[2] Paul, writing to the church in Rome two decades later, assumed that Jesus' intimacy with God was now an everyday reality for believers:

> When we cry "Abba, Father!", it is the Spirit himself bearing witness with our spirit that we are children of God. (Romans 8:15)

Like Jesus, these Greek and Latin speaking Christians addressed God as 'father', using the Aramaic that Jesus used, *'abba* (Mark 14.36; Galatians 4.6). Paul's practice of interceding is as familiar as breathing (so Romans 1.8–10; 2 Corinthians 1.8–11; Ephesians 1.15–23; 3.14–19). In the Spirit, believers found the barriers between them and God removed (e.g. Romans 5:5; 1 John 3:24). The Spirit knows our hearts and desires, our 'spirit', and the innermost being, or 'spirit', of God, 'translating' between them. As Paul put it,

> The Spirit helps us in our weakness. For we do not know how to pray as is right, but the Spirit intercedes for us with inexpressible cries. And the one who searches hearts knows what is the mind of the Spirit, because the Spirit intercedes for the saints according to God. (Romans 8:26–27)

Intercession thus arises not so much from human initiative, as from the prompting of God's Spirit. And we not only need divine prompting and help in praying: we need divine guidance to pray according to the will of God.

---

2   'Father' used of God is rare in the First Testament, but characteristic of Jesus. His distinctive practice is represented in each Gospel, though the 'father' imagery works differently in each: Matthew 11.25–27, 26.9–42 (heavenly father); Mark 14.36 (the 'sonless' father); Luke 10.21; 23.24 (the compassionate father in parables); John 11.21, 12.27–28 (Father of the Son). See further Charles Sherlock, *God on the Inside* (Melbourne: Acorn, 1991) Chapters Six and Seven.

In short, Christian prayer is the practical outworking of belief in the Holy Trinity. We pray to God our Father on the basis of the example and ministry of the Lord Jesus Christ, enabled by the Holy Spirit. It is not so much our praying that matters, as our being drawn into the Trinitarian 'conversation' of boundless, caring love. Prompted by the Spirit, our Advocate on earth, we bring into God's holy presence "all desires known", joining in the prayer life of Son, Father and Spirit, filled with praise, intercession, lament, blessing. This perspective shines through the prayers which open Ephesians (1.3–22) and 1 Peter (1.3–20).

Intercession: the Christian privilege

Christian prayer includes the distinct privilege of uncomplicated intercession.[3] But this has become so familiar that many see prayer as merely asking God for things. Prayer is often then spoken of in terms of getting 'answers' – typically 'yes', 'no' or 'wait'. Starting with 'wait', and looking for *responses* rather than answers, is a better way. It will likely involve 'pools of silence', quietness before God, and frequent struggles to know what to pray – yet with boldness in asking when just an inkling of God's way forward is given. God as revealed in Christ is of "infinite goodness and mercy", patient to hear all prayers, whatever their nature or motivation. Christian prayer therefore begins, not so much telling God our needs, as seeking to know what God wills to give. And all this involves the work of the Spirit, who gives the desire to pray.

Further, our praying is set within the communion of all God's people: God's will for me / us is all of a piece with the whole 'counsel of God' (Ephesians 1.11). Our praying takes place within the divine conversation of Spirit, Son and Father, and by extension among the praying of all who are 'truly alive' in their presence (2 Corinthians 1.11; Colossians 4.6; Hebrews 12.22–24). We pray with and for the whole people of God in 'common prayer'.

The Lord's Prayer

The classical Christian pattern is seen in the Lord's Prayer (Matthew 6.9–13; Luke 11.2–4). Addressing God as "our Father", we ask first that the divine name, kingdom and will may be shown "on earth, as in heaven". We begin with God, God's rule and desires, not ours, before making just three requests:

> First, for God to give us not just "daily bread", but "bread for tomorrow" (as the Greek is), the bread of heaven that truly gives life.

---

3   Classically, intercession is divided into supplication (for oneself) and petition (for others: cf 1 Timothy 1.22): 'common prayer' by definition centres on the latter. In *APBA*, 'intercession' includes all prayers of request, most being petitions but with some supplications in pastoral services.

Second, that God would forgive our sins **as** (not 'if') we forgive others: that we forgive is evidence that we are forgiven, not a condition of it.

Third, with eyes on ultimate matters, we pray "deliver us from evil / the Evil One, save us from the time of trial / temptation".

In some Greek manuscripts, Matthew's version continues with the 'doxology': "For the kingdom and the power and the glory are yours forever. Amen" (NRSV). In *BCP*, it is included in contexts of praise, but not intercession. In *AAPB* and *APBA* it is always used, though in Holy Communion (Second Order) a blank line is left, presumably out of deference to Anglicans who wish to include an embolism (#27, *APBA* page 141).[4]

Aspects of prayer in *APBA*

Collect-ed praying

Structure

A classical form of intercession in the Western Christian tradition is the 'collect', a way of praying shaped by the plain-speaking culture of the Latin world. As Evan Burge explains, "The term 'collect' implies the collecting of individual prayers in a single prayer by the leader on behalf of the gathered assembly, which responds with a corporate **Amen**."[5] In turning the Latin collects into English, Cranmer made them memorable classics.[6] In time many came to be associated with particular Sundays and feasts: the 'Prayer of the Day / Week' in *APBA* terms.[7]

---

4   Roman Catholics use a modified *BCP* version, less the doxology. At the end of the eucharistic prayer, however, the Lord's Prayer is followed by an 'embolism' (extending "deliver us from every evil") before the doxology is said by all, in modern English.
    APBA uses the *ELLC* version (see Note 1, 'The Lord's Prayer', page 820), but General Note 11 (page xi) allows "the following traditional form to be used" – the Roman Catholic version with *BCP* doxology. The change from 'them that trespass' (*BCP*) to 'those who trespass' is unarguable. But changing 'which' to 'who art in heaven' raises questions. 'Which' could be heard as making the Father impersonal, but 'who' suggests that the Father is 'personal' in the same way we are. God transcends all creaturely existence, however, being *at least* personal, a concept that 'which' is intended to preserve. That said, no translation is perfect: what matters is that we pray "as our Saviour Christ has taught us".
5   *A Practical Commentary*, 106.
6   Martin R. Dudley, *The Collect in Anglican Liturgy. Texts and Sources 1549–1989*. Alcuin Club Collection 72. (Collegeville, MN: Liturgical Press, 1994) analyses the source and revisions of collects in Anglican use to 1990, including those in *AAPB* and *Alternative Collects 1985* (Sydney: AIO, 1985).
7   Dr Burge was a member of the Liturgical Commission that prepared *AAPB* and its later publication, *Alternative Collects 1985*, and held the 'collects' portfolio for *APBA*. In *A Practical Commentary*, 107 he noted:
    Following a tradition a thousand years old, Archbishop Cranmer provided in *The Book of Common Prayer* 1549 a collect for each Sunday and Holy Day ... Most were translations of Latin prayers included in the Sacramentaries of Popes Leo and Gelasius in the fifth century and Pope Gregory at the end of the sixth. Many of those for Saints' Days were new in 1549, as were those for [some Sundays] ...

The collect structure reflects the theology of prayer sketched above: they begin with God's being and action, setting our concerns within this. Praying out of God's nature rather than our needs promotes godliness, and keeps us from self-centredness.

A full collect has five parts:

1. **Address**: God is approached directly, typically using a biblical title.
2. **Attribute**: An aspect of God's character or action extends the address to God.
3. **Petition**: What we seek is set in the light of God's being and acts.
4. **Purpose**: Our petitions are not ends in themselves, but have a goal. This is especially important when praying for healing: how will the restored person use their God-given renewed well-being? Not knowing to what end we should pray points to waiting in patience, trusting God's Spirit to prompt us.
5. **Ground**: We pray on the basis of Jesus' ministry, not in our own strength. Ending "in Jesus' name" or the like can be seen as a mere formality. But never to include such a phrase reflects too cheap a view of the Christian privilege of intercession.

Not all parts need to be present in every case – strict rules about how we pray are likely to get in the way of good praying. A classic example of a 'partial' collect is this:

> Lighten our darkness, Lord, we pray: and in your great mercy defend us from all perils and dangers of this night; for the love of your only Son, our Saviour Jesus Christ. **Amen.**

Amen

'Amen' is an another Aramaic word, characteristic of Jesus's usage, who according to John's gospel typically repeated it at the beginning of important sayings: "Amen, amen I say to you ..." (John 1.11, 3.3, 5, 11 for example: this is rendered 'Verily, verily' in the *KJB*, 'Very truly' in the *RSV* and *NRSV*).

In the letters of the New Testament, the 'Amen' is typically uttered by communities rather than individuals (1 Corinthians 14.6; Revelation 5.14, 19.4), and frequently expresses unrestrained praise (Romans 9.5; Ephesians 3.21; 1 Timothy 6.16; Hebrews 13.21; Jude 25; Revelation 1.6).

Paul wrote to the Greek-speaking Corinthians as if using this foreign word were familiar in their worship:

In *APBA* the Collects or Prayers for the Day for years A, B and C are largely taken or adapted from a three-year series drawn from many sources and published in an American Presbyterian book, *The Book of Common Worship* 1993. This rich selection has been supplemented in *APBA* by several new compositions and by prayers from Uniting in Worship, Janet Morley's *All Desires Known*, and *A New Zealand Prayer Book* 1989.

Whatever may be the promises of God, they find their 'Yes' in Christ. For this reason it is through him that we say the 'Amen' to the glory of God.
(2 Corinthians 1:20)

This use of 'Amen' points up again the scriptural idea that prayer is more than an individual matter, even when we are alone. It includes all who share the divine 'conversation', whether in the new creation or this age: the people of God of every time and place. And 'Amen' is the New Testament's last word (Revelation 22.21).[8]

Themes

Henry Speagle outlines five 'themes' across *BCP's* collects.[9] This summary expresses my own assessment of the abiding value of the Anglican heritage of collects:

1. Their most fundamental teaching is that *the only real world is Eternity*: existence beyond time and space, or any other measurement via the senses.

2. If Eternity is the reality we discern by faith, then our lives take on a serious, perhaps almost sombre, reality ... *the Christian faces the world with a steadfast purpose, to bring the light of Eternity into daily life*.

3. The link between time and Eternity is prayer, joined to a faithful life which issues in good works ... *The deepest belief inherent in the collects [is] the worshipper's deep and unending relationship with God* ... a mysterious but close relationship between us and God, or better, between God and us.

4. Grace under God's Providence is a major theme: they assume *God's continuing involvement in the human and cosmic situation* ... the working of grace in individual lives and the working of divine Providence on the larger canvas of existence.

5. In view of Providence it is fitting to keep praying for protection, guidance, and defence from hurtful events in the light of our essential frailty ... *The uncertain times we live in are perhaps a blessing to point us to the steadying trust in God's Eternity*.

The collect is not a perfect or compulsory form. But being familiar with it can give shape to 'free' praying, as well as the prayer of God's people to our Father, in the Spirit, through Christ. Learning to write a collect is a useful discipline. Starting from a psalm or biblical passage is likely to prompt you to intercede for things you might never think of otherwise.

---

8 A striking example of the significance of 'Amen' for Christian faith can be found in ARCIC II, *The Gift of Authority. Authority III* (London: SPCK / CTS, 1998).

9 Henry L. Speagle, *Pools of Peace. Reflecting on the Collects* (Melbourne: Prayer Book Society, 2012). This work offers an introduction to the 'spirituality' of collects, and a reflection on each collect in *BCP*.

Examples

APBA has many prayers in collect form.[10] A traditional collect is this (#18, page 3):

> O God, the author of peace and lover of concord, in knowledge of whom stands our eternal life, whose service is perfect freedom; defend your servants in all assaults of our enemies, that, surely trusting in your defence, we may not fear the power of any adversaries, through the might of Jesus Christ our Lord. **Amen.**

Modern collects use a more direct, even bold, style:

> Judge of all the earth,
> God of justice,
> we bring before you all who abuse others.
> Turn the hearts of the violent from the way of evil.
> Fill them with a hatred of the damage they do,
> so bringing them to true repentance
> and amendment of their lives,
> for Jesus Christ's sake. **Amen.**

The first prayer uses relative clauses (whose, whom, who) to express God's actions: typical *BCP* usage, describing God's actions 'objectively'. But the resulting sentence is long, and needs care when read aloud. In *APBA*, many prayers are written more directly, as in the second prayer. Often the third person 'who' is replaced by the second person 'you': "Almighty God, you proclaim your truth in every age ...".[11]

Here is a 'full' collect from *BCP*, *AAPB* and *APBA*, with its parts numbered, to show how pruning, reshaping and moving to a 'direct' style has taken place.

> BCP: Almighty God (1), who hast promised to hear the petitions of them that ask in thy Son's Name (2); We beseech thee mercifully to incline thine ears to us that have now made our prayers and supplications unto thee (3); and grant, that those things, which we have faithfully asked according to thy will, may effectually be obtained, to the relief of our necessity, and to the setting forth of thy glory (4); through Jesus Christ our Lord (5). **Amen.**

---

10   See *APBA* pages 462–463 for notes about 'The Collects'. Most conclude with reference to Jesus Christ only (as in both examples above), but permission is given to add a trinitarian doxology, such as "who lives and reigns with the Father and the Holy Spirit, one God, now and for ever". The length of this, however, can sometimes "overshadow the prayer itself", as the Note indicates.

11   Dr Burge comments regarding on the use of second person clauses for the divine attributes: "Such expressions are not to *inform* God, but gratefully to *acknowledge* some aspect of God's nature or of God's saving acts." *A Practical Commentary*, 107.

AAPB: Almighty God (1), you have promised to hear the petitions of those who ask in your Son's Name (2): mercifully accept us who have now made our prayers to you (3); and grant us those things which we have asked in faith according to your will (4); through Jesus Christ our Lord (5). **Amen**.

APBA: Faithful God (1),
you have promised to hear the prayers
of those who ask in Jesus' name. (2)
In your mercy, accept our prayers. (3)
Give us what we have asked in faith, according to your will; (4)
through Jesus Christ our Lord. (5) **Amen**.

For each Sunday, the 'Prayer of the Day' is intended for use with the three-year cycle of readings used at the Main service. (When a reading is to be omitted, it is a good idea to check whether this prayer is linked to it.) But it may not be suitable for other services, especially during the week, so a Prayer of the Week (or Season) is provided. These are included as an Appendix to the Shorter Edition (green) of *APBA*, so that all that is needed for daily Morning and Evening Prayer is at hand.

Addressing God in prayer

A major issue in drafting *APBA* was gendered language (see pages 32-33 in this book). *BCP* prayers use a high proportion of (masculine) royal metaphors, and 'Almighty' is the default way God is addressed. In *AAPB*, this was balanced by commencing many new prayers with 'Father'.[12] However, this came across to many as too direct, even disrespectful, and gave the impression of **defining**, rather than **describing** or **relating to** God as 'our Father'.

In drafting *APBA*, traditional forms of divine address were reduced in number, but not eliminated. 'Father' alone is rare: examples are the post-communion in HC2, "Father, we offer ourselves to you ..."; Litany #3 (*APBA* page 186); and Ministry with the Dying, "Father, into your hands I commend my spirit" (Luke 23.46; #4, *APBA* page 697). Elsewhere 'Father' is filled out, for example "Father of lights" (James 1.17), "Heavenly Father" (cf the Sermon on the Mount, Matthew 5-7), "Father of all mercies".

---

12 Dr Burge (ibid.) notes that
   In *AAPB* 1978, all the *BCP* 1662 collects were included in a modernised 'you' form, but redistributed. They were supplemented by an alternative one-year set devised by the Roman Catholic *International Committee on English in the Liturgy* for use with the three-year cycle of readings.
   The new set was the source of many which begin with 'Father'.

'Almighty' – the English translation of *'El Shaddai* – is retained in familiar prayers like the Prayer of Preparation and absolutions, but reduced in frequency. A significant decision was **never to combine paternal and power imagery**, thus excluding 'Almighty Father' and 'Father Almighty' in prayers.

Positively, a greater variety of scriptural divine attributes is introduced: Great Shepherd, God of the nations, God of justice and mercy, God of all comfort, God of wisdom, God our refuge, together with variations on 'Lord'. An address with strong Australian echoes is "God of holy dreaming, Great Creator Spirit"(#3, page 281). Occasionally prayer is addressed to the Spirit: Spirit of justice and truth (#4, page 202), Creator Spirit (#5, page 391), Healing Spirit (k, page 692), but the more typical use is invocation of the Spirit.

Particularly sensitive is the trinitarian formula, Father, Son and Holy Spirit, which could not be changed in baptism. It remains in "Glory to God: Father, Son and Holy Spirit" and many blessings, and opens the Great Litany and Litany for Ministry. The imagery is refreshed in the marriage blessing (#15 on page 662), and non-gendered forms are used in Blessing #2 (page 221), at the end of the Marriage (Second Order: #28 on page 674) and a psalm collect (#5 on page 397).

APBA thus opens a dialogue around how we address God, while respecting the long tradition of Christian praying, especially the *BCP* heritage.

Responsive participation

A major concern of the English Reformers was that the people should not only be present as watchers or hearers, but participate actively. With low literacy levels and high printing costs, depending on books was for many years impractical. A way forward, reflected in *BCP*'s rubrics, was to have the minister 'line out' longer texts such as the Lord's Prayer, confessions, canticles and psalms. These would quickly become memorised, and pass into the English spiritual heritage.

Another method, not new in *BCP*, was to employ 'versicles and responses' (*preces*). The minister says or sings the first half (versicle), which the people complete (response), echoing the 'parallelism' of Hebrew poetry. So in *BCP* Holy Communion, the Ten Commandments are recited by the minister, then internalised as the people respond, "Incline our hearts to keep this law" and "Write all these thy laws on our hearts".

The use of responses is seen as 'old fashioned' or 'churchy' in some circles today, but they offer a rich way of encouraging *congregational* participation. They become familiar through repeated use, freeing people from having their faces "in the book" (or on the screen), and enabling instinctive participation. Yes, there is the danger of over-familiarity and formality – but familiar words give rich opportunities for 'godly ruts' to be engraved on our hearts.

APBA provides a wide range of responsive prayers. Those in the Eucharist are likely to be the most familiar: "Lift up your hearts. **We lift them to the Lord**." In Holy Baptism many responses are made, by the people as well as candidates (pages 52–60). Morning and Evening Prayer contain rich resources for responsive prayer, at the beginning (#7, page 5, #8–9, page 22) and in the intercessions (#16, page 13; #19, page 25; cf #3, pages 186–187). Then there are five litanies and five confessions in responsive form (pages 188–201).

The 'Prayers of the People' in Holy Communion (Second Order) include six responses for use in intercessions (#19, page 124). Apart from enabling all to join in, by separating the main topics they keep those present alert. Each has a distinctive ethos: 'Lord, in your mercy' presumes that we are in need, while 'Lord, hear us' is more confident. 'Let us pray to the Lord' best introduces rather than follows a petition. 'Father' and 'God of grace' draw attention to key attributes of God related to praying, while 'For your love and goodness' is designed for use with thanksgivings. Most congregations will tend to use just one pattern, but encouraging variety, such as using one for some weeks, can deepen participation and avoid formalism. And further responses can be constructed from the readings.[13]

Prayers 'free' and 'set'

The historic battles over 'set' and 'free' prayer in services had been left well behind by the time *APBA* was authorised. 'Free' (*ex tempore*) prayer in midweek meetings was a feature of evangelical circles, but all Anglicans observed *BCP*'s rubrics, in which the only freedom was the choice of prayers "after the third collect" in Morning and Evening Prayer. And all were read by the minister only.

The charismatic movement of the 1960s, along with more relaxed social attitudes, saw 'free' prayer become more widely acceptable. In *AAPB* Holy Communion (Second Order), 'Church militant' was replaced by a litany covering similar topics, each with suggestions for local variation and a response. It was not long before 'variations' began to replace the printed forms. By 1995, across the national church the 'prayers of the people' had become that: intercessions prepared and led by one or more parishioners rather than the clergy. As Gilbert Sinden put it, "Prayer *for* the Church has become the prayer *of* the Church".[14]

---

13   This is an outstanding feature of Janet Nelson, *Let Us Pray: Intercessions Following the Revised Common Lectionary* (Sydney: HarperCollins, 1999).
14   *When we meet for Worship*, 123.

APBA makes significant provision for 'free' prayer in each Sunday and daily service. 'Set' forms continue to be provided: in collect form in First Order services (#21, pages 14-15; #15, pages 106-107; cf #4, page 187), and in litany shape in Holy Communion (Third Order: #12, pages 172-173; cf #1-2, pages 184-186). In Second Order services no forms are given, just lists (#21, page 26; #16, page 40) or a rubric (#19, page 124): it was presumed that in these services the intercessions would be prepared afresh for each occasion, whether offered *ex tempore* or from a written text.[15]

One consequence of the widespread acceptance of 'free' prayer by Australian Anglicans is that all clergy are expected to be at ease and capable in praying *ex tempore*, whether at a bedside or in church. Clergy leading the intercessions on Sundays is now unusual in many places, however: it is widely assumed that these will be led by parishioners, but clergy leading the intercessions from time to time allows them to model good practice.

Sometimes the difference between 'Prayers of the People' and those appropriate in private or a small group is not recognised. Too many words distract, and it is tempting to focus on just the immediate concerns of those present. The intercessions are not an opportunity for notices, breaching privacy, another sermon or pushing the prayer's agenda. As Gillian Varcoe writes,

> It is here more than anywhere else where our gathering to worship is most explicitly on behalf of the world. The prayer leader needs to have a sensitive ear to the pains and joys of those for whom we pray.[16]

Forms of prayer in *APBA*

An old mnemonic for types of prayer is ACTS – adoration, confession, thanksgiving, supplication. While useful, some biblical ways of praying are missing, notably lament and invocation. A more adequate list might be:

> Praise, thanksgiving, contemplation, blessing, remembrance, meditation, confession, invocation, supplication, lament, petition, protest …

Such a long list runs the risk of making overly precise distinctions. But the order is significant: prayer begins with the reality of God, who draws us on by acts of costly love, calling us to acknowledge our sin and need, and turn toward the plight of others.

---

15 A secondary reason for the absence of a list in HC2 was that General Synod members could not reach agreement on how the faithful departed should be included. This is provided for in other services, however (#15, *APBA* page 107; #12, page 173, and in each of the 'Prayers for Sunday Services' (*APBA* pages 183-187). Significant resolution of the issue was able to be reached in the Funeral Services: #20, *APBA* page 722, #12, page 747, #11, page 763.

16 *A Practical Commentary*, 79.

Importantly, this list points up that *APBA does not include every possible aspect of prayer*. Contemplation is by its nature intensely personal, and does not 'fit' with common prayer. Meditation can be encouraged by incorporating silence in the Ministry of the Word: on Sundays this will be limited by time, but in daily services less so (cf #3, #4 and #6 in each). Lament and protest are hinted at in a few prayers (#4, page 200; #28, page 210; #17–#19, pages 769-770), but are available through 'difficult' psalms – which are often left aside on Sundays.

So, what forms of prayer **does** APBA offer? 'Prayers for Various Occasions' (pages 181-222) brings together a diverse collection, but the range is wider. The list above is taken as a guide in considering the ministry of prayer across *APBA* as a whole.

Praise

Each Sunday and daily service in *APBA* praises God for who God is, not just for what God does (thanksgiving). Two prominent forms are the 'Hymn of Praise' which begins or concludes Holy Communion, and the response which opens each daily Morning and Evening Prayer service:

Glory to God: Father, Son and Holy Spirit: **As in the beginning ...**[17]

Sentences of scripture expressing sheer praise dominate the opening of 'Praise, Prayer and Proclamation', as the name implies it should. The same is true of Morning and Evening Prayer (Second Order). Morning Prayer (First Order) and Sunday Morning Prayer open with Psalm 95, calling worshippers to "sing out to the Lord ... a great king above all gods" and respond by taking heed of God's voice.[18]

'Holy, Holy, Holy' (the *Sanctus*), the song of praise offered by "all the company of heaven", has a central place in Morning Prayer in the 'Song of the Church' and in Holy Communion is the heart of each Great Thanksgiving prayer.

"Worthy to be praised and exalted for ever" runs the refrain in the Song of Creation (*Benedicite*, pages 427-428). In *BCP* it is an alternative to the Song of the Church, but is relegated in *APBA* to 'Additional Canticles'. Portions are used on Tuesday Evening Prayer and Saturday Morning Prayer, but this Song merits being better known.

The most frequent expressions of praise are found in the psalms. Having explored the depths and heights of God's ways, they reach their climax in Psalm 150, the one psalm in which nothing but praise is expressed, with no reason but God's own being. Walter Brueggemann suggests that singing it be left until the age to come.

---

17   On this form, distinctive to the Anglican Church of Australia, see page 101 in this book.
18   Psalm 95 opened the medieval Mass: Cranmer's revision saw it continue as the opening song of the reformed Sunday service of Morning Prayer, Litany and Holy Communion, typical of his sensitivity to human familiarity while adjusting doctrine.

Thanksgiving and remembrance

Thanksgiving – praise arising from remembrance of "the mighty acts of God" – likewise pervades *APBA*. 'Thanksgivings' (pages 218-220) opens with one of the most loved prayers in the Anglican tradition, the General Thanksgiving (#1; #2 is an abbreviation in 'direct' style).[19] Every *APBA* service, from 'Thanksgiving for a Child' to 'Funeral for an Infant', includes significant elements of thanksgiving, whether through canticles such as the Songs of Zechariah and Mary, in the psalms, prayers or provision for hymns.

Thanksgiving *precedes* intercession in each section of 'The Prayers of the People' (#21, page 26; #12, pages 172-173; #1, pages 184-185). When asking comes before offering thanks for what God has already given, priorities are out of order. And 'eucharist' means 'thanksgiving', expressed in what is *done* as well as said: we "*do* this for the remembrance ('*anamnesis*)" of Christ's victorious passion. *APBA* provides eleven Great Thanksgivings, together with significant seasonal material (pages 147-163). Similarly, in Holy Baptism the prayer offered over the water is 'eucharistic': "We give you thanks that …. **Thanks be to God.**" (#21, pages 57-58).

'A Thanksgiving for Australia' (#3, pages 218-219) was written during a committee meeting by Ms Lenore Parker, an Aboriginal Anglican "under evident inspiration" as one person present described it.[20] The prayer was sent to the Liturgical Commission, who were struck by its depth, generous honesty about the story of this land, and distinctive imagery. However, out of concern for possible reaction to the phrases 'Great Creator Spirit' and 'Mother Earth', an edited form was included in the draft book. In the General Synod debate, some members asked that the original be restored. After contributions of various worth, the Revd Rob Haynes (CMS Northern Territory and Nungalinya College) warmly supported this change, articulating the deep meaning of the contested terms for Aboriginal Christians – and Lenore Parker's words were restored. When a Liturgical Commission gets it wrong, it is a sign of God's goodness that the wrong is made right.

---

19 The General Thanksgiving was one of the few additions to *BCP* in 1662. It was written by the Puritan leader Edward Reynolds, who had accepted a bishopric. Puritan emphases are seen in "creation and preservation, and all the blessings of this life" (the concept of Providence), and "means of grace, and hope of glory". The *APBA* version makes minimal changes to *BCP*: 'and humble' is omitted before 'hearty' in line 2; 'all people' in line 4 replaces 'all men'; and 'immeasurable' in line 7 replaces 'amazing' in *AAPB* (alluding to Wesley's hymn), which replaced *BCP*'s (hard to say) 'inestimable'.

20 Lenore Parker was later ordained deacon and priest for the Diocese of Grafton.

Blessing

'Berakah' prayer

The characteristic way to offer thanksgiving in ancient Israel was offering a 'blessing' (*berakah*) prayer (e.g. Genesis 14.19–20; Ruth 4.14). The person or object for which God's blessing was sought was then set apart for God's service. The introduction to the Ordinal (page 781) takes this up:

> The shape of the ordination prayers in early centuries was a *berakah* ('blessing') prayer. God is blessed for the gospel ministry given by Christ, and for the ministries of those being ordained. In this context of thanksgiving, prayer is made for the Spirit to come upon each ordinand for their particular ministry in the Church of God.

A *berakah* prayer is found at the 'offertory' in Holy Communion (Second Order):

> Blessed are you, Lord, God of all creation.
> Through your goodness we have these gifts to share.
> Accept and use our offerings for your glory
> and for the service of your kingdom.
> **Blessed be God for ever.**

In blessing God for them, our offerings are set aside (dedicated) to God's service.

Blessing things

Reflections such as these allowed the Liturgical Commission to bring some resolution to a long-standing issue over blessing 'things'. Significant numbers of Anglicans (and other Christians) reject this as encouraging an unscriptural divide between 'blessed' and 'ordinary' things: a sacred / profane or created / redeemed dualism.

When *AAPB* was being drafted in the 1970s, the 'blessing' prayer over the water in baptism was the one point on which the Commission could not agree, so the wording of *BCP* was retained: "sanctify this water for the mystical washing away of sin". In *APBA*, this became "Pour out your Spirit in blessing, and sanctify this water so that ...", blessing by invoking the Spirit (*epiclesis*: compare Thanksgiving 2, page 132).

Forms of blessing

Blessing in the scriptures is much more commonly declared or pronounced on people, however. The 'Aaronic' blessing is an oft-used example: "The Lord bless you and keep you ..." (Numbers 6.24: *APBA* pages 28, 704). In Israel of old, calling down blessing upon a person is a great privilege (see Deuteronomy 33). Blessing can also be declared *of* someone: the Psalter opens with the words, "Blessed is the person who ...", and the Sermon on the Mount begins with the Beatitudes (Matthew 5.1–12).

Blessing can thus be a means of dedication (*berakah*), be pronounced, declared and prayed for. *APBA* provides for each:

- As well as in the ordination and offertory prayers, a significant *berakah* prayer is in Holy Communion (First Order), using words from *BCP*: "We also bless your holy name for all your servants departed this life in your faith and fear" (#15, page 17). In this blessing, the faithful departed are dedicated to God's service of praise: see pages 380–381 in this book.

- Blessing is pronounced in the Triune Name on the congregation at the 'end' of each Eucharist: 'end' in the sense of its goal as well as conclusion. Pastoral Services offer further forms (pages 674, 704, 734), one being non-gendered (#2, page 221).

- Blessing #3 (page 222) comes from the Church of the Province of Kenya. There, the people point to the cross as they exclaim the first three responses, and then towards the heavens for the fourth. Blessings with accompanying actions like this one encourage active participation.

- The fullest prayer of blessing in *APBA* is "A blessing of the whole person" (#1, page 221).[21] The pronouns are italicised to allow flexible use: for example, "Bless *Robin* through and through, that *we* may delight …". It could be used to bless a newly-engaged or married couple, people leaving a congregation and the like.

Who may bless?

Traditionally, pronouncing blessing is a bishop's ministry (#43, page 69), usually delegated to the presiding priest. In services led by deacon or authorised minister, the 'Grace' or a prayer of blessing is used (e.g. #28, page 28).[22]

Theologically, however, the difference in outcome between a blessing pronounced by a bishop or delegate, or prayed by another minister, may be hard to spot. But when my bishop is present I both expect and want him or her to pronounce blessing, representing the wider Church.

---

21 This form originated from repeated requests by a woman from the Diocese of Sydney for resources supporting people who have suffered abuse to be included in *APBA*: it was placed under Blessings since it has wider usage beyond that context. Her importuning saw three prayers relating to abuse included (#26–28, pages 209–210).The post-APBA Liturgical Commission has provided further resources for this agonising area of ministry: https://www.anglican.org.au/seasonal-resources

22 In the Solemnisation of Matrimony in *BCP*, the 'minister' rather than priest pronounces the blessing on the newly married couple. This could be an authorised lay person: the tradition in some places was for the bride's father to do this.

Confession

Christians make confession in two ways: of faith, and of sin. They are discussed in this order because without faith we are much less likely to be aware of sin.

Confession of faith

Confessing faith is an act of corporate prayer: that is why Creeds conclude with 'Amen'. Scholars can articulate the precise meaning of each phrase, but a creed is affirmed in the first place as a communal act *towards* faith. So in Baptism and Confirmation, the candidate is not asked to pass an exam, but "to affirm as yours the faith of the Church" (#22, page 58; #18, page 89). The expectation is that personal faith will grow in heart, mind and lifestyle, as is presumed in the prayers for the newly baptised (#19, page 57; #22, pages 80-81), and in their Christian formation through engaging with The Catechism (pages 815-818).

All three historic Creeds are included in *APBA*: the Apostles' in Holy Baptism (in question form) and in Morning and Evening Prayer; the Nicene in Holy Communion; and the Athanasian in the Supplementary Material. Some knowledge of the historical contexts which gave rise to these Creeds is likely to deepen an appreciation for the beauty of Nicene faith – but this is beyond the scope of this book.

"An Affirmation of Faith" (#9, page 37) is the outcome of requests for a straightforward Christian confession, suited to occasions (other than Baptism) when children or visitors are present. Written with a narrative structure, all the verbs are of one syllable, there are no adverbs and just one adjective (true). Doctrinally, it gives similar weight to the ministries of the Son, Spirit and Father, and concludes with a strong trinitarian response (based on the Church of England's *Patterns of Worship*).[23]

All these confessions of faith are corporate, as appropriate for 'common prayer'. But they do not exclude personal forms: 'An Act of Faith' in Ministry with the Dying (#4, page 697) offers models for a variety of situations, expressing faith in God in heartfelt intimacy, or by divine grace just hanging in there.

A note on the 'filioque' clause in the Nicene Creed

Note 1, 'Common Forms' (pages 820-822) explains issues in the translations employed. Though General Synod did not authorise it, implicit permission is given in this Note for omitting 'and the Son' (*filioque*) in line 26 of the Nicene Creed. This was recommended by the Lambeth Conferences of 1888, 1978 and 1988, and more recently by the *Inter-Anglican Liturgical Consultation*. It remains an issue between Western and Eastern Christian traditions.

23　The Affirmation was drafted by me on behalf of the Liturgical Commission. Before inclusion in the draft book it was submitted (with a commentary) to the Doctrine Commission, who approved the text.

The phrase does NOT mean that the Spirit proceeds "from the Father and from the Son" (*patri et filii*) separately, but from their union: "from the Father-and-Son" (*filioque*). This, as Augustine beautifully taught, is the work of the Spirit, who constitutes the "bond of love" between the Father and the Son.[24]

Confession of sin

The more Christians contemplate the goodness of God, the deeper our sense of sin. Yet the more believers reflect on the costly love and justice of God in Christ, the more this sense of sin is taken up into an even greater awareness of the peace of God. Sin is serious, corrupting the way we see the world, and crippling our capacity to do what is right. Yet God's grace, "abounding in steadfast love", is far greater. Both truths matter, but their order in liturgy can vary, depending on the context and congregation. In *BCP*, confession of sin comes first in Morning and Evening Prayer, clearing the way for praise and responding to the scriptures; in Holy Communion, it comes in response to the Ministry of the Word, leading into the Lord's Supper.

Confessing sins is often confused with our being finite creatures. But there is nothing sinful about being limited and finite. Nevertheless, sins turn harmless limitations into the tyranny of frustration, and ultimately death. '*Kyrie eleison*' responses – 'Lord have mercy' – have our weakness rather than our sin in mind: they are not so much a confession of sin, as a plea for God to 'come to our aid' (the literal meaning of '*eleison*').

Services in *APBA* typically open with praise, setting our eyes on God rather than ourselves. It is this that brings us to confess our sins and seek forgiveness. Different forms of confession and absolution are provided in each Sunday service, allowing considerable flexibility (#5-6, page 4; #6-7, page 21; #14, pages 38-39; #5, pages 52-53; #19-20, page 109; #22-23, page 126; #14-15, page 174). In each case the confession is 'general' rather than 'personal': I acknowledge my being caught up in the 'cussedness' of life and society, however few or many sins of recent days I may bring to mind.

Five 'Prayers of confession' are found on *APBA* pages 198-201. The first two are suitable for any service. The third, from the Koori Commission of the Anglican Diocese of Canberra and Goulburn, seeks to foster reconciliation in this land. The fourth and fifth are from *All Desires Known* by Janet Morley, and need congregational preparation before use. The fifth confession is appropriate for use on Ash Wednesday, provided such preparation has taken place.

---

24 My own practice, following a suggestion by a Russian Orthodox theologian, is to say (quietly) "proceeding from the Father *of* the Son". This avoids the issue of abstract ('patriarchal') ideas about 'the Father' when 'and the Son' is omitted, while preserving the Eastern concern that the Spirit be confessed as proceeding immediately rather than indirectly from the Father.

Intercession

Intercession takes its place in *APBA* through both the corporate 'Ministry of Prayer' or 'Prayers of the People' in Sunday services, and personal prayer in the pastoral and daily services. The latter offer opportunities for meditation as well as intercession, and selections can be made for use in family prayers (Note 10, *APBA* page 433).

'Prayers for Various Occasions' begins with 'Prayers for Sunday Services'. The first two forms, and those on pages 172–173, are litanies; the fourth is a revision (from South Africa) of the 'Church militant' prayer from Holy Communion in *BCP*. As Gillian Varcoe comments, these wide-ranging intercessions

> begin with prayer for the world rather than prayer for the church. The public prayer of the church is ordered so as not to be too parochial or personal. Its focus is first outward, to the world and the nation and the universal Church, then to the local community, the local church and individual needs, closing with a thankful acknowledgement of the communion of saints and the hope set before us.[25]

The ordering of the 'Occasional Prayers' follows through on this point. They begin with the world and society, then people in need, before praying for the Church.

Further intercessions are found in the pastoral services (pages 46–47, 652–653, 663–666, 689–692, 701–703, 758–762, 765–770). These prayers cover a far wider range of topics than *AAPB* or *BCP*: from intercessions for peace, police and priests to abusers and AIDS sufferers. The intention was not to be exhaustive, let alone suggest that only these prayers may be used. Rather, the aim was to offer models for setting the breadth of human experience before God in prayer.[26] Some of these prayers were newly written, some taken from other prayer books (see the Acknowledgements, *APBA* page 847).

The Great Litany begins with prayer for deliverance, but is likewise world-ranging: one or more of its sections can be used by themselves.[27] It has been observed that, when the Great Litany has been prayed as a whole, all the areas of life commended to be set before God in the scriptures have been covered. The litanies that follow have specific foci – ministry, peace, unity and the Spirit – while the Psalm Litanies offer variations to the 'lesser litanies' in Morning and Evening Prayer.

And don't forget the collects: they offer a wealth of scripture-related prayers for use on many occasions, whether personal or communal. To see what *APBA* offers, use the Index (pages 839–843).[28]

---

25   *A Practical Commentary*, 79.
26   An unintended gap is the lack of a prayer about sport, Australia's most followed religion after shopping.
27   The *Great* Litany is from the Anglican Church of Canada, used with permission.
28   This excellent resource was prepared by Gillian Varcoe, the editor of *APBA*.

Further reading

ARCIC II, *The Gift of Authority. Authority III* (London: SPCK / CTS, 1998)

Coggan, Donald, *The Prayers of the New Testament* (Sevenoaks: Hodder & Stoughton, 1967)

Dudley, Martin R., *The Collect in Anglican Liturgy —Texts and Sources 1549–1989*. Alcuin Club Collection (Collegeville MN: The Liturgical Press, 1994)

Morley, Janet, *All Desires Known*, expanded edition (London: SPCK, 1992)

Nelson, Janet, *Let Us Pray: Intercessions Following the Revised Common Lectionary* (Sydney: HarperCollins, 1999)

Sherlock, Charles, *God on the Inside* (Melbourne: Acorn, 1991) Chapters Six – Nine

Speagle, Henry L., *Pools of Peace. Reflecting on the Collects* (Melbourne: Prayer Book Society, 2012)

The Liturgical Commission of General Synod, *Alternative Collects* (Sydney: Anglican Church Trust Corporation, 1985)

Part C

Services of the Word

The *BCP* heritage

For centuries after the Reformation most Anglicans used 'Services of the Word' drawn from *BCP*. The English Reformers wanted to see Holy Communion celebrated each Sunday, as the provision of collects and readings shows. But a millennium of the Mass in Latin, and popular (mis)understandings of what it meant, saw few people receive communion more than the obligatory three times yearly.

Only after the *Uniformity Amendment Act* 1872 was it legally possible for the three parts of the Sunday service in *BCP* – Morning Prayer, Litany, Ante-Communion – to be held separately. It is from then that the pattern emerged that many older Anglicans remember: 8am Holy Communion, 11am Morning Prayer with sermon and hymns (the main service), sometimes with the Litany. The 8am Eucharist was favoured by both 'ends' of churchmanship: Evangelicals knew that only committed people would come at this early hour, Anglo-Catholics that bishops would tolerate more 'advanced' practices then. And as artificial lighting spread, Evening Prayer, with sermon and hymns, gradually shifted from its stipulated afternoon time to around 7pm.

The staple liturgical diet until the 1960s for many if not most Australian Anglicans was thus *BCP* Morning and Evening Prayer. These services include considerable singing and responses, positive reasons for their popularity.

Changes in Sunday patterns

This all changed quickly in the 1970s. Television led to the demise of Sunday evening services, while sport and community activities on Sunday mornings encouraged 'once-ing'. The re-combining of *BCP*'s 'triple service' in *AAPB* HC2 made Morning Prayer redundant: except for cathedrals and a few parishes, Morning and Evening Prayer on Sundays died. Few Anglicans under retirement age today have a sense of their 'rhythm': indeed, in my experience few ordinands since *APBA* was published have ever been to one.

Morning Prayer on Sundays gave way in some places to 'family services', or 'praise and prayer' times with little liturgical structure. Services became less formal, with music increasingly shaped by popular and folk styles: chanting was largely left behind. *AAPB* therefore included 'Another Order of Service' (page 39), drafted by (the then young) Lawrence Bartlett. This offered a framework more than content, anticipating the 'principle of coherent diversity' of *APBA*.

Daily Morning and Evening Prayer, in contrast, were given new life. The Lectionary had been revised in 1872 to separate Sunday and weekday readings, but using the same canticles each day was wearing thin. In *AAPB*, two 'Forms' of Morning and Evening Prayer were included: First Forms were a translation of *BCP* into modern English for Sunday use, while Second Form services were shorter, and shaped for each day of the week. These new daily services were well received, along with an updated Calendar and daily Lectionary.

Services of the Word in *APBA*

An evident need was for a new Service of the Word, suitable for use as the main service on Sundays, that would do for Morning and Evening Prayer what *AAPB* Second Order had done for Holy Communion. The Liturgical Commission prepared a rite that could serve for morning or evening, with the canticles placed to allow its use at any time of the day. Drafts received helpful feedback from churches, mainly in Melbourne, who gave it 'trial use'.

The outcome was Morning and Evening Prayer (Second Order – M&EP2). This offers spiritual substance, and has a coherent and flexible structure that is cognate with HC2, while being distinctive. Later, when it was decided to include modern-language *BCP*-based services in the new book, Morning and Evening Prayer (First Order – M&EP1) was prepared.

Some Anglicans, however, saw M&EP2, with its options and 'good English', as 'middle class'. They looked for a 'direct' service with few options, but fuller than 'page 39' in *AAPB*, and with a stronger emphasis on praise: this led to 'Praise, Prayer and Proclamation' (PPP) being prepared. Meanwhile, Archbishop Harry Goodhew had set up a Liturgy Committee in the Diocese of Sydney that began to draft new services. The national Liturgical Commission met with this Committee, and adjustments were made to the drafts of M&EP2 and PPP.

The daily services in *AAPB*, though in wide use, were regarded by many as too cerebral: a more meditative tone was sought. In 1992, the (Anglican) Society of St Francis in the UK issued *Celebrating Common Prayer:* this was immediately seen by the Liturgical Commission as offering a model for revision. The outcome was 'The Daily Services', to which was added 'Prayer at the End of the Day' (unchanged from *AAPB*) and 'A Service of the Light'.

Part C therefore has this structure:

Chapter Eight explores Services of the Word for Sundays

Chapter Nine considers Services of the Word for daily use.

Chapter Eight

Services of the Word, mainly for Sundays

'Services of the Word' are about much more than just words. The living Word of God, the Lord Jesus Christ, calls, addresses and inspires us as the Spirit illuminates the written Word of God, the holy scriptures. Engaging with the scriptures in readings, psalms and songs, God's people are built up, 'edified'.

Background

Biblical and historical roots

Praise and prayer at morning and evening in ancient Israel were associated with the daily sacrifices, when God "will meet with you, to speak to you" (Exodus 29.38-44). When the Temple was no more, the praises and prayers associated with these 'three-dimensional prayers' (see pages 226-228 in this book) were taken up in Jewish synagogues, in which the focus was on reading the scriptures. The occasion when Jesus took part (Luke 4.15-16) is the earliest known record of synagogue practice. Since early Christian communities began in the synagogue, it is not surprising that their gatherings were shaped by its forms (Acts 13.5, 15; 14.1; 17.1; 18.4, 26; James 2.2).

The synagogue pattern of daily and weekly praise, with systematic reading and reflection on the scriptures, continued and developed in the early centuries of the Church. Two broad patterns for corporate reading emerged: the proclamation of the Word in the Eucharist, and a more meditative approach in the daily 'office'.[1] The latter developed into the 'hour' services of monastic communities, held at eight times of the day and night with short scripture readings, prayer and psalms. Bishop George Hearn summarises these developments as follows:[2]

---

1 Details of the way the 'hours' services developed, and were taken up by Cranmer into *BCP*, is beyond the scope of this book. Analysis can be found in the standard *BCP* commentaries, notably Francis Proctor and Walter Frere, *The Book of Common Prayer with a Rationale of its Offices* (London: Macmillan; Third Impression, 1905) Chapter Ten; and Charles Neil and J.M. Willoughby (edd), *The Tutorial Prayer Book* (London: Church Book Room; Third Impression, 1912) 116ff.

2 *A Practical Commentary*, 85-86. Bishop Hearn held the Daily Services portfolio for *APBA*.

By the fourth century, two patterns of daily prayer had developed in the life of the Church. The first was centred in cathedrals, where the daily services had become an office for most Christians. These services were simple in content and fixed in form, with a small number of psalms constantly recited, short portions of Scripture read alongside canticles, and prayers of intercession usually culminating in the Lord's Prayer. They were celebrated with exuberance with the emphasis on praise and thanksgiving. Parallel to this was the development of the monastic style of daily office ... [where] the focus was upon the recitation of a large number of psalms and Scripture readings in sequence, with little attention to the time of the day or season of the Church year. Eventually these two forms of daily services were blended, so that the number of daily services increased.

Offices in the *Books of Common Prayer*

By the time of the English Reformation, the office services had become so complex that they were unusable for ordinary folk. After the monasteries were dissolved, Cranmer condensed the eight 'hours' offices into two forms, Morning Prayer and Evening Prayer, designed for all, not just for clergy. More radically, Cranmer invented a daily lectionary which covered almost all of the Bible in a systematic manner (see Chapter Three in this book). Bishop Hearn continues:

> In the fifteenth century, the daily offices became increasingly complex in character. Scripture was read at Matins and Vespers and often only single verses repeated each day were used as the lection at other times. The regular reading of the Bible was frequently interrupted by a number of Saints' and holy days, and non-scriptural readings were often substituted on these days. In the West, all of these services were in Latin, and intelligible only to the well educated.

> The English Prayer Books of the sixteenth and seventeenth centuries simplified this complexity by reducing the number of daily offices from eight to two—Morning and Evening Prayer. There was a deliberate return to the tradition of the monastic office with the sequential reading of the Psalter each month and the Bible over a period of a year. At the same time some aspects of the cathedral office were maintained, with fixed canticles (Venite, Benedictus, Te Deum, Magnificat and Nunc Dimittis), the lesser litany, Lord's Prayer and the morning and evening collects.

> The 1549 *BCP* describes these services as 'Matins' (the monastic morning office name) and 'Evensong'. In the *BCP*s which followed, an introduction was added,

and the names became 'Morning Prayer' and 'Evening Prayer'. Though there seems to be no significance in the usage, some Anglicans use 'Matins' and 'Evening Prayer' to refer to services taken in a meditative style, usually without introduction or music, and 'Morning Prayer' and 'Evensong' to describe a full service with the introduction, music and a sermon.

One *BCP* service likely to still be in use in the centuries ahead is Evensong. A Victorian age writer once compared Morning and Evening Prayer thus:

> As in the Morning Service intensity and vigour are the characteristics, so throughout the Evening Service there breathes a tranquil spirit, which is well embodied in the aged Simeon's soothing hymn, after his active day was past, and the shades of life's evening cheered by the assurance of Jesus' salvation were gathering round him.[3]

Many Anglicans, and others, continue to feel the same way.

Services of the Word in *APBA*

Ethos and structure

Each Sunday Service of the Word in *APBA* has a distinct ethos. This needs to be taken into account so the appropriate service can be chosen for a particular situation. For example, when canticles are to be sung, First Order is most appropriate, but Second Order would also be suitable. If the service moves towards an act of repentance and faith, then 'Praise, Prayer and Proclamation' is tailor-made. When an extended time of mutual ministry is anticipated, however, Second Order stands out, while a small group meeting in the evening may well find the Daily Service for Sunday Evening best.

The structure of these services is one of coherent flexibility, as elsewhere in *APBA*: **gather, listen, pray, do, go** (see pages 37–41 in this book). Each service begins by declaring the wonder of God's nature, calling forth our response of praise. First and Second Orders offer opportunity to state the purpose of the service, followed by confession and absolution to 'clean the slate' before the Ministry of the Word. 'Praise, Prayer and Proclamation' focuses on confession and absolution in response to the Ministry of the Word.

The order of readings, psalms, creed, and sermon varies between the services, but all move towards a time of intercession. Second Order makes the fullest provision for this, encouraging active participation (#21 on *APBA* page 26).

---

[3] Canon Fausset, cited in Neil & Willoughby, 116.

The Psalms

The Psalms play a significant part in each Service of the Word. They are songs, made to be sung, but in daily services they will typically be said.

Hebrew poetry has a 'parallel' structure, shown by the 'colon'. Each half-verse is spoken alternately, by one half of the congregation and then the other half. This allows all present to both proclaim and attend to the psalm. Leaving a pause long enough to breathe in and out at the colon or between verses, avoids this, and helps the psalm to be 'breathed in'.

Whatever method is used, allow the psalm to be entered into joyfully and / or meditatively, as appropriate to its content, whether recited in its own right, or as a response or preparation to reading other scriptures.

NB: 'Glory to God' concludes psalms and canticles in M&EP1, but is optional in daily services (Note 5 on *APBA* page 431): see page 101 in this book.

In the commentaries below there is some repetition, since this book will be used for reference purposes. Overall matters are considered first, then commentary: it is assumed that you have a copy of *APBA* open at the relevant place.

Morning and Evening Prayer (First Order): M&EP1
Ethos

M&EP1 follows the *BCP* service shape, though it opens with praise before moving to confession. Like *BCP*, it 'works' best when its time-honoured shape is trusted by those who lead it. There are no headings beyond 'Introduction', and few alternatives beyond the choice of opening sentences (#1, #3). As such, M&EP1 is not suited to data projection: it works quite well from the book itself.

M&EP1 uses contemporary 'good' English, with a mix of second and third persons in addressing God: in the terms of Chapter Three, 'Modern English (*AAPB*) style'.

M&EP1 is printed as one service, so it can be used at any time of the day. To enable this, the canticles are printed in succession on their own pages (6–8 and 10 for Morning Prayer, 9 and 11 for Evening Prayer). Their Latin names are placed in brackets, since *APBA* avoids non-English words, but including them in this 'closest to *BCP*' service was deemed appropriate. Ecumenically-agreed translations are used, but as Note 4 on *APBA* page x provides, other versions may be used when sung (usually from *BCP*).

The placement of canticles follows that of *BCP*: this order is not merely a succession of 'well-known songs', but leads participants to engage with the 'story' of God's saving work.

- In the morning, after the Introduction, Psalm 95 opens the service, as a 'call to worship' for the day. In Eastertide, the Easter Anthems, a tissue of New Testament passages, perform a similar function. The psalms of the day lead into a reading from each Testament, joined by the trinitarian 'Song of the Church' (MP). They are followed by Zechariah's song of blessing for the 'economy of salvation' from Abraham to Christ (MP).
- In the evening, a new 'call to worship' is not needed, so the psalms follow the Introduction. The 'Song of Mary', following the First Testament reading, enables us to join with her in praising God for fulfilling "the promise made to our forebears". (It could on occasion be replaced by the 'Song of Hannah' (page 429) on which it is based.) The New Testament reading is followed by a similar song, that of Simeon, rejoicing over the gift of the Word, and allowing us to "go in peace" to our rest.

This sequence of canticles, readings and psalms is a major reason why Morning and Evening Prayer were found by generations of Anglicans to be spiritually satisfying, and why Evensong continues to be the most used *BCP* service.

The *APBA* rubrics permit 'a similar hymn' instead of each canticle: good practice will respect the intention of their placement.

Commentary

Introduction

#1–3   The order of these sections might in practice vary, but the placement of the hymn at #2 between sentences which declare God's character (#1), and those which call us to repentance (#3), is deliberate. *BCP* includes many more sentences related to confession, which could be used in modern translation at #3.

If the Sentence of the Day is used, in most cases it will fit best at #1.

#4   This exhortation condenses *BCP* by reducing its 'image pairs', and constructing separate sentences. If a statement of purpose is needed, Second Order #4 (page 20) can be adapted.

Confession and absolution

#5   This is the first 'posture' rubric in *APBA*, and follows *BCP*. Such rubrics are kept to a minimum in *APBA* (see General Note 2 on page x and Note 4 on page 822).

The form of confession is a modern translation of *BCP*. As with all congregational confessions in *BCP* and *APBA*, it is 'general'. That is, it is not in the first place about my individual sins, but our being caught up in the disordered 'cussedness' of this world as it has become: injustice, pettiness, false priorities, lack of compassion ... our communal participation in 'corporate' sin.

#6 The 'Absolution' said by the priest is likewise a modern translation of *BCP*. (Its alternative title, 'or Remission of sins', added in 1604, is omitted as serving no purpose today.) It takes the form of a general 'declaration' of forgiveness, rather than a 'pronouncement' of pardon, as in Holy Communion. The priest stands since this is a declaration made with divine authority, an example of God's 'authoring' forgiveness.

The alternative declaration by a 'minister', presumably not a priest, takes the form of reading scripture sentences declaring God's forgiveness. This extension of *BCP*'s provision has become acceptable across the Anglican Communion. However, neither sentence includes the petition at the end of the Absolution asking God to change our attitudes and living. It is therefore recommended that an additional sentence be said, for example,

After 1 John 2.1-2:
> Since Christ laid down his life for us, we ought to lay down our lives for one another. Little children, let us love, not in word or speech, but in truth and action. 1 John 3:16,18

After 1 John 4.10:
> Clothe yourselves with love, which binds everything together in perfect harmony. And let the peace of Christ rule in your hearts, to which indeed you were called in the one body. And be thankful. Colossians 3:14-15

Note 1 on *APBA* page 17 allows the use of the 'declaration' on page 21 instead of either option here, whether read by a minister or priest.

#7 This rubric allows M&EP1 to work easily on weekdays for use as a daily office.

When sung, the *BCP* version of these responses can be used (see General Note 4 on *APBA* page x). The usual 'Ferial' and 'Festal' melodies will work with the modern words, but new compositions are not to be discouraged!

On the wording of 'Glory to God', see page 101 in this book.

The Ministry of the Word

#8 Psalm 95 (Venite) is included in full in *APBA*: the draft book omitted verse 10 (as did *AAPB*), but this was restored in the 1995 General Synod debate.

#10, #10a The introduction and response to the readings are as in *BCP*: these take an 'objective' stance as to the contents and theological standing of the scriptures. But no-one is likely to object if the responses in Second Order services are used.

#11 The (delightful) alternative canticle in *BCP*, The Song of Creation (*Benedicite*), can be found on pages 427–428.

The tradition of including an 'office hymn' at this point is hard to object to, but a better place for a hymn related to the occasion is at #2.

#13 The alternative canticle in *BCP*, Psalm 100, can be found on page 410.

#14 On the wording of the Apostles' Creed, see Note 2 on *APBA* pages 821–822.

Note 2 on *APBA* page 17 allows that the Apostles' Creed may be omitted if 'The Song of the Church (Te Deum)' is used.

As regards the custom of turning to the front ('east' in a church building traditionally aligned), Gilbert Sinden comments:

> The really important symbol here is the turning about, an acting out of the biblical meaning of repentance. This might have some application during the recitation of the Apostles' Creed, the baptismal creed …
>
> A further explanation of the custom, that it is a matter of turning to the east, either towards the sunrise as representing the rising of Christ, or towards Jerusalem, seems more appropriate to Islam than to Christianity.
>
> In any case, we need to ask what such a symbolic movement communicates today. Turning one's back on other people deliberately and unnecessarily seems somewhat rude. To stand in a sanctuary and face a blank wall seems faintly ridiculous. The continuance of this custom is not recommended.[4]

The Prayers

#15 In *BCP*, this familiar greeting only occurs here, and after the act of confirmation. Correspondingly, this is the only place in *APBA* that it is not optional. For further discussion, see page 243 in this book.

#16: The 'traditional' Lord's Prayer can be used instead of the version here (see General Note 11 on *APBA* page xi). When people from varied linguistic backgrounds are present, participants can be invited to pray it in their mother tongue.

The 'lesser Litany' is based on *BCP*, with two major changes: the *BCP* form,
  O Lord, save the Queen / **And mercifully hear us when we call upon thee**.
becomes (understandably, though #21 on page 14 prays for the monarch)
  Keep our nation under your care / **and guide us in justice and truth.**

---

4   *When we meet for Worship*, 47. The immediate context is turning to the east during 'Glory to God:', but on page 50 he writes, "For the custom of turning east for the Creed, see" the comment quoted.

Less helpful, I believe, is the change from *BCP*'s challenging, and neo-pacifist,
> Give peace in our time, O Lord,
>
> **Because there is none other that fighteth for us, but only thou, O God.**

to the insipid
> Give peace in our time, O Lord,
>
> **for you are our help and strength**.

A better alternative might look like this:
> Give peace in our time, O Lord,
>
> **for you alone, O God, can be trusted for our defence.**

It is in keeping with the overall ethos of M&EP1 for these responses to be sung, where this is appropriate for the occasion and they can be sung clearly and well.

#17 On collects generally, see pages 113–117 in this book.
If sung, those who do so need to know how to sing them as prayers.

#18 This Collect for Peace (#18), from *BCP* Morning Prayer, is also used at Evening Prayer. The *BCP* Evening Prayer collect is used in *APBA*'s daily services.

#18–19 These collects are modern translations of those in *BCP*, keeping its relative clause structure and punctuation. Rather than following strict grammar, the punctuation indicates the length of pauses: short for a comma, longer for a semi-colon.

#20 'Anthem' means a choral piece sung to, rather than by, the people. In *BCP*, in whose time 'hymns' as we know them were unknown, this is the only reference to singing other than a canticle, psalm or responses.

#21 The order of prayers follows that used across Sunday services in *APBA*: the world, including the wider creation and human society; church; and all people.

Each prayer here is based on those in *BCP* Morning and Evening Prayer. Shorter versions of the General Thanksgiving in *APBA* are found at #1, page 35 and #2, page 218.

As Note 3 on page 17 provides, "A sermon may be preached during or after the service". Typical practice (not noted here, surprisingly) has been this order:
> the prayers
>
> a hymn
>
> sermon
>
> concluding hymn (often with a collection: see Note 4 on *APBA* page 17)
>
> the Grace.

Morning and Evening Prayer (Second Order): M&EP2

Ethos

M&EP2 provides a full Sunday service in a flexible structure, using a pattern based on *BCP*, but reshaped for contemporary settings.

- Mainstream modern English is used, with shorter sentences and a more direct style than M&EP1. Apart from scripture passages, both minister's and people's words are lineated to assist reading aloud.
- The structure is one of flexible coherence, following the headings used across *APBA*, so that users can quickly sense the 'rhythm' of the service.
- The rubrics encourage active response, lest the service become 'wordy' and so move away from being a contemporary Service of the Word.
- The traditional canticles are provided, though not in the main text to allow the service to be 'user-friendly'.
- The service ethos is similar to that of HC 2 and HC3, so that congregations who use either of these along with M&EP2 can move from one to the other smoothly.

If M&EP1 is best used straight through, M&EP2 requires thoughtful and imaginative preparation, especially when the various opportunities for action and symbolic elements are taken up. M&EP2 is suitable for data projection.

Commentary

Gathering in God's Name

On the significance of this heading, see pages 40-41 in this book.

#1   The sentences of praise that open M&EP2 work best when pronounced with vigour. Since an opening hymn is at #3, they may need a 'signal' to introduce them: e.g. a word of welcome or cessation of music.

#2   Singing the responses can be achieved by using *BCP*-based forms, scripture choruses, or newly composed tunes. The Easter greeting gives a distinctive flavour to this focal season of the Christian year.

#3   The placement of the opening hymn (or three) here is designed to avoid it being seen as merely 'what gets us into the mood'. But it can be placed elsewhere. As the rubric indicates, whatever is sung at this point should continue the offering of praise, or shift towards invoking God's presence.

#4   This short statement of why this congregation has been called together by God, at this place and for this occasion, is designed to be filled out with the particular purpose of the service (see Note 1 on *APBA* page 33). Crafted from *BCP*, it summarises the twin reasons why we gather: "to meet with God' (sanctification), and "to take our part in the building up of his Church" (edification). It then turns to our need of forgiveness, not out of fear, but based on God's "boundless goodness and mercy" shown in Christ.

The contents of this section can be expressed "in these or similar words". Good practice will retain the directness and brevity of what is here.

#5   The call to confession can be strengthened by one or more of the sentences provided, or with suitable alternatives, e.g. #3 on *APBA* page 3 or #13 on page 38.

#6   Silence is suggested here in *APBA* for the first time. It reduces the 'noise' which may have built up, and provides space for reflection on God's mercy towards us mortals. The silence needs to be long enough for people to get beyond the "has the minister forgotten something?" stage: ten seconds is a good start. Writing for Roman Catholics, Jim Hews comments helpfully:

> Silence is not an absence of noise, but rather, sacred quiet which opens us to God's Spirit. It is out of such moments that God can really get through to us and move us to truly uplifting vocal praise and song. These silent moments serve to embrace and emphasize the words or phrases that went before. It allows us a chance to catch our breath. Silent pauses allow us to reflect on what we are really doing. It gives us a chance to listen to God in our heart.[5]

The confession, based on the *AAPB* 'page 39' form, is noteworthy for its rich intermingling of biblical images of sin, forgiveness and restoration. The variation in sentence length calls for thoughtful, unhurried reading: a slight pause after 'You alone can save us' can help mark the transition to petition.

#7   This form is an abbreviation of the 'Absolution' declared by the priest in *BCP* Morning and Evening Prayer. As in M&EP1, it is a general 'declaration' of forgiveness, rather than a 'pronouncement' of pardon as in Holy Communion. It is said by 'The minister', who stands since this is a declaration made with divine authority, an example of God's 'authoring' forgiveness.

The scripture sentences used in M&EP1 to declare forgiveness, plus Romans 8.38–39, can be used instead of, or in addition to, the declaration. In the latter case, as with the 'Comfortable Words' in *BCP* and HC1, they give a strong sense of assurance of God's full provision for those in Christ.

---

5   http://www.mikejohnpat.org/index.cfm/our-liturgy-and-silence/

#8   The mood now turns to thanksgiving through this praise response. We greet one another as forgiven people, the first of several active elements in M&EP2.

The form of words for the greeting, based on the introductory greetings in many of Paul's letters, is distinct from 'the Peace' given in Holy Communion. There it carries the note of reconciliation; here it has a sense of greeting and welcome.

#9   These responses are the first elements distinctive to a morning or evening time for this service. The morning form blends Psalm 95.1, used to open *BCP* Morning Prayer and M&EP1 (see page 137 in this book) with Psalm 100:1. For the evening, the short Psalm 134 is provided.

Sung settings in a variety of styles are available, or "A hymn or song of praise and thanksgiving" – an unusual breadth of description for an *APBA* rubric.

The Ministry of the Word

On this heading, see the opening paragraph of this chapter. The section is structured flexibly, both to encompass a 'traditional' format of psalms, readings and canticles, and also a more 'contemporary' style involving less formal elements, including provision for personal and communal response at #16-17.

#10 This ministry begins with prayer, asking that worshippers may 'hearken to' rather than merely 'hear' the living Word. It reflects the central importance of reading and responding to the scriptures, the written Word, in this service.

'Suitable alternatives' could include #4 (*APBA* page 36) or #48-49 (page 216), changing the past to the present tense ("the words we hear today"), or written prayers prepared beforehand. While *ex tempore* prayer is not excluded by the rubric, its use at this point could draw attention away from the scriptures.

Encouragement is given for a variety of responses to the readings, whether here or at #13: "silence, music, meditative response, discussion, dialogue or testimony". This gives considerable permission for creative participation using 'passive' responses: 'active' responses are encouraged at #16.

'Children's ministry': whatever form this takes, a clear link to the readings is essential if children are to participate meaningfully in this Service of the Word: 'Godly Play' or Scripture Union resources are examples of what is intended. Some churches place this ministry *before* a reading, to prepare children to hear it. Others use a skit to follow up a particular point or involve young folk in a dramatic presentation. These and similar methods require preparation and skill – and have the benefit of engaging God's children of every age.

#11 No provision is made to omit the Psalm(s), though they may be placed before (the 'office' position) or after (the 'eucharistic' position) the First Testament reading. On how the psalms may be sung or recited, see pages 97–103 in this book.

On the wording of 'Glory to God', see page 101 in this book.

#12, 14 When canticles are used, in the morning people turn forward from page 23 to 29, then on to 30, and back to 24. In the evening they turn from page 23 to 31, and back to 24. This is the only time in *APBA* that people 'turn back' (i.e. pages).

'Third person' forms of the canticles are given on *APBA* pages 29–32, in each case with musical settings. The following canticles should be added to these:

Song of the Church: *Together in Song* 98, 99, 127
Song of Zechariah: in second person *APBA* page 425; *Together in Song* 284
Song of Mary: in second person *APBA* pages 424-6; *Together in Song* 161, 172, 173
Song of Simeon: *Together in Song* 324
Easter Anthems: *Together in Song* 359.

#13 Note 2 on *APBA* page 33 authorises standing for the gospel reading, as in the Eucharist: this is especially helpful when M&EP2 and HC2 are used regularly by the same congregation. On this, see pages 242–243 in this book.

#15 A sermon is always included in this service, unlike M&EP1 where it is optional. Its placement at this point keeps it close to the readings, and corresponds to where it comes in Holy Communion. The traditional position is at #24, which tends to make it the climax of the service.

#16 This provision, while similar to that at #10, encourages active engagement with the scriptures and their exposition. Each place and style complements the other.

#17 On the wording of the Apostles' Creed, see Note 2 on *APBA* pages 821–822.

Where "another hymn declaring the Christian faith" is used, reference to the Church and Christian hope should be present. The Affirmation of Faith (*APBA* page 37) is another alternative.

The Ministry of Prayer

This distinctive heading emphasises the corporate nature and pro-active ethos of time of common prayer. #18–20 form a sound base for this ministry: there is plenty of room for creativity to build on, once this foundation is laid.

#18 On the translation of the Lord's Prayer, see Common Forms, Note 1 on *APBA* page 821. A 'traditional' form can be used (General Note 11 on *APBA* page xi).

#19 This 'lesser litany', constructed of responses beginning from Psalm 57.6, widens into a spiral of petition broader than that in *BCP*. It comes from *AAPB*, with "Have mercy on the poor and oppressed. / **Hear the cry of those in need.**" added.

#20 If the readings are from the 'Main' set, the Prayer of the Day is appropriate, or the Prayer of the Week could be read. On collects, see pages 113-117 in this book.

#21 This section is technically optional, if the rubrics are read strictly, but its omission in anything but a short service without music would be drastic. The opening response keeps petitions inseparable from thanksgiving, as specified in the rubric introducing the list: compare the full form on *APBA* pages 172–173.

The list follows the emphasis in *APBA* on 'common prayer' moving from the widest realm to the local: Chapter Seven explores the range of prayers in *APBA*. That the 'faithful departed' are not commemorated may surprise some, but in *BCP* this is provided for in Holy Communion, but not at M&EP.
'Similar responses' can be found at #19 (*APBA* page 124).

#22 Further provision is made here for active participation, and not by the minister alone: it offers a 'doing' of the sacramental Word through prayer with the laying on of hands. This ministry does not have to wait until people are in need: hence the naming of positive opportunites for which God's strengthening is sought. Further prayers for use with the sick can be found on *APBA* pages 689–692.

The mention of "silence, music or songs" encourages such a time to be sensitive to the cultures and personalities of those present.

#23 This pair of prayers illustrates the way contemporary and traditional forms are set out in *APBA*: both are based on a prayer from the 'Liturgy of St John Chrysostom', and both address God in the second person. The first form is lineated, has strong verbs and uses direct grammar and short sentences; the second uses continuous wording, longer sentences and dignified phrasing, and is punctuated to indicate the length of pauses rather than strict grammar.

The Sending Out of God's People

The service concludes with a strong outward-looking orientation, grounded in the "shape of God's mission" structure for *APBA*'s Sunday services: God's people are sent out to worship the Lord in our lifestyles.

The form of dismissal will need to be adapted to the particular occasion and congregation: hence the – technically unnecessary – rubric allowing hymns and songs being used "at any appropriate point in this section".

#24 Notices provide an opportunity in the service to bring out aspects of the mission of God beyond liturgy (see Note 3 on *APBA* page 33, and page 294 in this book).

#25 Likewise, the collection is a means by which believers offer their God-given resources for the service of God's mission. The 'offertory' prayer from HC2 makes a further link between the two Second Order rites.

#26 If notices and collection are not enough, more mission-oriented activity is provided for, filled out in Note 4 on *APBA* page 33.

#27 A familiar collect, used in several daily services, is provided as a form of communal response to all that has been experienced in this service. The briefer alternative focuses on evangelism, telling the world of God's saving love in action.

#28 Two traditional forms of concluding prayers are given: the 'Grace' (2 Corinthians 13.13) and a version of the 'Aaronic blessing' (Numbers 6.22).

#29 The dismissal is another element in common with HC2.

A Service of Praise, Prayer and Proclamation: PPP

Ethos

The order of words in the title is not what happens in the service: 'Praise, Proclamation and Prayer' would be more accurate, but does not have the 'ring' of the present title. But it says what needs to be said, assuming that all three of the names sections are included: PPP is not intended to start a service that does not go beyond the sermon.

PPP has two distinctive features which the title may not reveal:

- First, the structure is 'direct', with few alternatives beyond a fairly 'open' Ministry of the Word. This can be helpful when people are beginning to participate in public worship. When used regularly, however, attention needs to be paid to preparation that avoids offering thin gruel rather than "milk" or "solid meat" (Hebrews 5.12–13).

- Secondly, its shape is that of the Liturgy of the Word in Holy Communion: 'Ante-communion'. The Ministry of the Word leads towards response to the gospel through confession and absolution. This evangelistic aspect can work well where participants are moving towards full participation in the church's life. Where the congregation is used to Holy Communion, however, PPP can feel like a truncated service unless thoughtfully prepared.

Commentary

Praise and Thanksgiving to God

#1 Nothing is said about an opening hymn: the intention is to begin with praise grounded in the scriptures. General Note 6 on *APBA* page x offers wisdom.

Some of these marvellous sentences are long, and call for care in reading, especially if visitors are expected to be present. More than one voice can assist this, or a contemporary Bible translation such as *The Message* can be used.

The sentences also vary in intention: some are praises, some thanksgivings, some exhortations to the congregation. They are not a mixed bag to make a general 'praisey' start, but should be chosen to 'fit' the focus of the service.

#2 This thanksgiving is one of the few set prayers in this service, giving a stable base for its 'Praise' aspect. A slightly longer form, and the General Thanksgiving, can be found on *APBA* page 218.

#3 This generous rubric gives space for a prepared transition from 'Praise' to attending to the Word of God.

The Ministry of the Word

#4 As in M&EP2, this ministry begins with prayer: see #10, page 142 in this book.

#5, 7 A reading from each Testament is required: it is the *response* which is optional.

#6 If the 'Main' set of Sunday readings is used, the psalm will already "enable the congregation to respond to the first reading". Whatever is chosen to be said or sung, this purpose needs to be kept in mind.

#8 Using a canticle might appear out of kilter with the ethos of this service, but it may deepen the scriptural focus, and keep continuity with other Services of the Word.

#9 On the wording of the Apostles' Creed, see Note 2 on *APBA* pages 821–822.

On the 'Affirmation of Faith', see page 125 in this book.

The sermon has its own rubric to indicate that Proclamation is the calling of ministers licensed to preach. But it and the next section may well overlap.

#11 A generous rubric, offering wide opportunity for reflection: good preparation will ensure that engagement with the scriptures is both authentic and open.

The element of 'warning' mentioned at #16 (*APBA* page 24) is omitted here, because of the 'Confession of Sin' section which follows.

Confession of Sin

Though confession of sin is part of every Sunday service in *APBA*, this service is unique in it having a distinct section. The reason is found in the structure of PPP, moving from praise, to proclamation that calls for response beginning with confession of sin.

#13 These sentences are unique to PPP: others can be found at #3 (*APBA* page 3) and #5 (page 20). As with the sentences at #1, choice should be made on the basis of what has been the focus of the Ministry of the Word.

This general confession reworks the imagery of *BCP*, with more explicit invocation of the Holy Spirit. It recognises that God's children can and do rebel, and so need to seek God's forgiveness, turn from sins, and seek the Holy Spirit's enabling to love the new life.

#14 This is based on the *AAPB* 'page 39' form: see #6 on page 141 in this book. The next sentences are distinctive to this service: see also #7 on *APBA* pages 21–22.

The Ministry of Prayer

The heading emphasises the corporate nature and pro-active ethos of this time.

#15 On the translation of the Lord's Prayer, see Common Forms, Note 1 on *APBA* page 821. The 'traditional' Lord's Prayer can be used (General Note 11 on *APBA* page xi): this might seem unusual in this service, but it could be appropriate if 'semi-churched' people are present.

#16 The list follows the consistent emphasis in *APBA* on 'common prayer' moving from the widest realm to the local. Chapter Seven in this book explores the wide range of prayers in *APBA*.

The 'faithful departed' are not mentioned here, since in *BCP* this is only provided for in Holy Communion.

No congregational responses to prayer are noted, but examples are given at #19 on *APBA* page 124. Nor is the Prayer of the Day ('collect') mentioned: this would be appropriate when PPP is the regular service of a congregation.

The Sending Out of God's People

The briefest form of this section in *APBA*, it maintains the emphasis on worshippers being sent out to perform the Gospel in their daily living, having done so in liturgy. Notices and commissionings 'fit' here: see Notes 3 and 4 (*APBA* page 33) and the commentary at #24 on M&EP2 above.

#17 This prayer was contributed by the Revd John Chapman (Diocese of Sydney). The minister's words hopefully match what has taken place in the service.

#18 This form, inaccurately described as a 'blessing', is from Hebrews 13.21.

A final note

The ideas suggested in 'The Ministry of the Word', 'The Ministry of Prayer', and 'The Sending Out of God's People' on *APBA* pages 23–24 and 26–28 can be used in other services.

In accord with the 'principle of coherent diversity' that undergirds *APBA* – expounded in pages 21–25 of this book – structured and flexible 'Liturgical Resources' are offered in these services, not uniform texts.

Chapter Nine

Services of the Word, mainly for weekdays

Background

To pray the Daily Services or Offices is to join in a tradition of prayer, recitation of psalms, and Scripture readings that Christians of all ages have seen as a privilege and duty. (The term Office comes from the Latin *officium* meaning 'duty').[1]

The English Reformers intended that Morning and Evening Prayer, with their extensive psalmody and systematic reading from the scriptures, would be offered "daily throughout the year". The rubrics of *BCP* require the minister in each parish or chapel to say the services publically, and to "cause a bell to be tolled so that people might come to hear God's word and to pray with him". No doubt some clergy prayed alone, and over the next century this spiritual discipline was let slip. One outcome of the Evangelical and Oxford revivals, however, was a return to daily scripture reading and the offices. And, as Gilbert Sinden, the Editor for *AAPB*, significantly observed:

> There has been one development in the intervening centuries which I think it is highly unlikely that Cranmer anticipated or desired. This is the use of the daily services by individuals, clergymen or laymen, by themselves. The quite considerable use of *preces* (responsive prayers or versicles and responses) in the 1662 Morning and Evening Prayer is a little peculiar when one finds oneself answering oneself.[2]

Corporate daily prayer is one of the great privileges of being part of a theological college. Sustaining it into the often isolated contexts in which clergy live is a challenge: one remedy is to find ways by which parishioners can come together to pray the offices.

---

1 Bishop George Hearn, *A Practical Commentary*, 85. Then the Bishop of Rockampton, he held the 'Daily Services' portfolio on the Liturgical Commission that drafted *APBA*.

2 *When we meet for worship*, 53.

As social culture changed in the West, *BCP* Morning and Evening Prayer were felt to be too rigid and 'wordy' for everyday use. From the 1960s, revisions were trialled in several Anglican Provinces, typically revising the daily lectionary, introducing a greater variety of canticles, attending to the 'mood' of each weekday, and having a more flexible roster for the Psalms.

AAPB (1978) took such ideas on board: "The first consideration in drafting," Sinden wrote, was "the needs of individuals and groups who regularly use the daily services". Distinct services were provided for each weekday, and the Psalms spread over eight weeks. A modern version of the 'hour' service for late evening, Compline, became 'Prayer at the End of the Day'. These changes led to a "widespread recovery of the daily office by many Australian Anglicans", as Bishop Hearn observed.[3]

AAPB's offices were fairly cerebral, however. The aim in *APBA* was to 'soften' them, and enable them to be used in a variety of settings. Then *Celebrating Common Prayer (CCP)* from the Anglican Society of St Francis appeared in 1992.[4] It was immediately taken up as a model for further revision.

Daily Morning and Evening Prayer in *APBA*

Development and aims

In the draft book presented to 1995 General Synod, the *shape* of each daily service in *AAPB* was largely retained:

- opening sentence, canticle and prayer
- the recitation of the psalms, and hearing from the scriptures
- intercessions and thanksgivings.

But a number of changes were made:

- a *theme* for each weekday was adopted, though lightly: see Note 7 on *APBA* pages 432–33.
- '*Glory to God:*' was placed in the opening section (#1)
- the *canticles* were re-arranged (#2, #7) to reflect the themes of each day
- the *transition* in *CCP* from the opening canticle to the psalms was adopted (#3)
- the *psalm prayers* from *AAPB* were simplified (#5)
- considerable care was paid to *layout*, with each service starting a new page.

A significant omission was the suggestions in *AAPB* for Thanksgivings and Intercessions. The Liturgical Commission believed that for the services to work in a wide range of contexts they were best left as clean as possible. A regular discipline of

---

3   *A Practical Commentary*, 87.
4   Society of St Francis, *Celebrating Common Prayer, A Version of the Daily Office SSF* (London: Mowbray, 1992).

prayer is provided by participants attending to the readings, the daily 'themes' and the prayer diaries from diocesan and other mission agencies.

The 1995 General Synod used services from the draft book for its daily morning and evening prayers. Just one change was made to the offices. The opening acclamation for Wednesday evening was altered from Isaiah 55.6 ("Seek the Lord while he may be found", as in *AAPB*) to Isaiah 40.5 ("The glory of the Lord shall be revealed"). A trifling point perhaps, but one that retains the sense of the evening opening sentences lifting our hearts 'upwards': see the commentary below at #1.[5]

For the daily services in *APBA* to be used well, Bishop Hearn makes these points:[6]

- They are designed to make daily prayer accessible to a wider number of people in a variety of situations. The Notes on *APBA* pages 431–33 identify options.
- Note 10 on *APBA* page 433 suggests a suitable arrangement for family prayers.
- *APBA* (in hardback editions) has coloured ribbons which can be used to mark the place for the service, psalms, collect, and any alternative canticle.
- Daily Morning and Evening Prayer are provided for Sundays to offer a more meditative and reflective style of public worship.
- A helpful focus for prayer may be an open Bible, a cross, a lighted candle, or other appropriate Christian symbol.
- In a prayer group or small congregation, it is preferable for the group to gather in a semi-circle around the lectern, or in an open space.

Commentary

The following list sets out the suggested daily 'themes' (Note 7 on *APBA* pages 423–433). Where none are provided, some ideas of my own are indicated by question marks.

Sunday	Resurrection
Monday	Holy Spirit
Tuesday	Blessing (?)
Wednesday	People of God (?)
Thursday	Incarnation
Friday	The Cross
Saturday	Creation and recreation.

---

5   In debate it was moved "That the opening acclamation in the Daily Services for Monday, Wednesday, and Friday evenings, and Sunday, Tuesday, Thursday, and Saturday mornings, be 'Glory to God: Creator, Redeemer and Spirit of grace'." The motion came under Part D Amendments, those "which the Liturgical Commission opposes, but believes raise significant matters of principle which General Synod alone could resolve, and under the procedure recommended by the Standing Committee, whose debate would require the support of 70 members." The necessary support was not given, so the motion lapsed.

6   *A Practical Commentary*, 88–89: these comments are drawn into 'bullets' from various places in his text.

Being aware of these themes can assist 'entering in' to each service, and shape the ethos – but only if this is helpful. They are kept light to avoid 'framing' how praise is offered, the scriptures are heard and prayer made.

#1 Of the 14 opening sentences, nine are as in *AAPB*. They generally reflect the day's 'themes', in the morning tending to look 'forwards', in the evening 'upwards':

Day	Morning	Evening
Sunday	Psalm 118.24	1 Timothy 1.2
Monday	Romans 5.5	Romans 15.13
Tuesday	Deuteronomy 32.3	Psalm 96.1
Wednesday	1 Thessalonians 5.16–18	Isaiah 40.5
Thursday	1 John 1.5	Revelation 19.6–7
Friday	Hebrews 13.15	Ephesians 2.17
Saturday	2 Corinthians 4.6	Ephesians 1.2

"Glory to the Father …" (*Gloria Patri*) in *BCP* was recited after every psalm and canticle. This was felt to be overly repetitive, and to 'Christianise' the Psalms too easily. So in *AAPB*, while "Glory to God:" was retained after each scriptural canticle, it was made optional after the psalms. With these factors in mind, "Glory to God:" opens each daily service: Note 5 on *APBA* page 422 provides that it may be used after canticles. (On its wording, see page 101 in this book.)

#2, 7 Each canticle has a 'non-technical' name, with any scriptural reference at the end. The Latin names from *BCP* are retained in M&EP1.

The selection and placement of canticles for daily services was made afresh, noting both the 'themes' and times of each day.[7] *CCP* was influential, but how they are used elsewhere in the Anglican Communion and ecumenically was also considered. Most translations are from *CCP*; psalms used as canticles were translated by Evan Burge (see Acknowledgements, *APBA* page 848).

Each opening canticle is a song of praise; each second canticle gives expression to the human response to God's work, as evidenced in the scripture readings. So on Sunday evenings, Psalm 134 calls worshippers to "praise the Lord" as they "stand by night in the house of the Lord".

---

7   Sinden notes that the choice of canticles in *AAPB* was based on 1970 draft Church of England services, in which the Monday ones repeat those for Sunday: *When we meet for worship*, 58. A useful commentary on many contemporary canticles, explicating their scriptural texts, history and modern translations, is available at https://issuu.com/churchofireland/docs/comm11
    A list (with texts) of canticles used in the Roman Catholic tradition, many of which will be familiar to Australian Anglicans, can be found at http://www.liturgies.net/Prayers/canticles.htm

After the readings, the Song of Mary invites us to join with her in celebrating the "greatness of the Lord", whose nature and deeds have been heard in them.

Day	Opening canticle	Second canticle
Sunday am	A Song of Triumph (Psalm 95)	The Song of Zechariah (Luke 1.68–79)
Sunday pm	The Praise of God's Servants (Psalm 134)	The Song of Mary (Luke 1.47–55)
Monday am	Song of God's Marvellous Acts (Judith 16.13–15)	A Song of Isaiah (Isaiah 12.2–6)
Monday pm	A Song of Hope (Isaiah 61.1–3)	A Song of God's Children (Roman 8.2,14, 15b–19)
Tuesday am	A Song of God's Mercy (Ephesians 2.4–7)	A Song of the Blessed (Matthew 5.3–10)
Tuesday pm	The Song of the Three Song of the Three 28–34	The Song of Simeon (Luke 2.29–32)
Wednesday am	A Song of God's Grace (Ephesians 1.3–6)	The Song of the Church (*Te Deum*)
Wednesday pm	A Song of Praise (Psalm 67)	The Song of Mary (Luke 1.47–55)
Thursday am	A Song of God's Herald (Isaiah 40.9–11)	The Hymn of the Word (John 1.1–5, 10–14, 16)
Thursday pm	A Song of Joy (Psalm 100)	The Song of Christ's Glory (Philippians 2.6–11)
Friday am	A Song of God's Grace (Hebrews 10.19–22)	Saviour of the World[8]

---

[8] This canticle is a modern expansion of a Latin antiphon from 'Visitation of the Sick' in the Sarum Manual, the priest's book used from 1085 in south England, set to music by Thomas Tallis in the 16th century:
> Salvator mundi, salva nos, qui per crucem et sanguinem redemisti nos.
> Auxiliare nobis, te deprecamur, Deus noster.

An English translation is included in the 'Visitation of the Sick' in each *BCP* from 1549:
> O Saviour of the world, who by thy Cross and precious Blood hath redeemed us,
> Save us, and help us, we humbly beseech thee, O Lord.

The Friday canticle "first appears in the Congregational Hymnal of 1860, and would appear to have been written by the editor of the book, Dr Henry Allon. From there it was taken into various Free Church Hymnals, and was included in the Daily Office produced by the [English] Joint Liturgical Group in 1968, and has since appeared in a number of Anglican Prayer Books." M.C. Kennedy, *The Study of Liturgy. Morning and Evening Prayer and the Litany in the [Irish] Book of Common Prayer Part I* (Dublin: Church of Ireland, 2011) page 42.

Day	Opening canticle	Second canticle
Friday pm	The Lord's Servant (Isaiah 53.3-6)	A Song to the Lamb (Revelation 4.11; 5.9b-10)
Saturday am	A Song of Creation (Song of the Three 35, 60-65)	A Song of Redemption (Colossians 1.15-20)
Saturday pm	A Song of the Shepherd (Psalm 23)	The Easter Anthems[9]

Note 6 on *APBA* page 432 provides a way by which the *BCP* pattern of a canticle after each reading can be followed, and the Song of Zechariah and Song of Mary ('gospel canticles') used daily: some add the Song of Simeon to this provision. Several alternative canticles are found on pages 425-30, including 'second person' versions of the Song of Zechariah and the Song of Mary: the effect is to reduce the frequency of masculine pronouns for God.

#3 The opening words for each morning and evening are taken from *CCP*. A significant period of silence is envisaged, allowing participants to become aware of anything concerning them, clearing the mind for what follows.

Confession of sin forms a part of each Anglican Sunday service. The Commission held, however, that confessing sin each weekday morning is unhelpful. But in the evening, acknowledging our part in what has transpired against God's will that day is fitting. So daily Evening Prayer provides for a general confession of sin at #3: Note 1 on *APBA* page 431 provides a form, which can also be used on Sunday mornings. Conversely, confession of faith is appropriate in the morning, as the day is entered: see #8 below.

#4 A rubric not always observed is "a pause after each". Bishop Hearn comments: Thoughts provoked by a psalm may be turned into silent prayer. Our Lord's spiritual life was nourished by the psalms, and Christians have traditionally found them a source of inspiration.

#5 These psalm prayers, based on *AAPB*, relate to the daily themes. They are optional, and alternatives are available from various sources, including the seasonal collects for Advent, Lent and Easter (see Note 3 on *APBA* pages 431-432).[10]

---

9 The Easter Anthems bring together 1 Corinthians 5.7, Romans 6.9 and 1 Corinthians 15.20. They were included from the 1552 edition of *BCP*, under Collects and Readings, to replace Psalm 95 at Morning Prayer on Easter Day. In the 1549 *BCP* they preceded Matins, and were said with Alleluias: Proctor & Frere (539-40) state that they accompanied a procession of the sacrament reserved on Good Friday.

10 In the Lent collect on page 432, please add 'worthily' before 'lamenting', as in the 'Prayer of the Season' on page 481. *AAPB* omitted 'lamenting', returned in *APBA* to avoid despairing prayer.

#6 The daily lectionary is explored in Chapter Three in this book.

A third opportunity for silence is provided here, 'for reflection'. But brief responses or comments will on occasion be appropriate, not least after a difficult passage. In my experience, these can be poignant, humorous or challenging.

"May your Word live in us" comes from an *AAPB* alternative which quickly became preferred by many to "This is the Word of the Lord" (*AAPB* page 45). In daily services, in which the scriptures are read in course, the latter response would often be inappropriate, and sometimes false or wrong, so was omitted.

#8 The Apostles' Creed is used on Sundays if the service is a congregation's regular one (Note 2 on *APBA* page 431). But it is available for recitation each morning. NB: The Maori version is close to a 'haka', whose rhythm renders the Creed as a 'gutsy' symbol of Christian faith.

#9 The Lord's Prayer is the *ELLC* translation (Note 1 on *APBA* page 820). General Note 11 on *APBA* page xi provides a 'traditional' form which may be used. When people from varied language backgrounds are present, it is good practice to invite participants to pray this prayer in their mother tongue.

#10 The weekday collects are printed at the end of the shorter (green) edition of *APBA*, so they are available for use in daily services.

#11 The rubric specifies 'Intercessions and Thanksgivings', though this order would be better reversed: we ask in the light of God's provision.

On the prayer resources in *APBA*, see Chapter Seven.

#12 Two morning collects (Eternal God, Lord our God) and two evening collects (Lighten our darkness, Be present) are used on alternate days.

#13 The closing prayers take account of the daily themes. Each is worded so that they may be read by whoever leads the service, ordained or not.

The 'Grace' is used on Sunday morning and Thursday evening, but Note 9 on *APBA* page 433 provides that it may be used for any service:

Bishop Hearn's words make a fitting conclusion:

> With imagination, preparation and commitment, the Daily Services of *APBA* can become an integral part of the life of a parish. Clergy can ensure that Morning and Evening Prayer are not seen as clerical offices, by offering them at times accessible to some other members of the congregation.[11]

---

11   *A Practical Commentary*, 91.

A Service of the Light, and Prayer at the End of the Day

Light and dark, evening and morning

Light is a mysterious aspect of reality. Scientists employ complementary wave and particle models in order to understand its workings. Artists delight to explore the complexities of how light 'works' on canvas, stage, screen and buildings.

"Let there be light" marks God's first act of creation: and "God called the light Day ... and there was *evening and there was morning*, the first day" (Genesis 1.3-4). The order is significant: rest comes before activity (see page 63 in this book). So in Jewish practice God is blessed when the evening lamps are lit for the new day, which starts not at dawn but sunset. The lamp-lighting is especially important on the eve of the fifth day (Friday in modern naming), so that the Sabbath's beginning is blessed in this ritual of light. Christians see the biblical concept deepened in the coming of the Light in the incarnation of the divine Word, the "Light of the world" (see John 1.1-4,9; 3.19-21; 8.12; 9.54; 12.35-36).

Early Christians continued the Jewish practice of blessing God for light at the eve of the day, seen in 'First Evensongs'. The custom of lighting lamps gradually took on a different meaning, of closing the day, when it came to be seen as starting with sunrise. 'Lights' became associated with the 'hours' service of Vespers, held as daylight dims, offering praise to God for the day past, in anticipation of rest for the day ahead.

On the other hand, before artificial lighting, the dark was widely feared, believed to be inhabited by the powers of evil, whether human or worse. Another focus for late evening prayer thus arose, initially in Benedictine circles: seeking God's protection through the night. This is reflected in the 'hours' service of Compline, traditionally used just before sleep.

There is truth in all these concepts: light as the symbol of divine creation and recreation in Christ; offering praise to God at daylight's end; and prayer for protection in the hours of darkness. Bishop Hearn notes,

> links with these earlier traditions continue in the evening collect of the *Book of Common Prayer*, 'Lighten our darkness we beseech Thee, O Lord', and in the evening hymns traditionally associated with Prayer at the End of the Day (Compline), 'Hail Gladdening Light' and 'O Gladsome Light'.

A Service of the Light

This service, new in *APBA*, was added to celebrate Christ's overcoming of all darkness in order to reveal the light of God's nature and presence.

Note 1 on *APBA* page 438 indicates that "there should be as little artificial light in the church building as possible": this applies wherever the service takes place. The Note also offers suggestions for seasonal procession with a light.

#1   This response combines John 8.12 with John 1.4, and alludes to John 12.46.

#2   On 'O Gladdening Light', see #4 in 'Prayer at the End of the Day' in this book. Any other hymn chosen should focus on 'light', and be suitable for a candle or other light to be lit during its singing (see Note 3 on *APBA* page 438).

#3   The introductory response echoes the beginning of each Great Thanksgiving prayer: indeed, each seasonal thanksgiving here could be used as a eucharistic preface. A practical issue is that each is copyright, as the Note indicates, so must be read from *APBA* itself.

#4   This responsive version of Psalm 141.1-4, 9, translated by Evan Burge, will be accompanied in some places by censing.

#5   The intention is that the service form a prelude to Daily Evening Prayer, as the reference to #3 indicates. Given its strongly eucharistic ethos, it may be 'too much' if used before Holy Communion: but there is no rule against this, nor the service ending at #4.

In sum, this new-yet-ancient service has several possible uses:

- On Saturday evenings, it can be used as a preparation for Sunday by having it followed by the collect, readings or Gospel (Note 4 on *APBA* page 438).
- When there is a major feast the next day, for example, a patronal festival, this short service can be used to introduce the First Evensong of the day.
- Households or small groups can use it to conclude or prepare for a special day of Christian or personal significance, such as a new home or a graduation.

Prayer at the End of the Day (also called Compline)

The inclusion in *AAPB* of a modern version of Compline, 'Prayer at the End of the Day', was warmly received and had widespread use. It was retained in *APBA* unchanged. It can be used in a variety of contexts, e.g. to conclude a Parish Council meeting.

#1 This opening responsive prayer expresses the twin themes of our wanting to be undisturbed in the hours of darkness, and graced towards our goal to be "with Christ". "Perfect end" alludes to a good death, should I not awake from sleep.

#2 Though this silence is optional, its observance fits well into late-night settings.

The form of confession provided is personal rather than general: the form in Evening Prayer should be used if a communal confession is appropriate.

#3 'Praise the Lord!' sustains praise rather than petition as the opening focus of the service.

#4 'Hail gladdening Light' is a translation made in 1834 by John Keble of *Phos Hilarion*, an early hymn written in *koine* Greek, and associated with lamp-lighting. It was already seen as ancient by Basil the Great and in the fourth century *Apostolic Constitutions*, and is possibly the earliest known Christian hymn in use. The rubric says it is optional, but I've never known it to be left out. The usual plainsong melody is easily learnt: the harmony sounds nicely 'Russian'.

#5 Psalm 4 reflects troubled circumstances from which sleep brings God-given rest.

Psalm 91 celebrates God's protection, including from "terror at night": it was cited by the devil at Jesus' temptation (Matthew 4.6).

Psalm 134 is one of outright praise of God in the night-time.

Whichever psalm is chosen, it should relate to the context of the service.

The rubric lists a daily psalm cycle to bring variety when the service is used daily.

#6–7 The sentences speak for themselves. If replaced, they should relate to the occasion, or anticipate the next morning: the sentence of that day may fit well.

The 'Into your hands' responses, and the way the Song of Simeon is used in #7, employ a complex process of identifying and praying with Christ in his hour of need. 'Into your hands' are the words uttered by Jesus at his end (Luke 23.46), and echo those of Stephen, the first martyr, as he died (Acts 7.59).

The 'Save us' words reflect the protective aspect of eventide prayer, recalling the disciples' failure to stay with Christ's in his pre-trial 'watch' (Matthew 26.26ff).

Two practical matters:

a) The square brackets around the Alleluias indicate that traditionally they are said or sung in Eastertide. But there is no law against using them at other times.

b) If the bracketed 'Save us' words at the end of the Song of Simeon are to be used, a (non-distracting) indication needs to be made.

#8 The Lord's Prayer printed is the *ELLC* translation (Note 1 on *APBA* page 820), but the 'traditional' form may be used, as General Note 11 on page xi provides. If people from varied language backgrounds are present, it is helpful to invite participants to pray this prayer in their mother tongue.
Since this service will be used when people are about to go to bed, Thanksgivings and Intercessions are best kept to a minimum.

#9, 10 explain themselves, though it will be helpful if whoever leads the service takes a non-obtrusive lead in moving towards those present preparing for sleep.

Further reading

Christopher Cocksworth, *Renewing Daily Prayer. An Introduction to Celebrating Common Prayer*. Grove Worship Series 123 (Bramcote Notts, 1993)

The Society of St Francis, *Celebrating Common Prayer, A Version of the Daily Office SSF* (London: Mowbray, 1992), available at www.franciscanarchive.org.uk/b-ccp.html

The Anglican Church of Canada, *The Book of Alternative Services*, 36–43

M.C. Kennedy, *The Study of Liturgy. Morning and Evening Prayer and the Litany in the [Irish] Book of Common Prayer Part I* (Dublin: Church of Ireland, 2011), available at https://issuu.com/churchofireland/docs/comm11

Paul Roberts, David Stancliffe and Kenneth Stevenson (edd), *Something Understood – A Companion to Celebrating Common Prayer* (London: Hodder & Stoughton, 1994)

Part D

"Go and make disciples" Christian initiation

Jesus' last words to the disciples, according to Matthew's gospel, were

> Go and make disciples of all nations, baptizing them in the name of the Father and of the Son and of the Holy Spirit, and teaching them to obey everything that I have commanded you ... Matthew 28:19–20

Baptism is thus intrinsically linked to evangelism, identifying with the Name and people of God, and learning to live as Christian disciples. Such richness cannot be compressed into just one service. Being baptised entails entering into the life-long process of becoming a disciple mature in Christ. God's grace knows no bounds, so no minimum age for baptism was set by our Lord: for infants, learning what Christian living entails will follow on from their baptism, which will be confirmed when they are of age. Our baptism is completed liturgically at our funeral, when we are commended into God's care, and pass from faith and hope to sight and unqualified love.

How initiation into Christ takes place has varied over the centuries. Australian Anglicans inherited the 'Christendom' practice of the Church of England, which presumed that society was co-extensive with the people of God. Baptism was linked with birth and 'naming': in a society assumed to be 'Christian', for a child not to be baptised was a profound insult.

The Rev Dr Ronald Dowling held the Christian initiation 'portfolio' on the Liturgical Commission that drafted *APBA*. He describes the typical situation in Australian Anglican parishes half a century ago:

> On practically any Sunday afternoon the parish priest would be in the parish church with a small family group huddled around the font for the baptism of a family member ... Almost all candidates for baptism were infants, and in very many cases this was the last time the infant was in church for many years.

Along with this practice of baptism, confirmation often happened on a weekday night, and the newly confirmed would all turn up at the parish church on the following Sunday and 'make their first communion'. Confirmation was often the 'graduation ceremony' from Sunday School, and the 'first communion' in many cases was often the only communion (for many years, at least).[1]

Church and society have steadily drifted apart since those days, bringing what some have called a 'crisis' of Christian initiation. Across the Anglican Communion and beyond there has been renewed theological work, provoked not least by weaknesses in existing rites.

The path to *APBA*
Principles

Work towards revising rites began in 1984–85 in a committee of the Diocese of Melbourne. It consulted the Doctrine Commission, explored work going on in the Anglican Communion and ecumenically, and kept in contact with the Liturgical Commission. Ron Dowling, who participated in the Melbourne group, summarised the "basic principles" that emerged:[2]

(a) There should be one rite of Christian initiation. *AAPB* contains four services, with two more in *BCP*.[3] Adult and infant candidates do not need separate services, since the gift of God in baptism is the same, whatever a candidate's ability to answer. Differences can be managed with rubrics.

(b) Baptism is a communal, not a private, event. Whenever possible it should be celebrated within the main service on Sunday when most parishioners are present.

(c) The renewal of baptismal promises should be available beyond confirmation for those who wish to affirm faith in Christ after a time of spiritual renewal.

(d) Baptism is complete sacramental initiation, so leads to participation in the Eucharist. The Doctrine Commission, while affirming confirmation, supported this position, as does the *International Anglican Liturgical Consultation*.[4]

---

1 *A Practical Commentary*, 51.
2 *A Practical Commentary*, 53.
3 *BCP*: 'The Order of Baptism both Public and Private'; and 'The Baptism of those of Riper Years and able to Answer for Themselves'.
   AAPB: 'Public Baptism of Infants', 'Public Baptism of Adults', each in First and Second Orders (as also for Confirmation).
4 *Growing in Newness of Life*, Grove Worship Series 118 (Bramcote: Grove, 1991), known as the 'Toronto statement'. It is available at
   www.anglicanliturgy.org/wp-content/uploads/2015/06/growing-in-newness-of-life.pdf

(e) Baptism should be administered after appropriate preparation, whether of the candidate or, in the case of infants, the candidate's sponsors and family.

Processes

The Melbourne group drafted an integrated rite, bringing together baptism, for candidates of any age, and the laying on of hands, whether confirmation, reaffirmation or reception into the Anglican Church, in a eucharistic framework. The Liturgical Commission took this up, in 1990 issuing it for 'trial use': feedback shaped the initiation services in *APBA* approved at the 1995 General Synod.

'Holy Baptism, Confirmation in Holy Communion' was the first official integrated rite of Christian initiation in the Anglican Communion. At the request of the Bishops' Meeting, distinct services for Confirmation, and Holy Baptism in Morning and Evening Prayer, were included in *APBA* with identical wording to the relevant parts of the integrated rite.

Placement

Where Holy Baptism is placed in *APBA* is significant. In *BCP*, the Baptism and Confirmation services are set between Holy Communion and the Solemnization of Matrimony, implying that they are 'rites of passage' into a Christian society. *AAPB* continued this, placing them in 'Pastoral Services' section, from 'Thanksgiving for the Birth of a Child' to 'Funerals'.

In contrast, *APBA* locates these services in the middle of 'Sunday Services' (pages 51-98). In this way, Holy Baptism, Confirmation and admission to communion focus on Christian identity, rather than being regarded as 'rites of passage' around birth and puberty.

Given the social, cultural and liturgical shifts of the last half century, there are three chapters in this Part. While designed to be read in order, each stands on its own.

Chapter 10 explores the theology of Christian initiation, paying attention to issues of pastoral practice in the mission context of today's Australia.

Chapter 11 considers preparation for Christian initiation: candidates and sponsors, location, text, things and preparing for 'unchurched' guests.

Chapter 12 turns to a detailed commentary on the services of Holy Baptism, Confirmation, Reaffirmation and Reception in *APBA*.

Chapter Ten

Initiating Christians: theology and practice

Australian Christians live in a mission context. How does this affect our understanding of Christian initiation: Baptism, Confirmation and admission to communion? And how do these – and Reception and Reaffirmation – relate to practice, where context and theology interact?

The two sections of this chapter correspond to these questions. The first explores the theology of Christian initiation. The second locates key liturgical matters related to Christian initiation in the context of Australia today. Whether or not you agree with the positions put, the aim is to articulate the approach taken by the Liturgical Commission in drafting *APBA*.

But first, a crucial shift must be recognised. Until recently, baptism was often seen as part of a priest's ministry of pastoral care. This made sense in a Christendom age, but baptism is no longer the entry point for a new-born infant into a Christian society, a 'birth-right'. As in the early churches, it is being seen afresh as a 'rite of new birth', drawing a person into the household of God as a member of Christ.

Moreover, while clergy are called to 'make disciples', this is now more clearly viewed as a responsibility shared across the community of faith. As Ron Dowling puts it,

> Because baptism is a communal event, the first place to start is with the local Christian community.
>
> - Does the community see baptism as being of the greatest importance? Is there a local baptismal policy (or a diocesan one)?
> - Does the local community see that the whole community is responsible for making new Christians, and not just the priest?[1]

Recognising and practising this shared participation in the mission of God is fundamental to effective use of the Christian initiation services in *APBA*.

---

1   *A Practical Commentary*, 58–59.

Prologue: terms that may matter

Language frames the way we see the world. When it comes to words that express our identity as Christians, care in how we think and speak matters.

- Sometimes people ask for a baby to be 'christened'. This properly refers to anointing with oil (chrism) at baptism. Little is gained by insisting on using 'baptism', however, if this is clearly what is meant by 'christening'.

- The terms 'infant' and 'adult' baptism are in common use, implying that they refer to different 'baptisms'. Baptism is baptism, however, whatever a person's age or capacity. *BCP* uses 'The Baptism of Infants' and 'The Baptism of those of Riper Years, and able to Answer for Themselves'. Though awkward and lengthy, these titles state precisely what is in common (baptism) and what is different (the candidate's age) between the services.

- 'Believers' baptism' is usually shorthand for the baptism of someone able to answer for themselves, typically an adult. Yet what would 'unbeliever's baptism' look like? The *validity* of a baptism does not depend on a candidate's faith: that would make faith into a human work. Faith is itself the gift of God, as is baptism.

  This is of particular importance when the candidate is of limited intellectual capacity: as with a week-old infant, it is God's faith in them which matters (Genesis 17.12; Luke 2.21). Further, baptism involves the faith of the Christian community, not just the candidate: every baptism is 'believers' baptism'.

- 'Sponsors' is used in *APBA* rather than 'godparents' (as in *BCP*). The Liturgical Commission made this change because 'godfather' has taken on meanings that are some way from Christian use.[2] Also, 'sponsor' works for candidates of any age, and for both baptism and confirmation.[3]

- It has become customary to speak of 'baptismal vows', and their 'renewal'. 'Vows' conveys a legal sense, whereas 'promises' (the term in Anglican rites) has a more theological and personal sense (see Romans 4:13–25). 'Renewal of vows' can imply that baptism is about human action rather than God's grace. Despite the heading on *APBA* page 50, it is better to speak of 'baptismal promises' and their 'reaffirmation'.

---

2 Some see being a 'godparent' as accepting responsibility to raise the child should the parents die or become incapacitated. While laudable, this 'guardian' idea is not found in Anglican formularies.

3 See the *Canon on Holy Baptism* (1992), available at https://www.anglican.org.au/canons-and-rules

Christian initiation: what is involved?

Baptism: from washing to drowning

Christian initiation means making disciples of Christ, focussed in baptism (Matthew 28.18-20): plunged into water, we are symbolically drowned, buried to rise with Christ to new life (Romans 6.1-11) in the hope of participating in the new creation. Behind this dramatic symbolism is a profound biblical story.

Life, death and water

Scripture begins and ends with images of water (Genesis 1:2; Revelation 22:1-3, 17). Water is a universal symbol of both life and danger, of refreshing rain and destroying flood. The 'sea' is unpredictable, as Paul's experiences showed (Acts 27): for the Canaanites and Hebrews of old alike, 'sea' and 'deep' were fearsome images of the powers of chaos (contrast Revelation 21:1). No wonder that Jesus' calming the storm and walking on the 'sea' (Mark 4.35-40) terrified the disciples.

The Flood (Genesis 6-8) and Exodus (Exodus 14-15) became paradigms of salvation from water, through water, 'types' of God's people being saved through Christ's death and resurrection. So both baptism services in *BCP* open with this prayer:

> Almighty and everlasting God, who of thy great mercy didst save Noah and his family in the ark from perishing by water; and also didst safely lead the children of Israel thy people through the Red Sea, figuring thereby thy holy Baptism ... [4]

The prayer over the water in *APBA* takes up these motifs, beginning with the Spirit's moving over the waters of creation (pages 57-58 // 76-77).

Water and washing

Washing as a symbol of cleansing is found in the First Testament. Priests were strictly enjoined to wash their hands before offering sacrifice (Exodus 30.19-21), and to wash their clothes after contact with anything 'unclean' (Leviticus 13-17; Numbers 19). In the psalms and prophets, washing is an image of repentance (Psalm 51.2,7; Isaiah 1.16; Jeremiah 4.14).

But a person was born into the people of Israel, and if a male, was circumcised on the eighth day to mark this. Washing was not a symbol of initiation, though in inter-Testamental times a Gentile who wished to become a Jew would wash as a sign of repentance, and if a man, undergo circumcision.

---

[4] This so-called 'Flood prayer' was an innovation of Martin Luther in his first German language baptism rite in 1523. It came into *BCP* 1549 via Bucer's translation of the *Consultation* held in 1543 at Bonn by Herman, Archbishop of Cologne. However, its strong emphasis on baptism being necessary because of the transmission of Adam's sin in childbirth was muted in *BCP*.

The baptism of John

The symbolism of washing lay behind John the Baptist's baptising with "the water of repentance" (Matthew 3.11). When Jesus came to be baptised, John objected, since he believed that Jesus did not need to repent (Matthew 3.13-15). He saw Jesus as the one who would "baptise with Holy Spirit" rather than water, as each gospel testifies (Matthew 3.11; Mark 1.8; Luke 3.16; John 1.34). In receiving John's baptism, Jesus took his first public step in the divine mission to identify with sinful humanity, for whose sins his life will be given up. In response, the Spirit descends and a voice from the heavens identifies Jesus as God's suffering servant (citing Isaiah 42.1) and exalted Messiah / Christ (citing Psalm 2.7).

Water, new birth and death

Jesus took the image of washing much further than the First Testament and the Baptist. He spoke of 'living water' to depict the gift of the Holy Spirit (John 7:37-39), and of Jonah's 'burial' in water to interpret his death and resurrection (Matthew 12:40-41), Christ's 'baptism' for sinners (Mark 10:32-45). He told the theologian Nicodemus that "no-one can enter the Kingdom of God without being born of water and the Spirit ... born anew / from above" (John 3:3-5). Baptism is the sign and seal of this new birth.

The risen Lord Jesus commanded his disciples to "make disciples from all nations", baptising ('plunging') them into "the Name of the Father, the Son and the Holy Spirit" (Matthew 28:19). So Peter, on the day of Pentecost, called his hearers to "repent, and be baptised ... for the forgiveness of sins". They would receive the gift of the Holy Spirit and thus be joined to the Church, the renewed people of God (Acts 2:38-41).

In sum, baptism with water deepened from symbolising repentance (the baptism of John) to the radical symbol of dying in Christ, and so being born anew / from above by the Holy Spirit.[5]

Baptism: New Testament practice and images

Baptism soon came to be seen in early Christan communities as fulfilling circumcision, through the blood of Christ (see Colossians 2.11-12). This change allowed full entrance into the people of God for women as well as men, for Gentiles as well as Jews. The circumcision debates in the first Christian communities were so sharp because they were about the radically expanded boundaries of the people of God (see Acts 11-15; Galatians 1-3; Romans 9-11).

---

5   A close examination of what this 'radical' symbolism means for Aotearoa New Zealand Anglicans is Jenny Dawson, *A Radical Theology of Baptism* (Pukera Bay, Porirua A-NZ, 2011).

According to Acts, baptism was the invariable way by which people who responded to the apostles' preaching of the Gospel were admitted to the church (Acts 2:41, 8:12,38, 9:18 ...). Baptism is portrayed as what "now saves you" (1 Peter 3:21a), though as an 'instrument' of God's salvation, it is neither merely external (1 Peter 3:21b) nor automatic in effect (1 Corinthians 10:1-6). Baptism is a means of grace, to be received in trusting faith, and lived out in the works which "God has prepared for us to walk in" (Ephesians 2:10).

The Catechism teaches that each baptised person is made "a member of Christ, **the** child of God, and an inheritor of the kingdom of Heaven", so that he or she may "walk in newness of life". Baptism is a communal as well as personal event; a rite of commissioning as well as initiation, calling each baptised person into Christian ministry.

A wide variety of pictures to describe baptism is employed in the New Testament, as the 1982 'Lima Statement' of the *World Council of Churches* summarises:

> *Baptism is participation in Christ's death and resurrection (Romans 6.3-5; Colossians 2.12);*
> *a washing away of sin (1 Corinthians 6.11);*
> *a new birth (John 3.5);*
> *an enlightenment by Christ (Ephesians 5.14);*
> *a reclothing in Christ (Galatians 3.27);*
> *a renewal by the Spirit (Titus 3.5);*
> *the experience of salvation from the flood (1 Peter 3.20-21);*
> *an exodus from bondage (1 Corinthians 10.1-2) and*
> *a liberation into a new humanity in which barriers of division, whether of sex or race or social status, are transcended (Galatians 3.27-28; 1 Corinthians 12.13).*
> *The images are many but the reality is one.*[6]

The modes of baptism

As to how water is used in baptism, nothing is prescribed in the New Testament. A number of 'modes' have scriptural precedent behind them, however.

Submersion is the most dramatic mode, and is what the Greek *baptizein* means: the candidate is plunged wholly under the water. Strictly speaking, **immersion** refers to the candidate standing in water while more water is poured over them. Submersion brings out the symbolic meaning of baptism as being buried with Christ in his saving and cleansing death, to live his risen life (Romans 6.4).

---

6   Faith & Order, *Baptism, Eucharist and Ministry* (Geneva: WCC, 1982). This ecumenical text has received wide acceptance, and shaped practice in many western Christian traditions. As well as the New Testament evidence, it takes account of the varied history of Christian initiation rites: see Cheslyn Jones, Geoffrey Wainwright and E.J Yarnold (edd), *The Study of Liturgy* (London: SPCK 1978) Part II.

Affusion, pouring water on someone, is another scriptural image often related to baptism. It symbolises the love of God, "poured into our hearts by the Holy Spirit which has been given to us", for whom Christ died (Romans 5:5).

In *BCP*, submersion (being 'dipped' in water) is the normal way baptism is administered. In the Public Baptism of Infants, affusion is only provided as an alternative if the child is 'weak':

> *The Priest shall take the Child into his hands, and ... dip it in the Water discreetly and warily, saying,* N. I baptize thee in the Name of the Father, and of the Son, and of the Holy Ghost. Amen.

> *But if they certify that the Child is weak, it shall suffice to pour Water upon it, saying the foresaid words,* N. I baptize thee in the Name of the Father, and of the Son, and of the Holy Ghost. Amen.

Contrary to the idea that only a few drops of water should wet the child's head, in 1527 William Tyndale recounted the attitudes of English folk then.

> If aught be left out, or if the child is not altogether dipt in the water, or if, because the child is sick, the priest dare not plunge him into the water, but pour water on his head, how tremble they! How quake they! "How say ye, Sir John, is this child christened enough? Hath it his full christendom?"[7]

By the nineteenth century, pouring had become the usual mode of baptising. Sometimes this was done from a 'shell', the symbol of pilgrimage. The dramatic symbolism associated with water in the scriptures is minimised when only a few drops are used – hardly a sign of the costly generosity of God in Christ.

Sprinkling (aspersion) is not an authorised mode for baptism, and muddles the use of water for other liturgical acts. In the First Testament, 'sprinkling' with water, oil or blood was the sign of 'sanctification', the way by which the people of God were made 'clean' once more (see Leviticus 14; 16:14; Numbers 8:7; 19:18; and – famously – Ezekiel 36:25). Baptism is the sacrament of beginnings (justification); sprinkling is about ongoing spiritual life (sanctification), and so is not appropriate for baptism.

Should sprinkling then be forbidden? It has many other uses to strengthen faith in Christ: in rites of spiritual renewal, the reaffirmation of baptism promises at Easter, the dedication of a home, church or other buildings, or when entering church. Actions such as these reflect scriptural usage, and can helpfully recall our own baptism.

---

7   Cited in J.D.C. Fisher, *Christian Initiation: The Reformation Period*. Alcuin Club Collection 51 (London: SPCK, 1970) 80. Usual practice was to submerse an infant three times, on the left and right sides, then face down, at the naming of the Father, the Son and the Holy Ghost / Spirit respectively.

Baptism: the Gospel and pastoral ministry

The Anglican tradition accepts the approach to the sacraments that formed in the early church, developed in the Fathers and refined at the Reformation. This 'catholic and reformed' ethos is seen in several key theological issues that arise where the gospel and pastoral ministry meet.

Element, matter, virtue

Following Augustine, the Catechism describes a sacrament as "an outward and visible sign of an inward and spiritual grace, given to us by Christ himself, as a means by which we receive that grace, and a pledge to assure us of this" (*APBA* page 817). It thus entails three aspects: outward sign ('element'), inward grace ('matter'), and pledge of assurance ('virtue'). Understanding baptism as a "sacrament of the Gospel" holds these three dimensions together.

In baptising, we trust that God's Spirit is at work in both the church community and the candidate(s), whoever they may be. This can neither be presumed, as if baptism works automatically, nor despised, as if Christ's gift of baptism is empty. But in pastoral practice it is not always easy to keep this balance ... which brings the discussion to two sets of useful technical terms.

Validity, efficacy, intention

By 300AD, so much weight was placed on personal commitment that few candidates saw themselves having 'enough faith' to be baptised. It became common for people to delay their baptism, and so their participation in the Eucharist, until near death: the Emperor Constantine was a notable example. Conversely, when Christians do not live out their new life, does this mean that their baptism means nothing?

A distinction thus came to be drawn between a 'valid' (properly conducted) baptism, and an 'efficacious' one.[8] Baptism does not depend on the candidate's faith to be valid (genuine) baptism, but without faith, a baptism lacks efficacy.[9]

---

8   Around 258-260AD Cyprian, Bishop of Carthage, refused to recognise the baptism of Novatian Christians, who had separated from the Catholic Church during persecution. Stephen, Bishop of Rome, while agreeing that their teaching needed correction, insisted that they were truly baptised.

9   The delicate relationships between faith, works and grace was the original point behind the phrases *ex opere operato* (by the deed done) and *ex opere operantis* (by the deed of the doer) of scholastic theology. The first phrase guards the truth that only God's grace makes any means of grace available and effective. On the other hand, without faith the grace offered is not taken up, which is what *ex opere operantis* intends to teach, though any act of faith is not a human work, but the gift of the Spirit. However, *ex opere operato* came to be understood as if the mere giving of a sacrament ensured that grace was conveyed, unless hindered by a barrier (*obex*) of unbelief. This (mis)interpretation, rejected by the Reformers, was condemned in the 1553 edition of the 39 Articles. But such a condemnation could imply that the validity of a sacrament depended on human faith, so it was withdrawn in 1562.

A baptism is 'valid' when a person is has been baptised with water (the proper 'element'), 'in the Name of Father, Son and Holy Spirit' (the proper 'form'), and with the public (external) intention to baptise.[10] To assume that a candidate's 'inward intention' does not correspond to their outward profession is unChristian: God alone knows the heart.

As with element, matter and virtue, validity, efficacy and external intention normally belong together, but there are pastoral situations in which they need to be distinguished. A person might be anxious as to whether they are truly baptised, for example. Anyone baptised publically using the services of Baptism in *BCP*, *AAPB* or *APBA*, or privately under the conditions laid down in them, can have full assurance that they have been validly baptised into Christ.

NB: There is no such thing as 'Anglican' baptism. Baptism is into the whole Church of God, not a 'denominational' rite. The Anglican tradition recognises as 'valid' any baptism administered using water in the Name of the Holy Trinity with the public intention to baptise, even though it may sometimes be 'irregular'.

'Original sin' and the baptism of infants

The baptism of infants is sometimes linked with 'original sin', understood to mean that conception and childbirth are inherently sinful. Baptism is then seen as a way to make the child 'safe' or 'clean'. This goes back to Augustine's misreading of Romans 5:12, a major factor in later distortions of Christian understanding of sexuality.[11]

'Original sin' points to the reality that we humans, made in the image and likeness of God, nevertheless find ourselves as a race caught up in sin, evil and the powers of death. Stupid as it is to live this way, we keep doing so, both individually and communally. Sins are thus more than learned habits: they are the 'fruit' of a tree with sin-soaked roots (*origo*) and sin-tainted sap, encouraged by "the world,

---

10 'External' intention excludes things like a student prank where water is thrown over someone and baptismal words used: there was no intention to baptise, so it is not baptism.

11 Romans 5.12 reads: "Sin came into the world through one man, and death came through sin, and so death spread to all *because* all have sinned" (NRSV). The Greek behind 'because' is literally 'in that' (KJB 'for that'): the Latin version, however, transliterated this as *in quo*, 'in whom', so Augustine read it as "Sin came into the world through one man ... *in whom* all have sinned".

Article IX, 'Of Original or Birth Sin' (*APBA* page 827), is carefully worded to recognise the reality of sin in each of us, while refusing to be drawn into the riddle as to how 'original or birth sin' is *transmitted* from generation to generation.

The phrase "conceived and born in sin" in 'The Public Baptism of Infants' in *BCP* does not mean that birth is sinful, but that we are all sinners. This in part is why the *BCP* 1549 title, "The Purification of Women after Childbirth" was changed from 1552 to "The Thanksgiving of Women after Childbirth".

the flesh and the devil" around us and within. You don't kill a plum tree by stamping on the plums: you must dig out the root. Each of us – children, teens, adults and seniors alike – is caught up in a web of sin, injustice and abuse. That is why Anglican services include a 'general' confession: even if our sins seem trivial, we confess our corporate participation, however unaware of our part in it, in this deadly web. Each of us needs "new birth" in Christ through the Spirit: baptism is the sacrament of this "birth from above".

Baptism and faith

As a sacrament of the Gospel, baptism "doth not only quicken, but strengthens and confirms our Faith in [Christ]" (Article XXV). Such faith is more than an individual matter: it is embraced within the faith of God's people, the body of Christ, of whom the baptised person is made a 'member', a 'body-part' of Christ. The candidate is placed in a faith-relationship with new brothers and sisters, a relationship whose roots lie in the faithfulness of God in Christ. Baptism is thus 'into' faith, as well as 'by', 'in' or 'through' faith. And this faith has content, 'the faith', summarised in the Apostles' Creed, recited at baptism as "the faith of the Church" (*APBA* pages 59, 78).

At the time of baptism, the faith of *every* candidate is in its infancy, whatever their age or background. It unfolds over our life of faith in Christ, "until we come at last to his everlasting kingdom" (*BCP*). It is always 'on the way': even the most committed Christian is called to live by faith, looking in hope to when faith will pass into sight.

Baptismal faith being a communal matter, every candidate is supported by sponsors. For those unable to answer for themselves, these sponsors (the godparents) make the baptismal promises on the candidate's behalf. They also involve the family of which the candidate is a part: but an infant is not baptised because of who their parents may be (their bloodline), but because some Christians (their sponsors) trust that the child is called to grow up in Christ.

Confirmation: its place in Christian initiation

All Christians are called to live out the faith they profess in Christ. Those baptised when they could not answer for themselves should do so later before the church (see Note 1 on *APBA* page 94). Infants will most likely have been baptised by the parish priest, but their baptism transcends parish boundaries. In Anglican understanding, Confirmation offers the necessary opportunity for Christians, especially those baptised as infants, to profess their faith before the wider Church, represented in the person of the bishop, and to seek the strengthening of the Holy Spirit through prayer with the laying on of hands.

A mixed history

The rites of Christian initiation early on expanded to associate baptism by the bishop with hand-laying, anointing with oil, and participating in Holy Communion.[12] As bishops' responsibilities grew, baptism in the West was delegated to local priests, the bishop administering 'confirmation' (anointing and / or laying on of hands) at a later time.[13] Before Alcuin's work under Charlemagne, however, around 800AD, to 'confirm' meant to 'complete' or 'make secure' baptism. When described as a 'sacrament' in scholastic theology, 'confirm' was thus interpreted as 'strengthen' (by the Holy Spirit).[14] Baptised children received 'first communion' at around seven years of age, with episcopal hand-laying later.

Confirmation was rejected by many Reformers, as having no direct scriptural base.[15] The English Reformers retained it, however, seeing it as an opportunity for those baptised as infants, then almost everyone, to confirm their baptismal promises. Confirmation in *BCP* is tied to the Catechism, "An Instruction to be learned of every person, before he be brought to be confirmed by the Bishop". The Catechism formed part of the Confirmation service until it was made separate in *BCP* (1662). The bishop lays hands on "each candidate severally" with prayer for grace and the Holy Spirit: anointing is not mentioned.[16] Confirmation then became the means of admission to communion for those "who have come to years of discretion".[17] These emphases on Christian education, prayer for increase in the Holy Spirit, and admission to communion, continued in Anglican formularies until modern revisions.

---

12   *The Apostolic Tradition of Hippolytus* #20-22 offers an example from the early third century: the text is available in Geoffrey Cuming (ed), Grove Liturgy Study 8 (Bramcote: Grove, 1976) 17-20.

13   J.D.C Fisher, *Christian Initiation. Baptism in the Medieval West*. Alcuin Club Collection XLVII. (London: SPCK, 1965) has the telling subtitle, 'A Study in the Disintegration of the Primitive Rite of Initiation'. Appendix I, 'The Use of the Words 'Confirmare' and 'Confirmatio'", 141-148, is a close study of the meaning of these as technical terms, concluding that "although the term was used of the post-baptismal anointing and hand-laying by the bishop as far back as the first half of the fifth century, it did not become the normal term to use of this part of the initiatory rite before the ninth century" (148).
In the East, baptism (always by submersion) and 'consignation' (anointing with oil) are administred together for all candidates, of whatever age. The priest is the usual minister of both rites; the link with the bishop is through the oil having been consecrated by him for this purpose.

14   Fisher, 148 gives details.

15   1 Timothy 4.14 and 2 Timothy 1.6 are precedents for ordination rather than confirmation..

16   However, the confirmation formula changed from signing in the Name of the Trinity (1549), with which anointing could be associated, to the 'Defend O Lord' prayer for 'heavenly grace' (1552 on).

17   For those "of riper years" baptised, a new rubric in *BCP* 1662 provided that "It is expedient that every person, thus baptised, should be confirmed by the Bishop so soon after his Baptism as conveniently may be; *that so he may be admitted to the holy Communion*" (italics added).

The practice of Confirmation waned in the eighteenth century, notably in the American colonies, where there was no bishop for over a century. From the mid-nineteenth century, however, in the wake of the Evangelical and Anglo-Catholic revivals, Confirmation came to greater prominence in the Church of England. Bishops undertook more regular visitations, and preparation was taken with increased seriousness. A view of Confirmation as the bestowal (rather than increase) of the Holy Spirit became widespread, with Acts 8 as the scriptural warrant.[18]

If Baptism was viewed as a 'birth rite' of admission to a Christian society after cleansing from sin by Christ, Confirmation came to be seen as a rite of passage from childhood into adult Christian life, enabled by the gift of the Spirit. Evangelicals tended to regard it as a rite of 'conversion', Anglo-Catholics as a sacramental act 'completing' baptism. This 'two stage' approach to Christian initiation went largely unchallenged until the mid-twentieth century.[19] It came to be questioned not only by scholars, but from the experience of seeing young people regard confirmation as 'graduation' from church rather than into it.

Further, as society changed, communicants from other Christian traditions found themselves in Anglican congregations. Insisting on them being confirmed to be admitted to communion was ecumenically insensitive and pastorally unhelpful.[20] So in 1973 General Synod passed the Admission to Communion Canon that permitted communicants of churches "which hold the apostolic faith" to receive communion, though as guests. Remaining permanently as guests at the Lord's table, however, these unconfirmed Christians were excluded from holding church office. So in 1981 General Synod passed the Reception Canon that provides for baptised and communicant Christians to be 'received' into the Anglican Communion rather than confirmed, able to be full participants in its life.[21]

---

18 In Acts 8, the baptised Samaritans receive the Spirit when Peter and John lay hands on them. The text gives no hint of their act being one of initiation: rather, it would appear that the Spirit waits until the pair had dared to touch the (unclean) Samaritans before 'falling' upon them.

19 It was known as the 'Mason-Dix' line, "after Arthur Mason and Gregory Dix, two of its most influential proponents": Simon Jones, *Celebrating Christian Initiation*. Alcuin Liturgy Guides 7 (London: SPCK, 2016) xiii. The Mason-Dixon Line, surveyed in the eighteenth century to settle differences between US colonies, came to mark the border between its northern and southern states.

20 As a young adult I remember kneeling at the communion rail next to my devout Presbyterian elder but unconfirmed uncle. The priest administered communion to me, but passed him by: we had both been present at my grandfather's funeral a day earlier, in the same Anglican church with the same priest.

21 The Canons are available at https://www.anglican.org.au/canons-and-rules
The 1981 Canon included a service for Reception, included in *APBA* pages 95–98. The 1992 Canon concerning Confirmation sets it in the context of the 1973 and 1981 Canons on Admission and Reception.

Confirmation today

Theological work on confirmation has not stopped. A series of English and USA reports, and especially the 1991 'Toronto Statement' of the *Inter-Anglican Liturgical Consultation*, saw underlying issues clarified, not least in view of the mission situation in which Western churches live.[22]

The issues are often approached by debating "Who confirms?" In *BCP*, the *candidate* confirms their baptismal covenant, yet rubrics say the *bishop* confirms the candidate, a dual sense that has fuelled controversy. More recently, scholars suggest that the better question to ask is 'what?' rather than 'who?' is confirmed. Confirmation is then the candidate's *baptism* being confirmed in the wider church, represented by the bishop.[23]

In 1995, the Anglican Bishops issued a Statement, commending to all Anglicans the following statements concerning Confirmation:

- Confirmation is a 'sacramental' strengthening by the Holy Spirit for the ongoing Christian life;
- Confirmation is administered on the profession or affirmation of the baptismal promises;
- Confirmation is an opportunity for commissioning for the work of Christian witness to the world.

We believe that these three statements encompass important issues and that confirmation rites should reflect this importance: all who are confirmed should be able to recall the occasion as a liturgical celebration of these great truths.

Confirmation provides opportunity for baptised Christians, in the power of the Spirit, to embrace a considered commitment to Christian *diakonia*, ministry. Moreover, it is an occasion when a congregation, gathered together with its bishop, can recommit itself to be a 'ministering community'.

A Confirmation service should therefore be an effectual sign of personal and corporate growth in Christian faith and empowerment for Christian ministry.

The Liturgical Commission affirmed this positive view of Confirmation, but could not avoid the conclusion that "sacramental initiation is complete in baptism".[24]

---

22   See www.anglicanliturgy.org/wp-content/uploads/2015/06/growing-in-newness-of-life.pdf
23   In the Roman Catholic tradition, many confirmations are conducted by 'episcopal vicars', senior priests to whom the bishop has delegated this responsibility.
24   The title of the first Grove Liturgical Study, by E.C. Whitaker (Bramcote: Grove Books, 1975). It has had considerable influence across the Anglican Communion.

Confirmation matters, but is not a universal prerequisite for admission to communion. This position underlies the initiation services in *APBA*.

What then forbids baptised children receiving communion prior to their being confirmed? After a decade of discussion, in 1981 General Synod passed a Canon for the Admission of Children to Holy Communion, which provides for this "while awaiting confirmation". The 1995 Bishops' Statement cited above went on to clarify that

> it is imperative that those admitted to holy communion in one parish or diocese should not be excluded if they move to another parish or diocese; any resulting inconsistency is more tolerable than the exclusion of a person after admission.

Christian initiation: some issues of context

The churches no longer stand in the centre of Australian society, and fewer children are brought for baptism.[25] Positively, it can more clearly be seen as a sacrament of the gospel, a 'new birth rite', rather than a rite of passage, a 'birth right'. *APBA* thus sets baptism "within the regular pattern of congregational worship" (Note 1 on page 70).

Christian initiation at its fullest involves the baptism, confirmation and admission to communion of a person able to answer for themselves: the making of a disciple of "years of discretion". A full rite will integrate these aspects of Christian initiation, while recognising their foundation in baptism. This is the ideal behind "Holy Baptism, Confirmation in Communion" in *APBA* (pages 51–71), open to candidates of any age. But how does this ideal work out in the realities of modern life? A range of contextual issues come to mind.[26]

Baptism and birth

The pressures of modern life, and widespread loss of 'ritual-making' traditions, have seen a significant reduction in the celebration of birth.[27] This is a new shift in human culture: marking the gift of life has been universal, not least given the life-threatening dangers faced by mothers, now much reduced. This ritual 'hole' offers opportunities for Christian communities to make a positive 'pro life' contribution to society.

---

25   Alan Billings, "Why people want their babies christened", Chapter Three in *Secular Lives, Sacred Hearts* (London: SPCK, 2004) notes that in England the number of babies baptised per 1000 birth dropped from 602 in 1956 to 466 in 1970 and 211 in 2000 (page 44).

26   See further Charles Sherlock, *A Pastoral Handbook for Anglicans* (Second edition, Canberra: Acorn, 2001); Bradley Billings (Third edition: Mulgrave, Broughton Publications, 2018).

27   Interviews in the 1980s of 100 new parents in a Melbourne suburb showed that some 40% had the child baptised or dedicated; 30% held a welcome party, but 30% did nothing. A child's first birthday appears to becoming more significant. (I examined this work, but am not free to disclose details.)

Thanksgiving for a Child

'Thanksgiving for a Child' (*APBA* pages 43–48) acknowledges the natural human instinct to mark the awesome and mysterious arrival of a living human being. It is available to anyone who desires it, as a rite of birth or adoption, and includes naming. Ideally, every baptism of an infant will commence with elements from this service – which is not 'baptism lite': for further discussion, see Chapter 20 in this book.

That said, every request for baptism must be taken up positively and openly: perceptions of clergy saying 'no' do long-lasting spiritual harm. Further, Alan Billings notes that a child's birth marks a significant point in the parents' relationship, especially when not married. Baptising a child says something important about them, as well as affirming the importance of the wider human community.[28]

Naming is offered in Thanksgiving for a Child (#8 on *APBA* page 44).

Naming

The custom of an adult's name being changed when they are baptised is ancient, and continues in some places. But naming is not an essential part of baptism. Historically, a child's name was given during the pre-baptism rites, not at the baptism. In *BCP* 1549, the child is signed with the cross at the church door, using its name for the first time, before this name is used for the baptism at the font. When the church door rites were removed in 1552, the child's name was used for the first time at the baptism: in 1662, the priest says to the godparents, 'Name this child' immediately before the baptism. As Fisher concludes,

> It is the command to the godparents in the Book of 1662, "Name this child" – a command not found in the earlier books – which has done most to encourage among the ignorant the notion that baptism is primarily a naming ceremony, and that "to christen" means, chiefly if not entirely, "to name".[29]

This command was omitted in *AAPB* (pages 504, 523) and *APBA* (pages 59, 78: the candidate's name is stated in the Presentation, #14 on page 55; #7 on page 74).

The distinction between naming and baptism means that a baptised Christian may change their name without their baptism being called into question. They may have come to a life-changing experience of Christian faith, for example; be a woman recovering from a violent relationship; or be a transgendered person wishing to alter the gender of their name. It may be appropriate for the change to be recognised in church, with prayer for the person as they seek to live out a new identity.

---

28 Alan Billings, 52–56. He also notes that for non-churchgoers, arranging a baptism is often when "women take control" in getting the men to take life-issues seriously.
29 Fisher, *Medieval West,* Appendix II, 149–157.

The ministers of Christian initiation

Baptism is the act of the Church, rather than a personal rite: whoever administers it represents the Church, normally the priest given the 'cure of souls' of the congregation concerned. An exception may be the baptism of a priest's own children, where s/he may prefer to participate as a parent, with another deacon or priest administering the water.

But pastoral relationships cannot be brushed aside. An adult may have come to baptism through the witness and support of a parishioner; infants may have had sponsors and parents prepared by a baptism team. The *APBA* services offer several opportunities for such people to participate, in particular where 'minister' is found (#4, #5, #19, #25 on *APBA* pages 51ff) or 'priest' is not used (#3, #8, #9).[30] People involved in a candidate's preparation can take part as 'sponsors' at the Presentation (#12, #15, #16, #17), though not answering on behalf of candidates (#13, #16). Where the baptism is by submersion, people who have been part of the candidate's journey to baptism can assist them with their dress, and in helping them into and out of the water.

The minister of Confirmation and Reception is the bishop, who presides at a Eucharist in which these take place.

'Re-baptism'

Sometimes a person asks to be 're-baptised'. This is not surprising: not all people baptised as infants go on to live as Christians. When someone has come to a living faith in Christ, they may feel that their baptism as a child means nothing. Whatever the reason, the initial response must be to take the person's renewed sense of Christ seriously. The question is – how best to celebrate this without compromising baptism?

Baptism is unrepeatable. As Christ died and rose once for all, so we are baptised into that death and resurrection once for all (Ephesians 4:5). 'Re-baptism' to express renewed faith misunderstands what baptism is about: it is not so much about our commitment to God, but God's gracious commitment to us. Nor is the experience of baptism central, memorable though it ought to be for 'riper years' candidates. And no baptism 'takes' fully: the baptism of a mature adult convert is as much a matter of faith as that of the youngest baby. Likewise, no spiritual experience brings all God's blessings: we see "as in a glass darkly", and look to the future to see Christ "face to face" (1 Corinthians 13:12). Baptism sets us at the start of Christian life, calling us to "live as a disciple of Christ: fight the good fight, finish the race, keep the faith" (as *APBA* puts it).

---

30   The *APBA* rubric at the point of baptism reads 'minister' rather than 'priest' (#23 on *APBA* page 59; #16 on page 78). This is to allow for baptism in emergencies, where anyone may baptise.

The 1995 Statement from the Australian Anglican Bishops thus asserts that
> it is inconsistent with Anglican understanding of the theology of baptism to permit so-called re-baptism ... But we call upon all clergy and parishes to offer appropriate rites and symbols to those who, after baptism and confirmation, experience new found faith, so that they may celebrate their experience with the local congregation.

Celebrating Re-affirmation

APBA includes 'Re-affirmation' in the presence of the bishop (#30 on *APBA* page 62, #21 on page 91, Note 12 on page 71). This rite is quite brief, however, and needs to be filled out: but what 'appropriate rites and symbols' are helpful?

Whatever looks like repeating baptism is to be avoided. This might suggest that Re-affirmation not take place at a baptism service. Bishop Colin Buchanan, however, makes the point that distinguishing Reaffirmation from baptism

> is most easily achieved when there are actual baptisms as well as renewals to occur. For then there are, throughout the rite, two categories of candidates in view, sitting or standing at different places, and responding with different words.[31]

Further, different ways of administering water can be used. Rather than submersion or pouring (affusion), the modes for baptism, sprinkling (aspersion) can find a place in the Re-affirmation of baptismal promises, as might the post-baptism symbol of anointing. Words like these, derived from Buchanan, can accompany the act:

> N, as you have been baptised in the name of the Father, the Son and the Holy Spirit, so now, in commemoration of that baptism, I sprinkle water upon you [and anoint you] in the name of the Father, the Son and the Holy Spirit. Amen.

The post-baptismal words can follow, "Live as a disciple of Christ ..." and a candle be given. S/he could tell of their Christian pilgrimage, and how their re-affirmation relates to their baptism. An interview format can enable their testimony to be 'heard' by parishioners, and keep a discipline on time.

Including Re-affirmation with the corporate re-affirmation of baptismal promises on Easter Day may be helpful, though doing so with hundreds present would not be wise. The aim is to enable the person to enter this new stage of their walk with Christ by having both their baptism and their experience affirmed. It may well see other parishioners deepen their stance as disciples of Christ.

Each act of Re-affirmation is recorded in the Register of Services.

---

31 Colin Buchanan, *The Renewal of Baptismal Vows*, Grove Worship Series 124 (Bramcote: Grove, 1993) 20. This analyses the issues involved, and makes some very interesting suggestions for practical use.

Further reading

Billings, Alan, *Secular Lives, Sacred Hearts* (London: SPCK, 2004)

Buchanan, Colin, *The Renewal of Baptismal Vows*, Grove Worship Series 124 (Bramcote: Grove, 1993)

Dawson, Jenny, *A Radical Theology of Baptism* (Pukera Bay, Porirua NZ, 2011)

Fisher, J.D.C., *Christian Initiation: The Reformation Period*. Alcuin Club Collection 51 (London: SPCK, 1970)

Inter-Anglican Liturgical Consultation, Growing in Newness of Life. Grove Worship Series 91 (Bramcote: Grove, 1991), available at www.anglicanliturgy.org/wp-content/uploads/2015/06/growing-in-newness-of-life.pdf

Jones, Simon, *Celebrating Christian Initiation*. Alcuin Liturgy Guides 7 (London: SPCK, 2016)

Jones, Cheslyn, Wainwright, Geoffrey and Yarnold E.J (edd), *The Study of Liturgy* (London: SPCK 1978) Part II, especially Chapters One–Three, Five and Seven

Whitaker E.C, *Sacramental Initiation Complete in Baptism*. Grove Liturgical Study 1 (Bramcote: Grove Books, 1975)

WCC, *Baptism, Eucharist and Ministry* (Geneva: WCC, 1982), available at https://www.oikoumene.org/en/resources/documents/commissions/faith-and-order/i-unity-the-church-and-its-mission/baptism-eucharist-and-ministry-faith-and-order-paper-no-111-the-lima-text

Chapter Eleven

Initiating Christians: preparing the way

A millennium and a half ago, Cyril of Jerusalem wrote about the "awe-inspiring rites of initiation" into Christ as follows:

> What a strange and astonishing situation! We did not really die, we were not really buried, we did not really hang on the cross and rise again. Our imitation was symbolic, our salvation a reality.[1]

In Cyril's time, baptism followed a preparation of several months if not years. The rite was dramatic, typically enacted on Easter morning in such a way that the candidate would never forget it. But what took place was kept secret from outsiders. Today a baptism service will be held in public, though perhaps not be as dramatic. But why not? Infant, teenager or adult, the candidate symbolically dies to their old self, is buried with Christ, always a messy business, and is raised by the Spirit to begin a new life. When the bishop is present to confirm as well as baptise, and candidates testify to what Christ means in their lives, drama should be all around.

Funerals and baptisms echo one another in being about death and life, and both take place once. Funerals are universal, but it is the baptised who are "marked as Christ's own forever". Baptism is the sacrament of Christian identity, opening out into Christian living. It leads to admission to communion, and is confirmed in Confirmation.

The integrated rite of Christian initiation in *APBA* (pages 51–71) inevitably consists of words and instructions. These are true to the scriptures, offer good things from the Christian tradition, are sensitive to doctrinal matters and accessible to congregations. But putting flesh on these strong bones calls for sound preparation, creative choreography and user-friendly leading. Significant preparations are made for birth, the once-only event which begins each person's life. Why not for the event of new birth in Christ signified in baptism?

---

1   *Mystagogical Catechesis* 2.5, cited in Simon Jones, 1. For details of rites in the century after Constantine, when Cyril was writing, see Cheslyn Jones in Wainwright, Jones & Yarnold Part II, Chapter Three.

This chapter is structured in three sections:

- The first section focuses on **preparing the people** involved in Christian initiation – parishioners, sponsors, parents and candidates. The catechumenate is also noted.
- **The Catechism** is the traditional resource for preparing those baptised as infants for Confirmation, and is also useful in preparing older candidates for baptism.
- The third section explores **preparing the service**: place, contents, participation, things, and making ready the people involved, not least guests.

Preparing the people

The baptism of infants remains the most common initiation rite: Ron Dowling, who drafted these *APBA* services, suggests that preparation begin with the congregation.[2]

Preparing the congregation

Baptism should "take place within the regular pattern of congregational worship", states Note 1 on *APBA* page 70. But what if regulars stay away on 'Baptism Sunday'? Some might not like visitors in 'my seat', the noise of babies, or don't want to engage with new people. Regulars who understand what baptism is about help a congregation see the newly baptised "added to their number" (Acts 2.47) A service that feeds parishioners while being accessible to the baptism party, and is not too long, encourages positive attitudes.

A baptism policy and team

A parish baptism policy, 'owned' by the Parish Council, sets out matters such as the Sundays available, preparation and service arrangements. Two parishes in which I have been involved had many requests, two inner-city ones were delighted to have any. Policies varied correspondingly.

A baptism team bringing priest and people together is particularly important where enquiries about baptism are frequent. Young parents make ideal members: they know the context, joys and challenges of raising children today. Further, the priest is often seen by non-churched people as paid to deliver 'spiritual services': including 'ordinary' parishioners helps get across that baptism is a serious matter.

The 'first responder' needs preparation for this ministry. First impressions matter: stories abound of people angered because they 'heard' a church's response as refusing baptism for their child. An office volunteer will be helped by a 'script' based on the parish baptism policy: an ethos of 'rolling out the red carpet' to celebrate the life-changing act of baptism is ideal.

---

2   *A Practical Commentary*, Chapter Eight.

A preparation programme

Resources to help with preparation, both in printed and electronic form, are readily found by a web search. *First Steps* from the Church of England suits Australian contexts, but there are many others – *Credo, Christianity Explored, Emmaus* for example.[3]

A programme to prepare sponsors and parents for a child's baptism is ideally developed locally: balancing content, levels of spiritual understanding and relationships is an art. Alan Billings makes the point that, while we want enquiring parents to know what baptism is about, we don't always ask them how they see it.[4] Overdoing preparation can communicate that parents earn the right to their child's baptism; none at all makes grace cheap. It is easy to decry 'indiscriminate' or 'rigorist' extremes. It is harder to develop a theologically robust, liturgically sound and pastorally effective process. None can guarantee that a baptised child will go on to lead a Christian life: this is a matter of faith and hope, not sight.

A baptism 'kit' can include a welcome letter, a copy of the service, prayers for parents and sponsors to use, the Mother's Union 'Shine as a light' fridge magnet and so on. Making up a kit is a good baptism team project.

For the baptism of an infant, it is more likely that the parents rather than the sponsors will have taken part in preparation. But it is the sponsors who make the significant promises in the service (#13 = #8), and need to understand what this entails. So each sponsor, who may be a parent, needs to have seen a copy of the service before accepting the responsibilities involved: sending a DVD or web address of a preparation programme can fill this out.

Private baptism of an infant

Circumstances sometimes arise in which an infant is baptised privately. The child might be gravely ill in hospital, or suffer allergies which make being with many people dangerous. A parent might be in prison, or held in a refugee camp: Note 9 on *APBA* page 71 sets out the liturgical details. Urgent action may be called for, and preparation abandoned.

When the crisis is past, the new 'member of Christ' needs to be welcomed. The parents and sponsors, with the child if possible, are invited to a Sunday service, for which preparation is needed (see Note 9 on *APBA* page 71). The child's story can be told, and prayers of thanksgiving and for ongoing healing to be offered.

---

3   *First Steps: the journey to baptism*. Available from the (English) *Church Pastoral Aid Society* at https://www.cpas.org.uk/church-resources/first-steps/#.WpeiBOf-vDc
4   Alan Billings, 45ff.

Preparing candidates 'of riper years'

Preparing adults to live for Christ is a challenge in our 'post-Christendom' context. Working with them through the service (*APBA* pages 51–71) and Catechism (pages 815–818) is a good place to start. 'Confirmation class' manuals are available, though they are typically designed for teenagers: an annual confirmation class can form the backbone of a Christian education programme.

For adults, learning 'the faith' will focus on equipping them to live as Christian disciples: ***in**formation* in the service of ***trans**formation*. Here the practices of Christian life come to the fore: 'grace' at meals, regular times of prayer and scripture reflection (on the readings for the next Sunday for example). Flexible use of Daily Morning & Evening Prayer is helpful (see Note 10 on *APBA* page 433).

Involving other parishioners in such formation can see the candidate(s) supported as they make the demanding 're-orientation' to a Christian outlook. New disciples meeting with 'veterans' to share insights will help fold them together in the lead-up to their initiation, and in the weeks and months following. The fresh insights of the new, engaging the wisdom of the long-experienced, can invigorate a congregation.

The Catechumenate

The 'catechumenal' process brings together many of these aspects.[5] Over some months, candidates are taken through a process of formation in living as a Christian.[6] In the early centuries, baptism candidates came from Graeco-Roman backgrounds, with world-views and lifestyles far removed from Christian faith. Spiritual backbone was needed to survive the threat of persecution, so they underwent training over several years, learning to 'echo' the Word of God in their lives. When Christianity became official, this method fell into disuse, as baptism became entry to a Christian society. The Reformers' interest in catechisms applied some of these ancient methods to children.

---

[5] I acknowledge the insights of the Revd Dr Paul Dalzell in this section. He notes that in Greek, *katechein* means "to echo", and is used of the interaction between teacher and pupil. Luke wrote to Theophilus about what had been "echoed" to him (*peri hôn katechethes*: Luke 1.4).

[6] A modern form is the 'Rite of Christian Initiation for Adults' (*RCIA*) of the Roman Catholic Church: an Anglican analysis is Paul Tudge, *Initiating Adults. Lessons from the Roman Catholic Rite* (Bramcote: Grove Worship Series 102, 1988). On its use in the Anglican Communion see Peter Ball and Malcolm Grundy, *Faith on the Way: A Practical Parish Guide to the Adult Catechumenate* (London / New York: Mowbray, 2000). Several web sites offer resources for the catechumenal process, including those related to *RCIA*. Simon Chan, *Liturgical Theology. The Church as Worshipping Community* (Downers Grove Ill: IVP, 2006) Chapter Five brings Reformation Catechism practices into creative conversation with *RCIA*.

As churches and society in the West have steadily pulled apart, new life has come into the catechumenate.[7] The emphasis is on formation: an 'action and reflection' method supports candidates as they take on a Christian identity. Several stages are involved, through which candidates proceed as they are ready.

- **Gathering**: a church's witness sees people ask about baptism or look to renew their faith. At least annually those who might be invited into the process are identified.
- **Enquiry**: those gathered test whether the process is for them, by sharing information, responding to questions, and getting to know one another.
- **Formation**: an 'action and reflection' exploration of Christian faith and life, typically using the Sunday gospel readings. Areas covered are prayer, liturgy, the scriptures, service to and solidarity with people in need, and seeing daily life as a calling.
- **Intense formation**: when the 'catechumens' are ready for baptism, they receive sponsors, and begin more intense preparation. Lent is particularly suitable.
- **Baptism**: ideally this is at Easter, with the bishop present to baptise and lay on hands, and administer communion to the candidates for the first time. In many congregations it is also when baptism promises are renewed.
- **Post-baptism education**: over the next weeks, the newly baptised reflect on what has happened, discover 'holes' in their formation, and explore their calling to serve God in church and day-to-day living. An ideal time is the fifty days of Easter.

Each stage involves the catechumens with other parishioners: the aim is to see people folded in to a Christian community, not just instructed by clergy or a few lay leaders. Each stage can involve 'markers': enrolment, receiving a Bible, a formal welcome into the congregation and the like.

The Catechism

The concept of catechisms – manuals of basic Christian teaching – is ancient, but they received a considerable revival at the Reformation. The Reformers stressed the importance of sound doctrine being communicated to everyday Christians. Martin Luther's 'Large' and 'Small' Catechisms of 1529, the latter for children, reflected his strong pastoral sense. The Reformed tradition in England saw the Westminster Catechism issued during the Commonwealth, famously beginning with the question, "What is the true end of Man? Man's chief end is to glorify God and to enjoy him for ever."

---

[7] The five-syllable word 'catechumenate' can put people off, so names like 'The Journey', or 'The Path' are often used. Likewise, 'catechumens' can be referred to as 'learners' or 'on L plates'.

The Anglican catechetical tradition

BCP included a Catechism in its first editions, 1549 and 1552, as part of the Confirmation service. In contrast to Lutheran and Reformed Catechisms, it was not designed to stand by itself, but be part of the church's liturgical life. It was also much shorter, centred on the Creed, Ten Commandments and Lord's Prayer.

The 1604 *BCP* added a new section on the sacraments, given increasing doctrinal divergence in the Church of England. The 1662 *BCP* saw the Catechism separated into a separate rite, adjacent to the Confirmation service. As the concluding exhortation to the godparents in the Public Baptism of Infants states,

> YE are to take care that this Child be brought to the Bishop to be confirmed by him, so soon as he can say the Creed, the Lord's Prayer, and the Ten Commandments, in the vulgar tongue, and be further instructed in the Church-Catechism set forth for that purpose.

The Catechism thus plays a key part in the Christian education of children. No equivalent is found in 'Riper Years' baptism service, but significant preparation is presumed for any candidate:

> The Minister shall instruct such person, or cause him to be instructed, in the principles of the Christian religion, and exhort him so to prepare himself with prayers and fasting that he may receive this Holy Sacrament with repentance and faith.

Until a century or so ago it was assumed that each child born in England would be baptised: to be a citizen was to be a Christian. This can be seen in the lack of a rite for baptising adults until 1662, and the *BCP* rubrics urging that the baptism of infants not be delayed.[8] Until recent decades, Australian parents generally expected that every child would be baptised.[9] Though this assumption was not true in 1977, 'The Catechism' in *AAPB* is a close translation of the *BCP* one.

---

8   The opening rubric of the 'Private Baptism of Infants' in *BCP* states, somewhat embarrassingly today: "The Curates of every Parish shall often admonish the people, that they defer not the Baptism of their Children longer than the first or second Sunday next after their birth, or other Holy Day falling between, unless upon a great and reasonable cause, to be approved by the Curate."
    This was in the context of the Church of England being the national Church established by law, to which all citizens belonged.

9   On a humourous note, in the opening chapter of Dorothy Wall's children's classic, *Blinky Bill* (1939), the new baby koala is 'christened' by the Reverend Fluffy Ears, who is pictured in a voluminous surplice. The story assumes that this is the rite of entry to Australian life. Similar observations could be made of Banjo Patterson's poem, 'The Bush Christening'.

The Catechism in *APBA*

The Liturgical Commission for *APBA* took the mission context in which Australian Anglicans live with full seriousness. So Holy Baptism was drafted on the basis that the 'norm' is the baptism of someone able to answer for themselves, who would be confirmed and admitted to communion in an integrated service. It wrestled over whether 'The Catechism' should be included in *APBA*, and if so, what revision would be needed. Some Anglican Provinces had expanded it to reflect adult Christian faith and life, notably The Episcopal Church in the USA. The Commission came to the view, however, that such a revision would need more time than was available.

So the *BCP* Catechism was lightly revised, but adjusted so that it could be used by people of any age, and for other than Confirmation preparation. However, the draft book had no separate Confirmation service: this was added later at the request of the Bishops. So there was no rite to place the Catechism next to, as in *BCP* and *APBA*. It was therefore moved to the Supplementary Material. A disadvantage of this position is that it is not in the 'green' Sunday edition, so few parishioners have ready access to it.

Commentary

The revisions made in *APBA* allow the Catechism to be used by candidates who answered for themselves at their baptism. Thus the opening question in *BCP* about the child's name being given at baptism is removed. Headings are also introduced, outlining the Catechism's structure:

    The Covenant of Baptism
    The Christian Faith
    The Commandments
    Prayer
    The Sacraments

The Covenant of Baptism

The heading is significant: baptism is put forward as entailing a deep and lasting relationship between God and each Christian with profound consequences for their lifestyle. Half a dozen significant changes made to *BCP* point this up:

a) The *BCP* question, "What did your godparents do for you at your baptism?" is vastly improved: "N, what did God do for you when you were baptised?"

b) The response to this retains the startling affirmation, "I was made ... ***the*** child of God". But now it denotes a covenantal rather than a supportive relationship, as seen in the response to the next question about the promises made at their baptism, which is considerably reworked and shortened.

c) As in The Decision in Holy Baptism in *APBA*, the person says "that I would turn to Christ", ahead of "renounce all evil" (as in *BCP*). This latter phrase summarises "the devil and all his works, the pomps and vanity of this wicked world, and all the sinful lusts of the flesh" of *BCP*.

d) Instead of the content-oriented response in *BCP*, "that I should believe all the Articles of the Christian Faith", the person makes a personal confession of faith, "that I *would put all my trust* in God" (emphasis added).

e) Rather than promising to "keep God's holy will and commandments", as in *BCP*, the person commits to "strive to live as a disciple of Christ".

f) In the concluding question about relying on God's grace, the person gives thanks to God "for calling me to salvation" (*APBA*) rather than "to this state of salvation" (*BCP*).

All these changes not so much simplify what is entailed in Baptism, as restate it in a less formal, more personal and Christ-related way.

The Christian Faith

The Apostles' Creed expresses the faith confessed in Baptism. Now is not the place to exegete this Creed, and the Catechism does not attempt to do so. It takes a more personal approach to its teaching, summarised using *BCP*'s 'economic trinitarian' formula, "created … redeemed … sanctifies me". This personal "me" is not left alone, however, but paired with significant corporate realities: "me and all the world", "me and the whole human race", "me and all the elect people of God".

The Commandments

The second, third, fourth and tenth Commandments are abbreviated, though less so than in Holy Communion (First Order, #5). This avoids misunderstandings: in the second and third, lest God be thought of as jealous and guilt-inducing in their modern senses. In the third and tenth, it steps around the hierarchical relationships of class and gender implicit in *BCP*.

The "duty to God" is significantly reworked from *BCP*, again to avoid misunderstandings and espouse a more personal relationship between the believer and God. So to "believe in him and fear him" becomes "to respect and love him", while "to put my whole trust in him" is moved to be the first affirmation made. What "to worship" means is contested by some Anglicans: *APBA* rephrases this as "to offer him my praises, thanks and prayers".

One difficulty in the "duty to God" is the high number of masculine pronouns: removing them would have meant a major recasting, and is a task for another day.

The "duty towards my neighbour" is more radically pruned, to avoid the "I know my place" ethos of *BCP*. No mention is made of the sovereign, of "submit", "order myself lowly", or "that state of life to which it shall please God to call me". What remains does not improve with addition: yet the earthy truth of *BCP*'s "to keep my hands from picking and stealing" might bring a smile.

In sum, *APBA*'s revision retains the main emphases of *BCP*, but reworks them in positive ways that apply to believers of any age, not just youngsters.

Prayer

The Lord's Prayer is opened out with fresh language, though the omission of the opening stress on God's gift of grace in the *BCP* Catechism is regretful. The repeated "I ask" avoids the long clauses of *BCP*, but could reinforce the mistaken idea that prayer arises primarily from our activity, rather than God's initiative.

The Sacraments

The final section is a minimal reworking of *BCP*, whose phrases remain classics in Anglican spiritual life and understanding. Often forgotten, however, is the final phrase in the definition of 'sacrament': not only outward sign of inward grace, but also "a means by which we receive that grace, and a pledge to assure of this".

Some changes were made, however, each carrying doctrinal sensitivities:

- The reason given in *BCP* for the need of baptismal grace is that we are "by nature born in sin, and the children of wrath". This is capable of much misunderstanding, so in *APBA* it becomes "Because human nature is sinful".
- In the response as to why infants are baptised, *APBA* refers to Confirmation.
- In the response on the purpose of the Lord's Supper, "sacrifice of the death of Christ" becomes "his atoning death", avoiding issues around 'sacrifice', but retaining a strong sense of the objective benefits of Christ's work.
- The bread and wine are commanded to be received by the Lord "in remembrance of him", an improvement on *BCP*. And a possible dualism of body and soul is avoided in the "benefits" response by beginning "We ...".

A new question concludes the Catechism: "What do we look forward to as we participate in the Lord's Supper?" This leaves behind a 'Christendom' mindset in favour of the 'eschaton' of the reign of God proclaimed and lived by our Lord, Jesus Christ.

The Catechism in *APBA* deserves to be better known, not only by those preparing for Confirmation, but long-term parishioners, ordinands, and (dare I write it) not a few clergy. It represents a significant re-situating of *BCP* for mission contexts.

Preparing for the service

Making ready the place

The Easter (Paschal) candle is customarily placed in the church when a baptism is to happen, whatever the season, and kept alight throughout the service.

Places for Baptism and Confirmation

The 'baptismal space' in a church building will have the font as its focus, traditionally set near the entrance.[10] Enough room is needed around it so the baptism party can take part readily. The congregation needs to be able to see what is happening: turning around or gathering close by can be part of the drama. Moving the font to the centre or front achieves this, but can detract from it being a symbol of entering the church of God.

When the bishop is present, where will s/he sit? When the laying on of hands takes place, how does where this happens relate to the baptismal space? Baptism is the significant act, so the font should have first place. In a traditional building, candidates and ministers move from the font (near the door) to the bishop's seat (at the front). How and when this happens needs thought. If large numbers are present, how is communion best administered? Stepping over a wading pool in the aisle is not practicable.

Submersion / immersion

Arranging for baptism by submersion / immersion is not difficult: it is universal practice in the Eastern Christian tradition, typically involving infants. If the font is not large enough to 'dip' an infant fully, a baby bath can be laid on top. For this, the child is brought to the font naked, wrapped in a towel before and after the baptism itself, and then taken out to return for the Welcome in their 'chrisome' (christening gown): grandparents will be delighted to see it on display.

An adult can be covered by water if they lie down in a 'wading' pool: 30-40mm depth is enough. Most Anglican church buildings do not include a submersion font: a temporary one should be placed near the font. Wherever it is, people need to be able to move around it easily, and the inevitable – though welcome – water spills dealt with.

An important issue is ensuring privacy. Wearing a (modest) swimming costume underneath other clothing (traditionally white) is helpful: changing out of wet clothing can be done in a vestry or other room. Where the baptism takes place outside, a shelter shed, tent or vehicle will need to be ready. If the baptising minister stands in the water with the candidate, wearing shorts under their robes and removing footwear is practical.

---

10   On 'baptismal space', including where the font is best placed, see *Performing the Gospel*, 61–62.

Preparing the service

Shaping the contents

The full title, "Holy Baptism, Confirmation in Holy Communion together with provision for Reaffirmation of baptismal vows and Reception" shows that every possibility is covered. On most occasions quite a lot will be omitted (e.g. pages 61–62). A one-off booklet encourages participation, can give information about the candidate(s) and can function as a memento.

NB: when the bishop is involved, s/he will want to see a copy in advance, which increases preparation 'lead-time'.

Start by considering service length. When several infants are to be baptised, an hour should be more than enough. Two scripture readings, hymns that are not too long, and trusting the prayers provided (#19 on *APBA* page 57, #22 on pages 80–81) all help this. But curtailing the sermon too much upsets the balance of sacrament(s) and Word. Positively, a sense of drama and welcome is what matters.

If data projection is used, the service needs to be ready several days beforehand so that it can be used at a rehearsal.

Opportunities for active participation

Any baptism service involves more than the presiding minister. The candidate and sponsors are asked to say things in public, and some movement is needed. The suggestions below seek to enable key people to participate more actively.

- The 'Presentation' and 'Decision' can be accompanied by a 'riper years' candidate giving a short account of their faith journey to this point. When the candidate is an infant, a sponsor or parent can say a few words about their hopes and dreams for the child. Ideally, the words spoken will be read from a prepared script.
- The act of baptising is what guests have come for. It should form the climax of the service. Let the rubrics, Notes and text of *APBA* come to life in the way it is enacted.
- The movement of the baptism party to the font conveys a sense of 'journey'. The dramatic nature of the Thanksgiving Prayer can be made visible by a sponsor pouring the water into the font to the noise of splashing. Sponsors and parents can join in signing the newly baptised with the cross after the minister has done so.
- The Thanksgiving Prayers can be a challenge when there is a crowd. It is tempting for priests to whip through them as if they are embarrassed about all their 'God stuff'. But read well, with confident body-language and actions, supported by regulars responding actively, these prayers get across that what is happening matters.

- Well-planned administration of communion will ensure that it does not drag on. Those who give the cup need to be adaptable to a variety of communicants.
- Inviting parents and sponsors to bring the newly baptised infants to communion first – which has to be planned with them – not only points up the closeness of baptism and communion, but signals to visitors that this, too, matters to their friends.
- Notices that leave aside 'parish pump' topics, but sustain the welcome to the newly baptised Christians continue to communicate the Gospel. This is also a good time to present Certificates to candidates and sponsors, and for gifts such as a copy of the Bible, *APBA*, or a book of children's prayers.

Rehearsal

A rehearsal provides an opportunity to plan and prepare these elements of active participation, and work through the 'choreography' involved. For example, how will candidates and sponsors be welcomed and seated? Who says what at the Presentation, and where? Where and when will testimony and confirmation happen? How will communion be administered?

A sensitively conducted rehearsal will ease nerves, give opportunity for questions, and help those involved enter more fully into the service. The rehearsal can conclude with informal prayers, the daily office or Prayer at the End of the Day.

Preparing things

Water

Where baptism is by pouring, a suitable jug (ewer) needs to be filled with water. Where it is by submersion, it can take a while to fill the font / pool / bath, so starting this well beforehand is wise. Whatever the mode, the ewer is used to pour water into the font / pool / bath during the Thanksgiving prayer (#21 on *APBA*, page 57; #14 on page 76). As noted above, a sponsor can do this slowly as the prayer unfolds (see Note 3 on *APBA* page 70).

Should the water be warmed, lest the infant cry? No rule excludes it, but it reinforces the idea that baptism is 'nice'. The early document *The Didache* ('Teaching of the Twelve Apostles', bound up with some copies of the New Testament) states

> Baptise in the name of the Father and of the Son and of the Holy Spirit in living (running) water. But if you have not living water, then baptise in other water; and if you are not able in cold, then in warm. *The Didache* 7.2–3

When pouring is the mode, a towel to wipe away excess water should be at hand. When submersion is the mode, see the previous discussion on privacy.

Post-baptismal symbols: cross, oil, candle

APBA provides for several symbols to be used after the baptism, to show its meaning and implications. They also give opportunity for parents and sponsors to take part.

Signing with the cross (#24 on *APBA* page 60, #17 on page 79) is initially done by the baptising minister using water. **Oil** (of chrism) may also be used (Note 6 on *APBA* page 70): if so a vial and towel need to be ready at hand before the service.

Where a **candle** is presented (#25 on *APBA* page 60, #18 on page 79), it needs to be placed where it will be ready on hand. It can be lit from the Easter candle, and extinguished at the Greeting of Peace. Church supplies stores stock suitable candles, as well as transfers that can be applied to household candles. Cardboard stands are available that have space for the candidate and sponsors' names, and the date: these enable the candle to be lit on each baptism anniversary.

Certificates

Canon law requires that a Certificate of Baptism / Confirmation / Reception be presented to each candidate and sponsor, and the details recorded in the Service Register. Each Certificate needs to be prepared before the service, taking care that the names used are correct.

The 'welcome' (#26 on *APBA* page 60, #19 on page 79) is a good place for the presentation of Certificates – along with applause, baptised infants being paraded, older candidates greeting friends and so on.

Preparing for Christ's guests

All members of the baptism party – parent(s), candidate(s), sponsors – need to be asked to arrive well before the service starts. Someone familiar with the ministry of welcoming needs to be on hand to greet them, ideally a parishioner involved in their preparation.

Before the service, parents and sponsors will often want to meet the minister who will baptise their child. Where will they sit? Are they ready to make their responses? What movements will they need to make? They can be invited to stand around the gospel reader, as well as at the font.

Having guests in mind

Visitors, of whatever faith outlook, are not nuisances but guests, part of those "gathered in God's Name". They have taken time out for an occasion that matters to their friends, and will likely include the curious, perplexed, indifferent and perhaps hostile. Their presence should be appreciated: a baptism is an opportunity to show what being a Christian entails.

Visitors quickly pick up when they are unwelcome, regarded as a nuisance, looked down on or preached 'at'. Christian hospitality demands better. Some ideas were noted above: here are a few more.

- Welcomers have a vital ministry. They need to be natural in greeting, and know how to make straightforward responses to questions. Enquiries are more likely to be about practical matters, such as where the toilets are, than doctrinal niceties.
- Few visitors want to sit where they feel 'on view'. They can be taken to the font to see where the 'action' will be, especially if they want to video the baptism or take photos.
- People need to know when photos and video recording is (not) appropriate. Preserving memories is good, but it is the baptism that matters, not the album or movie about it.
- Parents and others with infants need to feel that a few noises are no problem. If there is a crying room, pointing this out may settle anxieties down.

The best witness is when 'regulars' throw themselves into the baptism as if their faith-lives depended on it. Active listening, joyous singing, full-throated responses help 'lift' the service. When visitors see that what happens in the service matters to others, they are more likely to go along with it. And don't despise the importance of good coffee and eats if visitors stay for a cuppa – though nothing puts off young adults more than poor-quality instant coffee and limp biscuits.

Further reading

Ball, Peter and Grundy, Malcolm, *Faith on the Way: A Practical Parish Guide to the Adult Catechumenate* (London / New York: Mowbray, 2000)

Simon Chan, *Liturgical Theology. The Church as Worshipping Community* (Downers Grove Ill: IVP, 2006)

Church Pastoral Aid Society, First Steps: the journey to baptism. Available at https://www.cpas.org.uk/church-resources/first-steps/#.WpeiBOf-vDc

Chapter Twelve

Initiating Christians using APBA

This chapter comments on the services of Christian initiation in *APBA*:
- The first section covers the Baptism parts of *APBA* (pages 51–71 and 73–82), and the changes made in Holy Baptism of an Infant (2009).[1]
- The second section takes up Confirmation and Re-affirmation (pages 51–71, 83–94).
- The third section considers Reception (pages 95–98).[2]

Holy Baptism

The service in outline

The commentary attends to a range of theological, liturgical and performance details. Sight can be lost of the overall shape of the service, and of its 'flow', so this section opens with an outline of Holy Baptism in Holy Communion. Items on the left are essential; those in italics are affected by rubrics or Notes; bracketed ones are optional.

    Gathering and Preparation
        [Hymn]
    Greeting
    Sentence / baptismal dialogue
    Explanation of baptism / confirmation
    Confession and absolution
        [Hymn of Praise – *Gloria*]
    Prayer of the Day
  The Ministry of the Word
    One or two readings
        [Psalm]
        [Hymn]
    Gospel reading
    Sermon

---

1 Available on the Liturgy page of the General Synod website: www.anglican.org.au/liturgy-worship
2 Holy Baptism in *APBA* is set both within M&EP and HC2. The distinctive elements of these 'framing' rites are considered in Chapters Nine and Sixteen respectively of this book.

The Presentation
- *Presentation of candidates*
- *Sponsors' acceptance of responsibilities*

The Decision
- Renunciations
- Apostles' Creed[3]
- Intention to live the Christian life
- Congregational support
- Litany for Christian initiation
  - [Hymn]

The Baptism
- Movement to the place of baptism
- Thanksgiving over the water
  - [Apostle's Creed]
- The baptising

After Baptism
- Cross-signing
- 'Light' prayer [candle]
- Welcome

Greeting of Peace (for baptism)

Great Thanksgiving
- *Preface for baptism*

The Breaking of Bread and Communion

The Sending Out of God's People
- *Blessing*

The overall 'movement' of the service thus centres around the baptism itself:

Gathering, with a baptismal focus
  Ministry of the Word
    Presentation, Decision and prayer leading to
      the baptising,
        explicated in symbols and welcome
  Holy Communion, with a baptismal tinge
The Sending Out of God's People.

---

[3] The placement of the Creed is discussed below.

In the commentary which follows, where section numbers for the two Holy Baptism services differ, those for pages 51–71 are suffixed HC; those for pages 73–82 are suffixed M&EP. Parallel sections are numbered with an equals sign (=) between them.

Gathering and Preparation

#1 Where parts of 'Thanksgiving for a Child' are included (a good thing), they are best placed after an opening hymn, or after the welcome in #4. In this way God's gift of life is marked before we celebrate God's gift of new life in Christ.[4]

#2 M&EP The rubric under the title, 'Holy Baptism in Morning and Evening Prayer', has it follow the second scripture reading: *this service is not intended to be used on its own*. In this way, the baptism is set within the Ministry of the Word, whether in M&EP1 or M&EP2, or in Daily Morning or Evening Prayer for Sundays.[5]

#3 The response printed is based on Ephesians 4.4-6. Other suitable sentences include John 3.3, 5; Romans 6.3-4; Galatians 3.27-28. They could be read by one of the sponsors, or put into responsive form.

Introducing baptism

#4 Considerable work went into this section. It makes no distinction about the age of the candidate (as *BCP* and *AAPB* do), and aims to be as straightforward as possible. But it is probably the most questioned aspect of the service. The rubric says that "these or similar words" may be used, so ministers are free not to use it, or construct their own. This is quite a challenge: and the Liturgy Commission would love to see alternatives. When doing so, please consider these points:

- In Chapter Ten it was noted that baptism, while having First Testament precedents, is a distinctive New Testament rite, commanded by Christ. The first two sentences make this point clearly, using a minimum of words, concluding with the purpose of the service.

- The next paragraph states tersely what baptism entails: sin, Christ's death and the Spirit. Replacement wording is likely to be longer, but could well be more imaginative, and use bolder metaphors.

- The final paragraph states the outcomes of baptism, summarising biblical teaching as reflected in the Articles and Catechism. More creative wording is welcome, but length needs to be watched.

---

4 Note 5 on *APBA* page 48 relates to services other than baptism.

5 'Praise, Prayer and Proclamation' is difficult to use with baptism: it opens with long sentences; confession and absolution will follow the baptism, an odd conjunction; and there is no provision for a greeting.

NB: Note 1 on *APBA* page 70 requires that if the sermon does not concern baptism, then #4 "shall be read" after it, so as to introduce the baptism rites.

The paragraph about children is more complex, and is not optional.[6] It states why children are baptised, spells out the responsibilities of parents and sponsors, and concludes with the child's response. Having it read by different voice(s) from the earlier words can be helpful.

After the words of welcome, the candidates, sponsors [and families] can be introduced briefly, perhaps by someone involved in their preparation. This personalises the welcome, and lets the congregation identify who is to be baptised. (Testimony and the like is better kept for the Presentation.)

Confession and absolution

#5 HC This distinctive form of confession and absolution is not optional. Though brief, it is a 'general' confession: contrast page 157, a personal form of confession.

The Ministry of the Word

Scripture readings

#8-9 HC The number of readings can be reduced if time is tight – but planned beforehand, not during the service. Note 8 on *APBA* page 71 provides readings focused around baptism, though normally they will be those of the day.

Keeping in mind visitors, an active Ministry of the Word works well. A reading can be performed by several voices in dramatic form; candidates and sponsors can be asked to stand around the gospel reader, as a sign of their listening to Christ; and children's ministry could be offered (#10 *APBA* page 23). Preaching when visitors are present is a challenge, but also a wonderful opportunity. But saying something worthwhile in six minutes takes more preparation than thirty.

#5-6 M&EP The New Testament reading relating to baptism is optional because Holy Baptism follows the Morning or Evening Prayer readings.

The Presentation

#11-12 HC = #7 M&EP Where the candidate and sponsors stand is not stated: what matters is that they can be seen and heard by the congregation.

All candidates have sponsors, including those able to answer for themselves (Note 11 on *APBA* page 71). The parent(s) of an infant, in bringing the child for baptism, act as sponsor(s) even if not officially named as such.

---

6   In 'Holy Baptism of an Infant' (2009) this paragraph is moved to introduce the Presentation (#13 HC, #8 M&EP).

The words of invitation at #12 can be varied so that candidates and sponsors feel 'at home' (see Note 2 on *APBA* page 70). When an infant is presented, the sponsors and parents are likely to be young adults, for whom informal words will be appropriate. For an older person, keeping things more formal may be better.

NB: Note 2 on *APBA* page 70 and #7 M&EP allow the 'inviting' to be omitted: there may be occasions when this is appropriate, but this Note is best ignored.

#13 HC = #8 M&EP "Children are baptised" (*APBA* page 52 or 73) can be placed here.

The sponsors need to know what they are promising: there is no future in someone making a hypocrite of themselves in public. The three questions address

- the criteria for being a sponsor (accepting responsibilities placed on them);
- their willingness to fulfill this role now, in this service; and
- their willingness to do so in the future.

The Decision

#16 HC = #9 M&EP For candidates able to answer for themselves, the responses to these key questions apply to them. Taken literally, they would appear also to apply to the sponsors of other candidates (typically infants). This is no bad thing, but as indicated in #13 HC = #8 M&EP, the sponsors answer on an infant's behalf.

When a child is able to answer for him/herself, but too young to do so 'independently' (e.g. a six year old), s/he and the sponsors can respond together.

The order of questions is significant. Logically, it might seem that rejecting evil should precede turning to Christ. But repentance is a fruit of God's grace, made possible only in the strength of Christ: so *theo*-logically, turning to Christ is prior.

Renunciations

The renunciations take up the widening circles of evil that spread out from sin:

- personal sins (the flesh)
- communal sin: false ways of living (the world)
- demonic evil (the devil).

BCP expresses this three-fold renunciation in a single question, and in the opposite order: devil, world, flesh. In *APBA* the questions move from the personal to the communal and the demonic, using distinctive verbs: repent, reject, renounce.

The change from 'devil and all his works' (*BCP*) to 'Satan and all evil' (*APBA*) was made after careful consideration. Both 'devil' and 'Satan' are mentioned in the New Testament, but 'devil' is popularly felt to be unreal, even a joke. 'Devil' does not appear in the First Testament, where 'Satan' (accuser) appears as a creature whose role is to accuse people before God, Job being the clearest example (Job 1-2; the other occurrences are 1 Chronicles 21.1 and Zechariah 3.1-2; John 13.37 and Acts 5.3 are similar). Accusation, it appears, soon turned to deceiving (Revelation 12.9). Christ's temptation showed up this creature in a darker light: rather than being an agent of God, it works against God's purposes. The deepest challenge to Christ's mission came unexpectedly: when Peter 'rebuked' Jesus for explaining that he must suffer and die, Jesus replied sharply, "Get behind me, Satan!" (Mark 8.31-33). *APBA* thus employs this scriptural naming of this quasi-personal focus of cosmic evil.[7]

The prayer which follows is not an 'absolution', a pronouncement of forgiveness, but an 'embolism', a prayer for rescue from the "powers of darkness" that we are helpless of ourselves to overcome.

The Apostles' Creed

The Apostles' Creed was placed here in the draft of *APBA* considered by the 1995 General Synod. The Minutes indicate that it was moved to #22 HC = #15 M&EP, but Liturgy Commission members believe that this was a mistake, discovered when preparing *Holy Baptism (2009)*. In this the Creed is placed to conclude The Decision, as in *BCP*. This also eases the baptism party's having to stand at the font for the Creed and Thanksgiving over the water, which can be stressful.

It is strongly recommended that the Apostles' Creed be said at the end of #16 HC = #9 M&EP, rather than where it is printed at #22 HC = #15 M&EP in APBA.

Intention to lead a Christian life

#17 HC = #10 M&EP Some question whether asking about how the candidate will live before they are baptised undermines the truth that we are saved by grace. But

- the question follows the Decision, 'embolism' prayer (and Apostles' Creed);
- Christ taught that we must "count the cost" of following him (Luke 14.25-33);
- Paul taught that faith and its outcome in 'good works' are alike God's unearned gifts (Ephesians 2.8-10);
- the question is about living out the two 'great' commandments given by Jesus (Matthew 22.36-40).
- the response concludes "with God's help": the believer's "I will" is not an isolated or autonomous act, but is itself God's grace-gift.[8]

---

7   See Charles Sherlock, *The Overcoming of Satan*. Grove Spirituality Series 17 (Bramcote: Grove, 1997).
8   Article X: "We have no power to do good works pleasant and acceptable to God, without the grace of God by Christ preventing us, that we may have a good will, and working with us, when we have that good will."

- The 'warrant' for baptising someone is the declared intention that they will live as a disciple of Christ. This final question is wholly consistent with this.[9]

Testimony is appropriate at this point, 'personalising' The Decision. This can help visitors as well as 'regulars' understand more fully the significance of what is about to happen. Adult candidates can speak for themselves: parents and sponsors may wish to express their hopes and dreams for their child. This is best done from a prepared text, both to keep an eye on time, and to encourage preparation. An interview format can work well when people are nervous or reluctant (or too keen …) to speak in public.

Congregational response

#18 HC = #11 M&EP Baptism is not an isolated individual matter, but personal and communal, involving a two-way relationship between candidate and Church. The candidate has affirmed their commitment to Christ, and so to the body of Christ: now the congregation expresses its support to the candidate.

NB: The question is phrased 'these our brothers and sisters' and 'them'. When one peson is to be baptised, the question is phrased 'our brother' or 'our sister': the reference is to the candidate only, not the sponsors.[10]

Applause sometimes happens at this point: no bad thing, but is better placed at the 'welcome' after the baptism: #26 HC = #19 M&EP.

The Prayers

The Litany in HC

#19 HC = #12 M&EP

This brief Litany is sometimes felt to be inadequate, so that 'prayers of the people' are offered as well. There is nothing 'wrong' with this, provided that the petitions here are offered, but it adds time pressures, and can disrupt the flow toward the baptism. These brief petitions bring before God what matters in all common prayer. If expansion is needed, adapting the final petition is the place to do it: so in *Holy Baptism in Communion (2009)*, this petition is added:

> We pray for the world in which we live,
> **for peace and harmony among all people.**
> Bring healing and wholeness to the sick [especially …],
> **to those who mourn and to all in need.**

---

9 In *BCP*, the question is wider: "Wilt thou keep God's will and commandments, and walk in the same all the days of thy life?", alluding to the divine will in general, the Decalogue, and Ephesians 2.10.

10 I thank Bishop Greg Anderson (Northern Territory) for drawing my attention to this point.

'These persons/their/them' changes to the singular when one candidate is baptised.

The opening prayer derives from the first pair of petitions in *BCP*: the scriptural allusions include Romans 6.4 and Galatians 5.22–26.

The bracketed words in the second prayer, "and their families", will usually be included when infants and young children are baptised, but may be applicable for other candidates. The bracketed phrase is omitted in 'Holy Baptism in M&EP' because similar petitions come in the prayers after the baptism.

The third (bracketed) petition, "for those who come to affirm their baptism", is included when the laying on of hands is part of the service.

"May they know …" is a positive expression of *BCP*'s prayer for those baptised to "triumph over the devil, the world and the flesh". It makes explicit the baptismal call to participate in God's people and mission.

The next petition recalls the other side of the mutuality involved in baptism: having prayed for the candidates, the ministry of Christ's members to one another is brought before God.

The final prayer looks to the ultimate horizon of God's reconciling work celebrated in baptism, the new creation (2 Corinthians 5.17ff).

Moving to the font

#20 HC = #13 M&EP Having a hymn at this point not only 'sings up' baptism, but allows the baptism group to move to the font. This is the candidate's final step in their journey to the font, supported by their sponsors.

Those involved will now be on even more public display than during The Decision, so they need to know where to go, and feel supported.

NB: If the Apostles' Creed is (unfortunately) said at #22 HC = #15 M&EP, the baptism groups will need to have copies of the service or *APBA* with them.

The Baptism

Thanksgiving over the water

#21 HC = #14 M&EP This responsive Thanksgiving over the water echoes the opening of the Great Thanksgiving in the Eucharist. It brings together several *BCP* prayers, shaping them into a narrative of God's work: creation; Exodus and land-gift; Christ's baptism, death and resurrection; and the Spirit's transforming work.

Two practical points:

a) The response has no 'tag-line' to signal the congregation's response, 'Thanks be to God'. This can be signalled by the minister raising hands, changing the tone of voice, or ending each section with "and so we say". In *Holy Baptism (2009)* the response is omitted, the prayer then being said as a whole.

b) Each thanksgiving can be led by a minister other than the priest. This allows for a change of voice, and is helpful where a deacon or Authorised Lay Minister has been associated with the candidate's preparation. Using the name(s) of the candidates may be impracticable where many candidates are being baptised. The petition said by the priest, "Pour out your Spirit in blessing" widens the similar prayer in *BCP* by invoking the Spirit. This goes a good way to resolving debates about what constitutes appropriate '*epiclesis* of the Spirit.

The Apostles' Creed

#22 HC = #15 M&EP **As noted above, this is best said at #16 HC = #9 M&EP to conclude The Decision.** On the translation, see Note 2 on *APBA* page 821. The Creed is recited by the candidates, and sponsors of those unable to answer for themselves. Having others join in will not cause a disaster, but was not intended by the Commission. The final response, **This is our faith** ... is the congregation's affirmation both of the Creed, and of the candidate's confession of it.

The baptising

#23 HC = #16 M&EP "Each candidate *is brought to* the water" because none comes as an isolated individual, acting under their own steam, but as a person drawn to Christ by the Spirit of grace, supported by 'members of Christ'.

'The minister' who baptises will normally be the bishop, or the priest to whom the bishop has delegated the 'cure of souls'. 'Minister' is used because there are occasions when other than the priest or bishop will do so.

The baptism formula, which must not be changed, begins with *Name*. There is no instruction in *APBA* to "Name this child" (as in *BCP*), since the name is already known, and naming is not a part of baptism itself (see page 177 of this book).

The baptising is by 'dipping' (submersion or immersion) or 'pouring', but not sprinkling (see pages 168–169 of this book). For submersion, care must be taken to protect the candidate's privacy: see page 190 in this book. A "significant amount of water" is to be used (Note 3 on *APBA* page 70). Clean water will not damage a heritage gown ...

After Baptism

Signing with the cross

#24 HC = #17 M&EP The heading 'After Baptism' is significant: it indicates that signing with the cross, giving a candle and the welcome, are not part of Baptism itself, but explicate its meaning. The cross-signing was a matter of some controversy at the Reformation. That is why the final rubric in *BCP* 'Public Baptism of infants' points to Canon XXX of MDCIV (1604): Note 3 on *APBA* page 822 summarises the issues involved.

This and the next two sections are set out so as to take place once all the candidates have been baptised. However, Note 5 on *APBA*, page 70 expresses this as a 'should', so the cross-signing can be used after each baptism, as in *BCP*.

The cross is signed by the priest on the candidate's forehead, using the thumb or finger: it can be done dry, with water from the font, or using oil of chrism (Note 6 on *APBA* page 70).

After the priest has signed the candidate, the sponsors, and parents of an infant can be invited to sign the newly-baptised person using water from the font: this gives a powerful sense of them being 'owned' by their fellow 'members of Christ'.

The wording associated with the cross-signing raised a number of issues for the Liturgical Commission, not least the masculine, military and servant imagery employed in *BCP*:[11]

> We receive this Child into the congregation of Christ's flock, and do sign *him* with the sign of the Cross, in token that hereafter *he* shall not be ashamed to confess the faith of Christ crucified, and manfully to fight under his banner, against sin, the world, and the devil; and to continue Christ's faithful soldier and servant unto *his* life's end. Amen.

The outcome of much discussion was to place the Welcome ("receive this child") later and employ positive imagery for the signing: "to show that you are marked as Christ's own for ever". In the charge that follows, "good fight" (1 Timothy 1.18, 6.12; 2 Timothy 4.7) is retained, but set within two other New Testament images for Christian life: a learner (Luke 6.40; 14.27 etc.) and athlete (1 Corinthians 9.24; 2 Timothy 4.7 again), ending with a strong imperative to "keep the faith".

The congregational response echoes the "Christ has died / is risen / will come again" acclamation in the eucharistic Great Thanksgiving.

---

11 For further discussion see *Performing the Gospel*, Chapter Four.

Celebrating Christ's light

#25 HC = #18 M&EP This responsive greeting / command picks up the New Testament image of light in Christian life (2 Corinthians 4.6; 1 Peter 2.9; 1 John 1.5-7; see also John 1.4-9).

A 'lighted candle' may be presented to each candidate (Note 7 on *APBA* page 70). The *Mothers' Union* provides a fridge magnet with the response words: it can be presented with the candle, or with the Certificate of Baptism.

People are not always sure when to extinguish the candle: it is a good idea to suggest that it be blown out during the next hymn.

NB: A helpful custom is to have the candle lit on each baptism anniversary, accompanied with prayer for the candidate's life in Christ.

The Welcome

#26 HC = #19 M&EP This is best left until all have been baptised and signed: it allows congregational applause to happen at the one time for all the baptised. Having each newly baptised infant paraded around the congregation is often helpful, but check with the parents first.

The Welcome is another opportunity for (prepared) testimony by a newly-baptised adult, or for the parents / sponsors of an infant to say something of their hopes and dreams for the child.

The hymn that follows allows candidates and sponsors to greet others in the congregation, as well as resume their usual places.

The service continues ...

Baptism in Holy Communion

The service continues at #33 on *APBA* page 63, with a distinctive introduction to the Greeting of Peace, special Preface and post-communion. Since there are likely to be visitors, care needs to be taken as to how communion is administered. The words of invitation to communion (#38) can be preceded or followed by words such as these:[12]

On this special occasion, communicants from all Christian churches are welcome to receive holy communion: please hold out your hands to show that you intend to receive. All are welcome to come forward for a blessing: to indicate this, leave your hands by your sides.

---

12 The 1973 General Synod *Admission to the Holy Communion Canon* stipulates that "A person who has been baptised in the name of the Holy Trinity and is a communicant member of a church which professes the apostolic faith" may receive communion in an Anglican service.

Communion should first be given to candidate(s) able to answer for themselves, and the sponsors and parents of other candidates.

The Sending Out, pages 68–69, includes the lovely "Go forth" bishop's traditional blessing (#43), derived from a tissue of scriptural allusions (1 Chronicles 22.13; 28.20; 2 Chronicles 28.20; Romans 12.17; Philippians 4.4; 1 Thessalonians 5.14–15; 1 Peter 2.17).

Baptism in Morning or Evening Prayer

The Lord's Prayer (#21) leads into the prayers (#22), to which others may be added (#23). Then comes the sermon (#24), hymn (#25) and the Grace (#26), but as the rubrics recognise, this order can vary, depending on the context and circumstances.

Holy Baptism for an infant (2009)

This is a light revision made by the Liturgical Commission in response to a request from some bishops for a rite of Holy Baptism that is only for candidates who are infants. The Liturgy page of the General Synod website offers two versions: one in the context of Holy Communion, one in Morning & Evening Prayer.[13] Changes made to *APBA* in this service have been noted above, but are summarised here.

a) "Children are baptised …" is moved (forwards) to introduce the Presentation.

b) The Apostles' Creed is moved (backwards) to conclude The Decision, and said by the congregation as a whole. The sponsors then answer, on behalf of the candidate, "I do" to the question "Do you affirm this faith as yours?"

c) When Baptism takes place in Holy Communion, the prayers include an additional petition. When set in Morning & Evening Prayer, the Lord's Prayer concludes rather than introduces the prayers, which are unchanged.

d) "Thanks be to God" is omitted in the Thanksgiving over the water.

This has been a long and sometimes 'bitty' discussion, but what is at stake is the meaning and implications of the Gospel.

Confirmation and Re-affirmation

The laying on of hands is the symbolic act associated with blessing, reconciliation and the renewal of Christian faith. *APBA* provides for these ministries in Confirmation and Re-affirmation. The theological and pastoral issues involved were considered in Chapters Ten and Eleven. This next section comments on the services themselves.

The minister of these rites of renewal is the bishop, representing the wider church into which the candidates have been baptised.

---

13   Available at www.anglican.org.au/liturgy-worship

APBA assumes that Confirmation will take place with a candidate's Baptism and admission to communion: pages 51–71.

What matters most is that the occasion be a memorable one for all involved. As the 1995 Australian House of Bishops' Statement concludes, "all who are confirmed should be able to recall the occasion as a liturgical celebration of great truths".

Adult confirmation candidates baptised previously

The Liturgy Commission was in 2008 asked by Melbourne's Anglican bishops to address liturgically the situation where a person is confirmed some time after their baptism. The Commission indicated its support of the principle that normally adults should be baptised, confirmed and admitted to communion in an integrated rite. But it also adapted #11 in the Confirmation service to address the bishops' concern. Having received a positive response, the text below was sent to all diocesan bishops, and placed on the General Synod website.

#11 *The bishop says these or similar words.*

> Some of you were baptised as infants or young children. You will now affirm for yourselves the promises made on your behalf at your baptism. Some others of you have more recently been baptised, making your promises in your own name. You will reaffirm these promises with us today.
>
> We will pray for the Holy Spirit to strengthen all of you.
>
> I invite the sponsors to present the candidates now.
>
> *The sponsors answer*
>
> We present *name(s)* who come(s) to be confirmed.

Confirmation: commentary

At the 1995 General Synod, the Bishops had requested that *APBA* include a separate Confirmation service (pages 83–92). For ease of working, the commentary below is based on this, with the relevant sections of the integrated rite marked by 'IR'.

Gathering and Preparation, The Ministry of the Word

#1–5, 7–9 the corresponding sections of both rites are the same.

> Note 3 on *APBA* page 94, provides that the readings of the day will normally be used, but if not, it suggests suitable ones: significantly, these do not include Acts 8.14ff (see footnotes 18 and 19 on page 174 of this book).

#4 The explanation of confirmation is omitted in IR since it is unnecessary there.

#6 This collect, invoking the Holy Spirit, affirms that the Spirit is already active in the candidate(s), since they have been baptised.

The Presentation

#10-11 (#14 IR) requires at least one sponsor for each candidate (see also Note 2 on *APBA* page 94). The Decision each makes personally is thus supported by other members of Christ, rather than being the act of an isolated individual.

Note 4 on *APBA* page 94 allows for variation in how the Presentation is done.

The Decision

#13-15 and #16-18 IR are identical. This is a good place for each candidate to offer a brief testimony as to how God has drawn them on their Christian journey. It is best read from a prayerfully drafted text, or conducted by planned interview.

#16 It is appropriate for this hymn to be an invocation of the Holy Spirit.

#17 The prayers cover major aspects of mature Christian living: deliverance from evil, the Spirit's gracing, living in communion with God's people, witnessing in deed and word, and looking towards the new creation. These prayers are always to be used, but as the rubric indicates, others may be added, and silence kept.

The Profession of Faith

#18 and #22 IR are identical, apart from the additional heading.

NB: a) The Decision includes all candidates who are to receive the laying on of hands.

b) The Apostles' Creed is appropriate at this point, as the heading implies, though in the integrated rite it comes best at the conclusion of The Decision.

The confirming

#19 and #28 IR are identical, rendering *BCP* into modern English. As at #6, the Spirit is assumed to be already active in these baptised candidate(s): it is their *baptism* that is being confirmed.

#20 and #29 IR are identical. The words vary from *BCP*: the bishop first prays for the Spirit to "strengthen" each candidate, before bishop and congregation join together in the (traditional) "Defend, O Lord" prayer over them all. In this way the bishop's distinctive ministry is blended with that of the congregation. The rubric allows the *BCP* practice of the bishop alone praying the "Defend" prayer.

"Hand" is in the singular in the rubric (as in *BCP*), though in practice many bishops place both hands on a candidate's head. Some hold that this singular is significant, the use of both hands being appropriate for re-affirmation, healing and ordination.

After the Laying on of Hands

#23 and #32 IR are identical. That the post-confirmation prayer from *BCP* is abbreviated is significant, omitting "Let your fatherly hand be over them", and "(after the example of thy holy Apostles)". The confirming bishop need not be male, and the doubtful exegesis of Acts 8 is avoided.

The Greeting of Peace

#24 opens with the responsive affirmation from Holy Communion (Second Order), whereas IR uses a baptismal one (#33 on *APBA* page 63).

#26 offers a newly drafted statement of our Christian calling, recalling the prayers at #17, but its use is optional.

#27 is the traditional bishop's blessing (see #43 of the integrated rite).

Re-affirmation of faith

The amount of text and rubrics may be small, but the occasion will matter much to those involved (see page 179 of this book). It best takes place when others are being baptised and/or confirmed.

A person re-affirming faith in Christ joins in these sections:

#1–3, 5–10 (IR) = #1–9 (Confirmation)

#4 (IR) needs a sentence added to indicate that Re-affirmation will happen.

#15 (IR) = #12 (Confirmation): as with Baptism and Confirmation, the Decision that the person re-affirms is supported by other believers.

#16–18 (IR) = #13–15 (Confirmation)

#17 (Confirmation): the prayers remain appropriate.

#22 (IR) = #18 (Confirmation)

#30 = #21 (Confirmation) The prayer alludes to Philippians 1.6. The person could be sprinkled with water or signed with oil.

Testimony is appropriate at this point, though in order to save possible confusion as to what is happening, this is best done at a separate time in the service from testimony by candidates for baptism or confirmation.

#32ff (IR) = #23ff (Confirmation): those who have re-affirmed their faith in Christ join in all that follows.

Reception into Communicant Membership

This short service, *APBA* pages 95–98, is of increasing significance in a context where several Christian traditions exist alongside one another. The Anglican tradition was until fairly recently quite intolerant of those outside it. Only in 1973 did General Synod make official provision for Christians "of churches which hold the apostolic faith" to receive communion. In 1981, the Reception Canon provided for communicants of such churches to be received rather than being (re)confirmed in order to play a full part in the Anglican Church.

The Notes on *APBA* page 98 indicate that the service, of which the bishop is the minister, may take place in Holy Communion. It is best set in a service other than Baptism or Confirmation, so that it is clear that the person is not being 're-initiated'.

The service is straightforward, but some language issues arise from its origins in a General Synod Canon: the repairs below do not touch its substance.

a) Each Christian is a "member of *Christ*", not of a particular Christian tradition or congregation. Moreover, 'Membership' is an abstract concept, so "Reception into the Anglican Communion" would be a better title.

b) 'Candidate' is used in the rubrics at #1, #2 and #5, with 'person' in #3. In this non-initiation context, this is an unfortunate word: 'person' is to be preferred.

Providing opportunity for a brief testimony of how God has called the person to this point may be appropriate, but not where there are ecumenical sensitivities, or if it is painful for the person. Whenever the rite is used, and whatever the context, what matters is that the occasion is a significant one for the person concerned.

Further reading

Buchanan, Colin (ed.), *Anglican Confirmation*. Grove Liturgical Study 48 (Bramcote, Notts: 1986)

Billings, Bradley (ed.), *A Pastoral Handbook for Anglicans*. Third Edition (Mulgrave: Broughton, 2018)

Holeton, David (ed), *Christian Initiation in the Anglican Communion. The Toronto Statement* (Nottingham: Grove Worship Series 118, 1991), from *IALC*. Available at www.anglicanliturgy.org/wp-content/uploads/2015/06/growing-in-newness-of-life.pdf

Part E

Holy Communion
The Eucharist
The Lord's Supper

As the day of his death began at sunset, Jesus shared a final meal with his friends. This, his 'Last Supper', was no ordinary meal, but shot through with meaning from Israel's Passover tradition.[1] During the evening Jesus gave two commandments to his followers. One was "do this for the remembrance of me" (*touto poiete 'eis tën 'emën 'anamnesin*).[2] Of this Gregory Dix famously wrote,

> Was ever command so obeyed? For century after century, spreading slowly to every continent and country and among every race on earth, this action has been done, in every conceivable human circumstance, for every conceivable human need, from infancy and before it to extreme old age and after it, from the pinnacles of earthly greatness to the refuge of fugitives in the caves and dens of the earth.[3]

The other command was "a new commandment, that you love one another.[4] Just as I have loved you, you also should love one another" (John 13.34–35). Tragically, Christians have found it much harder to obey this command, not least in how they treat fellow believers who have different understandings of Christ's other commandment.

A rose by any other name?
Australian Anglicans have not been free from strife around the Eucharist. Differences are reflected even in the name of the service: 'The Administration of the Lord's Supper or HOLY COMMUNION', is the title in *BCP* (1662), names derived from 1 Corinthians 11.20 and 10.16–17 respectively. The first edition in 1549 included at the bottom of the

---

[1] 'Last Supper' is not strictly scriptural, but is a useful and familiar term to identify this distinctive meal.
[2] 1 Corinthians 11.24–25, the earliest account, written by Paul about 54AD.
[3] Gregory Dix, *The Shape of the Liturgy* (London: Dacre, 1945) 744.
[4] In the Latin New Testament, the word for 'commandment' is *mandatum*, from which 'Maundy' is derived.

title, in small print, "commonly called the Masse". This name, used by Roman Catholics and some Anglicans, is fiercely repudiated by others. Since Christ frequently 'gave thanks' before breaking bread (Matthew 15.36; John 6.11, 23), in particular at the Last Supper (1 Corinthians 11.24), Eucharist ('thanksgiving' in Greek) is now widely used.

These observations about names give a clue as to how the Liturgical Commission approached drafting the services in *APBA*. "The Holy Communion, also called the Eucharist and the Lord's Supper" is the overall title for them all (page 99): the *BCP* main title, 'Holy Communion', is used for each service (pages 100, 118, 167, 669, 685, 725, 812). This signals that, in accordance with the Constitution of the Anglican Church of Australia, the Liturgical Commission adhered to the "principles of doctrine and worship" of *BCP*: see Chapter Two of this book. The Commission also benefited from insights from the post-War Liturgical Movement and ecumenical dialogue, notably the work of the *Anglican-Roman Catholic International Commission* (ARCIC).

NB: 'Lord's Supper' is used by liturgists to refer to the communion rite, rather than as a title for the service overall, as in *BCP*. This reflects classic understandings of the Eucharist as celebrating the two 'tables' of the living Word, audible and visible: so Augustine, John Calvin and the Second Vatican Council. As scholars would put it, Eucharist = Synaxis plus Lord's Supper.

Resources and works cited

Members of the Commission were able to participate in two scholarly bodies, one national, the other global: the *Australian Consultation on Liturgy*, and *Societas Liturgica*. It also kept in close touch with the *Inter-Anglican Liturgical Consultation* (IALC), which brings together scholarly practitioners from across the Anglican Communion.[5] Three scholarly works are cited frequently in this Part.

- Gregory Dix, *The Shape of the Liturgy* is a landmark work of liturgical scholarship: a long book, it is eminently readable. An Anglican monk of Nashdom Abbey, England, Dix was instinctively 'conservative' on many matters, but his book challenges many 'received' opinions. World War II isolated English liturgical scholars, so Dix worked independently in seeking to understand and chart how the complex eucharistic rites of the various Christian traditions developed. His research led him to identify the 'four-fold shape' of the Lord's Supper which has influenced revisions across the Anglican Communion and beyond.

---

5   See David R. Holeton (ed), *Revising the Eucharist: Groundwork for the Anglican Communion* (Grove Books: Bramcote, Notts, 1994); *Renewing the Anglican Eucharist* (Grove Books, Bramcote, Notts, 1996); and *Thanks and Praise: International Anglican Liturgical Consultation on the Eucharist* (Toronto: Morehouse/ABC, 1998). *IALC* Conference Reports may be found at https://anglicanliturgy.org

- ARCIC's "Agreed Statement on Eucharistic Doctrine" (1971) was issued with an Elucidation in *The Final Report* (1981).[6] Its conclusions were accepted by the 1988 Lambeth Conference as "consonant in substance with the faith of Anglicans", and assisted the drafting of Holy Communion services in both **AAPB** and **APBA**.[7]
- Gilbert Sinden is frequently cited for two reasons. First, his *When we meet for Worship* is a detailed commentary on **AAPB**, of which he was Editor, written with deep knowledge of the Australian Anglican context. Secondly, as a monk of the *Society of the Sacred Mission*, Brother Gilbert wrote from a scholarly Anglo-Catholic background, complementing the 'Prayer Book Evangelical' heritage and ecumenical involvement of the present writer.

BCP (1662) is also cited regularly, as the Constitution-based liturgical authority for Australian Anglicans. Familiarity with using the services in this book is now lost to all but a few, but every sentence, rubric and even punctuation mark has been debated in the past. Access to these discussions is available in the classic 'Prayer Book Commentaries' of Neill and Willoughby (representing a 'Prayer Book Protestant' tradition) and Proctor and Frere (representing an 'Oxford Movement' position).

Reference is sometimes made to the 'Sarum Rite'. This is a collection of medieval (hand-written) Latin services introduced at Salisbury ('Sarum' in Latin) by Bishop Osmund around 1085AD, one of several local 'uses' in England.[8] In turn, it was based on the revision of the Roman Rite made by Alcuin of York (c. 800AD).[9] The Sarum Rite became used widely across England, and was the basis for Archbishop Cranmer's English revisions.

6   ARCIC, *The Final Report* (London: CTS / SPCK, 1981), 'Eucharistic Doctrine', included, with related documents, in Christopher Hill and Edward Yarnold sj (edd.) *Anglicans and Roman Catholics: the Search for Unity* (London: SPCK / CTS, 1994). ARCIC's Agreed Statements are available at www.iarccum.org

7   I was a member of ARCIC II (1991–2005), during which I took part in the discussion on *Clarifications*, its response to the Official Vatican Response to *The Final Report*, and ARCIC III (2011–2017).

8   Evan Daniel, *The Prayer Book: its History, Language and Contents* (26th edition, Redhill: Well Gardner, Darton & Son, 1948; first edition 1901); William Maskell, *The ancient Liturgy of the Church of England according to the uses of Sarum York Hereford and Bangor and the Roman Liturgy arranged in parallel columns with preface and notes* (Oxford: Clarendon, 1882). My copy was once owned by Barry Marshall, dated Lent 1, 1948.

9   Charlemagne, having united Europe as the Holy Roman Empire from 800AD, found himself faced by debates over the Eucharist, so commissioned Alcuin to establish the rite that Jesus gave to the Apostles. The scholarly society of Anglican liturgists is the 'Alcuin Club', founded in 1897 with 'Anglo-Catholic' roots. In 1987 it merged with the ('Evangelical') Group for the Renewal of Worship (GROW), which from 1971 had issued the Grove booklets. The renewed Alcuin Club publishes the *Joint Liturgical Studies* quarterly, plus an annual scholarly volume.

How these chapters are structured

Issues around the Eucharist are many and varied, from historic divisions over the presence of Christ, to questions of practice: What sort of bread should be used? How best can an alcoholic parishioner participate? This Part therefore opens with two chapters exploring key theological and liturgical issues that shaped the Liturgicl Commission's work. They are followed by five chapters of detailed commentary on the services in *APBA*, and materials issued since it was published. To understand what is distinctive about each service, and why the text and rubrics are what they are, the chapters are best read in sequence.

Chapter 13 faces the key question: What does it mean to obey Christ's command, "do this for the remembrance of me"? The New Testament witness to the Last and Lord's Suppers offers a context for considering the historic issues. The aim is not to resolve them all, but to articulate the theology given shape in the Holy Communion services in *APBA*.

Chapter 14 considers how doctrine plays out in liturgical practice. A key outcome of the Liturgical Movement was the 'four-fold shape' approach that undergirds HC2 and HC3. But classical issues also need attention: sacrifice and offering, what is involved in presiding, administering communion and more.

Chapters 15, 16 and 17 comment respectively on HC1, HC2 and HC3.

Chapter 18 considers the Eucharist in pastoral ministry, including Holy Communion at weddings and funerals, where significant numbers of non-communicants are likely to be present. Areas where dispute has long been the case are also considered, notably extended communion, reservation of Holy Communion for the sick, and private confession.

Chapter 19 looks at eucharistic materials issued by the Liturgical Commission since *APBA* was published in 1995.

You do not have to agree with the perspective put forward.

I have sought to write with sensitivity to the variety of 'churchmanship' assumptions and practices that have developed over the past half-century or more. No doubt at some point I will give offence, for which I ask your understanding. The intention is to show why the 'Liturgical resources' offered in *APBA*'s services of Holy Communion are what they are.

Bibliography for Part E

Placing a reading list at this point is unusual for a book of this kind. It is done for two reasons. First, the issues across all seven chapters in Part E reflect ongoing debate in the Anglican Church of Australia. Gathering the resources used at the beginning aims to reassure readers of varied perspectives that a wide range of viewpoints was considered by the Commission. My hope is that this will assist the current book, and *APBA*, in furthering the well-being of the national Church. Secondly, in practical terms several items would be repeated across chapters were Further Reading given after each.

I acknowledge the generous understanding of the Editor in taking this step.

Texts from Anglican sources

Papers from IALC conferences related to the Eucharist

Holeton, David R. (ed), ***Revising the Eucharist: Groundwork for the Anglican Communion*** (Grove Books: Bramcote, Notts, 1994)

– – – – ***Renewing the Anglican Eucharist*** (Grove Books, Bramcote, Notts, 1996)

– – – – ***Thanks and Praise: International Anglican Liturgical Consultation on the Eucharist*** (Toronto: Morehouse/ABC, 1998)

Key resources for the Liturgical Commission's work on Eucharist

ARCIC, 'Eucharistic Doctrine', 'Ministry and Ordination', ***The Final Report*** (London: CTS / SPCK, 1981), with Elucidations. Available at www.prounione.urbe.it/dia-int/arcic/e_arcic-info.html, and www.iarccum.org

Dix, Gregory, ***The Shape of the Liturgy*** (London: Dacre, 1945)

Dowling, Ronald, 'Eucharist', ***The Oxford Guide to the Book of Common Prayer*** (Charles Hefling and Cynthia Shattuck edd; Oxford: OUP, 2006) 460–475

Shaver, Stephen R., ***Eucharistic Sacrifice as a Contested Category: a Cognitive Linguistics Approach.*** Alcuin/GROW Joint Liturgical Studies 85 (Norwich: Hymns Ancient and Modern, 2018)

Sinden, Gilbert, ***When we meet for Worship*** (Adelaide: Lutheran Publishing House, 1978): Chapter Four, on the Eucharist, is full of wisdom

Richardson, David, and Varcoe, Gillian, 'The Holy Communion', Chapter Nine in Dowling, Ron; Richardson, David; and Varcoe, Gillian (edd), *A Practical Commentary on APBA* (Melbourne: Dwyer, 1998)

WCC Faith & Order Commission, ***One Baptism, One Eucharist, and a Mutually Recognized Ministry*** (Geneva: Faith & Order, 1975): the 'Lima' document

Prayer Book commentaries

Daniel, Evan, *The Prayer Book: its History, Language and Contents* (26th edition, Redhill: Well Gardner, Darton & Son, 1948; first edition 1901)

Lowther Clarke, W. (ed.) *Liturgy and Worship. A Companion to the Prayer Books of the Anglican Communion* (London: SPCK, 1932): a collection of detailed essays, issued in the wake of the 1927–28 'Deposited Book'

Maskell, William, *The ancient Liturgy of the Church of England according to the uses of Sarum York Hereford and Bangor and the Roman Liturgy arranged in parallel columns with preface and notes* (Oxford: The Clarendon Press, 1882)

Neill, C. and Willoughby, J.M., *The Tutorial Prayer Book* (London: Church Book Room, 1963; first published 1912)

Proctor, F. and Frere W.H., *A History of the Book of Common Prayer with a rationale of its offices* (London: Macmillan, 1961; first published 1905): http://justus.anglican.org/resources/bcp/Procter&Frere/index.htm

Other significant resources

Anglican scholars

Bradshaw, Paul, *Eucharistic Origins.* Alcuin Club 80 (London: SPCK, 2004)

Buchanan, Colin, *What did Cranmer think he was doing?* Grove Liturgy Series 7 (Bramcote, Notts: Grove, 1976) a brilliant, ground-breaking analysis

Gregg, David, *Anamnesis in the Eucharist.* Grove Liturgy Series 5 (Bramcote, Notts: Grove, 1976)

Sherlock, Charles, *Words and the Word* (Melbourne: Mosaic / Morningstar, 2013) Chapter Six on sacrifice and atonement

Williams, Rowan, *Eucharistic Sacrifice: the Roots of a Metaphor.* Grove Liturgical Study 31 (Bramcote Notts: Grove, 1982)

Other scholars

Catholic Institute of Sydney, *The Eucharist: Faith and Worship* (Sydney: St Pauls, 2001) consists of readable essays by CIS faculty, taking up all the issues positively

Marshall, I.H., *Last Supper and Lord's Supper* (Vancouver: Regent, 2006)

Welker, Michael, *What Happens in Holy Communion?* (SPCK: Marylebone / Eerdmans: Grand Rapids, 2000)

Willimon, William, *Word, Water, Wine and Bread* (Valley Forge: Judson, 1980)

Chapter Thirteen

'Do this for my remembrance': theological foundations

When Christians celebrate the Eucharist, what 'remembrance' (*'anamnesis*) are we doing? This question undergirds both the spiritual fruitfulness and the controversies around this sacrament of the Gospel. Christ's ministry of teaching, healing and proclaiming the kingdom of God is recalled at every Christian service. At Holy Communion, with the Lord Jesus as host, they find their crux in the *'anamnesis* of his passion.

The final book of the New Testament resounds with praise to "the Lamb who was slain", the "Lion of Judah", by whose blood there was "ransomed for God saints from every tribe and language and people and nation" (Revelation 5). In the Eucharist, it is the exalted Lion-Lamb's victorious death that is proclaimed, until Christ's return (1 Corinthians 11.23–26).

It is against this background that an examination is undertaken in this chapter of the theological issues around "The Holy Communion, also called the Eucharist and the Lord's Supper" by considering the 'Last Supper' and 'Lord's Supper' in the New Testament; reviewing the nature of 'The presence of Christ' in the Eucharist; and, finally, by exploring 'Sacrifice and the Eucharist.'

Last Supper and Lord's Supper

Eating with the Lord

Sharing a meal is a basic expression of human community. In ancient Israel, eating together in the presence of God was the climactic expression of *shalom* – well-being, peace. Exodus 24 is the classic example: at the meal where the covenant was sealed, the elders "ate and drank with God" as they joined in "offerings of well-being".

Jesus ate and drank with others time and again. Not just with his disciples and family, but with civic and religious leaders, the politically incorrect, morally dubious and downright criminals: in Luke alone, see 4.38–39; 5.29–39; 7.31–50; 9.10–17; 11.37–44; 14.1–24; 19.1–10. After being raised to new life, Christ spent time at the meal table (Luke 24, John 21, Acts 1.14). Their Lord's practice struck a deep chord with the first Christian communities. They told and retold the stories of Jesus' table fellowship, and lived out of a like hospitality: to misuse these meals was to sin against their Lord, a theme running through Acts chapters 2-6.

The Passover (*pascha* in Greek)

As conflict between Jesus and his enemies drew to a climax, he chose to take his last meal in the context of the Passover (Matthew 26.17-19; Mark 14.12-16; Luke 22.7-13; John 13.1). There is debate as to whether the Last Supper was an actual Passover meal:[1] whatever the case, the meal was imbued with Passover meanings, just as an office party in December is filled with Christmas echoes.

Passover is **the** feast of identity for Jews, commemorating God's rescue of Israel from slavery in Egypt. As a 'domestic' feast, celebrated in household groups, it is distinct from the regular sacrifices of Leviticus chapters 1-7. At this springtime feast, the dramatic story of God's saving acts is told, and food is eaten that recalls the suffering and hasty departure at the first Passover: bitter herbs, unleavened bread and roast lamb / goat (Exodus 12.1-28; Deuteronomy 16.1-8).[2] The Passover meal (*seder*) is much anticipated in Jewish families, and great care is taken in preparing it and its special foods.[3]

How the Passover was celebrated in Jesus' day is not fully known. Later evidence indicates that it was structured around four cups of wine, with questions and response, hymns and psalms. It opens with the singing of a hymn and lighting of candles.

---

[1] Matthew, Mark and Luke each read this way, but do not mention a lamb, and speak of the bread as if it were ordinary rather than unleavened. John, on the other hand, writes that Jesus was crucified on "the day of Preparation" (John 19.31), which implies that "the Lamb of God, who takes away the sin of the world" (John 1.29) died as the Passover lambs were killed in the Temple precincts. Evidence suggests that the Pharisees and common people marked Passover a day earlier than the Sadducees and Temple officials: see I.H. Marshall, *Last Supper and Lord's Supper* (Vancouver: Regent, 2006) Chapter Three.

[2] After the Exodus deliverance, Passover is next mentioned in Numbers 9, the first anniversary; Joshua 5.10-11, at the entry to the land; 2 Chronicles 30, Hezekiah's reform; and 2 Chronicles 35 // 2 Kings 23.21-23, Josiah's reform. The latter text states that "No such Passover had been kept since the days of the judges who judged Israel, even during all the days of the kings of Israel and of the kings of Judah" (2 Kings 23:22). This surprising scarcity may reflect decline in observance during the judges' period, or that the relevant texts were only finalised in the Exile.

[3] *The Passover Haggadah, with English translation* (New York: Schocken, 1969) provides the traditional Hebrew text, and introductory essays, including "Jesus and the Last Supper" by Solomon Zeitlin.
The foods are *matzoth* (unleavened bread, in three layers); portions of roast lamb or goat, together with *zeroa* (a lamb shank, seen by some as representing God's mighty arm); *maror* (bitter herbs – horseradish and lettuce, representing the bitterness of Egypt), along with *karpas* (green vegetables dipped in salt water or vinegar); *charoset* (sweet fruit mince, seen by some as representing the clay of the bricks made in Egypt); *biytsah* (the egg, seen by some as representing God's unity and kindness). All are arranged on a *seder* plate, which has separate sections for each food.

- The ***first cup of wine*** is drunk, giving thanks for God's work in creation.
- The ***'four questions'*** are asked by the youngest person present able to do so:
    Why is this night different from other nights?
    Why on this night do we eat only bitter herbs?
    Why on this night do we dip our herbs twice?
    Why on this night do we all recline?
- In response, t**he Passover story (Haggadah)** is told by the adults, with actions.
- The ***Hallel*** ('Praise God', Psalms 113 and 144) is sung.
- The ***second cup of wine*** is drunk, recalling Israel's oppression in Egypt.
- The ***bread is broken and shared,*** the herbs are dipped in salt water and vinegar, and the ***meal is eaten***.
- The ***third cup of wine*** is drunk, blessing God for Israel's rescue from Egypt.
- ***Lament*** is made, arising from persecution, and prayers for deliverance are offered.
- The ***Great Hallel*** (Psalm 136) is sung
- T***he fourth cup of wine*** is drunk, in hope: "Next year in Jerusalem" became the cry. The meal closes with another hymn.

The 'Last Supper'

As a Passover meal

Four New Testament passages describe the Last Supper: in likely chronological order of writing, they are 1 Corinthians 11:23–25; Mark 14:12–26; Matthew 26:17–30; Luke 22:7–30.[4] These three gospels name the meal as a Passover, which, Paul writes, took place "on the night in which Jesus was betrayed". Setting these texts in a Passover structure suggests the following analysis of the Last Supper:

After an opening hymn, the first cup was drunk, 'toasting' creation.[5] According to Luke, Jesus says, "I have eagerly desired to eat this Passover before I suffer, for I will not eat it until it is fulfilled in the Kingdom of God" (Luke 22.15-16). The Exodus story (*haggadah*) was presumably then recited using the questions, setting the 'background' for what was about to take place. Giving the (second) cup to the disciples, Jesus says, "From now on I will not drink of the fruit of the vine until the

---

4   These texts need to be read side by side, with an eye to their similarities and differences. Albert Huck, *Synopsis of the First Three Gospels* (Oxford: Blackwell, 1959), translated by F.L. Cross, gives the Greek text with critical notes. An online synopsis (in English) is available at http://sites.utoronto.ca/religion/synopsis/meta-6gv.htm: each column can be scrolled through to line the texts up side by side.

5   The New Testament texts speak of 'the cup' but not its contents. At a Passover, however, it would have contained wine, probably as a cordial (strong drink) diluted with water. Wine, bringing joy and gladness out of a process of decay, is an effective symbol of death turned to life, of suffering to deliverance.

kingdom of God comes" (Luke 22:18). This Passover will be the final meal before his passion: if the suffering of Gethsemane is in the 'foreground', the 'messianic banquet' is also in view.

The bread ritual followed: Jesus took the bread, gave thanks over it,[6] broke and shared it. The usual Passover words associated with sharing the bread were something like "This – the bread of affliction which our forebears ate in the land of Egypt." Jesus relates them to his impending suffering (Luke 22.21–23; Matthew 26.21–25):

"This is my body" (as Matthew and Mark record it).

"This is my body, which is (given) for you" (Paul and Luke).[7]

After the meal,[8] Jesus took the third cup ('of blessing': so I Corinthians 10.16), gave thanks over it (as with the bread), and shared it. Again Jesus' words were startling:

"This is my blood of the covenant, poured out for many for the forgiveness of sins" (Matthew).

"This is my blood of the covenant, poured out for many"(Mark).

"This cup is the new covenant in my blood" (Paul, Luke).

Jesus thus interprets the Passover meal, and the covenant it commemorates, in terms of his own atoning death. The promised 'new covenant' (Jeremiah 31.31) will be ushered in as his blood is poured out 'for many', an allusion to the sin-bearing ministry of the 'suffering servant' (Isaiah 53:12). A wealth of First Testament hopes are drawn together and interpreted in terms of Jesus' costly self-offering.

The meal concluded as Jesus and the disciples sang a hymn (Matthew 26.30: the Hallel?) and departed (note John 14.31), though now to suffering.

Do this ... ('anamnesis)

Luke and Paul record Jesus adding, "do this for my remembrance (*'eis tën 'anamnësis*)" (Luke 22.30; 1 Corinthians 11.26). The Greek phrasing is important: Jesus did not say "do this to remember me", as if *our* remembering is what matters (the ultra-'protestant' view). Nor did he command his followers to "offer a memorial", as the Latin text has sometimes been understood (the ultra-'catholic' view). Two observations from scholarly work and ecumenical dialogue have proved valuable:

---

6   This thanksgiving ('eulogizing', Matthew and Mark; 'eucharisting', Paul and Luke) is a *berakah* ('blessed be') prayer: 'Blessed be God for ... '. In the scriptures, things are not blessed directly, but God is blessed for them: see pages 123–124 in this book.

7   Though the Greek is "This is my body / blood", Sinden renders as "This – my body / blood", deliberately omitting "the word 'is' since there is no such word in Aramaic or Hebrew," the language Jesus spoke: *When we meet for Worship*, 72.

8   No mention is made of the paschal lamb being eaten, presumably since early Christian communities saw Jesus as the "lamb that would take away the sins of the world" (John 1.29; Revelation 5.6).

a) In keeping Passover, Jews do not 'repeat' the Exodus: that remains the historic basis for Israel's faith. Rather, as participants share in the meal, with its story and symbolic foods, they find themselves 'taken back' to that foundational event, whose saving power reaches 'forward' to them in the present. As one scholar puts it, "We are as if there", *not* "It is as if here".[9] This perspective recognises the once-for-all character of both the Exodus and Christ's passion, his 'Exodus' (Luke 9.31). Celebrating Passover, whether Jewish or Christian, enables the power of the unique events commemorated to be brought into the present.[10]

b) Jesus spoke the "This ..." words *while giving* the bread and cup. In each case, 'this' (*touto*) is neuter case, whereas 'bread' ('*artos*) is masculine. The 'this' thus refers to the **actions** of giving and eating the bread, of giving and drinking the cup, rather than to the bread or cup in and of themselves. So the 'literalness' involved is not of 'body and blood' as static, impersonal 'things', but of Christ's personal self-giving, offering believers a personal encounter with their Lord. This understanding coheres with Jesus' strong words in John's gospel about eating and drinking his "flesh and blood", that is, putting our whole trust in (believing 'upon', '*eis*) Christ's dynamic words, which are "spirit and life" (John 6.52–63).

After analysing the Aramaic behind the Greek texts, Gregg concludes that in saying "do this for the remembrance of me", Jesus re-interpreted the *meaning* of the Passover *seder*. Gregg suggests "act of commemoration" as a helpful translation of '*anamnesis*: this keeps the focus both on the *action* involved, "DO this", and its *significance*, "for the remembrance of me", while excluding any sense of 're-enacting' Christ's unique work.

The Lord's Supper

The Lord's Supper (1 Corinthians 11.20) continued the pattern of eating and drinking with the risen Christ, present through the Spirit after his exaltation. In writing to the Corinthians, Paul assumes that this was the regular practice of each church – though he probably would not have done so but for their misuse of this privilege. He calls this meal a *koinonia*, a sharing / participation / fellowship in Christ's body and blood, a 'holy communion'. As he wrote, "The cup of blessing that we bless, is it not a sharing (*koinonia*) in the blood of Christ? The bread that we break, is it not

---

9   David Gregg, *Anamnesis in the Eucharist*. Grove Liturgy Series 5 (Bramcote, Notts: Grove, 1976). He goes on to analyse two important ecumenical agreements: that of ARCIC, and *One Baptism, One Eucharist, and a Mutually Recognized Ministry* (Geneva: Faith & Order, 1975). The Passover *Haggadah* puts it like this: "I was present in the loins of my ancestors when the Lord brought *me* out of the land of Egypt".

10 So ARCIC, 'Eucharistic Doctrine,' paragraph 5.

a sharing (*koinonia*) in the body of Christ?" (1 Corinthians 10:16). This *koinonia* brings about unity among the 'members' (body-parts) of the 'one body' of Christ, who share in the 'one loaf', excluding anything demonic (1 Corinthians 10:17-21).

Past – present – future

At the Last Supper, Jesus pointed 'forward' to his imminent suffering and death, interpreting them as fulfilling God's promises. Conversely, in the 'Lord's Supper' a church celebrates this (once-for-all) saving work in the present "until he comes" (1 Corinthians 10.15-22). The Lord's Supper does not repeat the Last Supper, but looks 'forward' to Christ's return and 'back' to Christ's death, to which the Last Supper looked 'forward'. It recalls both the Last Supper, and the risen Lord's custom of eating with his disciples, "known to us in the breaking of the bread" (Luke 24.30-35; 24.36-42; John 21.1-14).

A striking aspect is the tenses involved. When Jews celebrate the Passover, they tell of their historic *past* rescue by God from slavery in Egypt. The power of God's saving work is brought into the *present*, laying ground for hope in a transformed *future*: "next year in Jerusalem".[11] Likewise, in the Eucharist we proclaim Christ's once-for-all death as we eat and drink in the presence of our exalted Lord, looking for his coming again. The past and present dimensions of Holy Communion are all of a piece with hope in God's future. When the Lord returns, we will eat and drink at the wedding banquet of Christ and the Church (Revelation 19.6-9; Matthew 22.1-4 and parallels).

Paul concludes his letter to the Greek-speaking Corinthian church by urging them to pray "*Marana Tha* – come, Lord!" (1 Corinthians 16.22), using an Aramaic phrase from the earliest days of the church. This transient age, when we see by faith, "as in a mirror, dimly", will give way to the full presence of the kingdom of God, where we will see "face to face" (1 Corinthians 13.12) and walk by sight.

In sum, each Eucharist takes us *back* to Christ's death (we are as if there); enables us to encounter our exalted Lord in the *present*; and through the Spirit is an *anticipation* of Christ's future reign, the "marriage supper of the Lamb". As ARCIC put it,

> Receiving a foretaste of the kingdom to come, we look back with thanksgiving to what Christ has done for us, we greet him present among us, we look forward to his final appearing in the fullness of his kingdom."[12]

---

11 A Jewish-Christian colleague informs me that when the Passover meal is in Jerusalem, the words used are, "next year in Jerusalem *rebuilt*"; that is, in the heavenly / new Jerusalem.

12 ARCIC, 'Eucharistic Doctrine', paragraph 4.

The presence of Christ

Time and eternity

The sense of God's future being anticipated in the Eucharist was faint for much of church history. In the early centuries, when being Christian meant facing social pressure and persecution, hope is prominent. But over the centuries of Christendom the kingdom of God came to be seen as accomplished: the Westminster Confession, for example, identifies this kingdom with the visible church (Chapter XXV #3).

The medieval and Reformation debates over the Eucharist thus largely revolved around the relation of its present and past dimensions: how does what we do in the present relate to what Christ did in history? The 'future' aspect was blunted in the West, though less so among Eastern Christians, many of whom live their faith in minority contexts. It is receiving new emphasis as the gospel is carried to unevangelised peoples, as some churches face totalitarian regimes, and others find themselves under pressure from a 'me first' consumer culture. In the wake of these challenges, the future dimension of the Eucharist is being taken more seriously.

It is against this background that the nature of Christ's presence is helpfully considered.[13] In Matthew's gospel, Christ's last words are "I am with you always, to the end of the age" (Matthew 28.20). Yet "we walk by faith, not sight" (2 Corinthians 5.7). We live in the hope of Christ's full presence, one anticipated by the Spirit (Romans 8.24-27; 2 Corinthians 5.1-6). Christ is with us at all times, but we do not always appreciate or sense this: the day will come when the presence of Christ with us, known now by faith, gives way to sight (1 Corinthians 13.8-13).

When the future aspect of the Eucharist is downplayed, the temptation is to identify Christ with the elements. Cranmer held that this "overthroweth the nature of a sacrament" (Article XXVIII, critiquing the 'catholic' tendency); modern scholars would see it as "over-realised eschatology". The spiritual danger in such literalism is that it views Christ's blood and body as impersonal 'things'. In Holy Communion we encounter the *living* Lord Jesus, at least as 'personal' as when he walked around the Holy Land.[14]

---

13 At the time of the Reformation, *prasesentia realis* (real presence) was closely associated with 'literalist' (carnal) identification of the bread and wine with Christ's body and blood. The English Reformers rejected this, while affirming the 'true' presence (*prasesentia veritas*) of Christ. The shift in meaning of 'real' can be seen in the so-called 'Black Rubric' on kneeling to receive communion: "That thereby no adoration is intended, or ought to be done, either unto the Sacramental Bread or Wine there bodily received, or unto any **Real** Presence of Christ's natural Flesh and Blood." Omitted in the 1559 version, it was (surprisingly) re-included in the 1662 book, with 'Real' changed to '**Corporal**', i.e. 'fleshly' presence.

14 Michael Welker, *What Happens in Holy Communion?* (Grand Rapids / London: Eerdmans / SPCK, 2000) Chapter Five, drawing on Lutheran-Reformed dialogue.

The contrasting danger is focussing so much on Christ's past work that his living presence is downplayed, typically in Protestant reaction to 'transubstantiation'.[15] The bread and wine are then treated as mere reminders of Christ's atonement, but not "means of grace" which anticipate, in his living presence, the wedding banquet of Christ and his body.

Christ's living presence

In this age God is known to us mortals only through indirect means, the "outward and visible signs" of scripture, sacraments and the community of faith. "Given to us by Christ himself", they are "means by which we receive God's grace, and pledges to assure us of this" (The Catechism, *APBA* page 817). Identifying the sign with what it signifies runs the risk of idolatry (the 'catholic' danger). Conversely, separating what is signified from the sign runs the risk of evacuating it of meaning (the 'protestant' danger). The sacraments 'work' as means of grace, not automatically; through faith, not certainty; in hope, not sight; and in personal rather than impersonal ways. As ARCIC put this,

> It is the same Lord who through the proclaimed word invites his people to his table, who through his minister presides at that table, and who gives himself sacramentally in the body and blood of his paschal sacrifice. It is the Lord present at the right hand of the Father, and therefore transcending the sacramental order, who thus **offers to his church,** in the eucharistic signs, the special gift of himself.[16]

---

15 Article XXVIII rejects tran*substant*iation when understood as "the change of the *substance* of Bread and Wine" (*APBA* page 831). In scholastic theology, grounded in Aristotelian philosophy, 'substance' is what makes a thing what it is, *but has no local property*: 'tableness' can be seen in a table, for example but has no existence of itself. So ARCIC, 'Eucharistic Doctrine' Note 2 makes this important clarification:

> The word *transubstantiation* is commonly used in the Roman Catholic Church to indicate that God acting in the Eucharist effects a change in the inner reality of the elements. The term should be seen as affirming the *fact* of Christ's presence and of the mysterious and radical change which takes place. In contemporary Roman Catholic theology it is not understood as explaining *how* the change takes place.

That there is a change in the way the bread and wine are regarded, used and spoken of is not the issue, but the ways in which they are related to what they signify and communicate, the body and blood of Christ.

Sinden, *When we meet for Worship* 77-78 offers a helpful discussion of Roman Catholic teaching. A more recent account is Gerard Kelly, "The Eucharistic Doctrine of Transubstantiation" in *The Eucharist. Faith and Worship.* The Catholic Institute of Sydney (Sydney: St Pauls, 2001) Chapter Four.

16 ARCIC, *Eucharistic Doctrine*, paragraph 7, emphasis added. That Christ's self-giving and offering in the Eucharist is seen here as towards God's people, rather than towards God, is particularly significant.

Christ's sacramental presence

The relation between the bread and Christ's (broken) body, between the wine and his shed blood, is thus not one of sheer identity, but sacramental.[17] Gilbert Sinden writes,

> To share in Christ's physical body and blood would bring us only into communion with the incarnate Lord: we need to share his risen and glorified life, too.[18]

'Transubstantiation' was carefully defined at the Fourth Lateran Council in 1215AD. In the popular mind, however, it was understood to teach an identity between the elements and Christ's physical body. Ordinary folk came to fear the elements as dangerously sacred: by 1250AD the cup ceased to be given to other than the priest, to avoid spillage.[19] Until then, all the baptised received, infants receiving a sip of wine from a spoon in which a fragment of bread had been placed. They were now excluded. Most folk, fearful of these 'awe-full' realities, avoided receiving, therefore doing so at least three times a year was prescribed. The Reformers had their work cut out in seeking to restore weekly reception of the sacrament.[20] Their insistence that the communion be administered in 'both kinds' reflected a return to ancient practice.[21]

Christ's 'body' and 'blood' are not static, impersonal 'things', but dynamic realities: in being given and received they are 'effective signs' of his living presence, conveying what they signify, God's transforming grace. As noted above, a key word in Paul's teaching on the Lord's Supper is 'participation' (*koinonia*): "the cup of blessing" and "the bread which we break" are neither identified with, nor dissociated from, Christ's body and blood. Rather, in the bread and wine being drunk and eaten in faith, they are a *koinonia* (participation, sharing) respectively in the blood and body of Christ. As Article XXVIII states, citing 1 Corinthians 10.16:

> to such as rightly, worthily, and with faith, receive the same, the Bread which we break is a partaking of the Body of Christ; and likewise the Cup of Blessing is a partaking of the Blood of Christ.

---

17 Similar analysis can be applied to words and meaning. The 'fundamentalist' danger is identifying them (literalism); overdoing 'deconstruction' leads to their relationship becoming arbitrary. Seeing words as the 'sacrament of meaning' is more helpful: see Sherlock, *Words and the Word*, Chapter One.
18 *When we meet for Worship*, 77.
19 To justify this, it was argued that since a person's body includes the blood, the change of the substance of the bread into the body of Christ includes the substance of his blood.
20 *BCP*'s rubrics require reception three times annually, including Easter and Christmas. A century later, Charles and John Wesley failed to persuade most Methodists to receive the sacrament weekly. In much of the Anglican Communion, it was not until the 1960s that this was accepted as normal.
21 See Article XXX, *Of both kinds*, APBA page 832.

Each celebration of the Eucharist – the Ministry of the Word, Prayers of the People and Lord's Supper – has present, past and future aspects. On the one hand, appreciation of the Passover background has eased debates over the relation of God's once-for-all past work to the eucharistic presence of Christ. On the other hand, reflection on Holy Communion as anticipation of God's future, rather than its realisation, clarifies its nature as a sacrament, celebrated in hope, love and faith, rather than sight. The reality of Christ's living presence, and the *mysterion* ('sacrament' in Greek) of his offering us his body and blood, is most clearly expressed for Anglicans in the 'Prayer of Approach':

> We do not presume to come to your table, merciful Lord,
>
> trusting in our own righteousness, but in your manifold and great mercies.
>
> We are not worthy so much as to gather up the crumbs under your table.
>
> But you are the same Lord, whose nature is always to have mercy.
>
> Grant us, therefore, gracious Lord,
>
> so to eat the flesh of your dear Son Jesus Christ,
>
> and to drink his blood,
>
> that we may evermore dwell in him, and he in us. Amen.[22]

Sacrifice and the Eucharist

At the Reformation, it was (wrongly) assumed on all sides that 'sacrifice' entailed human-initiated actions, often involving violence, by which relationship with God is restored. All agreed that Christ's sacrifice was sufficient: the great divide was over how its benefits are brought into the present. Rome maintained that it took place through the 'sacrifice of the mass', as the priest offers the consecrated bread and wine to the Father. Protestants saw this as repugnant, replacing divine with human initiative.

How, then, does the concept of sacrifice relate to the Eucharist today? To respond, some unravelling of common ideas is needed.

The sacrificial system of ancient Israel

'Three-dimensional prayers'

Sacrifice lay at the heart of Israel's worship.[23] According to the key First Testament texts (Leviticus chapters 1–7 and 22–23; Numbers chapters 28–29):

---

22 For analysis, see pages 243–246 in this book.

23 'Sacrifice' is much debated: what follows stays close to the biblical text to clarify the differences between Hebrew and Graeco-Roman perspectives: see further Sherlock, *Words and the Word*, Chapter Seven. Stephen R. Shaver, *Eucharistic Sacrifice as a Contested Category: a Cognitive Linguistics Approach*. Alcuin/GROW Joint Liturgical Studies 85 (Norwich: Hymns Ancient & Modern, 2018) surveys contemporary discussion, notably the importance of excluding violence from Christian ideas of sacrifice.

- any offering could only be of what a person possessed (a 'sacrificial' act);
- it must be unblemished or 'whole'; and
- any association with magic or superstition must be excluded.

The various types of sacrifice are catalogued in Leviticus chapters 1–7:

- Burnt offerings (*'olah*) expressed dedication, as something precious was wholly burnt up, a tangible symbol of self-offering to God.
- Cereal or grain offerings (*minhah*) represented a 'thank-you' gift to God, especially of the harvest first-fruits.
- Offerings of well-being (*shelamim*, 'peace-offerings') celebrated peace with God and one another through communal sharing of a meal in God's presence. These sacrifices were *not* about 'making peace' with God, but enjoying the gift of peace, the outcome of the covenant.[24]
- 'Sin' and 'guilt' offerings (*'asham* and *hatta'th*) dealt with **unwitting** religious and civil wrong. They did not atone for "sin with a hard heart and a high hand" (Numbers 15:30–31), but were acts of humility, recognizing that personal and communal life never fully correspond to God's ways.[25]

The absence of reference to the forgiveness of serious sins is striking. These sacrifices did not achieve anything 'Godward'. They can helpfully be described as "three-dimensional prayers" of dedication, thanksgiving, celebration, repentance and humility. Practising them supported a lifestyle of justice: otherwise they were worthless (Psalm 51:16–17; I Samuel 15.22–23; Amos 5.21–24).[26]

The Day of Atonement

Serious sins were dealt with on the 'Day of Atonement' (*yom kippur*, Leviticus 16). On this solemn day, the High Priest, after careful preparations involving washing, *'olah* (burnt-offerings of dedication) and *'asham* (for unintentional sins), confessed Israel's 'real' sins over the head of one of a pair of goats. This goat was not offered as a sacrifice, but chased away to die 'naturally' in the wilderness, a sign that only God can take away sin. The blood of the other goat, described as an *'asham*, was smeared on the Ark, but its body was burnt outside the camp, not on the altar.

---

24 *Shelamim* were when the Israelites ate meat, but not blood, which represented the life taken (Leviticus 17).

25 Different animals are listed for different classes of people, indicating differing levels of responsibility. The ironic paradox of Luke 2.24 is delicious: Mary and Joseph make the minimal offering in presenting the "Saviour, Messiah, who is the Lord" (Luke 2.10).

26 Other occasions of sacrifice are described, not all of which fit neatly into the above schema, but none are inconsistent with it: see for example Judges 20:26, 21:4, 1 Samuel 7; Numbers 19; 1 Kings 8.62–64.

The 'Day of Atonement' rituals thus moved beyond the means and motives of the regular sacrifices. The extensive preparations underscored the seriousness of dealing with sins, as did the post-ritual washings for the three men involved. But the ceremony itself was not a 'sacrifice'. Leviticus thus acknowledges that sins, no matter how serious or light, must be dealt with – but only God can do the dealing.

In sum, Israel's sacrificial system distinguished between "three-dimensional prayers" (sacrifices) and rites of atonement. When this distinction between sacrifice and atonement is observed, several issues around 'eucharistic sacrifice' are clarified.

Atonement and sacrifice in the New Testament

In the world of the first Christians, sacrifice stood in sharp contrast to Israel's life. The Graeco-Roman gods were seen as capricious, delighting to interfere in human life: sacrifices were offered to 'appease' or 'propitiate' them (*hilaskomai*). Sacrifices were not offered to sustain relationship with the gods, but to keep them happy, at a distance, so that life could proceed normally.[27] Tragically, such ideas continue to influence how sacrifice is understood in Christian faith and practice. As a letter writer to an Anglican magazine once put it, "Paul and the author of Hebrews interpreted Jesus' death as a sacrifice in the tradition of those in Leviticus, designed to appease the just wrath of God against sinners."[28] The writer had neither studied Leviticus, nor how Paul and the author of Hebrews used the concepts of sacrifice and atonement.

'Pagan' ideas of sacrifice were utterly contrary to the nature of God as revealed to Israel. It was the *Lord* who took the initiative to rescue and forgive, not Israel. Under the 'First/Old' covenant (Testament), the sacrificial system was the God-given means by which Israel celebrated and sustained relationship with their Lord. Under the 'New' covenant (Testament) a similar perspective is taken: 'sacrifice' is used to interpret and proclaim Christ's death, notably in the letter to the Hebrews. But its reference point is not the sacrifices of Leviticus 1–7, but the Day of Atonement (Leviticus 16), which transcended these (Hebrews 9). Israel's sacrificial system 'worked' due to God's grace, as the 'shadow' of the only 'true' atoning act, that of Christ crucified and ascended (Hebrews 8.5).

The "three-dimensional prayers" of Leviticus 1–7 are applied to Christian life by the New Testament writers. Paul asks believers to "offer your bodies as a living sacrifice" (*'olah*: Romans 12.1), and speaks of the Gentiles as a "thank-offering, sanctified

---

27 Some biblical texts can be read like this, such as Noah's reaction when the flood subsided (Genesis 8:20–21). Yet the outcome of his *'olah* was the Lord's resolution never to destroy the earth, and a deeper relationship between God and all creation, the covenant whose sign is the rainbow (Genesis 9:8–17).

28 'Doctrine of Atonement with contradictions', *TMA* Sept 2007. Shaver cites similar examples.

by the Holy Spirit", a *minhah* arising from his ministry (Romans 15:15-16). Christian Jews and Gentiles eating together in God's presence evoke the *shelamim*: peace has come both "to those who were far off and those who were near" (Ephesians 2:13ff). The author of Hebrews urges Christians to "continually offer a sacrifice of praise to God ... and not neglect to do good and to share what you have, for such sacrifices are pleasing to God" (Hebrews 13:15-16).

Nevertheless, a few New Testament texts employ the Graeco-Roman idea of *hilaskomai*, 'propitiate', making an offering to appease a testy deity.[29] It was daring to use such an image from 'pagan' life: but in each New Testament case, God is the *subject* of the verb, not its *object*, as in Graeco-Roman use. Paul wrote to the Romans,

> *God* put forward Christ Jesus as a sacrifice of atonement (*hilasmon*) by his blood, effective through faith (Romans 3:23).

And, most significantly, John writes,

> In this is love, not that we loved God, but that God loved us and sent his Son to be the atoning sacrifice (*hilasmon*) for our sins. Beloved, since God loved us so much, we also ought to love one another (1 John 4:10-11; see also 1 John 2.1-2).

The popular caricature of a loving Son placating an angry Father to gain forgiveness for sinners finds no place in the Bible. Rather, the scriptures bear witness to what *God* has done in taking costly initiatives of divine love to rescue a lost creation. The seriousness of sin and its consequences ('wrath': John 3.36; Romans 1.18; Colossians 3.6), and the unbearably high cost of this rescue and healing (1 Corinthians 6.20, 7.23; 1 Peter 1.18-19) are presented without apology. But there is not the slightest hint that atonement is initiated from the human side – not even by Jesus as a man. It is in and through God's initiative of costly love, hinged around Christ's death, that atonement is made.[30]

The New Testament writers thus employed the biblical language of *sacrifice* for a range of ministries: but the language of *atonement* solely for the distinctive ministry of Christ. Further, God's motive in making atonement is one of costly love, doing whatever was necessary to deliver us from death, Satan, evil and all the consequences of the

---

29 Some translations, notably the RSV, sensitive to pagan notions of 'propitiation', render *hilasmon* as 'expiation'. But the difference is not insignificant. 'Propitiation' involves doing something to change a relationship from one of enmity or anger to being friends. To 'expiate' means to scrub off a stain, or fix a fault, an impersonal process. That God in Christ 'scrubbed off' sins is not untrue, but did far more, forgiving sinners and making them friends.

30 A classic discussion of these issues is Leon Morris, *The Apostolic Preaching of the Cross* (Leicester: IVP, 1955), especially the chapters on 'Blood' and 'Propitiation'.

corruption of our relationship with God. And this reconciling work not only concerns humankind: a 'new creation' is being brought about in Christ, of which the Spirit is our *arrabon* (guarantee, downpayment: 2 Corinthians 5.5, 14-21).

In sum, both Testaments see **atonement** as God's actions to forgive sinners and heal broken relationships, a divine initiative that takes shape in the covenant (Old and New alike). Conversely, both Testaments understand **sacrifice** as God-given "three-dimensional prayers" that enable God's people to live as God's children. This distinction lies at the heart of what it means to "do this for the remembrance of Christ" in the Eucharist. And it is closely related to the ministry of bishops, priests and deacons.

Sacrifice and ministry

Priests in ancient Israel

In ancient Israel, priests were men descended from Aaron, born rather than 'called' to their ministry.[31] Their significant tasks were to pronounce blessing (Numbers 6:22-27), and especially to 'give Torah', to offer divine guidance on the basis of what was already revealed (Deuteronomy 33:8-11): examples include Eli, Abiathar, Isaiah, Jeremiah and Ezekiel.[32] Surprising as it may seem, offering sacrifice was not their key ministry. Distinctive tasks appear in some sacrifices, for example burning each *'olah* (Leviticus 1:8), throwing blood on the altar (Leviticus 3:2), and eating parts of the *'asham* (sin) and *hatt'ath* (guilt) offerings (Leviticus 6:25,7:6). Such tasks were forbidden to other Israelites, but priest and people offered sacrifice together, notably in laying hands on what is offered.

Priests in Israel mediated the Lord's covenanted presence: as 'windows' to God, they enabled the people to receive divine guidance and blessing. They were in no sense 'turnstiles' through which one had to pass to gain access to God's presence, as in "the nations round about". Further, this mediating role epitomised the calling of all Israel, to be a "kingdom of priests" (Exodus 19), a "light to the nations" (Isaiah 49:6). So in the New Testament these priestly roles are ascribed to the Church, the "royal priesthood" called to proclaim God's truth and bring God's blessing to Jew and Gentile alike (1 Peter 2:11).

Jesus went about doing the tasks of a priest in Israel, 'giving Torah' in ways that respected yet re-interpreted the scriptures (Matthew 5.17-48), and blessing people (Matthew 19.13-15; Acts 3.26). Yet nowhere in the New Testament is Christ called 'priest' directly. Indeed, since Jesus was not descended from the tribe of Levi but

---

31   The Hebrew word for priest is *cohen*. As Judaism dispersed, the ministry of priests became dislocated from the Temple: a priestly heritage is seen in a person's surname being Cohen, Cohn or similar.

32   Hence texts arising from 'giving Torah' being termed the 'Priestly Document', 'P' by many scholars.

from Judah, he was disqualified from being one. Hebrews chapters 5–7 describes Christ as our 'high priest', 'great high priest', 'great priest', comparing him to the priest-king Melchizedek of pre-Israelite Jerusalem, who brought bread and wine to Abram and blessed him, and to whom Abram paid tithes (Genesis 14:18–20; Psalm 2.7). Melchizedek represents an older and more universal royal high priestly ministry than Aaron's, signifying that Christ's high-priestly and kingly calling extends beyond Israel to all humankind.

Post-apostolic shifts

Each local church, often with several congregations, had one bishop, who presided and preached, assisted by deacons.[33] The deacons prepared people for baptism, supported them in the liturgy, and looked after practical ministries: since most could read and write, they often became bishops. Each congregation had some older Christians (*presbyteroi*, i.e. 'seniors', elders: 1 Timothy 4.14) who acted as a 'sounding board' for the bishop, yet had little liturgical role. Dix describes the relation of presbyters to the bishop before 325 AD as an 'executive committee' to its 'chairman'.[34]

Persecution of Christians was sporadic until the imperial persecutions of 250–258 (Decian) and 303–313 AD (Diocletian). The bishops, as key leaders, were attacked and decimated: their ministry of presiding was delegated to presbyters. As churches grew in number when persecution ended, bishops came to have oversight over larger areas, and this practice of a priest presiding was normalised.[35] The bishop's ministry shifted from presiding in person over a local church, to a corporate office of regional 'managing' (1 Timothy 3.4–5). Conversely, presbyters' ministry moved from 'managing' to a personal one of presiding in one place. Barnett calls this the 'great exchange' of ministries between the Councils of Nicea (325) and Chalcedon (451). In the process, the distinctively Christian order of ministry, deacons, was reduced to a formality.

Alongside this exchange, Graeco-Roman ideas about sacrifice slowly permeated Christian understanding. As Roman Catholic theologian Robert Daly writes,

> Instead of looking first to the Christ event and then asking, from that perspective, what it was that Christians were calling sacrifice; instead of allowing the Christ event to define the Eucharist, Protestants and Catholics all

---

33 James Barnett, *The Diaconate: a Full and Equal Order* (New York: Seabury, 1981) Chapter Six makes a clear case for this summary. A brilliant picture of second-century Christian worship, set in a London suburb of the 1930s, which reflects both this 'ordering', and its dangerous social setting, is in Dix 142–145.

34 Dix, 270.

35 The Council of Ancyra (314) forbade presbyters to preside, which probably means that some were doing so; the Council of Nicea (325) normalised the practice: Barnett, 100.

took the opposite route. They all looked first to define sacrifice phenomenologically [i.e. from human experience and 'natural religion'], and then apply that definition to the eucharistic rite of the church.[36]

Even so, second-century churches took up with relish Malachi's vision that "in every place a pure sacrifice is offered among the nations" (Malachi 1.11), seeing this as a sign of the universal salvation won by Christ. Following New Testament usage, sacrificial imagery was initially applied to worship generally, as "the sacrifice of praise and thanksgiving". This gradually became focussed around the Eucharist, then with offering the eucharistic elements. A 'representative' understanding of Eucharist and ministry moved towards a 'substitutionary' one.[37] Rather than the eucharistic prayer being offered by the president *on behalf of* the people, it comes to be offered *in place of* the people.

But the most significant change was that a presbyter, presiding as the bishop's delegate, came to be called 'priest'. As Dix writes,

> It was a great loss when the idea of the corporate priesthood of the whole church in the Eucharist was obscured by attaching the title of the eucharistic 'priest' especially to the celebrant-presbyter.[38]

A new constellation of priestly imagery emerged, mixing scriptural and Graeco-Roman impulses. 'Priesthood' began to be understood in the pagan sense of 'gatekeepers' who give access to the divine, typically by offering sacrifices to gain favour with God. Priests were seen as 'turnstiles' to God's grace and the basic 'order' of ministry. For much of the Middle Ages this 'sacerdotal' concept dominated the popular mind. It was strengthened when the confession of (serious) sins shifted from being made in public, before the congregation, to being made to the priest in private, who held the power of granting absolution.[39] And that Latin remained the language of liturgy, when it had long ceased to be the language of daily life, deepened the idea that priests had exclusive access to divine truth, including the Bible.

---

36 Cited in Neil Ormerod, 51–52. Compare ARCIC, *The Final Report,* 'Ministry' #13.

37 Tertullian responded to the (possibly heterodox) Montanists by expounding a 'representative' view of presiding. A generation later, Cyprian opposed the (probably orthodox) Novatians by arguing for a 'substitutionary' one. Conversely, the ministry of Christ came to be seen as not only representative (on our behalf), but also substitutionary (in our stead). This latter concept needs great care, but points to the truth that Christ did for us what we cannot do for ourselves.

38 Dix, 270.

39 Individual confession was introduced by Irish missionaries in the 600s to assist evangelism, and grew steadily across Europe. Private confession of sins to a priest at least once a year was made mandatory in 1215 at the Fourth Lateral Council, the same Council that defined transubstantiation.

The reformed Church of England

The English Reformers were harshly critical of medieval abuses, but revived the classic 'three-fold order' of bishop, priests and deacons as embodying unfolding dimensions of responsibility for the gospel. Bishops were retained as an apostolic ministry, with the distinctive task of ordaining other ministers; deacons continued to be ordained to a ministry of advocacy and pastoral support.

Most reformed churches rejected 'priest' in favour of 'presbyter' or 'pastor'. Yet Archbishop Cranmer, a liturgical conservative, retained 'priest' in *BCP* 1549 and 1552, and in the 1550 Ordinal, retrieving its First Testament sense. He rejected any idea of mass-sacrifices, "in the which it was commonly said, that the Priest did offer Christ for the quick and the dead, to have remission of pain or guilt" (Article XXXI). According to the reformed Ordinal, the ministry of a Christian priest is to be a "watchman, steward and messenger of the Lord", alluding respectively to Ezekiel, Jeremiah and Isaiah, priests who 'gave Torah' in their prophetic calling.

The Church of England thus retained and reformed the 'three-fold' orders of ministry – though the tradition of regarding priests as the central ministry continued. Bishops came to be seen as regional administrators, whose distinctive identity was ordaining rather than presiding, which minimised the ministry of deacons. This outlook sustained misunderstandings of 'priestly ministry' across the Anglican Communion on all sides. Some identify the priest's ministry as an extension of Christ's, forgetting that Jesus is not a 'priest' in biblical terms. Others see it as particularising the 'royal priesthood' of the Church (then denoted 'ministerial priesthood'),[40] while a few reject the word entirely. These confusions came to the fore as the question of women being ordained priest emerged, drawing attention to the work of scholars like Dix, and the ecumenical progress made by ARCIC and the BEM document.

The 'episcopal-diaconal' dialogue in liturgy

Presiding is not a one-(wo)man band. It takes place within and through the body of Christ. A body has structures, sinews, heads and toes: it is is 'ordered' (1 Corinthians 12). 'Ordered' ministry means more than filling out rosters, as if anyone could be that week's ears, eyes, prophets, revealers or singers (1 Corinthians 14). Rather, the Spirit calls and sends some to minister in Christ's name, typically through the laying on of hands by those in ministry (Acts 6.6; 1 Timothy 4.14;

---

40 As ARCIC famously stated, the priest's "ministry is not an extension of the common Christian priesthood but belongs to another realm of the gifts of the Spirit" (Ministry and Ordination , #13).

2 Timothy 1.6).[41] This is the ideal set out in *BCP*, the Ordinal and *APBA*, where ordained ministers bear responsibility to ensure that God's people are gathered, taught, fed and equipped for ministry.

When Christians 'assemble' – the root meaning of 'churching' – the bishop, or priest delegated to act on the bishop's behalf, represents God's initiative. In presiding over the ministries of scripture and supper, s/he proclaims the Word of God, and speaks God's words of greeting, forgiveness, peace, and blessing. Complementing this ministry of presiding is that of deacons, who enable the people's response: leading in confessing sin and faith, inspiring prayer, gathering offerings, preparing the Lord's table, sharing the bread and wine, and sending those present to worship the Lord in daily life.

This episcopal / diaconal dialogue embodies the responsive and participatory ethos of Christian liturgy, especially the Eucharist. The congregation is not just an audience, watching the 'experts', but God's 'royal priesthood', given shape by presiding and enabling ministers. When put into practice, this 'dialogue' ethos of call and response expresses the truth that "corporate worship is to be corporately led".

Conclusion

The Lord's Supper / Holy Communion / Eucharist has many levels of meaning. Christ as the host of this holy meal comes to us in the ministry of Word and Sacrament. We obey his command to "do this" as we offer the sacrifice of thanksgiving, and proclaim Christ's atoning death as we partake, by faith, in the paschal communion of his body and blood, a Spirit-inspired foretaste of the new creation.

This was the overarching understanding of the Liturgical Commission in drafting the 'trial use' booklet of Holy Communion services circulated in 1993–94, and the rites presented to the 1995 General Synod.

ARCIC's words are a fitting way to conclude this chapter:

Christ instituted the Eucharist as a memorial (anamnesis) of the totality of God's reconciling action in him. In the eucharistic prayer the Church continues to make a perpetual memorial of Christ's death, and his members, united with God and one another, give thanks for all his mercies, entreat the benefits of his passion on behalf of the whole Church, participate in these benefits and enter into the movement of his self-offering.[42]

---

41 This traditional stance (so Article XXIII) has more scriptural grounding than is often realised. 'Minister' (*diakonos*) is only used in the New Testament of believers authorised to take up ministry (*diakonia*): see John Collins, *Are All Christian Ministers?* (Melbourne: EJ Dwyer / Harper Collins, 1992).

42 *The Final Report*, 'Eucharistic Doctrine', 6.

Chapter Fourteen

'Do this for my remembrance': liturgical implications

How is the Eucharist best celebrated? A range of liturgical issues arise from the doctrinal focus of Chapter Thirteen. The commentaries in Chapters Fifteen through Nineteen take up the details of each rite: common elements across *APBA*'s services are considered in this chapter.

There are five sections. The first is arguably the most significant outcome of the Liturgical Movement, 'four-fold shape' theory. This is followed by presiding at the Eucharist, then exploring common elements across all Holy Communion servies in *APBA*. The final two sections take up sensitive issues in eucharistic celebration and administering communion. But first, an overarching question:

The Lord's Supper: part of a 'real' meal?

Bread was broken at every Jewish meal. But when Jesus commanded the disciples to "do this", it was the *reason* for the meal that mattered, "for my remembrance". Problems arose early on when the Lord's Supper took place during a meal: indeed, this is why Paul wrote 1 Corinthians 10–11, less than two decades after the Last Supper. It soon became customary to hold a 'love feast' (*agape*) as well as the symbolic meal which celebrates Christ's passion (Jude 12; 2 Peter 2.14).

Congregations can find it liberating to celebrate the Eucharist in a meal setting, not least if regular services have become overly formal or complex. Holy Communion on Maundy Thursday is held in the context of a simple meal in many places for example. But the meaning of the Eucharist is what matters, not the meal itself.

The 'four fold shape'

For much of the twentieth century issues around the Eucharist in the Anglican Communion remained shaped by the controversies of the Reformation and Restoration, as the 1927/28 debates about revising *BCP* showed.

Since 1945, however, ecumenical awareness, often arising from cross-cultural experience, has had significant impact on prayer book revision, along with the writing of Gregory Dix. A recurrent theme in Dix's research is that the Eucharist is something *done*, not just said: Jesus did not tell us to "say this for my remembrance". Dix showed that no known early rite re-enacts the Last Supper: in the Eucharist, we celebrate in Christ's risen presence what his death achieved. Doing so, Dix argues, is not about using particular words or actions, but setting these within a particular 'shape'.

From seven actions to four

The Last Supper had seven basic actions:

Jesus took bread
> gave thanks ('blessed God' for it)
> broke the bread
> shared the broken bread (with Passover-related words).

[then, after the meal]

Jesus took wine
> gave thanks ('blessed God' for it)
> shared the cup (with Passover-related words).

Each early Eucharist we know of, Dix argues, has two parts, and stands apart from its original meal context. The first is the 'synaxis': gathering, scripture, preaching and prayers, a pattern derived from the synagogue. The second is the 'Lord's Supper': now held outside a meal context, the seven acts of the Last Supper are condensed into four:

> Taking the bread and cup ('Preparation of the Table')[1]
> Giving thanks for God's saving work in Christ
>> ('The Thanksgiving', hinged around Christ's passion)
> The breaking of the bread
> The sharing of the bread and wine.

Why reduce seven actions to four? It is not the meal itself, but its *significance*, that is enduring: proclaiming the Lord's death and feeding by faith on Christ's body and blood in his living presence. When this is understood, and the focus falls on what we *do*, several controversies are seen in a new light.[2]

---

1   The traditional technical names – Offertory, Consecration, Fraction, Communion – raise a variety of issues, especially 'Offertory'. The names here go back to the English Anglo-Catholic scholar, Arthur Couratin, who first espoused Dix's insights for Church of England use: see Buchanan and Lloyd, 44.

2   Dix opposed the admission of bishops from the newly-formed Church of South India to the 1948 Lambeth Conference. Ironically, the freedom from Anglican 'control' this gave CSI enabled it to issue a Liturgy for Holy Communion in 1950 that employed the 'four-fold shape', the first modern rite to do so.

The 'shape' of *BCP* Holy Communion

The Sunday service prescribed in *BCP* – Morning Prayer, Litany and Holy Communion – followed the twin parts of early Eucharists, synaxis and Lord's Supper. But its 'shape' is far from Dix's thesis, due in large part to its history. The edition of 1662 is an updated version of three revisions (1604 / 1559 / 1552) of a reformed translation (1549) of a mixed-language transitional rite (1548) based on the Latin Mass in its Sarum form (1085) that goes back to Alcuin (800, under Charlemagne), who unified the work of Gregory the Great (596) that derived from the Roman rite, whose origins can be traced in the *Apostolic Constitutions* (fourth century) and *Apostolic Tradition* of Hippolytus (c. 220AD), whose precursor was the service described by Justin Martyr (c. 150) …

This complex history does not mean that Holy Communion in *BCP* is invalid or spiritually ineffective. Its several gentle 'swings' from the sober heights of God's praise, to humble acknowledgement of our finite mortality, commend the gospel to people of English sensibilities. In view of the historic eucharistic controversies, every word and punctuation mark is precisely placed – but this did not get in the way of generations of 'ordinary folk' and nobility alike communing with their Lord. In Anglican debates over Holy Communion from the mid-nineteenth century, all sides took *BCP* as their starting point. Few took up the need to respond to the social changes brought by the Industrial Revolution: missionaries assumed that *BCP* was appropriate for churches emerging in the growing Empire, for example.

Dix's work brought clarity to the core action of the Eucharist. God's people, having engaged with God's Word, take bread and wine, give thanks, break the bread, and share the broken bread and wine.[3] Most modern-language Eucharists follow this 'four-fold shape', including HC2 in *AAPB* and HC2 and HC3 in *APBA*.[4]

Presiding at the Eucharist

Faith, grace and effort

Some clergy try to "make something happen" in the Eucharist, as if human effort is what matters, rather than God's grace. This temptation is especially present when a priest is the only ordained minister, and few others seem suited to 'up front'

---

[3] Further analysis of Dix's thesis has shown that some actions are more significant than others: it is widely agreed that the 'taking' and 'breaking' are primarily practical, leading into the two central ones, offering thanks and sharing.

[4] Buchanan and Lloyd, 43–47 give an account of how Dix's work, supported by Arthur Couratin, influenced the Church of England. Though several aspects have come under question, they note that the 'four-fold shape' has continued to be used "not because it is commanded, nor because they follow Dix to the letter, but because, once this particular shape was adopted, it has served a pastoral purpose".

ministries. It is all too easy to impose one's own liturgical ideas, or fail to use others' insights and skills. A celebration intended to embrace the congregation as a whole, over which the priest presides, becomes an audience-oriented performance. But *God* is the 'audience' in liturgy

On the 'low' side, clergy can try to "make it happen" by being overly earnest in the way words are read, or adding chatty explanations. "Now we are going to stand and say the Creed. I want you all to think about each sentence as we read it together so that we really believe each phrase in our hearts ..." Or worse, "As you each take communion, remember that, as the song says, only if you truly believe will you a pardon receive ..."

On the 'high' side, this sense of effort can see the priest adding formulae to those provided in the liturgy, as if the prayer book lacks something vital. Symbolic actions are multiplied at every possible point and made fussily, as if their accompanying words were ineffective. Presiding is replaced by performing (of the wrong sort).

Both examples describe presiding characterised by effort rather than graced skill. The efficacy of the Eucharist does not depend on clergy performance (or lack of it): it is God's gracious gift, "effectual because of Christ's institution and promise" (Article XXVI). And similar comments apply to preaching.

In persona / loco Christi

Given the 'democratic' culture of the West, some clergy, and not only on the 'low' end, are embarrassed about leading. They try to do as little as possible 'up front', their body language is casual and awkward, and anything that smacks of the formal (including robes) is avoided. Such attitudes fail to accept that being ordained to the ministry of Word and sacrament means being called to act *in persona Christi* – as public representatives of Christ. Ordained ministers, whatever their feelings, are called to accept the responsibilities placed upon them, not least in liturgy.[5]

In contrast, other clergy, and not only on the 'high' side, act like father/mother knows best 'control freaks'. Ministry is seen as their sole responsibility, assisted by others only when unavoidable. Over-confident about their words and actions, services are led as if their performance were crucial for parishioners' spiritual benefit. This runs the risk of clergy seeing themselves acting *in loco Christi* – in the place of Christ – as public substitutes for Christ.

---

5   Sociologists point to the mechanism of 'transference' onto those in a position of responsibility, in which a person 'transfers' hopes and ideals onto them, whether they realise it or not. A priest may not realise it, but some parishioners will 'transfer' their attitudes towards God or Christ onto them: better to accept the responsibilities involved rather than allow spiritual dependencies to develop.

A remedy for both errors is taking seriously the dialogical ethos of Christian presiding and enabling, the complementary ministries of bishop / priests and deacons.[6] This does not mean that there must be two clergy for a service to take place, as in Eastern Orthodox churches. Every bishop and priest is a deacon, and where s/he is the only ordained minister present, the deacon's tasks can be delegated to others who are licensed by the bishop for such ministries. Most congregations today are accustomed to this: yet it is not so much that "we need more volunteers to help with the prayers", as discerning who should be called and equipped for 'up-front' ministries.

Participating in Christian worship, especially in Holy Communion, whatever our role 'up front' or otherwise, involves the amazing realisation that Christ *wants* to come to us, the motley collection of odd folk who make up his body. The Eucharist is a means of grace, to be celebrated in an ethos of grace. When those who preside and 'deacon' accept the responsibilities to which God has called them, trusting that in the ministry of Word and sacrament our Lord delights to meet, feed and empower us, things do happen. This ethos is beautifully expressed in the 'Prayer of Preparation':

> Almighty God, to whom all hearts are open, all desires known, and from whom no secrets are hidden: cleanse the thoughts of our hearts by the inspiration of your Holy Spirit, that we may perfectly love you,
> and worthily magnify your holy name, through Christ our Lord. **Amen.**

Familiar elements in *APBA* Eucharists

The Prayer of Preparation

This prayer, known as the 'Collect for Purity', is one of the few distinctively 'Anglican' elements in Christian liturgy. Attending to its origins and theology also illustrates how Cranmer retained and reformed the heritage of Catholic faith.

Origins and translation

This collect was part of the priest's preparation for the Sarum Mass: it is not found in other rites (e.g. York, Bangor or Roman). But its origins are earlier still: Daniel notes that "it is found in a Sacramentary of Alcuin, Abbot of Canterbury about 780".[7] The Latin text is:[8]

> Deus cui omne cor patet et omnia voluntas loquitur, et quem nullum latet secretum; purifica per infusionem sancti Spiritus cogitationes cordis nostri; ut perfecte te diligere et digne laudare mereamur. Per Dominum Christum.

---

6   See 'The 'episcopal-diaconal' dialogue in liturgy', pages 235–236 in this book.
7   Daniel, 345.
8   Maskell, 6.

Translated literally:

> God to whom every heart is open and each will addresses, and before whom nothing lies secret; purify by the infusion of the Holy Spirit the reflections of our heart; that we may merit to perfectly value and worthily praise you. Through Christ the Lord.[9]

Cranmer enriched the terse 'Deus' to 'Almighty God'. Today this carries ideas of power, "God all-mighty". But 'Almighty' is the English rendition of the divine Name revealed to Abraham, Isaac and Jacob: 'El-Shaddai' (Genesis 17.1; 28.3; 35.11; 48.3).

'Heart' was a favourite term of Cranmer's.[10] With deep roots in the scriptures (Exodus 28.29-30; 35.21-22; Deuteronomy 6.5-6; 1 Samuel 16.7; Matthew 5.8; 6.21; Romans 10.8-10) and Augustine ("our hearts are restless ..."), it sidesteps 'body / soul' issues, and gives a firm Anglo-Saxon sense of fleshly reality. 'Heart' is threaded through *BCP* Holy Communion: from "incline our hearts / write thy law on our hearts" to "that their hearts may be truly thankful" to "Lift up your hearts". The Prayer of Preparation is where this eucharistic journey begins.

Reforming shifts

Cranmer's rendition displays typical 'reforming' shifts. The Latin *omnia voluntas loquitur* carries the sense that the will (*voluntas*) takes the initiative towards God. Rendering this by "desire" reflects Augustine's notion of the will being intrinsically directed to God and the good, though weakened and (apart from grace) made incapable of re-direction once diverted to creaturely things. Translating *loquitur* – active in meaning, though passive in form – by the passive "known" returns the initiative to God. And the active "lies secret" of the Latin is turned into the divine passive, "are hid(den)": God knows our pasts, our present ('hearts') and hopes ('desires').

"All desires known" is quintessentially English, echoing the spirituality of mystics such as Julian of Norwich: "all manner of things shall be well". If "hearts are open" has a sense of God's present action, "desires" brings into view God's knowing our hopes at their best. And it is not each or every (*omne*) but "*all* hearts" and "*all* desires", giving a corporate rather than collective sense.

---

9   One English rendition is known before Cranmer's time, "on a blank leaf between two treatises in English, forming part of a volume of religious tracts" from a York monastery of around 1420: Maskell, 7.

10 This paragraph owes much to a sermon preached in Durham Cathedral by Bishop Stephen Sykes at a 1989 conference to mark the 500th anniversary of Thomas Cranmer's birth, 2 July. He was born and raised at Aslockton, near Nottingham, where I was on study leave. On that day Peta and I went to the village to toast the good man at the local hostelry, The Cranmer Arms, only to find fellow Australian (now Bishop) Paul Barker already there

Even so, we sinful mortals need to be 'purified' in order to worship aright. But 'purified' carries unhelpful cultic connotations: "cleanse" avoids this, echoes Psalm 51 and is strong English. Such cleansing happens by the Spirit's *infusionem*: translating this as 'inspiration' avoids the idea of grace being 'imparted' – and English ears hear 'infusion' as about making tea. As to what is cleansed, 'thoughts' may seem a bit weak for *cogitationes*: 'reflections' is my attempt to render this. But 'thoughts' is ordinary English, and these are where sin has its beginnings.

A further reforming shift was omitting 'merit', a concept which represented the chasm between medieval and Reformation understandings of human-divine relationships. The purpose clause of the collect ("so that ...") is then grounded in the work of the Spirit, rather than in human activity.

What then is the 'end' (aim) of this praying? That we may "perfectly love" God, not in the sense of eros or mere feeling, but with committed affection (*diligere*), echoing the "first and great commandment"(Matthew 22.38). A pleasing filling out of the Latin calls us to "worthily magnify your holy name", alluding to the opening words of the Song of Mary (Magnificat, Luke 1.46–55), and identifying the object of our praise.

'The Lord be with you / And also with you'

This greeting occurs just once in the scriptures: "Boaz came from Bethlehem. He said to the reapers, 'The Lord be with you.' They answered, 'The Lord bless you'" (Ruth 2:4).[11] The New Testament letters include many greetings, typically beginning "Grace and peace ...", but none take this form. "The Lord be with you [plural]" first occurs in the *Apostolic Tradition* of Hippolytus, the earliest known full eucharistic prayer (c. 215AD). It is not an opening greeting there, but introduces *Sursum corda* ("Lift up your hearts"). This usage continued in successive Latin rites, including Sarum, down to the present. It was omitted at this point in *BCP* Holy Communion, since it would break the crucial link between 1 John 2.1 ("we have an Advocate with the Father") and "Lift up your hearts" (to this Advocate). It appears just twice in *BCP*: to introduce the 'Lesser Litany' after the Apostles' Creed in Morning and Evening Prayer, and as the bishop's greeting after confirmation. Its inclusion in more places in the 1928 book began the increase in its use. Today it is over-done: I have heard it called the 'liturgical hello', and even seen it used, in my opinion irreverently, just to get people's attention ...

The response, *Et cum spiritu tuo*, is rendered "And with thy spirit" in *BCP*. Taking the singular "thy spirit" to refer to the distinctive charism of Christian bishops and

---

11   In 2 Chronicles 15.2, the prophet Azariah greets King Asa saying, "The Lord is with you" (*Dominus vobiscum* in the Latin Vulgate). "May the Lord be with you" occurs thrice, all associated with David: 1 Samuel 17.37 – Saul to David; 1 Samuel 20.13 – Jonathan to David; 1 Chronicles 22.11,16 – David to Solomon.

priests, some argue that "The Lord be with you" should only be said by them. In the New Testament, however, Paul ends several letters by praying that the Lord, or the Lord's grace, may be with the 'spirit' (singular) of 'you' (plural). This implies that all the faithful, not only its leaders, share 'spirit',[12] as seen in Paul's many prayers that the Lord's grace "be with you [plural]".[13] So in modern English ecumenical texts the response became "And also with you", reflecting New Testament usage and intentions. This was adopted across the Anglican Communion, and by the Roman Catholic Church in the wake of the Second Vatican Council.[14] In 2008, however, its new English version of the mass changed the response to "And with your spirit", rendering the Latin literally, but raising questions about whether 'your' is singular or plural.

What matters most about this familiar versicle and response, however, is that it is used in meaningful ways, rather than being triviliased by over-use.

Standing for the Gospel

The rubrics about standing for the Gospel in each Eucharist are rare examples in *APBA* of specified posture. "All stand" points up the significance of the congregation acting together as a whole, the 'body of Christ'.

Sitting allows people to follow along from a Bible or pewsheet. This is appropriate when the passage is an unfolding argument or list of principles: proverbs, prophets or New Testament letters. If the psalm is said, or sung by a choir, most congregations will continue to sit, but when the psalm is sung standing feels natural.

What then of standing for the Gospel, carried over from *BCP* Holy Communion? Does this lend greater importance to the Gospels than to other parts of Scripture? Well, yes – but which scriptures would you translate first into the language of a people who have just begun to have the Gospel preached to them? Which scriptures would you recommend to a person enquiring about Christian faith? The obvious answer is a Gospel, since they speak directly of Jesus Christ. What Jesus said and did is central to Christian faith and life: theologically, the living Word is the key to the Word written.

Standing also has a liturgical value. This movement by the congregation as a whole points to a *communal* hearing of the Word. Standing together to listen to the words and deeds of Christ symbolises that we hear *as a body*. Further, in the context

---

12 So Galatians 6:18; Philippians 4:23; Philemon 25. The exception to the plural is 2 Timothy 4.22, which has "The Lord be with your (singular) spirit (singular)", as appropriate for a letter addressed to an individual. The final greeting, however, addressed to Timothy's community, is "Grace be with you [plural]".

13 So 1 Corinthians 16:23; 2 Corinthians 13:13; 1 Thessalonians 5:28; 2 Thessalonians 3:18; Colossians 4:18; 1 Timothy 6:21; Titus 3:15; compare Ephesians 6:13.

14 Note 1 on *APBA* page 820 refers to *Praying Together*, now available in an updated version at https://irp-cdn.multiscreensite.com/a42fbdb2/files/uploaded/praying.pdf

of the Eucharist, standing to attend to Christ together indicates the sacramental character of the Word read, the "outward and visible sign of an inward and spiritual grace, given unto us by Christ, as a means whereby we receive that grace", as the Catechism puts it (*APBA* page 817). And it undergirds the unity of the 'two tables' of the Word, audible (the Bible heard) and visible (Holy Communion received).

'Hear the word of the Lord'

What response is best made to readings from scripture? In *BCP* the reader concludes with "Here endeth the First / Second lesson / Epistle", with no response. This 'objective' ending, retained in HC1, reflects the importance of no particular scriptural interpretation being endorsed in public worship.

By the 1970s, however, this was felt to be too 'matter of fact'. So in *AAPB* daily Morning and Evening Prayer the readings may conclude with "May your Word live in us / **And bear much fruit to your glory**", a form that continues in *APBA*. In *AAPB*'s Second Order services, however, the readings are followed by "This is the Word / Gospel of the Lord / **Thanks be to God**". While true of the scriptures as a whole, this raises sharp questions when it follows many biblical passages: see for example Deuteronomy 7; Proverbs 3; Ezekiel 34; Luke 14.15-33; 1 Timothy 2; Jude 5-16. Roman Catholic rites have readings followed by "The Word of the Lord", rendering the Latin *Verbum Domini*, but this is not grammatical.

The draft of *APBA* sought to fix both problems with "For the word of the Lord", but many General Synod members saw this as allowing too loose a relationship between the Bible and the words read aloud. "Hear the word of the Lord" was proposed from the floor by the Archbishop of Perth, Peter Carnley, and was quickly accepted. It echoes the modern responses referred to above, but more significantly, picks up prophetic usage: Isaiah 1.10; Jeremiah 2.4; and most famously, Ezekiel 37.4. It is used in all Second and Third Order services, Holy Baptism and Praise, Prayer and Proclamation.

The Prayer of Approach (Humble Access)

Distinctive to Anglican liturgies, this is one of most loved prayers in *BCP*. It has fallen out of favour more recently, notably due to the phrase "we are not worthy".

Origins

In the Sarum mass, and in Cranmer's initial revision (1549), the intercessions follow the *Sanctus*, reflecting the desire that they be associated with the consecrated elements. From 1552, Cranmer returned the intercessions to their place in the early church, to follow the Ministry of the Word. This meant that a 'gap' would have been felt between the *Sanctus* and the eucharistic prayer. The 'Prayer of Approach', drafted originally by Cranmer for the 1548 'Order of Communion', filled the gap beautifully.[15] Colin Buchanan notes that this placement reflects the successive experiences of the prophet in Isaiah 6: the vision of God 'lifted up' and the 'Holy, Holy, Holy' song leading to a sense of unworthiness, eased by the seraph touching the lips with a live coal.[16] Perhaps more than any other prayer in *BCP*, it articulates its sense of reserve in God's presence: "we do not presume".

The Syrophoenician woman

The phrases "come to your table", "crumbs under your table", and the reference to God's nature as "always to have mercy", allude to the account of Jesus healing the daughter of a "Gentile woman of Syrophoenician origin" (Mark 7.24). Matthew's account records that Jesus refused to act on the woman's behalf, saying "I was sent only to the lost sheep of the house of Israel" (Matthew 15.21–28). But the woman

> came and knelt before him, saying, "Lord, help me." He answered, "It is not fair to take the children's food and throw it to the dogs." She said, "Yes, Lord, yet even the dogs eat the crumbs that fall from their masters' table." Then Jesus answered her, "Woman, great is your faith Let it be done for you as you wish."

Not only was the daughter "healed instantly", but this Gentile woman's faith would seem to have led Jesus to widen his understanding of those to whom he was sent: not only to the lost sheep of Israel, but to all who are under the power of evil or in need, since "God so loved the world" (John 3.16), the 'Comfortable Word' that introduces this prayer.[17] For Cranmer, it would seem that this episode in Jesus' ministry expressed the essence of eucharistic encounter: humble, not arising from our being or action, but the merciful gift of God to those desperate enough to come to the Lord's table for crumbs. Feeding thus on Christ's body and blood "in your heart by faith with thanksgiving" (the words of administration), Christ dwells in us and we in him: a deeply personal sense of "holy communion" with our Lord. Further, Gilbert Sinden notes that

> In Biblical as in Tudor times these 'crumbs' were fair-size hunks of bread used to soak up gravy to wipe your plate ready for a new dish, and to wipe your fingers. Such pieces of bread (TEV rightly calls them 'leftovers') which survived

---

15 The 1548 'Order' was material in English – Exhortations, Invitation, General Confession and Absolution, Prayer of Humble Access – inserted into the Latin mass as a temporary measure to prepare participants to receive communion. (Edward VI had just become king, launching the Reformation in England.) This material was taken up into *BCP* 1549: to clarify sveral doctrinal issues, its elements were moved around in the 1552 revision, where they remained in the 1559, 1604 and 1662 editions.

16 *What did Cranmer think he was doing?* 27.

17 For an analysis which contests the use of the scriptural texts in the prayer, see Alan Cadwallader, *Beyond the Word of a Woman: Recovering the Bodies of the Syrophoenician Woman* (Adelaide: ATF, 2009).

the greed of the dogs were commonly collected after the meal and given to the poor. This picture, though a little earthy, suggests rather more nourishment in the 'crumbs' than that word implies to us today.[18]

We are not worthy …

This phrase is criticised as being demeaning. But the 'not' accurately reflects Paul's words in 1 Corinthians 11.27, and it is hard to imagine what Christian would claim "we are worthy". The accusation of being demeaning has more force in relation to the additional invitation to communion in *APBA*, page 146: "Lord, I am not worthy to receive you, but only say the word and I shall be healed". Though derived from scripture (Matthew 8.8), these words are individual rather than communal, and make a sudden and unhelpful return to penitence just before communion is administered.

Some contrast "we are not worthy" with "you have deemed us worthy to stand in your presence" in the early eucharistic prayer attributed to Hippolytus. But "deemed us worthy" recognises that, of ourselves, we are not worthy to stand before God. Because of God's act in Christ, however, we may, and Christ calls us to do so. Acknowledging that "we are not worthy" does not stop us from going on to the Lord's Table, but is an honest beginning to asking God that we might feed on Christ's flesh and blood.

Eat the flesh … drink the blood

One might expect that the dramatic wording, "to eat the flesh of … Christ, and to drink his blood", would see offence taken by some, concerned that it made Holy Communion sound like a cannibal feast.[19] This has not been the case for Anglicans, however, for whom the strongly personal nature of holy communion is in view – and know that the phrase was drafted by Cranmer.

But "flesh and blood", rather than "body and blood", points to John 6.53–57, where they refer to "believing on the one whom God has sent" (John 6.30).[20] Jesus compares 'flesh' with 'spirit': "It is the spirit that gives life; the flesh is useless. The words that I have spoken to you are spirit and life" (John 6.63). The 'Prayer of Approach' thus deflects 'carnal' ideas about feeding on Christ, while offering

---

18 *When we meet for Worship*, 133. A further allusion to these 'crumbs' is made in Luke 16.21.

19 In *BCP* (1662) the penultimate sentence reads "that our sinful bodies may be made clean by his body, and our souls washed through his most precious blood". This is omitted in *AAPB*, *APBA* and other modern rites, to avoid an implicit dualism between 'body' and 'soul', and a naïve association of body with bread and wine with soul. But 'body' and 'soul' speak of the whole person being involved, and convey in earthy terms the spiritual benefit of receiving the sacrament of Christ's body and blood.

20 Cranmer delighted in John 6, taking it to refer to believing in Christ through the ministries of Word and sacrament alike, rather than having a primarily eucharistic reference. See Charles Sherlock, "The Food of the Soul. Thomas Cranmer and Holy Scripture", *Australian Journal of Liturgy* 2/3 (1990) 134-141.

a profoundly positive understanding of believers' personal encounter with their exalted Lord in the Eucharist.

Placement

In *BCP* and HC1, the Prayer of Approach comes between "Holy, Holy, Holy" and the Prayer of Consecration. To those used to the 'four-fold shape' this seems to interrupt the Preface, so in the 1993 'trial use' draft of HC2, it was moved to an Appendix. This provoked considerable negative responses, so it was returned to the service text, but placed with the Comfortable Words to begin the (optional) Preparation.

Sensitive issues in eucharistic celebration

Sacrifice and atonement

The distinction between sacrifice and atonement, explored in Chapter Thirteen, had by the time of the Reformation become wholly blurred. To both Cranmer and the Council of Trent, sacrifice was understood as actions initiated by human beings by which the relationship between ourselves and God in Christ was restored. As a result, in *BCP* Holy Communion any mention of a sacrifice we offer is left until after the sacrament has been received. Indeed, moving the post-communion 'prayer of oblation' to precede administration in the 1927–28 Deposited Book was a major reason for the book being rejected: 'eucharistic sacrifice' is a sensitive matter for Anglicans.[21]

The Final Report of ARCIC (1981) had considerable influence on revision of the Eucharist across the Anglican Communion. Particularly significant is its stressing that the 'movement' of eucharistic offering is Christ's taking the initiative, not us:

> When his people are gathered at the Eucharist to commemorate his saving act for our redemption, **Christ** makes effective among us the eternal benefits of this victory and elicits and renews our response of faith, thanksgiving and self-surrender ...
>
> In the whole action of the eucharist, and in and by his sacramental presence given through bread and wine, the crucified and risen Lord, according to his promise, ***offers himself to his people***.[22]

In view of this, when the scriptural distinction between sacrifice and atonement is made, eucharistic sacrifice can be acknowledged, but eucharistic atonement excluded. This has several significant implications:

---

21 Sinden 81–88 discusses carefully the changes in 'oblation' from the Sarum rite through the editions of *BCP* Holy Communion. Though he is explicating HC2 in *AAPB*, the point is applicable to HC2 in *APBA*.
22 'Eucharistic Doctrine', 3, emphasis added.

1. Holy Communion can properly be spoken of as a 'sacrifice' in the senses of Leviticus 1–7: dedication, thanksgiving, celebrating peace, and acknowledging our need of forgiveness and restoration (social as well as with God). These sacrifices are personal, focussed in the Spirit-inspired self-offering of God's people.

2. The Eucharist, interpreted against the background of the Passover deliverance, "makes available in the present" (ARCIC) the unique self-offering of Christ "as the propitiation … for the sins of the whole world" (1 John 2.2).[23]

3. But the Eucharist does not have an 'atoning' action independent of the once-for-all work of Christ, as if it were akin to *yom kippur* (Leviticus 16). This excludes the popular medieval understanding of the "sacrifice of the mass".

As a consequence, a variety of references or allusions to sacrifice were spread across HC2 in *AAPB*, a practice continued in *APBA*. This gives a significant lift to the sense of praise and thanksgiving in the service overall.

Consecration

This term was introduced in *BCP* 1662, when the eucharistic prayer was (unhelpfully) named the 'Prayer of Consecration'. Cranmer understood consecration as "the separation of anything from a profane and worldly use unto a spiritual and godly use".[24] He drew a parallel between the water of baptism and the bread and wine of Holy Communion as elements 'consecrated' by prayer that employs Christ's words.[25] Modern liturgists include 'thanksgiving' as a necessary aspect of consecration, but see the idea of a particular 'moment' as encouraging a 'static' understanding of Christ's presence. Using the 'four-fold shape' offers a better understanding, as Sinden summarises:[26]

---

23 Cranmer rejected the idea of the mass involving sacrifice (as Trent affirmed), seeing this as nullifying the atoning work of Christ. So "sacrifices of Masses, in the which it was commonly said, that the Priest did offer Christ for the quick and the dead, to have remission of pain or guilt, were blasphemous fables, and dangerous deceits" (Article XXXI, *APBA* page 832). Yet he retained 'propitiation' in the service, placing 1 John 1.2 immediately before "Lift up your hearts", lest the fullness of Christ's work be blurred.
Conversely, in its Official Response to ARCIC's Agreement on the Eucharist, the Vatican insisted that it has a "propitiatory dimension". ARCIC's response, *Clarifications* (CTS / SPCK, 1994), noted the distinction between sacrifice and atonement, in the light of which both Cranmer and Rome could agree that in the Eucharist "the benefits of Christ's passion" are made available in the Eucharist, without distorting Christ's unique, once-for-all atonement. See Charles Sherlock, "Eucharist, sacrifice and atonement: ARCIC's *Clarifications*", in IALC, *Thanks and Praise*.

24 Thomas Cranmer, *On the Lord's Supper* (London: Parker Society) 177.

25 This continued the scholastic view that the substance of the bread changed when the priest said *Hoc est meum corpum* ("This is my body"), one of the few words spoken aloud by the priest and heard by the congregation. These words led to the (blasphemous) expression 'hocus pocus' for something false.

26 *When we meet for Worship*, 91.

What consecrates ... what makes this meal and the bread and wine at its centre a means of grace, is not just any one thing, but the whole prayerful action in which bread and wine are taken, thanks are given to God for Christ over them, the bread is broken, and the broken bread and wine are distributed and received.

This perspective also gives opportunity for the Spirit's work to be acknowledged in the Thanksgiving Prayer, as in HC2. In *BCP* this is explicit only in the Exhortation, which was read rarely during the service.[27]

Manual acts

The Liturgical Commission decided not to include rubrics in HC2 and HC3 about 'manual acts' with the bread and wine. But Note 14 on *APBA* page 164 states that "it is customary during the narrative of the Last Supper (commonly called the Words of Institution) for the priest to take hold of the bread during the words concerning the bread, and likewise the cup". Other possibilities exist, however.

In each Great Thanksgiving, the 'Words of Institution' is followed by a 'Therefore we ..." clause that expresses what we are 'doing':

> ... we celebrate, with this bread and this cup,
> his one perfect and sufficient sacrifice
> for the sins of the whole world.   (Second Order)

> We eat this bread and drink this cup
> to proclaim the death of the Lord.   (Third Order)

Given the Commission's use of the 'four-fold shape' and the approach taken to 'eucharistic sacrifice', these words are congruent with the presider lifting the bread and cup, a focal point in our offering of thanks. Another possibility, again optional, is to lift them at the end of the prayer during the "Blessing and honour ..." doxology, symbolising our "sacrifice of thanksgiving".

These actions are neither specified nor forbidden.[28]

---

27 Some argue that without the Spirit being invoked on the elements ('*epiclesis*), a eucharistic prayer is defective. But such a criticism would apply to most classical prayers, and raises issues about the validity of invoking the Spirit on things. Sinden cites the Eastern Orthodox theologian Alexander Schmeman to show that the East does not understand the Spirit's work in the Eucharist, '*epiclesis* in 'causality' terms, i.e. making a change in the elements due to invoking the Spirit: *When we meet for Worship*, 90.

28 Article XXVIII states that "The Sacrament of the Lord's Supper was not by Christ's ordinance reserved, carried about, lifted up, or worshipped." The association between 'lifted' and 'worshipped' (the doctrinally objectionable point) here bears no relation to lifting the elements in a 'four-fold shape' Eucharist.

The sign of the cross

Closely related to the idea of a 'moment' of consecration is use of the sign of the cross during the Thanksgiving Prayer. Specified to be done many times in the Sarum rite, it was omitted in *BCP*, but taken up again in the wake of the Oxford Movement. As with bowing at particular times in the Thanksgiving, it remains an unauthorised practice.[29] The following comments are offered, not to advocate or restrict use of the sign, but to inform principled practice.

1. *BCP* Holy Communion's provision for supplementary consecration implies that the institution narrative is the 'moment' of consecration. This also suggests that the bread and wine be signed at the words "This is ...".

2. HC2 and HC3 employ the 'four-fold shape', in which the central action is 'giving thanks'. Archbishop Keith Rayner would therefore make the sign of the cross when these words are said over the bread and the cup. If the sign is used, this seems to me the most appropriate position.

3. Some make the sign at "may be partakers of his body and blood" (or equivalent words). While this makes instinctive sense, it precedes the institution narrative, and concerns our 'partaking' of Christ, not the bread and wine of themselves.

4. In Thanksgiving 3, 'sanctify' refers to the elements themselves, though in reference to the Spirit's work. This suggests that the relevant action at this point may be to extend the hands over the elements rather than make the sign of the cross.

The elements of Holy Communion

Preparation customs: mixture, lavabo

The bread and wine are 'taken' and 'placed' on the Lord's Table by the priest (#14 in HC1, #26 in HC2, #18 in HC3), the first 'action' of the 'four-fold shape'. Neither *BCP*, *AAPB* or *APBA* associate words with this action, since it is distinct from the preceding 'offertory' and is a necessary preparation for the Great Thanksgiving.

A number of customs not mentioned in *BCP*, *AAPB* or *APBA* have come to be associated with the preparation, typically by servers assisting the presider. Whether or not they take place is a matter of local custom, with significant provisos:

- doctrinal ideas associated with them must be consonant with the rest of the service;
- how they are performed should avoid fussy, 'churchy' actions that mystify; and
- they should not imply that what happens 'up front' is all that matters, rather than the celebration embracing the assembly as a whole.

---

29   Gilbert Sinden, writing from an Anglo-Catholic perspective, comments in detail on these and related practices in *When we meet for Worship* Chapter Five, e.g. page 175 on genuflecting.

A little water is mixed with the wine in many places, meaning that two 'cruets' are provided: one for water, one for wine.[30] Sinden says that this practice "goes back to the time of our Lord when wine was never served unmixed with water" because it was a thick cordial. Liturgical actions originating from practical necessity typically attract a meaning: this 'commixture' came to be seen as symbolising the union of the humanity and deity of Christ, or the water mixed with blood that flowed from the crucified Christ's side (John 19.34). Today wine comes ready to drink, so diluting it is not needed, but as Sinden wryly states of such meanings, "there is no harm in such a thought".[31]

Having the hands of the presiding priest or bishop washed (*lavabo*) is another custom that re-emerged in the wake of the Oxford Movement. In the medieval mass, it symbolised the priest's need to be cleansed before handling the sacred elements. Today such hand-washing is associated with healthy practice, and should take place before all offerings are handled, and include all sacramental ministers.

The House of Bishops recommends using disinfectant gel rather than, or in addition to, water: see 'Occupational Health and Safety' below.

What sort of bread?

Note 13 on *APBA* page 164 restates the rubrics of BCP in modern terms: "It is sufficient that the bread be such as is normally eaten". From the 1552 edition on, ordinary leavened bread was customary Anglican usage, as in the Eastern and in most Protestant traditions, until the Oxford Movement saw the re-introduction of unleavened bread in the form of wafers.[32] This is an issue about which feelings can run high, but, as in *BCP* 1549, it has come to be widely accepted.[33] Unleavened bread can evoke

---

30 In medieval times this was seen as symbolising the humanity and deity of Christ. In 1890, the Bishop of Lincoln, Edward King, was brought before the Archbishop of Canterbury and assessors on eight charges related to liturgical practices arising from the Oxford Movement. One was 'commixture', present in *BCP* 1549 but omitted from then on. The 1899 Lambeth Opinions of the Archbishops of York and Canterbury, which arose from the trial, allowed it, provided no words are associated with it.

31 *When we meet for Worship*, 136–7. Sinden goes on to note that where two cruets are used, "it is hoped that [the priest] will not attempt to bless the water".

32 Referring to the wafers as 'hosts' is most unhelpful: apart from being 'churchy' language, this muddies the truth that *Christ* is the 'host' of the meal, which is the *Lord's* supper.

33 The rubrics at the end of Holy Communion in *BCP* (1549) state:
    It is meet that the bread prepared for the Communion, be made, through all this realm, after one sort and fashion: that is to say, unleavened, and round, as it was afore, but without all manner of print, and something more larger and thicker than it was, so that it may be aptly divided in divers pieces: and every one shall be divided in two pieces, at the least, or more, by the discretion of the minister, and so distributed.

This rubric was changed from 1552 to the one in 1662, but the 1899 Lambeth Opinions affirmed the 1549 rubric as a guiding principle.

the Passover background of the Last Supper, and having wafers on hand is practical, not least because, kept in an airtight container, they do not go mouldy.

Few wafers meet the requirements of the 1549 rubric, however, that they be "without all manner of print, and something more larger and thicker than it was", or of the Holy Communion Canon (General Synod 2001) #5 that "the bread offered must be wholesome". A principled way of meeting these requirements is, as in *BCP* 1549, for each wafer to be "divided in two pieces, at the least" before it is given. Communicants then receive broken bread, and the unhelpful sense of being given 'spiritual plastic' is avoided.

A loaf, perhaps baked by a parishioner, can be used to link God's creative activity in nature and the gospel, especially at harvest time. Note 13 on *APBA* page 164, begins, "The symbolism of one bread and one cup has great value. It is suggested that one loaf of bread and one chalice of wine only be placed on the table for the Great Thanksgiving." (NB: This excludes the loaf being cut into small pieces before the service.) When the loaf is too large to be consumed, a slice can be cut in the middle and placed on the paten before the Thanksgiving begins, the rest being set aside. The slice should be large enough to be seen by the people at the breaking of the bread, and not so fresh that it is difficult to break for distribution: being a day or two old helps this.

The public breaking of the bread takes place as the third action of the Eucharist. A 'badge' sized wafer (the 'priest's wafer') is often broken at this point (the 'fraction') and then administered to the priest and a few others. This has the unfortunate consequence of the bread distributed being distinct from the bread broken at the third action. Large wafers (a 45rpm record or a CDROM size) are available which are sufficient for thirty or so communicants, and can be 'stacked'. Using such bread allows both the fraction to be seen by all, and each communicant to receive bread broken as part of the eucharistic action.

Some communicants may not be able to tolerate bread containing gluten. The presider needs to know when any are present, and so include gluten-free bread in the 'taking' (#14 in HC1, #26 in HC3, #18 in HC3). Additionally, those who administer the bread need to know to whom gluten-free bread is to be given, a matter of good pastoral relationships. Alternatively, all the bread used can be gluten-free.[34]

---

34 In parts of the Anglican Communion, bread and wine as known in the West are not available, or expensive. On these issues see *Eucharistic Food and Drink*. A report of the *Inter-Anglican Liturgical Consultation* to the [2007] *Anglican Consultative Council*, available at https://www.anglicancommunion.org/resources/document-library.aspx?subject=Liturgy+and+Worship&language=English

What sort of wine?

In the scriptures, wine is viewed in contrasting ways. On the one hand, it is dangerous to health, and symbolises the Lord bringing disaster on the unfaithful (e.g. Proverbs 20.1; 23.31; Psalms 60.3; 75.8). On the other hand, it "makes the heart glad" and symbolises joy and feasting (e.g. Psalms 4.7; 104.15). This paradoxical usage points up that wine is the fruit of decay, undergirding the core meaning of the Eucharist, that it is through the Lord's fruitful death that new life comes.

What colour wine is more fitting – red or white? Red wine runs the risk of encouraging 'literal' ideas about Christ's blood. White wine is therefore in general use in the Eastern churches. In the Western Church, in the wake of the 1215 transubstantiation decision, the wine was only given to clergy: the Second Vatican Council (1962–65) made the cup available again to others, with white wine in general use.[35] At the Reformation, when the cup was restored to all communicants (Article XXX) red wine, typically port, came into use, but Anglican formularies do not specify the colour.[36]

Unfermented grape juice is used in some places, but *BCP* and the Holy Communion Canon (General Synod 2001) stipulate that wine "of good quality" be used, defined as "the fermented juice of the grape". What then of communicants for whom alcohol is a problem? As with gluten-intolerant people, while the presider is likely to be aware of those affected, the cup may be administered by another minister. A straightforward approach is for communicants who cannot drink alcohol to take the cup, hold it as the words of administration are said, but not drink from it. (This also protects the communicant's privacy.) Such 'spiritual communion' is genuine sacramental participation in Christ (see Note 4 on *APBA* page 693).

Some advocate the use of de-alcoholised wine, though placing this in a separate vessel muddies the symbolism of 'one cup' (Note 13 on *APBA* page 164), and such wine still contains minute quantities of alcohol. People who are taking medications, particularly strong antibiotics, may become ill by receiving de-alcoholised wine.

---

35 Orvieto Cathedral was erected by order of Pope Urban IV to commemorate the 'miracle of Bolsena'. After the definition of 'transubstantiation' in 1215, a troubled Bolsena priest in 1263 found a consecrated wafer bleeding onto the cloth beneath, the corporal, which is now held in an Orvieto Cathedral chapel. The story is told by pictures set up high, with Latin text, but no other information was provided when I visited in 1989: for visitors, the story would seem to have passed into history. But for locals, the corporal is paraded around the city with much fanfare on Corpus Christi, the Thursday after Trinity Sunday.

36 Reformation era priests were instructed to ensure that sufficient wine was provided for all to communicate, since medieval chalices were typically tiny, holding only enough for the priest to sip. Conversely, the wine being offered to all raised the risk of drunkenness – and can still do so, not least in schools and colleges.

Why bread *and* wine ('both kinds')?

Today the Holy Communion is celebrated weekly in most Anglican congregations, with an 'open table' ethos of hospitality. Ecumenical progress has allowed communicants from other Christian traditions to receive as guests at an Anglican service, and baptised children are admitted to communion in many places. This welcome generosity runs the danger, however, of the Eucharist being seen as only a 'fellowship meal', rather than the sacrament of Christ's life-giving death. Bread by itself symbolises the 'staff of life': 'breaking bread' is synonymous with eating in peace. Wine by itself a symbol of celebration, though the dangers of its over-use are well-known. When body and blood are conjoined, they sustain life; when separated, however, death is in view. As Article XXVII begins,

> The Supper of the Lord is not only a sign of the love that Christians ought to have among themselves one to another; but rather is a Sacrament of our Redemption by Christ's death ...

The wonder of Holy Communion is that bread and wine, signifying the body and blood of Christ, when used together yet separately, give us access to the "benefits of his passion". The Eucharist is a sacrament of fruitful death: that is why communicants being offered 'both kinds' matters, whatever pastoral adjustments may be needed.[37]

The breaking of the bread

What does the bread-breaking symbolise?

In the New Testament, the phrase 'body of Christ' can refer to the physical body of Jesus (Matthew 26.12; 27.58–9), to the Church (1 Corinthians 12.12–13, 27; Ephesians 4.12) and to the bread of Holy Communion. Paul sees the breaking of the bread as weaving together these various meanings: "We who are many are one body in Christ, for we all share in the one bread" (I Corinthians 10.17).

In *The Didache* ('Teaching', dated between 70 and 130AD) a prayer runs, "As this broken bread was once many grains, which have been gathered together and made one, so may your church be gathered from the ends of the earth into your kingdom" (an alternative at #28 in HC2). This points to the hope of full unity in Christ, contrasted with the scattered nature of this age (1 Corinthians 11.26).

The breaking of the bread thus points to the privilege of sharing in the body and blood of Christ, as members of his body, and to acknowledging the brokenness of our world and ourselves in the hope of Christ's return. As Richardson and Varcoe write,

---

[37] The Holy Communion Canon 2001 (4) stipulates that "The sacrament must normally be offered separately in both kinds to every communicant." 'Normally' permits of appropriate pastoral adjustments.

the faithful receive the benefits of Christ's sacrifice, and in turn offer themselves in worship to God. Here our Lord takes us and blesses us, breaks and remakes us. Then he sends us out in renewed service to the world for which he died.[38]

A practical note

In Holy Communion (*BCP* and First Order), the bread is broken during the words of institution. In HC2 and HC3, however, based on the 'four-fold shape', the bread is broken as the third eucharistic action, the 'fraction'.

Perhaps recalling *BCP*, or thinking that the Lord's Supper repeats the Last Supper, or just not understanding the 'four-fold shape', some clergy when presiding at HC2 'crack' the bread during the words of institution, before breaking it properly at the 'fraction'. If you do this, please reconsider.

The Agnus Dei – when is it appropriate?

It is devotionally understandable to link the death of Jesus with the breaking of the bread: choruses such as 'Broken for me' reinforce this notion. But, in accordance with prophecy, Jesus' body was not broken (John 19.36). More seriously, the idea that in the breaking of the bread the risen and exalted Lord Jesus is somehow 'broken' again contradicts the 'once-for-all' achievement of his death (Hebrews 7.27; 9.12, 26–28; 10.2, 10).

Agnus Dei is the Latin name of the ancient hymn, "Lamb of God … ". In *BCP* 1549 it was provided as an anthem during the administration of communion. From 1552 it was removed, though its petition occurs in the *Gloria*.[39] HC2 returns the *Agnus Dei* to the 1549 position as a communion anthem, translated "Jesus, Lamb of God …".

Agnus Dei is fittingly sung as those who administer the sacrament themselves receive. But saying or singing it while the bread is broken fosters the spiritually disastrous idea that the fraction symbolises Christ's being broken again.

When bread or wine is insufficient

What if bread or wine run out? *BCP* 1662 assumes that consecration takes place when the words of institution are recited, requiring 'supplementary consecration' by repeating the appropriate words. While understandable in the context of Restoration debates, it interrupts the administration of communion, and in a 'four-fold shape' rite it fragments the eucharistic prayer.

---

38   *A Practical Commentary*, 47.
39   Allowing the *Agnus Dei* "to be sung immediately after the consecration of the elements at a celebration of the holy communion" was another charge against Bishop King. The Lambeth Opinions, noting that it was impossible to regulate hymn choices, allowed the *Agnus Dei* as a hymn during communion. But this is distinct from the fraction, which in *BCP* had already taken place in the Prayer of Consecration.

APBA is (deliberately) silent on the matter, but given the Constitution, the provisions of *BCP* apply. If it seems that the bread or wine might run out, some liturgists recommend that more be added before this happens. This avoids interrupting the eucharistic action as a whole, and associates the additional bread or wine with that over which thanks has been given. Gilbert Sinden offers wise words:

> It is always better for the priest to consecrate too much bread and/or wine than too little: the peculiarly Anglican provision for supplementary consecration ought never to be required; its theological and liturgical legitimacy is open to serious question.[40]

Sensitive issues in administering Holy Communion

The words of administration

For centuries before the Reformation only clergy received both bread and wine. Other communicants usually had the bread placed on their tongue, lest it be soiled, but were not offered the cup, lest the wine be spilled. This emphasis on the objective truth of the sacrament also encouraged a passive attitude: the grace offered was felt to work 'automatically'. The English Reformers sought to balance this by emphasising the importance of active faith, and the subjective truth of its involving personal encounter with Christ.[41]

The rubrics of *BCP* direct the minister to deliver the bread and cup "into their hands", so that each takes an active part in receiving. Such 'subjective' reception of the body and blood of Christ is 'by faith' (Article XXVIII). Correspondingly, receiving the holy communion without faith is spiritually dangerous (Article XXIX, citing 1 Corinthians 11.27–32).

NB: Some communicants may wish to have the bread placed on their tongue, or have the minister hold the cup. These wishes are to be respected, but not imposed: where communicants are likely to request them, those who minister the bread and cup need to be trained both to identify the request, and meet it respectfully.

From BCP 1559 onwards, the words of administration combine 'objective' giving and 'subjective' taking, of actively feeding on Christ and giving thanks:[42]

---

40   *When we meet for Worship*, 173.
41   Behind this issue lie the concepts *ex opere operato* (by the deed done) and *ex opere operantis* (by the deed of the doer) which developed in scholastic theology: see footnote 9 on page 170 of this book.
42   The 1549 Holy Communion service, reflecting Sarum, had the first (objective) sentence only. The 1552 service, reacting against medieval abuses, had the second (subjective) sentence only. It was the wisdom of Queen Elizabeth (I) to see both sentences combined in the 1559 edition, continued in 1604 and 1662.

> The Body of our Lord Jesus Christ, which was given for thee, preserve thy body and soul unto everlasting life. Take and eat this in remembrance that Christ died for thee, and feed on him in thy heart by faith with thanksgiving.

In each Holy Communion rite in *APBA* these words remain the standard form (#26, page 113; #29, page 142; #20, page 178; #26, page 672; #17, page 687; #17e, page 728). Given their length, however, they are commonly said while giving the bread or wine to two communicants. If both hear the full words, the intended objective / subjective pairing is met, but in practice this has proved to be awkward. So shorter (objective) words of administration are provided in HC2 and HC3, in each case preceded by 'subjective' words of introduction, and concluded with 'Amen':

Second Order
> [The gifts of God for the people of God]
> Come, let us take this holy sacrament of the body and blood of Christ in remembrance that he died for us, and feed on him in our hearts by faith with thanksgiving.
>
> The body of Christ (the bread of heaven) keep you in eternal life. Amen.
> The blood of Christ (the cup of salvation) keep you in eternal life. Amen.

Third Order
> Draw near with faith, to feed on Christ in your hearts with thanksgiving:
>
> The body of Christ keep you in eternal life. Amen.
> The blood of Christ keep you in eternal life. Amen.

In the 1993 'trial use' booklet the words of administration were "The body of Christ, the bread of heaven. Amen" and "The blood of Christ, the cup of salvation. Amen". Alluding to John 6.31–58 and Psalm 116.13, these derive from the *Apostolic Tradition* of Hippolytus. Responses, however, saw these forms as too 'objective' (and ungrammatical). So in the 1995 draft book the familiar *AAPB* words were printed: "The body / blood of Christ keep you in eternal life. Amen."

The two sets were combined by General Synod: as well as enriching their meaning, the longer forms 'slow down' the administration, which is helpful in giving the cup. When the shorter words are used, it is important that the appropriate invitation is given first, so that both the subjective and objective aspects of Holy Communion are acknowledged.

NB: "The body / blood of Christ" is not a form for administering communion authorised by General Synod for use in the Anglican Church of Australia.

Receiving communion

'Worthy reception'?

Paul warned self-satisfied Corinthian Christians not to "eat the bread or drink the cup of the Lord in an unworthy manner ... For all who eat and drink without discerning the body, eat and drink judgment against themselves" (I Corinthians 11.27–29). This is often seen as requiring participants to be 'worthy', whether by being 'good', or holding correct doctrine.

But Paul's point was the exact opposite. 'Unworthy' eating or drinking happens when we come to the Eucharist as if we are already well-fed, 'unbroken' people. 'Worthy reception' means acknowledging our brokenness before God, both personal and communal – yet still coming, in faith and hope.

Further, "discerning the body" is not about having enough faith to see the bread as Christ's body, but realising that we are part of Christ's body, the Church, whatever its faults and oddities. That is why Communion services in the Anglican tradition include a general confession and absolution: Christ came to call sinners, not the righteous (Matthew 9.13; Mark 2.17; Luke 5.32).

Standing, kneeling, sitting?

The presider first administers communion to him / herself, standing. In *BCP* HC and HC1, however, the people receive kneeling: this was controversial at the time, since some took it to imply adoration of the sacrament, to which the 'Black Rubric' responded.[43] Other Reformers had communicants sit around tables, but the liturgically conservative Cranmer retained kneeling, as signifying humility. Communion rails were introduced in 1633 (to keep animals away from the holy table): until fairly recently, kneeling to receive communion was standard practice across the Anglican Communion.

No mention of a posture to receive is made in HC2 and HC3, and in some church buildings there is no longer a 'communion rail'. Standing to receive is now widely accepted, while in some contexts people are gathered around tables, and thus sit to receive. When hundreds are present, or at a parish camp or beside a sick-bed, practical necessity will govern the posture for receiving.

The place and posture adopted to receive holy communion – standing, kneeling at a communion rail, sitting in a pew or wheelchair, lying down in bed – is of itself a thing indifferent. Several issues arise in pastoral practice, however.

---

43   See footnote 13 on page 223 of this book. Note 5 on *APBA* page 117 and Note 4 on *APBA* page 822 also relate to this matter..

- Sustaining a corporate sense matters: we receive as a congregation, mortals 'levelled out' in Christ's presence. The traditional practice of people of varied occupations, ages and lifestyles kneeling alongside one another evokes a strong sense of communal humility in Christ. Large numbers may mean that several 'stations' are used (for both bread and wine), with communicants standing to receive. A reverent communal ethos is encouraged by unobtrusive directions and suitable music.
- Provision for kneeling to receive should continue, respecting the spiritual heritage of each communicant. In modern buildings, this can be facilitated by providing a short 'communion rail' next to a step.
- Where a communicant cannot move from their seat to receive, the bread and wine should be to be brought to them, without hurry or fuss.
- In a household setting, communicants sitting around the dinner table can evoke both the similarities and differences between meal-times and the Eucharist: how the different thanksgivings offered 'speak' to one another, for example.
- The 'spirituality' of administration matters. Each minister needs to show respect in the way the bread or cup is given to each recipient, so they can receive the holy communion with reverent thanksgiving. Some will expect the minister to make eye contact, for example; some may wish only the minister to hold the cup. Care with hygiene is important here (see further below).

When should ordained ministers receive?

The rubrics of *BCP* stipulate that all ordained ministers receive first, as does the Holy Communion Canon (2001) #3. In *APBA*, the same provision is made in HC1 #26, is implicit in HC2 #29, but no direction is given in HC3.

It feels 'natural' to most priests to receive first, but does it matter? Any idea of 'my clergy rights' to receive first is not according to the mind of Christ. Some clergy, influenced by democratic ideals, prefer to receive last, after all have communicated. Yet there is good theological reason behind the presider, and those who will minister the sacrament, receiving first. Sharing any means of grace without having received it raises questions about a person's dependence on God's enabling. Gratitude, humility and thankfulness should characterise each communicant who receives the sacrament of Christ's self-giving, especially those with the humbling privilege of sharing it.

Should only priests administer the bread?

Administration is often shared between the presider and other ministers. Though it is common for the priest to distribute the bread, this is not essential. As Gilbert Sinden writes,

> There is a rather curious Anglican notion that the 'junior' minister should always distribute the chalice ...
>
> Where the 'junior' minister is a lay person ... it is obviously better for them and more courteous to the congregation if they distribute the bread of the Eucharist rather than the cup.[44]

Further, if sharing the bread is seen as the prerogative of the presiding priest as 'senior' minister, the bread comes across as more important than the wine. This implies that the bread and wine have different sacramental significance: the scholastic justification for communicants receiving the bread only was that the substance of blood is included in the substance of the body, for example.

It is thus desirable that the distribution of 'both kinds', wine and bread, is shared across all those authorised to administer Holy Communion.

Occupational Health and Safety in the Eucharist

Communicants who are ill should be sensitive to the danger of others becoming infected by them, e.g. by coughing, shaking hands or hugging. Behind this is the question as to whether they should be at church at all, and if so, whether they should share the Peace and receive communion. (A person who is ill, including the presider, must stand side from distributing communion or taking part in the laying on of hands.) Most regular worshippers are aware of these issues, but sharing the common cup raises health concerns for many.[45]

Hygiene in distributing the elements is important, and pandemics have increased the awareness in the community of health issues. Being over-scrupulous over cleanliness is unhelpful, but lack of attention to good hygiene puts obstacles in the way of people receiving naturally, and brings the gospel into disrepute.

Clean vessels

All vessels that hold bread, wine, water or oil must be clean, and kept clean. Storing wafer bread and alcoholic wine in water-tight containers for short periods of time is sufficient to keep them fresh and in healthy condition. But vessels containing water must be emptied after use, and fresh water supplied for each service.

---

44   *When we meet for Worship*, 161.
45   This discussion draws on work done for *IALC* on medical issues.

Cups (chalices) used for administering the wine are to be made of metal, not wood or pottery, washed thoroughly, and rinsed in very hot water, after each use.

Clean hands

The Greeting of Peace gives ready opportunity for infection to be transmitted among those present, especially when hand-shaking is augmented by hugging. In some cicumstances, such as on a cruise ship or during a pandemic, the greeting should be communicated verbally, without people touching one another.

The Australian House of Bishops recommends that, before the elements are prepared, disinfectant gel – not just a few drops of water – be used to cleanse the hands of all who will administer the bread or wine, not just the presider.

A positive symbol of this shared ministry is the presider, having had her/his hands washed and disinfected, cleansing the hands of each one who will administer the sacrament.

Similar considerations apply to anyone who will lay on hands in association with the administration of communion, e.g. during prayers for healing.

Cleaning the cup

Medical research has shown that the traditional practice of the (metal) cup being wiped with a close-weaved cloth – linen is ideal – after each communicant, when alcoholic wine is used, does not transmit infection.

The minister needs to wipe both the inside and the outside of the cup, and should rotate slightly the part of the cloth used after each wipe, and change the cloth itself when it is soiled – typically after the cup has been adminstered to 25 or so communicants. Cloths used for wiping the cup must be washed after each use with very hot water, and rinsed thoroughly.

Intinction

Some communicants wish to receive by 'intinction', that is, by dipping the bread in the wine. (For this to work, it must be wafer bread: regular bread will fall apart in the wine.) The practice is not supported by Anglican formularies, since it might appear not to fulfil Christ's command to "drink this cup". But neither is it banned, and it has become accepted in some places. There are, however, significant health risks in doing so, since the recipient's fingers are likely to touch the wine.

Where a person wants to receive by intinction, the practice recommended by the Australian House of Bishops is that the communicant give the bread to the minister of the cup, who touches it in the wine, and returns it to them. Being able to do this effectively may need some practice by the minister.

Conclusion

You do not have to agree with everything written here. The aim of this chapter has been to show why doctrinal, liturgical and pastorally sensitive aspects of *APBA*'s services of Holy Communion are what they are.

Written text like this can provide scholarly information and put forward helpful suggestions. But only real people in real places with real scriptures, hymns, prayers, wine and bread can celebrate "The Holy Communion, also called the Eucharist and the Lord's Supper".

The five chapters that follow apply the theological and liturgical perspectives of this and the preceding chapter to the range of eucharistic services in *APBA*, and resources issued by the Liturgical Commission in the quarter century since *APBA* was published.

Chapter Fifteen

Celebrating Holy Communion using First Order

The structure of the service

BCP Holy Communion remains the 'classic' Anglican eucharistic rite, but its structure and ethos is quite different to modern services. HC1 represents a new 'translation' of the *BCP* rite, with minor adjustments, that is closer to the original than the equivalent service in *AAPB*.

Though modern English is used throughout HC1, General Note 4, *APBA* page x, provides for traditional translations to be used when sung.

The service in outline

Outlining HC1 is perhaps pointless: as in *BCP*, each part flows onto the next, with few optional elements. But setting it out helps people familiar with HC2 who encounter HC1. **Bold italics** identify major differences from HC2 and HC3.

Gathering in God's Name	[Hymn]
	Greeting
	[Sentence]
	Prayer of Preparation
	Ten Commandments / Two Commandments
	Collect
The Ministry of the Word	Reading(s) other than the Gospel
	[Psalm, hymn or canticle]
	Gospel reading
	Sermon (if not later)
	Nicene Creed
	Sermon (if not earlier)
The Offertory	Sentences
	Collection of alms and offerings
	Placing of bread and wine

The Prayers	[Biddings]
	The Intercessions
	[Hymn]
Preparation for the Lord's Supper	**[Exhortations]**
	Invitation
	Confession and Absolution
The Lord's Supper	**Words of Assurance**
	Preface, *Sanctus*
	Prayer of Approach
	Prayer of Consecration
	Administration of communion
	[*Supplementary consecration*]
	Covering of remaining elements.
After Communion	Lord's Prayer
	Prayer of Oblation or Thanksgiving
	Glory to God (Gloria)
	Blessing
	Consumption of remaining elements.

Distinctive elements and ethos

- The (edited) Ten Commandments near the beginning, with distinctive responses
- The place and meaning of the Offertory (and no Greeting of Peace)
- The form and ethos of the Intercessions
- *BCP*-based Preparation for the Lord's Supper
- The Words of Assurance and Prayer of Approach bracketing 'Lift up your hearts'
- The use of 'manual acts' during the Prayer of Consecration, identified as such
- 'Glory to God' at the conclusion, rather than as an opening Hymn of Praise

HC1 and a Eucharist shaped by the Liturgical Movement differ widely. Yet HC1 carries a pervasive ethos of 'godly quietness', of reverence towards God, "King of kings, Lord of lords, the only Ruler of princes". Like *BCP*, HC1 focuses on Christ's saving passion: to 'celebrate' the Eucharist means that all is done 'decently and in order'. To 'celebrate' in today's culture, however, tends to focus more on the joy of Christ's presence, in an ethos of friendly inclusion. Further, in *BCP* and HC1, 'highlights' are followed by 'declines' in feel: the effect is one of 'waves' that slowly build, until finally 'released' in the Hymn of Praise, the *Gloria*, our 'sacrifice of praise and thanksgiving'. The joy in Christ is real and deep, but restrained.

Taking these differences of structure and ethos into account is especially important for clergy who usually preside at HC2, and to a lesser extent HC3.

Commentary

#1–6   Gathering in God's Name

BCP HC begins with the priest saying the Lord's Prayer quietly. HC1 assumes that the congregation expects a public opening, hence the provision for a "psalm, hymn or anthem", a greeting (#2) and "sentence of scripture appropriate to the day" (#3).

NB: Psalm 95 began the Sarum mass. Cranmer transferred it to begin the new Sunday service of Morning Prayer, Litany and Holy Communion. This Psalm may be thus appropriate to begin HC1. The *BCP* rubrics about intending communicants giving notice, the exclusion of immoral and malicious people, and how the Table is set, omitted from *APBA*, were updated by the 'Holy Communion Canon 2001' of General Synod.

#1   The rubric "The priest may begin the service at …" clarifies the much-debated 'north side' issue of *BCP*'s opening rubrics, now eased by the widespread adoption of the 'westward' position.

#2   On the origins of this greeting and response, see pages 241–242 in this book.

#4   *The Prayer of Preparation* ('Collect for Purity'): see pages 239–241 in this book.

#5   *The Ten Commandments*

Reading the Ten Commandments ('Decalogue', Exodus 20.1–17) is a distinctive aspect of HC1. Cranmer placed them here in 1552 to enable the congregation to first celebrate the First / Old Covenant, before coming to celebrate the New.

Reciting the Decalogue is often seen as an act of penitence, but in *BCP* this had already taken place in Morning Prayer: repentance as preparation to receive holy communion comes later. Reciting the Commandments here is an act of covenant commitment, as the responses show: not "forgive" us, but "incline our hearts to keep this law". The final response, "write your law in our hearts by your Holy Spirit", echoes the promise of the 'new covenant' (Jeremiah 31.31–33).

The text is shortened to avoid misunderstandings about what God's 'jealousy' (2) and 'hold guilty' mean (3); about six-day literalism (4: Deuteronomy 6.14–15 gives celebrating freedom as a motive for sabbath-keeping); seeing land as a reward for family loyalty (5); and husbands 'owning' women (10). A sobering example of the need for ongoing interpretation and re-reception of the scriptures …

Reading Jesus' summary of the Law (Matthew 22.37-40) as an alternative to the Decalogue was proposed by Archbishop William Laud in his 1637 revision for Scotland. Taken up in the 1927-28 Deposited book, it has been adopted in most modern Anglican books, but is typically used to introduce the confession of sins, as in HC2 and HC3. In HC1 the 'two commandments' alternative is not linked to confession: there is nothing 'wrong' with this, but it does not convey the sense of covenant renewal that responding to the recitation of the Decalogue enacts.

#6 *The Collect*

On this form of prayer, see pages 113-117 in this book.

On the location of the Collect in the service, see page 279 in this book.

In *BCP* the Collect is preceded by a collect for the sovereign, omitted in *APBA*.

#7-12 **The Ministry of the Word**

Chapter Three considers this Ministry, and the pattern of readings in *APBA*.

#7 *BCP* only provides for an Epistle, since readings from each Testament, and psalms, have been heard in Morning Prayer. HC1 is a service in its own right, so provision is made for further readings, and a "psalm, hymn or canticle". This also allows the full set of four readings provided in *APBA* to be used.

The words introducing each reading are those of *BCP*, and are not optional. The words following each reading are taken from HC2, and are optional.

On "Hear the word of the Lord", see page 243 in this book.

#8 Sometimes this is called the 'gradual hymn', from the custom of the Epistle and Gospel being read from different sides of the sanctuary, meaning the reader had to go up and down steps (*gradus* in Latin). This rarely applies today: a useful contemporary form of words is "We sing hymn NN to welcome the Gospel".

#9 The rubric states that "The people stand for the Gospel", as in *BCP*.

On standing for the Gospel, see pages 243-244 in this book.

#10, 12 In *BCP*, the Sermon follows the Notices and Nicene Creed, distancing it from the readings. HC1 thus provides for it to precede (#10) or follow (#12) the Creed. Note 3, page 117, offers a variety of positions for Notices, including at this point.

#11 On the translation of the Nicene Creed, see Note 1, 'Common Forms', *APBA* pages 820-821.

On the place of creeds in liturgy, see page 125 in this book.

On the custom of turning to the front for the Creed see page 138 in this book.

#13–14 The Offertory

The 'Offertory' in *BCP* refers to the "alms and other gifts" of the people being received as appropriate sentences of scripture are read aloud. Singing as the collection is made has become commonplace, but hearing these sentences has an impressive effect.

Does the 'offertory' include bringing up the bread and wine? The rubric in *BCP* after the collection requires the priest, "when there is a Communion", to place sufficient bread and wine on the holy table, on which the alms have just been put. If there is no Communion, then five prayers, printed after the blessing, are said "after the offertory". This implies that the collection of alms, and the preparation of the elements, are separate actions. This interpretation was disputed as the Oxford Movement developed: the practical effect was to have the bread and wine brought up with or after the collection.[1]

The Liturgical Commission's response to this debate is careful. On the one hand, the final offertory sentences move beyond giving money to commending "a sacrifice of thanksgiving", alluding to the eucharistic action, and both rubrics are placed in the same numbered set. On the other hand, the 'offertory' is not in any sense depicted as our offering bread and wine to God, who then returns them to us transformed (the objectionable point).

NB: In HC2 and HC3 the bread and wine are 'taken' much later in the service, after the Greeting of Peace. Clergy used to these rites need to ensure that when presiding at HC1 the bread and wine are made ready at this earlier point, or nothing will be at hand for the Great Thanksgiving.

#15–16 The Prayers

The ethos of HC1

As in *BCP*, these take the form of a single prayer of intercession offered by 'the minister'. In today's 'democratic' culture this is likely to be experienced as formal and clerical, though its advantage is that it carries an ethos of the intercessions as 'common prayer'. Note 4, *APBA* page 117, provides for a response to be made after each section: this is designed to bridge this cultural divide somewhat. Using another pattern of intercession is not forbidden, but failing to respect the ethos of HC1 may be a spiritual hindrance to participants.

The prayer may be preceded by biddings of "special prayers and thanksgivings". Rather than giving thanks or praying for particular topics directly, they are presumed

---

1   For full discussion, see Colin Buchanan, *The End of the Offertory. An Anglican Study*. Grove Liturgy Series 14 (Bramcote, Notts: Grove, 1978). By 'end' here is meant its purpose.

to be taken up as the single prayer is offered. The use of 'biddings' reflects the sense of 'reserve' in Anglo-Celtic cultures, and has the benefit of preserving personal privacy, which can be invaded when public intercessions go into too much detail about those for whom prayer is offered.

The topics for prayer

The introduction asks for prayer for "the Church throughout the world", a gentler version of "the Church militant here on earth" of *BCP*. The reference in the prayer to "the universal Church" thus refers to the Church 'visible' rather than 'mystical'.

The prayer opens by asking that "our alms and oblations", where present, may be received along with our prayers "which we offer to your divine majesty": explicit mention of the bread or wine is not made. It then proceeds with intercessions for a range of topics, derived in part from 1 Timothy 2.1–2:

- the nations and their rulers, notably "our Queen Elizabeth II" and her representatives in this land. Such prayer for the sovereign means interceding for the whole 'commonwealth' of administration and government represented in the monarch, not so much for Elizabeth Windsor as an individual;
- the universal Church;
- "all bishops and other ministers", not just Anglican ones;
- "all your people" to be given grace, receive God's word, and live holy and just lives; and
- "all who in this transitory life are in trouble, sorrow, need, sickness or any other adversity", a sensitive and comprehensive list from *BCP*.

The faithful departed

The prayer concludes with what seems to be thanksgiving for the faithful departed. In the First Testament, explicit intercession is rare, but "blessing God" for something or someone is commonplace, and is how they are blessed: the *berakah* structure of Jewish prayer: see pages 110, 123–124 in this book.

"We bless your holy name" is a strong *berakah* form: "holy name" speaks of the whole divine nature and being. Blessing God "for all your servants who have departed this life in the faith of Christ" thus does more than give thanks for them. They are already "partakers of [God's] heavenly kingdom", so interceding for them is pointless, or dangerous if it is thought that our prayers can change a person's standing before God. The prayer here avoids this, but offers more than thanking God for the faithful departed: "we leave them in God's care" might be a modern way of understanding this.

#17-20 Preparation for the Lord's Supper

The 'Preparation' has three parts: exhortations, confession and absolution, and leads into the 'Words of Assurance' that open the Lord's Supper.

#17 *BCP* provides three 'Exhortations': one as notice of a forthcoming celebration of the Holy Communion; one when the priest "shall see the people negligent to come to the holy Communion"; and one to be read at this point in every Holy Communion service.[2] All have long ceased to be used except on rare occasions.

The Liturgical Commission, having resolved to include First Order Sunday services, agreed to make them closer to *BCP* than their *AAPB* equivalents. The first Exhortation is new, based closely on the third Exhortation in *BCP*, with its citation of 1 Corinthians 11.28-29 and welcome emphasis on thanksgiving. The second is the Exhortation included in *AAPB* at this point: this has the costly love of God as its keynote, lightens *BCP*'s emphasis on repentance and self-examination, and omits its teaching about the benefits of the Eucharist.

#18 "You who truly ..." is always read. A 'translation' of *BCP*, this – and the following confession and absolution – retains its word-pairs: "truly and earnestly", "love and charity", "following ... walking", "wrath and indignation", "serve and please", "confirm and strengthen". These pairings work well in an oral culture – if you miss one, your ear catches the other – and deepen the meaning, as one image engages with another: see page 35 in this book.

Moreover, this address, much-loved by traditional Anglicans, covers the future as well as past and present tenses of Christian life: communicants are to confess sins past, sustain present neighbourly good relations, and "intend to live a new life".

#19 The 'general confession' follows. Such a confession is not in the first place about confessing my individual sins, but our being caught up in the disordered 'cussedness' of this world, the 'corporate' sin of our locale, nation and the human race as a whole. In this sense, 'general confession' comes close to lament. The text, based on *BCP*, is one of the strongest forms of confession in *APBA*. However, "the remembrance of them is grievous unto us; the burden of them

---

2   These Exhortations, composed at the first stage of what would become *BCP*, the 1548 'Order of Communion', show how the Reformers (1549 and 1552), 'establishers' (1559 and 1604) and Restorers (1662) understood the doctrinal and spiritual dimensions of Holy Communion.
    The first is significant for its reference to communicants, whose conscience cannot be quieted by personal reflection and general confession, making a private confession of sins to a "discreet and learned Minister of God's Word": in *APBA* this is taken up in 'Reconciliation of a Penitent' (pages 773-778).

is intolerable" (*BCP*) is omitted. To my mind this omission, made by the Liturgical Commission in the draft book, was unfortunate, though it is used as the response in Confession 4 on *APBA* page 200.

Conversely, the *BCP* line, "provoking most justly your wrath and indignation against us", not included in the draft book, was put back in during the General Synod debate. The Liturgical Commission had removed the line because the doctrine of God implied is questionable.

#20 Unlike the 'declarative' form in Morning & Evening Prayer, this absolution pronounces God's saving work in unfolding verbs: "have mercy on you" (in our weakness); "pardon and deliver you" (from our sins); "confirm and strengthen you" (for our earthly living), and "keep you in eternal life".

#21-28 The Lord's Supper

#21 These 'Words of Assurance' make the transition from confession and absolution to invitation. In *BCP* they are termed 'Comfortable Words', 'comfort' in its old sense of strengthening (*con* + *forte* in Latin).

The final 'word' takes us to Christ's "perfect offering [propitiation, *BCP*] for our sins", now as our "advocate with the Father". On the one hand, this contrasts with the Council of Trent's teaching that the Eucharist is a "propitiary sacrifice": see pages 229-230 in this book. On the other hand, it points away from Christ's past to his *present* work "with the Father" – to which heavenly Advocate we are now called to "Lift up your hearts!" *Sursum corda!* – "up, hearts!" – has a strong sense of exuberance.[3] This lovely conjunction of 1 John 2.1-2 and the *Sanctus* also meant that Sarum's "The Lord be with you" was omitted.

#22-23 For those used to HC2 and HC3, the Preface is abrupt: it is only filled out for Principal Festivals and saints' days. HC1 continues *BCP* with minor word changes: 'Holy Father', omitted in *BCP* on Trinity Sunday, is left out, and 'Almighty' becomes 'Mighty Creator' (not quite the same as 'El-Shaddai).

#24 *The Prayer of Approach ('Humble Access')*: see pages 243-246 in this book.
The rubric says the priest kneels at the Lord's Table: this assumes that after the offertory s/he has remained close to the Table, or moved there after the prayers. It also states, as in *BCP*, in which low literacy levels are assumed, that the priest reads the prayer "in the name of all who to receive the communion". Literacy

---

[3] *Sursum corda* continues to be used in art and poetry. A striking example is its use on the front of the La Sagrada Familia church in Barcelona: the eye is drawn above the incarnation scene, through *Sursum corda* to *Sanctus Sanctus Sanctus* ('Holy, holy, holy'), to the heavens.

is rarely an issue for those using this service, but the priest alone reading this prayer fits the ethos of HC1, though as in HC2, the congregation may join in.

#25 *The Prayer of Consecration*

The rubric says nothing about the priest's position at the Lord's Table, thus side-stepping the 'north end / eastward position' debates. Apart from its opening ("All glory to you") being more positive than *BCP* ("Almighty God"), the prayer is identical to *BCP*, including 'manual acts': see page 248 in this book. The 'Amen', said by all, draws the whole congregation into the prayer.

#26 *The administration of holy communion*

Chapter Fourteen above covers liturgical and practical issues, including ministers receiving first, modes and words of administration, and recipients kneeling.

#27 On 'supplementary consecration', see page 254-255 in this book.

#28 This follows *BCP*: its effect is to have consecrated bread and / or wine left on the Lord's Table during the prayers which follow, potentially associating them with the 'prayer of oblation' (see #30). Some have seen in this prayer a material form of 'eucharistic sacrifice', albeit after reception, but since it is not required to be said this idea is unsustainable.

#29-33 After Communion

#29 *The Lord's Prayer*

Prayed at this point, the Lord's Prayer gathers together communicants' participation in the Lord's Supper. In *BCP*, the people repeat each phrase after the priest, reflecting the low literary ability in most congregations; here it is said together.

#30 *The prayers of oblation and thanksgiving*

These prayers are renditions of *BCP*, and, as there, are alternatives to one another. Neither *BCP* nor HC1 specifies who says them, though they are customarily prayed by the presider. Several aspects of both are significant. Only after communion has been administered is reference made to any 'sacrifice' that we offer, reflecting the abiding concern in *BCP* about 'mass-sacrifice'. Further, this sacrifice is not material but one of 'praise and thanksgiving', epitomised in the *Gloria*.

The 'prayer of oblation' includes three petitions:

1. First, we pray that our "sacrifice of praise and thanksgiving" may be accepted by God, and forgiveness of sins granted. This request is not limited to the congregation present, but is for "we and your whole Church", and goes beyond forgiveness to include "all other benefits of [Christ's] passion".

2. Secondly, we offer "ourselves, our souls and bodies" (that is, all we are, individually and collectively) as a "reasonable, holy and living sacrifice" (Romans 12.1) with prayer for the fullness of divine blessing (benediction).

3. Thirdly, while reserve is again expressed about sacrifice, and recognising that we are unworthy (because of our many sins, not our human nature) we pray for these offerings to be accepted.

The 'prayer of thanksgiving' has two distinct sections.

1. First, we give thanks for the profound privileges of receiving "these holy mysteries": feeding on Christ, assurance of divine favour, being members of Christ's body, and heirs of the kingdom of God. There are echoes here of the Catechism answer about the benefits of being baptised.

2. Then the prayer turns to living out what we have performed liturgically: continuing in the Church, and doing "all such good works as [God has] prepared for us to walk in" (Ephesians 2.10). A striking aspect of this prayer is the range of images employed for holy communion and for the Church.

Both prayers conclude with a strong trinitarian doxology, drawing together the whole eucharistic action, from "Lift up your hearts!" to this point.

#31 The *Gloria*

The placement of this 'Hymn of Praise' is an clear example of the difference in structure between HC1 and HC2. Opening HC2, it forms a climax in HC1, as our 'eucharistic sacrifice'. Indeed, in *BCP* only here is congregational singing mentioned! Reciting the *Gloria* at this point in HC1 is its emotional highpoint, the growing 'wave' of praise finally not subsiding, but allowed to break out in song.

#32 The Blessing

This deeply-loved blessing opens with the 'peace', pronounced on our 'hearts and minds', then moves to a form which combines the classic First Testament naming of God, "God Almighty" (*'El Shaddai*), with the New Testament trinitarian form, "Father, Son and Holy Spirit" (Matthew 28.19).

#33 This rubric means that on occasion the 'After Communion' prayers will have been enacted with consecrated bread and/or wine on the Lord's Table (see #28). Its main purpose, however, is to exclude any use of them apart from the administration of communion.

On setting aside bread and wine for communicants who are not present due to illness, see pages 306–308 in this book.

A final note

The Notes on *APBA* page 117 that related to HC1 have been discussed at the appropriate place in the service.

Given the ethos of HC1, it is unsuitable for data projection: congregations are likely to be long-term Anglicans, and the service works quite well from the book itself.

As was said of M&EP1, HC1 'works' by being led with confidence in its time-honoured shape. Though headings provide a 'gather / listen / pray / do / go' structure, each section flows on from the previous and into the next, there are few substantive alternatives, and a high proportion of the text is said by the priest.

Chapter Sixteen

Celebrating Holy Communion using Second Order

The structure of the service

Common shape

Anglican scholar Dom Gregory Dix identified a 'four-fold' shape as the foundation structure for the Lord's Supper, paired with the 'synaxis' of Word and prayer: see Chapter Fourteen. As David Richardson and Gillian Varcoe note,

> The Lambeth Conferences of 1958 and 1978 produced guidelines for the reform of the eucharistic liturgy throughout the Anglican Communion which commended this common shape as the basis for liturgical revision.[1]

This common shape is found in *A Modern Liturgy* (1966), **Australia 69, 73** and HC2 in **AAPB**. It has thus had over a half-century of use. "The shape remains familiar to Australian Anglicans". In **APBA**, therefore, "verbal changes in congregational responses have been kept to a minimum". But the placement of alternatives in **AAPB** was complex. So, Richardson and Varcoe continue,

> The initial aim with the publication of the trial services in 1993 was to achieve greater simplicity. The response from the Church, however, while commending greater simplicity, rejected all attempts to slim the liturgy down by leaving out some of the more familiar and well-loved Anglican prayers. In fact the cry was for both simplicity and flexibility and it proved impossible to achieve both aims in the one liturgy. The Second Order offers flexibility in a way that is easier to use than its predecessor in **AAPB**. Third Order aims at simplicity.

Alternatives and pagination are kept as 'clean' as possible, and with a 'shadow line' on optional pages. Great Thanksgivings are printed sequentially, with 'Additional Prayers and Anthems' and 'Seasonal Variations' after the service. The content of 'Prayers of the People' was taken out and printed separately.

---

1   *A Practical Commentary* 65. For Lambeth 1958, see Resolutions 73–76; for Lambeth 1978, available at http://www.anglicancommunion.org/structures/instruments-of-communion/lambeth-conference.aspx

The service in outline

HC2 follows the 'gather / listen / pray / do / go' one used for Sunday services in APBA – see Chapter Two – with a four-fold shape structure for the Lord's Supper. In the outline below, essential elements are on the left; items affected by rubrics or Notes in italics. Options are in [square brackets].

Gathering in God's Name

    [Hymn, sentence, acclamation]
Greeting
    [Prayer of Preparation]
    Confession and absolution (if not later)
    [Lord have mercy /Kyrie]
    [Hymn of Praise]
    [Trisagion]

The Ministry of the Word

Collect
First reading
    [Psalm, hymn or anthem]
New Testament reading
    [Hymn or anthem]
Gospel reading
Sermon
Nicene Creed

The Prayers of the People

    [Notices]
Intercessions and thanksgivings
    Lord's Prayer (if not elsewhere)

Preparation
    [Comfortable words]
    [Prayer of Approach]
    Confession and Absolution (if not earlier)

The Greeting of Peace

Greeting
    [Hymn, Notices]
Bringing up the gifts of the people
    [Offertory prayer]

The Great Thanksgiving
    Placing of bread and wine
    The Great Thanksgiving
        Lord's Prayer (if not elsewhere)

The Breaking of the Bread and the Communion
    Breaking of the bread
    Invitation to communion
    Administration of communion
    [Anthems]

The Sending Out of God's People
    Post-communion prayer
    Prayer of self-offering
    [Hymn, Notices]
    Blessing and Dismissal

Commentary

Note 1 on *APBA* page 164 is the only comment in *APBA* on furniture: the Holy Table is to be spread with a white cloth. How the people, ministers and other furniture are arranged is left open.[2]

HC2 is notable for phrases like "may be said". This variety does not mean that 'anything goes', but assumes that creative practice will respect the overall structure, and what each element does in context.

#1-11 Gathering in God's Name

We gather in response to God's call, as people 'dripping wet', baptised "in God's Name": see pages 40-41 in this book. This section can be brief: only the greeting and collect are essential, a terseness appropriate for weekdays. It can be fulsome, as the rubric at the top of *APBA* allows – but thought is needed as to how new variations are introduced.

#1   Singing does not have to be a 'hymn'. An anthem or psalm, for example 95 (see page 264 in this book). And the rubric does not restrict singing to just one song.

#2   *Blessed be God* ... : on this *berakah* form see pages 123–124 in this book.

Richardson and Varcoe helpfully note that the forms offered "adapt a phrase from the Byzantine liturgy and immediately set the stage for the eucharistic journey ... the Eucharist for which we gather is a journey into the kingdom of God."[3]

---

2   *Performing the Gospel*, Chapter Two, 'Setting the scene', Part C explores these issues.
3   *A Practical Commentary*, 66.

#3 Gilbert Sinden helpfully observes:

> The opening Greeting is very important. It unites priest and people for their common corporate worship, and reminds us that we come to the Eucharist not as separate individuals, but as a gathered family.[4]

The grace ... : This is often used to conclude a service, but in the New Testament 'grace' phrases are used both to open (1 Corinthians 1.3; 2 Peter 1.2) and close letters (2 Corinthians 13.13; 1 Thessalonians 5.28). Its use to open a service is especially helpful when a fuller greeting is appropriate.

*The Lord be with you / **And also with you***: see pages 241–242 in this book.

*Christ is risen / **He is risen indeed***: This ancient Easter greeting of Eastern Christians is traditionally accompanied by a kiss. It echoes the angel's greeting to "Mary Magdalene and the other Mary" as they arrived at the tomb to anoint the body of Jesus (Matthew 28:6; compare Luke 24.34).

Christ ***is*** rather than ***has*** risen reflects how English grammar employs the Greek perfect tense, when a past action continues into the present. That Christ ***was raised*** is true, but not the whole Easter message: truly alive now, our living Lord Jesus Christ ***is*** risen.

#4 *The Prayer of Preparation*: see pages 239–241 in this book. Most congregations will expect this distinctive Anglican prayer to be used on Sundays.

#5–7 *Confession and absolution* – their placement.

The Two Great Commandments (#5), the Ten Commandments or "other suitable passages", can be used at this early point "when the confession follows". Placing the Commandments here derives from them being recited at this point in *BCP* Holy Communion: see pages 264–265 in this book. But that this material is in small type with a shaded line indicates that the Liturgical Commission recommended that confession and absolution come in response to the Ministry of the Word, as the standard size font there indicates (#22–23).

Confession early reflects the structure of MP, which in *BCP* led into the Litany and Holy Communion. It can give the sense of 'cleaning the slate', appropriate when significant action follows the Ministry of the Word, as in baptism, marriage and ordination. Some variation in the place of confession can be helpful: if the 'standard' position is used in 'ordinary time', having it early in Advent and Lent may help a congregation sense what is distinctive about these seasons.

---

4   *When we meet for Worship*, 107.

Anglicans are used to every Holy Communion service including confession and absolution: the rubric at #22 requires this on "Sundays and other Holy Days". As Richardson and Varcoe point out, however, "The corollary of this is that the confession may be omitted on week days." Explaining this, they write:

> Some have suggested that the result of this is to reduce the sense of sin, but that is not the intention. The reasons for this permission are two-fold: one psychological, the other liturgical. First, the standard repetition of the words of confession day in and day out may itself have the effect of reducing the seriousness with which the community confesses its failures in following Christ. Second, the confession of sin on every possible occasion of eucharistic celebration may serve to contradict the very event being celebrated. On Easter Day, for example, the Church celebrates our forgiveness and new life in the risen Christ who died for our sins.[5]

#5 *The Two Great Commandments:* the text opens with Deuteronomy 6.4-5, out of respect for the ancient people of God.[6] Known as the ***Shema***, 'Hear' in Hebrew, this is the core of Israel's faith, recited often by faithful Jews. Jesus' affirmation of this confession of faith follows, joining the "first and great commandment" with "a second like it" (Leviticus 18.19).

The translation "the Lord is one" reads Deuteronomy 6.4 as affirming God's nature. The Hebrew also carries the sense of "the Lord is our God, the Lord alone", and "The Lord our God is one Lord".

#6-7 *Confession and absolution*

Introducing the confession with a 'seasonal introduction' or appropriate sentence can give context to what is confessed. Silence allows worshippers to have time to reflect on their lives: the minister who introduces this needs to be comfortable with this, however: awkwardness is quickly communicated.

The confession at #6 and #22 is from *AAPB*, shaped as a response to the Two Great Commandments. Line 5 is new: "and in what we have failed to do". Including 'sins of omission' was suggested at consultations, but a letter from a laywoman gave the Commission the 'right' words.

The confession is 'general' rather than 'personal': see page 126 in this book.

---

5 *A Practical Commentary*, 71-72. The Easter Day service issued by the Liturgy Commission in 2003 contains a Renewal of Baptismal Vows: since this reiterates the renunciations of sin and Satan made at baptism, a separate confession of sin is unnecessary.

6 In *AAPB*, following 1928, these words are introduced by "Our Lord Jesus Christ said".

The absolution is from *BCP* Holy Communion, itself derived from Sarum. The presider stands to pronounce it *in persona Christi*, with divine authority: not due to his or her own holiness or status, but as an occasion of God's 'authoring' forgiveness and healing in Christ: see pages 237–239 in this book.

#8 *Lord have mercy / Kyrie eleison*

The *Kyrie* is one of the few Greek liturgical elements found in Latin rites, and now English.[7] In the Greek translation of the First Testament, the Septuagint, the divine Name, YHWH, is rendered *kyrios* ('Lord'), the term used for Graeco-Roman deities and Roman Emperors. The earliest New Testament 'creed' is "Jesus is Lord" (*kyrios*: 1 Corinthians 12.3; Philippians 2.11), so whether *kyrios* refers here to the Godhead or Christ is nicely ambiguous. In everyday speech, *kyrie*, the vocative case, was a courtesy address ('Sir ...': see Matthew 27.63; Luke 13.8 and 14.22 of human superiors; Mark 7.28; John 4.11, 6.34, 12.21, 20.15 of Jesus). This ambiguity points to believers' privilege of being able to address our Lord as to a fellow human being.

When *Kyrie, Christe, Kyrie* is prayed, it is not forgiveness for sins that is sought: this would call into question that God's nature is "always to have mercy". Pardon is offered to sinners; mercy (*'eleison)* to the weak and helpless. *Kyrie eleison* is a plea for divine assistance more than forgiveness: "Lord, come to our aid". This is why rubric at the top of *APBA* page 120 indicates that it may be used anywhere in this section, whether or not the confession is used.

#9 *The Hymn of Praise ('Gloria')*

The rubric implies that this is always to be used, except in Advent and Lent, yet Note 4 on *APBA* page 164, sees it as optional. Nice to know it is not perfect ...

The *Gloria* derives from the angels' song to greet the birth of the Saviour (Luke 2.14). It developed into a New Testament 'psalm', and by the fourth century in the East was included in daily 'hours' services. In the West it came to be recited near the beginning of the Eucharist, as in Sarum and *BCP* 1549. In *BCP* 1552 Cranmer moved the *Gloria* to follow the post-communion Prayer of Oblation or Thanksgiving: see page 271 in this book. It thus became the offering of praise and thanksgiving, the 'eucharistic sacrifice'.

Given their 'four-fold shape' structure, modern Anglican services have returned the Hymn to its classical position, as an opening song of praise.

---

7   Other original language forms retained in Christian rites are 'Amen', 'Alleluia' and 'Maranatha' (1 Corinthians 16.22; compare Revelation 22.20). Each is Aramaic, the language of the earliest communities.

The *APBA* version is from the ecumenical *English Language Liturgical Consultation*. Others can be used, not least when sung: General Note 2 on *APBA* page xi.[8]

#10 *Trisagion* ('thrice holy'): This short prayer for aid (*'eleison*) expands the angelic song in Isaiah 6.3 and Revelation 4:8. The stress on God's holiness and power, transcending death ('immortal'), reflects how the gospel was experienced in the early centuries of the Church, as a minority under pressure in a dying culture.[9]

The Trisagion was used at the Council of Chalcedon (451AD), so was familiar before then.[10] In the Roman Rite it was used on Good Friday, in both Greek and Latin; in Eastern rites it leads in to the Epistle. While appropriate for Lent and Advent, as the rubric indicates, it can be used at any time.

#11 *The Prayer of the Day* (Collect): see pages 113–117 in this book.

Evan Burge notes that "The term 'collect' implies the collecting of individual prayers in a single prayer by the leader on behalf of the gathered assembly, which responds with a corporate Amen."[11] As such it concludes the 'Gathering'. As the 'Prayer of the Day', it is linked with the readings, so looks forward to the Ministry of the Word.

The rubric requires that the prayer be offered by the presider, since it gathers together the prayer of the congregation as a whole. As Richardson and Varcoe note, however, it "is not the spoken prayer of the priest alone but a combination of silent and spoken elements in which all have a part".[12]

Allowing significant silence before the prayer is offered gives space for worshippers to acknowledge what is on their minds, and focus on attending to the Word of God: see Note 10 on *APBA* page 164.

---

8   Choirs using *BCP* should note that in its version, the line "thou that takest away the sins of the world, have mercy on us" is repeated. *ELLC* and other modern versions do not repeat the equivalent line.

9   The earliest Christian sign, the fish, appealed to believers intellectually because the Greek '*ichthus* was an acronym for Jesus Christ (IX), God (TH)'s Son (U), Saviour (S). Existentially, it symbolised their being able to survive in their alien environment of persecution as 'fish' survive in the deep.

   Archaeological evidence for the cross as a Christian symbol is found only from Constantine, when all and sundry flooded in, and the forgiveness of sins became salvation's core. See Graydon Snyder, *Ante Pacem. Archaeological Evidence of Church Life before Constantine* (Mercer University Press, 2018).

10 "Christ, who was crucified for us, have mercy on us" was added in some places in the fourth century, in reaction to Arian teaching. This form, addressed to the Son rather than the Trinity, soon fell away.

11 *A Practical Commentary*, 106.

12 *A Practical Commentary*, 67.

#12–18 The Ministry of the Word

Chapter Three in this book explores the wider issues involved in this Ministry, including the readings used in *APBA*.

#12, 14 No direction is given as to how the readings should be introduced, but Note 6 on *APBA* page 164, provides for the same pattern as in M&EP1, following *BCP*: "A reading from [the book], [chapter ..., beginning at verse ...]" If the full reference is not given in a pew sheet, then chapter and verse as well as book should be named aloud, to allow people to identify the reading and follow it in a Bible.

On "Hear the word of the Lord" see page 243 in this book.

#13 *The psalm* is chosen to assist the assembly respond to the First Reading. In this context, adding "Glory to God:" is not helpful: see Note 7 on *APBA* page 164.

#15 Calling the song at this point the 'gradual hymn' is anachronistic. It derives from the Epistle and Gospel being read from different sides of the sanctuary, which saw the reader going up and down steps (*gradus*). A useful contemporary form of words is "To welcome the Gospel, we sing hymn NN".

#16 As in *BCP*, no provision is made in *APBA* for 'acclamations' introducing the Gospel – a deliberate omission. Preceding scripture readings by more than their reference 'frames' its interpretation, the place for which is the sermon.

On "The Lord be with you", see page 242 in this book.

The rubrics "All sit for the Reading (#12)", "All stand for the Gospel" (#16), are rare examples in *APBA* of specified postures: see pages 242–243 in this book.

The words after the Gospel are both more ("This is ...") and similarly ("[For] the ...") precise than "Hear the word of the Lord". This reflects the Gospels' distinctive place in the scriptures, giving immediate access to the living Word, Jesus Christ.

#17 *The sermon*: only on rare occasions, and for significant reasons, should a sermon be omitted: see Note 8 on *APBA* page 164. As Richardson and Varcoe note, it

> is an integral part of the Ministry of the Word by which the word of God is applied to the pastoral situation of a particular community at a particular time and place ... It is appropriate that there be some reflection on the word of God at every eucharist, including weekday celebrations.[13]

But a brief homily can require more preparation than a 30-minute address. Note #9 on *APBA* page 164, "A time of children's ministry" could be observed more often: see #10 on page 23: again, this can take more skill and insight than a sermon.

---

13   *A Practical Commentary*, 69.

#18 *The Nicene Creed*: on the place of creeds in liturgy, see page 125 in this book. On the translation, see Note 1, 'Common Forms', on *APBA* pages 820–821. On the *filioque* clause, see page 126 in this book.

On turning to the front (liturgical east), see page 138 in this book.

The Nicene Creed, largely drawn up at the Council of Nicea (325 AD) to exclude Arian teaching, took a permanent place in the Eucharist of East and West from the sixth century. Richardson and Varcoe note that

> Some early commentators, while seeing the Creed as describing right faith, saw it more as a hymn of praise ... It is as responsive exulting to the word proclaimed and expounded that the Creed comes, the objective response to the Ministry of the Word.[14]

Few parishioners, and by no means all clergy, could exegete every clause. Some will have questions about its teaching, perhaps omitting some lines. The introduction, "Let us affirm the faith of the Church", does not call each person to give intellectual assent to all its statements, but to affirm as theirs what the Church as a whole believes. Our corporate recital of Creed is like 'flying the flag' of Christian faith: as much believing towards deeper faith as it is about informed assent.

#19 The Prayers of the People

On Christian prayer and its communal practice, see Chapter Seven.

The minister's introduction, "Let us pray for the world and for the Church", are in that order "as that seems to be the order of God's priorities" (Richardson and Varcoe).[15] They are not variable, but changing them is hardly a liturgical crime. Additions such as "and for ourselves" imply that the congregation is not part of the world or the Church ...

The rubrics encourage participation by others than the presider, notably "a **deacon** and/or other **members** of the congregation" (emphasis added). Leading the intercessions, and/or assisting in preparing those who do, is a classic deacon's ministry of enabling – and every priest and bishop is also a deacon. The plural members encourages a variety of voices: hearing prayers led by a range of accents and gender tones opens our eyes to the diversity of God's people. Where people whose mother tongue is other than English are present, their language(s) can be used in the prayers, with translation both ways where the context calls for it.

---

14 *A Practical Commentary*, 69.

15 *A Practical Commentary*, 70.

An obvious omission from this section is a list of topics: compare #12, page 26. This is due to members of General Synod being unable to agree on how to include reference to the 'faithful departed': see page 267 in this book.

In many congregations the Prayers of the People are prepared afresh for each service, using the topics on *APBA* pages 172–173. This reflects the pattern of the 'Prayer for the Church Militant' in *BCP* Holy Communion, based in part on 1 Timothy 2.1-2. It is 'common prayer' that is offered, rather than individual petitions, and ranges beyond the immediate life of those present to "the world and the Church" (capital 'C').

Silence in common prayer helps the petitions offered 'breathe' rather than being crowded.

Two possibilities are offered to conclude the prayers: both are congregational. If "another suitable form" is used, it should likewise gather together the prayers offered: those on *APBA* page 27, for example #23.

Then Lord's Prayer offered at this point gathers together the prayers offerred.

#20-21 Preparation

As the shaded line and brackets around this heading implies, the Liturgical Commission assumed that these elements would not be included in every celebration. Derived from *BCP* Holy Communion, they are much loved by many Anglicans. As the heading indicates, these sentences are not penitential, but preparatory. This makes their inclusion always appropriate, not only in Advent, quieter services and Lent.

#20 Other 'Comfortable Words' (as *BCP* speaks of them) or 'Words of Assurance' (as HC1 describes them) can be found at *APBA* page 110, #21.

#21 *The Prayer of Approach:* see pages 243–246 in this book.

This much-loved prayer is difficult to place in a 'four-fold shape' Eucharist. The Liturgical Commission considered returning it to its 1549 position, immediately prior to the administration of communion, but realised that this would deflect from the high point of praise of the Doxology. In this place, prior to the confession and absolution, it works quite well as Preparation for the eucharistic action as a whole.

#22-23 *Confession and Absolution*

The Liturgical Commission sees this as the 'standard' place, as the font size indicates: see page 277 in this book.

#24-25 The Greeting of Peace

#24 Such a greeting goes back to the Church's earliest days, associated with a 'holy kiss' (Romans 16.16; 1 Corinthians 16.20; 2 Corinthians 13.12; 1 Thessalonians 5.26). As time went on, it came to be shared between the clergy only, just before communion was administered. Omitted in Reformation rites, it was transferred by Cranmer to precede the blessing in *BCP* Holy Communion.[16] The Liturgical Movement paved the way for its restoration. Roman Catholic rites set it just before communion is shared; Anglicans follow Justin Martyr's *First Apology* (c. 155AD) where it is opens the way for the Lord's Supper.

Given Anglo-Saxon reticence, and sensitivities about 'duty of care', Note 11 on *APBA* page 164 suggests that the greeting be accompanied by "a handshake or other suitable sign of reconciliation". This last word is significant. The Greeting is not one of welcome, as at the beginning of a service (see #8 on *APBA* page 22), but expresses our reconciliation in Christ, and so with one another.

The *APBA* form has a two-fold structure: a declaration of Christian identity (the body of Christ / in one body), followed by the greeting itself. The former is appropriate to be given by a deacon or authorised minister; the greeting itself, representing Christ's initiative in offering peace, is made by the presider. This pairing forms a visible sign of our corporate identity as those who practice reconciliation in Christ's name.

#25 *The presentation of the gifts*

The song at this point is traditionally called the 'offertory' hymn, since the "gifts of the people are brought to the Lord's Table". These usually involve the collection of money, but items for sharing with refugees, local people in need or organisations of advocacy and care are often presented.

The rubric speaks of 'gifts' rather than 'alms' (i.e. money, as in *BCP*), thus including the bread and wine, which symbolise the 'stuff' of human life in many cultures. The prayer offered at #25 ("Blessed are you ...", a *berakah* form) expresses this well, as should any other 'suitable' one.[17]

---

16 The opening rubrics of BCP Holy Communion provide for the minister to exclude intending communicants who will not be reconciled with their fellows, so avoiding the absence of peace in the congregation.

17 On the *berakah* form, see pages 123-124 in this book. The 'Blessed are you' prayers over the bread and wine in the pre-2010 Roman Catholic English mass were problematic, and do not reflect ARCIC's work. They overemphasise human initiative ('fruit of human hands'), and what is prayed, that the elements will 'become' the body and blood of Christ, is made without qualification (e.g. 'may be for us', as in *BCP* 1549, or 'the sacrament of'). The new translation of 2010 improves on the former issue, but not the latter.

The offertory is distinct from first act of the 'four-fold shape', the action of 'taking' or 'setting the table' (#26). Seeing it as part of the eucharistic action implies that we offer "a sacrifice of material elements to God", which, as Sinden asserts,

> suggests a pagan (rather than Biblical) notion of sacrifice, in which we offer to God something of value to us, in return for something we need or desire which he alone can provide. Such a sacrifice is not only excluded, but would be an act of blasphemy.

As in *BCP*, the 'offertory' comes in response to the Ministry of the Word, not as the first step of the Lord's Supper. That would put the initiative with us rather than God.

All the gifts of the people are "brought to the Lord's Table". The bread and wine are always placed on the Table, but in some places the money is set aside elsewhere, as if it were 'unholy'. However, as *BCP* directs,

> the Deacons, Churchwardens, or other fit person ... shall receive the Alms for the Poor, and other devotions of the people, in a decent bason ... and reverently bring it to the Priest, *who shall humbly place it upon the holy Table*.

As Sinden puts it, "Money-gifts are not be regarded as 'filthy lucre', but as having a sacramental character: effective outward and visible tokens of the people's love and care for their neighbours".[18]

#26 The Great Thanksgiving

On doctrinal issues, see Chapter Thirteen; on liturgical, see Chapter Fourteen.

Nothing is said in *APBA* about how communicants and ministers are arranged for the Lord's Supper. The Liturgical Commission deliberately avoided assuming any particular setting, to give freedom for creative responses in diverse contexts.

Preparing the Table

The 'taking' of the bread and wine is the first eucharistic action: the rubric at #26 covers both 'taking' and 'thanking', showing the close relationship between them. The elements are 'taken' by the presider, who 'places' them on the Lord's Table.

It is customary in some places for a deacon or servers to "set the Table". The key ministry of deacons in the Lord's Supper is to administer the wine and / or bread, however. In whatever ways they (or others) might assist the presider, it is important that the one who acts *in persona Christi* presides over each of the four 'actions', starting with the 'taking'.

---

18   *When we meet for Worship*, 137.

In some places the bread and wine are brought forward from the congregation. Where this happens, Sinden urges that "they go right into the sanctuary and hand to the priest first the paten(s) or ciboria, and then the chalice(s). The intervention of servers ... is not necessary".[19]

Structure

In the earliest eucharistic prayers a 'moment' of consecration is left undefined. In *BCP* Holy Communion, however, continuing medieval tradition, the Thanksgiving is named the 'Prayer of Consecration', and the rubrics for supplementary consecration identify the institution narrative as the 'moment' (see page 254-255 in this book).[20] However problematic this is seen to be by scholars today, it was spiritually satisfying to generations. Further study, notably by the *Inter-Anglican Liturgical Consultation*, has seen two developments since *AAPB* was approved. As Richardson and Varcoe summarise,

> First, the shape of the Thanksgiving prayer has been more clearly delineated as having two main parts: thanksgiving for God's saving work, climaxed in Christ, followed by supplication, especially for those about to share the sacramental meal. Secondly, the 'four-fold shape' actions are not of equal significance: the 'taking' (offertory) is primarily preparation for the Thanksgiving, and the 'breaking' (fraction) a preparation for receiving the bread.[21]

The transition from thanksgiving to supplication was in *BCP* marked by the "Holy, holy, holy" (*Sanctus*, the song of heaven: Isaiah 6.3; Revelation 4.8). But in the East the example of Israel was followed, rehearsing the significant 'mighty acts of God' from creation to the incarnation and redemptive life, death and resurrection of Christ before the *Sanctus*. In some Eastern prayers a further transition marks the shift from thanksgiving to supplication: this is where the inclusion of "Christ has died ..." originated.

Richardson emphasises that, "Faithful to the tradition of *BCP*, the thanksgivings in *APBA* strongly assert the [biblical] understanding of Christ's once-for-all and 'full, perfect and sufficient' sacrifice."[22] The recital and proclamation of God's atoning work in Christ thus forms the 'hinge' around which each prayer turns.

---

19 *When we meet for Worship*, 136.
20 Puritans and Restoration scholars, following medieval tradition, alike tended to see the Lord's Supper as repeating the Last Supper: this in part explains why five 'manual acts' were introduced in *BCP* (1662).
21 *A Practical Commentary*, 73.
22 *A Practical Commentary*, 73.

This is the overall structure of the Great Thanksgiving prayers:

'Lift up your hearts' (*Sursum corda*)	[all]
Preface, recalling God's work	
in Christ	[1, 3]
in creation and First Covenant	[2]
in creation and Christ	[4, 5]
'Holy, Holy, Holy ...' (*Sanctus*)	[all]
['Blessed is he ... ' (*Benedictus*)]	[1, 2, 3, 4]
Prayer for right reception	[1, 4, 5]
for God's saving work in Christ	[2, 3]
Institution narrative	[all]
'Christ has died' (or later)	[all]
Therefore ...' / 'Fill ...' (*'anamnesis*)	[all]
'Christ has died' (or earlier)	[1, 2, 4, 5]
Praise in the Spirit (*'epiclesis*)	[all]
'... Amen'	[2a, 3a]
'Blessing and honour ... ' (doxology)	[1, 2b, 3b, 4,5]

Four sets of responses (set in quotation marks above) bracket three sections recited by the presider on behalf of the whole congregation: Preface; Institution and *'anamnesis*; *'epiclesis*. These sections proclaim the transforming work of Father, Son and Spirit respectively: this Trinitarian structure is clearest in Thanksgiving 2.

Blessed is he ... (Benedictus)

In the medieval mass, these words from Matthew 21.9 followed the *Sanctus* and led into the intercessions, before the consecration prayer. In *BCP* 1549 this pattern stayed, but when in 1552 Cranmer removed the intercessions to follow the Ministry of the Word, this 'gap' was filled with the Prayer of Approach (see pages 243-246 in this book). The function of the *Benedictus* was then unclear, and so was omitted.[23] When its reintroduction was sought in the wake of the Oxford Movement, it was strongly opposed, because "it seems to point to a 'coming' of the Lord Jesus at a particular moment of consecration" (as Sinden puts it).[24] In a 'four-fold shape' structure this tension disappears. In HC2, the **Sanctus,** the song of heaven, followed by the **Benedictus,** leads into the fickle

---

23 Queen Elizabeth 1 approved a Latin *BCP* in 1560, used in the two universities and various colleges: this retained *Benedictus* after the *Sanctus*.

24 *When we Meet for Worship*, 150. "Come, Lord Jesus!" in HC3 is open to a similar objection.

crowd's acclamation of Christ before his passion: "Hosanna to the Son of David!" (Matthew 21.9). As Sinden continues,

> The sanctus and benedictus together remind us of two things: that we are privileged in Christ to share the worship of heaven; and at what price that privilege was won for us. The benedictus points us to the passion of Christ and warns us of the fickleness of his human followers.

The Liturgical Commission thus included the *Benedictus*, but made it optional because it recognised that it remains sensitive.[25]

The place of the 'memorial acclamation'

'Christ has died ...' and similar acclamations are found in some Eastern rites, the Syrian / Antiochian Orthodox liturgy for example. They were introduced into the Roman Mass in 1969 in the wake of the Second Vatican Council.[26] This was taken up in HC2 in *AAPB* to conclude the institution narrative. In the 'trial use' booklet (1993), and the draft of *APBA* presented to the 1995 General Synod, however, this acclamation was printed in the later position, for three reasons:

- it marks the transition from thanksgiving to supplication;
- it enables the people to conclude the "act of commemoration" (*'anamnesis*) for God's saving work;[27]
- it emphasises that 'consecration' takes place across the Great Thanksgiving as a whole, rather than happening at a specific 'moment'.

Even so, many Synod members wished to maintain the *AAPB* (early) position of 'Christ has died'. Indeed, some saw this affirming the institution narrative as the 'moment' of consecration. General Synod thus voted to print it in the early position, but (except for Thanksgiving 3) by rubric allowed it in the later place.[28] In this later place, 'Christ has died' concludes the *'anamnesis*, and so functions as

---

25 Thanksgiving 5 does not include the *Benedictus*. This is because it was placed in Third Order in the 1995 draft book; when it was transferred to HC2, the absence of *Benedictus* was missed: since the presence of children is in mind, however, this simplifying is not unhelpful.

26 In the 2010 Roman Catholic Mass in English, 'Christ has died ...' was replaced by other acclamations, still in the early position. Unfortunately, the new ones correspond but loosely to those in the 1969 Roman English Mass, made available for Australian Anglicans in *AAPB*.

27 The sense of this as a "communal *'anamnesis*" is made visible where the presider holds up the bread and cup as the memorial acclamation is said or sung: see page 248 in this book.

28 Changing the acclamation to the early position was moved thirteen hours into the General Synod debate. Sitting with Lawrence Bartlett, I asked him whether we should explain to the Synod why the Liturgical Commission strongly preferred the later position. "Charles, nothing that matters has been lost thus far," he responded. "At this late stage I judge we best leave this one alone." So we did, a rare regret on my part.

a 'memorial acclamation' that needs no introduction. But in the early position its function is less clear, and a 'tag-line' is needed: some are provided on page 145.[29] **The Liturgical Commission recommends that the 'memorial acclamation' be used in the later position.**

Alternative acclamations are printed on *APBA* page 145: "Dying, you destroyed ...", with its strong verbs, works well with Thanksgiving 5. "Lord, by your cross and resurrection ..." is suitable in the Easter season.

Posture

Sitting is rarely mentioned in *BCP*, since until around the 1860s few church buildings had seats. In *BCP* Holy Communion the people kneel from the General Confession to the end of the Prayer of Consecration, the priest standing except for the Prayer of Humble Access. The ethos is one of reverent quietness, those present humbled at the wonder of God's saving love enacted in Christ's passion. In services shaped by the Liturgical Movement, however, the ethos shifts to the pre-Christendom sense of celebrating Christ's victory over death, sin and evil. So the presider stands throughout, and it is presumed that the congregation does likewise. Recalling *BCP*, some people prefer to kneel from the institution narrative. Nothing in *APBA* forbids this, but as Note 12 on *APBA* page 164 states,

> The Great Thanksgiving is a single prayer. Its unity may be obscured by changes in posture in the course of it; standing for the whole of the prayer is recommended.

Distinctive aspects of each Thanksgiving

Each Thanksgiving in HC2 follows a 'four-fold shape' structure. Significant place is given in each to the Spirit's work (*'epiclesis'*), but in different ways.

Thanksgiving 1 is close to its *AAPB* equivalent. It carries forward language familiar from *BCP*, and is designed to be 'normative': the other prayers are thus called 'Additional Thanksgivings'. In *AAPB*, the shortest Thanksgiving was #4, intended for situations where time is of the essence, such as communion with the sick. Though inappropriate for Sunday use, its brevity saw it used regularly in some places. So the Liturgical Commission decided that no Great Thanksgiving in *APBA* would be longer than the first.

The Preface celebrates God's saving work in creation and Christ, and is designed to be replaced by seasonal ones, *APBA* pages 147–163.

---

29 "Let us proclaim the mystery of faith", in Thanksgiving 3 as well as on *APBA* page 145, is questioned by some, since *mysterium fidei* in the Tridentine (Latin) Mass is part of the institution narrative.

The *'anamnesis* uses scriptural phrases familiar from *BCP*, with a brilliant bringing together of the 'evangelical' and 'catholic' impulses of the Christian tradition: "we celebrate *with this bread and cup* [my emphasis] his one perfect and sufficient sacrifice for the sins of the whole world." As argued above, it leads beautifully into the 'memorial acclamation' by the assembly as a whole.

The Spirit's work is taken up in three places: Christ being born of Mary; in praying that we may be fed with Christ's body and blood; and that the congregation may be renewed, united and brought to the 'eternal kingdom'.

Thanksgiving 2 was newly drafted, by David Richardson. Its imagery expresses biblical faith in terms which echo with Australians: the slowing of the rhythm in "and the new day dawned" is a prime example. In its shape, it reflects the structure of classical eucharistic prayers: as David explains,

> The old covenant is rehearsed before the Sanctus, and the new covenant after it, culminating in the institution of the Lord's Supper as a remembrance of Christ's death, followed by a statement of what we now remember and celebrate. The 'thanksgiving' then turns to supplication, asking the Holy Spirit to be active among us, and that communicants may receive the benefits of communion.[30]

How the Holy Spirit is invoked breaks new ground. That the Spirit enables our effective participation in the Eucharist is recognised on all sides. But debate takes place as to whether the Spirit is properly invoked on the bread and wine directly, as well as on the communicants.[31] This choice is side-stepped here: the Spirit is invoked "upon us and our celebration": not on the communicants and elements in isolation, but on the community celebrating Christ's saving work by eating and drinking at the Lord's Table, a dynamic invocation on everything involved.

Several phrases in Thanksgiving 2 deserve comment:

"Dawn of time" evokes 'light' emerging, God's first creative act.

"Wrought from nothing" brings together in striking paradox God' working *ex nihilo* and a term associated with iron, that very solid element, 'wrought'.

"Endowed us with creative power" is a strong affirmation of human dignity, male and female, which arises from our being made "in the image of God". This is picked up later in referring to Christ as the "bright image of God's glory".

---

30 *A Practical Commentary*, 74.
31 This is closely related to whether justification can be given for invoking God's blessing on things, as distinct from people: see pages 123–124 in this book.

"You called us by name ..." expresses the whole sweep of the First Covenant in just two dozen words: created ... searched ... covenant ... prophets.

"Breaking the power of evil" states God's victory in Christ over not only sin, but evil and its power, an emphasis in the earliest known eucharistic prayers.

"Com-panions" are those who eat bread (*panos*) together (*con/m*): doing so "on the way" alludes to the earliest name for Christians, "the Way" (Acts 9.2; 18.5).

"With this bread and cup" is an even clearer *'anamnesis* than Thanksgiving 1, and again invites being followed by the 'memorial acclamation'.

NB: Given its structure, seasonal Prefaces do not 'blend' with Thanksgiving 2.

Thanksgiving 3 follows the structure of Thanksgiving 1, and can be used with a seasonal Preface. Drafted during the 1995 General Synod meeting, it is the longest prayer: see pages 19–21 in this book.

Thanksgiving 3 was the main reason for the Canon for **APBA** being defeated in the Synod of the Diocese of Sydney, and questioned elsewhere.[32] Both its method of its composition and contents raise issues. It was negotiated to please various factions, and never prayed in drafting, so is awkwardly expressed and difficult to perform. It is unclear when the bread or wine might be taken up, and the concluding doxology is subjunctive rather than indicative. Surprisingly, no reference is made to Mary, and the *'anamnesis* does not include the bread and cup, in contrast to Thanksgivings 1, 2 and 4.

Richardson and Varcoe conclude that Thanksgiving 3

> represents a departure from the usual Australian practice of writing liturgy that represents a consensus of the Church as a whole which neither suppresses nor exaggerates particular doctrines. It is not a difficult exercise to find within it 'code' words representing the doctrinal positions of different factions within the church. Australian Anglicans have valued both diversity and unity, and it is to be hoped that this is a departure that will not become the norm.

But its inclusion was authorised by General Synod, and so is available for use.

---

32 Sydney Synod subsequently moved to allow its Archbishop to authorise **APBA** (without change) in parishes which requested this. The main objection was the reference to "accept our sacrifice of praise" in Thanksgiving 3; others found "sanctify this bread and wine" an unacceptable form of *'epiclesis,* despite the parallel to "sanctify this water" in *BCP* Holy Baptism; and some wondered what eucharistic theology is implied in the double "commemorate and celebrate his saving passion and death".

Thanksgiving 4 is a light revision of Thanksgiving 2 in ***AAPB***, and closely similar to 'Alternative Prayer of Thanksgiving A' in *Uniting in Worship*.[33] God's work in creation is taken up more fully in the Preface than in other Thanksgivings, while God's people being called to live in peace and love is given focus in its second and third parts. The *'anamnesis* is identical to Thanksgiving 1.

NB: replacing the fulsome Preface with a seasonal one defeats its purpose.

Thanksgiving 5 is based on the 1988 *Outline Order of Holy Communion*, composed afresh by the Liturgical Commission. The focus is directly on Jesus: his life, example, saving death and continuing ministry through the Spirit. Many verbs are used, and the language is direct: 'another', 'everyone' and 'remember' are the only three-syllable words. Together with the response that runs though the Preface, this gives the prayer an energy that makes it suitable for use when children are present.

Provision is made for "special thanksgivings appropriate for the occasion" to be included: where this is done, they should be written in similar style, and so 'fit' the context of where they are placed. The following example was written for celebrations of the Coming of the Light to the Torres Strait Islands (July 1):

> We thank you for the coming of the Light to the people of the Torres Strait.
> As we keep following Jesus,
>> we praise you that the Light of Christ is always present to lead and guide us.
>
> Lord our God, **we give you thanks and praise**.

NB: Another Thanksgiving based on Thanksgiving 5, taking up God's work in creation more fully, is available on the General Synod website.[34]

#27 *The Lord's Prayer*

This prayer was placed at this point in the liturgical reforms of Pope Gregory the Great (590–604), who sent Augustine to England. In *BCP* 1549, Cranmer left it there, but in 1552 moved it to conclude the whole eucharistic action, from "Lift up your hearts!" to receiving communion, which ended with its 'Amen'.[35]

---

33 This commonality is in large part due to the Thanksgiving being drafted by the Congregational liturgist Harold Leatherland. See Robert Gribben and Charles Sherlock, "Anglican-Uniting Church covenanting: liturgical aspects", *Australian Journal of Liturgy* 9/3 (2009) 71–79.

34 https://www.anglican.org.au/holy-communion, click on 'Great Thanksgiving for use when children are present - creation theme'.

35 See *What Did Cranmer Think he was doing?* for detailed exposition of this point.

When Queen Elizabeth 1 added 'Amen' to the Thanksgiving prayer in *BCP* 1559, the Lord's Prayer came to have the sense, familiar to many Anglicans, of communicants "saying together the family prayer after we have shared in the Lord's Supper" (Sinden).[36]

The rubric notes three places at which this prayer may be used in HC2: to conclude the Prayers of the People (#19), to follow the Thanksgiving (#27) or administration (as in *BCP*). As Burge notes, "One of the extraordinary things about the Lord's Prayer is the way its petitions take on a different kind of relevance according to the context in which it is being used".[37]

The use of the 'four-fold shape' for the Lord's Supper is also significant for the placement of the Lord's Prayer. At #27, it joins the flow from Thanksgiving to bread-breaking, and the petition about "our daily bread" takes on the 'eschatological' sense of the Greek: "give us today the bread of tomorrow".

This position is preferred by the Liturgical Commission, since it bids communicants, "as our Saviour Christ has taught", look forward in prayer to the messianic banquet. The prayer is therefore printed at this point in full, but not between #29 and #30, the *BCP* position, where it may also be used.

#28-29 The Breaking of Bread and the Communion

On the meaning of the breaking of the bread, what bread and wine are to be used. and matters relating to their administration, see pages 251–255 in this book.

#28 The bread-breaking is the third action in the four-fold shape. Though preparatory to the administration of communion, it should be performed without haste, and "broken in the sight of all": Note 15 on *APBA* page 165.

The rubric says the words "may be used", so the breaking can be done in silence.

The first set of words begins with an optional statement of the purpose of the breaking, followed by a versicle and response, all based on 1 Corinthians 10.16-17. The second is taken from one of the earliest non-canonical texts, *The Didache* (Teaching of the Twelve): see page 253 in this book. Another form is provided in Marriage (Second Order) #25 on *APBA* page 672. Other responses may be helpful, provided they do not associate the fraction with Christ's self-offering: see page 255 in this book.

---

36 *When we meet for Worship*, 145.
37 Evan Burge, *Proclaim and Celebrate* (Sydney: AIO, 1973) 47. This was a guide to the just-released *Australia 73* 'trial use' services, which would be included in *AAPB*.

#29 *The administration of Holy Communion*

On the practical and sensitive issues involved, see pages 255–260 in this book.

The Liturgical Commission took considerable care in drafting the words used to invite communicants and administer the sacrament, to ensure that the classical balance of 'objective' and 'subjective' aspects of the Eucharist is preserved. This is overturned when clergy take it upon themselves to omit or vary the invitation or change the words of administration, whether by abbreviating them to just "The body / blood of Christ" (the 'catholic' tendency) or making them up 'off the cuff' (the 'evangelical' habit).

Communicants look to encounter their Lord and know "the benefits of his passion" as they receive the elements. Having their 'doctrinal antennae' waving at this profound moment can cause deep offense.

The 'Invitations to Communion' on **APBA** page 146 were included from responses to the 'trial use' booklet, though with lukewarm support from the Liturgical Commission: indeed, they are not strictly 'invitations'. The first, from the Western tradition, is an act of penitence that is pastorally unhelpful here, even though it is loosely based on Luke 7.6–8. The second is an Eastern affirmation of Christ's deity, but its function here is unclear. Either "may precede the invitation on page 142", but are not alternatives to it.

The 'Anthems' on page 146 are for use "during the communion" (as the final rubric on page 142 provides). **Agnus Dei**, highly problematic when linked with the fraction (see page 255 in this book), is well-suited to be said or sung as the sacrament is given to those who will administer it. Conversely, the anthems "especially appropriate during the season of Easter" could be used more often.

On setting aside bread and wine for communicants who are not present due to illness, see pages 306–308 in this book.

30–34 **The Sending Out of God's People**

The heading points up a contrast with *BCP* Holy Communion, which assumes that communicants return to Christendom in "The peace of God". In HC2 and HC3, however, our self-offering is directed to living in a world where Christ's ways are known but in part. The service ends quickly: we are almost hurried out "to love and serve the Lord". This puts the emphasis on moving from worship in liturgy to worship in daily life.

As Richardson and Varcoe put it,
> Our worship together is not primarily for our own sake, but for strengthening for the mission to which God sends us in life, in our homes, schools, work and leisure places.[38]

#30 Post-communion prayers

The four options reflect aspects of the mission of God in which believers participate:

#30a) picks up *BCP*'s Prayer of Oblation (see pages 270-271 in this book), turning its focus to praying "that we may serve [God] in the world", with an eye to "that table where all your saints feast for ever".

#30b) is based on a prayer of Elizabeth Smith, opening up *BCP*'s Prayer of Thanksgiving (see page 271 in this book) with more active words, whose rhythm embodies what is prayed.

#30c) is a shorter version of the above, starting rather than concluding with 'hope'. The voice is a more active, the prayer being driven by "the power of your love".

#30d) was composed by Professor David Frost for the **Alternative Service Book** (1980) of the Church of England, and has become an Anglican classic. We pray as 'prodigals' in Christ met by our Father, while the striking inversion "Dying and living" picks up eucharistic proclamation of his saving passion and new life.
The final three lines are in **APBA** set in bold, as words appropriate for all to say. As the rubric following notes, when so used "#31 may be omitted", since the bolded words function in a similar manner.

#31 The first offering prayer became deeply familiar to Australian Anglicans in **AAPB**, reworking *BCP*'s Prayer of Oblation. The "living sacrifice" image is from Paul's exhortation in Romans 12.1, expressing the complete dedication to God of the "whole-burnt offering" (*'olah*) of Leviticus 1, not now through death, but in living (see pages 226-230 in this book) empowered by the Spirit of God.

The second prayer reinterprets the first "into more contemporary form".[39] A new composition, it was included late in drafting, perhaps to avoid misunderstandings of 'sacrifice' today. To my mind, however, its rather general biblical allusions lack the strength of the first prayer.

Seasonal post-communion prayers are provided on **APBA** pages 147-163.

#32 Songs at this point will reflect the mission ethos of the 'Sending Out'.

---

38 *A Practical Commentary*, 76.
39 *A Practical Commentary*, 76.

The Notices

Yes, these can be too long, unduly chatty or just repeat the pewsheet. But they signal the 'hinge' or transition between our worship of God 'in church' (liturgy) and 'in the world' (lifestyle). They are not placed at the end of the service as an 'afterword', but before the blessing and dismissal, or with the intercessions (#24 on **APBA** page 27 and Note 17 on page 163). These locations signal that worship continues in the days ahead in the activities of the community, not just the clergy.

The integration of liturgy and lifestyle that true worship involves can be furthered by using the 'Sending Out' to mark anniversaries, forthcoming events, to bless those who are moving on or facing a time of special need, to commission people for new ministries and so on. Notes 3 and 4 on **APBA** page 33 offer suggestions.

#33 *"The peace of God …"*

Pronouncing 'peace' before the blessing is another Anglican distinctive. As noted at #24, Cranmer moved the 'peace' to end the service, enriching it by citing Philippians 4.7 and alluding to Ephesians 3.19. As a pronouncement of God's peace it is more than a prayer (as in "May the peace …"): it is a 'performative' word, enacting the blessings of the Gospel.

The rubric provides for "an appropriate seasonal blessing": this wording implies that "The peace …" is always used in ordinary time.

"And the blessing …"

Some scholars believe that since the greatest blessing is receiving communion, no further one is necessary. Congregations disagree, however, desiring to go out with God's blessing on their hearts. The Liturgical Commission agreed with them (and Cranmer), so a blessing is specified except in Lent: see **APBA** page 152.

"… the Father, the Son and the Holy Spirit"

Sensitive to ideas of God as power-mongering, some clergy omit "almighty" or change it to phrases such as "all loving". Though this misunderstands 'El-Shaddai and is contrary to the rubrics, it is scarcely a hanging offence.

Changing "the Father, the Son and the Holy Spirit" to non-gendered terms is a serious matter, however. Such terms tend to be sub-personal and functional, for example 'Creator, Redeemer, Sanctifier' (as in a Tuesday MP prayer). But replacing 'Father' by 'Creator' implies that the Word and Spirit are not involved in creation, and assumes that Israel's God is the Father rather than the Trinity acting as One, a confusion which lay at the heart of the Arian controversy.

The Liturgical Commission held that the Trinitarian blessing in its apostolic form is how the people of God are to be blessed. So the 'Sending forth of God's People' harks back to our having been 'Gathered in God's Name' signified in our baptism: see pages 39–41 in this book.

#34 *The dismissal*

Two aspects of the rubric are significant:

First, "the *deacon* may say". The heart of a deacon's ministry is being an ambassador for Christ: see Chapter Twenty-Four in this book. In having the last word, the deacon embodies the calling of all Christians to worship the Lord "not only with their lips, but in their lives".

Secondly, "the deacon *may* say". There are occasions where the dismissal is not appropriate: a house communion where a cuppa will follow, for example.

The first form, continued from *AAPB*, echoes the words of Jesus and the apostles to those whose faith had saved / healed them (Mark 5.34; Luke 7.50, 8.48; Acts 16.36). But this peace is given so we may "love and serve the Lord" (James 2.16). We do so "in the name of Christ", as often in Acts (2.21, 2.38, 3.6, 3.16 and especially 4.10-12). The second form is a traditional version in modern English.

The 'Alleluia' rubric for Easter not only marks this season as distinctive, but is echoed with cheers and whistles in some places ...

Seasonal Variations: pages 147-163

Most include four elements: Invitation to Confession, Preface, Prayer after Communion, and Blessing, reflecting the theological themes of the season.

The inclusion of Variations for other than Principal Festivals is a significant enrichment of *AAPB* and *BCP*, notably for Saints, The Blessed Virgin Mary, Australia, and Ordination.

Notes on *APBA* pages 164-5 have been considered in the commentary.

A final note

HC2 is a liturgy designed to be mainstream, flexible and mission-shaped. Given the wide range of options, it can be celebrated in as little as 15 minutes and as long as you like. The opportunities for creative adaptation are many.

Thoughtful planning that is sensitive to the congregation and its context, involving others as appropriate, and ongoing review, will help make what is offered a truly eucharistic performance of the Gospel.

Chapter Seventeen

Celebrating Holy Communion using Third Order

Why a Third Order?

When the Liturgical Commission came to revise *AAPB*, it sought greater simplicity, but most responses to the 'trial use' booklets of 1990–94 looked for greater flexibility. Even so, parishes in the western suburbs of Melbourne and Sydney wanted a 'direct' service with minimal variation. As Richardson and Varcoe note,

> it proved impossible to achieve both aims in the one liturgy. The Second Order offers flexibility in a way that is easier to use than its predecessor in *AAPB*. Third Order aims at simplicity.[1]

The Liturgical Commission recognised that it was not good enough to simply cut HC2 down: a Third Order was called for with its own ethos. In 1988, the previous Liturgy Commission had issued *An Alternative Order for Holy Communion*. Baptised children were being admitted to communion, so this was designed for use when children are present. The *Alternative Order* was also sensitive to inclusive language, an issue that has emerged since *AAPB* was authorised in 1977. It thus made a start towards a 'direct' order. As it happened, the Anglican Archbishop of Sydney, Harry Goodhew, had in 1996 set up a Liturgy Committee for that diocese. Some members of this body were on the national Commission, so work was shared on the drafting of HC3.[2]

In the draft book presented to the 1995 General Synod, HC3 contained two Great Thanksgivings. One derived from the shared drafting work: *APBA* pages 176–177; the other from the 1988 *Alternative Order*. But responses showed that two Thanksgivings ran against the intended 'direct' ethos of HC3. The only change made to HC3 at General Synod was to move the alternative Thanksgiving to HC2, as the fifth one.

---

1 *A Practical Commentary*, 65.
2 On the Liturgical Commission, the 'portfolio' for HC3 was held by Lawrence Bartlett, supported by Evan Burge and David Peterson. It had 'trial use' in Melbourne and Sydney parishes.

HC3 thus has the same overall structure as HC2, but with many less alternatives. A full set of Prayers of the People is included, with confession and absolution following, as in *BCP*; the Great Thanksgiving is distinctive; and the *Gloria* is printed as part of the Sending Out. Overall, these features make HC3 'feel' somewhat like *BCP* Holy Communion in its 1928 form in modern English, adapted to the 'four-fold shape' with the Peace included.

The service in outline

The overall structure follows the 'gather / listen / pray / do / go' one used for Sunday services in *APBA*: see pages 37–40 in this book. In the outline below, essential elements are on the left, with options in [square brackets].

Gathering in God's Name
>   Greeting
>   >   [Hymns or songs of praise]
>
>   Two Great Commandments [or sentences]
>   Prayer of Preparation
>   >   [*Gloria* or other hymn of praise]
>
>   Collect

The Ministry of the Word
>   Bible readings from each Testament
>   >   [Psalm; hymn or song]
>
>   Gospel reading
>   Sermon (or after the Creed)
>   Nicene or Apostles' Creed
>   >   [Hymn or song]

The Prayers of the People
>   Litany of thanksgivings and intercessions
>   Lord's Prayer

Preparation for the Lord's Supper
>   >   [Sentences of exhortation]
>
>   Confession and Absolution
>   >   [Sentences of assurance]

The Greeting of Peace
>   Greeting
>   >   [Hymn or song]
>
>   Bringing up the gifts of the people

The Great Thanksgiving
>Placing of bread and wine
>"Lift up your hearts!", Preface
>Holy, Holy, Holy
>Prayer for reception
>Institution narrative – bread
>>[Breaking of the bread, with response]
>
>Institution narrative – cup
>Memorial Acclamation
>Invocation of the Spirit
>Doxology (Revelation 5.12)

The Breaking of the Bread and the Communion
>Breaking of the bread
>Administration of communion

The Sending Out of God's People
>Post-communion prayer
>Prayer of self-offering
>*Gloria* [or alternative]
>Blessing and Dismissal

Commentary

APBA provides no Notes to HC3, but those on pages 164–165 give guidance. Two are directive: the Holy Table is to be spread with a white cloth (#1), and any remaining consecrated bread and wine is to be reverently consumed (#16).

#1–4 Gathering in God's Name

#1 The priest's greeting is the first act of presiding. However formally or informally this greeting is given, s/he acts *in persona Christi*: see pages 238–239 in this book.

#2 On the Two Great Commandments see pages 264–265 in this book. They do not have their 'covenant recitation' function here, as in *BCP* or HC1, nor do they introduce the confession of sin, as in HC2. Rather, in HC3 they function as a 'call to worship'. When this is not appropriate, other sentences may be used: as well as those for the day, suitable ones can be found on *APBA* pages 3, 19 and 35.

On the Prayer of Preparation, see pages 239–241 in this book.

#3 On the *Gloria* and its placement, see pages 271 and 278 in this book.

#4 On Collects, see pages 113–117 in this book.

#5-11 The Ministry of the Word

On the Ministry of the Word, including the readings in *APBA*, see Chapter Three.

#5-8 The rubric allows a wide range of reading patterns, while requiring at least two readings including one from the Gospels.

On 'Hear the word of the Lord', see page 243 in this book.

On standing for the Gospel reading, see pages 243-244 in this book.

#9 On creeds in liturgy, and their translation, see Notes 1 and 2 on *APBA* pages 820-823, and page 125 in this book.

#12 The Prayers of the People

The intercessions in HC3 are the fullest in *APBA*. They are based on the litany form introduced in HC2 in *AAPB*, whose structure follows that of the Prayer for the Church Militant in *BCP*, itself based in part on 1 Timothy 2.1. An important aspect is that thanksgivings precede petitions in each section. These prayers are often replaced by forms prepared locally: see pages 127 and 281-282 in this book.

#13-15 Preparation for the Lord's Supper

The structure of this section follows that of *BCP*, but with new elements.

#13 These sentences are longer than those in HC1 and HC2 because they are intended to function as brief exhortations, corresponding to the "Ye that do truly and earnestly repent" of *BCP*.

On 'worthy reception', see page 245 in this book.

#14 This newly composed form of confession is from the Sydney Committee.

"Heavenly Father" is the characteristic divine naming in Matthew's gospel.

"loved you with an everlasting love" is from Jeremiah 31.3.

"broken ... have done" abbreviates the confession in *BCP* M&EPrayer.

"We are ... died for us" is a modern restatement of repentance, based on *BCP*.

"forgive us, cleanse us and change us" in three strong verbs brings together the progressive aspects of God's work in us, leading into reference to the Spirit:

"By your Holy Spirit ... ", who leads us on to perform the gospel in daily life.

This fresh reworking of scriptural and *BCP* motifs is available for use in all services in *APBA*.

#15 The absolution, another new composition, brings together *BCP*'s 'declarative' (M&EP) and 'pronouncement' (HC) styles in a commendably short space.

The next sentences correspond to the 'Comfortable Words' in *BCP* Holy Communion, placed to follow the absolution as in M&EP2: #7, *APBA* pages 21-22.

#16–17 The Greeting of Peace

These sections are a shorter form of #24–25 in HC2.

#18 The Great Thanksgiving

This Thanksgiving is noteworthy for the use of material from Revelation, worked into familiar phrases from *BCP* Holy Communion, in a 'four-fold shape' structure.

The Preface gives thanks for God's work in both creation (Revelation 4.11 plus Genesis 1.26) and Christ (abbreviating Thanksgiving 1 in HC2), but no provision is made for seasonal Prefaces. The function of the *Benedictus* (omitted here) is taken up boldly in the later response, "Come, Lord Jesus!" (Revelation 22.20).

The Institution narrative is close to HC1 and *BCP*, using simpler grammar, but with one regrettable change: "On the night in which he was betrayed" (1 Corinthians 11.23) is weakened to "On the night before he died".

Further, given the provision in *BCP* for manual acts, there is the option of breaking the bread at this point. This adds complexity, and runs the risk of muddying the 'four-fold shape', but the accompanying response avoids the idea that the Lord's Supper repeats the Last Supper, let alone that the fraction symbolises Christ's death.

The *'anamnesis* responses are direct and strong: one of proclamation, one of expectation. The doxology echoes both aspects, with a 'communion' *'epiclesis*, leading into the dramatic conclusion from Revelation 5.12.[3]

#19–20 The Breaking of the Bread and the Communion

#19 On issues around the 'fraction' see pages 253–254 in this book.

#20 On the words of invitation and administration, see pages 255–256 in this book. The invitation which precedes the shorter words abbreviates the "Ye that do truly" of *BCP* HC with an impressive economy of space.

The rubrics indicate that the minister "may say" the words of administration, but no mention is made of other words. Given the reference to silence at #19, if neither set of words is said, then nothing is.

#21–25 The Sending Out of God's People

#21 Following *BCP*, provision is made for the Lord's Prayer to be said following communion: see page 270 in this book.

The post-communion prayer abbreviates considerably *BCP*'s Prayer of Thanksgiving: compare the one in HC1, *APBA* page 115.

---

3   A further Great Thanksgiving and post-communion for HC3 is available on the General Synod website, based on Joel's prophecies. They are appropriate for occasions when an environmental focus is sought.

#22 The congregational response, identical to that in HC2, abbreviates considerably *BCP*'s Prayer of Oblation: compare the one in HC1, *APBA* page 114.

#23 The *Gloria* here enables the people to offer the eucharistic 'sacrifice of praise', as in *BCP* HC: see page 271 in this book.

The final line on page 127 allows the HC3 Thanksgiving to be used in HC2: this also enables the *Gloria* to be used after communion without undue page-turning.

#24–25 are identical to the forms in HC2: see pages 295–296 in this book.

A final note

The ethos of HC3 is 'direct', with few alternatives offered. So this is not the rite in which to get overly creative, or use many variations. That it retains several elements from *BCP* is consistent with this ethos. If HC1 suits congregations who appreciate *BCP* but want to use modern English, HC3 may suit those who wish to use a contemporary structure as well.

Chapter Eighteen

Celebrating Holy Communion in Pastoral Services

Holy Communion: Outline Order (HCOO)

This Order, set out on pages 812–813 in *APBA,* is most likely to be used in less regular pastoral situations: a parish camp, youth service or the like. You might respond, "But these aren't pastoral services, aren't they just normal ones in a different setting?" – which raises the issue of what 'pastoral' means. It is commonly taken to refer to situations of need or 'rites of passage': re-active contexts. But every "Gathering in God's Name" offers the pro-active pastoral care of the means of grace that communicate the Christian gospel.[1]

This Order "is not primarily intended for use at the principal Sunday celebration" (*APBA* page 812). This does not stop it forming the basis for other services, however: a Sunday evening Eucharist in Taizé style, for example. Such occasions typically require more planning than a 'usual' service, which is why the rubric opens by stressing the importance of "careful preparation by the participants", not just the leaders.

The standard headings from HC2 provide the 'Outline'. It is not intended to allow an 'anything goes' Eucharist, so some minimum requirements are listed.

Gathering in God's Name: however this begins, it ends with the Collect.

The Ministry of the Word: two or more readings, one being a Gospel, encourages a 'conversation' between them, and hearing them in 'stereo' (see page 54 in this book).

Confession and Absolution: are in the 'standard' position, "as a response to the word of God and in preparation for the celebration of Holy Communion". But their early use is allowed, albeit referring to a draft heading later abandoned, "The Gathering of the People" (see pages 39–40 in this book).

---

[1] William Willimon, *Worship as Pastoral Care* (Nashville: Abingdon, 1979), gives a North American perspective, while Robin Green, *Only Connect: worship and liturgy from the perspective of pastoral care* (London: DLT, 1993) writes from a Church of England context. Both employ the tools of psychology in pro-active and nuanced ways.

Preparation of the Lord's Table: "some of those present" is very open wording. This is sometimes seen as the deacon's ministry, but the rubrics of *BCP* and *APBA* specify that it is the presider who 'places' the bread and wine on the table, as the first of the actions in the 'four-fold shape'. S/he can be assisted, however.

The Great Thanksgiving: the terse wording could mistakenly be taken to mean that the Thanksgiving "The priest" offers is personal, rather than made on behalf of the congregation. "Using an authorised prayer" allows Thanksgivings beyond *APBA*, for example those issued by the Liturgical Commission since 1995 (see Chapter Nineteen in this book).

The Breaking of the Bread and Communion: The "words of distribution" will be those used elsewhere in *APBA*. The communicant's response of "Amen" is specified.

The Sending out of God's People: Post-communion prayers, blessing and dismissal are specified, but not their contents.

Holy Communion in a Wedding

Changing contexts

From early on in the Church's life, the wedding of a Christian couple was typically celebrated in the Eucharist. The English Reformers continued this: the Solemnisation of Matrimony from the 1549 to 1604 *BCP*s followed the order of the Sarum 'nuptial mass', the wedding leading into the Gospel reading. Their rubrics stipulated that "the new married persons (the same day of their marriage) **must** receive the holy communion" (emphasis added). But in *BCP* 1662 the service stands on its own, ending with this rubric:

> **It is convenient** that the new-married persons should receive the holy Communion at the time of their Marriage, or at the first opportunity after their Marriage.

So until quite recent times, few weddings held under Australian Anglican auspices were solemnised in the context of Holy Communion.

The *Family Law Act* (1973) crystallised the changing attitudes to marriage in Australian society. In its wake, 'church' weddings declined: by 2000 it was around half, and the proportion in which the couple are active believers grew, so that the number in which communion is celebrated became more common. *AAPB* included two Forms, both following the order of *BCP*; provision for communion is made in both by complex but identical Notes. *APBA* Marriage (First Order) is in 'office' shape, and provides for communion only by Note. Second Order reflects a more egalitarian understanding of marriage, and is in eucharistic shape. From the 'hinge' page 668, the service may conclude with a blessing, or continue to Holy Communion, *APBA* pages 669–674.

Distinctive aspects of Holy Communion at a wedding

NB: Comment on the Marriage services is found in Chapter Twenty-One. The focus here is on issues related to weddings in the context of a Eucharist.

Gathering in God's Name, pages 657–658, is arranged for a nuptial context. There is no seasonal material, Prayer of Preparation, *Gloria* or *kyrie*, and no provision for confession and absolution at this point. The blessing prayer, page 658, functions as the prayer of the day, whose responses 'collect' in the people's blessing.

The Ministry of the Word leads into the Wedding. No provision is made for a Creed, since those present will likely include other than Christian folk.

The Prayers of the People letters a–i, *APBA* pages 663–665, all relate to married life. As the rubric at #17 notes, j on page 666 is used "When Holy Communion follows", giving a wider context to the intercessions, which end as in HC2.

#20 the Confession and Absolution is optional, since it may not be appropriate to have these at a wedding that includes communion.

#21–22 are as in HC2.

#23 The Preface relates to marriage; the Great Thanksgiving is the first one in HC2.

#25 offers an alternative response for the breaking of the bread, worded so non-communicants can join in.

#26 Communion is given to the couple first. It may be appropriate for them to share in administering the bread and wine: this will depend on their being prepared and ready to do so, their state of mind, and their relationship with those present. The words of invitation and administration are from HC2. As with other pastoral services, there are likely to be visitors present, so care in how communion is administered will be appreciated. Some may be Christians of a tradition other than Anglican; others may not hold the Christian faith. The invitation to communion (#38) can helpfully be preceded or followed by words such as these:

> On this special occasion, communicant members of all Christian churches are welcome to receive holy communion: please hold out your hands to show that you intend to receive. All are invited to come forward for a blessing: to indicate this, just leave your hands by your sides.[2]

#27 The first post-communion prayer may be long, but read well it is dramatic and

---

[2] The General Synod *Admission to the Holy Communion Canon* (1973) stipulates that "A person who has been baptised in the name of the Holy Trinity and is a communicant member of a church which professes the apostolic faith" may receive communion in an Anglican service.

inspiring.

Holy Communion in Ministry with the Sick and Dying

NB: Detailed comment on 'Ministry with the Sick' and 'Dying' is found in Chapter Twenty-Two. The focus here is on these ministries in the context of a Eucharist.

Communion with the Sick

'Ministry with the Sick' is not so much a service, as a sequence that follows the order of HC2. A visit to a sick person for Holy Communion typically entails at least 20 minutes. Time is needed for listening to their situation, hearing from the scriptures – however briefly – and unhurried confession and prayers. This also applies when the 'reserved sacrament' is used: see below. Normative Anglican practice, however, is for the presider to perform all 'four fold shape' actions with those present: taking, giving thanks, breaking the bread and administering communion.

BCP's rubrics require at least two communicants in addition to the priest.[3] So Note 2 on *APBA* page 693 provides, "There should normally be at least two or three others to join with the minister and the sick person". Being accompanied by others enables the visit to be a communal act of worship, and sustains the bonds of friendship in a context of mutual ministry. This norm is not always possible, and the sick person may request the provision that "the minister alone may communicate with him or her". When only the minister and sick person are present, the celebration should carry the sense that it enacts the worship of God's people in microcosm.

Communion from 'reserved' bread and wine

BCP's rubrics appear to exclude taking the bread and wine from a regular Eucharist to a sick person who cannot be present: that is, administering communion from the 'reserved sacrament' (both bread and wine). The matter is more complex, however. Justin Martyr, writing around 155AD, states that

> When the president has given thanks, and all the people have expressed their assent by saying Amen, those who are called by us deacons give to each of those present to partake of the bread and wine mixed with water over which the thanksgiving was pronounced, and to those who are absent they carry away a portion.[4]

The practice of taking the bread and wine from a regular celebration to those unable to be present thus has an ancient pedigree. It was provided for in *BCP* 1549,

---

3   This excluded the pre-Reformation practice of a priest offering the mass alone. The one exception is *BCP* is during a plague, when others will not want to be present with the sick person.

4   *First Apology*, 65

and not forbidden in the 1552, 1559 and 1604 *BCP*s.[5] This reflected the Reformers' concern, not so much with reservation for the sake of communion, as to exclude the elements being used for other purposes, such as veneration and processions (see Articles XXV and XXVIII).

BCP 1662, however, stipulates that after communion the priest is to "place" on the holy table "what remaineth of the consecrated elements", which "shall not be carried out of the Church," but be eaten and drunk "immediately after the Blessing". These new provisions reflect debates in the Commonwealth period, and the possibility of the consecrated elements being put to 'secular' use. At the Offertory earlier in the *BCP* service, the priest was to "place upon the Table so much Bread and Wine, as he shall think sufficient": but sufficient for whom? Since notice of intending to communicate had to be given days beforehand, this 'placing' could include bread and wine being set aside for sick people unable to be present. Again, if the intention was only to communicate those present, why not consume the elements after communion, rather than after the blessing?

These rubrics, taken in the light of the pre-1662 situation, would thus seem not to exclude reservation for those who had notified their names but could not be present, and for whom the priest 'placed' elements. So in my opinion the practice is not unconstitutional, and illuminates the Ordinal for Deacons attached to *BCP* that depicts their ministry of "assisting the priest when *he* ministers the holy communion".

In sum, *BCP* 1662 does not exclude the practice of authorised minister(s), within a short space of time after a service of Holy Communion, taking the bread and wine to a communicant who is unable to be present, but has close links with the congregation from which the minister(s) came.

NB: *BCP* assumes that bread "such is usual to be eaten" is used. This goes stale fairly quickly, which may be one reason for the short time-frame in the rubrics of *BCP* 1549. Wafers, being unleavened bread, do not face this problem, but their continuous reservation is very difficult to square with Anglican formularies.

---

5   The *BCP* 1549 rubrics allow those who had notified their intention to communicate, but were absent due to sickness, to have the bread and wine brought to them before noon of the day following.

   For detailed discussion, with reference to Roman Catholic, Eastern Orthodox, Lutheran and Reformed practice as well as the Anglican tradition, see Charles Harris, "Communion of the Sick" in W. Lowther Clarke (ed.) *Liturgy and Worship. A Companion to the Prayer Books of the Anglican Communion* (London: SPCK, 1932), especially 589–596.

Ministry using the reserved sacrament

Reserved elements are used to set the communion of a sick person in the context of their faith community. So the resources used will be similar to a full celebration of the Eucharist at home or bedside, with readings and prayers. With this in mind, it is helpful for others to accompany the minister, and take parts of the service.[6]

When the bread and wine are ready to be shared, words of introduction which set a context for what is to happen should be used. For example,

N, at a celebration of the Eucharist at St George's today, this bread and wine was taken, thanks were offered to God for Christ's saving work, the bread was broken, and the bread and wine shared among the people. This sacrament of Christ's body and blood has been brought from St George's to be shared with you, as a member with them of the body of Christ.

The Prayer of Approach (#21, *APBA* page 125) can be used, and a time of silence observed. Many communicants appreciate the full words of administration being used in this context, the first option at #17, *APBA* page 687.

After a further time of silence, the Lord's Prayer can be prayed together. The resources on *APBA* page 688 can then be used to conclude the visit.

Extended communion

By 'extended comunion' is meant bread and wine being taken from a congregational celebration to a group of well people, for example at a small centre in a multi-congregation parish. It arose in the Roman Catholic Church following the reforms of the Second Vatican Council that saw regular reception of communion restored, but made impracticable due to a shortage of priests.

Among Australian Anglicans, in the 60s the Eucharist came to be the usual Sunday service rather than Morning Prayer. As regular reception of the sacrament came to be expected, 'extended communion' was experimented with in some rural dioceses.[7] Moreover, women were ordained as deacons from 1986, initially in Melbourne, with the expectation that most would be ordained priest in a year or two, but this stretched into years. A few male priests began to encourage these deacons to act as proto-priests, by presiding at 'extended communion' services, but it put the women concerned under pressure. The (then) Archbishop of Melbourne, Dr David Penman, appointed a representative group to examine the issue, and make recommendations: I was its secretary.

---

6   If the sick person wishes to have Reconciliation of Penitent, this will take place with the priest alone.
7   *When we Meet for Worship*, 166–167 provides "Extended Communion Ministered by a Deacon". Brother Gilbert met with the Melbourne committee (see below), but his proposal was not endorsed.

It took some time, however, for the group's members, coming from a range of Anglican traditions, to trust one another sufficiently so as to share heart-felt convictions about this sacrament of the Gospel. As time went on, it became clear to all that 'extended communion', while understandable as an innovation in emergecncy situations and unusual circumstances, was not helpful:

- from a 'liturgical' viewpoint, three of the four-fold actions were missing – taking, thanking and breaking;
- from a 'catholic' perspective, the Godward action of offering thanks is absent;
- from an 'evangelical' one, it encourages a overly 'localised' view of Christ's presence, leaving the door open to superstitious attitudes.

The Committee came to the view that 'extended communion' is a step too far. Moreover, all its members came to see the practice furthering the danger, in our individualist culture, of the Eucharist being seen as 'spiritual consumerism'.

Communion with the Dying

APBA does not provide specifically for Holy Communion with a dying person: it is presumed that the provisions in 'Ministry with the Sick' apply.

The final administration of communion is traditionally known as *viaticum*, medicine "on the way", the 'last rites'. The medieval emphasis on purgatory and divine judgement led to superstitious attitudes: ordinary folk would become distressed if they learnt that a friend was not 'shriven' (absolved after confession) or given the 'last rites'. The successive impacts of the Reformation, Renaissance, Industrial Revolution and modern science have seen these fears largely disappear, at least in popular culture, and along with them much *viaticum* ministry among Anglicans. But the reactions of modern humans to the approach of death have not gone away, as the work of Elizabeth Kubler-Ross has disclosed.[8]

As a Christian approaches their dying days, being able to receive holy communion should be seen by clergy as having a high priority in ministry. A person's final Eucharist can take into account their life-story and Christian testimony, and their present context. On specific aspects of such a rite, see 'Communion with the Sick' above, and the discussion on funerals that follows.

---

8 Elizabeth Kubler-Ross, *On Death and Dying* (New York: Routledge, 1969); *On Grief and Grieving: Finding the Meaning of Grief Through the Five Stages of Loss* (London: Simon & Schuster, 2005). Her precise 'stages' has come under criticism, but not the seriousness of modern humanity's approach to death.

Holy Communion on the Day of the Funeral

NB: Comment on each section of the Funeral service is found in Chapter Twenty-Three. The focus here is on their significance in the context of a Eucharist.

A new inclusion

APBA, in including this resource, breaks new ground for Australian Anglicans, since no such rite is provided in *BCP* 1662 or *AAPB*.[9] Why not?

The medieval requiem mass was offered on behalf of the dead person, with the intention that their days in purgatory might be minimised. Such ideas were rejected by the Reformers, though the Burial service in *BCP* 1549 provided a collect and readings for Holy Communion "when there is a burial of the dead".[10] But concern about misunderstandings saw the reference to Holy Communion with a burial removed in *BCP* 1552, and not restored in subsequent editions. The collect was taken up largely unchanged into the Burial service, and prayed at its conclusion. The lovely phrase "as our hope is this our brother doth" has spoken to many grieving hearts over the centuries.

When drafting Funeral Services for *APBA* began, the Liturgical Commission accepted that false ideas about what a funeral Eucharist entailed had passed. More positively, it believed that it is deeply fitting for the funeral of a practising Christian to be set within the Holy Communion. There we "proclaim the Lord's death until he comes", and receive "the benefits of Christ's passion". Laying the body of a believer to rest in Christ in the Eucharist sets our loss in the context of Christ's once-for-all fruitful death, where he drew its poisonous sting (1 Corinthians 15.55–57).

I have participated in the funerals of several members of the Liturgical Commission which drafted *APBA*. In each case they were conducted with Holy Communion, as I trust my funeral will be. It was both a spiritual privilege and an evangelical encounter to sense our communion in Christ across the bounds of time, and join with them in the song of heaven, "Holy, Holy, Holy". On each occasion, as I passed the coffin on the way to receive the sacrament of Christ's body and blood, I touched it as an act of thankful remembrance. Coffin and communion spoke to one another sacramentally, setting my own mortality against the reality of the "blessed hope" that is ours in Christ.

---

9   Gilbert Sinden, *When we meet for Worship*, 281–285, gives a fascinating account of the then Liturgical Commission's discussion of a proposal to provide for Holy Communion at a funeral in *AAPB*. While other aspects of the draft *APBA* Funeral services were questioned at the 1995 General Synod, the inclusion of Holy Communion was accepted without comment.

10 The provision was also included in the 1560 Latin *BCP* authorised by Queen Elizabeth I.

Distinctive aspects of Holy Communion at a funeral

The title, "Holy Communion on the Day of the Funeral" means that these resources can be used during the funeral, at a Eucharist on the funeral day, or as part of a Memorial Service: see Note 10 on *APBA* page 772.

'A Funeral Service' has a 'pilgrimage' structure, but follows the headings of HC2, whether or not the Eucharist is celebrated. For clarity, #17 is used both on *APBA* page 721 and for all parts of the Lord's Supper, pages 725–729. At a funeral Eucharist, the Farewell rites, pages 722–723, follow the post-communion prayer, #17f, page 729: since a personalised pewsheet is usual at a funeral, this should not present difficulties.

It was not envisaged that "A Funeral Service for a Child" be conducted with Holy Communion, though #17a–#17f of the Funeral Service could be used after #12, *APBA* page 746. It is also not appropriate for "A Funeral Service for an Infant" to be conducted with Holy Communion. This service is typically held with just the parents and immediate friends present, and is "powerfully intimate" (*APBA* page 753). A separate Eucharist with a wider circle of friends present, using appropriate elements of *APBA* pages 754–762, is recommended.

The funeral itself can be preceded by "Reception of the Body" and "Placing of Christian symbols". Since a funeral in the context of the Eucharist will most likely be of a regular communicant, it would be natural for these elements to be used.

As with Holy Communion at a wedding, there is no seasonal material, Prayer of Preparation, *Gloria* or *kyrie*, and no provision is made for confession and absolution at this point. The Psalm(s) are placed before the Ministry of the Word because they mark the transition from the story of the person's life, recounted at #9, to aspects of the story of God in that Ministry.

The Ministry of the Word offers readings that can work as the First, New Testament and Gospel readings for a Eucharist, though the Psalm may fall in a different place. No provision is made for a Creed: mourners may find it difficult to say many words, and those present will likely include other than Christian folk. The two canticles from Easter Morning Prayer (#13, *APBA* page 718) have a credal aspect, and nothing prohibits a hymn being sung instead.

The Prayers are set out fairly fully, and since a funeral is a sensitive time for all involved, the rubrics do not include "or other suitable prayers". The second prayer of thanksgiving is appropriate when the person has been a regular communicant, so would normally be used in a eucharistic funeral, as would the litany at #15, *APBA* pages 720–721. On where the Lord's Prayer is said, see #17, page 721 and #17c, page 727.

#17a *The Greeting of Peace* marks the transition to the Lord's Supper.

#17b *The Great Thanksgiving* has a strong Easter ring in the Preface, which includes an additional congregational response, similar to that in Thanksgiving 5: "With all your saints / **we give you thanks and praise**". This brings out our corporate celebration *with* the saints, in fellowship with the deceased person, their name being included at "N and ...". The response may be said by the presider as part of the prayer, or omitted.

The institution narrative and concluding section ("Renew us ...") are as in HC2 Thanksgiving 1, but the *'anamnesis* is shortened to give a clear Easter focus.

In the draft of APBA, the memorial acclamation followed "victory over the grave" as a corporate *'anamesis*, but General Synod moved it to its present position: see pages 287–288 in this book. The Liturgical Commission strongly recommends that the later – original – position be used.

#17d–e The fraction, invitation and administration words are as in HC2. With visitors likely to be present, care in how communion is administered is needed (see 'Holy Communion at a Wedding', pages 304–305 in this book).

#17f The eschatological dimension of the Eucharist is to the fore in the post-communion prayer, pointing those present to the Easter hope.

No prayer of self-offering is included for the congregation, since it is likely to include a mix of worldviews. The service moves immediately to the Farewell, *APBA* pages 721–722, which begins with a hymn to mark the transition.

With an unpredictable number of communicants, significant amounts of bread and wine may be left over. Rather than taking time at the end of the administration, what remains is best set aside reverently to be consumed later.

Ministers need to be aware of the pressures of ministering in the face of death. Strong expressions of emotion may be evoked as communion is administered. Presiding in this situation means being graced to be "the still point in a churning universe", while recognising that ministers are not 'above' grief.

Chapter Nineteen

Celebrating Holy Communion using post-APBA rites

In the 25 years since *APBA* was published, the Liturgical Commission has issued, with the approval of the General Synod Standing Committee, further 'Liturgical Resources' related to celebrating Holy Communion. This chapter introduces and comments on these rites, both to show their consistency with what General Synod has approved, and to encourage their use.

Lent, Holy Week and Easter

Historical background

Holy Week has been central to the Christian year from the earliest days. By the mid-second century, Christ's saving passion was being marked in the week of Passover as God's victory over death and sin.[1] By the third century, this Christian Paschal celebration had come to be preceded by a vigil for people preparing for baptism on Easter Day. This vigil soon lengthened to three days, and eventually the 47 days of Lent – including Sundays, which are 'in' but not 'of' Lent's 40 days – with services held daily in Holy Week.[2] By the Middle Ages, prominence was given to fasting, penitence and dramatic enactments: in the West, these became mixed with the springtime festival, Easter. In places touched by the Reformation, Holy Week ceremonies were abolished, sharply reduced or replaced by meditation on appropriate scripture readings.

In the reformed Church of England, the traditional Christian year was retained. Collect, Epistle and Gospel were provided for Ash Wednesday and Holy Week, and the Monday and Tuesday of Easter Week, meaning that Holy Communion was expected to be celebrated on each of these days. A Preface was provided for Easter Week, and 'Easter Anthems' for use at Morning Prayer. Alongside *BCP*,

---

[1] The earliest evidence for Easter is the 'Quartodeciman' controversy around 140AD, in which it was debated whether Easter should be kept on the fourteenth (quartodecima) day of the first month of the lunar year (Exodus 12.5, 16; Leviticus 23.25) or the following Sunday. The latter prevailed because it was the day of resurrection, and avoided copying the Jewish date.

[2] The journal kept by Egeria documents her observations of the rites of the week in Jerusalem around 380AD: an English translation is available at http://users.ox.ac.uk/~mikef/durham/egetra.html

some long-standing customs continued: pancakes on Shrove Tuesday (the eve of Ash Wednesday), simnel cake on Mothering Sunday (the middle Sunday of Lent), and hot cross buns on Good Friday (though *BCP* specifies it as a Fast).

Under the influence of the Oxford Movement, some pre-Reformation ceremonies were re-introduced: many are now observed across the Anglican spectrum. One is decorating church buildings with palms on 'The Sunday next before Easter' (*BCP*), with a palm procession preceding the service. Another is observing a vigil on Easter Eve, entering into the progress of God's saving work through readings, psalms and meditations, reaching its climax in the celebration of the paschal Eucharist. Questions are sometimes raised about some aspects of these practices. Can palms, as inanimate things, be blessed? Is foot-washing or a 'Passover' celebration on Maundy Thursday legitimate? Is it appropriate to celebrate the Eucharist on Good Friday, or use bread and wine set apart on the night before ('pre-sanctified' elements)?

The Roman Catholic rites for Holy Week were simplified by Pope Pius XII in 1955, in the wake of the Liturgical Movement. In the USA, Holy Week has no place in the civic calendar, as it does in England and Australia. In 1970, Episcopal (US Anglican) scholars issued Holy Week services that took this context into account. These resources have had steadily increasing influence across Western churches, so that over the past half-century Holy Week has come to new life across the Anglican Communion.

Australian Anglican provisions – and issues

With such questions and resources around, and in the wake of *AAPB*, some Australian Anglican dioceses began to issue their own Holy Week services, notably Wangaratta and Melbourne. Having seen *APBA* through General Synod, the national Liturgical Commission took up the task of preparing Lent services which could be used in all dioceses. Five rites were drafted: Ash Wednesday, Passion / Palm Sunday, Maundy Thursday, Good Friday and Easter Vigil. These were authorised for 'trial use' by the General Synod Standing Committee in 2005, and published on the General Synod website.[3] Each has a substantial introduction, giving context to the text and rubrics or the service, with suggestions about practical matters: so there is little need for commentary on them here. Two overall issues recur, however: how past and present relate, and how symbols 'work' with their associated words.

---

[3] Electronic rather than print publication was sought by the Liturgical Commission since each service is an annual 'one-off', and needs localising. The Standing Committee was cautious about approving a book, which might be seen as exercising an authority belonging to General Synod itself. In the event, the five services proved to be the precursor of the growing range of resources being issued by the Liturgy Commission on the web, available at https://www.anglican.org.au/lent-holy-week-and-easter

Re-enact or re-member?

Holy Week is sometimes seen as re-enacting the events leading to Jesus' death. But these were once-for-all, unrepeatable. A better way is to think in terms of 're-membering'. As the introduction to the 2005 Passion Sunday service puts it,

> In Holy Week we need to be particularly careful not to try and 're-enact' the events of the days before the death of Jesus. Liturgy is about celebration and commemoration rather than re-enactment.

Nevertheless, something about the story of Jesus draws people in when it is told. The drama of his final week, on which each gospel spends a disproportionate amount of space, calls for active engagement with it. In observing Holy Week, the Christian tradition has sought to focus on God's saving work in Christ as a whole. So the Holy Week re-telling of this central story centres on **who** more than **what** we remember: Jesus Christ, crucified and risen. In doing so, we are ourselves 're-membered' in his body, the Church: this is why Easter Day includes the renewal of baptismal promises.

An example of this re-enact / re-member dialectic is the name used for "The Sunday next before Easter, commonly called Palm Sunday" (*BCP*). Matthew 27 is the Gospel reading, orienting hearers to the coming week as a whole. *APBA* continues this perspective, naming the day as "Passion Sunday (Palm Sunday)", and setting the whole passion to be read from each synoptic gospel in its 'year'. Alongside this, readings for a distinct 'Liturgy of the Palms' are provided on *APBA* page 494, recognising 'Palm Sunday' customs, but keeping the focus on Christ's work as a whole.

The larger challenge is how the 'Three Days' (*triduum* in Latin) are observed: Good Friday, which starts on Thursday at sundown, Holy Saturday and Easter Sunday. It is helpful to move through these days accompanying the disciples, as it were: but we cannot repeat Christ's work, nor pretend that the Lord is not risen. The key is to keep an eye on the story as a whole, while engaging with each of its movements.

The symbols of Holy Week

The spiritual genius of the Church of England tradition has on the whole been 'plain', centred around attending to the (magnificent) words of *BCP* and the *King James Bible*. In *BCP*, minimal reference is made to symbols: the water and crossing of baptism, the bread and wine of Holy Communion, and the laying of hands in confirmation and ordination. One reason for the Oxford Movement's success was its breaking out of this scarcity into the Romantic world of colour and movement. But widespread antipathy also arose to the changes sought, seen as 'unEnglish' or 'Romish'. Protestant suspicion of symbols is still around, though colour television, the charismatic movement and today's highly visual culture has eased this: the use of candles, flowers and symbolic acts in public rituals is now nigh universal.

Symbols evoke something of the ineffable realities beyond words, and enable a strong sense of communal oneness. They can speak to a wide variety of personalities, and to those on the fringes of the Church. Symbols are threaded through the traditional services for Lent and Holy Week. So the Liturgy Commission, in drafting rites for use across all dioceses, saw the opportunity to 're-receive' symbols, while sensitive to the doctrinal and pastoral concerns surrounding their use, seen in two main ways:

a) The wording of prayers of blessing

The symbols employed, rather than being 'blessed' irrespective of their use, are related to those who receive them. In the scriptures inanimate things are not blessed, but God is blessed for them (*berakah*: see pages 123–124 in this book). So on Ash Wednesday,

> *The ashes are placed on the Lord's Table, and the priest says*
> Blessed (*berakah*) are you, God of all creation.
> You are eternal, we are mortal, formed from the dust of the earth.
> As we receive these ashes, make them a sign for us
> of repentance and returning to you.
> Breathe into us again the breath of life.
> **Blessed be God for ever.**

And in the Liturgy of the Palms,
> Sovereign God, we thank you for these branches [and crosses] of palm.
> By your blessing may they be for us signs of the victory of your Son.
> May we who carry them in his name ever hail him as our Messiah,
> and follow him in the way that leads to eternal life.

b) The wording associated with symbolic acts

A symbol enacted only in silence is open to misinterpretation, but too many words detracts from its working. So the words associated with symbolic actions in these services are brief and clear, giving a basic sense of the meaning, but avoiding over-interpretation. In some cases, more than one set of words is offered, to give space for particular meanings to be related to different circumstances. Thus on Ash Wednesday,

> *The ashes are placed on each person's forehead in silence, or with the words*
> Remember that you are dust and to dust you shall return.
>   *and/or* Repent and believe the gospel.
>   *and/or* Turn away from sin and be faithful to Christ.

Practical matters

Lent as a season is explored in the 'Liturgical Notes and Suggestions' accompanying the Ash Wednesday service. Holy Week overall is considered in the 'Liturgical Notes' for Passion (Palm Sunday), and the unity of the Three Days in those for Good Friday. The comments below complement these Notes.

Ash Wednesday: burning palm crosses

The Liturgical Notes suggest that people

> bring back last year's palm crosses or fronds and burn them to make the ashes for Ash Wednesday. This represents a little death, a letting go of the past in order to embrace God's future. The burning of the palms is best done in silence.

The intention is not that each parishioner burns their own palm ... but nothing is said about where or how the burning takes place. This is a matter for the priest to determine, playing close attention to safety. Burning the palms in the service, in a heat-proof container (pottery is good) on the Lord's Table, is symbolically powerful: it can take place as Psalm 51 is read. But you don't want the Fire Brigade turning up because an alarm was set off (yes, this has been known to happen). Further, a little water will be needed to cool the ashes down to make a paste suitable for signing with. This may take a little time, but there is no need for hurry.

Passion Sunday (Palm Sunday): procession practicalities

The 'Liturgical Notes' encourage palm processions to "take a route that will cause it to be public". If this involves crossing roads, local police will need to be informed – but officers put on Sunday morning duty for just a few folk may not be impressed.

Opportunities for the rainbow of Christian traditions present in Australia to worship together are few. So the Notes suggest that palm processions "can be occasions for ecumenical co-operation," with the different congregations involved then going to their own Sunday service. An ecumenical procession is more likely to be an act of public Christian witness in the late morning or early afternoon, following regular Sunday services. But whatever works locally is good: public processions in the name of Christ, as the Notes conclude, offer "all sorts of imaginative possibilities". And police co-operation is more readily given when local churches approach them as a group.

Palm Sunday processions have evolved into peace rallies, especially in cities. People of goodwill join with church folk to support peace-making being given higher priority in the agenda of society and government. This is a significant aspect part of the mission of God, but is distinct from processions of Holy Week witness.

Maundy Thursday: the holiness of mess

The 'Liturgical Notes' for this special evening mention that the liturgy can take place in the context of a meal, and may include foot-washing. But the mess involved is not mentioned: the challenge is to mix the natural bustle of preparations, serving and conversation with the profoundly spiritual significance of the occasion. This is a first-rate opportunity for people of different temperaments to work and pray together amid the necessary mix of moods.

The Gathering can be followed by the meal itself, during which the Ministries of the Word and Prayer can be shared, followed by foot-washing, with the Great Thanksgiving and communion concluding the meal. For some, sharing Eucharist in the context of a 'real' meal is a moment of wonder; for others it can be uncomfortable. Attention to the 'choreography' of the various elements will pay dividends: how the elements are administered is particularly sensitive.

Foot-washing, if overly formalised, can work against the rawness of Jesus' action. Those who have experienced it, or washed others' feet, find it to be deeply humbling. It must not be 'forced' on people: it can be quite sensuous, and some may find exposing their feet in public to be embarrassing. Again, the messiness involved – the floor getting wet, people moving around, where to put a growing pile of towels – is an opportunity for reflection on Christ's work rather than a 'problem'.

NB: hand-washing, carrying echoes of Pilate's actions, is not appropriate.

Traditionally, hot cross buns are only baked on Maundy Thursday and eaten on Good Friday. When one Anglican priest found that his local bakery followed this tradition, he offered to take a short 'blessing God for buns' service as work started on Thursday morning. The offer was gladly accepted, and dozens of people came for a brief time of readings, prayers … and buying buns for the morrow.

Good Friday: mood and stations

The 'Liturgical Notes' addressing Good Friday services state that they

> should not give the impression of being 'Jesus' funeral', complete with gloomy hymns. Moreover, the austerity of the liturgy should not preclude a note of triumph and joy, for the community gathers on Good Friday to *celebrate* the Lord's triumph on the cross – an event that can only be understood from the viewpoint of Easter.

This is why it is 'Good', that is, 'God's' Friday. Theologically, this is the day when "the strife is o'er, the battle won", though the reality of Christ's passion and dying cannot help but be to the fore. Conjuring up a sense of gloom, as if we did not know that

Christ is risen, reflects the worst side of a re-enactment mentality. The service will be most helpful when it is quiet in tone, with a sense of "solemn joys and lasting treasure".

The service makes provision for bringing in a large cross, to which people are invited to come "to make appropriate acts of devotion to the Crucified One". The cross as symbol points to the "Lord of glory" (1 Corinthians 2.8), not to itself alone. 'Appropriate acts' could include touching the cross, smearing fragrant balm on it, placing symbols used during Lent nearby, lighting candles in an adjacent sand tray and the like.

A long-standing tradition is processing the "stations of the Cross", symbols of the passion story. Where these are placed around the church building, the procession will take place inside. But Good Friday offers further opportunities for a public, ecumenical procession of witness: using all fourteen of the traditional stations may be too much, but a selection of readings, prayers and songs appropriate to the setting can work well.[4] The re-enact/re-member dialectic needs to be kept in mind, but the 'stations' are an effective way telling the story of the passion as a whole, while embracing our human dramatic instinct.

Significant periods of silence should form part of any Good Friday observation. Its dignified seriousness can be balanced by the eating of hot cross buns afterwards.

NB: A traditional service for Evening Prayer from Wednesday to Friday of Holy Week is Tenebrae (shadows). It consists of 14 scripture readings with responses and music, each section marked by a candle being extinguished until only one remains, whose putting out is accompanied by a loud noise, and then silence. Tenebrae is especially appropriate for the evening of Good Friday.[5]

Holy Saturday: the Great Sabbath

Holy Saturday can be a puzzle. In the medieval period, the classic emphasis on Christ's victory came to be imagined as his descent to the dead to defeat Satan on Holy Saturday—the 'harrowing of hell'.[6] The danger here is thinking in terms of 'might is right', rather than the New Testament emphasis on Christ overcoming these evils through suffering, 'absorbing' them and rendering them harmless for believers. Christ's last word, according to John's gospel, is *tetelestai*: "finished!"

---

4   A traditional form is in the *Book of Occasional Services* of The Episcopal Church: the 2018 version is available at https://www.riteseries.org/brain/bos. See Further Reading for contemporary rites.

5   A traditional form can be found in the *Book of Occasional Services*.

6   The phrase *descendit ad inferos*, included in the Apostles' Creed to affirm that Christ went through all that humans do in death, was translated as 'descended into hell' in BCP. In Hebrew thought, Hades, Sheol or the Pit was the place of the departed, a lifeless place but not one of punishment (Psalms 88, 142.8). Considerable debate took place in the Reformation on the *descensus*, evidenced in its separate treatment in Article III of the 39 Articles, abbreviated considerably from Cranmer's 42 Articles.

He *dies* victorious, having taken on all that could be thrown at him. As Matthew's gospel puts it:

> Jesus cried again with a loud voice and breathed his last. At that moment the curtain of the temple was torn in two, from top to bottom. The earth shook, and the rocks were split. The tombs also were opened, and many bodies of the saints who had fallen asleep were raised. (Matthew 27:50–52)

Matthew affirms that full access to God's presence was obtained in Christ's death, signified in the earth releasing those imprisoned in its depths. This description, however difficult for modern ears, places the victory of Christ in his suffering and dying, not in a post-death test of strength. So Holy Saturday is not about Christ's going into battle with the forces of darkness. It is the great Sabbath, the day which marks the divine rest after death and Satan were paradoxically overcome in Christ's obedience "to death, even death on a cross" (Philippians 2.11). As God rested after the work of creation (Genesis 2.2–3), so Christ rested after the work of redemption, of re-creation.

No commentary or resources are provided for Holy Saturday in the 2005 services, however. *APBA* includes only a sentence, two collects and readings. These recognise the reality of Christ's death, and his sharing with us mortals all its consequences, focussing on the importance of our 'waiting', in liturgy and lifestyle alike, in the hope of resurrection.

So, while much of Holy Saturday may be filled with busy preparations for Easter Day – setting out furniture, polishing brass, arranging flowers and so on – the day is best kept in the spirit of resting with Christ, joining Joseph and the two Marys in honouring his victory over death.

Easter rites: time and focus

The scriptures point to the early morning as a significant 'resurrection' time, when the women encountered the empty tomb and the risen Lord. On the other hand, in biblical thought the day begins at sunset, so 'The Great Vigil of Easter' opens as darkness falls on Holy Saturday. The idea of Christ revealed at Easter as the divine light soon saw a Service of Light develop, during which the 'paschal candle' is lit in the dark from 'new fire', and marked with signs of the new year.

The 2005 service is thus designed for use late at night or before dawn. But a near midnight or dawn start is for 'keenies', and is impractical for regulars with disabilities. So a 'usual time' service will likely be needed where larger numbers are likely to be present. Its ambience and symbolism will need to be thought afresh, taking into account visitors present, and families with children. If one distinctive element stands out, it is the reaffirmation of baptismal promises, with lots of water splashed around, whether or not a baptism takes place.

A practical way for people from dawn and later services to share together the joy of Easter is to have an open breakfast in between them, perhaps croissants with a glass of champagne. People can be encouraged to greet one another warmly with the traditional Easter shout: "The Lord is risen! He is risen indeed!"

Helpful resources for marking Holy Week include the following:

Holy Week Services, ed. Donald Gray (SPCK, 1983): English and ecumenical

Lent, Holy Week, Easter (Church House / CUP, SPCK 1986): Church of England rites, now taken up in *Common Worship*

The Episcopal Church, *The Book of Occasional Services* (New York: Morehouse, 1976): an updated electronic version is available at https://www.riteseries.org/brain/bos.

Two practical guides, grounded in theological and contextual awareness:

Akehurst, Peter, *Keeping Holy Week* (Bramcote, Notts: Grove Worship Series 41, 1976)

Lloyd, Trevor, *Celebrating Lent, Holy Week and Easter* (Bramcote, Notts: Grove Worship Series 93, 1985)

The Easter Holiday Book (Lion, 1985): lots of ideas for children

Two Australian 'stations of the cross', strikingly illustrated, are:

Moore, Brian sj, *His Cross and Ours: Praying the Stations* (Melbourne: Collins Dove, 1989)

Ungunmerr-Baumann, Miriam-Rose, *Australian Stations of the Cross* (Melbourne: Collins Dove, 1984): this is from the Daly River Mission, and brings a profound Australian Indigenous perspective.

Celebrating the Holy Communion using post-*APBA* rites

In Living Use

This booklet was issued by the Liturgical Commission alongside the draft of *APBA* in response to requests from The NSW Prayer Book Society that 'thee / thy' language forms be included. These were not present in *AAPB*, and the Commission for *APBA* saw no reason to change this policy. However, it was appreciated that copies of *BCP* were increasingly scarce, and that *BCP* services were often celebrated with changes of varying usefulness, especially Holy Communion.

Two members of the Liturgical Commission, Evan Burge and Charles Sherlock, believed that much good could be done, and potential tensions eased, if a book of *BCP* services was prepared that retained their integrity, set them out as they are typically used today, and revised dated expressions. The pair were given permission to pursue this project, and the result was *In Living Use: Revised Services from the Book of Common Prayer (1662)*. It contains forms for Morning and Evening Prayer, Prayers and Thanksgivings, the Collects, and Holy Communion. In the latter, the *Agnus Dei* was included (in brackets) "as a communion anthem": this was the only aspect of the book questioned at the 1995 General Synod.

In Living Use continues to be available to congregations who wish to have accessible versions of *BCP* services.

The Great Thanksgiving (HC2) based on the *Apostolic Tradition* of Hippolytus

In the draft book submitted to the 1995 General Synod, Thanksgiving 3 was based on the *Apostolic Tradition* attributed to Hippolytus (c.200).[7] The oldest known text of a eucharistic prayer, it preceded the controversies of the ninth, sixteenth and recent centuries. But in the Synod debate it was replaced by the newly-minted Thanksgiving 3, apparently because six Thanksgivings were thought too many.

When the Liturgy Commission began work on further Thanksgiving Prayers, an obvious start was the 'Hippolytus' one.[8] It has several notable features:

- It includes the first known use of "Lift up your hearts!" in a eucharistic prayer.
- The Preface celebrates God's work in Christ from creation, through incarnation to ascension. The key image is one of victory: Christ "won" a holy people by giving up his life to "break the chains of evil and death, and banish the darkness of sin and despair".[9] This 'classic' motif of God's overcoming evil, rather than forgiving sins, was dominant in the early centuries. Christians lived as a pressured minority in a death-drenched culture: the good news was that Christ delivered them from death and the powers of evil. This has renewed appeal today, where church is increasingly counter-cultural, and fear of 'the bomb' and climate change threaten extinction.
- The *Sanctus* is not in the *Apostolic Tradition*, but its omission would be felt as quite odd by Anglicans today, so it was included.
- In the institution narrative, the future tense is used: "this is my body / blood, which will be given / shed for you". A possible reading of the Greek text, it emphasises that the Last Supper looked forward to the passion of Christ.

---

7 Geoffrey Cuming, *Hippolytus. A Text for Students*. Grove Liturgy Series 8 (Bramcote, Notts: Grove, 1976) gives a critical text and commentary. The version for *APBA* was prepared by Evan Burge.

8 https://www.anglican.org.au/holy-communion

9 The full text of the *Apostolic Tradition* reads at this point, "when he was delivered to voluntary suffering, in order to dissolve death, and break the chains of the devil, and tread down hell, and bring the just to the light, and set the limit, and manifest the resurrection".

- The *'anamnesis*, "with this bread and this cup we give you thanks", is in line with the equivalent phrases in other Thanksgiving Prayers in *APBA*. The original, "we offer you the bread and cup, giving thanks", though doctrinally innocent in ancient times, is not available for Australian Anglicans given later controversies.
- The next phrase, that "in Christ you have counted us worthy to stand in your presence and serve you", does not say "we are worthy", but that our worthiness comes from God, and is attributed to ('counted', or 'deemed') rather than inherent in us.
- The *'epiclesis* invokes the Spirit on "the celebration of your Church", as in Thanksgiving 2, before doing so on the communicants. In the original, the Spirit is invoked "on the offering of your Church in their gathering".
- The concluding doxology, celebrating the Trinitarian presence of God "in the holy Church", shows the growing early sense of the Trinity, though the formula is not so precise as to exclude Arian ideas that emerged a century later.

Great Thanksgivings for use in HC2 and HC3

The Liturgy Commission, appreciating that the overall shape of non-*BCP* Eucharists has changed little since 1973, has issued several Great Thanksgivings for use with HC2 and HC3. At the time of writing, five were available for download on the Liturgy page of the Anglican Church of Australia website, each with explanatory notes:

- Great Thanksgiving (HC2), Wisdom in Creation theme
- Great Thanksgiving 5 (HC2), Creation theme for when children are present
- Preface, Great Thanksgiving 5 (HC2), for The Coming of the Light (July 1)
- Preface, Great Thanksgiving 1 (HC2), Marriage theme
- Great Thanksgiving (HC3), based on themes from the prophet Joel

Each 'theme' flavours the relevant Thanksgiving as a whole: as eucharistic prayers, each continues to hinge around commemorating the atoning passion of Christ.

New Eucharists

At the time of writing, two post-*APBA* Eucharists had been issued by the Liturgy Commission: each section, from Gathering to Sending Out, has been rethought.[10]

The 'Shepherd' Eucharist

The Notes state that this "has been prepared keeping in mind situations when children are present". This affects both the structure and language of the service, but the readings can be from any Festival.

---

10   Available at www.anglican.org.au/liturgy-worship. Both rites include explanatory notes, and make the HC3 regrettable change to the institution narrative: "On the night in which he was betrayed" (1 Corinthians 11.23) is weakened to "On the night before he died".

Contextually, the 'shepherd' theme relates to many places in Australia and the scriptures. Theologically, it expresses the focal purpose of Holy Communion, to "proclaim the Lord's death until he comes". The Good Shepherd "laid down his life for the sheep", so that there might be "one fold and one shepherd".

Holy Communion (2009)

This service breaks new ground for Australian Anglicans: **it is the first Eucharist issued by the Liturgy Commission in which there is no 'Cranmerian' material**. An initial draft received sharp critique from clergy devoted to *BCP*. The outcome is a new rite in which the Commission has listened closely to Australian needs, the Liturgical Movement and the *BCP* tradition.

In some ways Holy Communion (2009) can be seen as blending the approaches of HC2 and HC3. Like the latter it is 'direct', with few options and short sentences, though a more creative approach is taken to images involving gender. And it follows the Liturgical Commission's preferences in HC2, in particular setting both the confession of sin, and the memorial acclamation, in their 'later' positions.

I would be most surprised were another printed, 'hard copy' prayer book put before General Synod for consideration. The future for liturgical provision is resources released electronically, of which *ePray*, and the services considered in this Part, are a foretaste. This is "one big step" for Australian Anglicans, since it means trusting ministers and local liturgy committees to shape 'Liturgical Resources' for local use.

A long way from the "principle of uniformity" that governed the Anglican tradition for four centuries ...

Part F

Marking Rites of Passage using *APBA*

'Rites of passage' is how sociologists describe rituals through which humans face and respond to the main turning-points of life, especially ones that are challenging or dangerous.[1] Typical ones are rites associated with birth, marriage, illness and death, but moving house, losing or changing jobs and divorce are others.

The Church of England, as the 'established' religion of England, has for centuries been closely involved in providing rites of passage. The CofE arrived in this land on the First Fleet in 1788 in the person of a chaplain, the Revd Richard Johnson. His ministry was tolerated more than welcomed, and the Church he represented was anything but 'established' here. But he and his successors were expected to officiate at rites of passage for the nascent colony, and then the emerging nation.

Since World War II this expectation, and the opportunities it affords, has steadily waned. The proportion of weddings taken by Christian clergy has dropped below 50%, and funerals are increasingly replaced by 'celebrations of a life' led by civil celebrants. When the Liturgical Commission set to work on the Pastoral Services for *APBA*, this shift from the world of *BCP*, and even *AAPB* (1978), was very much in members' minds.

Four 'needs' called for careful work.

1. **The need for a Christian rite of birth distinct from baptism**

In Chapter Ten in this book the claim is made that

> Baptism is no longer the entry point for a new-born infant into a Christian society, a 'birth-right'. It is seen afresh as a 'new birth rite', drawing a person (of whatever age) into the household of God as a member of Christ.

A corollary is that a 'rite of passage' for birth, distinct from baptism, is needed. *BCP*'s 'The Churching of Women' offered a precedent, but it focuses on the women's coming safely through the dangers of childbirth. *AAPB* included 'Thanksgiving for

---

[1] Rites of passage analysis pays attention to the three-stage processes involved in 'liminality': people separating from normal life; crossing a significant boundary (limen); and resuming life changed.

the Birth of a Child', but this is just two pages, mostly consisting of Psalm 27 and the General Thanksgiving.

A rite related to birth was thus needed that offered more fulsome resources to celebrate God's gift of life, and the dangers involved. 'Thanksgiving for a Child' was the outcome: see Chapter Twenty.

2. **The need for a wedding service that responds to changing gender roles**
Marriage (Second Form) in *AAPB* (1978) took on board the increasingly egalitarian view of husband-wife relationships in Australian society, but its language and structure largely remained that of '*BCP* translated'. The impact of the *Family Law Act* (1973) had not been fully felt, and *de facto* marriages had not become as common as now. And the divisive intra-Anglican debate on the ordination of women, that would see 'headship' ideas of marriage both espoused and ridiculed, was just getting going.

A rite of Holy Matrimony was thus needed that set Christian understandings of marriage in the light of these contextual changes, and theological responses to them. A Service for Marriage (Second Order) was the outcome, accompanied at the request of General Synod members by a First Order rite: see Chapter Twenty-One.

3. **The need for a rite for personal confession and absolution**
The 'Visitation of the Sick' in *BCP* includes a form for a person troubled in spirit to confess their sins to a "minister learned in God's Word" and be absolved. However, such 'auricular' – that is, private – confession, practised by a few Anglican clergy, was opposed or viewed with suspicion by many others.

The revelation in recent years of sexual abuse by some clergy, however, and the possibility of this being covered up in the confessional, put the practice in a new context. State laws allowed 'client confidentiality' for doctors, lawyers and others to be breached in specific circumstances. In 1995, such 'mandatory reporting' was required of priests for crimes disclosed in pastoral conversation, but not for those disclosed in confession, provided an official form was used.[2]

A rite was thus needed which made provision for personal confession and absolution that was appropriate to the new context, and consistent with Anglican formularies. The outcome was 'Reconciliation of a Penitent', considered on pages 372-374 of this book.

---

2   The General Synod *Canon Concerning Confession* (1989) set out grounds under which a priest who reported matters disclosed in confession might not be disciplined. General Synod revised the Canon in 2014 and 2017, allowing a priest under certain conditions, and without penalty, to disclose to authorities the abuse of a child or vulnerable person that was confessed in confidence.

4. **The need for funeral resources that relate to changing views of death**
Cremation arrived in Australia soon after World War II, and is now widely accepted. Rites of passage for death then take place in two stages: the funeral, near the time of death and typically public; and the interment, some weeks later and usually private. Further, the proportion of funerals taken by 'civil celebrants' has increased steadily, typically in the form of 'celebration of a life'. These tend to divert attention from the grief and loss around death, and can be dominated by eulogies.

Within the Anglican Church, sensitivities around 'prayers for the dead' have continued, though what this means is not always clear. Conversely, a growing number of church funerals incorporate Holy Communion (see pages 310-312 in this book).

A rite was thus needed that took into account these changes in funeral practice and social context, and offered ways forward on theological issues of long standing. The outcome was Funeral Resources, considered in Chapter Twenty-Three.

How these chaptes are structured
The chapters in this Part are thus:

Chapter 20	Thanksgiving for a Child
Chapter 21	Celebrating Marriage using *APBA*
Chapter 22	Ministries of Wholeness:
	Ministry with the Sick,
	Ministry with the Dying,
	Reconciliation of a Penitent
Chapter 23	Resources for Funeral Ministry

Chapter Twenty

Thanksgiving for a Child

The safe arrival of a child is a time for great thanksgiving. On the one hand, the mother has survived one of the most dangerous times in a woman's life, though possibly with ongoing injuries: this was the focus of Christian rites until recent decades. On the other hand, there is rejoicing in God's gift of a new life, with its promise and hopes: this is the dominant emphasis in contemporary rites, within and beyond Christian circles. The contrast is seen in Jesus' words:

> When a woman is in labour, she has pain, because her hour has come. But when her child is born, she no longer remembers the anguish because of the joy of having brought a human being into the world. (John 16:21)

Rites marking childbirth

Historical background

Rites associated with the birth of a child are found in all human societies, but not all are consistent with Christian faith. When this faith permeated the Roman Empire from the fourth century, evils such as infanticide were outlawed. Prayers for and by women who gave birth were offered, with a focus on their post-natal 'cleansing'. In Christendom, baptism came to be the way an infant was welcomed into society as well as church, effectively becoming a 'rite of passage' for birth.

In the reformed Church of England such ideas at first continued. *BCP* 1549 required clergy to "admonish the people, that they defer not the Baptism of infants any longer than the Sunday, or other holy day, next after the child be born", and included 'The Order of the Purification of Women'. Liturgical Commission member Margaret Collison, who held the portfolio for this service, notes its significant changes of name.

> In 1552, the service became 'The Thanksgiving of Women after Childbirth, commonly called the Churching of Women'. Modern Prayer Books have names such as 'Thanksgiving for the Birth of a Child', 'Thanksgiving for the Gift of a Child' or, as *APBA* simply has, 'Thanksgiving for a Child'.[1]

---

1 *A Practical Commentary*, 49.

The increasing separation of churches and Australian society from the 1960s has seen declining numbers of children being brought for baptism.[2] While this has made space for deeper understandings of Christian initiation, explored in Chapter Ten, it left a significant gap in rites of passage for birth. The Liturgical Commission thus saw an opportunity to develop a Christian rite in which thanks is offered to God for a child, whether new-born, adopted, baptised, fostered, orphaned …

Childbirth and the purification of women

Why discuss 'purification', when 'Thanksgiving for a Child' has nothing remotely linked to this idea? Folk-religious ideas continue around rites of passage for birth, while new insights into gender roles illuminate attitudes and actions that harm women. The Liturgical Commission was also aware of new pressures on Christian women, for example revulsion at menstruating or pregnant women administering communion, or 'headship' ideas that exclude women from vocations beyond mothering.

Margaret Collison, writing of the English liturgical heritage, says:

> The rubrics which direct the place of the woman during the ceremony also reflect the attitude of the church. In the Sarum rite … used in England immediately before the Reformation, the first part of the office was celebrated at the church door, and it was not until the woman was sprinkled with holy water that she entered the church. The rubric of 1549 said "The woman shall come into the church, and there shall kneel down in some convenient place, nigh unto the quire door". The rubric of 1552 substituted "nigh unto the place where the table standeth". The 1662 book has "in some convenient place as hath been accustomed, or as the ordinary shall direct".

Despite the implication in the 1549 rubrics and 'Purification' title that the mother was 'unclean', the service itself gave no hint of this, but consists of thanks for safe deliverance offered in psalmody and prayer. The final collect asks that the woman may "walk in her vocation in this life", a positive view of her (unspecified) calling. The 1552 service goes further, welcoming the mother into the 'sacred space' of the church, near the holy table. As Collison concludes, "The idea of pollution and needing to be purified has been replaced by thanksgiving for the child."

Why did the idea of child-birth involving mothers being unclean arise? And why have so many down the ages feared an infant remaining unbaptised? Part of the answer is false understandings of 'original sin' (see pages 170–171 in this book). This

---

2   The decline is slower in rural areas and 'ethnic' churches, but baptism numbers have dropped steadily in all Christian traditions in Australia: in the 2016 Census, 52% of the population identified as Christian.

led to the popular idea that sexual union was itself sinful, so that sin was transmitted through childbirth. Despite Jesus' teaching that "to such as these (infants) belongs the kingdom of God" (Mark 10.14), mothers came to believe that an unbaptised child "went to some fearful place called limbo".[3] Paul in Romans 5, however, is emphasising that in Christ, the 'new Adam', sin has been overcome, rather than speculating about the riddles around sin's beginning and spread.[4]

The Reformers understood Augustine's teaching on sin in a nuanced way, as a careful reading Article IX, *Of Original or Birth-sin*, shows. Our new-born nature "*deserveth* God's wrath and condemnation", but the Article stops short of saying that new-born infants receive them. Nevertheless, the opening clause of each 'Public Baptism' service in *BCP*, "Forasmuch as all men are conceived and born in sin", meant that the popular idea that children were baptised to wipe away original sin continued.

A related issue is the meaning of 'unclean'. For English speakers, the term carries highly negative connotations of contagious disease. In ancient Israel, however, it referred to any 'non-normal' – not 'abnormal' – state of life which temporarily excluded a person from playing a full part in communal life (Leviticus 10–12). This mostly involved contact with blood, the symbol of life, which was only to be shed under specified circumstances. Its presence at 'non-normal' times of life was resolved by an appropriate rite of 'cleansing', or 'return': this conveyed assurance of God's presence rather than absolution from sin. Thus in menstruation and childbirth, the release of a woman's blood rendered her 'non-normal', usually translated into English as 'unclean', though sometimes prefixed by 'ceremonially'. Leviticus 12 provided rites of return, not forgiveness, for women after childbirth, protecting her and enabling her to come back from this 'non-normal' (and dangerous) aspect of life.[5] All this said, however, as Collison writes,

---

3 *When we meet for Worship*, 209. The change of context between 1977 and 1995 is well illustrated in Gilbert Sinden giving less than a page to comment on *AAPB*'s 'Thanksgiving for the Gift of a Child'.

4 There is no 'origin' for sin. Seeking one leads down the pointless path of laying blame, as the man and woman in turn act in Genesis 3. How sin and evil entered creation remains a horrible riddle: as the scholastics would say, the *material* cause of evil is the good, but it lacks *formal* and *final* causes and has a *deficient* rather than *efficient* cause. This analysis points up the need for care in how evil is dealt with, lest opposition multiplies it. The scriptures only affirm that there was a 'beginning' to sin, i.e. "there was a then when sin was not" (to paraphrase Arius). See Charles Sherlock, *The Doctrine of Humanity* (Leicester / Downers Grove: IVP, 1996) 61–66, and Appendix 1 on 'The Transmission of Sin'.

5 'Unclean' and 'common' are neutral terms in the First Testament: 'profane' and 'holy' are their extension into dangerous areas, whose extremes are seen in the 'ban of utter destruction' and 'holy of holies'. See *Words and the Word*, Chapter Eight; on blood in women's experience, see *Humanity*, Chapter Eight.

In the New Testament, there is a new perspective given on this matter by the teaching of Jesus. Although Mary is ritually purified after the birth of Jesus (Luke 2.22–39), later on Jesus says that what truly defiles a person is not external uncleanness but the thoughts and behaviour that come from within. Paul continues this line of thought by warning against being obsessively preoccupied with the traditional calendar (cf. Galatians 4:10f). No life experience by itself makes a person more or less holy. It is ethical behaviour that matters.

Childbirth today: celebrating in context

Childbirth in Australia today is much less dangerous than a century ago. A network of doctors, midwives and baby-health centres cares for mother and child(ren) in pregnancy, through birth and recovery. But giving birth remains dangerous. The focus of the *BCP* service was 'Thanksgiving for Women after Childbirth': the child is not mentioned, nor the father. After a difficult and dangerous birth today, and/or a child born with special needs, the relevant elements in a 'Thanksgiving for a Child' will be needed, and the service may best be conducted in private. But safe births are now the norm in the West: perinatal mortality comes as a bolt from the blue for Australian couples, not least those who have struggled with infertility.

With baptism rates declining, how is new life celebrated in Australia? Research in a middle-class Melbourne suburb in the 1990s explored how parents marked the birth of their first child. Planned interviews with some hundred couples showed that around 35% had a Christian or Jewish rite; around 35% had a party, usually at home; but some 30% found themselves too busy to do anything. One consequence has been increased importance of the first birthday: but overall, there is a growing drop in the practice of rites of passage around birth.

'Thanksgiving for a Child' is a Christian resource to fill this gap. On the one hand, as a *birth* rite it allows the baptism of an infant to be a *new birth* rite. On the other hand, 'Thanksgiving' can stand on its own as a Christian rite of birth for all children, whether or not they have church links. Many parents see their newborn child as a 'gift from above', whatever their faith stance. And not a few mothers (and fathers) see childbirth – pains, dangers and all – as a deeply spiritual experience: as one told a Melbourne priest, "the spiritual vibes in the birthing room were everywhere!"

Why not arrange with other churches in the area for a 'baby blessing' service every few months? 'Thanksgiving for a Child' is ecumenically open, and can readily be adapted to a public setting such as a park, perhaps with a barbeque. Such a service can be a positive demonstration of the Holy Spirit's work, as the 'Lord and giver of life'.

NB: Some children are folded into their long-term family some time after birth, typically through adoption. That is why the title has been kept brief, and the Additional Prayers include those for an adopted child, their birth and adoptive parents. Adjustments can be made to the service depending on the circumstances.

Some clergy require parents to be regular worshippers before they will consider the baptism of their child.[6] 'Thanksgiving for a Child' is then wrongly viewed as a 'baptism alternative'. For the couple, offering this is typically heard as a 'no', or as the offer of a 'dry baptism', whereas they want the 'real thing'.

Thanksgiving for a Child in Holy Baptism

Note 1 on *APBA* page 48 emphasises that "This service does not replace baptism, but provides the congregation with an opportunity to welcome the arrival of the child." Margaret Collison fleshes this out, writing,

> [T]his thanksgiving service is not one of Christian initiation. It is rather an opportunity for the parent(s) and other family members to give thanks for the birth or adoption of a child, for a mother to give thanks for a safe delivery and for the extended family of relatives to also give thanks. It provides an opportunity for parents and others to pray for concerns such as a sick mother or a child born with special needs.[7]

Elements of 'Thanksgiving for a Child' can helpfully be included at the beginning of the baptism of an infant. Note 5 on *APBA* page 48 indicates how it can be included in Holy Communion or a Service of the Word. Another possibility, building on the 'catechumenate' approach to Christian initiation, is to use it as an 'enrolment' rite a few weeks before the baptism. The provisions for naming of the child, and the public presentation of a Bible, can be included. In this way a sense of anticipation towards baptism is built, not only for the parents and sponsors, but in the congregation.

---

6 This is contrary to long-standing Anglican policy, which encourages preparation but requires only that the godparents be themselves baptised, and are willing to make the baptismal promises on behalf of the child. The *Canon Concerning Baptism* (1992) #6 specifies, "no minister may refuse or, except for the purpose of preparing or instructing the parents or guardians or godparents, delay baptising a child who has a parent or guardian who professes to be a Christian."

7 *A Practical Commentary*, 49.

The service in outline

Below is an outline of the services in *AAPB* and *BCP*:

BCP	AAPB
Introduction	Introduction
Psalm 116 or 127	Psalm 127.1–4
Lord / Christ / Lord have mercy	Prayer for the parents
	General Thanksgiving
Lord's Prayer	Lord's Prayer
Responses	
Prayer for the woman	Blessing / The Grace

Both rites are brief and follow a similar pattern, but have different foci, as their respective titles show: 'The Thanksgiving of Women after Childbirth' (*BCP*) and 'Thanksgiving for the Gift of a Child' (*AAPB*).

The *APBA* service is much fuller:

Welcome and Thanksgiving:	Words of welcome
	Prayer of thanksgiving (said by all)
	Psalm
Ministry of the Word:	Bible reading(s)
	Address
	Hymn
	Presentation of a Bible
	Presentation of other gifts
Welcome for the Child:	Naming
	Blessing of the child
The Prayers of the People:	Prayer for the parents
	Prayer by the parents
	Other prayers
	Lord's Prayer
	Blessing

The services in *BCP* and *AAPB* were envisaged to be part of a pastoral visit or existing service. As the above outline shows, however, and as Note 4 on *APBA* page 48 assumes, the *APBA* service is designed to be taken in its own right. Given their high level of participation, and since there are many options (Note 3), preparation with the parents – and others with close links to the child – is needed (Note 2).

Commentary

#1–2 The purpose of the service, thanksgiving and prayer, assumes that the child has been born safely, and that the mother is well: this will need to be adapted for other circumstances.

#3 Having a congregational prayer so early may seem unusual, but those involved will want to be present and active.

Additional Prayer 1 on *APBA* page 47 could be used after a difficult birth.

#4 Note 6 on *APBA* page 48 lists other psalms, which focus on thanksgiving for human dignity. A notable absence is Psalm 116, the first alternative in *BCP*, which speaks strongly to a woman who has survived a difficult birth.

#5 Suggested readings from scripture are given in Note 7 on *APBA* page 48, but consultation with the parents may lead to others being chosen.

#6 This is the only mention of singing, but hymns can be used anywhere: congregational song will work better in some situations than others. Recorded songs or music might be more appropriate for families unused to church.

#7 This gift can speak volumes, evoking the 'sacramentality' of the Ministry of the Word. The Bible translation chosen should be one the child can use across their life as a whole, a 'traditional' version such as the *NRSV*, or a 'contemporary' one such as *The Message*. If a 'children's Bible' is to be given, it should be additional.

#8 On the place and meaning of naming, see page 177 in this book.

#9 This act of blessing can be moving, especially for a first child, or one delivered after difficulties, so Note 2 on *APBA* page 48 refers to 'expressions of affection'. For some it may be a step too far, however, so preparing with the family is important. In a service with several families present, participation should clearly be voluntary.

#10 The rubrics do not provide for an alternative prayer, but adaptation to the pastoral circumstances will shape what is offered.

#11 As with the blessing, whether or not this is used will depend on the circumstances. The wording given is a model rather than to be followed strictly.

#12–13 see below on the Additional Prayers.

#14 This form, based on the 'Aaronic blessing' (Numbers 6.22), can be pronounced by any authorised minister.

Additional Prayers

1   is appropriate as an alternative thanksgiving at #3, as noted there;

2   assumes that both mother and baby need prayer;

3   was crafted late and is rather awkward, not least the abstract 'fatherhood', but avoids the idea that dad is 'head of the household';

4   a child is a gift to more than the parents, so this is a model prayer, deliberately inviting adaptation;

5–6   imply that similar adjustments should be made elsewhere in the service;

7   was crafted in consultation with those involved in the care of children with special needs.

This chapter may seem to be overly long for this uncontroversial rite. But clarifying the distinction between Christian rites of birth and new birth is of growing significance for the mission of God in third millennium Australia. As Margaret Collison concludes, "Used sensitively and appropriately, this service will only add to the richness and variety of our liturgy."

'Thanksgiving for a Child' is in large part an opportunity waiting to happen.

Chapter Twenty-One

Celebrating Marriage using APBA

Solemnising Holy Matrimony in Australia today

Marriage and weddings

Marriage is known and practised in every human society, with a 'nuptial lifestyle' that typically includes shared domestic life, faithfulness and the raising of children. A wedding is a public rite that marks the formal and public commencement of a marriage. The name of the wedding service in *BCP*, the 'Solemnisation of Holy Matrimony', reflects the serious nature of the occasion for both the couple and wider society. In *BCP* marriage is described as "an holy estate, instituted of God".[1]

Yet while there is much reflection on marriage in the scriptures (e.g. Deuteronomy 24–25; Ezekiel 16; 1 Corinthians 7.1–16 and most notably Ephesians 5.21–33), there is no example of a wedding rite. That Jesus attended one early in his ministry is seen in *BCP* as his "adorning and beautifying" the married estate (John 2.11), but beyond much wining and dining, no details of what took place are given. Some wedding customs are noted (Genesis 24 of Isaac and Rebekah; Ruth 4 of Ruth and Boaz; Tobit 7–9 of Tobias and Sarah), but these are the only named non-polygamous couples in the Bible. So liturgists looking for scriptural resources to draft a wedding rite have little to work with! Correspondingly, they have opportunity for considerable flexibility. Marriage is what matters theologically, how it is entered much less so.

Nuptial lifestyles in today's Australia

An increasingly egalitarian view of husband-wife relationships has emerged in Australian society. The idea that the man is 'head of the house' and the woman his 'helpmeet'[2] might still be around, but is widely ridiculed. The coming of the 'pill' in the 1960s made reliable birth control accessible: families could be planned, and careers for women beyond the home opened up.

---

1 *BCP* continues, "in the time of man's innocency". Perhaps with issues about an 'historic Fall' in mind, this phrase was unfortunately replaced in the 1928 book with "by God himself", an attribution of the divine origin of marriage that goes beyond the scriptural data.

2 'Helpmeet' is a contraction of the *KJB* translation of Genesis 2.18 as "I will make a helper meet for him".

A significant change of the past half-century is more couples living together without a wedding – *de facto* marriage in legal terms – or doing so before being wedded.³ In 1978, when *AAPB* was issued, 22% of Australian couples took the latter course; by the time *APBA* was drafted in 1994 this had grown to 68%, and in 2019 was estimated to be 77%. A further change is the increase in the age of first marriage. In 1978, 87% of men and 94% of women marrying for the first time were 30 or under; by 1998 this had dropped to 66% and 79%: in 2016 the average age for first marriage was 30 for men and 28 for women. Related to this is the steady increase in life expectancy. In 1918, "till death us do part" was promised with the expectation of 25 years or so of life together: by 1995 this had doubled to 50 years or more. Many people now experience two, three or more medium-term marriage relationships over their lifetime. And most recently, same-sex marriages have been legally recognised. A consequence of all these changes is the sharp drop in the proportion of weddings in Australia conducted by clergy, down to 27% in 2016.

The vast majority of couples today thus live a nuptial lifestyle before their wedding, and many do so without being wedded. This relative informality in long-term relationships means that a person may have been married *de facto* several times before approaching a church about a wedding. In the wake of the *Family Law Act* (1973), the Anglican Church of Australia agonised over the conditions under which a divorced person could have a 'church wedding': official practice continues to vary across its dioceses.⁴ The reality of couples seeking a wedding in church having had prior nuptial relationships calls for sensitive discernment about their intentions, rather than the strict application of church law.

---

3   For this and the statistics following, see the McCrindle Report, https://mccrindle.com.au/insights/blog/fast-facts-marriages-australia, accessed February 7 2019, and the earlier analysis by Luke Slattery, *The Weekend Australian*, 25–26 September, 1999, citing *Australian Bureau of Statistics* figures.

4   The 1981 General Synod passed three Canons relating to Marriage. Two update the relevant 1603 Canons to take account of Australian law, and specify that adoptive relationships are included within those prohibited. *The Marriage of Divorced Persons* (Provisional) Canon (1981), passed in 1985, makes the following provisions, within which each dioceses forms its policy:

   3. (1) The marriage of a divorced person shall not be solemnised according to the rites and ceremonies of this Church or by a minister of this Church during the life of the person's former spouse unless, upon application made by the proposed celebrant, the bishop of the diocese in which the marriage is to be solemnised has consented to the solemnisation of the marriage.

   4. Consent shall not be given by a bishop under this canon unless the bishop and the proposed celebrant are satisfied that the marriage of the divorced person would not contravene the teachings of Holy Scripture or the doctrines and principles of this Church …

   6. A minister of this Church may refuse to solemnise the marriage of any divorced person during the life of the person's former spouse.

Pastoral issues such as these are beyond the scope of this chapter, which is concerned with weddings conducted under Anglican auspices, rather than marriage, or who is eligible to be wedded. But they are never far from the ministry of preparing any couple for their wedding, and thus their marriage.[5]

Wedding rites for Australian Anglicans

Wedding services have changed in response to these developments. As long ago as 1928 'obey' in the woman's pledge was made optional.[6] The two Forms for Marriage in *AAPB* (1978) were shaped in the wake of the *Family Law Act* (1973) which had eased the requirements for divorce.[7] The Second Form provided identical words for the man and the woman, and allowed rings for both, but its language and structure remained largely that of '*BCP* translated' (as First Form was). Further, in 1978 the divisive intra-Anglican debate on the ordination of women was barely on the horizon: this would see 'headship' ideas both espoused and ridiculed.

The Marriage portfolio in the Liturgical Commission for *APBA* was held by the Revd Dr William (Bill) Lawton. A former Lecturer at Moore College, he was then Rector of St John's Darlinghurst, which included Kings Cross, Sydney, facing daily both the dark and delightful sides of human sexuality. He sought to offer a rite of Holy Matrimony that set Christian understandings of marriage in the context of changing attitudes to sexual relationships, taking with full seriousness both the scriptural data and contemporary theological and pastoral explorations of marriage, especially ecumenical work.[8] Lawton summarised this approach in writing,

---

5   Bradley Billings (ed.), *A Pastoral Handbook for Anglicans*. Third Edition (Mulgrave: Broughton, 2018) Chapter Two considers the wider pastoral as well as liturgical issues.
6   The Solemnisation of Matrimony in the 1928 book varies from BCP in three main ways:
    1. The language in the opening address about marriage being instituted "to satisfy men's carnal appetites, like brute beasts … and as a remedy against sin, and to avoid fornication" is softened to "that the natural instincts and affections, implanted by God, should be hallowed and directed aright".
    2. 'Obey' is omitted in the woman's 'troth' (vow and promise), while the man 'shares with' rather than 'endows' the woman with his worldly goods.
    3. Thirdly, the prayer for couple adds the italicised words below to BCP, reflecting the bishops' concerns about divorce: "O God, who hast *taught us that it should never be lawful to put asunder those whom thou by Matrimony hast made one, and …*"
    The structure and Christendom ethos of 1928 remained unchanged from that of *BCP*, however.
7   In *AAPB*, sacramental services are called 'Orders', other are 'Forms', a distinction removed in *APBA*.
8   "The Commission was particularly interested in liturgical developments taking place in the Roman Catholic Church, the Presbyterian Church in the USA and the Lutheran Church … and *Uniting in Worship*." *A Practical Commentary*, 112. The *Australian Academy of Liturgy* in 1990 issued *Celebrating Christian Marriage Together: an ecumenical marriage service for Australia*. This influenced the draft Marriage Service issued in 1992 by the Liturgical Commission: see *Aust Journal of Liturgy* 2/2 (October 1990) 183–206.

The Bible extols marriage as a gift and creation of God and any service true to its biblical foundations must locate this theme at its centre. But the changed nature of family life and the expectations of women and men for greater independence of action and lifestyle have to be recognised. Some of these changes have placed marriages under great stress; they are fragile relationships able to be broken, but with divorce or separation come grief, bitterness and hostility.

Our generation needs a liturgy that sympathises with people's predicament and offers God's love and healing presence. Services must have language and style that aid the process of reconciliation, while still maintaining God's hatred of estrangement and impenitence.[9]

A Service for Marriage (1990)

These principles undergirded the 'trial use' rite, *A Service for Marriage* issued by the Liturgical Commission in 1990. (It was known as the 'silver service', given its cover.) As in *AAPB* Second Form, the same words are said by the man and woman, but the possibility of two, one or no rings was offered. More significantly, as Lawton notes,

> The prayers were new and evocative, exploring facets of contemporary family life. They acknowledge the wide range of life experience that people bring to marriage, the realities of blended families, and the tragedy of divorce and separation.

The most significant liturgical change was structuring the service in a eucharistic rather than office shape, as in *BCP* and both Forms in *AAPB*. This was done for several reasons: to incorporate a Ministry of the Word, absent in *BCP*; to provide a better place for the prayers; and to bring Holy Communion within the service, though without requiring it. Overall, as Lawton explained,

> The service needed to be flexible enough to make an outsider comfortable and yet to enable the celebrant to affirm the essential nature of marriage according to Christian principles. The major exegetical difficulty was the dominant role given to Ephesians 5.21–33 in classical Anglican liturgies … The use of the text, however, was complicated by debates current in the Church about 'headship'.

Responding to these debates about the roles of women and men in marriage,

> [T]he Commission constructed the new marriage service around the theology of Genesis 1 and 2. This text underlays Jesus' statement about marriage and divorce in the gospels and it seemed to the Commission that this text

---

9   *A Practical Commentary*, 111.

was also fundamental to the ideas raised in Ephesians 5 – indeed, Genesis 1 is quoted at Ephesians 5.31. They believed that by taking this action, they would continue to give biblical underpinning to the marriage service while, at the same time, sidestepping the debate which was engaging the mind of the whole Australian Church.[10]

General Synod 1995

The Liturgical Commission planned for there to be one Marriage service in the draft book, based on the 1990 rite. Several General Synod members, however, requested that the Second Form in *AAPB* also be included. Provided that both Orders were sensitive to issues around gender, the Liturgical Commission eventually agreed to this, recognising that the two services were differentiated by distinct structures. First Order is in 'office' shape, while Second is eucharistic.

Having made the decision to offer two rites, the structure and linguistic style of First Order was made more 'conservative'. An optional 'giving away' of the woman is in the text, for example, with the wording changed to "brings" rather than "gives", to avoid ideas of male ownership. Second Order is more contemporary in style, encourages significant participation by the congregation, and the 'giving away' is replaced by a provision for the family to "give your blessing to this marriage", not in the text but in Note 3 on *APBA* page 675.

In the 1995 General Synod debate on the wedding services, no changes were proposed to Second Order. But in First Order, as well as a slight expansion of Note 5 on *APBA* page 654 on legal impediments, an amendment was proposed to have different wording in the 'vow and promise' for the man and woman, but not the Consent. After some back-room dialogue between women synod members from Sydney and Melbourne dioceses, it was agreed that in the Consent the man would say "to love and to cherish", while the woman would say "to love, *honour* and cherish". Conversely, in the (compulsory) ring-giving by the man, he says, "with all that I am and all that I have, I *honour* you". These changes, though not sought by the Liturgical Commission, were not unacceptable because both man and woman commit themselves to honour each other, though in different places.

But the general media, who had taken little interest in the Synod proceedings thus far, latched onto this change. It came in the last hours of debate on the draft book, just before the dinner break on the third day of discussion. After the break, the key vote on the book as a whole took place, seeing well over 75% approval in all

---

10   *A Practical Commentary*, 113.

three Houses, and nearly 90% in favour overall, a far better result than the Liturgical Commission had hoped for, and very good news. As my 'General Synod Diary' in *Church Scene* for the day reports,

> I get up early to finish the Commission minutes, and hear the 6.30am ABC news: not good news about reconciled Anglicans having a prayer book, but bad news about us having (apparently) forced all women to be chattels, due to the revisions in First Order Marriage to retain asymmetrical vows! Turning into media mode instantly, I get onto 3LO [now 774, ABC Melbourne] to explain the situation. Listeners seem to agree, but the 7am bulletin is unchanged. Ring ABC news, whose editor listens: the 7.45 (national) bulletin changes slightly. But while Channels 7 and 10 are OK, ABC TV will keep getting it wrong until the 7.30 Report.

The wedding services in *APBA*

The distinctives of each Order

An initial task is to identify the distinctive aspects of the two Orders in *APBA* so that ministers can assist couples identify which service is appropriate for them.

First Order is a minor revision of *AAPB*'s Second Form. As such, it reflects some of the changes from *BCP* made for twentieth century contexts: 'banns' are not mentioned, the man as well as the woman may receive a ring, and the words said by the bride and groom are, with the one exception discussed above, identical. Yet *AAPB* Second Form, though more 'progressive' than *AAPB* First Form, was more 'conservative' than its drafters wished. Gilbert Sinden identified three points around which agreement could not be reached for *AAPB*:

1) Does the Bible teach that marriage is in essence a hierarchical relationship ... or a mutual sharing relationship between husband and wife?

2) Is the prime end of marriage procreation ... or a relationship [of] sharing companionship, faith and strength in a unique way?

3) Is the marriage bond by its very nature indissoluble, so that divorce and remarriage are theologically not *possible* ... or is a life-long union an ideal, and are divorce and remarriage ways of dealing with particular situations?[11]

Sinden states that the 1977 drafting group, based in Western Australia, leaned towards the second answer to each of the questions, but "were constrained not to embody their answers in the rite itself because they felt that ... the Church cannot have two different doctrines of marriage in two different marriage services."

---

11 *When we meet for Worship*, 244-5.

This position was that of the Liturgical Commission for *APBA*: as noted above, its decision to accept two Orders was made on the basis of them having distinct 'shapes', rather than diverse understandings of marriage and gender roles. This is best seen by comparing the structures of both rites:

First Order	**Second Order**
Assembly in the church entrance	*Gathering in God's Name*
	[receiving of man / woman], welcome, greeting, sentence
Preface (close to *BCP*)	Preface, *berakah* response
	The Ministry of the Word
	scripture readings
	address
The Consent: 'I will'	
['Who brings this woman?']	
hands, corporate prayer	
The Wedding:	*The Wedding*: 'I will'
	people's witnessing
vows, ring(s)	vows, [ring(s)]
declaration	declaration
	[couple's prayer]
nuptial blessing	nuptial blessing
[Scripture readings]	
Sermon, or Ephesians 5.20–33	
The Prayers	*The Prayers of the People*
Psalm	intercessions
Lord's Prayer	Lord's Prayer
intercessions	
	[*The Holy Communion*
	Greeting of Peace
	Great Thanksgiving
	Breaking of Bread and Communion]
	The Sending out of God's People
	[Post-communion prayer]
	Congregational blessing

First Order, as with *BCP* and 1928, falls into two parts: the 'social' and 'church' rites, hinged at the nuptial blessing. This assumes that weddings typically take place in church rather than elsewhere: it thus has an 'office' shape.

Second Order, whether Holy Communion is included or not, blends the social and church roles, presuming that a wedding 'in Christ' is throughout an act of Christian worship: it thus has a 'eucharistic' shape.

Further, the language style of First Order is more 'traditional', whereas Second Order is more 'contemporary', notably in the prayers.

Beginnings, aftermath – and rehearsal

One matter that arises in every wedding is how the couple arrive. Sinden comments:

> Where the groom slips in with his best man via the vestry, and waits at the front for the arrival of the bride ... the wrong impression can be given that this is her day. It is her day, but it also the bridegroom's.
>
> I suggest that it is much better for the bride and groom to meet at the door of the church, and for them both to be brought in by the priest. They would, of course be accompanied by their various attendants ... Where this happens, the bride and groom bring up the rear of the procession (with the exception, perhaps, of the bridesmaids responsible for the bride's train) to mark the fact that they are the principal celebrants of this rite and the ministers of their own marriage.[12]

No doubt the tradition of the bride's 'moment of glory' will continue, but how the couple enter sets the tone for the wedding, and raises significant issues about what is thought to be going on. No Anglican rite prescribes how bride and groom enter, or leave: this is left to the pastoral discernment of those preparing the couple for their wedding.[13]

One practical matter is where the bride and groom, and their attendants, having come to the front of the assembly, will sit for scripture readings, address and prayers. When the wedding takes place outside a church building, such issues of choreography multiply. These matters point to the importance of a rehearsal. Moreover, few young couples have much experience in 'public' roles, speaking life-changing words in front of a crowd.

---

12 *When we meet for Worship*, 247.
13 Other possibilities include the bride coming halfway 'up' the aisle (perhaps brought by her father) and the groom halfway 'down' (perhaps brought by his mother), the couple meeting in the middle. I know of one wedding where the bride's father accompanied her halfway, from where her step-father took over.

First Order: commentary

#1 Note 2 on *APBA* page 654 gives a little more weight to the greeting, which will happen whatever the rubrics may say.

Note 7 provides that the placing of psalms and hymns, and directions as to posture, may be determined by the priest.

The Preface opens with the teaching of Jesus about marriage (Matthew 19.4-5, citing Genesis 2.24). Marriage is viewed in the first place as a symbol of God's rather than human love (Isaiah 55.1-10). Paul's teaching is summarised carefully, and the status, responsibilities and 'goods' of marriage are stated in contemporary terms: all this reflects a considerable shift from the social context of *BCP* 1662 or 1928. Like them, nevertheless, the Preface concludes with asking if there is any objection to the couple being wedded: see Note 5 on *APBA* page 654.

Omitted from *BCP* and *AAPB* is the 'charge' to the couple to declare if they know any reason why the wedding should not proceed: the signing of the Declarations required by the Australian Government covers this.

#2-3 The Consent, identical for both man and woman, makes a significant word change from *BCP*: 'take' is replaced by 'have' to avoid a sense of 'possessiveness'.

NB: The response is *not* "I do", as in Hollywood, but "I will". Whether the couple love one another is not the point. What matters is that their coming together is a free and deliberate act of the will (*voluntas* in Latin), not mere feelings.

#4 This section is optional not only due to changes in social context, but because the woman leaving one home for another contradicts Genesis 2:24, where the man does. Note 3 partly corrects this by allowing the man to be likewise 'brought'. Given time-honoured custom, however, the woman being 'handed over' is allowed, yet with another significant word change from *BCP*: the father or friend (whose gender is not specified) does not 'give' but 'brings' her to the man.

#5 Preference for the right hand remains, and only the woman's hand is mentioned: but the initiative in it being taken – 'causes' – is that of the priest, not the man. The congregational prayer that follows goes beyond gender difference, and again affirms that love has its origin in divine rather than human activity.

#6-7 The rubrics have the man 'holding' the woman's right hand, whereas she 'takes' his, because the man was given the woman's hand by the priest at #5.

Instead of 'troth', the double term 'vow and promise' is used. Though the link with be-troth-al is lost, few would understand "plight thee my troth" today. The double term 'vow and promise' avoids 'vow' being seen as merely a legal, contractual term: 'promise' points to the covenantal character of the relationship being entered. The words for the woman and man differ, as noted above: she promises to 'honour' the man, a promise he makes in the ring-giving, #9.

The expectation that the marriage will be lifelong is expressed more positively than in *BCP*: "as long as we both shall live" rather than "till death do us part".

Some couples learn the words of their 'vow and promise', whereas others are happy to have each phrase 'lined out', the man and woman repeating each after the priest in turn. Sinden suggests that a card with the words in large type, held by the priest so that only the couple sees it, is a better way. Such matters can be taken up at the rehearsal.

#8 The rubric is minimal: "The priest receives the weddings rings(s)". *BCP* is much fuller: the ring is first placed on the Prayer Book "with the accustomed duty" (fee), then given by the priest to the man, who puts it on "the fourth finger of the woman's left hand". The man holds the ring there while saying his ring-words. Many see such customs as a key part of the rite – this is another matter for discussion with the couple.

The prayer over the ring(s) is optional: there is none in *BCP*. The prayer avoids seeing them as things 'blessed' (see pages 123–124 in this book), but rather in sacramental terms, as "token and constant sign" of the couple's mutual love.

#9–10 The wording in *BCP* – "with all my worldly goods I thee endow" – until a century or so ago contradicted English law, which saw the property of a married couple as belonging to the man. *AAPB* and *APBA* changed this to "with all that I am and all that I have I honour you", and the woman may respond, #10. A further change from *BCP* is that the man's ring-words conclude "in the name of God" rather than an explicitly trinitarian formula.

#11 This rubric needs to be read carefully. If the woman gives the man a ring, she is not required to say the same words: this may not sit well with her.

#12–13 The Declaration names the evidence that the marriage has begun: consent, promise, ring-giving and receiving, hand-joining and mutual acceptance. It is made not only in the name of society, since the minister has been licensed by the State to officiate at weddings, but more particularly in the Name of God.

No posture is mentioned at this point in either of the *APBA* rites, but in *BCP* and *AAPB*, the couple kneel for this Declaration and the following blessing.

Many priests wrap their stole around the couple's joined hands while pronouncing Jesus' words from Matthew 19.6, signifying the strength of the marriage bond here covenanted.

#14 This lovely nuptial blessing is more explicitly trinitarian than the equivalent in *BCP*. It is set out with three distinct verbs (enrich / make holy / strengthen) and outcomes (grace / love / joy), concluding with the Lord's blessing, and a congregational *berakah* response of blessing.

#15 That scripture readings are optional may seem surprising, but this was the case in *BCP*, which assumed that Holy Communion would follow. The reading of Ephesians 5.20-33 "at least" is only required if a sermon is not preached. Note 4 on *APBA* page 654 points to Note 4 on *APBA* page 675 for suitable readings.

#16 Note 6 on *APBA* page 654 follows the requirement in *BCP* that the newly married couple come to the Holy Table. This movement is an effective symbol that their first act together is one of moving to pray. If Holy Communion follows, as provided for in Note 1, this will position them appropriately to participate.

Psalm 67 is perhaps the most common used at weddings: *BCP* also provides for Psalm 128, though today this could be seen as rather 'husband-focussed'. Others are suggested at Note 4 on *APBA* page 675.

#17 The prayers open with the Lord's Prayer, as in an 'office', then follow *BCP*'s topics for intercession: eternal life, referring to Abraham and Sarah; the blessing of children, omitted where "the couple is unable to have children", Note 9 on *APBA* page 654; and mutual love and faithfulness, but omitting *BCP*'s reference to Isaac and Rebekah.[14]

#18-19 This congregational prayer is new, engaging those present in prayer for their own living. The final blessing is for all present, rather than for the couple only.[15]

---

14 Sinden, 252 notes that the phrase "the *couple* are unable to have children", taken from the General Synod *Canon on Marriage*, spreads responsibility for this inability, relieving the burden felt by some childless women: *BCP* allows the prayer to be omitted where "the woman is past child-bearing". Since only the couple will know their situation, they decide if the prayer is omitted. The Anglican tradition rejects the "contraceptive mentality" implicit in omitting the phrase to suit the couple's lifestyle: see ARCIC II, *Life in Christ. Morals, Communion and the Church* (London: Church House/CTS, 1993) #78.

15 The equivalent blessing in *BCP* refers to "our first parents, Adam and Eve," seen as those whom God did "sanctify and join together in marriage", a debatable exegesis of Genesis 2.22-25.

Second Order: commentary

NB: comment on matters discussed in First Order is not repeated.

#1 This may seem to state the obvious, but two things are noteworthy:

1. The couple are present "in the presence of witnesses": a wedding is more than a private event, both legally and communally.

2. Both the man and the woman may receive their hand "from a member of the family or friend". Which hand, right or left, is not specified, nor that the father is the one who offers the hand of one to the other. No words are provided: such an act best takes place in silence: see First Order #4.

#2-4 explain themselves, but if the sentence from 1 John 4.16 could be misunderstood as God's love being about romantic feelings, another should be used.

#5 The Preface reshapes First Order using shorter sentences and direct verbs, and gives a positive view of what marriage should be based on Christian teaching.

A new element is its leading into prayer for the couple, in the form of a *berakah* in congregational form. If many of those present are unfamiliar with church, having some 'regulars' primed to lead the responses – and sing hymns (Note 5 on *APBA* page 675) – will encourage a lively opening to the service.

#6-8 The Ministry of the Word takes place as in a regular Sunday service, whether or not the wedding takes place in a eucharistic setting.

Note 2 on *APBA* page 674 provides for the presentation of a copy of the Bible to the couple, with appropriate words. Experience shows that this gift is appreciated, but the couple should be consulted about the translation given: see pages 58-62 in this book.

#9 The Consent is similar to First Order, with two changes. Each of the couple is asked whether they "will you *give yourself to*" rather than "will you *have*" the other; and the agreement of each to love, honour and protect the other is re-arranged, with 'comfort' added. The effect is a more 'human' question – and the response is "I will", *not* "I do".

Note 3 on *APBA* page 675 provides for the couple's families to give their blessing to the marriage: this may not be appropriate if only one family wishes to do so.

#10 This new section points up the role of others present as witnesses, clarifies that marriage, though enacted by the couple, is enfolded in wider relationships, and that every couple can do with support from 'outside' the marriage itself.

#11 These 'vows and promises' (troth) are the heart of the wedding: see #6–7 of the commentary on First Order. Their content remains unchanged from *BCP*.

The rubrics here do not specify which hand is taken, and leave the initiative of taking to the man and woman themselves.

#12 The rubric allows for no rings to be exchanged. This change was made because some couples view rings as signs of ownership rather than commitment.

The ring prayer has less of a sacramental character than in First Order, but is more direct in invoking God's blessing. As noted earlier, in *BCP* the ring was placed on the prayer book, and many priests continue this tradition.

#13 The rubric does not specify which is the ring finger, but traditionally it is the fourth finger of the left hand, now for men as well as women.

The wording of the ring-placing is a contemporary form of the traditional form, significantly including "honour you". The response echoes the symbolic function of the ring, and affirms the life-long intention of the marriage being entered.

#14 The declaration makes no reference to rings, since they are not required in this service: but where they are included the First Order form supplies wording.

The prayer provided for the couple to pray together is a wonderful enrichment of the service. But it should only be used where the couple has agreed to this, and is ready to say it – another matter for the rehearsal.

#15 This nuptial blessing, a new composition, is rich in trinitarian imagery, carefully 'appropriated' to each Person. It echoes the practice of 'crowning' the couple at this point in the Eastern Orthodox tradition, where they are celebrated as king and queen for the day. If the couple requests it, crowns can be prepared (e.g. from flowers) for each, and placed during the blessing.

#16 The signing of the Marriage Certificates within the liturgy blends the church and social aspects of the rite, rather than this being seen as an annoying 'extra'. Lawton suggests that "signing in a convenient part of the church rather than in the vestry enable maximum involvement of family and friends".[16] Having the Certificates signed on the Holy Table undergirds the solemnity of what is happening.

In many places music or singing accompanies the signing, which can take several minutes. Photographs are best done after the actual signing, to allow the couple to be fully engaged in this significant moment, with an 'arranged' signing for a picture or video once this is complete.

---

16 *A Practical Commentary*, 115.

#17 The first rubric notes that the litany at j, *APBA* page 666, should be used when the wedding takes place in Holy Communion: this ensures that 'common prayer' is offered rather than for the couple only.

The next rubric allows for people closely associated with the couple to lead the prayers. This not only gives opportunity for a variety of voices, but symbolises the spiritual support offered to the couple by their friends and families. As Lawton notes, "The effect is to make the service seem natural, earthy and embracing".

A wide range of prayers is provided, with headings that state their purpose, to help the couple and minister agree together on which is appropriate. Prayer (b) was included because the sexual aspect of marriage is often avoided in church, but dominant at the reception. Prayer (c) recognises a common situation today, where two households with children are blended, while Prayer (h) allows difficult pasts to be acknowledged without getting into judgement about them.

#18–19 provide for the closing of the service when Holy Communion does not follow. Three forms of congregational blessing are provided: the traditional trinitarian form; one drawn from the divine naming of the prophets of Israel (e.g. Isaiah 54.5); and the 'Aaronic' blessing of Numbers 6.22–24.

#20–29 Distinctive aspects of Holy Communion on the day of a wedding are considered on pages 304-305 of this book. Sections #20–29 are as in HC2, with Preface, fraction response and post-communion for marriage.

Communion is given to the newly wedded couple first. Sinden suggests that after receiving they remain kneeling or standing at the centre of where communion is administered, so that others have the sense of receiving with them.[17]

Resources issued since *APBA* was published
Some couples not wedded in church have requested a 'Blessing of a Civil Marriage'. The Liturgical Commission responded with a rite closely related to Marriage (Second Order). The main difference is that 'The Wedding' is replaced by 'Affirmations' in which the couple renew their consents, vows and promises.

To support marriage as the years go on, an annual renewal of marriage can be offered, whether corporately on a day such as February 14, or by a couple on their wedding anniversary: the Commission has issued prayers, blessing and 'Thanksgivings for Marriage ', prayers and blessings for both situations.

These resources are available on the liturgy page of the General Synod website.[18]

---

17 *When we meet for Worship*, 251.
18 https://www.anglican.org.au/liturgy-worship

Whatever service is used, each wedding is unique to each couple. Preparing and shaping it to their particular circumstances will enable their wedding to be a celebration with serious intent. But be courageous enough to prevent the rite dissolving into the couple looking into each others' eyes: let them stand 'back-to-back' as it were, looking outwards, to allow their union to be fruitful for God's good purposes for all creation.

Dr Lawton ends his chapter on Marriage in *A Practical Commentary* with these words.

> These services are offered to the contemporary Church as an experiment in the reaffirmation of marriage. In time, we may achieve a marriage rite common to all the major Christian churches; it will be a symbol of how far we have moved together in our understanding of God's interaction with human need. The marriage rite is a sign of Christ's incarnation – the intersection of the divine with our flesh.

Further reading

ARCIC II, *Life in Christ. Morals, Communion and the Church* (Church House /CTS, 1994)

Billings, Bradley (ed.), *A Pastoral Handbook for Anglicans*. Third Edition (Mulgrave: Broughton, 2018) Chapter Two

Kasper, Walter, *Theology of Christian Marriage* (New York NY: Seabury, 1980): a profound continental Roman Catholic perspective

Lawler, Michael, *Secular Marriage, Christian Sacrament* (Twenty-Third Publications, 1985): a positive US Roman Catholic perspective, attending to Vatican II

Meyendorff, John, *Marriage: An Orthodox Perspective* (St Vladimir's Press, 1984)

Ramsay, Paul, *One Flesh*. Grove Ethics Series 2 (Bramcote, Notts, 1980): an excellent brief theological treatment of marriage

Roman Catholic-Uniting Church in Australia National Dialogue, *Interchurch Marriages: their ecumenical challenge & significance for our Church* (St Paul/UCP, 1999)

Something to Celebrate. Valuing Families in Church and Society (London: Church House, 1997): a Church of England report, focussing on *de facto* relationships

Stevenson, Kenneth, *Nuptial Blessing. A Study of Christian Marriage Rites*. Alcuin Club Collections 64. (London: SPCK / Oxford: OUP, 1983)

Storkey, Alan, *Marriage and its Modern Crisis: repairing married life*. (London: Hodder & Stoughton, 1996): theological and realistic, using the social sciences

Varcoe, Gillian, 'Marriage', in Charles Hefling and Cynthia Shattuck, *The Oxford Guide to the Book of Common Prayer* (OUP, 2006): an excellent coverage of marriage rites and issues across the Anglican Communion

Chapter Twenty-Two

Ministries of Wholeness in APBA

Christian understandings of wholeness

Christian rites for ministries of healing are hard to find before 1900. Surviving infancy was a challenge, public health was patchy, doctors were expensive and going to hospital was dreaded.[1] 'Visitation' in the *BCP* rite for the 'Visitation of the Sick' meant the priest coming to call a seriously ill person to account for their life, and prepare them for death. Sinden describes the rite as "a hangover from the concept of extreme unction: the idea that the Church's ministry of healing is a ministry to those … about to die".[2]

In sharp contrast, in contexts of clean water and effective sewage, high life expectancy, good hospitals and doctors on hand, ministries of healing are seen as a natural outcome of the gospel, following our Lord's example. Unrealistic, even false expectations can be held about how 'easy' life in Christ is meant to be, with 'miracles' keeping believers comfortable. Western Christians face the temptation to forget that only our resurrection in Christ will bring true wholeness. Human beings, made in the image of God, are nevertheless mortal: we live now by faith, not sight. Authentic ministries of wholeness see our ultimate 'end' in Christ brought into the present through the ministry of the Holy Spirit – but with firm realism about "the changes and chances of this fleeting life" (Sunday Evening Prayer, *APBA* page 389).

Every act of Christian worship is a ministry of wholeness, as Word, sacrament and common prayer are enacted. Alongside these, and as aspects of them, particular ministries offer God's care and support in the crises of life, and the peace which only

---

[1] A rare positive example of a healing ministry was the "royal touch", where English monarchs from Edward 1 to Queen Anne would lay hands on sick people, typically those with tuberculosis, 'scofula', and hang a special coin around their necks with prayer for their healing. Charles II was particularly active, 'touching' thousands each year. The practice ceased in England from 1712 when George 1 came to the throne: the last to receive this ministry is reputed to have been Samuel Johnston, 'touched' by Queen Anne. Until then the service "Touching for the King's Evil" was unofficially included with some printings of *BCP*, with Mark 16.14–20 as the reading.

[2] *When we meet for Worship*, 259.

the gospel of reconciliation can bring the troubled soul. So *APBA* includes 'Ministry with the Sick', 'Ministry with the Dying' and 'Reconciliation of a Penitent'. The titles of the first two are significant: rather than ministry *to* those in need, as in *AAPB*, it is *with* them. So the introduction to 'Ministry with the Sick' (*APBA* page 678) states:

> Of first importance in this ministry is the relationship between those in need and those who care for them. It is a mutual relationship, in which vulnerable people minister to one another in and through the grace of Christ.

Those who minister Christ's wholeness cannot avoid the reality that they do so from a position of better health, but Christians are like "beggars telling other beggars where they food is to be found".[3] New contexts and situations where Christ's wholeness is needed continue to arise. Since *APBA* was published, the Liturgy Commission has continued to issue related resources, especially as concerns about climate change and the disclosure of sexual abuse have increased.

This chapter thus focuses individually on:
   Ministry with the Sick
   Ministry with the Dying
   Reconciliation of a Penitent
   Post-*APBA* resources issued by the Liturgy Commission

Ministry with the Sick

Healing, wholeness and the cross

When is it appropriate to offer explicit prayer for the restoration to health of a person affected by illness? All involved in 'Ministry with the Sick' face this challenging question. Space forbids more than a sketch: it is offered with a deep sense of the mystery of the workings of God's grace in human life.

The example of Jesus and the apostles sets precedents for prayer for healing, and Christian experience has seen the presence of God bring newness in bodily and mental life. But 'too-easy' or facile answers do harm: relief is not always given, which can lead to trust in God reaching breaking point. What does the New Testament tell us?

On the one hand, the verb 'to heal' is *sōzein* (to save) or *'iaomai* (to restore) rather than *therapeuo* (to cure). The apostle Peter summed up Jesus' ministry as "going about doing good, and restoring all who were under the power of the slanderer [the devil], for God was with him" (Acts 10.38). Sometimes Jesus healed whoever was before him (Mark 1.21–34) but at other times was selective: at the pool of Bethesda,

---

[3] Sri Lankan theologian Daniel Thambyrajah (D.T.) Niles, *New York Times*, May 11, 1986.

for example, he chose to heal only one of the many who were there (John 5.2–9). As Sinden concludes, our Lord "came to bring health, not just bodily or even mental cures, but wholeness for men and women, individually and together".[4]

On the other hand, Christian life gives a significant place to suffering. Jesus called disciples to "take up your cross" (Matthew 16.24), and the first thing done to a newly baptised person is to mark their forehead with this sign. Christ's victory at Calvary over sin, evil and death took away their power, and that of Satan, the 'great accuser'. Nevertheless, as the apostle Paul knew well, these tragic realities are not thereby removed from our experience (2 Corinthians 12.7–10; Colossians 1.24). Restoration of health in this age is partial and temporary, a Spirit-given anticipation of the wholeness that resurrection in Christ will usher in.

In this light, should prayer for the restoration of health include "if it be God's will" or "God willing"?[5] Never mentioning this could give the impression that God always wills to cure the sick, which is evidently not the case. Yet speaking of God's will too easily can lead to considerable distress, for example when a person for whom much prayer has been offered does not have their suffering relieved. Much of the difficulty arises from assuming that the will of God involves a simple 'yes' or 'no': rather, God's will for a person relates to the whole of their life, relationships and well-being. "God our Saviour (*sōtēr* – healer) desires everyone to be saved (*sōzein* – healed) and to come to the knowledge of the truth" (1 Timothy 2.4).

When, then, is it right to pray for a person's restoration to health? What signs are there that such prayer is according to God's will? Only once in the New Testament is the phrase "the Lord's will be done" found, at Acts 21.14. Paul had come to Caesarea, on the way to Jerusalem, to give account to the Jewish church of his ministry among the Gentiles (Acts 20.16; 21.17–19). When Agabus prophesied that this would lead to his arrest, those present urged Paul to think again.

> Paul answered, "What are you doing, weeping and breaking my heart? For I am ready not only to be bound but even to die in Jerusalem for the name of the Lord Jesus." Since he would not be persuaded, we remained silent except to say, "The Lord's will be done." (Acts 21:13–14)

Paul's companions accepted his conviction, and supported him by accompanying him as he journeyed further into the will of God, difficult though it would prove to be.

This episode suggests the following criterion for when it is right to pray for someone who is ill to be cured: when a ministry waits to be taken up by the healed

---

4   *When we meet for Worship*, 256, part of a long and detailed discussion.
5   *Deo volente* in Latin, often abbreviated to DV.

person. It could be a single mother with children who have no-one else to care for them; a church member whose insights are desperately needed for a congregation's well-being; a leader whose absence would see a significant organisation fall apart. Yet even in such cases, our prayer is not one of sight or certainty, but remains one of faith, of trust in God's good purposes.

'Ministry with the Sick': overall perspective

'Ministry with the Sick' is substantially new. The 'Visitation of the Sick' in *BCP* was about holding a seriously ill person accountable for their life, including a form of personal confession and absolution. In *AAPB*, following the 1928 book, 'Ministry *to* the Sick' suggested Bible readings, prayers and commendations, and resources for Communion of the Sick.[6] But no provision was made for the laying on of hands, anointing or reconciliation of a penitent beyond the sick-bed. The Liturgical Commission for *AAPB* drafted Forms for hand-laying and anointing of the sick, but these were not included in the book, since debate might have delayed its approval: they were issued later on cards for use in hospital and other contexts. By the 1990s, wide acceptance of healing ministries among Australian Anglicans meant that the inclusion of 'Ministry with the Sick' in *APBA* was welcomed. No amendments were proposed at the 1995 General Synod.

'Ministry with the Sick' is the first service in *APBA* to have an introduction (page 682). The Liturgical Commission provided introductions for each service in the draft book, but most were removed by the Synod on the grounds that they might influence a rite's interpretation, and that educational resources were inappropriate for a prayer book. The need for a pastoral introduction saw the first two paragraphs of the one for 'Ministry with the Sick' retained, but the third paragraph was deleted:

> The liturgical forms provided here offer resources for ministry with the sick in the name of Christ. They draw on the means of grace which God offers us: the Scriptures, prayer, the laying on of hands, anointing, and the holy communion. The material is set out in the form of a continuous service, but the various sections are designed to be adapted flexibly, according to pastoral need.

The service in *APBA* is thus "a resource to be drawn upon, rather than an order to be followed strictly or sequentially".[7]

---

6 Anointing of a sick person was retained in the 1549 *BCP*, but as Sinden notes, there was confusion as to its purpose: "was it for healing, remission of sins, or preparation for death and burial?" *When we meet for Worship*, 271. It was thus omitted in 1552, and not restored until recent times, focused on healing.

7 Bishop Owen Dowling (Canberra & Goulburn), *A Practical Commentary*, 117. Bishop Dowling held the portfolio for 'Ministry with the Sick' and 'Ministry with the Dying' on the Liturgical Commission.

Service structure

This outline shows how the various sections are set out in sequence as a full service, but each part can stand alone depending on the pastoral context.

Preparation

    Greeting and sentences
    Prayer of Preparation
    Prayer for the sick person
    Scripture readings
    Intercessions: *kyrie* form printed
    Lord's Prayer
    Confession (general) and absolution

Anointing and Laying on of Hands

    James 5.14–16
    Prayer over the oil
    Anointing
    Laying on of hands
    Prayers
    Return of thanks

The Holy Communion

    Prayer for knowing Christ's presence
    Great Thanksgiving (with special Preface and *'anamnesis*)
    Breaking of bread and communion
    Post-communion
    Blessing

Additional Prayers

Commentary

'Ministry with the Sick' is frequently carried out by a minister making a personal visit: it is traditionally a significant aspect of a deacon's calling. The following commentary assumes that others may be present, making the pastoral care involved an act of corporate worship, as the *BCP* rubrics in 'Communion of the Sick' prescribe. Bishop Dowling thus writes,

> An important part of ministry with the sick is to focus together – minister, sick person, family and friends – on the promises of God. They can do this in the opening sentences (at #2) and in the Scripture readings.[8]

---

8 *A Practical Commentary*, 118

Preparation

#1 In most contexts, the first words will be the minister(s) and sick person introducing one another, and perhaps some enquiry as to how the sick person is feeling. These optional greetings will be familiar to regular worshippers, for whom their use can signal that the liturgy itself is about to begin.

#2 Bishop Dowling comments that "the opening sentences … suggest tender mutuality: 'O praise the Lord with me: let us exalt his name together'".

#3 All present saying this prayer is particularly appropriate when Holy Communion is to be celebrated, but it is suitable for any occasion.

#4 This prayer seeks courage, confidence in God and peace for the person who is ill, but not 'healing' as such. When others are present with the minister, all except the sick person saying this prayer draws the community of faith together.

#5 The readings are printed to avoid ministers having to balance books, but the selection is left to their discretion. In part to facilitate Holy Communion, one is from each Testament, plus a Gospel reading.

Bishop Dowling sees the Isaiah 40 reading as "appropriate in many a pastoral situation, helping sick people and their carers to draw on the mysterious strength of God, the God who stands with us in adversity".

Nevertheless, Jesus' repeated promises in the Gospel reading, "ask whatever you wish, and it will be done for you" (John 15.7; see also Matthew 7.7, 18.19, 21,22; Mark 11.24; Luke 11.9) can raise doubts when a sick person is not restored in response to prayer. As Bishop Dowling writes,

> [although] we do not always receive the physical healing we ask for … [from] the relationship of faith and desire to rest in the ultimate will of God, it is natural and right to ask in faith for healing blessings – healing of body, mind or spirit, healing of relationships, the healing of forgiveness.

Though a sermon is not mentioned, "A time for reflection" encourages mutual engagement with the scriptures, as appropriate for the person's condition.

#6 Prayer is suggested not only for the sick person, but for those involved with them. As Bishop Dowling notes, asking the sick person and others what they would like to pray can "establish agreement *before* we pray – a powerful thing".

Using *ex tempore* prayer will come naturally to many ministers, but the prayers provided on 689-692 "are part of our professional equipment", Bishop Dowling notes. They should be "studied carefully to be drawn on in time of need … they give us the words to say when minds may well go blank." Those who are ill often appreciate the use of prayers drawn from the Christian tradition.

The threefold *kyrie* form printed is not a confession of sin: this is provided for at #7. It is an open-ended plea for God's help, on the basis of what we know of the ministry of Christ and his apostles (see page 278 in this book).

#7 This confession is the 'general' one from HC2, and will be familiar to most regular communicants. However, as Bishop Dowling writes,

> It may be appropriate to lead the sick person to the form provided in 'Reconciliation of a Penitent', especially if there is a need for this ministry. Privacy and confidentiality would be necessary in this case. The ministry of reconciliation and the provision of a definite, authoritative and personal form of absolution may indeed be the ministry that a sick person needs, though it should never be demanded.[9]

Anointing and Laying on of Hands

These ministries may be brief on the page, but must not be hurried. The acts of anointing and hand-laying are deliberately accompanied by "very simple formulae", as Bishop Dowling notes. "A profusion of words is not necessary: the action, done in faith and with simple trusting prayer, is sufficient in itself."

Care is needed with the 'choreography', the positioning of the minister and the sick person, so that the anointing – and hand-laying – can take place safely, and without awkwardness. This may take time in places such as Intensive Care Units, where the directions of medical staff must be followed. Sustaining a sense of quiet reverence can be challenging when the surroundings are noisy.

#8 The reading of James 5.14–16 can be done by a friend or family member.

The rubric requires that this passage be used when anointing is to take place. If it raises issues about 'unanswered' prayer, however, ignore the rubric.

#9 As with prayer over the water in baptism and the ring at a wedding (see pages 123–124 in this book), this prayer centres on the blessing of people through material things dedicated to God.

#10 These words echo those used with baptism in the New Testament (Acts 2.38, Matthew 28.19): 'anoint' is *christo* in Greek. Which words are used will depend on the circumstances, and any preference expressed by the sick person.

Have a towel or something similar at hand to wipe away excess oil.

---

9   *A Practical Commentary*, 119–120.

#11 The heading and rubrics could be interpreted to imply that hand-laying always happens with anointing, and never apart from it. This was not the intention of the Liturgical Commission: the laying on of hands can be used of itself.

The rubric states that "Those present may join in the laying on of hands". When several people lay hands, take care they do not apply pressure that causes discomfort and possible harm. Please lay on hands lightly.

NB: In emergency situations, when the sick person is facing death, anyone willing to do so – Christian or not – may pray for, baptise, anoint or lay hands on the sick person: communicating God's love and care is what matters.

#12 The words provided for use with the laying on of hands, and in this closing prayer, are simple and direct. When "similar words" are used or added, over-confidence as to the outcome of this ministry can be unhelpful.

#13 These words are an example of the sick person taking as active a part as possible for them, exemplifying that this ministry is *with* them. Even though s/he may have limited capacity, 'Ministry with the Sick' is one of mutual support.

The Holy Communion

Wider matters relating to Holy Communion with the sick, including the reserved sacrament and extended communion, are considered on pages 306-309 of this book.

#14 Communion will typically take place in a bedroom or hospital ward in a private setting. A collection is inappropriate, and the bread and wine will be to hand, so no 'offertory' prayer is provided. This prayer, tender in tone, opens the way to the celebration of Holy Communion in such a personal setting.

#15 The Preface, *Sanctus* and *Benedictus* are in parentheses to meet situations where time is short (Note 3 on *APBA* page 693). But the extra minute needed is well worth it, not least since it allows the communicants to join in the *Sanctus*.

The Preface expresses the saving work of Christ in terms related to suffering, alluding to Isaiah 52.4–5. The memorial acclamation leads into a shortened *'anamnesis* and invocation of the Spirit.

The Lord's Prayer is not printed after "Blessing and honour", but earlier at #6, to conclude the prayers. Note 3 requires that it always be used, even in extreme illness, whether at #6, #15 or after the administration of communion. This Note also addresses "cases of extreme illness".

#17 The bread and wine should be administered into communicants' hands, as usual, but variations from this may be necessary to meet pastoral circumstances.

Administering by intinction means the *minister* dipping the bread in the wine and giving the communion in both kinds together. This is desirable where there is danger of spreading infection, or where the sick person is lying down.

Note 4 on *APBA* page 693 assures communicants unable to eat the bread or drink the wine that, as repentant believers, they "truly eat and drink the body and blood of Christ". They may be able to touch the bread and / or hold the cup.

#18 These two sentences are appropriate for the sick person and minister to read in turn, expressing the mutuality of this ministry.

#19 Bishop Dowling writes that this post-communion prayer "sums up the approach to the healing ministry put forward by the *APBA* rite". Though the rubric indicates that the priest says it, it is appropriate that all present do so.

#20 This encouraging form of blessing derives from *BCP*, 'Visitation of the Sick'.

Additional Prayers

It may be obvious to say so, but these prayers do not limit the scope of what is prayed. Rather, they offer carefully crafted models of what can and should be brought before God, not least for situations in which praying is difficult.

a   *For healing*

Each of these prayers is a light revision of similar ones in *AAPB*. Each is in collect form: divine address, attribute, petition, purpose, ground (see pages 113–117 in this book). Prayer for healing is thus grounded in the being and action of God in Christ, rather than in the situation of the sick person: all these prayers are made through Jesus Christ, Saviour (Healer) and Lord.

Further, each prayer moves beyond healing of itself, whether by acknowledging ongoing pain, the importance of trust, or the person using their restored health to serve the Lord. "According to your will" is used in the third prayer, leading into thanks being returned to God.

b   *For healing for a child*

A fervent 'Prayer for a sick child' is included in *BCP* in 'Visitation of the Sick', it presupposes that the child is in danger of death, but includes this rich petition:

Visit *him*, O Lord, with thy salvation; deliver *him* in thy good appointed time from *his* bodily pain, and save *his* soul for thy mercies' sake: That, if it shall be thy pleasure to prolong *his* days here on earth, *he* may live to thee, and be an instrument of thy glory, by serving thee faithfully, and doing good in *his* generation; or else receive *him* into those heavenly habitations …

The Christ-based collect in *APBA* recalls Jesus' example of blessing, and then enacts it with the lovely phrase "hold *him* in your love", whatever the situation. "Make *him* well" is day-to-day language, always prayable because every child has the potential for divine service. Doing so alongside "fill *him* with your peace" is wise, since this is likely to be the immediate need.

c   *Thanksgiving for healing*

Perhaps surprisingly, this prayer is new. There is no equivalent in *BCP*, while one with the same title in *AAPB* is used as the post-communion prayer in *APBA*. The present prayer offers thanks not only for the sick person's healing, but also for others involved in this ministry.

d, j   *For those experiencing guilt and anxiety / For those in doubt and tested faith.*

The first prayer, d, is new: brief and direct in its simplicity. If prayed aloud, do so slowly. The second prayer, in collect form, is a helpful revision of one in *AAPB*.

Prayer j stands out by being written in the (plural) first person: **we** pray **with** those living with doubt and tested faith. To do so as if 'they' were over and against 'us' would be hypocritical: the line between faith and unbelief runs through the heart of every person. Further, the rare recognition of the feelings involved – angry, confused, fear, deceived, longing, assure – is significant, and highly relevant to the subject matter.

AAPB and *BCP* include 'A Prayer for persons troubled in mind or in conscience'. The latter is lengthy, but includes the memorable petition, "Break not the bruised reed, nor quench the smoking flax" (Isaiah 42.3). *APBA*'s prayer is 'For those experiencing guilt or anxiety' rather than 'conscience' or 'mind': does this reflect a contrast between pre-modern 'reason' and post-modern 'feelings', and the impact of psychology on pastoral ministry?

e, f   *For one facing / recovering from an operation*

Prayer e is a light revision of one in *AAPB*, a collect focussed on the person knowing God's presence as the remedy for fear.

Prayer f develops 'For a convalescent' in *AAPB*, but in a new direction. Rather than a focus on the outcome of the operation, it offers thanks for the skills and healing hands of the carers involved, whatever their faith.

g   *For one with a life-threatening illness*

This prayer is new: honest in what it does not ask, direct and realistic in what it does. *AAPB* includes two related prayers. 'For one believed to be suffering from an incurable illness' is vague about the sick person's state, and rather didactic about those involved in medical research. 'For the handicapped' assumes that being handicapped involves suffering, a position contested by many who live with disability. These prayers were not included in *APBA*, but that must not stop Christians from praying for such people: see Prayer k.

h, i *For those suffering from the process of ageing / For the aged*

Prayer h is a beautifully crafted collect: strong images contrast divine and human spans of life (see Isaiah 50.9; 51,6–8), leading to petitions that speak life into the experience of ageing.

Prayer i is confident in its requests, and realistic about praying for what is appropriate to the life experience of people experiencing 'increasing years'.

k *Prayer for those suffering severe illness*

This prayer brings together all the petitions for those experiencing illness offered in the preceding prayers. This welcome breadth was encouraged by the HIV / AIDS epidemic, but it is suitable for use in many circumstances.

In sum, 'Ministry with the Sick' is a resource rather than a rite, and a mutual ministry: those who offer care find themselves ministered to, the wonder of God's grace.

Ministry with the Dying

A tradition reformed and renewed

Rites associated with death are present in every human culture: Christian ones bear the mark of the "blessed hope" of resurrection in Christ (Titus 2.13). As Paul urged the Thessalonians to accept, we do not "grieve as others do, who have no hope. For since we believe that Jesus died and rose again, even so, through Jesus, God will bring with him those who have fallen asleep" (1 Thessalonians 4:13–14).[10]

In the early centuries of the Church, this hope came to be celebrated at places where martyrs had borne witness (*marturia*) to death. But when everyone in European society was embraced in Christendom, the Church came to be seen as more a refuge for sinners than a training ground for saints. This shift can be seen in the change in symbols of Christian identity. In the early centuries, when to be Christian was illegal, a prime symbol was the fish, '*ichthus*', whose letters spell out 'Jesus Christ, of God the Son, Saviour'. Closely linked with the 'sign of Jonah' (Matthew 12.38–41), this signifies

---

10 The New Testament authors consistently see believers as 'falling asleep' at their life's end, though modern English translations render this as 'died'. 'Falling asleep' is no euphemism, but discloses the early churches' instinctive resurrection outlook on life. Christ, on the other hand, died indeed, drawing the sting of death; this in sum is the argument of 1 Corinthians 15.

Christ's going down into the deep to rescue believers so they can survive in the alien environment of this age.[11] After Christian faith became the official religion of the Roman world, however, the sign of the cross, unknown in Christian art before 330AD, came to prominence, signifying Christ's work of forgiving sinners. 'Ordinary' believers came to see this as their central spiritual need, especially near death. Dying unprepared was feared, and rites associated with dying came to focus on being 'shriven'. These 'last rites' involved making a final confession of sins to a priest, being absolved and anointed (extreme unction, *viaticum*). The penitent might then enter heaven with minimal need fot their sinful soul to be purified in purgatory.

The Reformers strongly rejected such ideas, since they cut across the scriptural affirmation of God's work of justifying sinners (Romans 3.21-26 is the classic text). The practice of private confession to a priest was seen as particularly objectionable, since it was widely understood that priestly absolution was necessary for divine forgiveness to be obtained. Closely related to this was the practice of 'requiem' masses being offered for someone who had died, to reduce their time in purgatory: rich people would leave funds to erect a chapel (chantry) and pay a priest's stipend for an annual mass.[12]

In *BCP*, Archbishop Cranmer brought the focus of the funeral service back to God's saving work in Christ, while taking care not to make assumptions about the person's state of grace. But the only provision for ministry at the time of death in *BCP* was 'Visitation of the Sick'. There is much in its prayers that speaks of assurance, notably the traditional 'O Saviour of the world',[13] and 'A commendatory Prayer for a sick person at the point of departure'. But the tone remains one of being held to account for one's life, and the importance of dying with a clear conscience.

All this said, over the centuries Anglican priests would be present to support and pray with the dying. English versions of 'last rites' began to appear in the Anglo-Catholic revival, and the immense loss of life in World War I saw them taken up by many chaplains. In 'Visitation of the Sick' in the 1928 book, a 'Litany for the Sick and Dying' was included, along with the ancient *Paradisium*: "Go forth upon thy journey from this world, Christian soul". These resources, lightly revised, were included in *AAPB* (1978) with little debate: changes in attitude were beginning to take place.[14]

---

11 See further footnote 9 on page 279 in this book.
12 Sinden made the interesting argument that, since Holy Communion with a funeral would require several communicants, it would come "into head-on collision with a very long tradition that no-one (apart from the priest) received holy communion at a funeral mass": *When we meet for Worship*, 281-283.
13 See *APBA* page 414, and footnote 8 on page 153 in this book.
14 Even so, that Sinden saw the need in *When we meet for Worship* Chapter Eleven for a lengthy discussion of issues around 'last rites' shows that long-standing suspicions were alive and well in the 1970s.

Overall perspective

Against this sensitive background, the inclusion of 'Ministry with the Dying' in *APBA* was seen by the Liturgical Commission as uncontroversial. Care was taken to ensure that these resources are biblically, doctrinally and pastorally sound. The drafting was assisted by the ministry experience and sensitivity of Bishop Owen Dowling, and at the 1995 General Synod no amendments were proposed.

As with 'Ministry with the Sick', the title is significant: it is ministry *with* the dying. Likewise, what is offered is a set of resources which may be used as a continuous service. On the other hand, this ministry will always be offered at a crucial time in the dying person's life, and the processes around dying can be unexpected and unpredictable. It is assumed what is helpful will be selected, depending on the circumstances of those involved. Ideally, the dying person will be known to the minister, through 'Ministry with the Sick' having been shared over an extended period. In such cases death can be prepared for, including practical and spiritual matters (Note 1 on *APBA* page 706).

But when a minister is called to the bedside of a stranger, a car accident or emergency ward, 'spur of the moment' choices and actions will be needed. As Bishop Dowling wrote, 'Ministry with the Dying'

> will no doubt vary considerably, depending on whether the dying person is a practising and believing Christian or not, whether the person is conscious or not, where there can be an extended ministry spread over a period of time or … [it] has to be at the last minute, or even after the death of the person.
>
> Once it is recognised that the person is dying, then it is appropriate that prayer should specifically turn in that direction. Pastoral sensitivity is very much required at this point. The dying person may have come to a recognition of their condition, whereas some relatives or friends may not have come to that point. An open conversation about the matter may be very confronting, yet it is usually better to be open and honest than to engage in the illusion that the person is going to recover.[15]

Pastoral discernment is crucial. Bishop Dowling's suggestions about one element are indicative of the approach called for across ministry in the face of death:

> A person deemed to be unconscious may well respond to prayer uttered out loud. It is wise to speak to the dying person by name and for the pastor to identify himself or herself. The familiar words of the Lord's Prayer or Psalm 23 (provided at

---

15 *A Practical Commentary*, 122–123.

#6) may well be received and heard by the dying person, even if he or she does not give any outward response. It is certainly wise to say the words of prayers aloud even if the person is described as being deeply unconscious and the minister is alone with the patient. If family or friends are present, there is a very real ministry to them as well as to the dying person. Holding hands and the ministry of touch may also be an important means of communication and comfort.

And 'Ministry with the Dying' faces ministers with the prospect of their own mortality. It is not unusual to be thrown off-balance or become confused when facing "the last enemy" (1 Corinthians 15.26). Being aware of this, and having some understanding of the processes and riddles of dying and grief, is important. Even so, while Christians may have insights into palliative care, psychology and social work, the distinctive Christian contribution to the care of a dying person is God's gifts of the 'means of grace' – the ministries of Word, prayer and sacrament. Being familiar with the resources available, and humbly confident in their use, equips Christian ministers for the distinctive contribution to human wholeness that 'Ministry with the Dying' offers.

Service structure

This outline functions as an 'index' to the resources in *APBA*. While they follow the structure of a Sunday service, each element can be used on its own.

Preparation
    Greeting
    Sentences of assurance
    The Lord's Prayer

An Act of Faith
    Expressions of trust in God
    Prayer together

The Ministry of the Word – passages printed
    Psalm 23, Romans 8.38–39, John 14.1–3

Confession and Absolution
    [Reconciliation of a Penitent]
    Invitation to confession
    "I confess to you ..." / "I absolve ..."

Anointing
    Anointing
    Invocation of the Spirit
    Litany of light

Prayers
> For eternal rest
> "Support us ..."
> A Litany for use near the time of death

Commendations
> "Go forth ..." [*Paradisium*]
> "Give rest ... " [*Kontakion of the Departed*]
> Prayer of commendation

Blessings
> with a litany of blessing from Psalm 103

Commentary

#1–3 The first words said when greeting the dying person (and family and friends) are important. They will expect a Christian minister to offer prayer, but may not be familiar with responses, or be in a condition to use them. So it may be better to one of the sentences first, rather than the greeting printed.

The greeting is the typical way Paul greeted his readers (e.g. Romans 1.7; 1 Corinthians 1.3; Galatians 1.3). It is also used in the Funeral Services in *APBA*.

#3 Having the Lesser Litany and Lord's Prayer early may seem unusual, but as Bishop Dowling notes,

> It is good to start with the familiar ... the Lesser Litany and Lord's Prayer may be pastorally desirable, allowing the sick person and any who are gathered at the bedside to participate. It may be wise to use the traditional form of the Lord's Prayer.

#4 These words are in an 'intimate' style (see page 36 in this book). They may not be suitable for everyone, but give permission for similar expressions. Some may prefer to say a familiar prayer in a more 'objective' style, for example the Prayer of Preparation from Holy Communion. "The words 'Father, into your hands I commend my spirit,' are a marvellous vehicle for the expression of trust when the dying person is conscious and able to speak" (Bishop Dowling).

#5 This modern collect, using a string of images and verbs, brings together core aspects of our life in Christ. It echoes the painful wrestling of Job 30:26, the prophet's hope cited in Matthew 4:16, the theological insight of John 1:5 and the calling of God's people proclaimed in 1 Peter 4:11.

#6 The passages printed are those that pastoral experience shows are familiar and appropriate to be heard by a person near death, and those supporting them. They are printed out to ease the practicalities of handling books, and have deliberately been kept brief. A favourite text of the dying person could be used, if known.

A response is provided for Psalm 23: after each use, a short space of quiet can 'slow down' the reading, allowing the comfort of these familiar verses to sink in.

#7 As the rubric indicates, 'Reconciliation of a Penitent', and any similar act of personal confession, must not be imposed by the priest, but must come from the request of the dying person.

The words of invitation, and the personal, not general form of confession, are traditional forms rendered into modern English.

The authoritative absolution comes from *BCP*, a delicate balance of a 'reformed' reading of 'catholic' practice. The traditional words of the priest, "I absolve you", are not grounded in a 'priestly charism', but express the power to absolve which Christ left to the Church as a whole. Further, this absolution comes as a consequence of the prayer that Christ "of his great mercy forgive you all your sins".

Many priests, when commending the dying person to God's care, will instinctively express its words with actions. So Note 2 on *APBA* page 778 provides that "During the words of absolution, the priest may extend a hand, make the sign of the cross, or lay hands on the penitent, as is pastorally appropriate".

#8 Anointing is today largely associated with prayer for healing, on the basis of James 5 (see #8–10 on page 357 in this chapter). Its traditional use for centuries, however, was as 'extreme unction', anointing a person at the point of death (*viaticum*: see page 307 in this book). Anointing for healing was restored in *BCP* 1549, but soon ceased, as did extreme unction. The 1988 Lambeth Conference commended the revival of anointing for healing, but made no mention of its use at the time of death. The return of the anointing of a dying person in *APBA* is thus significant. As Bishop Dowling writes,

> The anointing provided in *APBA* (at #8 and #9) is a different one from that provided in the Ministry with the Sick. Here the requests are rightly quite specific:
>> Of his great mercy may [our heavenly Father] forgive you your sins
>> … release you from suffering
>> … deliver you from all evil
>> … preserve you in all goodness
>> … bring you to everlasting life.

Nothing is said regarding the oil to be used. Traditionally it is aromatic olive oil: eucalyptus oil or balm are other possibilities. If the oil is from those that the bishop has dedicated in Holy Week, the oil for healing is used for the dying.[16]

#9   This litany is derived from Psalm 31, which includes "Into your hands I commit my spirit" (Luke 23.46, Acts 7.59). The response, as Bishop Dowling notes, "gives an opportunity for those who are standing by to utter a simple and positive prayer which fits well with the rite of anointing".

#10 The first prayer not only encompasses the dying person, but all those present. Based on a tissue of scriptural references, it comes from the Anglican Province of Canada. The second prayer comes from John Henry Newman: it has become much-loved, evoking the quiet English spirituality of 'Lead kindly light' (also Newman's work) and 'Abide with me'.

#11 This Litany is a revision of the one included in the 1928 book, brought closer to The Litany in *BCP* in the opening (trinitarian) and closing (*Agnus Dei*) sections. In both cases the response is "have mercy *on your servant*" rather than "on us". The central petitions ("hear us, good Lord") pray for the dying person along the lines of the *BCP* 'Prayer for a sick person at the point of departure'.

This Litany works well when the dying person, and those present, are familiar with traditional forms of prayer.

#12 The first Commendation is a modern rendition of the traditional *Paradisium*. It is addressed to the dying person rather than God, so it is not a prayer so much as a bold, confident 'send-off'. That the congregation may join in at the end heightens this sense of strong affirmation of God's purposes in Christ, reinforced by the concluding 'Amen'.

The dying person is addressed as "good Christian", evoking *The Pilgrim's Progress*, rather than "Christian soul", as in *AAPB* and earlier versions. This steps around the body/soul dualism of *BCP* and traditional rites.

NB: In the 1993 'trial use' Funeral service, this Commendation was placed between the Farewell and Committal (#20 and #12, *APBA* pages 722–3). Since some interpreted it as 'praying for the dead', it was moved to 'Ministry with the Dying' in the draft book presented to General Synod.

---

16   Surprisingly, many modern Roman Catholic commentators, in explaining the traditional three oils – for catechumens, the sick, and ordinations and dedications – make no mention of anointing the dying. Anointing the sick is frequently referred to as "formerly extreme unction". Anointing the dying nevertheless continues to be practiced by Roman Catholic clergy.

The second Commendation is a 'Kontakion of the Departed' from the Eastern Orthodox tradition: the version here comes from The Episcopal Church. The opening and closing refrain is sung or said by the people, the verse by a cantor. Though the refrain is addressed to Christ, 'Amen' is not added since it functions more as a statement than a petition. But no harm is done if it is said.

The third Commendation, based on Romans 8.38–39 and Jesus' last words, is a new prayer of petition, with a congregational 'Amen'.

Each of these Commendations may be accompanied by those present – not only the priest – "making of the sign of the cross ... on the forehead of the dying person, recalling our baptism into Christ" (Note 2 on *APBA* page 706).

#13 The range of blessings offered affirms the 'resource' rather than 'rite' ethos of 'Ministry with the Dying'. The rubric hints that more than one may be offered. The first blessing is a post-communion form; the second derives from the 'economic Trinity' expression of God's work in the Catechism. The third is from Holy Communion; and the fourth is the 'Aaronic' blessing (Numbers 6.24–26).

#14 On some occasions this ministry will end with a blessing, but on others the opportunity to conclude with an act of praise to God will be appropriate. That is what this litany, based on the opening verses of Psalm 103, offers.

Where it is desired to have Holy Communion celebrated with the dying person, the form provided in 'Ministry with the Sick' is used, as adapted to the situation.

Reconciliation of a Penitent

The practice of 'auricular confession' and authoritative absolution by a priest has a long history of controversy (see page 326 in this book). Even so, as stated on *APBA* page 774, a form for "the ministry of individual reconciliation is part of the Anglican tradition" in the "'Visitation of the Sick' in *BCP*". Ron Dowling summarises the history of this ministry:[17]

> In the early centuries, members of the Church who sinned gravely were publicly excluded from full fellowship, and subsequently publicly restored after a suitable period of penitence. Only after centuries of experimentation did rites of private, individual reconciliation emerge. By the end of the mediaeval period, it had become the rule that no one could receive Holy Communion without first making a private confession of sin and receiving absolution.

---

17 *A Practical Commentary*, 145–146. The Revd Dr Ronald Dowling, who served in the Dioceses of Melbourne, Adelaide and Perth, and chaired the *Inter-Anglican Liturgical Consultation* for some years, held the portfolio for this service and the rites of Christian initiation, since they are closely related.

Although confession and pardon are at the heart of all worship, no actual rite of confession and absolution was a public part of the Eucharist until Archbishop Thomas Cranmer introduced them in the *Order for Communion* 1548. They entered the prayer book of 1549 and have been part of the Anglican Communion service and other Sunday services ever since.

Changes in Australian law had mandated an official rite in order to protect the privacy of confession, so 'Reconciliation of a Penitent' was included in *APBA* without demur.[18] In view of past sensitivities, however, the Introduction included in the draft of *APBA* was largely retained.[19] The first paragraph sets out relevant biblical material, and emphasizes that the ministry of reconciliation "is proclaimed in all our forms of public worship".

It is important to recognise, however, that the form of confession offered in public worship is general: beyond our personal sins, we acknowledge that we are caught up in the cussedness, cruelty and injustice of this 'fallen' world (see page 126 in this book). So the second paragraph of the Introduction, while clarifying that "the priest exercises this ministry on behalf of the whole Christian community", emphasises that reconciliation involves relationships beyond the penitent and priest. As Ron Dowling explains, continuing his historical summary,

> While introducing this 'general' public reconciliation within the liturgy, the rite of private, individual confession and absolution was never removed. It has continued in Anglican prayer books, usually within the rite for the Ministry to/with the Sick (cf. *AAPB* pp. 576–77). Although it is private and individual, this ministry committed to the Church is a corporate act because sin affects the unity of the whole body. The rite prepared for *APBA* is available to all and is not restricted to times of illness.

Commentary

'Reconciliation of a Penitent' is a ministry in which privacy between priest and penitent "must be assured", not least since the penitent may be facing a spiritual crisis (see Note 1 on *APBA* page 778). Ron Dowling notes that

> Many confessions will be made in private homes, at hospital bed-sides, or in clergy studies / offices. Privacy should always be assured. This applies also

---

18 The 2017 General Synod *Concerning Confessions (Revision) Canon* and *Concerning Confessions (Vulnerable Persons) Canon* amended the *Concerning Confessions Canon 1989* to provide for situations where a penitent confesses a grave offence, or one which may put a vulnerable person at risk. These changes in Canons do not affect the rite of 'Reconciliation of a Penitent', but may see consequences arise from its use.

19 Notes 2 and 5 on *APBA* page 778 were in the Introduction in the draft book, but are better as Notes.

when a confession is made within a church building. It may take place at a communion rail, at a prayer desk, or with both priest and penitent sitting side by side, or kneeling together.[20]

Only #2, #5 and #8 are optional, so – unlike *APBA* elsewhere – there are no headings. The service proceeds best by being taken staight through, without hurry or fuss: "It may be necessary for the priest to lead the penitent step by step through this rite" (Note 4 on *APBA* page 778).

#1 The service begins with welcome rather than greeting. Given the profound nature of what is about to take place, this seeks to set the penitent at ease.
Note 3 applies to this opening section: "the penitent's name may be used … ".

#2 This optional selection from Psalm 51 will be appropriate when the penitent is a regular confessor, and so is familiar with the rite.

#3 The scripture passage is short, as the printed and 'other suitable verses' show: the penitent has come to confess, and needs assurance rather than exhortation.

#4 The confession comes in response to the Ministry of the Word. As the rubrics note, it may be in the penitent's own words: this is likely when a person is making a private confession for the first time, or has come to disclose a 'mortal' sin. Using the form printed – a modern English version of the traditional words – may help them bring this difficult and stressful act to completion.

#5 Though this brief rubric is optional, it points to what will be highly significant words in the rite, the priest's response to the penitent's confession. There are many resources to assist priests in this delicate ministry, which calls for skills of discernment which transcend liturgy. As Ron Dowling notes,

> Those who give counsel should be experienced and have received some training in this area. The priest may suggest some appropriate devotions or actions be performed by the penitent after the rite is concluded. Again, care and sensitivity are needed.

#6 These questions echo those asked in Holy Baptism. As Ron Dowling notes, "Reconciliation was sometimes known as 'second baptism' in the early Church because it restored the penitent to their baptismal state".

#7 The second form, a modern English rendition of the *BCP* 'Visitation' absolution, sees the priest – on behalf of Christ's Church, and doing so in the name of God – make the authoritative declaration, "I absolve you".

---

20 *A Practical Commentary*, 146–7, as are the quotations following.

The first form is a less direct pronouncement of absolution, emphasising that this ministry is exercised on behalf of the whole Church, on the basis of the atoning work of Christ and the grace of the Spirit.

Whichever form is used, the words spoken are "performative language": they not only inform, they *do* something, so invite accompanying actions. Note 2 on *APBA* page 778 therefore provides that "During the words of absolution, the priest may extend a hand, make the sign of the cross, or lay hands on the penitent, as is pastorally appropriate". As Ron Dowling writes,

> Reconciliation involves the whole person, and gestures may assist the penitent to know the forgiveness of God. The sense of touch can be very important in this regard, but does need to be used sensitively and responsibly.

Note 3 on page *APBA* 778 indicates that "The penitent's name may be used at the absolution": the priest would then say "... absolve you, N".

#8 These thanksgivings for pardon are optional, but will be especially appropriate when serious expressions of sin and evil have been laid bare before God.

#9 If ever the traditional words introducing the Lord's Prayer were fitting, they are so here. If the penitent is more familiar with the traditional form, this should be used (see General Note 8 on *APBA* page xi).

#10 Prolonging the rite once absolution has been given is unhelpful: these words of dismissal seek to encourage the penitent to "go, and sin no more".

The priest's request to the penitent at the end of the service must not be forgotten: "pray for me, a sinner". In words cited earlier, "we are all beggars showing other beggars where bread may be found".

Post-*APBA* Resources from the Liturgy Commission

The core Christian ministry of wholeness is the gospel itself, lived out by the grace of God through the Holy Spirit. When challenging events and issues in the life of churches and the wider world arise, gospel-grounded responses are called for. Since *APBA* was published in 1995, the Liturgy Commission has continued to make resources available, through the Liturgy page on the General Synod website.[21]

Resources related to a day or theme

Some of the resources on the website relate to particular days or events: Anzac Day, the *Week of Prayer for Reconciliation*, a parish anniversary, Safe Church training, White Ribbon Day, election campaigns, after a natural disaster.

Others relate to a broader theme, particularly climate change and the environment. It is not easy to discern what Christians should bring before God in these areas, where local effects and issues vary, long-term research continues, and the consequences of harmful action for the earth are dire. A wide range of liturgical resources are offered, relating to farming, rain, solar energy, salinity, sustainable cities, and a lament for drought, deforestation and flood. Resources suitable for use in the Eucharist include the themes of food and the stewardship of creation.

Resources related to sexual abuse

Drafting resources related to sexual abuse by clergy and others was difficult. Two prayers for people abused, and one for abusers were included in *APBA*: #26, #27 and #28 on pages 209–210. In addition, 'A Blessing of the whole person' (#1 on *APBA* page 221) arose from ministry with abused people (see page 124 in this book).

The following resources are found on the Liturgy page of the General Synod website:

- 'A Litany following sexual abuse' is for use in a congregation or community in which sexual abuse has just been disclosed. Structured on The Great Litany, it is designed for public use, and is 'objective' in tone. As the introductory Note explains,

    > Not only the individual offended against, but also the communities of the survivor and the offender have pastoral needs which may call for appropriate liturgical resources. For example, in the early stages of the community's journey, feelings of hurt, anger, and shock must be recognised and given expression. The community's dependence on God for present help and future healing needs to be affirmed. This litany is intended for use at this stage.

---

21   https://www.anglican.org.au/liturgy-worship

- Two 'Prayers of a companion' are personal and reflective in tone. One is for a companion to an abused person to use for her / himself; the other is prayer for the companion as s / he undertakes their ministry of care and support.
- 'A Service of thanksgiving and prayer for the journey of healing following sexual misconduct or abuse by a church worker' is a particularly sensitive resource. (It is named as 'Prayer for healing after sexual misconduct' on the website.) It is prefaced by significant Notes which set out the importance of understanding the context, and of good preparation. This service should only be held when these matters have been taken fully into account. Even so, the likelihood of causing further suffering cannot be excluded.

However powerful, relevant or insightful ministries of wholeness may be, we live by faith, not sight, utterly dependent on the grace of the living God.

Further Reading

Archbishop's Council, *A Time to Heal Handbook. The Development of Good Practice in the Healing Ministry* (London: Church House, 2013)

Evans, Sioned and Davison, Andrew, *Care for the Dying. A Practical and Pastoral Guide* (Norwich: Canterbury, 2013 // Eugene OR: Cascade, 2014)

Pickering, Sue, *Creative Ideas for Ministry with the Aged* (Norwich: Canterbury, 2014): explores ministry with the sick and dying as 'theology of the cross'

Raining, Hilary D., *Joy in Confession: Reclaiming Sacramental Reconciliation* (Forward Movement Publications, 2017): Raining is a priest of The Episcopal Church

Sherlock, Charles, "Rites of Reconciliation: the Anglican Tradition", *Australian Journal of Liturgy* 2/1 (1989) 43–50, written prior to *APBA*

Wilkes, Paul, *The Art of Confession. Renewing Yourself through the Practice of Honesty* (New York: Workman, 2011)

Websites:

General Synod Liturgy page: https://www.anglican.org.au/liturgy-worship

The Order of St Luke the Physician (Australia): www.osl.org.au/first.html

Chapter Twenty-Three

Funeral Services and Resources in APBA

The Funeral Services and Resources in *APBA* take as their basis God's gift of life, and of new life through Christ's death and resurrection. Further, they seek to honour both the human and gospel dimensions of Christian rites around death, as expressed in 'For the congregation' on *APBA* page 711.[1] They look forward in hope to believers being fully healed (saved) in God's presence, and call those who remain to courage, repentance, and renewed consciousness of God's grace and love.

A 'trial use' booklet was published by the Liturgical Commission in 1993. The draft book presented to the 1995 General Synod took account of responses received: no further amendments were made by the Synod to funeral-related material.

'A Funeral Service' is designed to meet a variety of circumstances for an adult who has died. It is complemented by 'Funeral of a Child', and the 'Funeral of an Infant', along with a wide range of Additional Prayers. This chapter therefore has the following structure:

- Perspectives on Funerals: theological, historical, pastoral and liturgical
- A Funeral Service in *APBA*, and Additional Prayers
- Funeral Services for Children

A personal note

The Funerals portfolio on the Liturgical Commission for *APBA* was held by me.

Drafting 'A Funeral Service' was not easy: difficult situations came to mind, but this was primarily a liturgical task.

Drafting 'Funeral for a Child' was difficult, though there are occasions when a child's death comes as a relief.

But drafting 'Funeral for an Infant' was heart-rending, since it would always be marked by dashed hopes and deep loss. The assistance of experienced chaplains at children's hospitals was of inestimable help.

---

1   A lively overview of funeral ministry, based in social research (including Australia) from a Christian perspective, is Tony Walter, *Funerals and how to improve them* (London: Hodder & Stoughton, 1992).

Funeral ministry in perspective

Theological perspectives

Death and life in Christ

Death is one of life's few certainties. It is marked in every society by rites of passage that reflect what is believed about death, and the extent to which life transcends it. A Christian funeral marks the liturgical expression of Christian beliefs about death: thanksgiving to God for the gift of life, mixed with the reality of grief, looking in hope to the resurrection of the body.

The return of the body to the earth is the ancient Christian tradition for disposing of the mortal remains, following Jewish practice. Along with Jews, Christians hold that we are whole persons, whose body, soul and spirit are inseparable (1 Thessalonians 5.23). In biblical terms, death marks the return of an 'earthling' (*adam*) to 'earth' (*adamah*: Genesis 2.7). The finality of this act is pastorally important, signifying the earthly finality of death. It is expressed liturgically in the presence and procession of the body, and especially in its committal, "earth to earth, ashes to ashes, dust to dust".

Christian hope revolves around the resurrection of Christ, in which we share as its "first fruits" (1 Corinthians 15.20), part of the "new humanity" (1 Corinthians 15.42-29) in the "new heavens and new earth" (Revelation 21.1-2). Burial or interment in the earth thus marks the finality of our participation in this creation, and identifies us with it in expectation of the new creation. So Christian faith does not despise the body, but regards it with deep respect.

A Christian funeral points to the fulfilment of our baptism: being symbolically buried with Christ to die to sin, receive the gift of the Spirit and live as those "marked as Christ's own for ever". The relationship begun in faith passes into sight as through death we pass to life. So, after the day of Pentecost, the New Testament writers never speak of a Christian as having 'died', except in baptism (Romans 6.1-11). As regards physical death, we "fall asleep" (1 Corinthians 15.18; 1 Thessalonians 4:13-14). Jesus Christ 'died' indeed, entering into the full pangs of death and dying, so that those who trust in Christ might share his risen life.

This "blessed hope" (Titus 2.13) does not obscure the fact that Christians share the sufferings of their Lord: we face death, as do all mortals. Death in human experience is complex, and each death is as distinct as the person who dies. It can come as a merciful release, a sudden tragedy, a victorious climax, a gentle end of a long life. Even so, a funeral shaped by Christian belief is not only a farewell, but celebrates our fellowship in the communion of saints with the person who has died

– or, better, who is in Christ now 'truly alive'. This is why provision is made for Holy Communion in a Christian funeral. The sacramental proclamation of the death of Christ interacts wonderfully with the realities of human death, and offers the grace of God to mourners in a way that transcends words.

NB: Some requests were made to the Liturgical Commission for the inclusion of a funeral for a non-believer. The difficulties involved show up quickly when the attempt to draft such a service is made – to start with, a Christian funeral is an act of worship. The required 'core' of the *APBA* services retains the balance of graced objectivity and charitable hope that characterises Burial of the Dead in *BCP*.[2]

Prayer and the faithful departed

'Prayers for the dead' has long been a matter of contention. Indeed, one reason that no list of topics for thanksgiving and prayer is provided in HC2 (*APBA* page 124) is that General Synod could not agree on how the faithful departed were to be included. The Liturgical Commission believed that pastoral situations demanded principled progress in this area, and that agreed texts are preferable to clergy 'doing their own thing'.[3]

No Christian tradition holds that human intercession can change a person's standing with God beyond death. Care is taken in *APBA* to avoid any sense in which human action overrides the judgement of God. Related to this is the division of 'soul' and 'body' that undergirds purgatory, where the souls of believers – who will be saved in due course – are believed to be made ready for God's full presence. This division is seen in the prayer of medieval origin, "May his / her soul, and the souls of all the faithful departed, rest in peace".[4] Biblical scholars have come to question this division, so it is avoided in *APBA*, where 'body' refers to the person as a whole.

Moreover, the New Testament portrays believers as 'truly alive' with Christ (Philippians 1.21–24), continuing to worship the Lord and offer praises and prayers. Revelation envisions these being offered by "every creature in heaven and on earth

---

[2] Sinden cites the response of the English Bishops to Puritan objections to statements of hope in *BCP*: "It is better to be charitable, and to hope for the best, than rashly to condemn": *When we meet for Worship*, 288.

[3] The Commission was assisted by the work of ARCIC II and AustARC on 'invocation': ARCIC II, *Mary: Grace and Hope in Christ*, Part D, #67–60: I was a drafter of this text, which drew on *The Saints and Christian Prayer* from AustARC, to which I was a consultant. The texts are available at
www.prounione.it/dia/arcic/Dia-ARCIC-16-II-Mary.pdf
https://www.cam.org.au/Portals/.../AustARCC_TheSaintsandChristianPrayer_1997.pdf

[4] The closest that the 1928 book comes to intercession for the faithful departed is in the Burial of the Dead: "Grant unto *him* eternal rest; / And let perpetual light shine upon *him*. Amen." This avoids a soul/body distinction by taking up the Eastern notion of 'perpetual light' as characterising God's presence. It is used by some clergy at the end of a service, though to my mind its vagueness is unsatisfying.

and under the earth and in the sea" (Revelation 5:13; 7.9–11), whose prayers "rose before God" (Revelation 8.1–4). We who "remain in the flesh" join with the communion of saints in prayer and praise as fellow members of Christ.

Thinking in terms of "praying for the truly alive" opens up possibilities beyond debates about "prayers for the dead". For those 'truly alive' in Christ, may we not pray that they enjoy the full presence of God, be transformed from one degree of glory to another (2 Corinthians 3.18), and realise that they pray for us? Further, that with them we may share the joys of God's new creation, and continue to grow in grace? It is realisations such as these which undergird the way in which the deceased person is held before God in prayer in 'A Funeral Service'.

Thanksgiving for the faithful departed, and praising God for them, form part of each of the 'Prayers for Sunday services' in *APBA* (see pages 184–187; 172–173). In the 'Prayer for the Church Militant' in *BCP* Holy Communion, however, stronger terms are used. The priest concludes it by saying, "we *bless God's holy Name* for all those departed this life in thy faith and fear". Blessing God for them transcends thanksgiving (see pages 123–124 and 267 of this book): they are commended into God's care, so that "with them we may be partakers of thy heavenly kingdom".

Further, all Christians pray for those who are dying, and the precise point at which intercession for them should change to commending them to God's care and blessing is difficult to say. Often it depends on when the person's death comes to be known. The attitude that prays in desperation for a deceased person's salvation is as unhelpful as one in which we must be wholly silent before God about someone dear to us whose earthly life has just ended.

There is a proper Christian instinct to entrust into our Father's hands one whom we trust is in Christ's care: this is reflected in *APBA*'s committal prayers.

Historical perspectives

The significance attached to honouring martyrs in the early churches led, as early as the second century, to their burial places becoming places of worship: the case of Polycarp, laid to rest in 155AD, is a famous example.[5] By the fourth century, their remains had begun to be placed in church buildings. In the medieval West, relics came to be placed under the altar as part of the consecration of a church building. The relics were not thought of as supplementing the saint's burial, but as bringing something of their participation in holiness into the present. Increasing focus on martyrs' suffering, however, would lead to a diminishment in the celebration of resurrection

---

5   *The Martyrdom of Polycarp* 18.3, available at www.earlychristianwritings.com/martyrdompolycarp.html

hope, the characteristic emphasis of a Christian funeral until the eighth century. Allied with this was the development of belief in purgatory, alleviated by a requiem mass being offered to reduce the soul's time there (see page 362 in this book).

The Reformers rejected relics, and replaced requiem masses with rites consisting of little beyond scriptural excerpts. Even so, 'rites of passage' instincts continued, typically in a vigil with the body overnight (separation), then the funeral and burial (*limen* – boundary crossing), followed by a wake (re-incorporation: see pages 38–39 in this book). In England until recently, common practice was burial of the body – wrapped in a shroud – in a church-yard, or under the floor of a church building or cathedral. Coffins were not in common use until the nineteenth century, hence the reference in *BCP* to "preparing the body". In Australia until World War II, the use of 'Burial of the Dead' from *BCP* was widespread among Protestants: apart from a few historic churchyards, burials took place in public cemeteries, divided into denominational areas.

Two significant changes have taken place in funeral ministry since World War II. First, the growing practice of cremation has forced a rethink of the funeral service, now divided into two parts. The main part takes place at the church or funeral chapel, the committal an hour or so later at the crematorium, while the ashes are interred some weeks later.[6] *APBA* provides resources for each part, but the result can be a dislocated experience for mourners. With this in mind, provision is made for the Committal to take place in the funeral itself: a rite at the crematorium is then not needed, though prayers may be offered if mourners accompany the body there. The interment, usually involving only immediate family and friends, will have a more private character.

Secondly, the proportion of funerals taken by 'civil celebrants' has increased steadily. In part this is a consequence of people having less church connections, or bad experiences at a church funeral. But it also reflects a widespread unwillingness to face death: funerals are seen as morbid, best replaced by the 'celebration of a life'. This shift, however, can divert attention from the grief and losses surrounding death.

---

6 On cremation, see J. Douglas Davies, *Cremation today and tomorrow*, Alcuin / GROW Liturgical Study 16 (Bramcote Notts: Grove, 1990). He notes that the practice of cremation is high in Australia compared to Europe, where memories of Nazi gas chambers persist. Some Christian bodies do not accept cremation: the Anglican tradition sees it is accelerating the natural processes of decomposition, provided that the mortal remains are interred. The use of columbarium niches to store ashes indefinitely is therefore generally resisted by bishops.

Pastoral perspectives

The minister and pastoral care

In ministry with the bereaved, Christians have opportunities to exercise unconditional caring. This calls for witnessing with integrity to the Christian hope, interwoven with support of the bereaved, whether faith be firm, frail or seemingly absent. Those ministered to include the family, friends and others who knew the deceased, funeral staff – and those who minister.

The effectiveness of pastoral care around a funeral is closely related to a minister's own facing of death and grief. A sense of earthy reality about the funeral details, and the often painful nature of grief, is healthy. A minister's own actions and attitudes speak most loudly of the ministry of Christ. With this in mind, wearing robes takes on pastoral as well as liturgical significance. They allow a minister to stand a little apart from the mourners, and reflect the "still point in a churning universe" that reflects Christ's presence in times of stress: *APBA* offers a wide range of resources for difficult situations. Where liturgical colours are used, white or gold points to the Easter victory, while red points to the redemptive suffering of Christ, though some find purple helpful, with its sense of solemnity.

Ministry that is unreal is disastrous. Hypocritical statements about the person are an obvious trap, but unreality about suffering, getting details of the circumstances of death wrong, or ignoring unresolved relationships all do damage.

Funerals and faith

A Christian funeral is in the first place an occasion of corporate worship in which divine promise and human loss meet. Whatever the situation, the Church must not deny to those present the one resource which the gospel alone offers: the presence, grace and love of God. Further, a Christian funeral must not avoid the reality of death: grief needs to be acknowledged, but mourners' responses will vary, so the liturgy must correspondingly be adaptable. Nevertheless, the focus of a Christian funeral is on God, and God's loving purposes, not solely on the needs of those present.

In drafting the funeral services for *APBA*, Commission members were surprised at pressure from not a few clergy and others to keep them 'pastoral'. A few wanted the negative aspects of death excised, others to have Christian distinctives played down, seen as embarrassing. So the 1993 booklet received objections to the inclusion of John 11.25, and "Yet Christians believe that those who die in Christ share eternal life with him" in the Gathering. Some of this concern, it would seem, arose from funerals where the deceased person's standing with God was dubious, which raises other issues.

Given the 'established' status of the Church of England, 'Burial of the Dead' in *BCP* had to be useable for all except those who had died "unbaptized, or excommunicate, or have laid violent hands upon themselves". Funeral services in the Anglican tradition thus stop short of using the language of certainty about the state of grace of the deceased. This avoids giving false hope or encouraging spiritual hypocrisy, while refusing to call into question the risen life of Christ promised to believers.

'A Funeral Service' in *APBA* assumes that the rite is for a Christian, but the required 'core' retains the 'objective' stance of *BCP* as regards the state of grace of the deceased person. The 'Funeral of a Child / Infant', however, is 'warmer' about the present state of the youngster who has died, taking account of Jesus' promise that "the kingdom of heaven belongs to such as these" (Mark 10.14).

Liturgical perspectives[7]

The funeral as a pilgrimage

The 'shape' of a Christian funeral corresponds readily to neither the eucharist or office patterns, in part due to its controverted Anglican history. It is helpfully understood as a 'pilgrimage', in which friends and family accompany the deceased person on their last earthly journey: this aligns with 'rite of passage' perspectives. As this was described on pages 38–39 of this book,

> A community group faces a situation of challenge by '***separating***' from regular life in order to ***cross a dangerous boundary or threshold*** ('limen') in safety, before resuming daily living as people '***re-incorporated***' in an adjusted identity.

As its fullest, a rite of passage around death sees people spend time with the body (vigil), conduct a rite of commemoration and farewell (funeral), and then join together in a celebration without the body (the wake). The funeral service in and of itself is rarely adequate to bear the weight of what is needed pastorally.

'A Funeral Service', therefore, does not seek to meet all that is needed by a group faced with death, but points to these needs. At a 'macro' level, the symbolic rites 'Before the Funeral' (*APBA* pages 708–709) point to the 'vigil' aspect. The funeral rite is the *limen*, concluding with the Committal. The 'wake' can be supported by good after-service eats and drinks – and is where projected photos can work well. At a 'micro' level, the Gathering establishes 'A Funeral Service' as an act of Christian worship (*APBA* pages 712–713), which is then shaped as a pilgrimage of several stages.

---

7   The 2007 *International Anglican Liturgical Consultation* meeting took up funeral liturgy: its work, edited by Trevor Lloyd, is known as the Palermo Statement: *Rites surrounding Death*. Joint Liturgical Study 74 (London: Alcuin Club, 2009). It sets liturgical issues in theological and pastoral contexts.

- The **'story' of the person** is told (*APBA* page 714 #9). Psalmody marks a transition to
- the **'story' of God's work** in giving life and new life, through scripture and sermon (pages 714–718).
- Both **'stories' join** in the prayers and Farewell (pages 719–722), and
- then **separate** after the Committal, as the body is taken out (pages 723–724): "we leave the deceased in God's care, and we continue life's journey" (page 711).

In this way the truths of human responses to grief, and the good news of Christ's life-transforming ministry, are performed in ways that respect and integrate them.

NB: The deceased person is not present but, for the congregation, the body represents the person. 'Memorial services' without the body may sometimes be necessary, as mentioned in Note 10 on *APBA* page 772. Where the body is not available, symbols of the person in view can to some extent make up for its absence.

The funeral location

Where the funeral takes place will affect how it is conducted. 'A Funeral Service' is designed for use in a church building or funeral chapel; Note 7 on *APBA* page 771 offers suggestions for when it takes place in a crematorium chapel, and Note 8 on *APBA* page 772 for funerals at home. When the funeral takes place at the graveside, those present may see themselves as observers rather than participants: the weather may be unpleasant and hearing difficult. The minister's part is likely to be more prominent than for a service in a building. This situation calls for prayerful clarity of purpose, care not to rush, and awareness of body-language.

What's in people's hands

What the congregation need to have in their hands needs thought. *APBA* itself (the 'red brick') is quite impracticable: it is designed for the minister's use. The Funeral card available from Broughton Publications will meet some situations, but the best resource is a leaflet, which can also be kept as a memento. Funeral directors are usually glad to prepare and produce these as part of their service.

For funerals without Holy Communion, the people's words will usually fit into the insides of an A5 booklet: the front and back can be used for photographs and details of the person's life. When the funeral includes Holy Communion, a fuller booklet will be helpful: this is permitted under the copyright terms for one-off services from *APBA*. A template will ease the workload for other funerals.

NB: Data projection of songs for a funeral can work, but showing photos during the service can draw attention away from the coffin and surrounding symbols.

A Funeral Service

Overview

A few 'core' elements are required for every funeral. As with *BCP*'s 'Burial of the Dead', these sustain an 'objective' tone about the state of grace of the deceased person. For a long-term communicant, a richer liturgy that is positive about their standing with God is called for: observing a vigil, a significant Ministry of the Word and Prayers, and Holy Communion being celebrated, along with hymns and anthems.

The overall structure of the service is set out below, omitting hymns, which may be placed at any suitable point. The 'core' elements are in ***bold italics***.

Before the Service
> ***The body is accompanied in***
>> Reception of the body
>> [Placing of Christian symbols]

A Funeral Service
> *Gathering in God's Name*
>> ***greeting*** and introduction
>> ***John 11.25;*** other sentences
>> prayer for those present
>> remembrance of the deceased person's life
>> placing of symbols, silence
>> ***psalm***
>
> *The Ministry of the Word*
>> ***scripture reading***(s)
>> ***sermon***, silence
>
> *The Prayers*
>> ***thanksgiving for the gift of life***
>> ***prayer for those who mourn***
>> further thanksgivings and prayers, Lord's Prayer
>
> [*Holy Communion*
>> Greeting of Peace
>> Great Thanksgiving
>> Breaking of Bread and Communion]
>
> *The Farewell*
>> prayer of dedication
>> ***prayer of entrustment***
>> [The Committal]
>
> *The Blessing and Dismissal*
>> ***blessing and dismissal***
>> ***procession of the body***

There is here a definite 'pilgrimage' movement. The corpse is brought in, and after an introduction and prayer for those present, the person's life may be recalled. The psalm leads into hearing Christian perspectives on death in the readings and sermon. The Prayers move on to give thanks for the person's life, and pray for those in need. The Farewell sees journeys part: the body being taken out marks the final earthly journey of the deceased, while others take up the journey of life without them.

Whatever local variations are made, this pilgrimage shape must be respected if the *APBA* funeral services are to have integrity.

At the Graveside or Crematorium
    Preparation
        Meeting of the body
        Greeting and sentences
    The Committal
        'In the midst of life' / Psalm 103
        Committal prayer and response
    The Prayers
        The Lord's Prayer
        Prayer for those gathered
        Dismissal sentence

Commentary

The ideal situation is where ministry has been taking place with the dying person. Discussion can then happen with family and friends about the funeral, as Note 1 on *APBA* page 771 encourages. Writing down reminiscences about the person not only has therapeutic value, but will help in framing words to be said at #9.

Before the Service

That the body is met by the minister is not optional. The tradition that it not be left alone is a worthy one, and is much appreciated by family members and friends. It may also mean that the minister is unavailable to greet others: this can be done by Funeral Director staff, parishioners, family and friends.

#1   This prayer gives voice to a minister when the body is received, briefly articulating Christian belief about life and new life in Christ.

     At a large funeral, the body can be processed to its place of rest, which should be visible to the congregation. This also provides opportunity for music, singing and sentences, as the rubric notes.

#2   This prayer is suitable for a funeral where the body is processed in. It exemplifies the approach explored in 'Prayer and the faithful departed' above, in which more than their earthly life is remembered before God. The words "as we remember before you" transcend thanksgiving, and the *brother / sister* is not said to have died, but is assumed to be 'truly alive'.

#3 Silence is provided for in a number of places. In a funeral, it gives space for sensing the mystery of death, and the depth of human loss entailed.

A pall is a large cloth, draped over the coffin as a mark of honour for the body: some churches have one for regular use. It has the advantage of avoiding costly coffins. Family members or friends sometimes provide one that evokes memories of the person. For members and former members of the *Australian Defence Forces*, the pall is usually an Australian flag.

The rubrics provide for flowers and "symbols of the person's life" to be placed "near or on" the coffin: see Note 1 on *APBA* page 771. The intention is provide for symbols that take up the human side of funeral liturgy: photographs, significant documents, medals and awards, symbols of work, hobbies or interests. The placing of Christian symbols follows at #4, taking up its gospel aspect.

Family members may wish to arrange symbols on the coffin before the service, which means that it needs to be received beforehand. Note 2 on *APBA* page 771 requires that "Any symbols placed on or near the coffin must be consistent with Christian faith". Where there is doubt, they can be placed elsewhere, or at a wake or reception that follows the funeral.

#4 Symbols are by their nature capable of interpretation. To fill out what is happening, and avoid misunderstanding, interpretive words are provided: their inclusion was done after wide consultation. As Note 2 on *APBA* page 771 indicates, they "may be used at any appropriate point in the funeral service".

The opening line(s) of each prayer affirm Christ's work as Light, Life-giver, Word and Saviour: the petition relates this to the congregation. The inclusion of the deceased person's name reflects 'Prayer and the faithful departed' above.

For the congregation

This resource summarises the rationale for a Christian funeral. It is not designed to be read aloud, but is suitable for inclusion in a service booklet.

Gathering in God's Name

#5 The greeting is the typical way Paul began his letters (e.g. Romans 1.7; 1 Corinthians 1.3; Galatians 1.3), a shorter form of The Grace. That it ends "the Lord be with you" is designed to pick up the instinctive response, "and also with you".

But it is long enough to work if the congregation does not make the response. That the service begins with a Christian greeting is important. More informal words of welcome can follow, but a Christian funeral is an act of worship, and a serious occasion at which some formality is expected.

The initial words of introduction say in brief form what is about to happen. These lead into a statement of our human mortality, Christ's gift of eternal life, and our turning to God. Its directness has been criticised, but it has the benefit of brevity – and it faces the reality of death. The minister may use "similar words": the Liturgical Commission's plea is that the intentions behind what is provided here are respected.

#6 Hymns can be placed wherever suitable in the service (see Note 6 on *APBA* page xi). Note 1 on *APBA* page 771 encourages family and friends to contribute choices, "provided they are not inconsistent with Christian truth".

#7 John 11.25 is always used. The original pronoun before "believe" and "die" is singular: it is rendered "they" to embrace all present. Some may wish to read "she" or "he", reflecting the deceased person's gender.

The other sentences relate to the variety of circumstances faced in funeral ministry. It may feel awkward to read aloud texts such as Ecclesiastes 5.15–16, but in situations of tragedy people deeply appreciate knowing that God knows about it. Others sentences can be found at #3 in 'Funeral of a Child', *APBA* page 739.

Who reads these sentences is not specified. This is an opportunity for family or friends to take a public part, as Note 1 on *APBA* page 771 encourages.

#8 This prayer is from *AAPB*, where it comes at the end of the service. Having those present join early on in praying for each other as mourners has proved its worth. As the rubric indicates, it can be said by the minister alone.

The phrase "life-giving Spirit flow through us" is widely valued, as are the strong verbs – fill, give, kindle, give way – and outcomes – compassion, calm, hope, joy.

#9 The inclusion of a place for 'eulogies' in the 1993 booklet was thought to be daring, but has become widely accepted, and works well at this point.

A major issue is keeping 'control' of the number and length of speeches. In preparing the service with the family, who will speak, and for how long, can be discussed. Asking what they do ***not*** want said not only helps the minister understand the situation, but often includes a request that the service not be too long. Too many speakers can lead to unease and discomfort in the congregation.

Note 4 on *APBA* page 771 is now dated: it assumes that the minister will read a text, thinking that family members will not want to speak in public. When there are disagreements about who should speak, and what might be said, however, the minister doing so can be wise, drawing on material provided by the family.

Placing "flowers or symbols on or near the coffin" allows for this to be associated with words spoken about the deceased person. If this has happened earlier, it may be inappropriate here: these are matters for pastoral discernment.

Projecting photographs of the deceased person is often associated with eulogies. This works well when blended into the addresses, but showing photos for their own sake is better before or after the service, at a vigil or wake.

The final rubric, mentioning silence and / or music, is often suggested by Funeral Directors as a fitting way to conclude this time of recalling the person's life.

#10 A psalm is always included. Some are printed in *APBA* to provide accessible resources and avoid the need for mourners to balance books: the intention is not to limit choice.

Psalm 23 is often used, with its familiar words and promise of God's presence. Sinden notes, however, that its brevity can mean that it is over before mourners realise it, and "its comfort can come across as somewhat superficial".[8] He therefore prefers Psalm 90, as in *BCP*, which reflects on human mortality, and calls all present to use our days wisely. (Psalm 128, used in *BCP*, is not included here.)

Psalm 121, a favourite of many regular worshippers, affirms repeatedly and helpfully that "My help comes from the Lord" (*not* the hills …).

Passages from Psalms 130 and 103 (*APBA* page 741), and 139.1–11 (*APBA* page 755) are printed in the Funerals for a Child and Infant respectively.

A response is provided with each psalm: this allows the congregation to join in without having to read words aloud, with a cantor or reader singing or saying the verses. A minister can signal when the response is to be used.

The Ministry of the Word

#11 At least one scripture reading is always used. As with psalms, some are printed to provide ready access to suitable passages: the intention is not to limit choice. A range of other suitable readings is listed with brief headings to guide selection: other passages may be ones that were favourites of the deceased person.

---

8 *When we meet for Worship*, 287.

Romans 6.3–9 sets out the Christian hope, its relation to baptism and relevance for daily living.

1 Corinthians 15.50b–58 is the conclusion of this magnificent chapter. A longer portion is set for reading in *BCP*, which some may request be used.

John 14.1–6 is a familiar passage of comfort and hope on Jesus' lips. Where Holy Communion is celebrated, this is an appropriate Gospel reading.

#12 The sermon is always given. Note 5 on *APBA* page 771 sets out five elements that it should contain. That the person's life has been addressed at #9 means that the sermon can focus on Christian faith, though some reference to the deceased may be appropriate.

Nothing should be said about the deceased person that is not known to be true. Inaccuracies grate, as do doubtful claims of a person's standing with God.

#13 These classic canticles, with their strong affirmation of Christ's triumph in death over death, are especially appropriate at the funeral of a long-time believer.

The Prayers

#14 Prayers prepared by family and friends should be considered in the preparation for the service with them.

There are two sections to the prayers, 'Thanksgiving' and 'For those who mourn': at least one item from each section is to be used.

After the minister's introduction, who offers these prayers is not specified: Note 1 on *APBA* page 771 encourages family and friends reading some.

Thanksgiving:

The first prayer includes a list of possible aspects of the person and their life for which thanks to God can and should be given. It is not exhaustive: family and friends should be consulted about what is prayed. The second prayer is appropriate for use with a long-term parishioner.

The rubric at the bottom of *APBA* page 719 points to two 'objective' collects, that for Easter, *APBA* page 502 or page 765 #1–3. These are useful when few are present, and / or the deceased person is unknown to the minister.

Other thanksgivings can be found at #4–7 on *APBA* pages 766–767.

For those who mourn:

The first prayer has long precedents in the Christian tradition, and is relatively 'objective'. The second, more 'subjective' prayer, is appropriate where the death has been difficult, unexpected or has elements of tragedy. Other prayers for those who mourn can be found at #8–10 on *APBA* page 767.

#15 This Litany, as the rubric notes, is particularly appropriate when Holy Communion follows. Beginning with thanksgiving, it includes a general confession (not included elsewhere in *APBA*'s Funeral services), petitions related to those touched by death – those present, those who mourn, the dying – and leads to praise for the saints, with the possibility of including the person's name.

#16 The Lord's Prayer concludes the prayers, unless used later in association with Holy Communion: the cross-reference is to 17c. A 'traditional' version may be used if this is appropriate for the congregation.

#17 This section is the turning point to the Greeting of Peace and Holy Communion: otherwise the service moves toward its third stage, the Farewell.

The Farewell

#18 A hymn here marks the transition to the climactic point of the service. The imminent removal of the coffin means that further congregational song is unlikely, so what is selected should take account of this.

#19 This prayer of farewell is for the congregation as they prepare to face their friend's departure. It assumes that the deceased was baptised, but nothing more, though it may be 'heard' as a fuller statement. This preserves both the 'objectivity' of *BCP*, and its 'charitable assumption' about the deceased person's faith. Where other words are used, they should have a similar function.

#20 This, the point of farewell, has two distinctive aspects:
a) It is congregational, drawing all present into this sacred moment.
b) It is doctrinally and pastorally sensitive. All those present know that the deceased has died, yet from their point of view this is the point of his or her transition from life to death. So the person is entrusted to "the mercy / merciful keeping of God", an action appropriate at this time, though a week later there might be objections about 'prayer for the dead'. The prayer is offered "in the faith of Christ", carrying the sense of Christ's faith in us, as much as ours in him.

NB: In the 'trial use' booklet, the Commendation at #12 on *APBA* page 703 was an option for closing The Farewell. Some saw it as 'prayer for the dead' so it was moved to 'Ministry with the Dying' (see page 367 of this book). Not a few ministers, including Evangelicals, find this *Paradisium* a great comfort, marking the deceased person's transition from the Church militant to the Church triumphant.

The Committal

The Committal of the body, as the climactic point of a funeral, is only to happen once. The wording of the rubric, that it "may take place at this point, if it is not to occur does at the graveside or crematorium," indicates that when the Committal is to happen needs to have been decided before the service.

Allowing the Committal to take place during the funeral itself recognises that in many cases the interment will take place elsewhere, with only immediate family and friends present. This allows the congregation as a whole to make their last farewell. But this is an option, as the shaded line indicates. When it takes place in the funeral, this excludes a second committal at the graveside or crematorium.

#21 The rubric requires the minister to face the coffin, since the prayer that follows relates closely to the body of the deceased.

The prayer of Committal, taken from *AAPB*, fills out the equivalent in *BCP* but avoids its implicit body / soul distinction: the body committed to the earth or sea, and so to God, stands for the whole person. The closing lines echo 1 Corinthians 15, leading into the response from 1 Corinthians 15.57.

The rubric allows for other prayers to be added, but it is not intended that these be many or long. Where an RSL or Masonic ceremony is requested, this may be the best place for it to happen.

The Blessing and Dismissal

#22 With the Farewell completed, the service moves to its close, with either the Grace or Aaronic blessing, followed by an optional dismissal.

#23 It is both liturgically and psychologically important that the body be taken from the congregation, rather than the people leaving the body behind. In pilgrimage terms, the departure of the body is the outward and visible sign of journeys dividing, as the deceased person and the congregation go their separate ways.

The tradition of friends and family members carrying out the coffin has much to commend it, but is not required by canon law. With safety matters in mind, Funeral Directors generally prefer that the coffin be wheeled out.

Many funerals will have well-known music played or sung as the body is taken out. Football songs are not uncommonly requested: what matters is that the lyrics are not inconsistent with Christian faith. However, the use of other than Christian hymns is contrary to policy in some places.

The first anthem printed is the Paschal *troparion*, an Eastern Orthodox Easter hymn in English translation. The second is the Song of Simeon (*Nunc Dimittis*, Luke 2.29–32) from Evening Prayer. Both work well at the funeral of a believer of long standing.

Note 6 on *APBA* page 771 underlines the corporate nature of the Farewell, by encouraging the congregation to "accompany the body to the hearse". This supports the tradition that the body is never left alone until buried or cremated.

Holy Communion on the Day of a Funeral: see pages 310–312 in this book

At the Graveside or Crematorium

Except in special circumstances, the gap between the funeral and the burial or cremation is typically only a matter of an hour or two. The numbering of the rubrics therefore continues from 'A Funeral Service', since liturgically a burial or interment continues the funeral.

NB: A funeral held at the gravesite or crematorium includes the Committal of the body: what follows is not relevant for these cases.

Preparation

#24 The funeral procession to the gravesite or crematorium is itself a significant 'rite of passage', as friends and family follow the hearse together. The custom of the minister and Funeral Director walking before the hearse for some distance is not only a mark of respect, but denotes the link between the service and the disposal of the mortal remains. This link is further shown by the minister meeting the body at the 'entrance' to the site, as the opening rubric states.

The rubric about a hymn or music is optimistic at a burial, which will take place in the open air: unaccompanied singing can work, and there are battery-powered music players. At a cremation, music will usually be provided by the Funeral Director: the family should be consulted as to what they do **and do not** want.

#25 The greeting, though used already in the funeral, takes into account that those gathered are in a new place, for a new purpose. The rite is short, unlikely to last more than a dozen minutes: using several sentences, with silence between them, may be helpful. The first three give assurance of the Christian hope, while the last two face the tragic aspect of death: both perspectives are needed.

The Committal

#26 The first statement is a shortened form of "Man that is born of woman" from *BCP*, alluding to Isaiah 40. The second is taken from Psalm 103.8–17.

Some resist using these statements, with their realistic assessment of our mortality. But without them, the rite fails to face the reality of death, the 'last enemy'. Many Australians are wary of using the words 'die' or 'death' today: the person has 'passed away' or even just 'passed'. Grief and mourning are hard places, yet Christian faith does not allow their pain to be sidestepped. God's grace gives strength to endure, looking to the Lord of life and death for remedy.

#27 See *The Committal* in 'A Funeral Service', and the commentary on #21 above.

At a burial, the rubric specifies that earth is cast on the body. It is assumed that the minister takes the lead – as in *BCP* – but others joining in is pastorally helpful, as mourners see the coffin in its final resting place.

At a cremation, the Committal takes places as the coffin (on a catafalque) is lowered.

The response after the Committal is from Revelation 14.13

The Prayers

#28 The Lord's Prayer is optional, since it will have been used not long previously. It should be used if the funeral was some time back.

#29 Both these prayers are for those present, the first for use of our remaining time as disciples of Christ, the second – based on *BCP* – for comfort and the hope of life in Christ. A time of silence is often appropriate.

#30 As well as these sentences of dismissal, those in 'A Funeral Service' are available.

The Interment of the Ashes

Practical matters include the hole to receive the ashes being dug before the service. It needs to be deep enough to avoid animals digging up the remains, which will take some years to decompose fully. A tool to fill in the hole afterwards is also needed.

The rubric numbers start afresh, since interring the ashes takes place some time after the funeral and cremation. This brief rite is experienced as a distinct service.

Gathering

#1 The greeting is the one that began the funeral, as is the opening sentence, connecting this second stage rite to its predecessor.

Other appropriate sentences can be found in 'A Funeral Service', while a favourite verse of the person whose ashes are to be interred could be used.

#2 This prayer links back to the thanksgiving for the deceased person's life in 'A Funeral Service'.

The Interment

#3 It may take a minute or two to arrange things around the site for the interment: that the minister does not hurry to do this conveys much.

The rubric does not specify who pours the ashes into the earth: some family members or friends may wish to share in doing so. The ashes may blow about if there is wind, so should be poured out as close to the hole – or water – as possible.

The prayer while the ashes are poured out has similarities to the prayer of Committal, though it rests on deepening aspects of God's gift of life generally. The gift of new life in Christ is evoked in the people's response (1 Corinthians 15.57).

#4 This passage from 1 Corinthians 15, read after the interment, speaks to those present of the resurrection of the body in a *changed* state. As well as affirming the Christian hope, it mitigates against unhelpful ideas about the fate of the ashes.

The Prayers

#5 The Lord's Prayer at this point brings the people together in prayer. The prayer following sets the sights of those gathered towards the hope of being united in the presence of God with their friend whose ashes have been interred.

#6 The service ends with a dismissal from the New Testament.

Additional Prayers

A variety of sources is drawn on for these. Some adapt prayers from the heritage of the Christian tradition, others come from modern prayer books (see the Acknowledgements on *APBA* page 850). A few are new compositions.

- The italicised gendered pronouns alternate between prayers: thus 'her/him' in prayer 4 is followed by 'him/her' in prayer 5.
- The main groups are shown by self-explanatory headings. Within 'Particular Situations', subheads indicate further categories.
- The inclusion of prayers 'After a suicide' was approved after consultation with the Doctrine Commission, in view of the *BCP* rubric that excludes use of 'Burial of the Dead' for those who "have laid hands violently upon themselves".
- The inclusion of 'Prayers of struggle' was questioned by some, but widely affirmed by most, and accepted by General Synod.[9]

Other prayers may be found in the two Funeral Services for children.

---

9   Prayer 21 is not a 'Prayer of struggle', but a litany whose sub-heading was lost as the number of prayers was reduced from the 1993 'trial use' Funeral Services booklet.

Funeral Services for Children

A Funeral Service for a Child

Introduction

A separate service for a child was included in *APBA* to take account of the fact that many children are likely to be present. The main differences from the Funeral Service are the 'warmer' theological statements about the standing of the deceased child with God, the choice of scripture sentences and passages, and generally simpler language.

"The death of any child is always the death of hopes and dreams", so that expressions of feelings are to be expected, as Note 2 on *APBA* page 772 indicates.

As the words on *APBA* page 739 note, this service is not designed for infants, or children old enough for 'A Funeral Service' to be used. Elements from the other funeral services may be included where this is helpful (see Notes 1 and 5 on *APBA* page 772).

"Flexibility is essential for a service such as this", as Note 3 states. The Committal is included in the service to allow the children present say goodbye to their friend.

The use of data projection in this service is only recommended during #5, where pictures may be helpful: elsewhere it may see too much focus on reading words.

Commentary

Only sections not covered in 'A Funeral Service' receive comment.

#2 In contrast to the introduction at #5 on *APBA* page 712, this is less 'objective', because the death of any child is a tragedy, and calls for immediate pastoral support. The final lines state the 'theology of children' which arises from Jesus' teaching in Mark 10.13-16, the scripture reading in 'The Public Baptism of Infants' in *BCP*.

#3 Similarly, these scripture sentences make positive affirmations about the place of the 'lambs' in God's kingdom, and our hope for what they will become in Christ.

The sermon may be offered here "to set the scene for what all are about to do together", as Note 4 on *APBA* page 772 states.

#4 These prayers and congregational response continue the acknowledgment of grief, alongside the assurance that the child is in God's care.

#5 This opportunity for speaking and symbols may take some time, especially where children present are involved. See the commentary at #9 on pages 389-390 in this book.

#6 The inclusion of Psalm 23 is familiar. Psalm 130 gives voice to the sense of loss, Psalm 103 to God's ongoing care and compassion. Responses are provided to make it easy for those present to join in, rather than them having to read a text.

#7–11   See the commentary on the equivalent sections of 'A Funeral Service'. The Additional Prayers contain others which may be helpful, especially 13 and 21.[10]

#12   Both prayers of Commendation are deeply personal, expressing a positive view of the child's relationship with God, reflected in the use of their name.

#13   The Committal is shorter and more personal than that in 'A Funeral Service'.

#14   The brief blessing and dismissal strike a strong note of God's peace.

#15   As in any funeral, that the body leave the congregation, rather than the people leaving it behind them, is liturgically and pastorally significant. The presence of children means that how this takes place needs careful attention.

At the Graveside or the Crematorium

As with 'A Funeral Service', the rubric numbering continues without a break.

#17   Greater emphasis is placed on the use of symbols than in 'A Funeral Service', both before and after the Committal when it takes place at this point.

#18   The prayer after the Lord's Prayer sums up the ethos of this service.

#19   The rubric notes that these sentences may be said by the minister and people together. Since only immediate family and friends are likely to be present, this may draw them together in prayer before they depart without the child they have lost.

A Funeral Service for an Infant

Introduction

This service, as with 'Ministry with the Sick' and 'Ministry with the Dying', is best seen as a set of resources arranged as a service, but available to be adapted for the circumstances encountered. That said, those with experience in this ministry report that parents find a short, well-structured rite is pastorally helpful: a drawn-out liturgy will be tiring, especially for the mother. They also report that the preparation, immediate pastoral care, and follow-up can take considerable time and spiritual energy.

The resources are structured in a similar pattern to 'A Funeral Service', without provision for a 'eulogy', with a wider range of prayers provided. Each service element has a more personal tone than the other Funeral rites, and the language is intimate in parts. The theological tone is wholly positive about the infant's standing with God, whether baptised or not: see Additional Prayers 13.

---

10   The Acknowledgements on *APBA* page 850 note that #12b and Additional Prayers 13 and 21 are from the (Roman Catholic) *ICEL*, Order of Christian Funerals.

Commentary

As with 'Funeral of a Child', comment is only made on distinctive aspects. The Introduction on *APBA* page 753 further reduces the need for commentary.

#1 This introduction, quite different from the other funeral rites, was difficult to be given 'trial use', so is more a model of what might be said than a proven text.

The use of the child's name (N) assumes that one has been given, as health professionals recommend.

#3 This section, drawing on a range of sources, is again more a model than text.

#4–5 These scripture readings speak to the mystery of tragedy in the face of God's love. Some relate to the child, some to the needs of the parents and close friends. They were chosen in hope more than confidence: use whatever is helpful from these or other passages, some of which are printed or listed in the other funeral services.

#7 'Words of comfort' are mentioned at #2: this could also describe the sermon.

#8 The Prayers are extensive, and specific to this service. Several are new, since suitable ones could not be found, e.g. that for a father.

#9 This Litany could also be used at a service in which the child is remembered.

#10 The Lord's Prayer can be prayed at any suitable time. The rubric implies that it is used somewhere in the service.

#11 The rubric implies that this prayer is optional, but without it – or something similar – the child is not entrusted to God's loving care.

#12 Where the Committal takes place is not specified, though it is assumed that it happens at the burial or cremation which soon follows. It is as brief as possible.

#13 As with 'Funeral of a Child', prayer at this point for those who grieve is appropriate: Additional Prayers 8 and 9 are suitable.

#14 The rubric is a little odd, since only one option is printed. Any of the prayers of blessing and dismissal from the other funeral services may be used.

Further reading

ARCIC II, *Mary: Grace and Hope in Christ*, Part D, notably #67–60, available at www.prounione.it/dia/arcic/Dia-ARCIC-16-II-Mary.pdf

AustARC, *The Saints and Christian Prayer*, available at https://www.cam.org.au/Portals/.../AustARCC_TheSaintsandChristianPrayer_1997.pdf

Davies, J. Douglas, *Cremation today and tomorrow*, Alcuin / GROW Liturgical Study 16 (Bramcote Notts: Grove, 1990)

ICEL, *Order for Christian Funerals, with Cremation Rite* (London: Catholic Book Publishing Company, 1991)

Lloyd, Trevor (ed.), The IALC Palermo Statement. *Rites surrounding Death*. Joint Liturgical Study 74 (Cambridge: Alcuin / GROW, 2009)

Walter, Tony, *Funerals and how to improve them* (London: Hodder & Stoughton, 1992)

Part G

Other resources in *APBA*

This Part picks up liturgical resources that are not strictly 'common prayer'. The Ordinal and Thirty-Nine Articles have traditionally been "attached to" rather than included in *BCP*. The Athanasian Creed was included in *BCP*, but has fallen out of general use, so in *APBA* was placed in the Supplementary Material. *APBA* is rounded out with an Index of Prayers, and Acknowledgements.

Chapter 24 focuses on The Ordinal.

Chapter 25 gives attention to the Supplementary Materials in *APBA*,
    apart from The Catechism, discussed on pages 185–189 of this book.

Australian Anglicans Worship concludes by returning to *APBA*'s opening, the Preface from the Chair of the Liturgical Commission in 1995, Canon Dr Lawrence Bartlett.

Chapter Twenty-Four

The Ordinal

The Ordinal is a keystone in the Church's self-understanding. Whenever someone is ordained, on public display is the meaning and significance of the ministries of the gospel that Christ entrusts to the Church. It is thus essential that any Ordinal revision, while responding to new contexts, remains in full continuity with existing teaching and practice.

This chapter falls into three main sections:
> Ordination in Australian Anglican contexts
> Theological issues around ordination
> Commentary on The Ordinal in *APBA*

Ordination in Australian Anglican contexts

Developments in understandings of ministry

The Fundamental Declarations of the Anglican Church of Australia state that "This Church will ever … preserve the three orders of bishops, priests and deacons in the sacred ministry". The Constitutional meaning of these 'orders', and what is required of candidates for each, are set out in the Ordinal attached to *BCP*.[1] The Ordinal in *APBA* stands by this commitment, while reflecting developments of the past half-century.

a) All Christian ministry proceeds from Christ. But fresh awareness has arisen in recent times that it involves the whole body of Christ rather than being the prerogative of the ordained – a 'baptismal ecclesiology'.[2] Deacons, priests and bishops are called and sent to enable the ministry of all Christians – to let them shine.

---

1. The first reformed Ordinal was issued by Cranmer in 1550 as a 'stand-alone' rite, separate from *BCP* 1549. The Ordinal has remained 'attached to' successive *BCP*s, in part because it is not 'common prayer' relating to the ongoing life of a congregation. Its being bound with *BCP*, however, means that all have access to the ministries to which their clergy have been are called.
2. This was first recognised in the Anglican Communion in Resolutions 24–27 of the 1968 Lambeth Conference. The WCC Faith & Order document *Baptism, Eucharist and Ministry* (Geneva, 1982 – the 'Lima text') put this approach into the public realm. Resolution 3 of the 1988 Lambeth Conference set 'baptismal ecclesiology' at the centre of Anglican reflection on ministry. Resolution 45 acknowledges "that God through the Holy Spirit is bringing about a revolution in terms of the total ministry of all the baptized".

b) The participation of women in ordained ministries has become a reality in the Anglican Church of Australia, as deacons since 1986, priests since 1992 and bishops since 2008. Associated with this development has come fresh appreciation that ordained ministries involve the ***being*** of clergy together with what they ***do***. Ontology and function are inextricably interwoven.

c) The context of ordained ministries has changed from supporting Christians in a largely Christendom environment to enabling them to survive and equipping them to thrive in a world that knows less and less of Christ. This shift to mission more than maintenance mode is leading to ordained ministries being exercised in a growing variety of ways.

d) The 1662 Ordinal requires those ordained to have an exclusive commitment to ministry in Christ's name, to "forsake and set aside all worldly cares". This was traditionally interpreted as entailing full-time ministry: a man was ordained to a 'living', with housing and stipend sufficient for basic needs.

Many bishops have now taken on more flexible ways for clergy to function and be supported, including part-time and honorary positions (in which women are at present disproportionately represented).[3] Being in 'full-time ministry' no longer means having a 'full-time' stipend: clergy are not employees, but remain 'professionals' in the sense of belonging to a group with shared skills, expertise and wisdom.

These developments are significant, but of themselves do not touch on the distinctive nature of each 'order' of ministry: bishop, deacons and priests / presbyters. Practical realities affect how they are understood, however.

- Most deacons are ordained priest after a year, in large part so that they may preside at the Eucharist, and thus be 'employable'. This reinforces the idea that priests are the central order of ministry, with deacons 'below' and bishops 'above'.[4]

- Most priests minister as 'the' cleric in a congregation. The resulting isolation is not helpful personally, and undermines the biblical idea that priests belong to the 'council of presbyters' (1 Timothy 4.15). The corporate nature of

---

[3] The possibility of other than full-time ministries was recognised in Resolution 89 of the 1958 Lambeth Conference, and reaffirmed in Resolution 33 of the 1968 Lambeth Conference.

[4] Even so, that every bishop and priest is also a deacon means that their vocation has its foundation in this primary order of ministry. Some Anglican scholars have advocated 'direct ordination' for priests, but this would displace the 'episcopal-diaconal' dialogue which lies at the heart of Christian liturgy (see pages 233-234 in this book), steps around the commission to be an 'ambassador for Christ', and the diaconal call to lowly service.

- their ministry is seen at each ordination, where priests join as a presbyteral college with the bishop in the laying on of hands.

- Many bishops today find themselves expending energy on administration, putting out media fires and coping with the latest crisis. Opportunities for teaching, public witness and support of colleagues must be found around these demands. Further, larger dioceses typically have several bishops, challenging the idea of 'the' bishop being the diocese in person – and where is the 'see' of a regional or assistant bishop?[5]

These realities cannot be swept aside, though they can be mitigated. **What continues to distort the way ordained ministry is understood and practised is the focus on 'priesthood' as central.** It is sustained by long-standing debates over 'sacrifice' in the Eucharist, despite ecumenical work bringing fresh insights (see pages 230–233 of this book). Scholarly research on *diakonia* (ministry) has given impetus to renewing the foundational order of Christian ministry, the deacon (*diakonos*). And the recognition by Vatican II of the episcopate as a distinct order, rather than a subset of the priesthood, has spurred new reflection on the bishop's ministry, not least by Lambeth Conferences and ARCIC.[6]

The *APBA* Ordinal reflects these developments. The introduction, pages 780–81, notes "the minister's role in a partnership with other clergy and the congregation", the dignity of the deacon's ministry, and ordination set in "the context of the ministry of the whole people of God, in the light of the unique ministry of Christ". These issues underlie almost every sentence of the Ordinal.

The process of revision

The Ordinal in *AAPB* (1978) rendered into modern English the Ordinal attached to *BCP* (1662), with minimal changes. The Liturgical Commission had prepared a 'Second Form' Ordinal, taking account of ecumenical scholarship, but in view of concerns about whether the new book would be accepted, this did not proceed. Ordinations continued for some years using *BCP* in some dioceses alongside others taking up the Ordinal in *AAPB*.

---

5 Traditional episcopal titles recognise the problem of there being more than one bishop in a local church (the diocese in classical ecclesiology). A 'coadjutor' bishop is usually someone who will succeed the diocesan, sharing their responsibility in the meantime. The title 'suffragan' (break-together-with, i.e. sharing the breaking of the bread with the diocesan) recognises the issue but does not resolve it.

6 See Resolution 18 of the 1978 Lambeth Conference, which details the 'public ministry of the bishop', and ARCIC, 'Ministry' in *The Final Report* (London: ACC / CTS, 1981). This is available at www.prounione.urbe.it/dia-int/arcic/doc/e_arcic_ministry.html

Growth of interest in a renewed diaconate, and the prospect of women becoming deacons, saw the 1985 General Synod approve a new service for the ordination of deacons. This followed the structure of HC2 in *AAPB,* with the welcome inclusion of an Exhortation, absent in the 1662 Ordinal. Further, the deacon's ministry is to be exercised "under the care of your bishop", as in the early centuries, rather than under the priest, as in the 1662 Ordinal. The description of a deacon's tasks is corresponding less parish focussed, and sensitive to the more egalitarian ethos of society today. Its use of 'service' as the focus of the deacon's ministry, however, would soon come into question.

Preparation of the *APBA* Ordinal began by considering the 1977 Second Order drafts and the 1985 deacons' rite. But it was soon realised that these leaned too much towards the 'functional' side of ministry, what clergy are to *do*. The Liturgical Commission sought to balance this with a reaffirmation of the 'ontological' (being) dimension of ministry.[7] Drafting proceeded in consultation with the Doctrine Commission, which examined the priests' service particularly closely, and asked for minor changes, which the Liturgical Commission adopted. The joint work of the two Commissions ensured that the Exhortations in each service were not only true to our formularies, but are distinctive and memorable so they would 'speak' to clergy as the years went on.

A presentation of the resulting draft Ordinal was made to the Australian House of Bishops at its 1994 meeting. The feedback received was taken into account in the draft book presented to the 1995 General Synod. Several Synod members paid close attention to the Ordinal, and a few amendments were adopted. The more significant were having newly ordained deacons and priests "take" rather than "receive" authority, and in the priests' service expanding the words at #19 to include John 20.23.[8] Attempts to remove 'Concerning the Ordinal' on page 780 and 'Liturgical principles' on page 781 failed, since they set down issues of theological and liturgical significance.[9]

Three issues which arose in the process of drafting call for further comment.

---

[7] A draft Ordinal for 'trial use' could not be issued for comment, since those ordained using it might have their orders called into question. Opportunity was taken at several Liturgical Commission meetings for the draft rites to be 'trialed', with already ordained members taking part.

[8] This addition was mistakenly omitted in the first printing of the full 'red brick' *APBA*.

[9] The 1999 (Kottayam, India) and 2001 (Berkeley, USA) meetings of *IALC* had ordination as the topic: the outcome was *To Equip the Saints*, known as the 'Berkeley Statement'. Some Liturgical Commission members were able to participate in these meetings, at which the *APBA* Ordinal was well received.

1. Terminology

In the 1550 and 1662 Ordinals a deacon is 'made', a priest 'ordained' and a bishop 'consecrated'. Archbishop Donald Robinson pointed out to the Liturgical Commission that the title of the 1662 Ordinal, "The Making, Ordaining and Consecrating of Bishops, Priests and Deacons" is set out in an 'ABC–CBA' structure. This implies that 'making', 'ordaining' and 'consecrating' are inclusive of all orders, rather than particular to each. The Constitution of the Anglican Church of Australia thus speaks of three 'orders', so that deacons, priests and bishops are all 'ordained'.

APBA thus uses 'Ordination' for all services, though 'consecration' is retained in the rubrics and prayers associated with the Laying on of Hands of a bishop-elect.

2. Gendered language

General Synod authorised the ordination of women as deacons in 1986 and as priests in 1992. In 1995, not all dioceses had adopted the respective Canons. It was not clear, however, as to when women might be authorised to be ordained as bishops: in the event, this would not happen until 2008. The Liturgical Commission meeting in 1994 noted that women had been ordained as bishops in the Anglican Provinces of the USA, Canada and Aotearoa New Zealand, and that recent episcopal ordinations in Australia had been of pairs of bishops. It therefore agreed that candidates in all three services would be referred to in the plural, using italicized pronouns.

3. Structure

Drafting began on the three 'orders' separately, but it was soon apparent that a common structure was the better way to proceed, and this commended itself to the House of Bishops. Each ordination rite in *APBA* thus follows the pattern for Sunday services.

> Gathering in God's Name
> The Ministry of the Word
> The Presentation of ordinands
> The Prayers
> The Exhortation and Examination
> The Laying on of Hands:
> > Hymn to the Spirit
> > Hand-laying with prayer
> > Equipping with the tools of ministry
> > Welcome of the newly ordained
>
> The Greeting of Peace ...

Liturgical resources related to ministry are placed in *APBA* so that they are readily available, beyond ordination services. The 'Litany for Ministry' is included in the Prayers in *APBA* (pages 192–3); the preface and post-communion prayers for ordination in the seasonal material for HC2 (pages 162–3). The Notes and Scripture Readings (pages 808–809) are common to all three services.

One outcome of this commonality is that the words associated with the laying on of hands, apart from the terms deacon, priest and bishop, are the same for each rite (#18 on pages 788 and 796; #21 on page 805). Most other modern Anglican rites do not include the middle line, "whom we set apart by the laying on of our hands": it was added after General Synod members expressed concern that this action needed explicit mention in the ordination formula.

The Liturgical Commission held that ordinations should take place at a distinct service for each 'order'. The practice of ordaining deacons and priests in the same service is therefore not provided for in the *APBA* Ordinal.

Theological issues around ordination

Deacons: ambassadors of Christ

The ministry of deacons has undergone significant changes in understanding in recent decades. For centuries, almost all deacons were ordained priest after a year or less, and the diaconate was seen as an inferior office of service.[10] The Anglican deaconess movement emerged in the 1860s as a Christian response to pastoral needs arising from the Industrial Revolution. Interest in a renewed diaconate since 1945 in large part drew on this 'service' focus.[11]

Three issues are relevant to the Ordination of Deacons in *APBA*.

1. Deacons have typically been viewed as 'servants', doing lowly practical tasks and undertaking pastoral care.[12] As a result, deacons in most non-episcopal traditions are not ordained, or, as in the Uniting Church of Australia, are ordained

---

10 In the concluding prayers in the 1662 Ordering of Deacons, the bishop prays for the newly-ordained deacons "that they may be worthy to be called unto higher Ministries in thy Church".
11 The 1968 Lambeth Conference recommended opening the diaconate to women, affirmed that priests and bishops are deacons, rejected the idea of it being an inferior office, and recognized deaconesses as deacons, but continued to see it as "combining service of others with liturgical functions" (Resolution 32).
12 For example, Ormonde Plater, *Many Servants. An Introduction to Deacons* (Cambridge MA: Cowley Publications, 1991), writing from a USA Episcopal background, and Christine Hall (ed.), *The Deacon's Ministry* (Leominster: Gracewing, 1992), a collection of essays from the Church of England. A more balanced but still 'servant-focussed' work is James Monroe Barnett, *The Diaconate. A Full and Equal Order*. Revised Edition (Valley Forge: Trinity Press International, 1995): the thorough grounding of Barnett's discussion in 'baptismal ecclesiology' is impressive.

to a ministry of social concern, 'parallel' to that of Ministers of the Word (presbyters). Along with this, reaction against triumphalism and clericalism led to welcome emphasis on the 'servant church'. However, beyond 'public servants', it is a century since servants were a reality in Australian society.[13] 'Servant ministry' thus lacks models, so what it means is open to misuse, whether encouraging passivity or being a code for keeping women in their place.

The meaning of *diakonos* in ancient times was 'sacred agent', one who gives skilled service as an ambassador for the gods or leaders.[14] It does not carry connotations of *lowly* service, though New Testament texts conjoin *diakonos* with 'slave' (*doulos*) to emphasise this aspect (Matthew 20.26–27).[15] So *doulos* and *diakonos*, while having some overlap in meaning, are not to be confused. A Christian deacon is a skilled 'go-between', called to cross boundaries to enable sacrificial communication of the gospel, Stephen being the exemplar, as in the 1662 Ordinal.

2. The meaning and status of a deacon's *diakonia* (ministry / service) derives from the identity of whoever commissions them, rather than from those who are served. To "serve the poor" is a part of every Christian's calling, but making this the focus of ministry leads to burn-out. To serve God is "perfect freedom", as Augustine of Hippo put it, life-sustaining: this service enables disciples to follow Christ "unto their life's end", serving others in need.

Jesus is presented in the scriptures as the servant of *God* (Matthew 12.18, citing the "servant of the Lord" of Isaiah 52.13–53.12, as does Acts 8.32–33).[16] Though being our "Lord and Teacher", he washed the disciples' feet (John 13.14) and rendered lowly divine service, even to death, through his atoning work of redemptive suffering (Philippians 2.9–11; Mark 10.45.). The deacon's ministry thus derives from Christ's redemptive *diakonia*, though, as with the ministry of priests, it must not be conceived in any way that would displace or rival Christ's unique work.[17]

---

13   The nouns 'servant' and 'service' are more problematic than the verb 'to serve', which makes sense in Australian culture, though care is needed about its object.
14   The research of Australian scholar John Collins has been central to this: see *Deacons and the Church: Making Connections Between Old and New* (Leicester: Gracewing; Harrisburg: Morehouse, 2003). For Anglican reception of his work, see The Church of England General Synod Report, *For such a time as this. A renewed diaconate in the Church of England* (London: Church House Publishing, 2001).
15   Mary's response to Gabriel begins, "Here am I, the *doulē* of the Lord" (Luke 1.38, 48): 'maidservant', not *diakonē*. Likewise, Simeon calls himself a *doulos* (Luke 2.29).
16   In Acts 3.13, 36; 4,27.30 Jesus is described by Peter as God's *pais* (servant / child of God).
17   It is ironic that some who deny the term 'priest' because 'Jesus is our priest', though he is not called that in the New Testament see no problem with 'deacon', though it speaks strongly of Jesus' atoning work.

3. Many see deacons having a 'passive' ministry, undertaken at the direction of others: this is often how the 1662 Ordinal for deacons is 'read'. But in the New Testament *diakonia* involves pro-active ministry. Thus Stephen saw the apostles' response to Christian Hellenist widows as a call to preach a Christian Hellenist reading of the First Testament, and have Luke include his whole speech in Acts. Moreover, only those set apart for Christian *diakonia* are called *diakonoi* in the New Testament, though every Christian is described as a *doulos* (slave). Such *diakonia* is *with* rather than *to* others, but bears its own authority. So in the 1662 Ordinal, the bishop exhorts the deacon to "search for the sick, poor and impotent", not to minister to them directly, but "to intimate their names ... unto the Curate, that ... they might be relieved with the alms of the Parishioners or of others". The deacon is to take a stance of pro-active advocacy, embodying the restorative aspects of justice.

The ordination service for deacons in *APBA*, especially in the Exhortation, takes up this positive understanding of their office. As 'Concerning the Ordinal' states, "The deacon's office derives its dignity from the Lord Jesus, the unique servant of God" (*APBA* page 780). The bishop exhorts the deacon "to be an ambassador of Christ", a skilled 'go-between' the church and the wider world.

As ambassadors, deacons are called and trusted to exercise the authority of the one who commissioned them, Christ. Only when this authority is accepted does the call to humility come into view: otherwise it fosters a 'doormat mentality', and can be oppressive. The deacon is charged in the first place with "serving *God*" rather than others or the Church, as in *AAPB*, doing so as they "serve others in Jesus' name".

Priests: 'pastors and teachers'

1. Priests and presbyters

The service's title (*APBA* page 792) has 'also called presbyters' after 'priests'. Members of the Liturgical Commission would have preferred 'presbyters' to be used in the service, but realised that this could have been misunderstood. There are several reasons for this addition:

- As 'Liturgical Principles' 4 notes, the use of 'presbyter' makes it clear that the rite is equivalent to ordinations elsewhere in the Anglican Communion, and "current Roman Catholic and Orthodox usage".
- The growing ecumenical use of 'presbyter' reflects biblical terminology, and encourages a corporate rather than individualistic understanding of this order, not least in the 'democratic' culture of western societies.

- 'Priests' are still understood by many in a false sacerdotal way, that is, as 'turnstiles' rather than 'windows' to God. 'Presbyter' helps avoid this distortion (see pages 239–240 of this book on *in persona / loco Christi*).
- 'Presbyter' enables a clearer distinction to be made between the ministry of priests and the ministry of all the baptised, the "royal priesthood" (1 Peter 2.9). It makes no sense to speak of "the presbyterate of all believers".

2. *Baptised into ministry*

In their baptism, disciples of Christ are called and commissioned to ministry that is exercised corporately. All the baptised belong to the "royal priesthood", described by Luther as "the priesthood of all believers". However, this (non-scriptural) term is often misunderstood to mean "the priesthood of each believer". This owes more to Western individualism than the New Testament image of God's people as "the body of Christ", interdependent on one another (1 Corinthians 12.14–27).

Each Christian is involved in ministry, but only those "called and sent" to have responsibility for the Gospel are properly called "ministers".[18] So in Anglican formularies the term 'minister' means someone "lawfully called and sent" to do or say the task or words specified. This is typically an ordained Christian, though not necessarily, provided that s/he is authorised for the ministry concerned: lay readers, communion assistants and others licensed by the bishop. The Anglican (and classical Christian) tradition does not provide for just anyone to read the scriptures or lead the prayers in church, for example. Article XXIII, 'Of ministering in the congregation', (*APBA* page 830) puts this position carefully:[19] it excludes the modern "every Christian is a minister" idea, while stopping short of identifying 'minister' with 'ordained'.

3. *Priests and the unique ministry of Christ*

The ministry of priests is often seen as continuing the work of Jesus Christ as 'priest'. But Jesus was not descended from Aaron, so was disqualified from

---

18 See John Collins, *Are All Christians Ministers?* (Melbourne: EJ Dwyer / HarperCollins; Collegeville MN: Liturgical Press, 1992), whose conclusion to his title is 'No'. The key biblical evidence is Ephesians 4.11–13, in which "the work of ministry", followed by a comma, then "to equip the saints" is traditionally understood as distinct tasks of office-bearers. 'Democratic' contemporary readings omit the comma: even then, the plural points to a corporate understanding of this ministry.

19 It is not lawful for any man to take upon him the office of publick preaching, or ministering the Sacraments in the Congregation, before he be lawfully called, and sent to execute the same. And those we ought to judge lawfully called and sent, which be chosen and called to this work by men who have publick authority given unto them in the Congregation, to call and send Ministers into the Lord's vineyard.

being a priest. Rather, as the letter to the Hebrews delights to point out, his ministry transcends that of ancient Israel's: it is universal, akin to that of Melchizedek, High Priest and King of pre-Davidic Jerusalem, whose origin and end is unknown, and whom Abraham honoured (Hebrews 7). The parallel with Aaron is that Christ is our perfect High Priest, whose unique atoning work is the key to God's saving work (Hebrews 9-10 – see pages 230-233 of this book).

Both 'protestant' objections to using the word 'priest' of ministers, and 'catholic' ideas of Christian priests following in Christ's steps, make this mistake. Over against both misunderstandings, Cranmer retained the term 'priest' in the 1550 Ordinal. It would seem that he did so because the primary ministry of priests in Israel was to 'give Torah', to make pastoral application of the scriptures for God's people in the present. This is why Ephesians 4.11 is prominent in Anglican Ordinals, including *APBA*: as the bishop says to the candidates in the Exhortation (page 793): "you are to live and work as a priest, a pastor and teacher".

The ordination service for priests in *APBA* thus recognizes that the description 'presbyter' is appropriate, and takes up more fully than the 1662 Ordinal that ministry is grounded in baptism. It continues its focus on the priest being "a pastor and teacher", setting aside false sacerdotal concepts. Such priests are responsible and accountable to God for the ministry of the means of grace: the scriptures, gospel sacraments, and prayer, set forward by "their life and teaching" as an integrated whole.

Bishops: chief minister and pastor

Drafting the Ordinal for Bishops saw practical more than theological issues arise: allowing for women candidates has been noted already. Further, though the Anglican tradition has sustained bishops and priests as distinct orders, the renewed recognition of this in the Roman Catholic Church since Vatican II has refreshed Anglican understandings.

Nevertheless, several elements distinctive to the ordination of a bishop meant that the service structure was adjusted to include the taking of oaths, and the complex way in which prayers and exhortation are mixed in the 1662 Ordinal. The Declarations required to be made are brought into the Presentation, while the Examination questions and post-ordination rites are fuller, as is appropriate for this office, the focus of unity and mission of a diocese.

Commentary

Sections common to all services

Sections #1-11 (#1-13 for bishops) and #20 (#23-24 for bishops) are identical for all orders, beyond changes of wording for the respective candidates.

Gathering in God's Name

This heading immediately indicates that the service structure follows that of *APBA* Sunday services.

#1-6 are as in HC2, with the bishop presiding. The rubrics say nothing about the entry of the candidates, presenters, bishop and others: this is left to local discretion.

#7 The collect for deacons and priests is based on the 1662 Ordinal: to the glory of God's name and the benefit of God's Church, we pray that deacons may "faithfully serve" (*diakonein*) and that priests may "faithfully minister" (*diakonein*)! The bishops' collect has the same objects, but emphasises the pastoral nature of the office: it speaks of "gifts" from Christ rather than "orders of ministry" from the Spirit. Typical of Anglican approaches, shaped especially by the Elizabethan theologian Richard Hooker, neither collect seeks to define what 'orders' or 'gifts' are given to the Church.

The Ministry of the Word

#8 The readings are presumed to be those of the day, but others suitable are listed on *APBA* page 809. Some bishops allow candidates to propose a reading.

#9-11 are as in HC2. The Nicene Creed is always used, even if the ordination does not take place on a Sunday or Festival (see Note 1 on *APBA* page 808).

The Presentation

#12 At least one presenter for each Order is a layperson. This recognises that the ordinand comes from the people of God, and is called to minister with them.

For deacons and priests:

In 1662, the candidate(s) are presented to the bishop "sitting in his chair near to the holy Table". Note 2 on *APBA* page 808 states that the bishop's chair "should be placed so that the laying on of hands can be plainly seen".

Note 3 on *APBA* page 808 lists appropriate presenters, and allows that the candidates "may be presented individually or as a group". Individual presentation is desirable, but becomes self-defeating when there are many candidates. This Note also provides that a priest candidate's ministry as a deacon may be recognised.

The bishop is addressed as "N, bishop in the Church of God", rather than "Reverend Father in God" (1662).

The archdeacon is the appropriate office-bearer to affirm the readiness of candidates for ordination, as in the 1662 Ordinal. The criteria named are twofold: "learning and godly living". This blending of academic and spiritual maturity runs across Anglican formularies: so in Prayers for Sundays 4 on *APBA* page 187, based on *BCP*'s 'Prayer for the Church Militant', we pray for clergy that "by their *life* and *teaching* your glory may be revealed" (emphasis added).

The presenters' response opens by noting that "the people of God" have been consulted about the candidates' suitability, and only then "those concerned with their preparation". This contrasts with the 1662 Ordinal, where only the archdeacon is involved in assessment of a candidate's readiness for ministry.

When the candidates have been presented, the bishop asks the congregation if they know any "adequate reason why we should not proceed". Note 6 on *APBA* page 808 notes that if this happens, "the bishop shall postpone the candidate's ordination", presumably until the allegation has been considered. NB: an unsubstantiated accusation may leave the objector open to a libel suit.

For bishops:

Note 4 on *APBA* page 808 stipulates that at least three bishops will lay on hands, and encourages the participation of representative priests, deacons, and laypersons. The rubric at #12 likewise encourages this for the presentation, which is followed by the reading of the Authority for Consecration (#12).

The form of Declaration and Assent (#13) to the relevant Constitution(s) and Canons, and the Oath of Canonical Obedience (#14) are then taken and signed in the presence of the congregation. These public acts point to the bishop's accountability to those in their charge for their ministry.

The public acceptance of the bishop(s)-elect by the people (#15) corresponds to the ancient practice of the people having the final say in the election of a bishop.

The Prayers

#13 Deacons and priests: the prayers being offered at this point is the Liturgical Commission's preference, since it keeps the Exhortation, Examination, Acceptance, hymn invoking the Spirit, and the Laying on of Hands together as one continuous act. But there is nothing 'wrong' with the Prayers coming after #16, between the Acceptance and hymn invoking the Spirit.

#17 Bishops: a prayer that associates the calling of bishops with the calling of the twelve apostles, Matthias, Paul and Barnabas is offered before the Litany for Ministry. But, as in the 1662 Ordinal, the prayer stops short of identifying bishops as successors of the apostles.[20]

The Greeting of Peace

This is preceded by the presentation of the newly ordained, who "*may* be welcomed with applause" ... but I have never known a service where applause has not happened.

The Holy Communion

For deacons and priests, the rubrics at #21 explain themselves.

For bishops, the rubric at #24 does not indicate how the newly ordained might take further part, but a special prayer of blessing for them is provided on *APBA* page 807.

The Exhortations

Each Exhortation was written with great care and repays careful study, not least by those considering ordained ministry, and candidates for all Orders. Each explicates the context of Christian ministry within the people of God, activated through the Spirit, and the distinctive nature and responsibilities of each 'order'. Candidates are encouraged to become in their own persons the ministers Christ calls them to **be**. In this way, balance is kept between the functional and ontological aspects of ordained ministries.

Particular attention was paid to ensure that the Exhortations read well, especially for deacons and priests. Spacing delineates sections, there is variation in the mood of verbs and sentence length, and the lineation is designed to assist reading.[21]

Deacons (#14 on APBA page 785)

The Exhortation opens with the unique ministry of Christ as the "servant of God", alluding to the "suffering servant" of Isaiah. Christ's saving work undergirds the call of every disciple to "serve God in the world", and sets the deacons' calling in the context of the people of God as a whole, reflecting a "baptismal ecclesiology".

---

20 Bearing witness to the resurrection was the criterion for choosing a replacement for Judas Iscariot in the Twelve (Acts 1.22). This has been seen as setting bishops among the apostles: but Matthias and Joseph had accompanied the twelve "during all the time that the Lord Jesus went in and out among" them. The Twelve are thus not so much a sign of the ordained ministry as of the Church as a whole, the new 'twelve tribes' (Revelation 21.9–21), who bear witness to the resurrection of Christ. Appreciating this point was a crucial step in debates about opening all orders of ministry to all the baptised, women and men alike.

21 The exception is the paragraph at the top of *APBA* page 794. After "Christ", General Synod replaced the draft words with these from *AAPB*, based on the 1662 Ordinal: "if it should come about that the Church, or any of its members, is hurt or injured as a result of your negligence, you know the greatness of the fault and the judgement that will follow." My problem is that I do not know what "judgement will follow".

The bishop then addresses the deacon candidate(s) directly. Their central ministry is to be an "ambassador of Christ", whose service to God is expressed in "serving others in Jesus' name". The charge to "Proclaim the good news" includes preaching implicitly, but embraces a wider range of ministries, whose outcome is seen in lives changed towards prophetic lifestyles (Micah 6.8). It is a proactive ministry of "transforming love," reaching out to all in need by "ministering among" them.

The third section turns to the deacon's responsibilities within the Church, again a ministry "with" others. Locally, this includes preaching, assisting with the sacraments, and prayer with an outward-looking focus, but it is not restricted to this: it includes participation in the "life and councils of the Church" (capital C).

The Exhortation ends with the call to "model your life according to the word of God". That "word" includes the scriptures, reflection upon which is to be a major concern "with God's people", the outcome being Christlike lifestyles. All of which involves faithful prayer, so that the race may be run well.

Priests (#14 on *APBA* pages 793–794)

The Exhortation opens with Christ's call to all believers, explicated in baptism, to live as a "royal priesthood". It avoids description of Christ as a priest, however, since this confuses a number of issues. And it sets the ministry of priests as one within rather than above the people of God.

The deacon(s) are then addressed directly by the bishop. They are responding to the call of "God and of the Church": this avoids the idea of a sense of call that is individual rather than arising from the discernment of others. The call is "to live" (being) "and work" (doing) as a "priest, a pastor and teacher" (Ephesians 4.11).

The bishop goes on to "exhort" the priest(s)-elect warmly in terms drawn from the prophets: as "the Lord's messenger" they are to proclaim, announce, warn and correct. This picks up the image in the 1550 and 1662 Ordinals of priests as "Messengers, Watchmen and Stewards of the Lord", alluding to the priest-prophets Isaiah, Ezekiel and Jeremiah.

The priests' tasks are then recounted. (This paragraph was assisted by comments from members of the Doctrine Commission.). Rather than being dot points, they are set within the overarching call "to encourage and build up the body of Christ". Again, these ministries are exercised "together with" others.

Strong words begin the next sentences. The first two explicate the twin identification of **being** a priest: "**be** a pastor ... **be** a teacher", according to the pattern of Christ. The next one embodies the style of a priest's ministry: "lead ... as a servant of Christ", "love and serve the people with whom you work": they are, after all, "Christ's spouse and body", whom "you *must* serve" and give account for.

A daunting range of disciplines is prescribed to enable this ministry to be fulfilled: humility, prayer, scripture reflection "with God's people", depending thankfully "on the Holy Spirit and the grace of God". While every Christian is called to *follow* the example of Christ, priests are to *model* it: failure to do so is quickly discerned by others, not least the general media. This implicit 'double standard' of lifestyle is expressed in the charge to "put away all that does not make for holiness of life".[22]

Bishops (#18 on APBA page 802)

The Exhortation to priests about to be ordained as bishops is shorter and more direct than those for deacons and priests, since the Examination is much fuller. It opens with the bishop's calling, to keep the Church 'on track', ensuring that it continues to witness to the resurrection of Christ, and that the gospel is kept pure. This is the calling of a "chief minister and pastor", whose work includes yet transcends the life of congregations.

The bishop is involved in a good deal of 'conserving' ministry, as shown in words like guard, faithful, duly, lead, guide, care, watch over, protect, govern. Yet it is also outward-looking, "to proclaim Jesus Christ as Lord" and "promote [the Church's] mission in the world". And it cannot be exercised apart from the people of God: the bishop "*must*, therefore, know and be known by them".

One phrase which I have heard several bishops affirm as highly significant is their charge to see "Christ's discipline applied justly, and with mercy". So much of their time has to do with facing the consequences of sinful behaviour, a life-sapping business. A bishop needs friends, encouragement, support and ongoing prayer.

The Examination

'Hurdle' questions

For each 'order' there are two 'hurdle' questions, which must receive positive responses before other questions about how candidates intend to exercise their ministry are put.

The first concerns each candidate's acceptance of God's call. The question shortens with each 'order', since the earlier Examinations are presumed. So deacons-elect are asked whether they be "moved by the Holy Spirit" – a separate question in the 1662 Ordinal – while they and priests-elect are asked if they are called "to this order and ministry according to the will of our Lord Jesus Christ and the order of this

---

22 As noted earlier, the 1662 Ordinal has "forsake and set aside (as much as you may) all worldly cares and studies", traditionally interpreted as excluding other than full-time stipendiary ministry.

Anglican Church of Australia". The double condition is significant: acceptance of the Lord's will and the particularity of this Church stand together. The answer is fuller than in the 1662 Ordinal, and is cast as a positive affirmation: "I (do) believe I am called to this ministry".

Bishops-elect are asked the shortest question: "Do you trust that you are called by God to the office and work of a bishop in the Church of God?". "Office and work" correspond to "order and ministry", but the widening of scope to "the Church of God" affirms Anglican belief that its ordained ministry belongs to the "one, holy, catholic and apostolic Church".

The second 'hurdle' question concerns acceptance of the canonical Scriptures as the basic resource for Christian ministry and key criteria for Christian faith and life. In contrast to the 'call' question, these lengthen with each Order, corresponding to the seriousness of the responsibilities entailed in them. Deacons are asked to accept the scriptures as conveying diverse divine revelation; priests and bishops whether they are "convinced that the holy Scriptures contain all doctrine necessary for eternal salvation", and will teach nothing that is not based in them.

Intention (Will you?) questions

The next questions begin, "Will you?" As in the wedding service, to say 'I will', is more than 'I shall': it puts into words that the person's will is directed to enact what is asked.

There is some repetition in the questions across the three Orders, but this is minimized: so the question about shaping their personal and household lifestyles is only asked of deacons. The main differences concern what is distinctive about each Order, reflecting growing levels of responsibility, and the exercise of discipline.

Deacons: read the Scriptures in church

(#15)   assist in the ministry of Word and sacraments

          be diligent in prayer and studies

          shape a Christian household life

          develop God's gifts, so as to serve all

          promote peace, love and others' ministries

          live out Christ's kingdom

          accept lawful authority.

Priests, in addition:

(#15)   minister Christ's doctrine, sacraments and discipline

          oppose false teaching

          build up the body of Christ

Bishops, in addition:

(#19)   proclaim the gospel and make disciples
administer discipline with mercy
ordain others and encourage them
show compassion and defend the helpless.

The responses to each question are identical for deacons and priests: "I will, by God's grace". For bishops, however, different aspects of the grace of God, and the significance of the office, are reflected in distinctive answers to each question.

Acceptance by the people

The Examination has taken place in public, before the people. For deacons and priests, the people's acceptance follows (#16); for bishops, however, their ministry is known, so the acceptance concludes the Presentation (#15).

Invoking the Spirit

"A hymn invoking the Holy Spirit is sung" at this point. This brief rubric speaks of a deeply significant part of the rite: it is customary for candidates to kneel or prostrate themselves while it is sung. For priests and bishops, those who will join in the laying on of hands gather around the bishop.

Veni Creator is printed in the 1662 Ordinal: other suitable hymns are listed at Note 8 on *APBA* page 808.

The Laying on of Hands

Practical matters

This, the climax of the service, needs detailed planning so that it is unhurried, and memorable for the candidates. When several candidates are involved, care with choreography and a rehearsal are important.

Reading the whole prayer for each ordinand is unwieldy: it is suggested that the first part is read by the bishop to the ordinands as a group, with each coming forward for the laying on of hands. For deacons, the bishop could move to each one as they kneel in their places.

When all have had hands laid on them, the prayer is completed with a significant **Amen** from the whole assembly.

NB: The unity of the ordination prayer needs to be respected. The 'Amen' is a corporate response offered by all at its conclusion, rather than coming after the laying on of hands. Similarly, vesting each candidate during the prayer breaks it apart.

The ordination prayer

As 'Liturgical principles' 3 on *APBA* page 781 explains, the ordination prayer is in *berakah* form (see pages 123-124 in this book). God is blessed for the ministry and gifts of Christ, with prayer for the Spirit to grace and empower each candidate for the ministry to which they are called.

Each prayer opens with the distinctive Christological basis of each Order: Christ, the Deacon of God offering divine riches as a "ransom for many" (deacons); Christ the Apostle, High Priest and Shepherd (priests and bishops). Each prayer then celebrates the gifts of the exalted Christ, the citation of Ephesians 4.11 increasing from deacons to priests to bishops. The words of thanksgiving are identical for deacons and priests: for bishops, "whom we consecrate in your Name" was added by General Synod.

The hand-laying words are the same for each Order except for their naming: this displays the unity of ordained ministries. The prayer concludes by asking for God's graced empowerment of those ordained, and that her or his ministries may be effective.

Porrectio instrumentorum ('handing over of the instruments')

The newly-ordained are customarily vested according to their Order.[23] Each is then equipped with and authorised to use the 'tools of ministry': for deacons a *copy* of the New Testament, a *copy* of the Bible for priests and bishops.

A change made at General Synod was especially significant for deacons: at #19, newly ordained priests and deacons "take" rather than "receive" authority from the bishop as the relevant copy of the scriptures is presented. Note 7 on *APBA* page 808 offers various ways by which this may be done.

The same, large volume being presented to each candidate emphasises that the Bible is not in the first place a personal but a Church book, from which the community's leaders are to teach and pray.[24] A personal copy for each of the newly ordained can be given afterwards, along with their certificate of ordination.

In the bishops' service, following Cranmer's 1550 Ordinal but omitted in 1662, the provision for the new bishop to receive their pastoral staff and other symbols is restored. A pectoral cross and ring are traditional, but see the second part of Note 7 on *APBA* page 808.

NB: Both vesting and presentations follow **after** the ordination: they do not complete it, but identify and equip the newly-ordained for their ministries.

---

23 Deacons who wear a preaching scarf will not be vested differently when ordained as priest, however.

24 Other symbols are not mentioned in the deacons' and priests' services, but it is not uncommon for items such as a towel, cup and paten or Prayer Book to be presented.

Creative planning will see each rite of ordination conducted with accessible reverence, allow all present to participate actively, see the actions that take place, and be inspired to fulfil their own vocation and support the newly ordained. It should be an occasion of that encouraged remembrance ('*anamnesis*') of their calling for those ordained, as the years unfold with their inevitable challenges and joys.

Re-arranging the Ordinal

Some bishops, noting suggestions in the 'Berkeley Statement' from *IALC*, and having been given permission at the meeting of the Australian House of Bishops to do so, have re-arranged the Ordinal for deacons and priests, without changing the text.

The intention is to 'spread' the several 'core' rites of ordination across the Eucharist in which each is set, e.g. by bringing the Presentation to the beginning, associated with a renewal of the baptismal covenant of all present.

Here is an example.

Gathering in God's Name
    Opening procession, hymn and greeting
    Reaffirming the Ministry of all Baptized Persons:
        The bishop invites all present to reaffirm their Christian ministry.
    The Prayer of Preparation (Collect for Purity)
The Presentation (APBA #12)
    The Collect (*APBA #7*)
    The first 'hurdle' questions about calling, and the Scriptures.
The Ministry of the Word
    Collect of the Day
    Readings
    Sermon
    Nicene Creed
The Prayers (or later)
The Exhortation
The Examination ('Will you' questions)
    Acceptance by the people
    Hymn invoking the Spirit
The Laying on of Hands
    Vesting and porrectio
    Welcome of the newly ordained
The Greeting of Peace ...

Further reading

ARCIC, 'Ministry' in *The Final Report* (London: ACC / CTS, 1981), available at www.prounione.urbe.it/dia-int/arcic/doc/e_arcic_ministry.html

Barnett, James, *The Diaconate: Full and Equal Order*. Revised Edition (Valley Forge: Trinity Press International, 1995)

Collins, John, *Are all Christians Ministers?* (Melbourne: HarperCollins, 1992)

Collins, John, *Deacons and the Church: Making Connections Between Old and New* (Leicester: Gracewing; Harrisburg: Morehouse, 2003)

Faith & Order Commission of the World Council of Churches, *Baptism, Eucharist and Ministry* (Geneva, 1982)

The Church of England General Synod, *For such a time as this. A renewed diaconate in the Church of England* (London: Church House Publishing, 2001)

Gibson, Paul (Ed.), *To Equip the Saints. The Berkeley Statement on Ordination* from the Sixth *IALC* Consultation, 2001 (Bramcote, Notts: Grove, 2002)

Chapter Twenty-Five

Supplementary Material

Some Supplementary Materials may appear to be of little relevance to the liturgical life of congregations, but all are significant for the wider life of the Church. Supplementary Materials offering liturgical resources have been considered in earlier chapters of this book:

Holy Communion Outline Order, *APBA* pages 812-3 – pages 303-4 in this book
A Catechism, *APBA* pages 814-818 – pages 185-189 in this book
Notes, *APBA* pages 819-823 – discussed at the relevant points in this book

The Articles of Religion

A full discussion of the 39 Articles is clearly beyond this book. Given their significance in the life of the Church of England and then the Anglican Communion, many commentaries have been written: see Further Reading.

In Australia, from 1891 the two Doctrine papers of the Licentiate in Theology (Th.L.), which almost all ordinands took until 1962, were based on Articles 1-19 and 20-39 respectively. Direct study of the Articles has faded since undergraduate degrees in Theology became available from the mid-1970s. But they remain constitutionally important for Australian Anglicans, hence their inclusion in *APBA*.

Historical background

When the Church of England was separated from Rome in 1534 under Henry VIII, Articles were needed to define what was required of clergy and other office-holders, and several sets were issued in his reign. When Edward VI ascended the throne in 1549, and the Church of England began to be reformed, 42 Articles were drafted by Archbishop Thomas Cranmer. It is unclear as to whether they were approved by Convocation (i.e. the clergy), but Edward VI died before they were adopted by Parliament.

The 39 Articles, a revision of the 42, were approved by Convocation in 1563 and issued in 1571 by Elizabeth I after the Pope had excommunicated her.[1] They were made with a view to the Church of England being comprehensive. That said, they

---

[1] The omissions relate to soul / body issues: Christ's descent into hell (Article 3) and the Christian hope (Articles 40-42: 42 condemned universal salvation). Oliver O'Donovan, *On the Thirty nine Articles: a conversation with Tudor Christianity* (Exeter: Paternoster, 1986) sets the 42 and 39 out side by side.

are "demonstrably Protestant as opposed to Roman Catholic and Anabaptist, and within the Protestant spectrum Reformed as opposed to Lutheran".[2]

After the Restoration in 1661, the (established) Church of England took tighter control of the nation's civic life. A key aspect was the Test Act (1672), which made adherence to the Articles a requirement for civil office, including Members of Parliament. This affected Roman Catholics, Dissident and Non-Conformist Protestants, a restriction lifted only in 1828 as part of the Reform Acts. These, however, would lead to Keble's 'National Apostasy' sermon of July 1833, which launched the Oxford (Tractarian) Movement. John Henry Newman, in the final *Tracts for the Times*, number 90, sought to interpret the Articles in a 'Catholic' manner, noting for example that XXXI condemns "the sacrifice of masses" rather that "the sacrifice of the mass". The Articles' moderate stance on many issues allowed Newman to 'read' them in this way, but this was widely repudiated: in 1845 he was received into the Roman Catholic Church.

Out of this debate arose the 'Subscription' controversy, in which the requirement for clergy to 'subscribe' to Articles at ordination and licensing was questioned. In 1865, the formula of Assent was changed to have clergy affirm that the doctrine in the Articles is "agreeable to the Word of God".

The Constitution of the Anglican Church of Australia refers to the Articles in #4, the 'Ruling Principles': that

> The *Book of Common Prayer*, together with the Thirty-nine Articles, be regarded as the authorised standard of worship and doctrine in this Church, and no alteration in or permitted variations from the services or Articles therein contained shall contravene any principle of doctrine or worship laid down in such standard.

The *Oaths Affirmations Declarations & Assents Canon* (1992) provides that clergy at their ordination(s) and on each occasion of licensing swear or affirm that "I, NN, do solemnly and sincerely declare my assent to be bound by the Constitution of the Anglican Church of Australia", which includes the Articles among its texts. But how they are interpreted remains a lively issue, as occasional debates at General Synod show.[3]

---

[2] Archbishops' Commission on Christian Doctrine, *Subscription and Assent to the 39 Articles* (London: SPCK, 1968) 9.

[3] It is instructive to compare the commentaries by Moore College Principals Nathaniel Jones (1904) and D. Broughton Knox (1964 and 1976) and that of the Canadian W. Griffith Thomas (1930, who was nominated to be Archbishop of Sydney).

The theological perspective of the Articles

It is not uncommon to hear the Articles being called old-fashioned, irrelevant or even fundamentalist.[4] Those who make such comments are unlikely to have studied them, however. As a student at the University of Sydney in 1966, I well remember an address by (then) Vice-Principal of Moore College, Donald Robinson, to the Anglican Society. He noted that the Articles

- start in the right place, with the Christian doctrine of God;
- have as their primary focus the spiritual well-being of believers, rather than doctrine in and of itself, as shown in the frequent use of 'we' and 'us';
- are minimalist about matters then in dispute, saying with nuanced precision only what must be said.

In the years since, teaching Theology to Anglican ordinands, I have come to value these insights. In 1647, the Church of England under the Commonwealth published the Westminster Confession, a core text for the Presbyterian tradition. It continues to warrant study, but a comparison with the Articles is striking, especially with Robinson's points in mind. The Confession begins with the doctrine of revelation rather than God, takes a polemical approach on disputed issues, and attempts to outline the whole of Christian doctrine: it is more than three times as long as the Articles.

Some claim the Articles to be an Anglican 'confession of faith' along the lines of Westminster. Articles I–VIII could perhaps be seen like this, but they conclude by affirming the three Creeds as sufficient, "for they may be proved by most certain warrants of Holy Scripture". The *nature* of the Thirty-Nine thus differs from that of the Westminster Confession, as seen in their naming as 'Articles'. They are not a statement of faith required of Christian people generally, but were formulated for the clergy, as a framework for their ministry in the 'national Church'.

A useful comparison is with lawyers: having completed their Law studies, they take their 'Articles', working as 'apprentices' in the profession they are entering. Likewise, those called to the ministry of Word and sacrament take up the Articles of their profession at ordination, and at each subsequent appointment. They are best seen as the framework for Anglican clergy to teach and live the Gospel as their 'profession'. This responsibility is exercised within rather than over the people of God, since "Baptism doth represent unto us our profession; which is, to follow the example of our Saviour Christ, and to be made like unto him" (*BCP*).

---

4   A cheap gibe is that the 39 Articles are for clergy what the "40 lashes save one" were to Paul (2 Corinthians 11.24).

The Articles in outline

NB: Throughout the Articles, 'Man' means humanity, 'man' and 'men' include both male and female human beings, and 'very' means 'true / truly' (*veritas* in Latin).

The Articles fall into groups of lessening significance. The titles below are my own: their order exemplifies the ethos of the Anglican tradition as "catholic and reformed". Brief comments are made about a few Articles of particular significance below: for full discussion, consult the commentaries.

I–VIII: The Catholic faith

These affirm historic statements on God the Holy Trinity, the authority and canon of the scriptures, and the three Creeds.

Article II, "Of the Word or Son of God, which was made very Man", takes up the Chalcedonian Definition of the 'two natures' of Christ. The language of 'substance' (*homoousios, substantia*) is used of Christ's relation with **both** the Father (as touching his divinity) **and** with Mary (as touching his humanity). This shows the Church of England's positive understanding of the place of the Virgin Mary in the economy of salvation. But "to reconcile his Father to us", a conventional expression in terms of sixteenth century doctrine, is problematic in the light of biblical studies, which show that the initiative in reconciliation lies with God (notably 2 Corinthians 5.18–20).[5]

Article III, "Of the going down of Christ into Hell", was much longer in the 42 Articles, which sought to articulate the soul / body relationships involved. This was omitted in the 1563 revision as speculative, and this Article cut down to the basics.

Article IV, "Of the Resurrection of Christ", states that Christ "took again his body, with ... all things appertaining to the perfection of Man's nature". This nicely avoids the (not uncommon) idea that Christ was raised back to his earthly body, akin to the re-vivification of Lazarus and the Nain widow's son.

Article VI, "Of the Sufficiency of the Holy Scriptures for salvation", is often read as affirming the final authority of Scripture in all things: its 'necessity'. As the opening words state, however, the focus is on what is "necessary *to salvation*", and that nothing that cannot be derived from Scripture can be required for this

---

[5] The Evangelical tradition rightly sets Christ's atoning work as central to the Gospel, but care is needed in how this is expressed. Emphasizing Jesus as taking the initiative to reconcile God to us runs the risk of making the Father appear unwilling to do so. Nathaniel Jones, *The Teaching of the Articles* (Sydney: Edgar Bragg, 1904) shows awareness of this, while defending Article II. The classic Evangelical discussion is Leon Morris, *The Apostolic Preaching of the Cross* (Leicester: IVP, 1955, with several reprints).

– a complex but significant triple negative. Articles XX and XXI fill out the Scriptures' authority in relation to that of the Church, likewise taking a 'double negative' approach.

The recognition of the (Western) Apocryphal books as having value for Christian living, but not being canonical, takes a similarly moderate stance. A comparison with the Westminster Confession, Chapter I, 9ff shows the very different approaches of the two documents.

IX–XVIII: *Theological issues at stake in the Reformation*

A succession of delicately phrased and moderate statements clarify points in dispute with Roman Catholic teaching as formulated at the Council of Trent (1545–63).

Article IX, "Of Original or Birth Sin", stays close to the Augustinian rejection of Pelagian ideas. But it is careful to avoid holding that infants, born into a corrupt human race whose nature "*deserveth* God's wrath", *receive* divine condemnation.

Article X, "Of the Justification of Man", touches the central issue of the Reformation. Having stated that we are *accounted* (Reformed) rather than *made* (Trent) righteous, one might expect it to insist that justification is true, right or correct (the way of controversy). But it merely goes on to affirm that it does one good …

Article XIV, "Of Works of Supererogation", takes up the delight of 'do-gooding' in British culture – very carefully. Such deeds are not said to be wrong, but lead inevitably to "arrogancy and impiety". One of the few scriptural quotations in the Articles, Luke 17.10 is cited in favour of keeping busy …

Article XVII "Of Predestination and Election" is the longest Article. (Article VI is filled out by its two lists.) Why? As fresh realisation that it is **God** who takes the initiative in salvation sunk in – that grace is primary – how this engages the human will became *the* existential issue for ordinary folk. The Article is thus a sermon on assurance and the danger of speculation more than a doctrinal statement. In stark contrast is the Westminster Confession Chapter III, 'Of God's Eternal Decree', whose awe-full logic I find terrifying.

Article XVIII "Of Obtaining eternal Salvation only by the Name of Christ" rejects the notion that we can be saved by living sincerely, seemingly taking a strict 'exclusivist' line. But the last phrase is vital: it is only by the Name (capital, the divine identity of the exalted Lord) of Jesus whereby we "*must* be saved". This use of the 'divine passive' again points to God's initiative, and that all salvation is in and through Christ.

XIX–XXXI: *Reforming the Church*

These Articles set out the implications of the theological issues of the Reformation for the public life of the Church: its nature, authority, ministries and sacraments.

Article XIX, "Of the Church" identifies the *visible* Church by the 'marks' of Word and gospel sacraments – but discipline is not included, as in Reformed confessions, or the papacy, as in Rome. This Church is seen with the eyes of sight. The 'mystical / invisible' Church, confessed in the Creeds, whose 'notes' are unity, holiness, catholicity and apostolicity, is seen with the eyes of faith.

The paragraph about the ancient Sees of Jerusalem, Alexandria, Antioch and Rome not only recognises that they have erred, but also excludes the view that the 'visible Church' only exists at congregational level.

Article XXV, "Of the Sacraments", is careful to respect both their 'subjective' and 'objective' aspects: see pages 170 and 255–257 of this book. They are not only badges, signs and sure witnesses, but are also effectual signs of grace that work invisibly in us, quicken (i.e. bring to life), strengthen and confirm faith in Christ.

The paragraph about the five "commonly called" sacraments is again moderate. They lack "the same nature" as Baptism and Eucharist, because they are not "Sacraments of the Gospel" (their 'inward' nature, as the Catechism states), and also lack "any visible sign" (their 'outward' character). But this does not exclude them from having a sacramental dimension. They are helpfully understood as graced signs of the *outworking* of the Gospel, in confirming baptism, showing the union between Christ and the Church in marriage, divine reconciliation in personal confession, the call to live and proclaim the Gospel in ordination, and the healing power of Christ in unction.

Article XXVI, "Of the Unworthiness of the Ministers, which hinders not the effect of the Sacrament", may have begun life in times of persecution to assure ordinary folk of God's love and grace when clergy failings were evident. But it gained new relevance in debates about the ordination of women: even if her gender made a female deacon, priest or bishop 'unworthy' (a false idea in any case), her ministry was valid and effective because she acts in Christ's name.

Articles XXVII, "Of Baptism" and XXVIII, "Of the Lord's Supper", sustain the classical 'objective / subjective' balance in the 'means of grace'. The concern is to exclude what gets in the way of healthy spiritual life, rather than make doctrinal points. Even transubstantiation, the most disputed idea in Reformation debates, is not said directly to be wrong, but is unsupported by evidence, contradicts what a sacrament is, and leads to superstition.

Article XXIX, "Of the Wicked, which eat not the Body of Christ in the use of the Lord's Supper", clarifies rather than contests Roman Catholic teaching that grace is communicated *ex opere operato* unless an *obex* (barrier) is put up by the recipient. It puts this in behavioural and relational rather than causal terms: we cannot be saved by good works, but can be condemned by wicked ones.

XXXII–XXXIX: Practical matters

A variety of issues had to be faced as the Church of England shaped its life apart from Rome (Article XXXVII). Positions had to be taken on married clergy, excommunication, Church traditions (XXXII–XXXIV) and the authenticity of English bishops (XXXVI). With many clergy uneducated, homilies were provided (XXXV). And 'Establishment' meant that matters related to social order called for decision: 'church and state' relations (XXXVII), private property (XXXVIII) and oaths XXXIX).

Further reading

Archbishops' Commission on Christian Doctrine, *Subscription and Assent to the Thirty-Nine Articles* (London: SPCK, 1968). This Report surveys the Articles' origins and history to 1968, and similar documents in other Christian traditions.

Bicknell, Edward John, *A Theological Introduction to the Thirty-nine Articles of the Church of England* (London: Longmans, Green 1925; reprinted 1955). A careful book, written with the needs of theological tutors in mind.

O'Donovan, Oliver, *On the Thirty nine Articles: a conversation with Tudor Christianity* (Exeter: Paternoster, 1986). A lively discussion, noting the lack of reference to creation in Articles 9 and 10.

Gibson, Edgar Charles Sumner, *The Thirty-nine Articles of the Church of England Explained*. Two volumes (London: Methuen, 1897). A thorough discussion based on the Latin text, citing patristic, Reformation and Roman Catholic sources.

de Satgé, John, Herklots, H.G.G., Lampe, G.W.H., and Packer J.I., *The Articles of the Church of England* (London: Mowbray, 1964). Essays written to illuminate the 1960s debate in England about subscription to the Articles.

Jones, Nathaniel, *The Teaching of the Articles* (Sydney: Edgar Bragg, 1904). Jones was Principal of Moore College, Sydney from 1897 to 1911. This small book, intended for parishioners, shows Jones' keen awareness of biblical scholarship.

Knox, David Broughton, *The Thirty-Nine Articles* (London: Hodder & Stoughton, 1964; AIO, 1976). This brief book sets out Knox's distinctive approach to divine revelation, the Church and means of grace.

Griffith Thomas, W., *The Principles of Theology: An Introduction to the Thirty-Nine Articles* (London: Church House, 1931; Eugene, Oregon, 2005). My copy was given to me by my mother, Emily Elizabeth Newth, who was presented with it by her home parish in Sydney following her marriage to the Revd Charles Henry Sherlock. It was presumably seen as suitable reading for a rector's wife.

The Athanasian Creed

No indication is given in *APBA* as to when this Creed (pages 835–837) is to be used. In *BCP* it is placed between Evening Prayer and the Litany, and described as "At Morning Prayer, *Quicunque Vult*" ("Whosoever will" in Latin, the opening words). It is specified to be used instead of the Apostles' Creed on Christmas Day, Easter, Ascension, Whitsun and Trinity, and on seven saint's days. That requirement soon fell into disuse, in part because of its length and complex language.

In the nineteenth century objections were raised to the clause "they that have done evil into everlasting fire".

More recently, its strongly 'western' expression of Trinitarian faith has raised issues around relationships with the Eastern and Oriental Orthodox traditions. Its inclusion in *APBA* was due to its presence in *BCP*, and the reference to it in Article VIII.

How, then, might this unwieldy Creed be used? The most obvious occasion is Trinity Sunday, though perhaps not in the main service, where it might be misunderstood. It has at least two things going for it, however.

First, its summary of "the Catholick Faith" is brilliant: "That we **worship** one God in Trinity, and Trinity in Unity". All that follows is but a footnote to this sublime truth. Further, the mutually referencing phrasing of One and Trinity could hardly be better done.

Secondly, the effect of saying it in church is overwhelming: the phrases roll over you, despite their complex and unfamiliar terms. By the end, one is overawed at the sheer magnificence of the Triune God, and the profound privilege of confessing the Catholick Faith.

The Index of Prayers

This invaluable aid, *APBA* pages 838–843, was prepared by the Editor of *APBA*, the Revd Gillian Varcoe. It covers not only the 'obvious' prayers such as those of the Day and Week, but prayers found in the daily and pastoral services. Well worth photocopying and sharing with parishioners licensed to lead intercessions.

Acknowledgements

This recognition of sources taken up in *APBA*, found on pages 844–850, was also prepared by the Editor. It was a time-consuming but necessary aspect of her work: failure to acknowledge sources is not only poor manners for a Christian body, but in some circumstances could lead to legal action. Her attention to detail, seen throughout *APBA*, is epitomized in these pages.

Two points should be noted:

- First, these Acknowledgements are not exhaustive. Liturgical texts by their very nature draw on the long heritage of Christian faith, and there is no need to acknowledge those that are in the Christian public domain, in particular *BCP* and much of *AAPB*.

- Secondly, as explained on pages 100-102 of this book, the copyright of *The Liturgical Psalter, 'inclusive language' version 1995*, was held by HarperCollins, as acknowledged on *APBA* page 847. This later reverted to HarperCollins Religious (Australia), who in 2001 released the copyright to the Trustees of the General Synod. The condition of 'one psalm only' being reproduced in a service thus no longer applies.

That said, it is courteous to acknowledge the work of David Frost, John Everton and Andrew Macintosh when psalms from *The Liturgical Psalter* are reproduced.

The translations of Psalms from elsewhere in *APBA* are the work of the Revd Dr Evan Burge: no copyright, beyond retaining integrity, applies to these. Again, acknowledgement of his work is courteous.

Back to the future: The Preface to *APBA*

This commentary on *APBA* concludes by going back to the Preface, pages vii–ix. It was penned by Canon Dr Lawrence Bartlett, who chaired the Liturgical Commission in the years leading up to the 1995 General Synod.

Lawrie was crucial in pressing on with the work *peaceably*, amid often tangled relationships and misunderstandings. All the while he fulfilled his ministry as a much-loved parish priest in the Diocese of Sydney and skilled musician in the wider Church and community. His patience in chairing Liturgical Commission meetings over several days, keeping us on track when details could lead discussion astray, and his calm responses to sometimes harsh and unfair criticism, evidenced his strong sense of depending on God's generous grace.

The Preface opens by tracing briefly the path from *AAPB* to *APBA*, drawing attention to the importance of making flexible services "easier to follow". A particular issue was the adoption of "inclusive language for human beings", with "a range of address for God which reflects the diversity and richness of biblical imagery". And in the pastoral services of *APBA* "there is a noticeable attempt to reflect the human role in life and liturgy".

The Preface's closing words still ring true, and I finish this book by citing them:

> The book contains the words for liturgy, but only the words. Liturgy is more than words. Words provide a framework to encourage worship, but the important thing is the spirit in which the words are used. No prayer book can determine that. It is our prayer that the use of this book will facilitate the worship of our Church, providing nourishment for experienced worshippers and a welcome for newcomers.

INDEX

A Service of Light	158	Augustine of Canterbury	81, 293
AAPB distinctives	12–14, 150, 310, 333, 337, 400	Augustine of Hippo	38, 46, 68, 126, 170–171, 212, 240, 329, 404
'abba	111		
absolution	137, 141, 300	auricular confession	326, 369–371
active participation	142–146, 191–192, 198	*Australian Academy of Liturgy*	17
		Australian Cons'n on Liturgy	17
Acts 8 and hand-laying	174	baptism	
administration of communion	255–256, 293	affusion (pouring)	169
Advent	69–71	and birth	176–177, 325, 332
Affirmation of Faith, The	71, 125, 143, 146	and faith	172
Agnus Dei (Lamb of God)	254, 367	and naming	177
Akehurst, Peter	67	believer's, of infants	165
alcoholic wine	252	of older child	199
All Souls	86, 93	intercessions in	201–202
Almighty / 'El Shaddai	30, 33, 61, 118, 271	location of	190
Amen	114–115	ministers of	178
'anamnesis – meaning of	220–221	New Testament on	167–168
Anderson, Greg	200	preparation / policy	182–185
'And also with you'	241–242	private (of an infant)	183
anointing	357–358, 368–369	submersion	168, 190
anthems during communion	297	water thanksgiving	202–203
Anzac Day	73–75	validity and efficacy	170–171
Apostles' Creed in baptism	200, 204	Baptism of John (June 24)	167
Apostolic Tradition, The	16, 18–21, 173, 236, 240, 245, 256, 322–323	Baptism of the Lord	87
		Barnett, James	233, 405
		Bartlett, Lawrence	v, 6, 14, 94, 103–104, 107, 130, 287, 297, 397, 427
ARCIC	5, 47, 90, 115, 212, 221–222, 224, 232–234, 246–247, 346, 376, 400		
		BCP (1549)	20–22, 44–45, 105, 113, 133, 153–154, 166, 171, 173, 177, 186, 211, 233, 243–244, 250–251, 254–255, 268, 278, 282–283, 286, 291, 304–307, 310, 331, 354, 366, 369, 398, 422
Article III	320		
Article IX	171, 330		
Article X	199		
Article XXII	89		
Article XXIII	234, 406		
Article XXIV	29		
Article XXV	171		
Article XXVI	238	BCP (1552)	22, 44, 154, 171–173, 177, 186, 233, 237, 243–245, 250, 254–255, 264, 268, 278, 286, 292, 307, 310, 328–331, 354
Article XXVII	253		
Article XXVIII	223–235, 248, 255		
Article XXIX	255		
Article XXX	227, 254		
Article XXXI	233, 247		
Ascension Day	87	BCP (1559)	44, 98, 223, 237, 244, 256, 269, 292, 307
Ash Wednesday	75, 317		
ashes	316, 391	BCP (1604)	44, 137, 186, 204, 237, 244, 255, 268, 304, 307
aspersion	169, 177		
Atonement, Day of	227–228		

BCP (1662)	21–23, 34, 122, 213	canticles	143, 153–154
baptism and birth	177, 328–330, 333	Catechism, The	185–189
confession of sin	268–269	Catechumenate	184–185
faithful departed	377	*Celebrating Common Prayer*	130, 150
heritage	129, 149, 186	certificates	179, 193, 348
Holy Communion	211, 223, 237, 241–247, 254–256, 262–271, 306–310,	Chan, Simon	184
		Chapman, John	148
		children's ministry	142
Holy Week and Easter	313–314	'Christ is risen'	276
language of	29–30, 34, 117	christening	165
Lectionary	45–46	Christmas	
M&E Prayer	133–134	date of	68–69
psalter	96	in Australia	77–78
BCP (1928)	9–10, 45, 338–346, 354, 362, 367, 378–79	Santa and Xma$	70–71
		Church of South India	23, 236
Beckwith, Roger	65	circumcision	167–167
Benedictus (Blessed is he)	286–287, 301	collection	145, 284
berakah prayer	123–124, 275, 349, 415	collects	113–117, 279
Billings, Alan	174–177, 181	Collins, John	234, 404, 406
Billings, Bradley	338	Collison, Margaret	6, 15, 19, 328–332, 335
Birth of John Baptist (June 24)	69		
birth-rites	327–331	Commandments (Decalogue)	188, 264–265
bishops and confirmation	176, 207–208	Commemorations	57, 83, 86, 88
bishops and deacons	233–234	Commendations of the dying	362, 367–368, 388
'Blessed be God, Father …'	275	committal of the body	389–391
Blessing of a Civil Marriage	349	communicants, minimum	306
blessings	123–124, 295–296, 316, 334, 346	communicant visitors	305
		communion in both kinds	253
Box, Reginald	98–99, 102–103	confession	
bread of Holy Communion	250–251	general	126, 136, 147, 154–156, 172, 198, 268–270, 300, 369
breaking of bread	251, 253–254, 292–293, 301		
Buchanan, Colin	11, 16, 179, 236, 244, 266	personal	156, 326, 369
		HC2 placement	276–277, 282
Burge, Evan	6, 13–22, 31–35, 50, 97, 100–101, 113–117, 152, 279, 292	Confession of Peter (Jan 18)	86
		confirmation of baptised adults	207
		confirmation prayer	208
Calendar in *APBA*	80, 85–87, 90	consecration of elements	246–249, 254–255
candles	193, 205	Conversion of Paul (Jan 25)	86
Canons		Cranmer, Thomas	1, 44–46, 53, 89, 106, 113, 121, 132–133, 213, 223, 233, 239–240, 243–247, 257, 264, 278, 283, 286, 292, 295, 320, 322, 362, 369, 398, 407, 415, 418
Concerning Baptism (1992)	332		
Concerning Confession (1989)	328		
Concerning Confession (Revision, 2017)	369		
Concerning Confessions (Vulnerable Persons, 2017)	369		
for APBA	290		
on Admission to the Holy Communion (1993)	205, 305	creeds	125–126
		cremation	327, 378
on Holy Communion (2001)	251–253, 257, 264	Cuming, Geoffrey	171, 322
on Marriage of Divorced Persons (1985)	337, 346	Curnow, Andrew	19–20
		Daily Offices, themes	151
on Oaths, Affirmations Declarations & Assents (1992)	419	Dalzell, Paul	184
		Davies, Douglas	378
on Reception (1981)	208	Davis, John	10

Dawson, Jenny	167	Great Thanksgivings	285–286, 288–291, 297, 301, 311, 322
Day of Atonement	227–229		
deacons	284, 296, 400–407	greeting, initial	276
deacons and bishops	233–234	Greeting of Peace	283
death	375–377	Gregg, David	223
Devil / Satan	199–200	'Hail Gladdening Light'	105, 158
Didache, The	191, 253, 292	Hall, Christine	403
dismissal, liturgical	296	Halloween	69
Dix, Gregory	66, 211–212, 231–232, 236–237, 273	hand-laying	208–209
		hand-washing	250, 260
Dowling, Owen	6, 14–15, 354–359, 363–367	Harris, Charles	307
		headings in services	39–41
Dowling, Ronald	v, 6, 14–17, 66, 85, 88, 158–162, 180, 369–371	healing	351–355, 359–361
		'Hear the Word of the Lord'	243
		Hearn, George	6, 15, 17, 132–133, 147–149, 152–154
Easter greeting	276		
Easter in Australia	75, 321	'helpmeet'	336
eating	217–218	Holeton, David	13, 212
electronic liturgy publishing	18, 32, 314, 323	Holy Baptism, explanation	197–198
Ember Days	80–81	*Holy Baptism for an Infant* (2009)	205
'epiclesis	20, 123, 203, 248, 286, 288, 301, 323	Holy Communion / Eucharist / Lord's Supper	
		at a funeral	309–312
ELLC	17, 28–29, 113, 155, 157, 281	at a wedding	304–305
		health care	259–260
Epiphany	78	in meal context	235
eulogies	385–386	institution narrative	220–221, 247–248
ex operato / operantis	170	insufficient elements	254–255
ex tempore prayer	119–120, 356–357	intinction	260, 361
Exhortations – HC1	268	invitations to	293
extended communion	308–309	manual acts	248
Family Law Act	302, 326	ministers of	258–259
'father'	14, 111, 117, 335	New Testament data	221–222
Festivals / Holy Days	87	place of Lord's Prayer	270, 291–292
filioque	125–126	posture	257–259
First Evensongs	63, 87, 156	preparing the Table	249, 284
Fisher, J.D.C	169, 173	presiding	237–239
'four-fold' shape	212, 235–236, 247–249, 285–286	title	211–212
		with sick	306–307, 358–359
Frost, David	31–32, 100–101, 294, 426	*Holy Communion* (2009)	324–325
		HC1, intercessions	266–267
funerals, non-believers	376, 379–380	HC2, intercessions	281–282
funerals, receiving the body	383–384	HC2, Post-communions	294
furniture	275	HC2, Great Thanksgivings	288–291
gender and God	32–33, 117–118, 151	HC Outline Order	303–304
gender and language	14, 31–32, 59–60, 402	Holy Saturday	76, 320
General Synod 1995	17–20, 24–25, 340–341	Holy Week	76–77, 313–316, 321
Gloria, placement	271, 278, 300	*Homily on Reading of Scripture*	46–47
'Glory to God:' (*Gloria Patri*)	101, 105, 135, 137, 152	Hours services	132–133
gluten-free bread	251	Humble Access, Prayer of	243–245
God willing	353	International Anglican Liturgical Consultation (IALC)	13, 17, 212, 247, 259, 401
godparents	165, 177		
Good Friday	319	*'ichthus*	288, 361
Goodhew, Harry	16, 297	*In Living Use*	6, 322
gradual hymn	265, 280	*in persona Christi*	238–239, 278, 284, 299, 406
Gray, Donald	9		

Jesus, High Priest	230–232, 406–407	mixture (of water and wine)	250
Jobbins, Boak	19	Morley, Janet	33, 35, 114, 126
Johnston, Richard and Mary	8, 321	Morris, Leon	229, 421
Jones, Cheslyn	165, 181	music	96, 103–108
Jones, Nathaniel	415, 417	for M&EP	105
Jones, Simon	174, 181	for Eucharist	105–107
Joseph (March 29)	86, 225	weddings and funerals	108, 389
Judd, Andrew	12	musicians	107–108
Kaye, Bruce	8, 21	naming of a child	177, 202, 332
Kelly, Gerard	224	Nelson, Janet	119
Knox, David Broughton	10, 419	new birth	164, 167, 172, 325, 331
Kyrie	278	new commandment	76, 211
Lambeth Conferences	23–24, 90, 125, 213, 236, 250, 254, 273, 366, 398–400, 403	Newell, Philip	19
		Newth, Emily Elizabeth	425
		Nicene Creed	33, 125, 281
language in liturgy	29–30	Nicholson, Adam	29
language styles in *APBA*	33–37	Nicholson, Sydney	98
last rites	309, 361–367	Notices	147, 295
lavabo	250, 260	Offertory in Holy Communion	268, 283–284
Lawton, William	6, 14, 338–341, 348–350	oil(s)	193, 357–358, 367
		ontology and ministry	399
Lectionary		ordained ministries	397–399, 400–409
daily	52–53	*Order of Communion* (1548)	44
Sundays	51	'Ordinary' time	88–89
Three-Year	47–48	ordination of women	14, 400
Lent	75–76, 313	original sin	171–172
Lesser Festivals	57, 83, 86, 88	*Oxford Guide to BCP*	22, 85
light	156, 204	Palm / Passion Sunday	315–318
liminality	38–39, 380–381	Parker, Lenore	3, 34, 122
litanies, short (lesser)	118–119, 138–139, 144	Passover	66–67, 218–220
		'performative' language	295, 371
'Liturgical Resources' subtitle	20	persecution	231
liturgical shapes	37–40	Peterson, David	6, 15–16, 19, 41, 297
Lloyd, Trevor	11, 16, 236–237, 380	pilgrimage	38–39, 380–381
Lord's Prayer, version	29, 112–113, 159	planning liturgy	91–94
marriage		Plater, Ormonde	403
and divorce	337	*porrectio instrumentorum*	415
certificate signing	348	posture	136, 257–258, 269–70, 280, 287, 345
General Synod 1995	340–341		
'giving away' of bride	344, 347		
in Australia today	336–338, 350	prayers	
nuptial blessing	346, 348	responsive	118–119
rings	345, 348	and faithful departed	267, 376–377
'vow and promise'	345, 348	for peace	139
Marriage, A Service for (1990)	339–340	for the Queen	138, 265
Mary, Mother of Our Lord	86, 227, 331, 378, 404	in the First Testament	110
Maundy Thursday	318	in the New Testament	111–112
McCall, David	19–20	of intercession	112, 127
'member of Christ'	172, 209	of praise	121
memorial acclamations	287–288	of thanksgiving	122
Michael & All Angels (Sept 29)	69	'three-dimensional'	226, 230
'minister'	25, 124, 178, 400–408	Prayer of Approach	243–245
		Prayer of Oblation	270–271, 300
Ministry of the Word	46, 52–56, 132	Prayer of Preparation	239–241
mission of God and liturgy	38–40	Prayer of St John Chrysostom	144

Praying Together	28, 106, 242	servant imagery	204, 403-404, 410-411
preaching	55-57, 94, 280, 387	sexual abuse	372
'priesthood of all believers'	406	Shaver, Stephen	226
priests		*shalom, shelamim*	210, 217, 227
Christian	233, 400, 405-407	*shema'*	277
in the First Testament	230	Sherlock, Charles	6, 8, 15, 17, 18, 21, 25-26, 31, 49, 74, 100, 111, 225-226, 245, 247, 291, 322, 330, 425
Graeco-Roman	231-234		
presbyters and	231-232, 405		
Principal Festivals / Holy Days	44, 57, 83, 86-87, 101, 269, 296		
'Principle of uniformity', the	22-24		
privacy	191, 369-372	Sherlock, Peta	v, 49, 71
propitiation	228-229, 247, 269	sign of the cross	204, 249
Psalm 95 (*Venite*)	137, 142, 264	silence	141, 155
Psalms		Silk, David	16, 18, 20
daily system	53-54	Sinden, Gilbert	12, 64, 85-86, 119, 138, 149-150, 152, 214, 244-250, 255, 259, 276, 284-287, 292, 310, 330, 343-354, 351-355, 362, 376, 386
Gelineau chanting	99		
in M&EP	135		
imprecatory	54, 101		
inclusive language	31-32, 100-101		
metrical	98		
pointing	102		
saying / singing	97-103	Smith, Elizabeth	48, 71, 76, 296
purgatory	362, 378	solstices and equinoxes	68-70
'Purification of Women'	328-329	Song of Creation (*Benedicite*)	121
Rayner, Keith	19, 249	Song of the Church (*Te Deum*)	121
re-baptism	178-179	Song of Simeon (*Nunc Dimittis*)	157
Reception	208	*Southern Cross*	15
Reconcilaion of a Penitent	326, 366	Speagle, Henry	115
'red-letter' days	85	Spinks, Bryan	98
renunciations	198-199	sponsors for initiation	165, 177, 200-201, 210
reserved sacrament	306-308	sprinkling (aspersion)	169, 177
Revised Common Lectionary	48-50	standing for the Gospel	143, 245-246
Richardson, David	6, 15-16, 273, 275-280, 285, 289-290, 297, 428	Sunday	65-66, 72-3, 83-84
		supplementary consecration	256-257
		Sydney, Anglican Diocese of	14, 16-24, 124, 130, 148, 290, 300, 428
rites of passage	38-39, 325, 378-381		
Robinson, Donald	12-13, 420	Sydney Liturgical Committee	16, 297, 300
Rogation Days	82	synagogue worship	132
Royal touch	353	testimony	142, 179, 192, 197, 200, 204, 207-209
Sabbath	64-66, 72-73, 83-84, 320		
		Thanksgiving for a Child	177, 196, 325-331
sacrifice in ancient Israel	226-228	Thanksgiving for Australia	34, 74, 122
sacrifice in the New Testament	228-230	Thanksgiving for Holy Communion (Lesser Festival)	86
saints, criteria for inclusion	85		
saints days	67-68, 89-90	'The Lord be with you'	138, 241-242
Sanctus	106-107, 121, 285, 323, 362	Thomas, Griffith G.	419
		time	
Sarum rite	215, 241-242, 243, 278, 304	and eternity	223-224
		'Ordinary'	88-89
Saviour of the world (canticle)	153, 362	seasons	72
Scripture sentences	36, 137, 141, 152, 392-393	the day	63-64
		the week	64-66
Scripture readings, how many?	54	the weekend	72-73
		the year	66-71

Together in Song	96, 100–101, 105–107
Transfiguration	49
trial use booklets 1990–1994	15
Trinity, Holy	118
Trisagion	279
troth	338, 344, 348
turning to the front (east)	138
Two Great Commandments	265, 276–277, 299
unclean	330
Varcoe, Gillian	v, 6, 15, 273, 275, 277, 279–280, 285, 297, 425
viaticum	311, 366
Visitation of the Sick, *BCP*	326, 351, 354, 362, 368
visitors	193–194, 198, 205, 305
vows	36, 163–164, 177, 189, 277, 341, 344–348
Wainwright, Geoffrey	163, 179
Walter, Tony	374
water in liturgy	164–166, 188, 190
'We are not worthy'	245–246
weddings and marriage	336
Week of Prayer for Christian Unity	86
Week of Prayer for Reconciliation	86
Welker, Michael	225
Wesley, Charles and John	122, 225
West, Fritz	48
Westminster Confession	420
wholeness, Christian view of	351–352
wine at Holy Communion	252
words of administration	255–256, 293
'worthy reception'	257
Yarnold sj, E.J.	165, 181

www.ingramcontent.com/pod-product-compliance
Lightning Source LLC
Chambersburg PA
CBHW060521010526
44107CB00060B/2644